MW01618531

The Complete Guidebook to Family Purity

for Men and Women

Rabbi Reuven Epstein

Based on the teachings of
Rabbi Yitzchak Berkovits

The Complete Guidebook to Family Purity for Men and Women

Rabbi Reuven Epstein

ISBN: **978-1-64570-941-1**

Published by:

www.adirpress.com

Distributed by:
Feldheim

Book design and layout:
Rochel Leah Black
Yocheved Herzog

Printed in the U.S.A

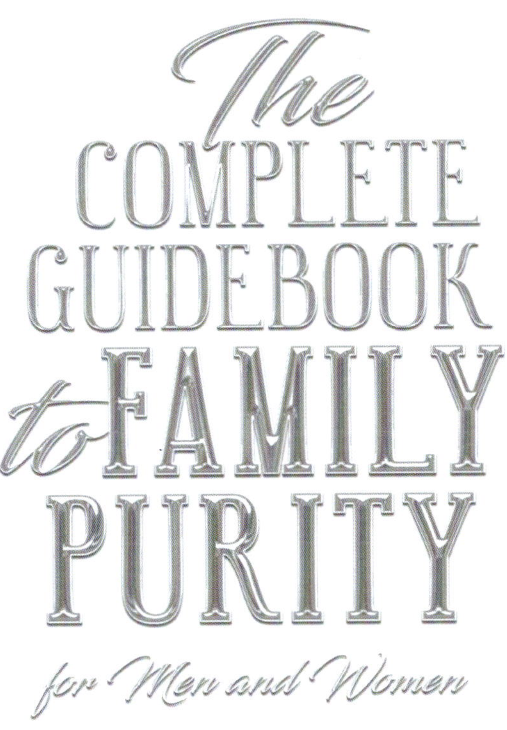

The Complete Guidebook to Family Purity

for Men and Women

Rabbi Reuven Epstein

Based on the teachings of
Rabbi Yitzchak Berkovits

UPCOMING BOOK TITLES BY THE SAME AUTHOR

SUBSCRIBE AT **MARRIAGEPRO.CO** TO STAY UP TO DATE WITH THE LATEST CONTENT!

The Marriage Project is an online and in-person project dedication to providing high quality content for those in the dating, engaged and married stages of life. To date The Marriage Project's dating, marriage and relationship seminars have been attended by hundreds of thousands around the world.

More information about The Marriage Project can be found online at MarriagePro.co (not .com)

RABBI YITZCHAK BERKOVITS

ROSH KOLLEL, **THE JERUSALEM KOLLEL**

Rabbi Yitzchak Berkovits
Sanhedria HaMurchevet 113/27
Jerusalem, Israel 97707
02-5813847

יצחק שמואל הלוי ברקוביץ
ראש רשת הכוללים לינת הצדק
סנהדרי׳ה המורחבת 113/27
ירושלם ת״ו

בס״ד ירושלם ת״ו כ״ב באלול תשע״ח

The world of Halacha is vast and complicated, yet it was designed by The Creator for every one of us. So much of Halacha grows on us from childhood, enabling us to carry with us a vast collection of Halacha without formal study.

The laws of Tahara in their entirety are to be acquired by every Jewish couple over the course of a very short period of time. To many this is a very tall order, and some struggle with many of the details.

Rabbi Reuven Epstein has compiled a comprehensive guide to all of the halaches on the subject in an organized and clear manner, making the task an enjoyable learning experience, and enabling retention of every detail.

Much of it is based on his years of dilligent study at The Jerusalem Kollel and continued toil as he moved on.

I appreciate this work as a great service to Klal Yisrael, and look forward to more such projects by the author.

בברכת הצלחה וחתימה טובה

לכב' המחבר ולכל כלל ישראל,

[illegible]

RABBI NOACH ISAAC OELBAUM

RAV, **CONGREGATION NACHLAS YITZCHOK**

TEL. (718) 520-0115
FAX (718) 268-0186

קהל נחלת יצחק ד׳הומנא

CONGREGATION NACHLAS YITZCHOK

141-43 73RD AVENUE
KEW GARDENS, HILLS, N. Y. 11367

נח אייזיק אהלבוים
בעהמח״ס מנחת חן
רב ואב״ד דק״ק נחלת יצחק
בקיו גארדענס הילס, נ. י.

NOACH ISAAC OELBAUM
RABBI
AUTHOR OF SEFORIM
MINCHAS CHEN

לעלוי נשמת

R' DOVID ELIEZER BEN R' ELCHANAN YAAKOV Z"L
MINDEL BAS YESHAYA SHMUEL A"H

R' HILLEL BEN R' MEIR Z"L
CHANA BAS R' ARYEH LEIB A"H

R' TZVI BEN R' ELIEZER YEHOSHUA Z"L
ZISEL BAS R' MORDECHAI A"H

R' MOSHE YESHAYAHU BEN R' YAAKOV DOVID HAKOHEN Z"L
CHANA BUNYA BAS HENOCH HALEVI A"H

JEFFREY AND MALKIE ZELL
MORDECHAI AND NECHAMA ETTINGER

לזכר ולעלוי נשמת

R' YISROEL BEN R' AHARON Z"L
MARAS SHOSHANA BAS R' YEHUDA A"H

R' YEHOSHUA MORDECHAI BEN R' YISROEL YITZCHOK Z"L

R' MOSHE MENACHEM TZVI BEN R' KLONIMUS KALMAN Z"L
MARAS BREINDEL BEN R' YITZCHOK EIZEK A"H

YISROEL AND SURI TABI

לזכר נשמת

YISROEL BEN YITZCHOK DAVID Z"L
YITZCHOK DOV BEN AVRAHAM ZT"L
SARAH BAS AVRAHAM A"H
YEHOSHUA AHARON BEN ELIEZER
YISACHAR DAVID ZT"L
FAIGA BAS ASHER CHAIM A"H
MALKA BAS YEHOSHA AHARON A"H

THIS DEDICATION WAS SPONSORED BY OUR LOVING AUNT

SHOSHANA LEFKOWITZ A"H,
CHAYA RAIZEL BAS YEHOSHA AHARON A"H

לעלוי נשמת

CHANAH BAS RAV AVRAHAM TZVI A"H
SARAH BAS RAV ASHER A"H
YITA BINA ERDMAN A"H

IN HONOR OF

MIRIAM SCHLANG

YITZCHAK AND ELLE LIEBLICH

לזכר נשמת

In loving memory of

LOTTIE VALBERG, A"H AND RUTH TENZER A"H

Loved and remembered everyday
Missed beyond words
May the learning of this sefer be an aliyah for their neshamos

SIMCHA AND RONIT VALBERG

AS A ZCHUR FOR
REFUAH SHELEIMA FOR

אסתר בת רוזיא

MOSHE AND RIVKI CALLER

TABLE OF CONTENTS

SECTION TWO

SECTION THREE

INTRODUCTION TO FAMILY PURITY

Of all the gifts Hashem has bestowed upon us there is one that oftentimes gets distorted and misunderstood.

Mankind was created with urges, needs, wants and desires. One may think that avoiding all impulses would make one "holy". Separate from your urges and you shall be elevated.

However our sages teach us differently.

There are three inherent *taivos* within man: the ambition to get close to Hashem, the yearning for food, and the drive for physical intimacy. Each of these drives must be digested and understood to fully appreciate the gift Hashem has given us by instilling within mankind these natural desires.

Adam L'amal 'Yulad (Iyov 5:7) man was created to work. When man works and accomplishes there is a wonderful feeling that overcomes him. When one sits at home, unproductive, he is overcome with depression, anxiety.

The purest "work" that this drive refers to is actually the purpose of creation itself: to work on our relationship with Hashem by undergoing a process of self-perfection and self-development. There's no greater feeling than learning Torah or a heartfelt prayer. There is an inner longing of every human being to find and achieve purpose in life through self-development and spiritual fulfillment.

This ambition is imperative, because it lays out the *purpose* of mankind- to get close to Hashem. The relationship we forge in this world continues with us for all eternity. Therefore we are created with a drive to work; to work on ourselves to strive toward the ultimate perfection, an emulation of the Perfect Being, Hashem. This ambition helps us maximize our spiritual existence.

The need for food is essential as well. Without it, man may forget to sustain his body. Simply by remaining in a state of being we are reminded to "refuel" ourselves, to have energy to live another day. This drive is imperative as it helps us maintain our existence in the physical world.

The third *taivah* is similarly as important as the first two, but is oftentimes misconstrued and misinterpreted. One look at Adam before the creation of Chavah shows a yearning for a helpmate (*Bireishis 2:20*). This desire was not based on a physical need, rather it was based on a spiritual quest Adam knew he was on to get closer to Hashem.

As Adam came to recognize the goal of life – to connect to Hashem- Adam felt lacking, inadequate. Man is distant from Hashem. His everyday thoughts, words and actions are so base, so physical. How was he to connect to Hashem without someone to assist in this journey? Chavah is created as the answer to his dilemma; she is created as a helpmate, that is, to help Adam fulfil the purpose of his creation. She is created a few steps closer to Hashem, and is someone who can balance man's intellect with a healthy dose of emotional connectivity.

This partnership would be the ultimate partnership: man is on his quest for a relationship with Hashem, along with Chavah who would help him navigate his journey through life. Since her purpose is intertwined with his, she is exempt from all time-bound positive commandments, as that would take her away from her ultimate purpose: to be the ever-present helpmate, support, for her husband and family.

The raw *taivos* that man has are incredibly important to his existence. The drives for Hashem, sustenance and marriage show us what the most important elements in life actually are.

But the *yetzer harah* has distorted these ideas. Instead of fighting our inborn ambitions, he simply redirects our focus. He tells us to paint a picture and bask in the sense of accomplishment, instead of striving to be more accomplished in our personal development or Torah knowledge. He tells us to eat the cheesecake instead of the whole wheat bread. He tells us to focus on other facets of the male-female relationship, rather than its true intended purpose.

Hilchos Niddah is the ultimate balance. It reminds us what our ultimate goals of marriage are: to develop *kesher*- connection with our spouses by focusing on their emotional, physical, mental and spiritual needs, wants and desires. We renew our commitment to giving them anything they would need, without expecting anything in return.

The renewal of *mikveh* is the physical expression of a newfound emotional connection and appreciation of our spouse. Adherence to these laws reaffirms our commitment to ourselves, more than anything else in our relationship, that the intent and purpose of our relationship remains altruistic. It reminds us that the goals of our marriage are not physical and base. Rather we are a nation bent on maximizing our lives. We recognize that nothing tastes as good as feeling good tastes. We remember that we are in control of our *taivaos* and we don't let ourselves get caught up in the physical. Month after month we reembrace the idea that the emotional connection is the prerequisite to any physical affection.

That's truly a one of a kind gift.

AUTHOR'S INTRODUCTION

This book is a unique book in many ways. The format of the book is intended to explain to the reader on many levels how each area of halacha pertains to them at their level of understanding. Each idea is presented clearly for the reader to grasp and retain the knowledge and understand how to apply this to their lives.

This entire book began with notes. While learning these important laws in The Jerusalem Kollel I thought it was important to record each concept clearly and methodically. As the manuscript came together, there were requests to print it as a small book. That book evolved over the years and more sections and layers of information were added.

One day I received a phone call from Rabbi Moshe Kormornick, an old friend from The Jerusalem Kollel, suggesting that I consider publishing as a full book. Adir Press has an excellent reputation, and from the inside, I see that it is well-deserved. With the talented Rachel Leah Black designing the book layout, the keen insight of the halachic editor, Rabbi Avraham Harstein, and the sharp eyes of Mrs Shira Hoffman, a book was formed.

Boruch Shehechyanu V'Kiyimanu V'higiyanu Lazman Hazeh. The Ribbono Shel Olam was kind enough to allow this *sefer* to come to fruition and it is our hope and prayer that many more such works should be produced and distributed in the coming years.

To thank Rav Yitzchak Berkovits and express what his guidance means to me would take an entire book. The trajectory of my life was altered in a positive way in every sense of the word from my first encounter with Rav Berkovits. It is a privilege to have learned in The Jerusalem Kollel and to be counted among his many Talmidim.

To my Rebbe, Rav Yitzchok Kalifon, there simply are no words to thank you for your constant guidance and devotion. You have helped shape the trajectory of our lives. We are overflowing with hakaras hatov for all you have done for us.

Rav Yossi Stilerman instils in his Chabburah clarity, sensitivity and Dikduk Halacha, which has made Halacha "come alive" for those who are fortunate to learn under his leadership. Extra special appreciation is due to R' Mati Friedman; your beautiful Middos eclipse your understanding of each part of the Torah. You're truly an inspiration those who are fortunate to know you. Without you, this production couldn't exist. Many areas in this book have been clarified by these two giants.

I am forever indebted to my Chavrusas, Yussi Breningstall and Dov Ber Cowan for sharing their knowledge, while prodding and leading us on the journey through Hilchos Niddah. I have learned so much from the two of you- in and out of the Sefarim we learned together. I will always be thankful for your friendships and the special bonds we created at the JKollel.

To R' Moshe Kormornick, you are the spark that ignited this powder keg. The idea to turn this manuscript into a sefer was yours and this should be a *zchus* for you and your family for all time.

A tremendous amount of gratitude is owed to Yocheved Herzog for accepting the responsibility to complete this project and for exhibiting an unlimited amount of patience in the final stages. The final typesetting, formatting and designs are a testament to your professional work.

To our dear patrons, Simcha and Ronit Valberg, Yisroel and Suri Tabi, and Yitzchok and Ellie Lieblich, your generosity and support allowed this project the wings it needed to take off. I am forever grateful for your friendship and encouragement. The Marriage Project and this *sefer* are only made possible by you.

Jeffrey Zell and Mordechai Ettinger, thank you for your overflowing support and friendship. This sefer became a reality only thanks to your generosity.

To Moshe and Rivky Caller, thank you for your generosity and encouragement. You took the time to get to know the project and how this book would impact the community. More than anything, you opened your hearts and completely embraced me in supporting this project. Generosity is an artform you have perfected.

My parents, Rabbi Binyomin and Sandy Epstein have always been guiding lights to me and my wife. By trailblazing a life of Torah and *chessed* we hope to make you proud with our own contributions to the *klal*. Thank you for always supporting and encouraging our decisions and projects.

Rabbi Dovid and Malky Saks, my in-laws, could not be more encouraging toward our project. Thank you for always keeping a positive tone, even through life's challenges. With you in our corner, sunshine is always a phone call away.

To my dear wife, Gitty, there really are no words that can thank you enough. Everything we have accomplished is in your credit. When Rabbi Akiva arrives home with 24,000 students in tow and his wife rushes forward to see him, Rabbi Akiva said the famous phrase "*sheli V'shelachem shelah hee*" (what's mine and yours is hers), in testament to his wife's dedication to his learning.

That phrase takes on extra meaning, as Rabbi Akiva was ignorant when his wife met him. Only through her belief in her husband's potential allowed him to soar to his great heights.

My wife gravitated to the cause we have dedicated our lives to, from early in our marriage. Her selfless dedication to me, my children and the *kallos* who are fortunate to learn under her allows us to grow into a better version of ourselves. She understands that a relationship takes constant dedication of time and effort and makes everyone around her feel like they are the only thing she has on her list of priorities. My life could not be more blessed to have such a dedicated partner in every area of life.

Thank you!

Rabbi Reuven Epstein

PUBLISHER'S PREFACE

One who learns the laws of family purity in depth will be struck by a phenomenon unparalleled by any other set of Jewish laws: stringency after stringency — from the earliest sources — have come to be codified into Jewish law. Why are these laws different, and from which source did the greatest *Rabbanim* throughout the generations initiate so many boundaries and protective fences for the Jewish people in this area? One answer can be found in the words of the Gemara that the women *themselves* took on these stringencies (*Niddah* 66a). Nothing was forced upon these righteous women, yet they themselves took exceptional care regarding the laws of family purity in order to beautify this mitzvah in which they played such a significant role. In fact, it was this incredible dedication and care for the mitzvah of family purity that led to great praise for the entire Jewish nation, with Hashem testifying to their righteousness (*Sanhedrin* 37a).

Working on this very special *sefer* with my dear friend Rabbi Reuven Epstein has been an immense pleasure. Having learned with Rabbi Epstein under the tutelage of HaGaon HaRav Yitzchak Berkovits *shlit"a* in Yerushalayim, I first came to know him as a *talmid chacham* who sought clarification after clarification regarding these laws. But when he left for New York, I came to know him as a dedicated educator, counselor, sought-after speaker, and pioneer in Jewish teaching who has literally helped hundreds — and probably thousands — of Jewish couples with his guidance and teaching in the areas of *shalom bayis* and the laws of family purity.

Therefore, it has been a great *zechus* for me to have been able to help Rabbi Epstein's furtherment of Jewish education in this area. And it is my sincere prayer that this *sefer* help to further Hashem's testimony to the care and dedication of the Jewish people to His Torah and mitzvos, specifically this precious mitzvah of family purity.

Bivrachah,

Rabbi Moshe Kormornick

Adir Press

SECTION ONE

Section One is a presentation of *hilchos niddah* for the beginner. The reader will find the basic application of applicable laws in an easy-to-read format. Background to each halachah is included so the concepts are easily understood.

Calendars, charts, and reference tables are disbursed throughout this section and can be used as aids to help the reader comprehend each topic.

The entire book follows the same chronology in terms of presentation: *Niddah D'Oraisa*, *Niddah D'Rabbanan*, *Harchakos*, *Taharah*, and *Vestos*. These chapters present the halachah according to the monthly calendar: how a woman becomes a niddah, the applicable laws while in the state of niddah, removing the niddah status, and anticipating the upcoming flow.

As one reads through each chapter, they are sure to have questions. Many of these questions are addressed in Sections Two and Three. References are provided at the end of various subsections with common questions which the reader will find answers to later in the book.

HOW A WOMAN BECOMES A NIDDAH

Introduction to How a Woman Becomes a Niddah

We have many laws, many rules, and many guidelines. Of all of these, there is a group that is less understood than the rest: that of *chukim*, laws of which we have no understanding.

To most people, the concepts of purity and impurity ring of good and bad. Purity sounds so white and clean. Impurity sounds so dirty.

The Arizal says this is not the correct understanding of purity and impurity. Rather, it is potential or loss thereof that deems something pure or impure. A woman who becomes a niddah is in a state of impurity simply because she lost the potential to create a baby during this menstrual cycle.

While this concept rings true on certain levels, in truth, we cannot comprehend the entirety of the reason behind these important laws.

One of the most famous of all Torah-related sayings states: "[God] gazed into the Torah and created the world." That is, the Torah was in existence before the creation of the world; God peered into the Torah and used it as a blueprint for creation.

This statement is puzzling on many levels. If the Torah is a rule book, how could the rule book have existed before the need for rules? Imagine traveling back in time and seeing speed limit signs along a dirt path, created by Native Americans in the 1700s! Who would create rules years before the need for their implementation?

Rav Elya Lopian explains that there are certain rules that are created as guidelines, and certain rules that are created as practicality. For example, there are rules of nature such as gravity. No one walks around upset at the existence of nature's rules. No one feels "chained" by these rules. They simply exist.

Such is the view on the Torah's laws. They represent the perfect existence. The world is a manifestation of Hashem's creation which is governed by these laws. Observance of these laws allows one to tap into the Creator of the laws. They should not be viewed as impositions. They should be viewed as existence itself.

Hilchos niddah are of the most severe laws in terms of punishment for transgressing them. That should tell us the severity of breaking nature's laws, and how important the balance between purity and impurity is viewed from the lens of the Torah, the ultimate guidebook for creation.

Understanding the Anatomy

In order to understand *hilchos niddah* properly, it is necessary to have a basic understanding of the structure and function of the female reproductive system. We therefore preface our halachic discussion with a brief biological discussion of this system and the monthly menstrual cycle. The female cycle works as follows:

1. An egg cell is created in the ovaries, which is released during ovulation.
2. After ovulation, the uterus builds up a lining called the endometrium, which absorbs and sustains the egg cell in preparation for fertilization and implantation of the fertilized embryo into the endometrium.
3. The egg cell ovulates, and travels down the fallopian tube into the uterus.

At this point one of two things happens. The first option is that the egg becomes fertilized, and then becomes absorbed into the uterine lining. The egg cells start multiplying, and begin to develop into a baby.

The uterus releases the HCG hormone which tells the body to change gears and sustain the pregnancy; this keeps the lining from falling out.

Alternatively, the egg may not become fertilized or may not properly attach to the lining. It instead falls out of the body. The body waits approximately 12 to 14 days, and, when it realizes that there is no pregnancy, releases the endometrium. This is called a period; it lasts approximately 3 to 9 days. Some women's periods are longer and some are shorter, with the average being 5 or 6 days. After the period, the body starts readying itself for the new cycle. When the lining is finally ready, she ovulates once again.

In summary, from the halachah-observant woman's perspective, a monthly cycle (unless she becomes pregnant) looks something like this:

- Day 1 — onset of the period
- Day 1 to Day 5 or Day 6 — bleeding
- Day 6 to Day 12 — *shivah nekiyim* ("7 clean days," which will be discussed later)
- Night of Day 13 — immersion in the mikvah
- Day 14 to Day 16 — ovulation
- Day 28 to Day 32 — a new cycle, with a new period, begins.

It is interesting to note that the egg cell, which is approximately the thickness of a strand of hair, lives a total of 12 hours unless it is fertilized. Sperm cells, however, live up to 72 hours from the time they enter the woman. Since, as we will later learn, the couple separates for at least 12 days from the time that her period begins, a woman generally ovulates within a few days after she goes to the mikvah. As a result of marital relations on the night she immersed in the mikvah, there should still be sperm inside of her to fertilize the egg at the time she ovulates.

Niddah D'Oraisa (Niddah according to the Torah)

We will learn that *Chazal* (the Sages) instituted many safeguards to Torah law in *hilchos niddah*. We will now discuss the situation that makes a woman a niddah on a *d'Oraisa* (Torah law, before the institution of Rabbinic "safeguards") level.

A *niddah d'Oraisa* is a woman who has experienced both of the following two criteria:

1. A flow of blood — even the smallest drop — from the uterus

and

2. A *hargashah* (sensation).

The *Poskim* speak about three different kinds of sensations that a woman may feel when blood begins to flow from her uterus, in description of the *hargashah* discussed by *Chazal*:

1. The *Rambam* explains that she feels her entire body quiver.
2. *Tosafos* and the *Terumas HaDeshen* explain that she feels her cervix opening.
3. The *Noda B'Yehudah* and *Chavas Daas* explain that she feels an internal flow.

It should be noted that a woman may discharge a wide variety of colors: clear, white, yellow, green, blue, pink, brown, amber, gold, orange, red, and black. Not all of these render her *temei'ah*. A *Rav* may need to be consulted to determine which colors are *temei'im* (impure), as we will soon discuss.

Many women experience PMS (premenstrual syndrome) which sometimes presents itself in the form of cramping or other pains. However, there are almost no women today who experience the *hargashos* discussed by the *Poskim* above. It would thus appear that nowadays, a woman who gets her period should not be a *niddah d'Oraisa*, for she did not experience the necessary accompanying *hargashah*.

However, this is not the case. The *Aruch HaShulchan* and Rav Moshe Feinstein explain that when *Chazal* tell us that a woman is a *niddah d'Oraisa* only when a *hargashah* accompanies the flow of blood, they are actually saying that that Torah law (before the Rabbinic "safeguards") only considers her to be a niddah when her body discharges blood in the "normal" way, which is accompanied by a *hargashah*. (The body's "normal" discharge of blood is termed *derech re'iyah* —literally, "'natural' seeing." This discharge is also called a *re'iyah* — literally, "seeing.") However, a woman who experiences an "unusual" emission of blood (which we will discuss in Basic Overview, How a Woman Becomes a Niddah, headline "Niddah D'Rabbanan: Kessamim", page 13), is not *temei'ah* (impure) on a Torah-law level. Experiencing the flow of a large amount of blood, such as what takes place when a woman gets her period, shows us that this discharge is normal. We will thus assume that a *hargashah* occurred as well, even though she did not feel it. We will soon learn what is considered "a large amount" of blood.

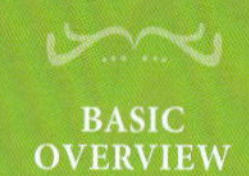

The *Baruch Taam* explains this idea. Let us use the example of someone who touches another person who is sleeping. It may very well be that the sleeping person may not have realized that they were being touched. But if they are afterwards shown a video of what took place, they will agree to what other people told them happened. The same is true in regard to a woman's *hargashah*: even though she did not actually *feel* the *hargashah* sensation, because women nowadays are generally not tuned in to these feelings, the accompanying large amount of bleeding makes it clear that it must have happened even though she did not notice. A woman who gets her period is thus considered a *niddah d'Oraisa*.

Sometimes a woman will notice that she has had a discharge of a smaller amount of blood, one that does not seem to be connected to her regular period. Unless she actually experienced a *hargashah*, this blood is considered a *kesem* (stain) which carries with it several leniencies, which will be discussed in Basic Overview, How a Woman Becomes a Niddah, headline "Niddah D'Rabbanan: Kessamim", pages 13 and 14. If we are concerned that a *hargashah* may have occurred, these leniencies will not apply, and she will be *temei'ah mid'Oraisa*, as stated above.

How much blood is considered "a lot"?

- Rav Moshe Feinstein rules that this amount is half the size of a dollar bill.
- Many *Poskim* in Eretz Yisrael rule that this amount is the size of 6–7 *gris*. (A *gris* is a Talmudic measurement, which is approximately the size of a penny or a one-shekel coin.)

When a woman gets her period, there will be a lot of blood. She is certainly a *niddah d'Oraisa*.

Mistaken Sensations

If a woman felt a *hargashah* but did not get her period, but she saw even a tiny amount of blood, she is considered a *niddah d'Oraisa* in the following three cases:

1. When she discovers blood after using the bathroom. The reason for this is that she may have experienced a *hargashah* and not felt it, because it was masked by the feeling of performing her bodily needs.

2. When discovering blood immediately after intimacy. This is because the physical feelings of intimacy may have masked the *hargashah* that took place.

3. When blood is discovered after something was inserted in the vaginal canal, for example, a *bedikah* cloth or a tool during a doctor's examination. In this case, too, perhaps the woman experienced a *hargashah*, which was masked by the feeling of the foreign object. For this reason, a woman should never perform a *bedikah* that is not one of the standard required *bedikos* (these will be discussed in which we will discuss in Basic Overview, Taharah, and Vestos), unless a *Rav* tells her to do so.

In all three of these cases we assume that a foreign sensation masked the *hargashah* that accompanied the discharge of blood. This blood that is discharged is thus treated as *tamei d'Oraisa*, and not as a *kesem*, with its leniencies which will be detailed in the upcoming pages.

 **Summary**

In summary, there are four basic cases that would render a woman a *niddah d'Oraisa*:

- When she gets her period
- If she finds any amount of blood immediately after intercourse
- If she finds any amount of blood immediately after using the bathroom
- If she finds any amount of blood on anything inserted vaginally, such as a *bedikah* cloth

A Hargashah Without Seeing Any Blood

A woman who thinks she had a *hargashah* — whether or not she actually found any blood —should immediately contact her *Rav*, as some halachic authorities may render a woman a niddah on the basis of the *hargashah* even if she is not bleeding.

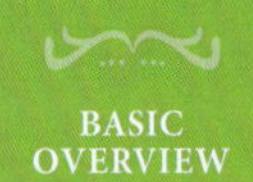

Niddah D'Rabbanan: Kesamim (Stains)

The Torah would prefer that a woman remains in a *tahor* (pure) state. She should therefore not do anything to make herself *temei'ah* unnecessarily. She should not look for stains on her sheets and her undergarments unless she was specifically instructed to do so. However, a woman who *notices* staining must tell her husband and contact their *Rav*. The sheet or garment on which the stain occurred may not be discarded or washed, but should be presented to the *Rav* for his halachic ruling.

Although, as we learned, Torah law does not consider a woman to be *temei'ah* unless she saw "a lot" of blood (as discussed above) or was in one of the situations in which she may have unknowingly experienced a *hargashah*, *Chazal* created a safeguard, and decreed that a woman is *temei'ah* after discharging even a smaller amount of blood, in certain circumstances. A discharge of a "small" amount of blood without a *hargashah* is called a *kesem* (stain).

However, *Chazal* included five leniencies in this decree. These include:

1. A *kesem* is only problematic when it is at least the size of a *gris*.
2. A *kesem* is not problematic when found on colored sheets or colored clothing.
3. A *kesem* is only problematic when found on something that is *mekabel tumah* (susceptible to *tumah*).
4. A *kesem* is only problematic when the blood cannot be attributed to something else.
5. Even when problematic, blood discharged as a *kesem* does not create a *vest* (pattern for future concern, which will be discussed in Vestos).

We will now discuss these points in greater detail.

Leniency 1: The Kesem's Size

The era in which *Chazal* instituted the edict of *kesamim* was one in which small insects (called *macholos*) were prevalent around people's homes. In order that a woman not be declared *temei'ah* based on blood found on her sheets or clothing that in truth came from an insect's body, *Chazal* instituted that a stain only makes a woman *temei'ah* if

the *kesem* is bigger than the amount of blood that could have possibly come from a louse.

This size is a Talmudic measurement called a *gris*, which is approximately the size of a penny or one-shekel coin. This leniency applies nowadays as well, and a woman who finds a stain smaller than this size remains *tehorah*. Very often, a *Rav* who is presented with a *kesem* rules leniently simply based on the size of the stain.

Point of interest: a *kesem* found on the body has different rules. See Advanced Rulings, How a Woman Becomes a Niddah, headline "Calculating the Gris", page 210.

Leniency 2: A Kesem Found on Colored Sheets or Colored Clothing

A woman who finds a *kesem* on colored clothing remains *tehorah*.[1]

Rashi explains that the reason for this leniency is that *Chazal* were lenient when we cannot determine exactly the color of the stain due to the coloring of the clothing.[2] Understanding like Rashi, Rav Yosef Shalom Elyashiv rules that this leniency only applies when the sheet or clothing that she is presenting the *Rav* is colored to the point that he cannot accurately tell the *kesem*'s color. If, however, the background material is one on which the color can still be determined, this leniency cannot be utilized.

The *Rambam* states that a woman is advised by *Chazal* to wear colored clothing in order to save her from having questions of *kesamim*.[3] Rav Moshe Feinstein understands from here that *Chazal* simply did not include a *kesem* that is found on colored sheets or clothing within the decree of *kesamim*. This means that when a sheet or article of clothing is not "white," any *kesem* found on it does not present a problem, and the woman remains *tehorah*.

Therefore, a *kesem* found on pastels and light colors can still be *tamei* according to Rav Yosef Shalom Elyashiv, but will be *tahor* according to Rav Moshe Feinstein.

---

1. Provided that the stain discovered is not larger than the amount of a "lot of blood" discussed earlier in this chapter, for this would no longer be considered a *kesem*; rather, it would be considered the onset of her period.

2. *Niddah* 61:72, "*Lehakel*."

3. Quoted in the *Rama*, *Yoreh Dei'ah* 190:10.

As a matter of practice, a woman should wear colored underwear, and the color should be one that is dark enough that the *Rav* to whom the couple brings their *she'eilos* will discount any *kesamim* that may appear on it. The same is true for nightgowns, pajamas, towels, and sheets, and any other place with which blood may come in contact. (The one exception is during the *shivah nekiyim*, when a woman must wear specifically white underwear so she will know with certainty that she has stopped bleeding, as will be discussed in Basic Overview, Taharah, headline "Shivah Nekiyim", page 48.)

Leniency 3: A Kesem Is Only Problematic When Found on Something That Is Mekabel Tumah

During the times that Bnei Yisrael were mindful of the halachos of *tumah* and *taharah* — when they would go to the Beis HaMikdash and eat sacred foods — a *kesem* would not only make the woman *temei'ah*, but would make the item on which it was found *tamei* as well. The *Chavas Daas* explains that *Chazal* found it difficult that an item that is not susceptible to *tumah* would not be affected by a *kesem* and remain *tahor*, yet the woman from whose body this stain emerged would become *temei'ah*. This being the case, they only instituted the decree of *kesamim* on garments and other items that are *tumah*-susceptible. As such, a *kesem* that is found on something that is not *tumah*-susceptible does not cause the woman to be *temei'ah* either.

Generally speaking, underwear and other "full" garments such as skirts and shirts are *tumah*-susceptible, and a *kesem* found on them is potentially problematic. Common questions arise regarding tights, pads, and toilet paper. When such a question presents itself, the item should be saved to be brought to the *Rav*'s attention.

Question

What happens if a woman finds a *kesem* that is larger than a *gris* on a white-and-blue patterned toilet seat, and the blood is clearly red?

See Advanced Rulings, How a Woman Becomes a Niddah, headline "Calculating the Gris", (page 210) and "Toilets and Bathtubs" (page 212).

Leniency 4: A Kesem Is Only Problematic When the Blood Cannot Be Attributed to Something Else

Chazal only instituted that a *kesem* may render a woman a niddah when the blood stain cannot be attributed to anything other than uterine bleeding. Attributing the stain to something else is called a *teliyah* (ascription). One of the most common *teliyos* which presents itself is when a woman has an internal cut that is producing blood. She may continually stain for weeks, yet so long as the origin of the blood can be attributed to a cut, she may avoid becoming a niddah from the staining.

When a woman presents the *Rav* with a *she'eilah*, she should say if she suspects she has a cut or if she feels any internal pains. In such a case, the *Rav* may send her to a *bodekes* (an examination nurse) to do a quick internal examination to see if something is there that could be the cause of the blood. This is a fairly common occurrence, and seeing a *bodekes* only helps the couple, by potentially avoiding unnecessary periods of separation.

 **Question**

"My kid was playing with paint and I found a stain on my skirt. Should I check the stain in a lab to prove it's not blood?"

See Advanced Rulings, How a Woman Becomes a Niddah, headline "Attributing the *Kesem* to a Different Source", (page 218).

A woman who finds a *kesem* that she suspects may be from an external source, for example, one of the children was playing with the laundry after having cut their finger, or someone close to her had a nosebleed, should mention this information to the *Rav*, and allow him to make the determination.

Leniency 5: Even When Problematic, Blood Discharged as a Kesem Does Not Create a Vest (Pattern for Future Concern)

We will soon learn that the halachah tells us that we may expect next month's period based when this month's period occurred, and are thus expected to take the necessary precautions on that date. This is called a *vest*. A *kesem*, though, is by definition not the normal flow of blood. Even when it makes a woman *temei'ah*, it does not indicate that

her period or another *kesem* will come on this date next month. This idea is a called a *vest* which will be discussed in Basic Overview, *Vestos* (page 59).

Before we continue learning about other forms of *niddah* it would be appropriate to summarize the five leniencies of *kessamim* as well as a quick review of niddah de'oraisa and how that compares to *niddah de'rabannan*.

Summary

If a woman finds a stain outside of one of the four cases stated above, then although she will not become a *niddah d'Oraisa*, she may be considered a *niddah d'Rabbanan*. In such a case, five leniencies must be considered:

1. If the stain is smaller than a *gris* (penny or one-shekel coin), or
2. If the stain is found on something that is not *mekabel tumah*, or
3. If the stain is found on a colored item, or
4. If the stain possibly originates from a source other than the uterus, then she will be *tehorah*.
5. Even if the stain does render the woman *temei'ah mid'Rabbanan*, she nonetheless does not observe any *vestos* the upcoming month as a result of the *kesem*.

Question

What is the status of blood that definitely came from her body — for example, she wiped herself in the external part of her vaginal area?

See Advanced Rulings, How a Woman Becomes a Niddah, headline "Vadai MiGufah" (page 223).

NIDDAH D'ORAISA

Blood WITH a Hargasha (Sensation)

SCENARIO	BLOOD FOUND	SIZE
Period	*Anytime*	*6-7 Gris in size*
Restroom	*Immediately after*	*Any visible amount*
Cohabitation	*Immediately after*	*Any visible amount*
Bedikah Cloth	*Anytime*	*Any visible amount*

NIDDAH D'RABANNAN

Blood WITHOUT a Hargasha (Sensation)

SCENARIO	LENIENCIES
Kessem	*1. Gris (Penny) in size*
	2. Colored garment
	3. Not Mekabel Tumah
	4. Teliyah (Attribution)
	5. No Vest Created

Additional Forms of Niddah

In addition to one who got her period, a woman who is in labor, delivers a baby, or has a miscarriage becomes a niddah as well. Additionally, a woman who underwent certain intrauterine procedures may become a niddah, as may a one who lies about becoming a niddah.

Each of these cases is discussed at length in Sections Two and Three.

A Niddah Rav

It should be quite clear that *hilchos niddah* play a central role in the life of a married couple. They are also some of the most important halachos in terms of observance and their severity, as well as the complex nature of the practical applications. Essentially, each area of

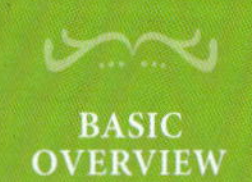

hilchos niddah is likely to be encountered by most couples, and questions often arise.

Question

"If I showed a *mareh* to a *Rav* and he said it was not good, may I go and ask another *Rav*?"

See Advanced Rulings, How a Woman Becomes a Niddah, headline "*Chacham SheHorah*" (page 201).

It is of utmost importance that each and every couple have a *Rav* they have a relationship with, to whom they can present their questions and receive an answer in a timely manner. Such a *Rav* should be reachable, relatable, and reliable. There is no need for embarrassment when asking questions related to these halachos. A competent *Rav* will often be of great assistance to a couple and will serve to maximize the *tahor* time in the relationship.

Review Questions on Niddah D'Oraisa and Niddah D'Rabbanan

1. If a woman got her period and all the blood was seen on a pad, is she *temei'ah*?
2. If a woman performs a *bedikah* and sees less than a *gris* of blood on the *bedikah* cloth, is she *temei'ah*?
3. If a woman sees blood in the toilet after going to the mikvah, what should be done?
4. If a *kesem* is found on white underwear but it is smaller than a *gris*, what is the status?
5. If a *kesem* is found on colored underwear but is larger than a *gris*, what is the status?

Answers

1. Yes. A woman who got her period is considered *temei'ah d'Oraisa*. She is *temei'ah* no matter what the blood is seen on.
2. Yes. A woman who found blood on a *bedikah* cloth is considered *temei'ah d'Oraisa* since it is inserted vaginally, regardless of how much blood she saw on the cloth.
3. A *Rav* should be consulted.
4. The woman is a *tehorah*. One of the five leniencies of *kesamim* is that a *kesem* is only *metamei* if it is larger than a *gris*.
5. The woman is *tehorah*. One of the five leniencies of *kesamim* is that a *kesem* is only *metamei* if it is found on white clothing.

HARCHAKOS

The "proverbial lollipop" is perhaps one of the most memorable lessons of Rabbi Yitzchak Berkovits. Imagine a child who wants candy. All he thinks about is candy. He dreams of candy. He desires candy. He really, really wants candy.

Finally, he gets candy. He's so excited! But then the candy falls from his fingers and onto the floor. The beautiful candy is covered in dirt!

A young child may pick up the candy and put it in his mouth, because in his eyes all he sees is candy. An older, more mature child may wash off the candy and then eat it.

But what about an adult? An adult doesn't want candy. He doesn't only think about food in terms of how it tastes. He thinks about food in terms of how it makes him feel. He asks himself, "Does this give me energy? Is this healthy for me?" With maturity comes the realization that one must think about life and its consequences in a real way on a consistent basis and make decisions based on that reality.

The adult who likes candy isn't a bad person. He just has less mature taste. His taste is for what feels good for the moment, not necessarily for what feels good in the long run. He fails to train his palate to enjoy healthy options so he can truly live a healthier, more energized, and more productive life.

The child's mind is not only stuck on the candy — he doesn't even see the dirt and grime even when it's caked all over his precious sweet.

This is the story of our lives. Many of us have immature taste. We see something we desire and we focus on that. We don't care that it's not good for us in the long run. We don't see that. All we see is our candy.

Harchakos are separations between husband and wife that exist when a woman is a niddah. These separations are there for many reasons, but primarily they are there to remind us that marriage is not candy. The Gemara says that a man should separate during the times his wife is a niddah so that there will be a renewal like the wedding day.

These separations ensure that the relationship between husband and wife is based on a mature outlook toward one another. They learn to confirm each other in a deep, emotional way, without glazing it over with a physical hug. They renew their emotional connection by spending quality time together, by walking and talking and discussing matters of the heart.

Niddah days are intrinsically "on" days. The marriage is on. The relationship is on. Dedication to these important halachos is a reaffirmation between the couple that they intend to treat each other with the respect that is due, while maintaining boundaries and exhibiting self-control.

Overview: Understanding Harchakos

Chazal established guidelines as to how a couple should act with each other during the times that the woman is a niddah. These are called *harchakos* (literally, "distances"). *Harchakos* are designed to distance the couple from reaching a situation in which they may come to physical intimacy, which is prohibited when a woman is a niddah. Halachah discusses twenty different ways that a couple may not interact when the woman is a niddah.

Two reasons are offered in explanation of why *Chazal* instituted *harchakos*:

1. The Rosh explains that in general, the laws of *yichud* do not allow a man to remain alone together with a woman with whom intimacy is forbidden. Although a wife is forbidden to her husband while she is a niddah, the fact that she will soon be permitted — after her *shivah nekiyim* and immersing in the mikvah — allows him to control himself from forbidden behavior. For

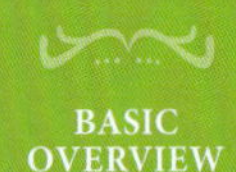

this reason, and because otherwise it would be impossible to maintain normal married life, the laws of *yichud* do not apply to a husband and wife even if she is a niddah. However, because we are lenient in the matter of *yichud*, to better ensure that they will not act wrongly while remaining alone together, *Chazal* added extra restrictions to preserve the proper atmosphere.

2. The Rashba explains that the close sense of familiarity between husband a wife means that even ordinary actions of closeness can potentially lead to intimacy. *Chazal* therefore instituted restrictions to ensure that this will not occur.

In general:

- *Harchakos* apply from the time that a woman becomes *temei'ah* until the time that she immerses in the mikvah, even if she for some reason waits a long time to do so.
- The laws of *harchakos* apply to every couple when the wife is a niddah, whether she became *temei'ah* because of her regular period, because she found a *kesem*, or due to any other cause.

Rav Moshe Feinstein points out that everybody knows that it is normal for a woman to be on a cycle and get her period approximately once a month. Keeping *harchakos* is therefore not considered to be something that is embarrassing, even when other people are around. Therefore, all *harchakos* must be observed even while in a public setting. Like all areas of halachah, *harchakos* must always be adhered to, even in difficult situations. A couple must contact their *Rav* before being lenient about a particular *harchakah* in a specific situation.

Question

"My wife is sick and there is no one around to help her. Must I observe the *harchakos*?"

See Advanced Rulings, Harchakos, headline "When the Wife Is Sick" (page 290).

A husband and his wife who is a niddah may not interact in the following ways:

Marital Relations Are Forbidden

- Intercourse with a niddah is a prohibition of the utmost gravity. As part of the *arayos* (forbidden relationships), it is included among the three cardinal mitzvos for which one must surrender their life rather than transgress.
- This prohibition carries with it the severe Heavenly punishment of *kareis* (extinction of the soul and its denial of a share in the World to Come).
- This prohibition is equally on the husband and the wife.

Hirhur (Thinking about That Which Is Forbidden)

- During the times that his wife is a niddah, a man may not think about her body in a manner relating to marital relations, or about the physical aspects of the relationship that they share during the times of the month when she is *tehorah*. Even thinking about hugging and kissing is prohibited because of the prohibition of "*v'nishmarta mikol davar ra*" (*Devarim* 23:10), which says that one should avoid engaging in prohibited behavior.
- This prohibition applies whether or not they are together in the same place.

A Man May Not Look at Parts of His Wife's Body That Are Normally Covered

- Rav Moshe Feinstein explains that the parts of the body that are normally covered are from a woman's neckline to her knees and down to her elbows.
- However, the husband may gaze at his wife's face even if he enjoys doing so, which is something that is forbidden in regard to other women. He must be careful, however, that this does not result in his thinking about her in ways discussed above.
- Rav Moshe Feinstein rules that a woman does not have to cover her forearm and lower part of her legs, even if she is accustomed to covering these areas of her body in the presence of strange men.

- Rav Moshe Feinstein rules that a woman does not have to cover her hair in her husband's presence when she is a niddah.

Question

Is it appropriate for a husband to be in the room when his wife is giving birth? Is he allowed to look at her at this time?

See Advanced Rulings, Harchakos, headline "*Histaklus*" (page 256).

A couple may play games and have a good time when the wife is a niddah. They may go on "dates," and they may eat out together. They may give each other gifts.

- They may not engage in passionate or overly frivolous activity to the point that they lose the awareness that she is in a state in which they are forbidden to each other.
- They may not talk to each other in an overly frivolous manner, or talk about intimacy.
- Included in this prohibition is that the husband may not smell his wife's perfume, even when she is not wearing it.

Question

"Can we play games together?"

See Advanced Rulings, Harchakos, headline "*Kalus Rosh*" (page 257).

- There are three types of touch:
  1. Intimate touch — a pleasurable, purposeful touch
  2. Incidental touch — a non-pleasurable, purposeful touch
  3. Accidental — a non-pleasurable, non-purposeful touch
- Intimate touch is included in the three cardinal mitzvos for which one must surrender their life rather than transgress. This includes play-touching, kissing, hugging, and the like.
- Incidental touch and accidental touch are also forbidden. A couple must be extremely careful that they do not touch each other in any way.

  Examples of prohibited touch include:

- He should not touch her finger or her clothing, or feel something that she is holding.
- He should not poke her with a pen or pull her hair.
- He should not blow something off of her shoulder.

› When traveling in an airplane or car, the couple must be very careful not to touch or bump into one another, even accidentally.

› A *Rav* should be called for guidance when one spouse is sick and requires the other one's physical assistance. (In a case of danger to life, they may be lenient.)

Question

"My husband is snoring and I can't sleep. I am not allowed to touch him. What should I do?"

See Advanced Rulings, Harchakos, headline "Practical Cases of Indirect Touching" (page 261).

A Couple May Not Hold an Item Together

Included in not holding an item together is that one spouse may not hand something to the other one. Rather, someone who wants to give something to their spouse when the wife is a niddah should instead put it down on a table, for example, and let them take it from there.

› Some examples of not holding something together include:

- He may not hand a serving bowl to her during dinner.
- They may not each hold one side of a jump rope so their child can jump rope in the middle.
- They cannot carry a box together up the stairs.
- They may not work together to push a table from one end of the room to the other.
- He cannot take something from her pocketbook when it is hanging on her shoulder.

› One spouse may not hand a very young child to the other, unless the child is able to stick out their arms to go from the arms of one parent to the other on their own. This is based on the principle that a living being "carries" itself.

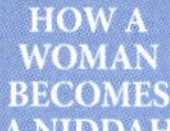

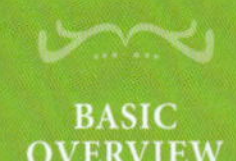

- It is customary to designate a couple to carry a newborn baby boy at the time of his bris. This designation is called *kvatter*. A couple should not serve as *kvatter* when the wife is a niddah. This holds true even if they first place the baby on two separate pillows, one on top of the other.

Question

"My husband fell asleep with my newborn baby. May I take the baby from him?"

See Advanced Rulings, Harchakos, headline "Other Forms of Passing" (page 262).

A Couple May Not Toss Something to One Another

Any form of tossing or throwing an object is prohibited.

Some common examples of tossing include:

- Throwing car keys
- Playing catch
- Playing ping-pong

A Husband May Not Listen to His Wife Sing

- A man may not be present when his wife is singing while she is a niddah.
- A woman may sing *zemiros* along with her husband because there are two voices singing together, in addition to the fact that *zemiros* are a *davar sheb'kedushah* (holy endeavor).

The following five *harchakos* are relevant when sharing a meal together:

A Heker at the Table

When the wife is a niddah, the couple must put some form of "reminder," called a *heker*, on the table at which they are eating. Seeing the *heker* during the meal serves to remind them of her status so they will not unthinkingly take some food off of each other other's plate, which is a form of affection reserved for a husband and wife.

- The *heker* must be:
  - Placed between them
  - Something that is noticeable to the husband
  - An item that has some height
  - Something that is not being used at this meal, or, if it is being used, it should be an unusual item that is usually not on the table
- Examples of a valid *heker* include:
  - An extra pitcher on the table that is not being used at this meal
  - The honey dish from Rosh HaShanah during the rest of the year, even if it happens to be being utilized during this meal

Sometimes the circumstances at the table serve as a *heker*, and nothing extra must be put on the table.

- Another person who is sitting between the husband and wife serves as a *heker*, alleviating the need for something on the table as well.
- Placemats serve as a *heker* for a couple that does not generally use them. If they do generally use placemats, another *heker* is still necessary.
- If the husband and wife each have a fixed place at the table, then changing to a different seat is also a valid *heker*.
- Many authorities rule that a *heker* between the husband and wife is not necessary when other people are also at the table, as it is unlikely that they will demonstrate affection in this setting. Other authorities maintain that nevertheless, a *heker* is still necessary. Each couple should follow their custom.

The Couple May Not Eat from the Same Plate

- A husband and wife not eating from the same plate when she is a niddah also means that they may not eat directly from the serving dish or serving plate. Rather, each must first put the piece of food on to his or to her own plate before eating it.

BASIC OVERVIEW

- Rav Moshe Feinstein notes that food that is generally eaten directly from the serving bowl, for example, popcorn, may be eat directly by both husband and wife. Most other authorities disagree with this leniency.

Question

Is a two-section dish counted as one or two plates? What about two different foods on one plate?

See Advanced Rulings, Harchakos, headline "Eating from One Plate" (page 271).

A Husband May Not Eat His Wife's Leftovers

- This *harchakah* is specific to the husband. He may not eat leftovers that remain on his wife's plate after she has finished eating.
- He may, however, eat the food after she has left the room and is not returning soon.
- He may also eat the food after it has been transferred to a "different plate."
  - Rav Moshe Feinstein states that for the above two methods to permit the food to be eaten, there is another condition: it must be no longer recognizable that this food was once his wife's. Aside from putting the serving of food onto a different plate, or her leaving the room, it must be made to look like new to the extent that a stranger would now eat it. Only then can the husband eat it as well.
  - Most authorities disagree, and say that the husband may eat any food as long as it is actually put on a different plate or the wife is no longer there.

  As noted above, a wife may eat her husband's leftovers directly from his plate after he has finished eating.
- Rav Moshe Feinstein does not allow the couple to share "individual portions," such as a can of soda.
- If another person takes from the food on the wife's plate, the husband may also partake of it, as this is indicative that this food is not particularly "hers."

 **Question**

"I drank some of my husband's Coca-Cola before I brought it to him. Do I need to tell him?"

See Advanced Rulings, Harchakos, headline "Leftover Food" (page 273).

A Wife May Not Serve Her Husband in the Usual Way

- When she is a niddah, a wife may not serve an individual portion of food or drink directly in front of her husband. Rather, some change, called a *shinui*, is necessary. (However, the serving bowl, which is meant for everyone at the table, may be placed directly in front of him in the regular manner.)
- Some examples of a *shinui* are:
  - Instead of putting the plate of food directly in front of her husband as she normally does, she places it slightly to the side of where it belongs.
  - He looks away when the item is served.
- This procedure also applies when the husband serves his wife.

 **Question**

What happens if she forgets and serves her husband? May he eat the food?

See Advanced Rulings, Harchakos, headline "The Woman Serving" (page 277).

A Husband May Not Send Alcoholic Beverages to His Wife

- Aside from the general restrictions against a couple's handing something to one another or serving each other directly when the wife is a niddah, a husband must also not "send" — that is, ask someone to give —alcoholic beverages to his wife, or move the serving closer to his wife.

- This restriction applies to wine, beer, grape juice, and other beverages with alcoholic content.
- This restriction does not allow a husband to send his wife a cup filled with wine or the like that is "for her." It does not apply to sending her a bottle of wine that is meant for everyone at the table.
- This applies to the wife as well as the husband.
- In many homes, everyone at the table drinks some of the Kiddush wine on Shabbos. This may be done in the following ways:
  - In a home where the Kiddush cup is passed around for everyone to take from, a man may put the cup down next to his wife even when she is a niddah, because this cup is not "hers." However, he should not pour wine from this cup into her cup.
  - A man may put the cup down on the table in front of where he is sitting, and his wife may take it from there and drink his leftovers, since, as stated, a woman may drink her husband's leftovers.
  - A man may pour many small cups and send them around the table even though one of them is for his wife, since no cup was specifically designated as "hers."

Question

"We were guests at someone's Shabbos table. The host passed me two small cups of wine, for myself and my wife. Am I allowed to pass her a cup?"

See Advanced Rulings, Harchakos, headline "Sending Alcoholic Beverages" (page 279).

A Couple May Not Sit on the Same Surface in a Way That They Feel Each Other's Movements

- Some examples of a surface that they may not sit on together are beds, couches, chairs, benches, and swings.

- This restriction only applies to a surface that is freestanding. They may both sit, however, on a bench or chair, for example, that is attached to the wall or to the ground.
- This restriction only applies when no one is sitting between them.
- Rav Moshe Feinstein explains that the back seat of the car is treated like something that is attached to the ground since a vehicle is large and heavy. They may therefore sit together in a car even if they feel each other's movements.
- A couple may sit on the same couch if they cannot feel each other's movements.
- A couple may not go row boating together when the wife is a niddah if no one else is with them in the boat. However, they may go on a large boat where they will not feel each other's movements.

The following four *harchakos* apply to issues that arise regarding the couple's beds.

A Woman May Not Arrange Her Husband's Bed Before He Goes to Sleep

- This restriction only applies when the woman arranges the bed in front of her husband.
- "Arranging his bed" in this context means that she may not prepare her husband's bed for him before he goes to sleep, for example, by fluffing the pillows as preparation for his sleeping in that bed.
- A woman may make the beds in the morning as part of the housework.

Question

May a husband make his wife's bed?

See Advanced Rulings, Harchakos, headline "Making the Beds" (page 282).

The Couple's Beds Must Be Separated

- The couple's beds must be separated by the distance in which a person can walk between them.
- There is no requirement to put anything between the beds to separate them.

A Husband May Not Sit or Lay on His Wife's Bed

- This applies even when she is not home, whenever she can easily arrive home.

A Woman May Not Lay on Her Husband's Bed

- This restriction only applies in front of him. If he is not present, she may even sleep in his bed.
- A woman may sit on her husband's bed, even in his presence.

A Couple May Not Prepare Water for Each Other to Wash or Bathe

- One may not start the water in the shower or bath for their spouse.
- One may turn on the boiler to heat up the water.
- One may not prepare their spouse's *netilas yadayim* (water for washing one's hands before partaking of bread).
- One may prepare their spouse's *negel vasser* (water for washing one's hands upon awakening).
- This restriction only applies if the spouse is present.

A Couple Should Not Go on a Trip Whose Purpose Is to Spend Time Together

- Traveling to spend time with each other, which is forbidden when the wife is a niddah, means that the couple is:

1. Traveling,
2. Alone, and
3. With no destination.

- The couple may travel alone together if they are going somewhere specific.
- The couple should avoid simply driving around with no destination.
- When traveling together toward a destination, the couple should avoid taking a big detour just to enjoy the route together.
- The couple may take a walk together.
- The couple may go on vacation.

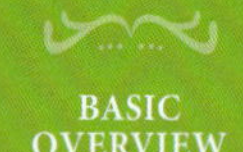

Summary of Harchakos

Intimate	Food	Bedding	Other Laws
Marital relations	*Heker at the table*	*Feeling each other's movements on a seat/couch*	*Preparing water to bathe*
Illicit thoughts	*Sharing plates*	*Arranging bedding before sleep*	*Traveling with no destination*
Looking at the wife's uncovered body	*He cannot eat her leftovers*	*Separate beds*	
Frivolous behavior	*Serving in an unusual manner*	*He may not sit or lie on her bed*	
Touching	*Sending alcoholic beverages*	*She may not lie on his bed*	
Passing			
Throwing			
Singing			

Review Questions for Chapter Two: *Harchakos*

1. Is a niddah couple permitted to hold hands?
2. May a husband hold the door open for his wife while she is a niddah?
3. Can a wife who is a niddah make her husband's bed while cleaning the house?
4. May a niddah couple sit on each other's bed?
5. May a niddah sing in front of her husband?

Answers

1. No. All forms of touching must be avoided.
2. Yes. Such an action is not considered frivolous behavior and is permitted.
3. Yes. Housework is permitted.
4. A husband may not sit on his wife's bed even if she is not present, and a wife may sit on her husband's bed even in front of him.
5. According to some authorities, a woman may sing *zemiros* along with her husband. All other singing should be avoided in front of her husband.

TAHARAH

A story is related about a pious woman who didn't have children for many years. She was due to immerse in the mikvah, and upon emerging from its waters, she noticed an impure animal. She knew, based on Kabbalistic sources, that the first thing a woman sees upon emergence from the mikvah should be someone pure, such as a Jewess.

This holy woman asked the attendant to supervise an additional immersion. Upon emergence from the waters, she noticed another impure source. Again and again she dunked, until she fulfilled this mitzvah to the highest degree possible.

In heaven, an angel stepped forward and beseeched Hashem on behalf of this woman to grant her a child. The angel was instructed to meet the woman and to prophesize about the child's imminent conception. When the angel met the woman, he related to her a special Name with which this child would be granted access to heights of Heaven. He was to use this name if he should need it.

This child was none other than Rebbi Yishmael ben Elisha, the *Kohen Gadol*. It was he who, when the Sages were approached by the Roman officers and threatened with a death sentence, uttered the Heavenly Name to discover whether they should be martyred or resist.

Our Sages teach that purity brings blessing. One must be committed to the observation of the purity process of *hilchos niddah* to the highest

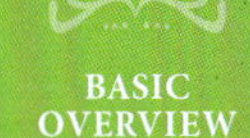

standard. Today, with all of life's conveniences, this is hardly a difficult challenge. Women no longer have to chisel through ice or risk execution to immerse in a mikvah. In most of the world, the mikvah is a beautiful sanctuary, testifying to the beautiful mitzvah apportioned to women.

How does one achieve a high level of purity? By prioritizing responsibility. There will be nights that it will be difficult to immerse on time. There will be challenges. There will be scheduling conflicts. By rising above the challenges and realizing that she is a link in the chain of women who have observed — and prioritized — these halachos for thousands of years, a woman can be confident in knowing that just as she performed this mitzvah to its fullest potential, the reward for this mitzvah on This World and the Next is immense.

Some key terms that will be discussed in this chapter:

Shivah nekiyim — the period of "7 clean days" in which a woman, through regular inspections, shows that she has absolutely stopped bleeding

Poletes shichvas zera — the 72-hour period after marital relations when *zera* (sperm) is emitted from a woman's body

Bedikah (plural: *bedikos*) — the inspection that a woman does to determine that she is clean from uterine bleeding

Bedikah cloth — the clean, white cloth that is used to check that bleeding has stopped

Mareh (plural: *maros*) — questionable *bedikah* cloths that are presented to a *Rav* for a halachic ruling

*Hefsek taha*rah — a *bedikah* that is performed to establish that a woman has stopped bleeding, which allows the *shivah nekiyim* to begin. This *bedikah* often includes a *moch dachuk*.

Moch dachuk — a *bedikah* in which the *bedikah* cloth is left inside the woman's body for a period of time

Chorin v'sedakin — literally, "cracks and crevices"; a thorough *bedikah* that establishes that blood has not been discharged from the uterus for some time

Tevilah — immersion in the mikvah

Chafifah (plural: *chafifos)* — the process that a woman undergoes to prepare for immersion in the mikvah

Chatzitzah — an interposition or separation; something present on the woman's body that prevents the mikvah waters from coming into contact with every area.

Getting "Clean"

Before a woman may immerse in the mikvah to become *tehorah* and be permitted to resume marital relations with her husband, she must first make sure that she is clean from blood for a period of 7 days. These days are called the *shivah nekiyim*. The *shivah nekiyim* are necessary to allow any woman to immerse in the mikvah *anytime* she becomes *temei'ah*, including when she became *temei'ah* because she got her regular period, saw a *kesem*, or is after childbirth. We will soon learn how a woman makes sure that she is in fact totally free of blood during these days.

The First 5 Days

However, the *shivah nekiyim* do not always begin as soon as the uterine bleeding has stopped. Even when blood is no longer present, a minimum of 5 days must pass from the time that the woman first experienced bleeding, before the *shivah nekiyim* may be commenced. The reason for this halachah is because, as we learned in Chapter One, the *zera* present in a woman's body remains for 72 hours following marital relations. Since she is unable to begin the *taharah* procedure as long as *zera* potentially remains within her, the *shivah nekiyim* may not begin within 72 hours of the time that marital relations were last permitted. (This principle is termed *poletes shichvas zera*.) The halachah does not differentiate between whether marital relations took place or not. As long as the blood arrives on a day when intimacy was permissible, she must wait for this time.

This being so, a woman who got her period on Sunday afternoon may not attempt to begin *shivah nekiyim* on any day that part of it is included within this 72-hour period. These days are Sunday (the day the bleeding commenced), Monday (24 hours after Sunday), Tuesday (48 hours after Sunday), and Wednesday (72 hours after Sunday), for a total of 4 days.

In addition, the Rama raises another concern.[4] We know, for example from the fact that Shabbos begins on Friday night, that the Jewish day begins and ends at *shkiah* (sunset). Thus, after *shkiah* on Sunday is halachically already Monday. This means that a woman who got her period on Sunday afternoon may not begin her *shivah nekiyim* until after Wednesday, as we just learned. But, if her period came several hours later, on Sunday *night* which is halachically Monday, her 4 days are now Monday, Tuesday, Wednesday, and Thursday. A woman who gets her period around sundown is not always attuned to whether the bleeding began before sundown — making Sunday her 1st day — or afterwards, which means that her 1st day is Monday, in which case she may not begin her *shivah nekiyim* until after Thursday. The Rama thus rules that every woman adds a 5th day to her pre-*shivah nekiyim* count, so we will always be sure that the *shivah nekiyim* will begin after a 4-day waiting period. A woman who gets her period on Sunday, that is, from sundown after Shabbos to sundown on Sunday, must wait 5 days — Sunday, Monday, Tuesday, Wednesday, and Thursday — before she may try to begin her *shivah nekiyim* at *shkiah on* Thursday, as we will soon learn.

To Summarize:

- The "day" on which the menstrual bleeding began is a "halachah day," which is calculated from *shkiah* to *shkiah*, and not from morning to morning.
- The 1st day of this 5-day period is the day that she got her period or saw a *kesem*, from the time that she began to bleed until *shkiah*. This is true even when the bleeding occurred right before *shkiah*. Thus, the length of "the 1st day" will vary depending on what time she began to bleed. When bleeding commences at night, the "1st day" will last many hours, until "tomorrow's" *shkiah*. If she begins to bleed in the late afternoon, "the 1st day" may only last for a few minutes. Either way, she waits another 4 complete days before *shivah nekiyim* may be begun.
- We observe an extra day before beginning *shivah nekiyim* out of the Rama's concern that a woman may err about which day the bleeding began. With the exception of very extenuating circumstances, this stringency is universally observed. A *Rav* must give explicit permission in order to be lenient in this area.

4. 196:11.

- If a woman got her period or saw a *kesem* during the time of *bein hashmashos* (the period of time immediately after *shkiah* until nightfall), she may be able to count the day before (i.e., from before *shkiah*) as the 1st day. Should this happen, she should make a note of the exact time the bleeding began and call a *Rav*.

- Every woman, irrespective of the last time that the couple actually had marital relations, must wait 5 days from the onset of bleeding before the *shivah nekiyim* can be started.

- The only exception to this rule is a woman for whom intimacy was not permitted beforehand, obviating the halachic concern of *poletes shichvas zera*. Examples include:
  - A kallah preparing to immerse in the mikvah before her wedding need not wait any period of time before beginning to count *shivah nekiyim*.
  - Similarly, a married woman who stains in the middle of *shivah nekiyim*, necessitating her to begin once again, can start again as soon as the bleeding clears up, and need not wait another 5 days.
  - A woman doing a *hefsek taharah* for the first time after childbirth may begin *shivah nekiyim* as soon as she is able to do so. Assuming that she is clear from blood, she may begin the *shivah nekiyim* at *shkiah* at the end of the 5th day after she began bleeding. If her bleeding has not yet finished, as is common with many women, she may begin the *shivah nekiyim* at *shkiah* of any day afterwards.

Hefsek Taharah

Before the *shivah nekiyim* start, we must establish that blood is no longer being discharged from the uterus. To do this, a woman performs a *bedikah* called a *hefsek taharah* right before *shkiah* on the day before Day 1 of the *shivah nekiyim*. The *bedikah* is afterwards inspected to make sure that it is totally clean of blood.

- The ideal time to perform the *hefsek taharah* is from *Minchah ketanah* (about two and a half halachic hours before sundown) until sundown. A *bedikah* done any time after *shkiah* is invalid as a *hefsek taharah*, as the *shivah nekiyim* must be a complete 7 days. (In the event that a woman mistakenly performed a *hefsek taharah* within the first few minutes after *shkiah*, a *Rav* should be consulted, as this may be considered the next day.)

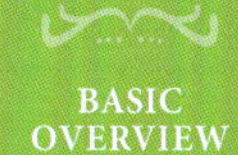

- A woman who is unable to perform her *hefsek taharah* during this time and needs to do it earlier should contact her *Rav*.

- The day of the *hefsek taharah* is not part of the *shivah nekiyim*. A successful *hefsek taharah* allows the *shivah nekiyim* to commence after *shkiah*.

- As with delaying immersing in the mikvah, the halachah disapproves of unnecessarily delaying performing the *hefsek taharah*. If it does need to be delayed, there are halachic ramifications, and this should therefore not be done without Rabbinical guidance.

Since the average menstrual cycle ranges anywhere from 3 to 9 days, it is clear that not every woman will get a clean *hefsek taharah* at the end of the 5th day after the bleeding began.

These are some halachic details regarding a *hefsek taharah*:

- Before performing the *hefsek taharah* a woman should wash the external vaginal area. This is called a *rechitzah*. Some women wash the entire lower half of their bodies, while others are careful to shower the entire body on days that this is permitted, as opposed to Shabbos and Yom Tov. The reason for washing is to ensure that she does not have any blood present from beforehand, which may unnecessarily jeopardize the *hefsek taharah*.

- The *rechitzah* should preferably be done with warm water. If this is not possible, she may wash with cold water, or even a baby wipe. On Shabbos, Yom Kippur, and Tishah B'Av, cold water should be used. On Yom Tov, warm water may be used.

- When a woman performs a *hefsek taharah* and it comes out unclean (i.e., it is not totally free of blood), she may wait a few minutes and try again if it is not yet *shkiah*, to see if she can get a clean one. ("Trying again" is a leniency unique to *hefsek taharah, that does not apply* to any other *bedikah* that a woman does, whether during *shivah nekiyim* or on the day of a *vest*, as we will soon learn.) The reason for this is as we learned above — the *bedikah* of *hefsek taharah* is not one of the *bedikos* of the *shivah nekiyim*. Its function is to show that the bleeding has stopped, thus allowing her to start the *shivah nekiyim* after *shkiah*. This being so, any clean *bedikah* that she gets before *shkiah* establishes that she is no longer bleeding, allowing her to begin the *shivah nekiyim*, provided that it is the last *bedikah* before *shkiah*. (Of course, if her body is still discharging blood, she should wait until the next day and attempt the *hefsek* then.)

As a matter of practicality, a woman should not try more than three or four times to get a clean *hefsek taharah*. Women are sensitive internally, and repeatedly doing *bedikos* will eventually irritate dry skin, possibly causing her to cut herself. Cut dry skin bleeds, and makes it more difficult to get into and through *shivah nekiyim*.

A *bedikah* is always performed using a *bedikah* cloth, which is a totally clean, totally white piece of material that a woman uses to check that she is clean from uterine blood.

The following is a list of halachos relevant to *bedikos*. The first section contains halachos that apply both to the *hefsek taharah* and to the *bedikos* of the *shivah nekiyim*. The second section contains halachos that are unique to the *hefsek taharah*.

How a Bedikah Is Performed

The following points apply to all *bedikos*:

- A *bedikah* should be done with a special *bedikah* cloth purchased for this purpose. A woman should not use ripped-up pieces of clothing unless directed by a *Rav* to do so.

 **Question**

"May I use a tampon for my *bedikos*?"

See Advanced Rulings, Taharah, headline "What to Use for the *Bedikah*" (page 325).

- A woman should check the cloth before the *bedikah* to make sure it is clean and has no red threads on it.
- To be able to fully insert the *bedikah* cloth into her body, the woman should either lie on her back with her knees by her chest, or stand with one foot up on a (toilet) seat.
- She should wrap the cloth around her finger.
- She should gently insert the cloth into her vaginal canal, as deeply as she can easily insert the cloth.
- Once it is inside, she should push the cloth around the internal vaginal walls, and then take the cloth out. Doing this establishes

that there has not been any blood inside of her for some time, and is called doing a *bedikah* in *chorin v'sedakin*, which literally means in "cracks and crevices."

- A *bedikah* that was not done in *chorin v'sedakin* is invalid, unless she left the *bedikah* cloth inside for some time.
- A *bedikah* is invalid if the woman did not get the cloth into her vagina, and just wiped the outside.

If the woman is not able to insert the cloth into her body (due to extreme dryness, for example), she should put some water or lubricant such as KY Jelly into her vaginal canal, and wait a few minutes. She should then try to do the *bedikah* again. Vaseline may not be used, and it is best not to put anything on the *bedikah* cloth itself.

The following points only apply to a *hefsek taharah*, done before the *shivah nekiyim* may begin:

The woman should look at the cloth after the *hefsek taharah* has been done.

- If the cloth is clearly not clean, she should try again, but, as we discussed, never more than three or four times. After that, if she still did not get a clean *bedikah*, she should wait until the next day to try again.
- If she is not sure if the *bedikah* is clean and she does not have the ability to consult a *Rav* and to do another *bedikah* if necessary before *shkiah*, she should try again, as above. If the last (third or fourth) *bedikah* is still unclear, she should wait until the cloth dries. She should then put all the unclear *bedikos* into envelopes to save them to present to the *Rav* for a ruling. She should mark the envelope clearly with her phone number, the time of the *bedikah*, and which *bedikah* it is (for example, "*hefsek taharah*, attempt #2").
- If the cloth is clearly clean, she should not do another *bedikah*. Instead, she should go on to the next step of the *shivah nekiyim* process, which is the *moch dachuk*.

There are many options for a woman who has or suspects she has an internal cut and cannot get clean. See Advanced Rulings, Taharah, headline "The *Bedikos* of *Shivah Nekiyim*" (page 315) and always consult a *Rav*.

Moch Dachuk

When the *bedikah* of the *hefsek taharah* has been done successfully, the woman inserts another *bedikah* cloth into her vagina a few minutes before

shkiah. This one, though, is left there throughout the *bein hashmashos* period, i.e., from before *shkiah* until nightfall (*tzeis hakochavim* – a local *Rav* should be contacted to determine the halachic time of *tzeis hakochavim* that is kept in that town). This additional *bedikah*, called a *moch dachuk*, shows that she entered and began the *shivah nekiyim* in a clean state.

- If the *hefsek taharah* cloth was clean, the woman should simply insert this second *bedikah* cloth into her vagina and leave it there throughout *bein hashmashos*.
- If she is not sure whether the *hefsek taharah* was clean and put it aside to present to a *Rav*, she should take a second cloth, do a thorough *bedikah* of *chorin v'sedakin*, and leave it there throughout *bein hashmashos*. If it turns out that the *hefsek taharah* was not good, the *moch dachuk* will be counted as a valid *hefsek taharah*.
- In the event that a *moch dachuk* causes irritation to sensitive skin, a *Rav* should be consulted. He may advise to skip the *moch*.

Any question regarding either the *hefsek taharah* or the *moch dachuk* should be presented to a *Rav* as soon as possible.

Question

When is the ideal time for inserting the *hefsek taharah* and the *moch dachuk* on *erev Shabbos*, and if Shabbos is being brought in early?

See Advanced Rulings, Taharah, headline "*Hefsek Taharah* and *Moch Dachuk* After Accepting Shabbos"(page 311).

Summary

- The day a woman's bleeding commences is the first of the necessary 5 days before she may do a *hefsek taharah* to begin *shivah nekiyim*, even if it only began shortly before *shkiah*.
- On the 5th day she washes and does a *hefsek taharah*, which is a *bedikah* of *chorin v'sedakin*, at any time between *Minchah ketanah* (about two and a half halachic hours before *shkiah*) and *shkiah*.
- After the *hefsek taharah*, she performs a *moch dachuk*, which remains inside her throughout *bein hashmashos* (from before *shkiah* until nightfall).

The Five Days

Sunday	Monday	Tuesday	Wednesday	Thursday	Friday	Shabbos
1 **DAY 1** *Period Begins* 2 P.M.	2 **DAY 2**	3 **DAY 3**	4 **DAY 4**	5 **DAY 5** *Rechitzah Hefsek Moch*	6	7
8	9	10	11	12	13	14
15	16	17	18	19	20	21
22	23	24	25	26	27	28
29	30					

Shivah Nekiyim

Now that she has established that she is clean of blood, and night has fallen, the woman's *shivah nekiyim* have begun. After inserting the *moch dachuk* (right before *shkiah*), she should change into white underwear. Many women also put a white sheet on their bed for the duration of *shivah nekiyim.*

Two *bedikos* of *chorin v'sedakin* are done each day — one in the morning and one in the afternoon. These *bedikos* done over the course of a week establish that she has certainly stopped bleeding, and are a halachic prerequisite to her subsequent immersion in the mikvah.

- One *bedikah* is done in the morning at any time between sunrise (*neitz hachamah*) and halachic midday (*chatzos*), and one *bedikah* is done in the afternoon, ideally between *Minchah ketanah* and sundown.
- A woman who missed a *bedikah* or foresees herself having to miss one should consult a *Rav*. The woman should inspect the *bedikah* cloth after every *bedikah* to make sure that it is clean and blood-free. Any questionable *bedikos* should immediately be taken to a *Rav*, marked with her phone number and a description of which *bedikah* it is (for example, "afternoon *bedikah* of the 5th day of *shivah nekiyim*"). Similarly, the woman should examine her white underwear at the end of each day to ensure that no staining took place.

In the event that a *bedikah* comes out unclean, or the woman begins to stain, the *shivah nekiyim* have been invalidated and may not be continued. She may try to begin again with a new *hefsek taharah* and *moch dachuk* in the late afternoon hours, just like she did the first time. If these are clean, that night and the following day are Day 1 of her new *shivah nekiyim.*

If a *bedikah* was inadvertently missed, a *Rav* should be consulted.

Summary

- The day a woman's bleeding commences is the first of the necessary 5 days before she may do a *hefsek taharah* to begin *shivah nekiyim*, even if it only began shortly before *shkiah*.
- On the 5th day she washes and does a *hefsek taharah*, which is a *bedikah* of *chorin v'sedakin*, at any time between *Minchah ketanah* (about two and a half halachic hours before *shkiah*) and *shkiah*.
- After the *hefsek taharah*, she performs a *moch dachuk*, which remains inside her throughout *bein hashmashos* (from before *shkiah* until nightfall).
- The woman should change into white underwear at *shkiah*.
- That night and the following day (which is, at the earliest, the 6th day following the time that she began bleeding) is Day 1 of *shivah nekiyim*. On the night after Day 7 of *shivah nekiyim* she immerses in the mikvah.
- A woman performs two *bedikos* of *chorin v'sedakin* every day of *shivah nekiyim* — one in the morning and one in the evening.
- There are thus sixteen *bedikos* in total: the *hefsek taharah*, the *moch dachuk*, and two *bedikos* a day for 7 days.
- The woman should check each *bedikah*, as well as her underwear for staining, throughout *shivah nekiyim*.
- The day of the week on which a successful *hefsek taharah* is done (during the day) will be the same as the day of the following week on which she will be able to immerse in the mikvah (in the night). This is obviously assuming that her *shivah nekiyim* are successfully completed. For example, if she performs a successful *hefsek taharah* on Thursday afternoon, then, after a successful *shivah nekiyim*, she will go to the mikvah on the following Thursday night.

Shivah Nekiyim

Sunday	Monday	Tuesday	Wednesday	Thursday	Friday	Shabbos
1 DAY 1 *Period Begins* 2 P.M.	2 DAY 2	3 DAY 3	4 DAY 4	5 DAY 5 *Rechitzah Hefsek Moch*	6 DAY 1 *Shiva Nekiyim* *2 Bedikos*	7 DAY 2 *Shiva Nekiyim* *2 Bedikos*
8 DAY 3 *Shiva Nekiyim* *2 Bedikos*	9 DAY 4 *Shiva Nekiyim* *2 Bedikos*	10 DAY 5 *Shiva Nekiyim* *2 Bedikos*	11 DAY 6 *Shiva Nekiyim* *2 Bedikos*	12 DAY 7 *Shiva Nekiyim* *2 Bedikos*	13	14
15	16	17	18	19	20	21
22	23	24	25	26	27	28
29	30					

Tevilah

Once the *shivah nekiyim* have been successfully completed, a woman immerses in the mikvah to complete her *taharah* process. Since a *hefsek taharah* may not be done until the end of the 5th day from the commencement of bleeding, and the *shivah nekiyim* are 7 days (a concept that is often referred to as "5 and 7"), the earliest that a woman may immerse in the mikvah is on the night beginning the 13th day of her cycle.

One should go to the mikvah at the first available opportunity and not push it off to the next night. Only very extenuating circumstances may justify this. See Advanced Rulings, Taharah, headlines "Prioritizing *Tevilah* on Time" and "Pushing Off Going to the Mikvah" (pages 338 & 339).

In order for her *tevilah* to be effective, a woman must immerse her entire body in the mikvah waters at the same time. If even one strand of hair remains floating above the waters, the *tevilah* is meaningless and she remains a *niddah d'Oraisa*.

Another important rule of mikvah immersion is that at the moment of immersion, the mikvah waters must be touching the person's entire body. Something that covers an area of the person's body in a way that blocks the water from coming into contact with this area is called a *chatzitzah*.

The halachah discusses three degrees of *chatzitzah* that a woman must be concerned with:

1. *Chatzitzah d'Oraisa* (a Torah-law *chatzitzah*)
2. *Chatzitzah d'Rabbanan* (a Rabbinic-law *chatzitzah*)
3. The Rama's ideal guidelines

We will now study these three categories.

1. A *chatzitzah d'Oraisa* is something that covers most of a person's body, that the person does not want to be there. (The halachic definition of something the person "does not want to be there" is that either she or most people do not want this object on their body, and they would not let a week go by without taking it off.) For example, a woman who immerses while wearing a wet suit would remain a *niddah d'Oraisa*.

Question

A woman is on vacation and there is no mikvah, only the beach. May she dip in her clothes?

See Advanced Rulings, Taharah, headlines Immersing in Clothing" (page 342) and "Immersing in a Public Place" (page 370).

2. A *chatzitzah d'Rabbanan* is when only one of these two criteria is present. It is either something that covers most of a person's body that the person does not mind having there, or it is some-

thing that covers part (less than half) of the body and the person does not want it to be there. For example, a Band-Aid that adheres to part of the body, which most people would not want on their body for a long period of time, is a *chatzitzah d'Rabbanan*.

3. The Rama writes that a woman should ideally remove anything that impedes the mikvah waters from coming into contact with part of her body, even if it only covers a small part of the body and she really does not mind that it is there. For example, although a woman may want to immerse with nail polish, she should remove it, even though she may want the nail polish on her nails for a long period of time.

Chafifah

In order to avoid anything being present on a woman's body that might constitute a *chatzitzah*, the halachah requires that she does her best to make sure that her body is absolutely clean before she immerses in the mikvah. This cleansing is called *chafifah* (plural: *chafifos*). Should a woman immerse in the mikvah without first doing *chafifos*, even if she assumes that she was clean, the immersion is invalid, and she must immerse once again after having done *chafifos*.

We will soon discuss examples of which things must be removed and how a woman should remove them.

Some things to remember about *chatzitzos*:

- A woman must immerse in the mikvah again if any type of *chatzitzah* is found.
- The halachos of *chatzitzah* apply to internal bodily orifices, called *beis hastarim* (discussed below in headline "Preparations and Immersing in the Mikvah [page 54] within the list of *chafifos*), as well.
- A couple that discovers a *chatzitzah* after the woman has already come back from the mikvah should call a *Rav*, whether or not they have already been intimate. These questions are relatively common, and in many cases the *Rav* can be lenient. There is no reason for the woman to have to return to the mikvah with all of the preparations it entails just because they were too embarrassed to call a *Rav*.

The Ideal Time to Prepare for Tevilah

The Gemara says that *chafifos* should be done close to the *tevilah*. There are three opinions as to when a woman should do *chafifos*:

1. *Rashi* — A woman should do *chafifos* during the day of Day 7 of *shivah nekiyim*. This is preferable to doing them at night before she immerses in the mikvah, because this way there is no concern of her rushing through her *chafifos* in her hurry to get home. Rashi holds that the *onah* (the day or night, which we will soon define, in Chapter Four) immediately prior to the *tevilah* is still considered "close to the *tevilah*."

2. *Tosafos* (*She'iltos*) — The *chafifos* should be done at night so they will be as close to her *tevilah* as possible. This way there is the least chance of having a *chatzitzah* when she immerses.

3. *Rosh* — The woman should begin doing *chafifos* during the day before *shkiah*, and continue through *bein hashmashos* until nightfall, when she may go to the mikvah for *tevilah*. This way her *chafifos* will be close to her *tevilah*, but, since she began when it was still daytime, there is no concern that she will rush and do a less than thorough job.

Ideally, we try to fulfill the Rosh's opinion, by beginning *chafifos* before *shkiah* and completing them at nightfall and immersing immediately after nightfall. When this is difficult, for example, a woman is at work during these hours, she may start her *chafifah* process by doing one *chafifah* at any time during the day (in line with *Rashi*), and do the rest of the *chafifos* at night (like the *She'iltos*).

When a woman cannot begin *chafifos* during the day at all, she may do everything at night. However, she must then spend a full hour on the *chafifos*. The reason for this is that we are concerned that she will rush through her *chafifos* in order to get home. When she knows that she must spend at least an hour preparing herself, she will take her time and do a good job.

Some women are taught that they must spend at least a half hour on the *chafifos* when they start during the day. Some are even taught that they have to spend a half hour in the bath alone. This practice is not brought in any source; rather, a woman may spend as long or as short as it takes her to properly remove all *chatzitzos* from her body. If she is spending too little time, however, she is probably not getting the job done, and she should be certain she is doing a thorough job for these important preparations.

Preparing for Immersion on or after Shabbos and Yom Tov

The halachos that we have just discussed are for a woman who is going to the mikvah on a regular night. On Shabbos or Yom Tov, when many of the procedures necessary for *chafifos* may not be performed due to Shabbos restrictions, the halachos are slightly different.

- When a *tevilah* occurs on Shabbos or Yom Tov night, the woman makes all of her preparations on *erev Shabbos* or *erev Yom Tov*, ties up her hair, lights candles, and walks to the mikvah. Once there, she immerses in the mikvah. She does nothing at the mikvah building to prepare. She should be careful to look herself over immediately prior to immersion (*iyun*) and should be careful to avoid coming in contact with anything that may cause a *chatzitzah* subsequent to preparing for the mikvah. The same applies if she is immersing on the second night of a 2-day Yom Tov, or when Yom Tov and Shabbos are next to each other (or the third night of a 3-day Shabbos and Yom Tov).
- Some *Rabbanim* allow women to wear Shabbat Makeup, which is specially formulated makeup that does not adhere to the skin well and is permissible to apply on Shabbos according to some authorities.
- When a *tevilah* occurs on Motzaei Shabbos or Motzaei Yom Tov, the woman does all of her *chafifos* on Friday or on *erev Yom Tov*, and just does a basic overall *chafifah* before she immerses. She should only wear easily removable makeup over Shabbos or Yom Tov.
- When a *tevilah* occurs following a 3-day Yom Tov, she should do something to prepare on *erev Yom Tov*, and should perform the bulk of the preparations after Shabbos or Yom Tov.

Preparations and Immersing in the Mikvah

The *chafifos* that a woman does to remove any possible *chatzitzah* from her body include the following:

- The woman removes all nail polish, jewelry, bandages and all of their residue, makeup, smoking or birth control patches, contact lenses, marks from pens, pencils, paint or markers, and temporary tattoos.

Question

What should a woman do if she has cuts, scabs, or blisters on the day of *tevilah*?

See Advanced Rulings, Taharah, headline "Calluses, Blisters, and Dry Blood" (page 353).

- She calls a *Rav* if she has retainers, stitches, casts, temporary fillings, or tattoos.
- She cleans all internal bodily orifices, called *beis hastarim*, including her ears, mouth and teeth, and naval, and removes vaginal birth control devices and the like.
- She cuts (and files) both her fingernails and toenails.
- She takes a hot bath.
- She makes sure not to use anything that leaves a film on the skin, for example, oils or residual soaps.
- On a regular night, the woman takes a shower, combs her hair well, and inspects her body for *chatzitzos* in the mikvah building before immersion. This inspection is called *iyun*, and it is an imperative part of the preparations. On Shabbos and Yom Tov nights, she combs her hair well before Shabbos or Yom Tov, and inspects her body for *chatzitzos* at home.
- As a piece of advice, a woman should do the second *bedikah* of Day 7 a bit earlier than usual (but not too early — from after the time of *Minchah ketanah*). This way, in case there is a question on the *bedikah*, she can bring it to the *Rav* early, and go straight to the mikvah when she finishes *chafifos*.

In general, a woman should stay away from foods and activities that may cause *chatzitzos* on the day that she will be immersing in the mikvah. The commentaries specifically discuss baking challah and eating meat and chicken. Some other examples are eating peanut chews, popcorn, and the like, and drinking orange juice with pulp.

Question

"I need to have a haircut. Must I do it before going to the mikvah, and may I do it on the day of the *tevilah*?"

See Advanced Rulings, Taharah, headline "*Chafifah* on Hair and Shaving Hair" (page 347).

At the mikvah there is an attendant, often known as a mikvah lady or *balanit*, who watches a woman immerse. The reason for this is primarily to be sure that no part of her body or hair remained above the water during *tevilah*, thereby invalidating the *tevilah*. The mikvah lady generally has a checklist, and asks the woman who is about to immerse questions to be certain that she did not forget any of the *chafifos*. A woman should not rely on the mikvah lady, however, and should make sure to take care of everything herself.

When in the mikvah waters, a woman should fully immerse under the water, come up and say the *brachah* with a hand across her midsection, and then fully immerse a second time.

For more detailed instructions regarding the mode of *tevilah*, see Advanced Rulings, Taharah, headline "The *Brachah* and the *Tevilah*" (page 371).

- A woman should look at the mikvah lady after immersing, in order that the first thing that she sees is something *tahor*.
- As a piece of advice, the woman should do something that causes a *chatzitzah* after she comes out of the water. This can include rubbing the towel hard against her body, messing up her hair, eating something sticky (for example, a peanut chew), or scratching her finger- or toenails on a tile. This will help her later if she finds a *chatzitzah*, as this gives the *Rav* something that he may attribute it to.
- A woman should not shower in the mikvah building after she immerses. She may, however, shower after she gets home, after interacting with her husband in a way that breaks the *harchakos*.
- The woman should change into dark underwear after *tzeis hakochavim*.
- Upon arriving home, she should tell her husband that she is now *tehorah*.
- If, after she has returned from the mikvah, a woman notices something that may have been a *chatzitzah* at the time of immersion, she should contact a *Rav* right away.

Mikvah Prep Chart

The Day of Immmersion

It is advisable to refrain from kneading dough, using glue, paint or any other substance which is difficult to remove.

Meat and chicken should not be eaten, except in honor of the Sabbath or a Jewish holiday.

It is preferable to shave/wax any body hairs prior to day of immersion to avoid residue.

Preparations (at home or at the Mikveh)

- ▢ **Remove all make-up.**
- ▢ **Remove nail polish, fingers and toes.**
- ▢ **Cut and file nails, fingers and toes.**
- ▢ **Clean inside ears and nose.**
- ▢ **Brush and floss teeth.**
- ▢ **Remove all jewelry, including necklace, braclets, earrings and rings.**
- ▢ **Soak in a warm/hot bath as long as it takes for any dried dirt to be removed. Wash entire body with soap and clean hair with shampoo.**
- ▢ **Remove any easily-removable calluses and scabs.**

At the Mikveh

- ▢ **Shower in warm/hot water.**
- ▢ **Comb all hair to remove knots.**
- ▢ **Visually inspect entire body for any chatzitzahs.**
- ▢ **Remove contact lenses or glasses.**

Review Questions for Chapter Three

1. What is the earliest time after a woman becomes *temei'ah* that she can perform a *hefsek taharah*?
2. Which three things should be performed the day a woman performs a *hefsek taharah*?
3. What should be done when one has a questionable *bedikah*?
4. When is the ideal time to begin preparations for immersion in the mikvah on a weeknight?
5. When is the ideal time to begin preparations for immersion in the mikvah on a Motzaei Shabbos?

Answers

1. The earliest a woman may perform a *hefsek taharah* is on Day 5 of the *tumah*, preferably between *Minchah ketanah* and *shkiah*.
2. She does a *rechitzah*, *hefsek taharah*, and *moch dachuk*.
3. It should be preserved, labeled, and presented to a *Rav* for inspection.
4. The majority of preparations should take place during the day. Finishing touches should occur at night.
5. The majority of preparations should take place during the day on Friday. A basic, overall *chafifah* should occur at night on Motzaei Shabbos.

VESTOS

When a woman emerges from the mikvah waters she is in a state of purity. This should not change until she sees blood again in the upcoming month. However, the Gemara warns, based on a *passuk* in the Torah, that one should separate from his wife as she nears the time of her anticipated flow. This is called a *vest*.

A woman gets her period based on one of many variables: it could be the length of time between her cycles, a specific date of the month, or any other such pattern. In fact, in the days of the Gemara women would see blood on a specific date or at a specific time, on a consistent basis. This idea is called a *vest kavua*, which literally means she has established that the anticipated flow and the actual flow actually occur in the same time three times in a row.

Nowadays, women see blood with less predictability than in yesteryear. Nevertheless, we are required to separate each month on the dates and times she expects the period to arrive, based on the previous month's date and time. This is called a *vest she'eino kavua*. It is observed one month at a time. Once the period has not arrived on the *vest*, the *vest* is uprooted and a new *vest* is created.

Should she see blood three months in a row in a specific pattern, she may create a *vest kavua*, which will then be observed for the upcoming three months.

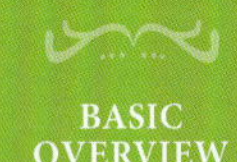

Hilchos niddah are so important that *Chazal* implemented these "blackout dates" to prevent one from being intimate with his wife and subsequently finding out that she was bleeding during intimacy.

Some key terms that will be discussed in this chapter:

Vest — a day on which we may assume that there is a significant chance that a woman will get her period

Vest kavua — a "fixed *vest*"; the set day that a woman gets her period each month

Vest she'eino kavua — a "non-fixed *vest*"; a day that a woman got her period once and therefore, even though she does not always get it on this day each month, there is a chance that she will

Onah (plural: *onos*) — literally, time; the part of the day from *shkiah* to sunrise, and the part of the day from sunrise to *shkiah*.

The Reason for Vestos

If a woman gets her period while the couple is in the middle of marital relations, and this may reasonably have been avoided, she and her husband have committed a severe sin.

In order to prevent this from happening, the Sages decreed that marital relations are forbidden on certain days of the month — although she has not yet gotten her period — because based on previous patterns, we must be concerned that she may get her period on that day. A day on which we may assume she may get her period is called a *vest* (plural: *vestos*). A *vest* is created when we detect something — a catalyst, sign, or trigger — that had caused the period to begin in a different month, which may trigger it once again.

In the laws of niddah, the halachah does not look at "days," but rather at "*onos*," which is the period of time from *shkiah* to sunrise, and the period of time from sunrise to *shkiah*. The Gemara says that a couple must separate for the entire *onah* that a *vest* occurs, which is the *onah* in which her period began last month.

For example, if she began bleeding last month on a particular date at eleven o'clock at night, marital relations are forbidden during the nighttime hours, from *shkiah* to sunrise the next morning, on the

upcoming *vestos*. Similarly, when looking for patterns from one month to the next, as we will soon discuss, we do not only look for the "day" on which the period occurred, but rather, the *onah* of a particular date.

To illustrate this example further: A period that occurs during the daytime hours of the 10th day of the Hebrew month creates a *vest*, as will be explained. A period that occurs during the nighttime hours of the 10th day of the Hebrew month will create a different *vest*. Although both periods occurred on the 10th day of the Hebrew month, since they occurred during different *onos* the *vestos* will be different, as we will explain.

A Vest That Came and Went Without Incident

Marital relations are prohibited on the *onah* of the *vest*, since we are concerned that the woman's period is about to come. If the *vest* passes uneventfully and the period does not commence, however, there is no need for the couple to separate any longer. The reason for this is as we explained; a *vest* is based on a concern that something will trigger the woman's period to occur, and does not come from the concern that she has one less day left in her cycle. This being so, when the trigger day passed without issue, there is no reason for further separation and concern.

For example, a woman's *vest* occurs on a certain Sunday during the day. Marital relations are prohibited on Sunday, but are permitted on Shabbos and Monday. Whatever reason we thought that Sunday might trigger her period has nothing to do with Shabbos or Monday.

Nevertheless, we will learn that certain precautions must be taken on days that are not *vestos* on which we suspect she might get her period, even when no actual *vest* has been created.

Vest Kavua

Up until several hundred years ago, almost every woman had a *vest kavua* (a fixed cycle), which means a woman would get her period on the same day each month. In the times of *Chazal*, women had a fixed cycle not only for the day, but could expect to get their period at a certain *time* of day, as well.

Vest SheEino Kavua

Nowadays, nearly every woman has a *vest she'eino kavua* (a non-fixed cycle). The woman knows that she will get her period approximately once a month, but not necessarily on the same day or at the same time as she did last month. Instead, one month her period may occur 28 days after it did last month, the next month on a 33-day cycle, the next month after 30 days, and so on.

What changed?

Everything! People's lifestyles and diets were much simpler a few hundred years ago than they are now. People's schedules were much simpler as well; they woke up at dawn and went to sleep at nightfall. Nowadays, we live in the age of prepared foods and technology. The foods we eat, the lifestyles we live, and the technology we have in our lives throws women's bodily clocks off track.

The *Chavas Daas* explains that a woman's cycle is regulated by the light of the sun. In the days when people woke up and went to sleep with the sun, they were regulated. Today everyone is on a different schedule, with electric lights on all the time. This constant change throws a woman's cycle off.

Although women nowadays cannot generally expect their period to begin on a precise day, the halachos of *vestos* still apply, as a *vest she'eino kavua.*

Here are some differences between a *vest kavua* and a *vest she'eino kavua*:

- A *vest kavua* is established through a pattern of a woman getting her period on a certain day, or following a particular pattern, three cycles in a row. A *vest she'eino kavua* is a cycle or pattern that has only happened once or twice.

The Number of Months That This Vest Must Be Observed

- A woman who has a *vest she'eino kavua* must "observe this *vest*," that is, separate from her husband on the day that the period is expected to begin, for the next month. If, for example, her period last month came during the daytime of the 5th day of the Hebrew month, marital relations will be forbidden the day onah *of t*he 5th day of the following month. (That is, the fact that she got her period at this time causes us to be concerned that she will get it next month at this time as well.) If, after this date during the second month, we see that the time has passed without incident and her period did not begin, she no longer needs to remain concerned about this time in the future.

- A *vest kavua*, however, must be observed for the next 3 months after it has been established. Only after this *onah* passes three times without incident may the couple resume marital relations during this time each month.

Vest Kavuah (Yom Hachodesh)

Month:	*1*	*2*	*3*
Actual Period Began *(Date of the month)*	**5 Nissan** *During the Day*	**5 Iyar** *During the Day*	**5 Sivan** *During the Day*

Upcoming Month:	*2*	*3*	*4*	*5*	*6*
Vest *(Expected Period)*	**5 Iyar** *During the Day*	**5 Sivan** *During the Day*	**5 Tamuz** *During the Day*	**5 Av** *During the Day*	**5 Elul** *During the Day*

Summary: The first three months, the period is not yet established, and the vestos therefore reflect a month-by-month expectation of the upcoming period. Once the period develops into a pattern, three months of the same vest being "fulfilled," three of the same vest are projected into the future.

Once a *vest* has been established three months in a row, it must be observed for the following three months. As we will soon see, although deviating from a *vest kavuah* three times in a row mitigates the requirement to observe the *vest kavuah*, the *vest kavuah* is not completely "uprooted" until a new *vest kavuah* is established, and may need to be observed if the period occurs on the date of the dormant *vest kavuah*. See Background and Analysis, Vestos, Headline "Creating a Vest Kavuah" (page 168).

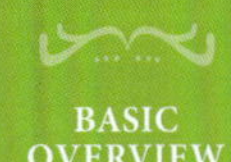

Vest She'eino Kavuah (Yom Hachodesh)

Month:	*1*	*2*	*3*	*4*	*5*
Actual Period Began *(Date of the month)*	5 Nissan *During the Day*	6 Iyar *During the Day*	4 Tamuz *During the Night*	7 Av *During the Day*	8 Elul *During the Day*
Upcoming Month:	*2*	*3*	*4*	*5*	*6*
Vest *(Expected Period)*	5 Iyar *During the Day*	6 Tamuz *During the Day*	4 Av *During the Night*	7 Elul *During the Day*	8 Tishrei *During the Day*

Summary: Since no pattern is detected, each vest is observed in the upcoming month only. Once that day is "broken" by the period arriving on an alternate date than what was anticipated, the vest is disregarded for future months.

Since almost every woman nowadays only has a *vest she'eino kavua*, we will first focus on the halachos pertaining to it. We will then discuss some halachos of *vest kavua* that a couple should remain aware of, so they can be on the lookout to see if a *vest kavua* arises.

These are some basic rules about *vestos*:

- *Vestos* are patterns that we infer from studying the times that a woman has recently gotten her period. We are concerned that something about this pattern triggers her period, which will cause her period to come once again, according to this pattern.
- *Vestos* are set using *onos*, which are the part of the day between *shkiah* and sunrise and the part between sunrise and *shkiah*. If one month a woman's period began at night, the couple must separate during this entire night *onah* the following month.
- Sometimes it is easy to know the *onah* that the period began, such as if it happened at a time that is clearly daytime or clearly nighttime. Sometimes it is more complicated, when it is close to sunrise and *shkiah*. It is very important to remember the exact time that a woman's period began, and is always best to write down the exact time and date when it happens. When it is unclear when the period began, for example, before or after *shkiah*, we generally rely on the pattern that she has previously

established to establish that the period came in the later *onah*. A *Rav* should be consulted when there is doubt.

- *Vestos* for future months are established based on the day and *onah* that a woman got her period and began bleeding. While she of course remains *temei'ah* during the times that she continues bleeding until she immerses in the mikvah after completing her *taharah* procedure, these days do not play a role in establishing a *vest* pattern of concern for the future.

Question

What happens if she wrote down the date and time of her period, but she lost the calendar?

See Advanced Rulings, Vestos, Headline "*Vestos*: Lost Calendar" (page 414).

Types of Vestos

What causes a woman to get her period?

The answer is, any one of several different factors. There are a few *vestos* that a woman who does not have a *vest kavua* must observe every month. We are concerned that any of these patterns is the catalyst that triggers her period to occur, in the same circumstances as it happened last month. Three of these *vestos* are required by halachah. Several others are stringencies that have been adopted by many Jewish communities.

The three *vestos* that the halachah requires a woman who does not have a *vest kavua* to observe are:

1. *Yom hachodesh* — the date of the Hebrew month
2. *Onah beinonis* — the average cycle of most women
3. *Haflagah* — the length of her most recent cycle

Yom HaChodesh

The *yom hachodesh* is the Hebrew date on which a woman got her period. For example, when a woman's period comes on 18 Tishrei during the day, a *vest she'eino kavua* is created for 18 Cheshvan during the day.

- Don't forget that the night preceeds the day in the Jewish calendar!
- The *yom hachodesh* is, at this moment, a *vest she'eino kavua*, for there is no immediate history of the woman's period beginning on this date. This being the case, when she deviates from the *vest* for 1 month — because her period did not begin on that date and in the same *onah* as it did in the previous month — this date becomes no longer relevant. (If the woman got her period on the same date and *onah* three times in a row, however, the *yom hachodesh* then becomes her *vest kavua*, which will be discussed soon.)

Sunday	Monday	Tuesday	Wednesday	Thursday	Friday	Shabbos
1 Oct *11 Tishrei*	*2 Oct* *11 Tishrei*	*3 Oct* *11 Tishrei*	*4 Oct* *11 Tishrei*	*5 Oct* *13 Cheshvan*	*6 Oct* *14 Cheshvan*	*7 Oct* *15 Cheshvan*
8 Oct ***18 Tishrei*** DAY 1 *Period* DAY 10 AM	*9 Oct* ***19 Tishrei***	*10 Oct* ***20 Tishrei***	*11 Oct* ***21 Tishrei***	*12 Oct* ***22 Tishrei***	*13 Oct* ***23 Tishrei***	*14 Oct* ***24 Tishrei***
15 Oct *25 Tishrei*	*16 Oct* *26 Tishrei*	*17 Oct* *27 Tishrei*	*18 Oct* *28 Tishrei*	*19 Oct* *29 Tishrei*	*20 Oct* *30 Tishrei*	*21 Oct* *1 Cheshvan*
22 Oct *2 Cheshvan*	*23 Oct* *3 Cheshvan*	*24 Oct* *4 Cheshvan*	*25 Oct* *5 Cheshvan*	*26 Oct* *6 Cheshvan*	*27 Oct* *7 Cheshvan*	*28 Oct* *8 Cheshvan*
29 Oct *9 Cheshvan*	*30 Oct* *10 Cheshvan*	*31 Oct* *11 Cheshvan*				

In our example, if this woman got her period any time other than 18 Cheshvan during the day, the daytime hours of the 18th of future months no longer need be observed as a *vest*.

Sunday	Monday	Tuesday	Wednesday	Thursday	Friday	Shabbos
			1 Nov 12 Chesvan	2 Nov 13 Cheshvan	3 Nov 14 Cheshvan	4 Nov 15 Cheshvan
5 Nov 16 Cheshvan	6 Nov 17 Cheshvan	7 Nov 18 Cheshvan Yom Hachodesh DAY	8 Nov 19 Cheshvan	9 Nov 20 Cheshvan	10 Nov 21Cheshvan	11 Nov 22 Cheshvan
12 Nov 23 Cheshvan	13 Nov 24 Cheshvan	14 Nov 25 Cheshvan	15 Nov 26 Cheshvan	16 Nov 27 Cheshvan	17 Nov 28 Cheshvan	18 Nov 29 Cheshvan
19 Nov 1 Kislev	20 Nov 2 Kislev	21 Nov 3 Kislev	22 Nov 4 Kislev	23 Nov 5 Kislev	24 Nov 6 Kislev	25 Nov 7 Kislev
26 Nov 8 Kislev	27 Nov 9 Kislev	28 Nov 10 Kislev	29 Nov 11 Kislev	30 Nov 12 Kislev		

Onah Beinonis

The *onah beinonis* (literally, average *onah*) is the span of the average menstrual cycle of most women, which the Gemara tells us is 30 days. As long as a woman has not established her own *vest kavua*, we are concerned that her next period will occur 30 days after her last one. The date that her last period started is Day 1. Day 30 is thus the *onah beinonis*, on which marital relations are prohibited. The *onah beinonis* is the same *onah* as the last period occurred, 30 days later. Therefore, if the last period began during the night, the *onah beinonis* is observed during the night of the 30th day. If the last period began during the day, the *vest* will be during the day.

BASIC OVERVIEW
HOW A WOMAN BECOMES A NIDDAH
Miscellaneous Laws
Niddah D'Oraisah
Period
Bedikah, Relations and Restroom
Niddah D'Rabbanan
Stains
Other forms of Tumah
HARCHAKOS
Intimate Separations
Eating Restrictions
Seats and Bedding
Additional Restrictions
TAHARA
The Five Day Wait
Rechitzah, Hefsek, Moch and Bedikahs
Shivah Nekiyim
Mikveh Preparations & Immersion
VESTOS
Understanding Vestos
Calculating Basic Vestos
Conduct on a Vest
Vestos Stringencies
Birth control and Vestos
Additional Vestos concepts

In our example, since the period commenced during the day of 18 Tishrei, *onah beinonis* will be observed 30 days later, on 17 Cheshvan during the day.

Sunday	Monday	Tuesday	Wednesday	Thursday	Friday	Shabbos
			1 Nov *12 Chesvan*	*2 Nov* *13 Cheshvan*	*3 Nov* *14 Cheshvan*	*4 Nov* *15 Cheshvan*
5 Nov *16 Cheshvan*	*6 Nov* *17 Cheshvan* DAY 30 ***Onah Beinonis DAY***	*7 Nov* *18 Cheshvan* ***Yom Hachodesh DAY***	*8 Nov* *19 Cheshvan*	*9 Nov* *20 Cheshvan*	*10 Nov* *21Cheshvan*	*11 Nov* *22 Cheshvan*
12 Nov *23 Cheshvan*	*13 Nov* *24 Cheshvan*	*14 Nov* *25 Cheshvan*	*15 Nov* *26 Cheshvan*	*16 Nov* *27 Cheshvan*	*17 Nov* *28 Cheshvan*	*18 Nov* *29 Cheshvan*
19 Nov *1 Kislev*	*20 Nov* *2 Kislev*	*21 Nov* *3 Kislev*	*22 Nov* *4 Kislev*	*23 Nov* *5 Kislev*	*24 Nov* *6 Kislev*	*25 Nov* *7 Kislev*
26 Nov *8 Kislev*	*27 Nov* *9 Kislev*	*28 Nov* *10 Kislev*	*29 Nov* *11 Kislev*	*30 Nov* *12 Kislev*		

The *vest* of *onah beinonis* applies every month when there is no *vest kavua*, whether or not the woman actually got her period on Day 30 of her last cycle.

Haflagah

The third *vest* that every woman who does not have a *vest kavua* must always observe is the *vest haflagah* — the interval of days between her last periods.

This is how the interval, and upcoming *vest haflagah*, is calculated.

1. A woman checks her calendar to ascertain the Hebrew dates of her two last periods. (Don't forget that the Hebrew date begins at nightfall.)

2. She counts the number of days between these two dates. The first date (that is, the day of the first of these two periods) is counted as Day 1, and the second date (the date of the second of these two periods being calculated) is the final date of the tally. This number of dates — that is, the length of her cycle — is the "interval." (The interval between the two dates is counted even when one period began during the daytime *onah*, and the other during the nighttime *onah*, or the opposite, as the focus is on the dates, not the *onos*.)

3. Using the number of dates that she has just calculated, the woman now counts again. This time, the latest period (the second of the two periods that were just calculated) is counted as the 1st day. The amount of the "interval" is counted from the date of the latest period (again, including the date of the latest period as Day 1). Since we are concerned that the future period will come after the same interval as the previous one, this future date becomes a *vest*, a day of concern.

The premise behind the *vest haflagah* is to calculate the upcoming anticipated date, the *vest*, based on the *actual* length of the previous cycle. Therefore, we must first calculate the amount of dates that occured in the previous cycle, by counting the first date of the last period, through the first date of the current period. That will determine the length of the cycle. We can now count that amount of dates forward toward the anticipated date for the upcoming period, the *vest haflagah*.

The *vest haflagah* is, in a way, more logical of a calculation, as compared with the *vestos* of *yom hachodesh* and *onah beinonis*, as it is specifically dependent upon each individual woman and the actual length of her monthly cycle. This is in contrast to the *vestos* of *yom hachodesh* and *onah beinonis* which are objectivly projected based on the "monthly cycle"

This calculation may sound complicated. But it's really not so hard. Let's continue with our previous example.

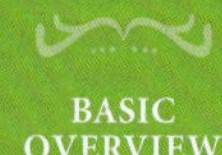

Sunday	Monday	Tuesday	Wednesday	Thursday	Friday	Shabbos
			1 Nov *12 Chesvan*	*2 Nov* *13 Cheshvan*	*3 Nov* *14 Cheshvan*	*4 Nov* *15 Cheshvan*
5 Nov *16 Cheshvan*	*6 Nov* *17 Cheshvan* DAY 30 *Onah Beinonis DAY* *Ohr Zaruah NIGHT*	*7 Nov* *18 Cheshvan* *Yom Hachodesh DAY* *Ohr Zaruah NIGHT*	*8 Nov* *19 Cheshvan*	*9 Nov* *20 Cheshvan* **DAY 33** *Period* **NIGHT 10 PM**	*10 Nov* *21Cheshvan*	*11 Nov* *22 Cheshvan*
12 Nov *23 Cheshvan*	*13 Nov* *24 Cheshvan*	*14 Nov* *25 Cheshvan*	*15 Nov* *26 Cheshvan*	*16 Nov* *27 Cheshvan*	*17 Nov* *28 Cheshvan*	*18 Nov* *29 Cheshvan*
19 Nov *1 Kislev*	*20 Nov* *2 Kislev*	*21 Nov* *3 Kislev*	*22 Nov* *4 Kislev*	*23 Nov* *5 Kislev*	*24 Nov* *6 Kislev*	*25 Nov* *7 Kislev*
26 Nov *8 Kislev*	*27 Nov* *9 Kislev*	*28 Nov* *10 Kislev*	*29 Nov* *11 Kislev*	*30 Nov* *12 Kislev*		

- A woman gets her period on the Hebrew date of 18 Tishrei, during the day, and again on the night of 20 Cheshvan. Let us first calculate the *vestos* we learned. *Yom hachodesh* from the new period will be observed the same date of the month, during the same *onah* as the period began. In our example, that falls on the night of 20 Kislev.

- Now let's calculate the *onah beinonis*. This is 30 days from the last period, and that also falls on the night of 20 Kislev. Since the month of Cheshvan has only 29 days, the *yom hachodesh* and *onah beinonis* in this case will be observed in the same *onah*.

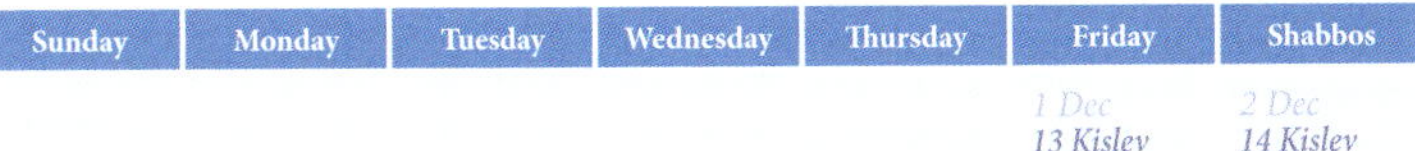

Sunday	Monday	Tuesday	Wednesday	Thursday	Friday	Shabbos
					1 Dec *13 Kislev*	2 Dec *14 Kislev*
3 Dec *15 Kislev*	4 Dec *16 Kislev*	5 Dec *17 Kislev*	6 Dec *18 Kislev*	7 Dec *19 Kislev*	8 Dec *20 Kislev* DAY 30 *Yom Hachodesh Onah Beinonis NIGHT*	9 Dec *21Kislev*
10 Dec *22 Kislev*	11 Dec *23 Kislev*	12 Dec *24 Kislev*	13 Dec *25 Kislev*	14 Dec *26 Kislev*	15 Dec *27 Kislev*	16 Dec *28Kislev*
17 Dec *29 Kislev*	18 Dec *30 Kislev*	19 Dec *1 Teves*	20 Dec *2 Teves*	21 Dec *3 Teves*	22 Dec *4 Teves*	23 Dec *5 Teves*
24 Dec *6 Teves*	25 Dec *7 Teves*	26 Dec *8 Teves*	27 Dec *9 Teves*	28 Dec *10 Teves*	29 Dec *11 Teves*	30 Dec *12 Teves*
31 Dec *13 Teves*						

- Now let's calculate the *haflagah*, the interval between the first period which started on 18 Tishrei and the second period which started on 20 Cheshvan. Counting 18 Tishrei as the first date of the cycle and 20 Cheshvan as the last, she counts the number of dates between these two dates and arrives at an interval of 33 days.
- Now, starting from 20 Cheshvan, she counts 33 days forward. We already learned how to calculate *yom hachodesh* and *onah beinonis*, which in this example both fall on 20 Kislev at night. Three days later, the 33rd day of the upcoming cycle, will be the

haflagah on the night of 23 Kislev. (Some advice: make sure to check the Jewish calendar to see if a month is 29 or 30 days, and always count twice.)

Sunday	Monday	Tuesday	Wednesday	Thursday	Friday	Shabbos
					1 Dec *13 Kislev*	2 Dec *14 Kislev*
3 Dec *15 Kislev*	4 Dec *16 Kislev*	5 Dec *17 Kislev*	6 Dec *18 Kislev*	7 Dec *19 Kislev*	8 Dec *20 Kislev* DAY 30 *Yom Hachodesh Onah Beinonis NIGHT*	9 Dec *21Kislev*
10 Dec *22 Kislev*	11 Dec *23 Kislev* DAY 33 *Haflagah NIGHT*	12 Dec *24 Kislev*	13 Dec *25 Kislev*	14 Dec *26 Kislev*	15 Dec *27 Kislev*	16 Dec *28Kislev*
17 Dec *29 Kislev*	18 Dec *30 Kislev*	19 Dec *1 Teves*	20 Dec *2 Teves*	21 Dec *3 Teves*	22 Dec *4 Teves*	23 Dec *5 Teves*
24 Dec *6 Teves*	25 Dec *7 Teves*	26 Dec *8 Teves*	27 Dec *9 Teves*	28 Dec *10 Teves*	29 Dec *11 Teves*	30 Dec *12 Teves*
31 Dec *13 Teves*						

- If the last period happened during the day, the *vest haflagah* of 23 Kislev will be a daytime *vest* as well. And, when the 20-Cheshvan period began at night, the night of 23 Kislev will be the time for concern.

Like the example of the *vest* of *yom hachodesh*, the *vest haflagah* in this example is a *vest she'eino kavua*. Should the period not come the following month on the day that it was anticipated (23 Kislev in our example), this interval of days between these two periods will no longer remain a concern for future months. However, if the woman gets her period based on the same interval for three consecutive cycles, this *haflagah* becomes her *vest kavua*.

Conduct during a Vest

Abstention

Marital relations are forbidden during the times that a woman's *vest* occurs, since the halachah is concerned that her period will begin during this time.

 **Question**

A couple realizes in the middle of marital relations that it is an *onas havest*. What should they do?

See Advanced Rulings, Vestos, Headline "*Marital Relations on a Vest*" (page 392).

Although other forms of intimate conduct are technically permitted, it is recommended and considered praiseworthy to avoid hugging and kissing. All other *harchakos* are permitted during a *vest*. For example, one spouse may touch the other, and there is no need to separate the beds as there is when the woman is a niddah.

However, as a matter of practicality, intimate contact should not occur to the point where if she does get her period, it will be difficult for the couple to go through the niddah days.

Bedikos during a Vest

The reason for *vestos* is the concern that there is something about this day that is the catalyst for the woman to get her period. This being the case, she must do a *bedikah* towards the end of the *onah* of her *vest* to ascertain whether or not this has occurred. A *bedikah* is done at the end of a day *vest*, close to *shkiah*. A woman does not need to wake up towards the end of the night to do a *bedikah* before dawn, during a night *vest*. Instead, she may do the *bedikah* before she goes to sleep at night.

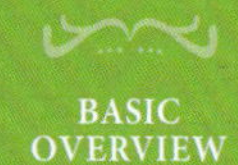

A woman who forgot to do a *bedikah* during her *vest* should call a *Rav* immediately. Depending on which *vest* it was, marital relations may continue to be forbidden even after the *vest* has passed, until a *bedikah* is done.

See Advanced Rulings, Vestos, headlines "A Woman Who Is Unable to Perform *Bedikos* on Her *Vest*" (page 389) and "A Missed *Bedikah* on a *Vest*" (page 390).

If the woman finds blood on the *bedikah* she has done — whether during the *vest* or after the *vest* — she is *temei'ah* immediately.

Some women wear white underwear during a *vest*. Strictly speaking, this is not something that is required.

After the Vest

After a *vest* comes and goes without incident and the proper *bedikos* are done, marital relations are once again permitted. As a matter of practicality, however, it is very likely that the woman will get her period during the upcoming days. It is therefore appropriate that before marital relations in the days following the *vest*, the woman should ensure that she has not started to bleed. A regular bedikah should not be done. Instead, the woman should wipe the external area with a colored (not white) tissue. Strictly speaking, if she finds a small amount of blood, it is not problematic because it is a *kesem* on a colored background (which is also not mekabel tumah according to many *poskim*). However, it may be indicative that her period will soon begin. The couple should thus wait to see what time brings. They should not have marital relations until she is sure the period has not begun. This should be done on all subsequent non-*vest* days, until the woman either gets her period or gets a positive pregnancy test. This should be done in the days following a *vest kavua* and *vest she'eino kavua*.

Other Vestos

Beyond the three *vestos* of *yom hachodesh*, *onah beinonis*, and the *vest haflagah*, which every woman without a *vest kavua* must observe each month, the commentaries discuss several other *vestos*. Many communities have adopted these other times of separation as stringencies.

These include the following "stringent" *vestos*. Each one is "named" after the *sefer* that is its leading proponent:

1. The *Ohr Zarua*
2. The *Pleissi*
3. The *Chavas Daas*

The Onah of the Ohr Zarua

When we take a look at the Gemara that discusses *vestos*, we see that the precise terminology is that the couple must separate during the "*onah* adjoining the monthly *vest*." The *Ohr Zarua* explains this to mean that besides for separating during the *onah* that a woman is "scheduled" to bleed, the couple must also observe the *onah* that immediately precedes it.

One of the reasons given for the observance of the *Ohr Zarua* is that nowadays a *vest kavua* is extremely uncommon. The chances of a woman actually getting her period on the day of her scheduled *vest* are low. Therefore, the *vest* is extended and moved up by one *onah* to deal with the very real chance that this month, the period will come during this time. The *onah* of the *Ohr Zarua* is always the *onah* prior to the time that the woman's period came last month.

Since the *onah* of the *Ohr Zarua* is only observed as a stringency, a *bedikah* is not required during this *vest*, and intimate conduct other than actual marital relations is permitted.

As we will soon see, the common practice in the United States is that the onah of the *Ohr Zarua* is observed on all three regular vestos — of yom hachodesh, onah beinonis, and the *vest haflagah*. In order to fully comprehend how to calculate the *onah* of the *Ohr Zarua* let us start with the calculations of the *vestos* we already learned, and add the *onah* of the *Ohr Zarua* on top of those calculations.

- For example: a woman who got her period during daytime hours on the Hebrew date of 18 Tishrei.

Sunday	Monday	Tuesday	Wednesday	Thursday	Friday	Shabbos
1 Oct *11 Tishrei*	2 Oct *11 Tishrei*	3 Oct *11 Tishrei*	4 Oct *11 Tishrei*	5 Oct *13 Cheshvan*	6 Oct *14 Cheshvan*	7 Oct *15 Cheshvan*
8 Oct ***18 Tishrei*** **DAY 1** ***Period*** **DAY** **10 AM**	9 Oct ***19 Tishrei***	10 Oct ***20 Tishrei***	11 Oct ***21 Tishrei***	12 Oct ***22 Tishrei***	13 Oct ***23 Tishrei***	14 Oct ***24 Tishrei***
15 Oct *25 Tishrei*	16 Oct *26 Tishrei*	17 Oct *27 Tishrei*	18 Oct *28 Tishrei*	19 Oct *29 Tishrei*	20 Oct *30 Tishrei*	21 Oct *1 Cheshvan*
22 Oct *2 Cheshvan*	23 Oct *3 Cheshvan*	24 Oct *4 Cheshvan*	25 Oct *5 Cheshvan*	26 Oct *6 Cheshvan*	27 Oct *7 Cheshvan*	28 Oct *8 Cheshvan*
29 Oct *9 Cheshvan*	30 Oct *10 Cheshvan*	31 Oct *11 Cheshvan*				

- As previously discussed, this woman creates a daytime *yom hachodesh vest* for 18 Cheshvan, and the *onah beinonis* will fall on 17 Cheshvan.

As we previously learned, on the *onah* of *yom hachodesh* and *onah beinonis* the couple must refrain from being intimate, affectionate touching should be kept to a minimum, and a *bedika* should be performed before the end of the vest.

In our example, the *onah beinonis* occurs on Monday, the 17th day of Tishrei and is observed from *netz hachamah* until *shkiyah*, while the *onas havest* of *yom hachodesh* occurs on Tuesday, the 18th of Tishrei during the day and is observed from *netz hachamah* until *shkiyah*.

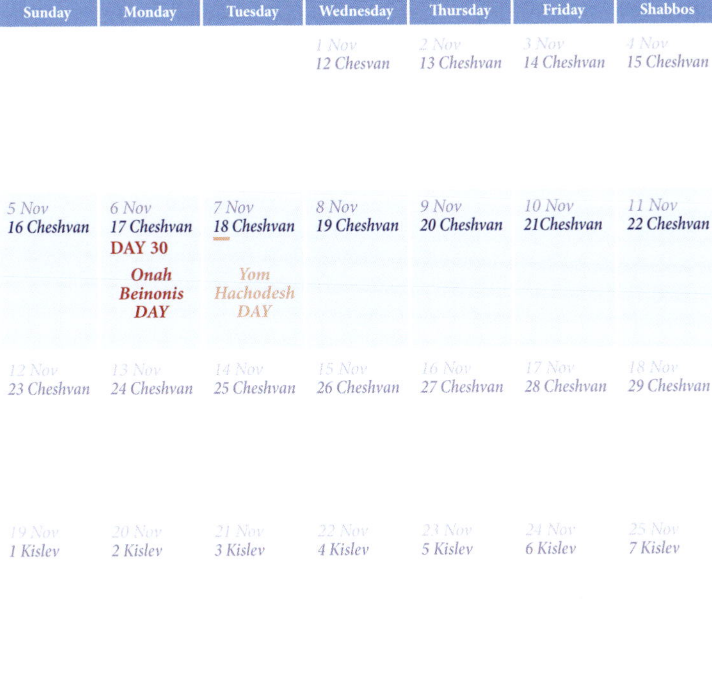

Sunday	Monday	Tuesday	Wednesday	Thursday	Friday	Shabbos
			1 Nov *12 Chesvan*	2 Nov *13 Cheshvan*	3 Nov *14 Cheshvan*	4 Nov *15 Cheshvan*
5 Nov *16 Cheshvan*	6 Nov *17 Cheshvan* DAY 30 ***Onah Beinonis* DAY**	7 Nov *18 Cheshvan* ***Yom Hachodesh* DAY**	8 Nov *19 Cheshvan*	9 Nov *20 Cheshvan*	10 Nov *21Cheshvan*	11 Nov *22 Cheshvan*
12 Nov *23 Cheshvan*	13 Nov *24 Cheshvan*	14 Nov *25 Cheshvan*	15 Nov *26 Cheshvan*	16 Nov *27 Cheshvan*	17 Nov *28 Cheshvan*	18 Nov *29 Cheshvan*
19 Nov *1 Kislev*	20 Nov *2 Kislev*	21 Nov *3 Kislev*	22 Nov *4 Kislev*	23 Nov *5 Kislev*	24 Nov *6 Kislev*	25 Nov *7 Kislev*
26 Nov *8 Kislev*	27 Nov *9 Kislev*	28 Nov *10 Kislev*	29 Nov *11 Kislev*	30 Nov *12 Kislev*		

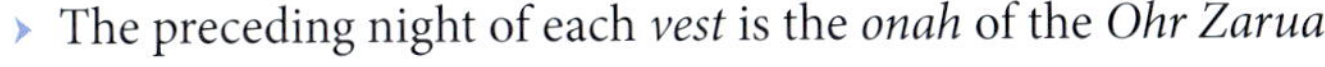

- The preceding night of each *vest* is the *onah* of the *Ohr Zarua.*

As we learned, the onah before the *onas havest* of *yom hachodesh* and *onah beinonis* the couple must refrain from being intimate, in observance of the *ohr zaruah*. In our example, since the *vest* of *onah beinonis* is observed on Monday, the 17th day of Tishrei from *netz hachamah* until *shkiyah*, the previous *onah*, which is the night before, from *shkiyah* until *netz hachamah*, is observed as the *ohr zaruah*. One should refrain from being intimate on this night.

Similarly, since the *vest* of *yom hachodesh* is observed on Tuesday, the 18th day of Tishrei from *netz hachamah* until *shkiyah*, the previous *onah*, which is the night before, from *shkiyah* until *netz hachamah*, is observed as the *ohr zaruah*. One should refrain from being intimate on this night as well.

BASIC OVERVIEW
HOW A WOMAN BECOMES A NIDDAH
Miscellaneous Laws
Niddah D'Oraisah
Period
Bedikah, Relations and Restroom
Niddah D'Rabbanan
Stains
Other forms of Tumah
HARCHAKOS
Intimate Separations
Eating Restrictions
Seats and Bedding
Additional Restrictions
TAHARA
The Five Day Wait
Rechitzah, Hefsek, Moch and Bedikahs
Shivah Nekiyim
Mikveh Preparations & Immersion
VESTOS
Understanding Vestos
Calculating Basic Vestos
Conduct on a Vest
Vestos Stringencies
Birth control and Vestos
Additional Vestos concepts

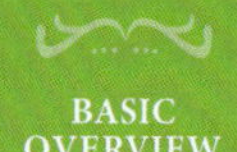

Sunday	Monday	Tuesday	Wednesday	Thursday	Friday	Shabbos
			1 Nov *12 Chesvan*	*2 Nov* *13 Cheshvan*	*3 Nov* *14 Cheshvan*	*4 Nov* *15 Cheshvan*
5 Nov *16 Cheshvan*	*6 Nov* *17 Cheshvan* DAY 30 *Onah Beinonis DAY* ***Ohr Zaruah NIGHT***	*7 Nov* *18 Cheshvan* *Yom Hachodesh DAY* ***Ohr Zaruah NIGHT***	*8 Nov* *19 Cheshvan*	*9 Nov* *20 Cheshvan*	*10 Nov* *21Cheshvan*	*11 Nov* *22 Cheshvan*
12 Nov *23 Cheshvan*	*13 Nov* *24 Cheshvan*	*14 Nov* *25 Cheshvan*	*15 Nov* *26 Cheshvan*	*16 Nov* *27 Cheshvan*	*17 Nov* *28 Cheshvan*	*18 Nov* *29 Cheshvan*
19 Nov *1 Kislev*	*20 Nov* *2 Kislev*	*21 Nov* *3 Kislev*	*22 Nov* *4 Kislev*	*23 Nov* *5 Kislev*	*24 Nov* *6 Kislev*	*25 Nov* *7 Kislev*
26 Nov *8 Kislev*	*27 Nov* *9 Kislev*	*28 Nov* *10 Kislev*	*29 Nov* *11 Kislev*	*30 Nov* *12 Kislev*		

- The couple abstains from marital relations on this night, but no other halachos of a *vest* are relevant. Daytime is her "real" *onah*, and the woman does a *bedikah* before *shkiah*, after which marital relations are once again permitted, unless that night is another *vest*, her period began, or the *bedikah* did not come out totally blood-free.

In the United States, Rav Moshe Feinstein established the practice that the *onah* of the *Ohr Zarua* is observed on all three regular *vestos* — of *yom hachodesh*, *onah beinonis*, and the *vest haflagah*. It is generally observed, unless a *Rav* specifically says tells a couple not to.

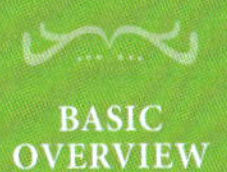

There are instances when even those who observe the *Ohr Zarua* will be lenient. See Advanced Rulings, Vestos, headline "When the *Onas Ohr Zarua* Should Not Be Kept" (page 396).

The Onah of the Pleissi

Many people in Eretz Yisrael, as well as some in the United States, observe an additional stringency of *vestos*, that of the *Pleissi*. The *Pleissi* explains that *onah beinonis*, which is the average 30-day cycle of most women, requires separation throughout the *entire* Hebrew date of Day 30 of the period — night and day — and not just during the *onah* that the period last came (like we learned above).

Sunday	Monday	Tuesday	Wednesday	Thursday	Friday	Shabbos
			1 Nov 12 Chesvan	2 Nov 13 Cheshvan	3 Nov 14 Cheshvan	4 Nov 15 Cheshvan
5 Nov 16 Cheshvan Ohr Zaruah NIGHT	6 Nov 17 Cheshvan DAY 30 Onah Beinonis DAY Ohr Zaruah NIGHT	7 Nov 18 Cheshvan Yom Hachodesh DAY	8 Nov 19 Cheshvan	9 Nov 20 Cheshvan DAY 33 Period NIGHT 10 PM	10 Nov 21Cheshvan	11 Nov 22 Cheshvan
12 Nov 23 Cheshvan	13 Nov 24 Cheshvan	14 Nov 25 Cheshvan	15 Nov 26 Cheshvan	16 Nov 27 Cheshvan	17 Nov 28 Cheshvan	18 Nov 29 Cheshvan
19 Nov 1 Kislev	20 Nov 2 Kislev	21 Nov 3 Kislev	22 Nov 4 Kislev	23 Nov 5 Kislev	24 Nov 6 Kislev	25 Nov 7 Kislev
26 Nov 8 Kislev	27 Nov 9 Kislev	28 Nov 10 Kislev	29 Nov 11 Kislev	30 Nov 12 Kislev		

BASIC OVERVIEW

HOW A WOMAN BECOMES A NIDDAH

Miscellaneous Laws

Niddah D'Oraisah

Period

Bedikah, Relations and Restroom

Niddah D'Rabbanan

Stains

Other forms of Tumah

HARCHAKOS

Intimate Separations

Eating Restrictions

Seats and Bedding

Additional Restrictions

TAHARA

The Five Day Wait

Rechitzah, Hefsek, Moch and Bedikahs

Shivah Nekiyim

Mikveh Preparations & Immersion

VESTOS

Understanding Vestos

Calculating Basic Vestos

Conduct on a Vest

Vestos Stringencies

Birth control and Vestos

Additional Vestos concepts

For example, if a period began on the night of 20 Cheshvan, her upcoming *yom hachodesh* and *onah beinonis* will both be observed the night of 20 Kislev, and the *haflagah* will be observed the night of 23 Kislev, as in the example before.

The *Ohr Zarua* will be observed the days before each *vest*.

Sunday	Monday	Tuesday	Wednesday	Thursday	Friday	Shabbos
					1 Dec *13 Kislev*	2 Dec *14 Kislev*
3 Dec *15 Kislev*	4 Dec *16 Kislev*	5 Dec *17 Kislev*	6 Dec *18 Kislev*	7 Dec *19 Kislev* **Ohr Zaruah DAY** Yom Hachodesh Onah Beinonis NIGHT	8 Dec *20 Kislev* DAY 30	9 Dec *21Kislev*
10 Dec *22 Kislev* **Ohr Zaruah DAY** Haflagah NIGHT	11 Dec *23 Kislev* DAY 33	12 Dec *24 Kislev*	13 Dec *25 Kislev*	14 Dec *26 Kislev*	15 Dec *27 Kislev*	16 Dec *28Kislev*
17 Dec *29 Kislev*	18 Dec *30 Kislev*	19 Dec *1 Teves*	20 Dec *2 Teves*	21 Dec *3 Teves*	22 Dec *4 Teves*	23 Dec *5 Teves*
24 Dec *6 Teves*	25 Dec *7 Teves*	26 Dec *8 Teves*	27 Dec *9 Teves*	28 Dec *10 Teves*	29 Dec *11 Teves*	30 Dec *12 Teves*

The *Pleissi* would be observed the day of 20 Kislev, as that is the date of the *onah beinonis*.

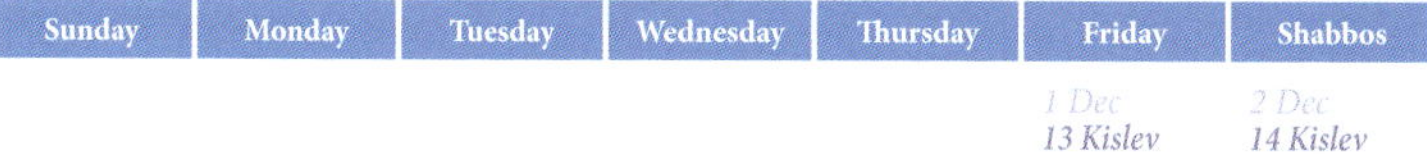

Sunday	Monday	Tuesday	Wednesday	Thursday	Friday	Shabbos
					1 Dec 13 Kislev	2 Dec 14 Kislev
3 Dec 15 Kislev	4 Dec 16 Kislev	5 Dec 17 Kislev	6 Dec 18 Kislev	7 Dec 19 Kislev Ohr Zaruah DAY	8 Dec 20 Kislev DAY 30 Plaisee DAY Yom Hachodesh Onah Beinonis NIGHT	9 Dec 21Kislev
10 Dec 22 Kislev Ohr Zaruah DAY	11 Dec 23 Kislev DAY 33 Haflagah NIGHT	12 Dec 24 Kislev	13 Dec 25 Kislev	14 Dec 26 Kislev	15 Dec 27 Kislev	16 Dec 28Kislev
17 Dec 29 Kislev	18 Dec 30 Kislev	19 Dec 1 Teves	20 Dec 2 Teves	21 Dec 3 Teves	22 Dec 4 Teves	23 Dec 5 Teves
24 Dec 6 Teves	25 Dec 7 Teves	26 Dec 8 Teves	27 Dec 9 Teves	28 Dec 10 Teves	29 Dec 11 Teves	30 Dec 12 Teves

In a daytime *onah*, the *Pleissi* (which says that separation is required for a complete 24-hour period of the *vest*) and the *Ohr Zarua* (which requires separation in the *onah* preceding the *vest*) are the same. They are both the night before the *vest*. In a nighttime *onah*, the *Pleissi*'s twenty-four *onah beinonis* is the following *onah* (the upcoming daytime hours), and the *Ohr Zarua*'s *onah* is the preceding day. Since engaging in marital relations is anyway not ideal during the day, often the compelling reason a couple has to permit relations during the day will allow them to not observe these stringencies either. A *Rav* should be consulted regarding practical application of this leniency.

As mentioned above, the practice in the United States is to consistently observe the *Ohr Zarua*, and in Eretz Yisrael the *Pleissi*

is followed on *onah beinonis*, with the *Ohr Zarua* followed on *yom hachodesh* and the *haflagah*.

The Onah of the Chavas Daas

The Chavas Daas is of the opinion that the *onah beinonis* discussed in the Gemara is not Day 30 of the woman's cycle, but rather Day 31.

Using the example above, *vestos* would be observed as follows:

Sunday	Monday	Tuesday	Wednesday	Thursday	Friday	Shabbos
			1 Nov *12 Chesvan*	*2 Nov* *13 Cheshvan*	*3 Nov* *14 Cheshvan*	*4 Nov* *15 Cheshvan*
5 Nov *16 Cheshvan* *Ohr Zaruah NIGHT*	*6 Nov* *17 Cheshvan* DAY 30 *Onah Beinonis DAY* *Ohr Zaruah NIGHT*	*7 Nov* *18 Cheshvan* *Yom Hachodesh DAY*	*8 Nov* *19 Cheshvan*	*9 Nov* *20 Cheshvan* DAY 33 *Period* NIGHT 10 PM	*10 Nov* *21Cheshvan*	*11 Nov* *22 Cheshvan*
12 Nov *23 Cheshvan*	*13 Nov* *24 Cheshvan*	*14 Nov* *25 Cheshvan*	*15 Nov* *26 Cheshvan*	*16 Nov* *27 Cheshvan*	*17 Nov* *28 Cheshvan*	*18 Nov* *29 Cheshvan*
19 Nov *1 Kislev*	*20 Nov* *2 Kislev*	*21 Nov* *3 Kislev*	*22 Nov* *4 Kislev*	*23 Nov* *5 Kislev*	*24 Nov* *6 Kislev*	*25 Nov* *7 Kislev*
26 Nov *8 Kislev*	*27 Nov* *9 Kislev*	*28 Nov* *10 Kislev*	*29 Nov* *11 Kislev*	*30 Nov* *12 Kislev*		

BASIC OVERVIEW

HOW A WOMAN BECOMES A NIDDAH
Miscellaneous Laws
Niddah D'Oraisah
Period
Bedikah, Relations and Restroom
Niddah D'Rabbanan
Stains
Other forms of Tumah

HARCHAKOS
Intimate Separations
Eating Restrictions
Seats and Bedding
Additional Restrictions

TAHARA
The Five Day Wait
Rechitzah, Hefsek, Moch and Bedikahs
Shivah Nekiyim
Mikveh Preparations & Immersion

VESTOS
Understanding Vestos
Calculating Basic Vestos
Conduct on a Vest
Vestos Stringencies
Birth control and Vestos
Additional Vestos concepts

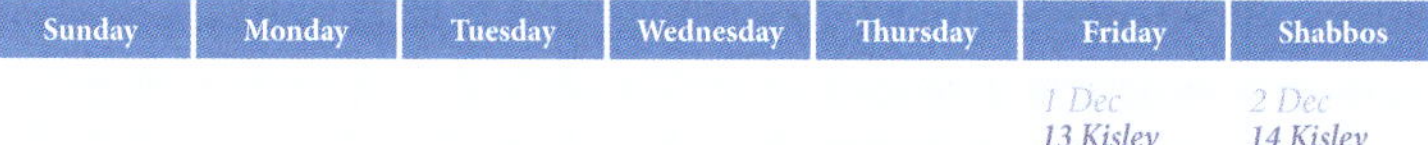

Sunday	Monday	Tuesday	Wednesday	Thursday	Friday	Shabbos
					1 Dec *13 Kislev*	*2 Dec* *14 Kislev*
3 Dec *15 Kislev*	*4 Dec* *16 Kislev*	*5 Dec* *17 Kislev*	*6 Dec* *18 Kislev*	*7 Dec* *19 Kislev* *Ohr Zaruah DAY*	*8 Dec* *20 Kislev* DAY 30 *Yom Hachodesh Onah Beinonis NIGHT*	*9 Dec* *21Kislev* ***Chavas Daas NIGHT***
10 Dec *22 Kislev* *Ohr Zaruah DAY*	*11 Dec* *23 Kislev* DAY 33 *Haflagah NIGHT*	*12 Dec* *24 Kislev*	*13 Dec* *25 Kislev*	*14 Dec* *26 Kislev*	*15 Dec* *27 Kislev*	*16 Dec* *28Kislev*
17 Dec *29 Kislev*	*18 Dec* *30 Kislev*	*19 Dec* *1 Teves*	*20 Dec* *2 Teves*	*21 Dec* *3 Teves*	*22 Dec* *4 Teves*	*23 Dec* *5 Teves*
24 Dec *6 Teves*	*25 Dec* *7 Teves*	*26 Dec* *8 Teves*	*27 Dec* *9 Teves*	*28 Dec* *10 Teves*	*29 Dec* *11 Teves*	*30 Dec* *12 Teves*

Many people observe this *onah* as well. Since the *Chavas Daas*'s opinion is only observed as a stringency, the *onah* of the *Ohr Zarua* is not observed in the *onah* preceding it, and intimate conduct other than actual marital relations is permitted during this time.

Vest Kavua

As we discussed, a *vest kavua* is a set cycle, i.e., a woman has seen that her period has come at the same interval, or on the same date, for 3 months in a row. Similarly, if she observes any other pattern that recurs three times, she will have a *vest kavua*. Should any of this happen, this *vest* must be observed during subsequent months, until 3 consecutive months pass when it did not occur. It is then uprooted, or canceled.

The overwhelming majority of present-day women do not have a fixed cycle. Creating a *vest kavua* is often a fluke occurrence, but one should be educated so that they can know what to look out for.

In order to create a *vest kavua*, the woman must have the same catalyst three times in a row. Here are some examples.

- *Yom hachodesh* — A woman gets her period on the same Hebrew date, and in the same *onah*, 3 months in a row.
- *Haflagah* — A woman gets her period after the exact same gap of days three times in a row, each time during the same *onah*. *Four* periods are necessary to create three equal gaps of days — the interval between the first time and the second time, the second time and the third time, and the third time and the fourth time.
- *Vest l'yemei hashavua* (a *vest* on the same day of the week) — A woman gets her period on the same day of the week, in the same *onah*, three times in a row. For example, she got her period Tuesday during the day 3 months in a row with the same interval. This means that a woman who gets her period after a 29-day interval (or 36-day interval, or any interval that is one more that a number that evenly divides into weeks: 22, 29, 36, 43, and so on) during *2* consecutive months has established a pattern of bleeding on the same day of the week. This *vest* may be the most common fluke *vest kavua*.
- *Vest hadilug* (a predictably changing cycle) — For example, one month a woman gets her period after a 34-day interval, the next month after a 35-day interval, and the third month after a 36-day interval, all during the same *onah*. Or, the opposite: 36, 35, 34, or even 31, 33, 35 or the opposite: 35, 33, 31. This may create a *vest* for the next number in the series during the next month. In general, it is always good to keep an eye out for patterns and discuss them with a *Rav*.
- *Vest haguf* (a *vest* connected to a bodily sensation) — This *vest* is when a woman gets her period at the same time every month after experiencing certain feelings. PMS is not a *vest haguf* because it is usually only vaguely related to the period, in terms of the timing and symptoms.
- *Vest hakefitzos hamurkav* (a *vest* connected to "jumping on a specific date") — This *vest* is created when there is a physical activity that the woman finds causes her period to come every month for 3 months in

a row. An example of this is she goes to an exercise class every month on a Tuesday, and gets her period during the class every month.

A woman who has created a *vest kavua* marks the calendar with this *vest* for next 3 months. For example, a woman who sees that she has a *vest kavua* for the *yom hachodesh* after getting her period during the same *onah* on the Hebrew dates of 5 Nissan, 5 Iyar, and 5 Sivan, circles this *onah* on the dates of 5 Tammuz, 5 Av, and 5 Elul. If she deviates from this *vest* during one of these 3 months by getting her period on a different date, she observes the *vest she'eino kavua* along with the *vest kavua*. The *vest kavua* must be observed until her period does not come on this day for 3 months in a row.

A couple who suspects a *vest kavua* should contact a *Rav*, who will guide them how to proceed.

We have learned the basic rules of *vestos*. For those who feel confident and are interested in observing some of the more widely accepted stringencies in *vestos* calculations, refer to Advanced Rulings, Vestos (pages 379–415).

Birth Control Pills

When a woman takes birth control pills that alter her cycle she takes active hormone pills (generally starting a week before going go the mikvah) which, when she stops taking them (and switches to placebos), cause her to get her period within a certain amount of time.

A *vest she'eino kavua* would not be calculated during these times, as the pill has been established to be the catalyst to bring her period about. *Onah beinonis*, however, should be observed if her period has not arrived by Day 30 of the cycle.

When she stops taking the pills, she should treat the days after as *yemei hamevuchim* (days during which a woman anticipates that she will get her period, but she does not know precisely when it will be), because she knows that she will get her period sometime after she stops taking the pills, although she does not know exactly how long afterwards the period will begin. She should perform an external wipe before intimacy with a tissue (which is not susceptible to *tumah* and therefore will not render her a niddah if a small amount of blood is detected) until the period comes. If blood is detected on the wipe, the couple should refrain from intimacy until the bleeding clears up for a few hours.

It must be noted that all women who want to take any form of birth control must discuss this matter with their *rav*. As there are various opinions about which birth control methods are permissible and which are problematic according to *halachah*, each couple must discuss birth control options with their rav prior to speaking to their doctor. Additionally, there is a Torah-mandated

requirement to have children. By actively preventing herself from conceiving a woman may be delaying this important *mitzvah*. Although circumstances may necessitate a woman pushing off having children, a *rav* should be the one to make this determination. Asking a *rav* about birth control is not only a requirement for newlywed couples. Anytime a couple would like to refrain from conceiving, they should only do so with the guidance of their *rav*. For those who have received a *hetter* to use birth control, and the method of contraception is the "month-to-month" pill, their calendar may look something like the following illustration:

Pills and Vestos

Sunday	Monday	Tuesday	Wednesday	Thursday	Friday	Shabbos
1 DAY 1 *Period Begins*	2 DAY 2	3 DAY 3	4 DAY 4	5 DAY 5 *Rechitzah Hefsek Moch*	6 DAY 1 *Shiva Nekiyim* DAY 1 *Active Pills*	7 DAY 2 *Shiva Nekiyim*
8 DAY 3 *Shiva Nekiyim*	9 DAY 4 *Shiva Nekiyim*	10 DAY 5 *Shiva Nekiyim*	11 DAY 6 *Shiva Nekiyim*	12 DAY 7 *Shiva Nekiyim* *Mikveh Night*	13 *Tehorah*	14 *Tehorah*
15 *Tehorah*	16 *Tehorah*	17 *Tehorah*	18 *Tehorah*	19 *Tehorah*	20 *Tehorah*	21 *Tehorah*
22 *Tehorah*	23 *Tehorah*	24 *Tehorah*	25 *Tehorah*	26 *Tehorah* LAST DAY *Active Pills*	27 *Tehorah* *External wipe required before Intimacy* *Treated as Yimei HaMevuchim*	28 *Tehorah* *External wipe required before Intimacy* *Treated as Yimei HaMevuchim*
29 *Tehorah* *External wipe required before Intimacy* *Treated as Yimei HaMevuchim*	30 *Onah Beinonis observed*					

Review Questions for Chapter Four

1. If a woman gets her period during the day on 5 Nissan, which *onas havest* will she keep the upcoming month?
2. How does one calculate the *onah beinonis*?
3. Is intimacy permitted on the *vest*?
4. When should the *bedikah* of the *vest* be performed if the *vest* occurs during the day? If the *vest* occurs at night?
5. Which *vestos* are observed while a woman is on birth control pills?

Answers

1. She keeps 5 Iyar during the day as *yom hachodesh*, 4 Iyar during the day as *onah beinonis*, and whichever is her *yom haflagah*.
2. The 30th day of the period, counting the day of the period as Day 1. The *vest* is observed during the day or night in which the period occurred.
3. No. Other *harchakos* need not be observed. Hugging and kissing are strictly permitted, but recommended to be avoided.
4. On a day *vest* the *bedikah* should be performed during the day, close to *shkiah*. On a night *vest* the *bedikah* should be performed before going to sleep.
5. *Onah beinonis* is the only *vest* observed while on birth control pills. After ceasing to take the active pills, a woman should perform an external wipe before intimacy to determine she is not actively bleeding (*yemei hamevuchim*).

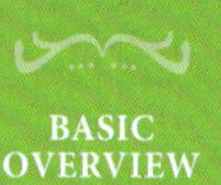

BASIC OVERVIEW

HOW A WOMAN BECOMES A NIDDAH
Miscellaneous Laws
Niddah D'Oraisah
Period
Bedikah, Relations and Restroom
Niddah D'Rabbanan
Stains
Other forms of Tumah

HARCHAKOS
Intimate Separations
Eating Restrictions
Seats and Bedding
Additional Restrictions

TAHARA
The Five Day Wait
Rechitzah, Hefsek, Moch and Bedikahs
Shivah Nekiyim
Mikveh Preparations & Immersion

VESTOS
Understanding Vestos
Calculating Basic Vestos
Conduct on a Vest
Vestos Stringencies
Birth control and Vestos
Additional Vestos concepts

SECTION TWO

Section Two is a review of *hilchos niddah* for the intermediate user.

The reader will find a more advanced presentation of the background for each halachah, as well as more details in terms of the development of the practical application of the halachah.

Specific questions will be addressed in this section, and will answer many questions the reader is likely to have after reading Section One.

Much time has been spent sourcing most of the opinions presented, while trying not to distract the reader with too much non-pertinent information.

It is imperative that the reader understand Section One before reading Section Two.

HOW A WOMAN BECOMES A NIDDAH

What Makes a Woman a Niddah D'Oraisa

The menstrual cycle of a woman is such that the ovary releases an egg cell which can potentially become fertilized. The uterus builds up a lining of blood called the endometrium in anticipation of this potentially fertilized embryo. If no pregnancy occurs after ovulation, the body waits approximately 14 days before "giving up" and releasing the endometrium. The endometrium falls out of the woman's body and causes bleeding, an occurrence that happens approximately every 28–32 days. This bleeding is called a period, and is a process that generally lasts between 3 and 9 days.

A woman who gets her period is called a niddah. The Torah discusses the laws of niddah in three places: in *Parashas Metzora* (*Vayikra* 19:24), in *Parashas Acharei Mos* (*Vayikra* 18:19), and in *Parashas Kedoshim* (ibid. 20:18). Marital relations with a woman who is a niddah are forbidden. In addition to the prohibition against cohabitation, the second *passuk* tells us that niddah in a form of *tumah*. In addition, the term "*temei'ah*" is also used colloquially to refer to the onset of niddah-bleeding as a way of saying that marital relations are now forbidden.

Chazal instituted many safeguards to Torah law in *hilchos niddah*. A woman who is *temei'ah* on a Torah-law level is termed a *niddah d'Oraisa*. A woman can also become *temei'ah* because of the safeguards of Rabbinic law. Such a woman is called a *niddah d'Rabbanan* (Rabbinic-law niddah).

This section will now expand upon what has been taught in the previous section.

Six conditions are necessary to render a woman a *niddah d'Oraisa*:

1. The blood that emerged from the woman's body came from the uterus, which *Chazal* call the *mekor* (literally, the source).
2. The blood left the *mekor* and touched another part of her body.
3. The blood does not come from a *makkah* (cut or wound).
4. The blood left her body in the normal way.
5. The blood is a specific shade of color.
6. The woman's bleeding was accompanied by a *hargashah*.

The Blood Came from the Mekor

The first condition for a woman to be rendered a *niddah d'Oraisa* is that the blood that emerges from the woman's body must have originated in the *mekor* — the uterus.[5] The uterus is an organ that is shaped like an upside-down pear, and is akin to a hot-water bottle. The top part of the uterus hosts the lining, the endometrium, while the narrower lower part is called the cervix. The cervix is a muscle which is almost always closed very tightly. When a woman gives birth, the cervix dilates to allow the baby to descend into the birth canal.

When describing the female anatomy, the Gemara discusses the "*prozdor*."[6] However, it is not clear from the Gemara exactly which part of the body this term is referring to. The *Rambam* explains that the *rechem*, which is another part of the body that the Gemara discusses, is another word for the *mekor*, which literally means "source," for this is where the blood originates, and the *prozdor* is the cervix, which dilates when a woman gives birth.[7] However, the next halachah in the *Rambam* appears to pose a problem with this approach,[8] as there the *Rambam* says that the *eiver* (the male reproductive organ) reaches the *prozdor*

5. שו"ע ס' קפ"ג וש"ך ס"ק א'.
6. נדה י"ז ע"ב "אשכחינהו רבה בר רב הונא דיתבי וקאמרי: החדר מבפנים, והפרוזדור מבחוץ, ועלייה בנויה על שתיהן, ולול פתוח בין עלייה לפרוזדור."
7. רמב"ם הל' איסו"ב ה, ג.
8. איסו"ב ה, ד.

at the *gemar bi'ah* stage (the climax) of marital relations. The cervix is too deep and closed, however for the *eiver* to reach there at any time.

In explanation, Rav Shlomo Zalman Auerbach says the Rambam means the *mekor* is the entire area from the cervix upward, and what the Rambam calls the *prozdor* is the vaginal canal.[9]

Most other *Poskim* explain the *Rambam* differently: the *prozdor* comprises the cervix *and* the vaginal canal.[10] When the Rambam says that the *eiver* enters the *prozdor* he means it reaches *part* of the *prozdor*, because it does enter the vaginal canal.

The blood discharged from a woman's body is only niddah blood, rendering her *temei'ah*, when it originates in the *mekor*. During a regular menstrual cycle the blood comes from the uterus, rendering a woman who gets her period a *niddah d'Oraisa* according to everyone. The question arises regarding a woman who is bleeding from her cervix. Rav Shlomo Zalman Auerbach considers the cervix to be part of the *mekor*, making her *temei'ah*, and other *Poskim* do not, making cervical bleeding non-problematic. The issue of cervical bleeding does occasionally arise, and a *Rav* should be presented with the question when it does.

The Blood Left the Mekor and Touched Another Part of Her Body

The second condition mentioned by the Gemara[11] for a woman to be rendered a *niddah d'Oraisa* is that the blood left her *mekor* by traveling to what the *passuk* calls "*bivsarah* (in her flesh)."[12] Only when the blood reaches *besarah* does it create *tumah*. The Gemara explains *besarah* to mean the vaginal canal. The Gemara then discusses the halachah that if the blood only traveled to a place in the female anatomy called *bein hashinayim* (literally, "between the teeth") she is still not *temei'ah*. After the blood has passed this point she is certainly *temei'ah*. Most *Poskim* understand the *Rambam* to define *bein hashinayim* as the area outside the cervix that the blood passes through on its way to the vaginal canal. The woman is thus *temei'ah* once blood passes out of the cervix into the vaginal canal, even though the blood has not yet left her body completely.[13]

---

9. שו״ת מנחת שלמה חלק ב׳ ס׳ ע׳ אות ל״ז ד״ה גם צ״ע.
10. שו״ת חתם סופר יו״ד ס׳ קס״ז .
11. נדה י״ז ע״ב.
12. ויקרא טו:יט
13. גמ׳ נדה מ״א ע״ב "תנו רבנן: בבשרה - מלמד שמטמאה בפנים כבחוץ, ואין לי אלא נדה, זבה מנין - ת״ל זובה בבשרה. פולטת ש״ז מנין - ת״ל יהיה" ע״כ, ס׳ קפ״ג.

Rav Shlomo Zalman Auerbach — who holds that the cervix is part of the *mekor* — thus needs another area to be called *bein hashinayim*. He says that *bein hashinayim* is the inside of the vagina, near the cervix. This area has skin that resembles teeth, and this is the place where the blood's passing through makes a woman a *niddah d'Oraisa*.

The Blood Does Not Come from a Makkah

The third condition that the Gemara discusses about blood that emerges from a woman's body is that she remains *tehorah* if the blood was caused by a *makkah*.[14]

However, the Gemara also brings a *passuk* stating that a woman can become *temei'ah b'oness* (inadvertent or forceful) should the *mekor* begin to bleed in an abnormal way.[15] Why? This bleeding was also caused by a problem or imbalance in the uterus, and is not regular uterine bleeding. Why does it make her *temei'ah*?

The difference between these two halachos is the following. The leniency of bleeding caused by a *makkah* not being problematic specifically applies when the blood came from a cut in the vaginal canal or the like, because the blood that emerged from her body does not originate in the *mekor* — it is not the endometrium breaking down. A woman who bleeds due to extenuating circumstances, however, is bleeding from the *mekor*, just like she does when she gets her period. The *passuk* brought in the second Gemara is telling us that although this bleeding was not caused by a regular period, but by an external catalyst, this bleeding is still coming from the *mekor*, and the woman is *temei'ah*.

The Shev Yaakov says a woman is only *temei'ah* when she gets her period in a regular way, not if she bleeds because she has a weak uterus or another condition that is classifiably abnormal.[16] In these scenarios, he holds she remains *tehorah*. The Noda B'Yehudah rejects this, and says that when the Gemara says that a *makkah* does not make her *temei'ah*, it is because she has an infection or a wound inside the uterus or vaginal canal. If her endometrium bleeds because of any reason, she is *temei'ah* as always.[17]

If something was inserted into the uterus and cuts the lining, the *Poskim* generally presume that that is a *makkah*, and the woman remains *tehorah*. Rav Yosef Shalom Elyashiv, however, disagrees, explaining that

14. נדה ט״ז ע״ב וסוע״א ובשו״ע ס׳ קפ״ג.
15. נדה ל״ו ע״ב ובט״ז ס׳ קפ״ג ס״ק א.
16. שו״ת שב יעקב ס׳ ל״ז.
17. שו״ת נו״ב מהדורה תנינה יו״ד ס׳ קי״ד.

although this bleeding was *caused* by a *makkah*, what is happening is that the *makkah* may have caused the endometrium to discharge. This woman is thus *temei'ah*, for this is (albeit off-cycle) menstrual blood.

One should be aware that many medical procedures entail inserting something into the uterus, and these instruments often cause bleeding. A *Rav* should be consulted whenever a woman has an intrauterine procedure performed that causes bleeding.

Sometimes a woman keeps on finding stains on her *bedikos*, past the point in the month when it would be expected for her to see blood. It may be that she cut herself, and a *Rav* may send her to a *bodekes* to determine where the blood originated from. If the blood came from an irritation (a polyp, cyst, cut, or the like) in the vaginal canal, these *bedikos* are *tehoros*, because the blood that was seen is not niddah blood. The same may apply if she finds a *kesem* and suspects that she has a cut. As we will soon see when we discuss *kesamim*, when there is a cut, a *Rav* may assume the *kesem* came from there and is *tahor*.

The Blood Left Her Body in the Normal Way

The fourth condition mentioned by the Gemara for *niddah d'Oraisa* is also learned from the word *bivsarah*: the blood must exit her body the normal way, which is by touching her flesh on the way out.[18] This means that if a tube going from the cervix to the bottom of the vaginal opening was to theoretically be inserted in her body, the woman would always be *tehorah*, because the blood never touched *besarah*.

If the uterus prolapsed to the point where the cervix is visible outside of her body, the blood can go straight out of her body without touching *besarah*. Nevertheless, we are generally stringent regarding any blood experienced by a woman with a prolapsed uterus. In such circumstances a *Rav* should be consulted for final halachic decisions.

The Blood Is a Specific Shade of Color

The fifth condition for *niddah d'Oraisa* is the color of the blood that left the *mekor*. The Mishnah states there are five colors of *tamei* blood, and everything else that comes out of the *mekor* is *tahor*.[19] (The Gemara[20] explains that this halachah is understood from the *passuk* that

18. ויקרא טו:יט – גמ׳ נדה כ״א ע״ב.
19. נדה י״ט ע״א.
20. שם.

tells us that we are to go to a *Rav* to rule — and thus differentiate — between types of blood,[21] implying that there are questions that should be asked regarding colors of blood, and not everything is *tamei.*) The Gemara says blood has to be red, and since the *passuk* mentions the word *damehah* (her blood) (which is plural) twice, we understand that there are four shades of *dam tamei*, all of which are red. The fifth shade of *tamei* blood is black, because when red blood oxidizes it turns black. Beis Shammai holds there are other shades that are *temei'im*, while Beis Hillel holds that besides for these five, all other colors are *tehorim*.

Akavyah ben Mehallel says the color *yarok*, generally translated as green, is also *tamei*,[22] and the Chachamim disagree, maintaining that it is *tahor*. Tosafos ask a question on Akavyah ben Mehallel's position:[23] we know that blood has to be red, so how can *yarok*, which contains no red elements, be *tamei*? Tosafos answer that indeed, the color that Akavyah ben Mehallel is discussing is not green, for green does not look red at all. Rather, the color *yarok* that he is referring to is the color of an esrog.

How does *Tosafos*'s answer solve the problem — we all know from Sukkos that the yellow color of an esrog is not any redder than green is! The answer is that the esrogim that we are familiar with from Sukkos time have been picked too early. *Tosafos* is saying that if an esrog would remain on the tree — or, for that matter, in a bag in the fridge — it would change to a bright orange color. Since we rule like the Chachamim, *Tosafos* is teaching us that orange is another color that is *tahor*.

The *Rosh* says *yarok* can refer to gold, orange, or egg-yolk color.[24] Depending what they feed the chickens, the yolk will be yellow, gold, or amber. These various shades of *yarok* are *tehorim* as well.

The *Rosh* says that nowadays we are unable to rule about the five *tamei* colors like they could long ago, so any shade that is *noteh la'admimus* (close to red) is considered *tamei*, except for *yarok*, which is amber gold, or orange — and white.[25] Since the Rosh cannot mean literally white, which is not even close to red, it is clear that he means whitish-red — that is, pink.

---

21. דברים יז:ח.
22. נדה י״ט ע״ב.
23. שם ד״ה הירוק.
24. רא״ש נדה פרק כל היד ס׳ ד׳ וז״ל ״הירוק עקביא בן מהללאל מטמא וחכמים מטהרין. פר״י דמכאן משמע דירוק סתם הוא צבע הדומה לחלמון של ביצה או לזהב הנוטה למראה אדמומית״ עכ״ל.
25. שם וז״ל ״ובדורות הללו אין בקי במראות דמים לישען על חכמתו ולהפריד בין דם לדם ואפילו בימי חכמי הש״ס היו מן החכמים שהיו נמנעים מלראות דמים. כ״ש האידנא שאין לטהר שום דם הנוטה למראה אדמומית אם לא שיהא לבן וירוק כמראה הזהב״ עכ״ל.

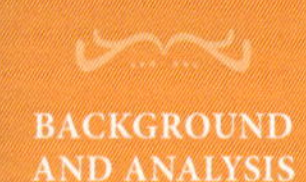

The *Tur* says the *yarok* of Akavyah ben Mehallel and white are *tehorim*, but he does not mention anything about anything that is *noteh la'admimus* being *tamei*.[26] The *Beis Yosef* says orange and white are not shades of red at all. There are different shades of red, and then there is a new color called orange.[27]

Today, anything with a reddish color is ruled *tamei*.[28] Orange, however, is *tahor*, because orange is not one of the five shades of blood. The exact colors of the shades that are *temei'im* and shades that are *tehorim* have been transmitted by *mesorah* (tradition), and *Poskim* often differ in their *mesorah*. Technically, a person can learn the topic and rule on his own, forbidding anything that remotely reminds him of a leaning towards redness, but what will happen is that he will end up being stringent unnecessarily. Sometimes colors that appear to be blood-red are in fact *tehorim*, for they are of the *tahor* shades of red, or are of the colors included in Akavyah ben Mehallel's discussion.

A person may rule on the status of a *mareh* for himself when he sees a certain color that he has come across before and his experience has shown him it is not a problem. However, shades and their nuances are varied, and the differences are often subtle. To be sure that what is before him is the same as the color he remembers is very difficult for the layman. *Rabbanim* often spend years gaining the experience necessary to rule on these colors. As a couple presents *maros* to a *Rav* and over time learn which colors are not problems and which colors are more difficult to determine, they do not have to continue bringing every single *mareh* that arises to a *Rav*. However, at the same time, one must be scrupulous in observance of these halachos and present a *she'eilah* to a *Rav* when necessary.

The Woman's Bleeding Was Accompanied by a Hargashah

The sixth condition for *niddah d'Oraisa* is that the bleeding must be accompanied by a *hargashah*, which means that the woman felt something happening in her body within some time of the blood emerging.[29] (We will soon discuss this feeling at greater length.) This too, explains Shmuel in the Gemara, is learned out from the word *bivsarah*: the bleeding must be felt "in her flesh," that is, in her body, in

26. יו"ד ס' קפ"ח.
27. שם ד"ה כתבו התוס' וד"ה ומשמע.
28. שם ברא"ש, שו"ע קפ"ח, א' – ועיין בח' הרמב"ן לנדה י"ט ע"א ד"ה ואנו עכשיו.
29. נדה נ"ז ע"ב.

order for it to be the *tamei* bleeding that the Torah is discussing. On a *d'Oraisa* level, a woman who discovers blood and knows that she did not experience a *hargashah* remains *tehorah*.[30] However, we will see that *Chazal* decreed that this woman is *temei'ah mid'Rabbanan*.[31]

Bleeding that was accompanied by a *hargashah* renders a woman *temei'ah d'Oraisa*, while blood that was discovered that was not accompanied by a *hargashah* is called a *kesem*, which literally means "stain." Besides for the basic difference between them — that a woman who experienced a *hargashah* is a *niddah d'Oraisa*, and a woman who discovered a *kesem* is "only" a *niddah d'Rabbanan* — a *kesem* carries with it several leniencies, which we will discuss shortly, in this chapter. If the bleeding is determined to have been seen with a *hargashah*, in ways that we will soon discuss, none of the leniencies of *kesamim* apply.

Rashi says an actual *hargashah* is not always necessary.[32] The purpose of a *hargashah* is to clearly establish that the blood came from the *mekor*, and not from some other place. But if we know that the blood came from the *mekor* (*vadai migufah*), the woman is *temei'ah d'Oraisa* in any case, whether or not she felt it by experiencing a *hargashah*. Tosafos disagree, saying that an actual *hargashah* is always a requirement for a woman to become a *niddah d'Oraisa*, in line with the plain understanding of Shmuel's statement.[33] The *Rosh* does not cite Shmuel at all.

The Sidrei Taharah in fact rules like Rashi, and holds that blood that definitely came from a woman's *mekor* always makes her a *niddah d'Oraisa*.[34] Most other opinions, however, agree with Tosafos, that a woman is only a *niddah d'Oraisa* when she experienced a *hargashah*.[35]

The accepted halachah is like the opinion of Tosafos, that a *hargashah* is necessary to make a woman a *niddah d'Oraisa*. For example, we find that the *Rambam* clearly mentions the requirement of *hargashah*, implying that he does not understand the Gemara in the way that Rashi does.[36] The *Shulchan Aruch* also states that a woman is *temei'ah d'Oraisa* when she experiences a *hargashah* together with her discharge of blood.[37]

Assuming that a *hargashah* is needed to make a woman *temei'ah d'Oraisa* puts modern-day women into an interesting position. Women

30. יו״ד קפ״ג.
31. ס׳ ק״צ סע׳ א׳.
32. נדה נ״ח ע״א ד״ה רב אשי.
33. שם ד״ה מודה שמואל.
34. ס׳ ק״צ ס״ק נד׳ ד״ה וטרם וד״ה וכבר.
35. תורת השלמים, גליון מהרש״א ס׳ קפ״ג שדינו דרבנן אלא שאין דין פחות מכגריס משום שודאי מגופה היא.
36. הל׳ איסו״ב ט, א.
37. ס׳ קפ״ג.

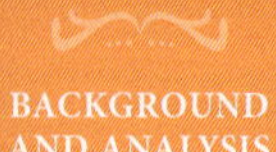

nowadays almost never feel a *hargashah* when their period comes each month. It would thus seem that every time a woman gets her period, she should only be a *niddah d'Rabbanan*. Below we will explain why this is not so.

Types of Hargashos

What is the *hargashah* that causes a woman to be *temei'ah d'Oraisa*? The *Poskim* give several different definitions in answer to this question.

Tosafos[38], the *Rashba*,[39] and the *Ramban*[40] explain that the sensation that a woman must feel to be the niddah whom the Torah discusses is that she feels her *mekor* (i.e., her cervix) opening. The *Rambam* says she feels her entire body shake.[41]

A third approach is taken by the Noda B'Yehudah,[42] who says that the *hargashah* required by the Torah is that the woman feel some sort of moisture flowing inside of her body. The Chasam Sofer disagrees with this definition of *hargashah*,[43] and says that feeling wetness is not a *hargashah* at all. In defense of the Noda B'Yehudah, the *Chavas Daas* explains that the wetness being discussed is the *hargashah* of wetness leaving the cervix, and does not refer to a feeling of moisture farther down in the vaginal canal or outside the woman's body.[44]

Women nowadays generally feel none of these sensations. At most, they feel wet outside of their bodies when they get their period, which is not considered a *hargashah*. The *Poskim* say if a woman were to feel something wet flow out of the uterus, she would be a *niddah d'Oraisa*. However, most women today will say that these *hargashos* simply do not exist.

Hargashos Today

The *Aruch HaShulchan* answers the problem that it would appear that women are no longer *temei'os d'Oraisa* by explaining that when the Gemara says that a woman needs a *hargashah* to become a niddah, it really means that she sees blood "*b'derech re'iyah*" — in the normal way

---

38. נדה ד׳ ע״א ד״ה והא אשה.
39. תורת הבית שער ד׳ הל׳ א׳.
40. הל׳ נדה לרמב״ן.
41. פרק ה׳ מהל׳ איסו״ב הל׳ יז׳.
42. נו״ב יו״ד ס׳ נ״ה מובא בפ״ת ס׳ קפ״ג ס״ק א׳.
43. שו״ת חת״ס ס׳ קמ״ה וקנ״ג וקס״ז וקע״א ג״כ מובאים בפ״ת שם.
44. שם בפ״ת ובס׳ ק״צ בביאורים אות א׳.

of seeing blood, that is, she sees blood in the usual way — i.e., she got her period.[45] Thus, a woman who gets her period is certainly experiencing a flow of bleeding that is *b'derech re'iyah*, making it no question that she is a *niddah d'Oraisa*.

Many *Poskim* explain that the Torah's including a *hargashah* within the description of "regular" niddah tells us that we may assume that part of a woman's getting her monthly period involves the experience of a *hargashah*. Women nowadays are simply less sensitive to what is happening in their bodies due to changes in lifestyles and eating habits which occurred over the generations. When a woman has her period, we assume that her body is experiencing a *hargashah* even though she is not sensitive to actually experiencing the feelings of a *hargashah*. A woman who gets her period is thus treated as a *niddah d'Oraisa* even when she did not actually feel any of the physical sensations that are mentioned above.

Assuming that blood that comes as a *re'iyah* is *tamei mid'Oraisa*, and blood found as a *kesem* is "only" *tamei mid'Rabbanan*, the *Poskim* discuss how much blood is called a *re'iyah*, such that it is assumed that a *hargashah* was present. Many *Poskim* in Eretz Yisrael rule that a *re'iyah* is the amount of blood that is at least the size of 6–7 *gris*. (A *gris* is a Talmudic measurement, which is approximately the size of a penny or one-shekel coin.) Rav Moshe Feinstein says a *re'iyah* is the amount of blood that is at least half the size of a dollar bill. We assume that a woman who bleeds this amount got her period, and is a *niddah d'Oraisa* even when she says she did not actually feel any *hargashah*, since we will assume that when she gets her period a *hargashah* is present.

Sometimes a woman will see stains over a period of time. Depending on the circumstances, a *Rav* may determine that the staining is in fact a *kesem*, as opposed to a period, subject to the leniencies associated with *kesamim*. A *Rav* must be consulted for specific guidance when such matters arise.

The Three Exceptions

A woman who experiences the discharge of less than a *re'iyah*'s amount of blood is not assumed to have experienced a *hargashah*, and, unless she clearly knows that she felt a *hargashah*, she is not a *niddah d'Oraisa*, but a *niddah d'Rabbanan*.

45. יו״ד ס׳ קפ״ג סע׳ א׳, ב׳, נ״ב.

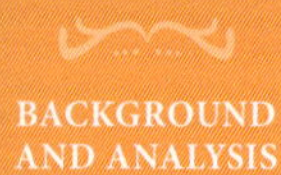

As we learned, Shmuel says a woman is only *temei'ah mid'Oraisa* when she experienced a *hargashah*.[46] The Gemara asks regarding Shmuel's statement: There are three cases in which although the woman did not experience a *hargashah*, she is *temei'ah mid'Oraisa*. One case is when a woman finds blood immediately after using the restroom, another is when she finds blood on a *bedikah* cloth that was inserted vaginally, and the third is when she finds blood immediately after marital relations. How is this so? The Gemara answers that in all three cases there *was* a *hargashah*, but it was masked — by the feeling of performing her bodily needs, by the feeling of the foreign object of the *bedikah* cloth, or by the *eiver* during marital relations.

The Gemara's answer may be understood in one of several ways. The *Rambam* explains that the Gemara is saying that according to Shmuel, we may assume that the woman had a *hargashah*, as women generally do when discharging blood. However, since she was not paying attention because the feeling of the *hargashah* was masked by the other, stronger sensation, she simply did not notice it.[47] The *Pleissi* explains differently: even when a woman *knows* that she did not have a *hargashah*, she is still *temei'ah mid'Oraisa* after seeing blood on a *bedikah* cloth.[48]

The accepted halachah is that a woman is a *niddah d'Oraisa* when she discovers blood immediately after marital relations, immediately after performing her bodily needs, or on a *bedikah* cloth even after time has passed.[49]

The Gemara says we are concerned about a *hargashah* in the cases of finding blood immediately after relations and using the restroom, and a discussion ensues to determine the amount of time that is still considered "immediate."[50] The conclusion is that "immediate" is within the time frame it takes for a woman to perform a *bedikah*.

The *Rama* says we are not sure exactly how long this amount of time is.[51] Many *Poskim* say this amount of time is approximately fifteen seconds. Thus, a woman who discovers blood within fifteen seconds of urinating is *temei'ah*, and is considered a *niddah d'Oraisa*; the blood she discovered is not subject to the leniencies of *kesamim* that we will

46. נדה נ״ז ע״ב.
47. הל׳ איסו״ב ט, א ״אין האשה מתטמאה מן התורה בנדה או בזיבה עד שתרגיש ותראה דם ויצא בבשרה כמו שביארנו ותהיה טמאה מעת שתראה ולהבא בלבד, ואם לא הרגישה ובדקה ומצאה הדם לפנים בפרוזדור ה״ז בחזקת שבא בהרגשה״ ע״כ.
48. יו״ד ס׳ קפ״ג ס״ק א׳.
49. חוו״ד חידושים ס׳ קפ״ג ס״ק ב׳ מובא בפ״ת ס׳ קפ״ג סוס״ק א׳.
50. נדה י״ד ע״ב: ״נמצא על שלה אותיום״.
51. ס׳ קפ״ז סע׳ א׳ ושם מדובר לענין רמ״ת.

discuss shortly in this chapter. The most common example of this happening is when a woman wipes herself and sees blood on the toilet paper.

Rav Moshe Feinstein says that in the case of a woman who discovers blood after urinating, the amount of time that is considered "immediately" is that she did not wait for the drops to finish falling.[52] This being the case, unless she was literally rushing out of the restroom, the leniencies of *kesamim* will generally be applied to any blood found after urinating, because we generally assume that she waited a few seconds between urinating and wiping herself. The same is true with regard to blood discovered after marital relations, where there is often a degree of latitude present that allows a *Rav* to view this blood as being found after the *shiur osyom* (immediate time frame), and therefore we treat it as a *kesem d'Rabbanan*.[53] However, if blood is found on a cloth used to wipe the husband's *eiver* after marital relations, this leniency will not apply.

The most common issue that arises is when a woman discovers blood on a *bedikah* cloth. In this case she is considered *temei'ah d'Oraisa*. Even if the *mareh* is only presented to a *Rav* hours after the *bedikah* was performed, we assume that at the time of the *bedikah* she experienced a *hargashah* that was not felt due to the presence of the foreign object of the *bedikah* cloth in her body, and she is therefore *temei'ah* even if there is only a small amount of blood.

52. בספר הל' נדה להרב שמעון איידר ס' י"ג.
53. ועיין בדרכי תשובה ס' קפ"ז ס"ק כ"ג.

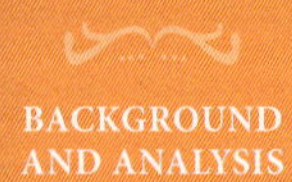

NIDDAH D'ORAISA

Blood WITH a Hargasha (Sensation)

SCENARIO	BLOOD FOUND	SIZE
Period	*Anytime*	*6-7 Gris in size*
Restroom	*Immediately after*	*Any visible amount*
Cohabitation	*Immediately after*	*Any visible amount*
Bedikah Cloth	*Anytime*	*Any visible amount*

NIDDAH D'RABANNAN

Blood WITHOUT a Hargasha (Sensation)

SCENARIO	LENIENCIES
Kessem	*1. Gris (Penny) in size*
	2. Colored garment
	3. Not Mekabel Tumah
	4. Teliyah (Attribution)
	5. No Vest Created

Other Types of Niddah D'Oraisa and Niddah D'Rabbanan

Until this point we have been discussing the *tumah* of niddah brought about by the breakdown of endometrium, which is what happens when a woman gets her period, as well as other cases of *niddah d'Oraisa*. The Torah also discusses several other types of *tumah* that are relevant to women.

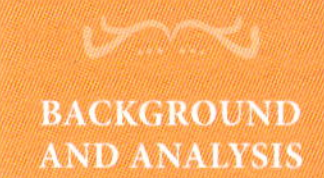

Birth

Tumas leidah is the *tumah* brought about by childbirth.[54] A woman is *temei'ah* after childbirth even if she were theoretically not to have bled at all. Giving birth to a boy makes her *temei'ah* for 7 days, and she is *temei'ah* for 14 days after the birth of a girl.

A woman only becomes *temei'ah* from the time she actually delivers the baby (*mid'Oraisa* most of it, and *mid'Rabbanan* as soon as part of it has come out). However, she is already *temei'ah* by that point in most cases because of the bleeding that accompanies the birth. The bleeding renders her *temei'ah* like every time blood comes out, i.e., with *tumas niddah*. In the event that she has a girl, *tumas leida*h makes her *temei'ah* for longer than the bleeding (*tumas niddah*) does, although this is usually irrelevant.

In summary, birth brings with it two types of *tumah*: *tumas niddah*, which starts when there is blood, and *tumas leidah*, which starts when the baby is born.

There is another possibility that we may assume that she is a niddah even before the blood is seen, which we will discuss in a few paragraphs. This is due to the rule that when the cervix opens for birth we assume that there is blood (*ein pesichas hakever b'lo dam)*. We will see that there is a debate about this stage, and that we are lenient.

Miscarriage

A miscarriage that occurred at least 40 days after conception is treated as a birth, i.e., the woman has *tumas leidah*. In the event that the fetus's gender is unknown, the woman must wait 14 days before she may immerse in the mikvah, out of concern that the fetus was a female.[55] The *shivah nekiyim*, however, may take place during the 14 days of *tumah*, but she may not immerse before Night 15. (The 7 days that a woman must wait before immersing in the mikvah after giving birth to a male are practically irrelevant, as she must anyway wait 5 days before the *hefsek taharah* and 7 days for *shivah nekiyim*.)

It should be noted that the halachic term "miscarriage" is only relevant when the woman discharged either a bone or some tissue.[56] Otherwise, any bleeding is considered to be regular *dam niddah*, which

---

54. ויקרא יב: א-ח.
55. ש״ך ס׳ קצ״ד ס״ק ב׳, ג׳ ובשו״ע שם סע׳ ג׳.
56. שו״ע קצ״ד ג׳ ובפ״ת ס״ק ו׳ שם.

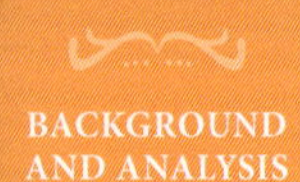

allows her to go to the mikvah after the regular *taharah* process of a *hefsek taharah* on the 5th day and *shivah nekiyim*.[57] Similarly, an early miscarriage that occurred less than 40 days from the time of conception is treated as a regular period; the woman may attempt a *hefsek taharah* at the end of the 5th day after the bleeding began.

Whenever a *safeik* (doubt) arises as to the timing of a miscarriage, a *Rav* should be consulted. Practically, a woman will have to wait for the bleeding to stop before undergoing the *taharah* process. This will almost always be in excess of the 14-day wait. She should ask a *she'eilah* regarding the status of an upcoming child with regard to *pidyon haben*.

Pesichas HaKever (Opening of the Uterus)

The Mishnah discusses a woman who discharged something that does not have a definitive shape.[58] The Chachamim say she is only *temei'ah* if there is blood; otherwise, she is *tehorah*. Rebbi Yehudah disagrees, saying that she is always *temei'ah*.

The Gemara explains that these Tanna'im are arguing about the halachah of of *ein pesichas hakever b'lo dam* — that any opening of the womb automatically discharges even a small amount of blood.[59] Rebbi Yehudah holds that blood is discharged whenever the uterus opens, and that blood is *dam niddah*, automatically making the woman *temei'ah*. The Chachamim disagree, saying that bleeding is not automatic when the uterus opens. A woman is only *temei'ah* when she specifically knows that blood is there.

The *Shulchan Aruch* rules like Rebbi Yehudah[60] — the halachah assumes that some blood came out any time a woman's cervix opens.

Internal Examinations

The *Noda B'Yehudah* says that the rule of *ein pesichas hakever b'lo dam* applies even when the uterus is forced open with an instrument.[61] The Baruch Tam disagrees; he holds it is only when the cervix opens to expel something from the inside.[62] From the fact that the *Poskim* discuss whether an instrument makes a woman *temei'ah* when it is

57. שו"ע קצ"ד, ב'.
58. נדה כ"א ע"א.
59. נדה כ"א ע"א.
60. יו"ד קפ"ח, ג'.
61. נו"ב תניינא יו"ד ס"ס ק"כ.
62. הגהות רב ברוך פריינקל לשו"ת נו"ב ס' ק"כ.

only inserted into the tip of the cervix and does not enter the uterus completely,[63] it seems that the halachah follows the stringent opinion of the Noda B'Yehudah. The discussions surround determining the exact specifications for the opening of the cervix that would render her *temei'ah*.

Another discussion revolves around how thick the inserted instrument must be to consider the uterus "open," thereby making the woman *temei'ah*. An instrument narrower than 18 millimeters is generally not an issue, and she will remain *tehorah*. Inserting an instrument thicker than 18 millimeters into the cervix will be very painful. The woman will know that something was inserted.

Most regular internal exams do not go into the cervix, and thus do not present any problem. An internal ultrasound does not present a problem either. A pap smear goes into the entrance of the cervix, but it is too thin to be considered a problem. A pap smear may cause abrasions on the cervix, so any blood found afterwards is *dam makkah* and is not *metamei*. As we discussed previously in this chapter, Rav Yosef Shalom Elyashiv considers bleeding that is caused by the uterine lining being punctured to be *dam niddah*. According to this, procedures that puncture the uterine lining are *metamei* a woman, even if they do not cause *pesichas hakever*. Pap smears, though, generally do not go past the cervix, which has no lining. They are not problematic, even according to Rav Elyashiv.

A common problem used to be when a laparoscopy (an internal photograph taken by a camera in a very slender tube inserted into the body) was performed. However, thin fiber optic cameras are used nowadays instead, so this generally is not an issue anymore.

An IUD

A woman who has an IUD inserted should speak to a *Rav*. Depending on the specifics of the procedure, it is generally *metamei* her when it is removed, but not when inserted, because of *pesichas hakever*.

63. ב"י ס' קפ"ח, גר"א ס' קצ"ב ס"ק כ"ב, אבני נזר ס' רכ"ד, אג"מ יו"ד א' ס' פ"ג, מנח"י חלק ג' ס' פ"ד, שיעורי שבה"ל, חוט שני.

Labor Contractions

The cervix of a woman in labor dilates when she gets contractions. There is a stage at which this dilation is considered *pesichas hakever.* The Gemara discusses the point from which one is permitted to desecrate Shabbos to help a woman in childbirth: is it from the time that she begins bleeding heavily, or from the time of the *pesichas hakever*?[64] Most *Rishonim* follow the latter opinion. The Gemara then describes certain signs that indicate that *pesichas hakever* has occurred. One is that other people have to carry her because she cannot walk on her own. According to another opinion, it only from when she is actually sitting on the birthing stool. When one of these signs occurs, one is allowed to desecrate Shabbos in order to help her. Practically speaking, one may desecrate Shabbos to assist a woman during childbirth from the time that she begins having regular contractions.

The *Poskim* debate whether the above halachah has ramifications on the *tumas niddah* that occurs with the flow of blood at the time of childbirth. Some conclude that when one of these signs happens, just as we may desecrate Shabbos, so we assume that some blood must have come out and therefore she is *temei'ah niddah.* Others disagree, based on a number of objections. First, maybe we are more lenient in regard to saving life and we do not have to be so cautious as to assume the time has come yet with regard to niddah until we actually see the blood. Second, there is a general debate as to when *pesichas hakever* is *metamei* a woman. Is blood assumed to come out as soon as the uterus opens? Or perhaps the reason that *pesichas hakever* is *metamei* is because it opened for a reason, to allow something to come out. This being the case, we assume that blood will come out together with whatever it is we are anticipating, which is the reason why the uterus opened in the first place. Accordingly, before the baby leaves the body, there is no reason to be concerned about blood.

The Noda B'Yehudah is lenient, saying that the woman remains *tehorah* until the baby comes out unless we clearly see blood.[65] Most *Poskim* rule like the Noda B'Yehudah. Although Rav Moshe Feinstein is stringent in regard to this issue, the accepted halachah is that dilation on its own is not *metamei* a woman. A woman only becomes a niddah during childbirth when she sees blood. (As said above, were there to be no blood she would become a niddah when the baby comes out.)

64. שבת קכ"ט ע"א, ועיין בפ"ת ס' קצ"ד ס"ק ח' בשם הנחלת שבעה שדנין יולדת לענין נדה כמו לענין שבת.

65. נו"ב קונטרס אחרון ס' קט"ז.

Practically, she will be *temei'ah* when she discovers a *kesem* that is ruled to be *tamei,* when blood is seen as a result of an internal exam, from the time she begins to bleed during the delivery process, or when she actually delivers the baby. She will not become *temei'ah* from dilation alone.

Blood during Birth

Some say that we assume that blood came out if a woman's waters broke, while others say we assume blood came out when she ejects the mucus plug. Practically speaking, we do not assume either. If the mucus plug falls out without blood, it is not *metamei* the woman. If there is blood on the mucus plug, the color of the blood should be checked to see if it is problematic. Blood that is found on the mucus plug is treated as a *kesem* with all of its leniencies.

The doctor will often perform an internal examination to check the woman's dilation. If there is any amount of blood on their glove after they are finished, she becomes *temei'ah.* Since the glove was inserted inside her body, this blood is treated as a *bedikah* — making her *temei'ah d'Oraisa* — and not as a *kesem* with its accompanying leniencies.

In general, if a woman does an unnecessary *bedikah* at a time that she has no reason to expect to discover blood (i.e., not during *shivah nekiyim* or on a *vest*), the *bedikah* need not be looked at; it may be discarded and ignored as long as she has not become aware of a problem on the *bedikah* cloth. This rule does not apply to an internal exam performed during labor. Since blood is common and may be expected under these circumstances, the woman should ask to see the glove.

Feeling a Hargashah Without Discovering Blood

The *Terumas HaDeshen* says a woman who feels a *hargashah* must assume that blood has come out, unless she can prove otherwise. Therefore, she must do a *bedikah* to see what came out of her body.[66] If she finds blood she is of course *temei'ah.* If she does not find anything she is *temei'ah* as well, because we assume that some blood was discharged from the *mekor* when it opened. If, however, she finds something that is a *tahor* color, she may assume that the *hargashah* she felt was associated with this discharge, and the woman remains *tehorah.* The Darchei Moshe disagrees with the Terumas HaDeshen's position

66. שו״ת תרומת הדשן ס׳ רמ״ו.

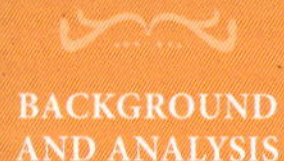

and says that until the time of the Terumas HaDeshen, nobody had thought to forbid a woman just because of a *hargashah*.[67]

The Shulchan Aruch rules like the Terumas HaDeshen.[68] However, it is not clear which *hargashah* the *Shulchan Aruch* is discussing, that would make a woman *temei'ah*. As we discussed earlier, women nowadays generally do not experience any *hargashos*, aside from an occasional woman who feels internal wetness. Rav Moshe Feinstein says if a woman *knows* she felt internal wetness, she should do a *bedikah*.[69] In practice, a woman who thinks she experienced a *hargashah* should *externally* wipe herself to look for blood, and not do a regular *bedikah*. If a *tahor* color is found on the wipe, the woman may assume that this was the cause of the *hargashah* she felt. If the wipe comes out clean, however, she should do a *bedikah*. If this too comes out clean, the practice is to be lenient as per the opinion of the Darchei Moshe, who says that the woman is *tehorah* if she looked and did not find any discharge. The reason for this leniency is that many hold that feeling internal wetness is a not considered a *hargashah*, so we do not add this stringency of the *hargashah* of feeling internal wetness to that of the *Terumas HaDeshen*. Also, the *Chavas Daas* adds that a woman can mistakenly think that she felt internal wetness when she really did not.[70] As a matter of practice, therefore, a woman may be lenient after experiencing a feeling of internal wetness when no blood was subsequently found.

The *Maharsham* says a woman may establish that she finds *tahor* colors after a *hargashah*, by doing a *bedikah* after each of three *hargashos* and finding a *tahor* color. In such a case, she does not need to do *bedikos* after each *hargashah* anymore.[71] Practically speaking, a woman who does a *bedikah* after experiencing a *hargashah* three times may ignore future *hargashos*. This case is rare nowadays, though.

Rav Moshe Feinstein says this is only effective until the woman's situation changes, for example, until she becomes a niddah again.[72] Rav Shlomo Zalman Auerbach disagrees, and holds this will work for her anytime she feels a *hargashah* again in the future.

Some *kallah* teachers teach their students about many different types of *hargashos*. This often results in women doing many unnecessary *bedikos* to establish that they are *tehoros* after every kind of suspected *hargashah*. They often hurt themselves in the process, see blood on

---

67. יו״ד ס׳ קפ״ח אות ב׳ ובשו״ת רדב״ז חלק א׳ ס׳ קמ״ט.
68. ס׳ ק״צ סע׳ א׳ וס׳ קפ״ח סע׳ א׳ ברמ״א.
69. בספר הל׳ נדה לרב שמעון איידר אות ח׳.
70. חוו״ד ס׳ ק״צ סע׳ א׳.
71. שו״ת מהרש״ם חלק א ס׳ קפ״ח.
72. בספר הל׳ נדה לרב שמעון איידר אות ט׳.

the *bedikah* cloth that comes from their now-irritated skin, and are generally stringent more than necessary. The whole concept of a *hargashah* without blood is a stringency of the *Terumas HaDeshen*. A woman should be taught not to do a *bedikah* even when she thinks that she feels something; she should do an external wipe instead. If she has a *hargashah* and actually discovers blood, she is *temei'ah*, as anytime she performs a *bedikah* and finds blood on the cloth, as discussed in Basic Overview, How a Woman Becomes a Niddah, headline "Mistaken Sensations (page 12). In general, however, a woman does not become *temei'ah* simply because she thinks she felt a *hargashah*.

Dam Mid'Rabbanan

The halachos discussed until this point are all cases of *niddah d'Oraisa*, where blood was discovered as part of a regular period, together with a *hargashah*, as part of childbirth, or because the woman's *mekor* was opened. We will now learn about cases of *niddah d'Rabbanan*. These include *dam chimud*, *dam besulim*, and *kesamim*.

Dam Chimud

The *Shulchan Aruch*[73] states that the *shivah nekiyim* and mikvah immersion that a *kallah* does in preparation for her wedding must be done after the time that the wedding date has been set and wedding preparations have begun.[74] The reason for this is the concern that the excitement of confirming the wedding date will cause the *kallah* to bleed. So, even if she has already been to the mikvah and will not be getting her period again until the wedding, since she might have bled at that point of confirmation, she must start again with a *hefsek taharah* and *shivah nekiyim*. This concern is called *dam chimud* — bleeding caused by longing.

If the wedding was called off completely after the *kallah* already counted *shivah nekiyim*, she needs another *shivah nekiyim* when they set a new date, since there is now a new *chimud*, that is, emotional excitement.[75] If, however, the wedding was never called off, but they just decided to change the date, no new *shivah nekiyim* are necessary, since no new *chimud* was created.[76]

---

73. ס' קצ"ב.
74. גמ' כתובות י', שו"ת מהרש"ם חלק א ס' צ"ה.
75. ס' קצ"ב סע' ג'.
76. ועיין בס' קצ"ב בש"ך ס"ק ו', ז' ובט"ז ס"ק ו'.

Dam chimud applies to every woman who is getting married, even if she is postmenopausal.[77]

There is a widespread custom that a *chassan* and *kallah* do not see each other a week before the wedding. Some say that the reason for this is because of a type of *dam chimud*; we are concerned that seeing her groom will cause the *kallah* to bleed and ruin the *shivah nekiyim* before the wedding. This is not the real halachic worry of *dam chimud* which only exists when the wedding date is set. Therefore, it is not treated as more than a custom, and many extenuating circumstances allow a meeting in that week. Other reasons given for this custom are so that the *chassan and kallah* will have more anticipation for the wedding night, or to make sure that the *chassan* does not speak to a nervous *kallah* and ruin things right before the wedding.

As a matter of practice, a *kallah* should immerse in the mikvah as close to the wedding as possible.[78] A *kallah* who immersed in the mikvah more than 4 days before the wedding must do *bedikos* every day until the wedding. Many *Poskim* necessitate *bedikos* even if she immersed less than 4 days before the wedding. The Rama, however, says she need not do any more *bedikos* if she went to the mikvah up to 4 days before the wedding.[79]

This halachah applies only to a *kallah*. A regular woman who did not immerse in the mikvah immediately following her *shivah nekiyim* does not need to do any additional *bedikos*, since no concern of *dam chimud* exists.

A second type of *niddah d'Rabbanan* brought in the *Shulchan Aruch* is *dam besulim* — virginity bleeding.[80] The bleeding that comes from the hymen being broken is actually *dam makkah*. However, *Chazal* nevertheless declared that it makes the woman *temei'ah*.[81] One explanation is that this avoids confusion between *dam besulim* and other forms of niddah, such as blood caused by marital relations (see Background and Analysis, How a Woman Becomes a Niddah, headline "Dam Chimud", page 109).[82] Another reason is the concern that some *dam chimud* may have come during the *bi'ah rishonah* (first intercourse).[83]

---

77. פ״ת ס׳ קצ״ב ס״ק ב׳.
78. ס׳ קצ״ב ברמ״א סע׳ ב׳.
79. ס׳ קצ״ב ברמ״א סע׳ ב׳.
80. ס׳ קצ״ג.
81. גמ׳ נדה ס״ה ע״ב.
82. שו״ת הרשב״א חלק ז׳ ס׳ קס״א.
83. אג״מ יו״ד א׳ ס׳ פ״ז.

A difference between these two reasons is seen in the following scenario. The *Poskim* discuss the case of a woman who inadvertently tears her *besulim* when doing a *bedikah* before the wedding — is this woman *temei'ah*? (A woman should never surgically remove her *besulim* before the wedding to save herself from *dam besulim*.[84] The *sefarim* discuss that the *chassan* should make the *kallah* into his *kli* [vessel]. A doctor should not remove the *besulim*, which are a woman's sign of purity, unless explicitly sanctioned by a *Rav* [sometimes necessary, as when she has a septated hyman].)

Some *Poskim* say the *besulim*'s breaking is *metamei* a woman even when they are cut surgically.[85] According to these *Poskim*, if the *besulim* were broken by a *bedikah* done either before or after the wedding, the woman is rendered *temei'ah*, even though the *besulim* were not torn during *bi'ah rishonah*. Rav Moshe Feinstein, however, says the reason that *dam besulim* is *metamei* is out of concern for *dam chimud*.[86] Accordingly, a woman is only *temei'ah* when her *besulim* were broken during marital relations, and not when she broke it in other ways, such as during a *bedikah* or through a medical procedure. Should this question arise, the practice in the United States is generally to follow Rav Moshe Feinstein's opinion.

At Which Point Is Dam Besulim Metamei?

A *kallah* is *temei'ah* after the first complete *bi'ah* that the couple had, even if they did not actually find any blood afterwards, on the chance that the *zera* covered over the small amount of blood that was there.[87] The *Raavad* adds that the *kallah* is *tehorah* in a case of *he'arah* (surface-level contact, with little penetration) — when her *chassan* was not successful in penetrating, but only "poked" her — and they did not find any blood.[88] The Rama rules to be lenient in regard to *dam besulim* in a case of *he'arah*.[89] *He'arah* is *kenissas atarah* (penetration of the crown of the male organ) and nothing more. If the *chassan* enters any more than that, the *kallah* is *temei'ah*, because this is considered *gemar bi'ah*.

In general, the average *chassan* has no idea what happened. The *kallah* doesn't either know; she just knows that she felt some pressure.

84. חוט שני ס׳ קצ״ג בסוף הסימן, שיעורי שבט הלוי ס׳ קצ״ג אות ג׳, ובמנחת יצחק.
85. שו״ת מנחת יצחק חלק ד׳ ס׳ נ״ח.
86. אג״מ יו״ד א׳ ס׳ פ״ז.
87. רא״ש נדה פרק י, ס׳ א.
88. עיין בבעלי הנפש להראב״ד סוף שער הפרישה, ועיין בהג״מ הל׳ איסו״ב פרק יא אות ג׳ ובשו״ע ס׳ קצ״ג סע׳ א׳ וברמ״א שם.
89. ס׳ קצ״ג.

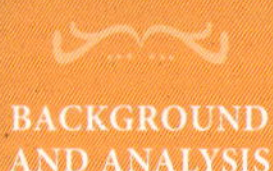

(Generally, any pain associated with *dam besulim* is caused by stretching muscles that are being used for the first time in her life, and is not caused by the actual *besulim* tearing.)

Some *Poskim* are stringent, saying that one must be concerned about *dam besulim* every time the couple thinks that the *chassan* penetrated a bit further than *kenissas atarah*, even when no blood was discovered, out of the concern for *gemar bi'ah*.[90] This, however, is a tremendous stringency. A *Rav* may ask the couple a series of questions to determine whether or not it appears that they have completely consummated the marriage. Taking their answers into account will help him determine whether they may continue trying for *bi'ah rishonah*.

Rav Moshe Feinstein says once *dam besulim* has been found, the couple does not have to look out for *dam besulim* again, even if the *chassan* just did *he'arah* the first time, and the second time there was a *gemar bi'ah*. The *kallah* is unquestionably *tehorah* if there is no blood the second time. If they do see blood the second time, this blood is considered *dam besulim* again, and she will be *temei'ah* according to both reasons cited above. Rav Moshe Feinstein says, however, that the couple does not have to *look out* for blood. According to Rav Moshe Feinstein, the couple should use colored sheets and underwear after *bi'ah rishonah* so the *kallah* will not become *temei'ah* unnecessarily.

Kesamim

The third area of *niddah d'Rabbanan* is *Chazal*'s institution of the laws of *kesamim*.[91] A *kesem* (stain) is the word used to refer to blood that a woman discovers that is not part of a regular period, is not accompanied by a *hargashah* or suspected *hargashah*, and is not one of the other types of blood that have been discussed previously that would make her a *niddah d'Rabbanan*. Although blood discovered as a *kesem* is *tahor mid'Oraisa* since it was not accompanied by a *hargashah*, *Chazal* nevertheless said that a *kesem* makes the woman *temei'ah*. However, *Chazal* included five leniencies within the edict of *kesamim*.

These leniencies are:

1. A *kesem* only makes the woman *temei'ah* when it is more than the size of a *gris*, which is approximately the size of a penny or one-shekel coin.

90. עיין מש״כ בזה בחכ״א, בבד״ה ובשי׳ שבט הלוי בס׳ קצ״ג.
91. גמ׳ נדה נ״ז ע״ב- נ״ח ע״א בדברי ר׳ ירמי-ה ובשו״ע ס׳ ק״צ א׳.

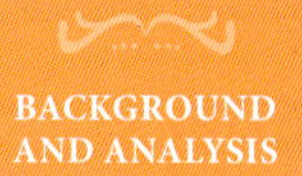

2. A *kesem* does not make the woman *temei'ah* when it is discovered on colored sheets or colored clothing.
3. A *kesem* is only ruled *tamei* when found on something that is susceptible to *tumah*.
4. A *kesem* is only ruled *tamei* when the blood cannot be attributed to something else. Attributing the stain to something other than coming from the *mekor* is called a *teliyah* (literally, ascription).
5. Even when ruled *tamei*, blood discharged as a *kesem* does not create a *vest*.

We will now discuss these points in greater detail.

The Size of a Gris

The first leniency of *kesamim* is that a *kesem* is only a problem when it is larger than the size of a *gris*.[92] (A *gris*[93] is about the size of a penny or one-shekel coin.[94]) The reason for this leniency is that lice were prevalent in people's homes and beds in the times of *Chazal*, and *Chazal* realized that no woman would ever remain *tehorah* if she would be declared *temei'ah* from every speck of blood that she discovers. The *Poskim* ask: If this is the case, how can we, nowadays, attribute the blood to these lice if these bugs are not commonly found in our homes and beds anymore?[95] Furthermore, today's bedbugs are much smaller than they used to be, and are not nearly the size of a *gris*. There are almost no lice today that produce blood stains the size of a *gris*!

In answer to these questions, the *Chasam Sofer* explains that originally, *kesamim* only made a person *tamei* for *Taharos* (the laws of purity, as kept until the time of the destruction of the Second Beis HaMikdash). Eventually, the edict of this *tumah* was extended to be *metamei* a woman to her husband as well.[96] Therefore, although we keep the edict of *kesamim* that were kept in the times of *Chazal*, we also keep the leniency of the times of *Chazal* — the institution of the leniency that the stain must be larger than a *gris* to be *metamei* the woman.

92. נדה נ״ח ע״ב במשנה וגמ׳ שם ועיין בשו״ע ס׳ ק״צ סע׳ ה׳– ח׳.
93. עיין ברמב״ם פ״ט מל׳ איסו״ב הל׳ ה׳, בשו״ע ק״צ ה׳, ובתוה״ש שם ס״ק ז׳ מש״כ בזה. ועיין עוד בלו״ש ס״ק יט׳ ובשו״ע הרב ס״ק י״ג ובחזו״א בקונטרס השיעורים ס״ק ט״ו ובחוט שני ששיעור הגריס הוא כ18 מ״מ. ויש שכ׳ שהוא כ19 מ״מ, וכ״כ באג״מ ובטהרת בת ישראל. ועיין בפתחי תשובות שהביא עוד דעות בענין.
94. אג״מ יו״ד ג׳ ס׳ נ״ו אות ב׳.
95. חת״ס ס׳ ק״נ מובא בפ״ת ס׳ ק״צ ס״ק י׳.
96. חת״ס שם וכן הוא עיקר שיטת האשכול בס׳ האשכול הל׳ נדה פרק א׳ ״גם מדיני כתמים וכו׳״ ע״ש, אע״פ דלא אמרינן כשיטתו שם לבטל כתמים בזמנינו שאין טהרות.

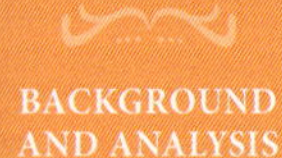

The Gemara says that several small *kesamim* are not joined together to reach the (problematic) size of a *gris*.[97] However, another Gemara discusses whether many small dots found together on her skin in unusual shapes, forms, or directions are *metamei*.[98] The *Rambam* resolves this seeming contradiction by explaining that *kesamim* discovered on a woman's clothing are not combined to reach the size of a *gris*, but a *kesem* found on her body is *metamei* her even when it is less than a *gris*, because it is not common to find lice on the body. In other words, according to the *Rambam*, the leniency of the *gris* does not apply to a *kesem* found on a woman's body.[99]

Tosafos answer differently.[100] A few stains found on her clothing are not joined together to become a *gris*. Since lice are commonly found on clothing, it makes sense that the different stains of blood came from separate lice. Therefore, if each individual *kesem* is smaller than the size of a *gris*, the woman remains *tehorah*, even if all the stains together amount to more than a *gris*. On her body, though, where it is not so common to have lice, we do not assume that the various stains came from more than one louse. This being so, the different stains *do* join together to the size of a *gris*.

The Rashba has a third approach.[101] He says that when a woman discovers a *kesem* on her body, she will only be *temei'ah* if it is larger than a *gris*, and a few smaller stains are not joined together. He explains that the Gemara that discusses whether small dots found together on her skin in unusual shapes, forms, or directions are *metamei* her is speaking about a case in which some dots are larger than a *gris* but come in a specific shape. The Gemara's question is thus: does this shape indicate that this blood came from a source other than her *mekor*, giving her an innate *teliyah* that she is *tehorah*?

The halachah is like the opinion of Tosafos.[102] *A kesem* is always *tahor* when it is smaller than a *gris. Kesamim* discovered on clothing are not combined to make up the size of a *gris. Kesamim* that a woman discovers on her body are joined together, but she remains *tehorah* if the *kesem* found on her body is smaller than a *gris*.

A woman who discovers a *kesem* on her body should estimate its size, and transfer it to a *bedikah* cloth or tissue. If it is a dry stain, she

97. נדה נ״ט ע״א.
98. נדה נ״ח ע״א.
99. הל׳ איסו״ב פרק ט׳ הל׳ ו׳ והל׳ כג׳.
100. נדה נ״ח ע״א ד״ה כשורה.
101. תורת הבית בית ז׳ שער ד׳.
102. שו״ע ק״צ ו׳.

should use clear scotch tape and put the stain on the tape so the *Rav* can see the shape, size and color.

When measuring a *kesem* that includes several shades of color and only part of it is *tamei*, the size of a *gris* is calculated, taking only the *tamei* parts into account.

The size of a *kesem* is measured only by its length and width. The thickness is not considered. A thick *kesem* whose area is less than a *gris* is *tahor*.[103]

A Kesem Discovered on a Colored Item

The second leniency of *kesamim* is that a *kesem* discovered on a colored background is not *tamei*.[104] *Rashi* explains that "colored" means that one cannot see what color the blood is, because it is distorted by the color of the fabric upon which it is lying.[105] Rav Yosef Shalom Elyashiv rules that, following *Rashi*'s explanation, if the background color is light enough to allow the *kesem*'s color to be viewed clearly, this leniency no longer applies.

The *Rambam* says that *Chazal* did not institute that a *kesem* on a colored background is *tamei*, no matter how light a shade of color it is. Rav Moshe Feinstein's ruling is that if something is not "white," it is called "colored," and is automatically *tahor*.[106] This is ostensibly learned[107] from *Rashi* in a different place,[108] where he says that blood that is seen on clothing that has any color other than white will distort the color of the blood. Most American *Poskim* rule like this. Consequently, a *kesem* found on pastel underwear is problematic according to Rav Yosef Shalom Elyashiv, and always *tahor* according to Rav Moshe Feinstein, even if it is larger than a *gris*.

The *Shulchan Aruch* says a woman should wear colored underwear when she is *tehorah* to avoid *kesamim*.[109] According to Rav Moshe Feinstein she can wear pastel colors or darker. Rav Yosef Shalom Elyashiv says she should wear something with real color. But he adds that a woman should not wear black, because she can get her period and

103. עיין בפ״ת ס׳ ק״צ ס״ק ט׳ מש״כ בזה בשם הס״ט.
104. גמ׳ נדה ס״א ע״ב.
105. שם ד״ה להקל על כתמיהן.
106. איסו״ב ט׳ ז׳.
107. שו״ת מעיל צדקה ס׳ ס״ב.
108. נדה י״ז ע״ב ד״ה ולא.
109. ס׳ ק״צ סע׳ י׳ ברמ״א.

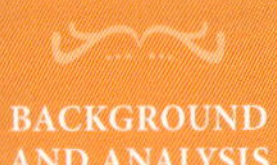

simply overlook it. Rather, she should wear something that will distort the color, but allow her to see if she in fact starts to bleed.

If a *kesem* is discovered on a background that is partially white (or, according to Rav Yosef Shalom Elyashiv, light-colored) and partially colored, the part on the white should be examined, and the part on the color disregarded. In a case of a white background with a black stripe on it, and the *kesem* is on both sides of the stripe, the *kesem* should be examined, and the parts on the white will join together to make the size of a *gris* assuming the stain is one large stain. The part appearing on the color is not taken into account.[110] If the colored portion of the clothing cuts the stain in half, we only combine the parts of the stain on the colored parts of the clothing if it is determined that the stain is one large stain rather than two stains.

An Item Than Is Susceptible to Tumah

The third leniency of *kesamim* is that a *kesem* is *tahor* when discovered on something that is not susceptible to *tumah*.[111] One explanation for the reason behind this leniency is that the edict of *kesamim* originated because of *taharos*.[112] *Kesamim* are only dealt with leniently for a woman, who is only a *niddah mid'Oraisa* if she has a *hargashah*. However the blood itself, even if it came without a *hargashah*, makes a vessel it touches *tamei*. There thus emerged a situation in which a woman would see blood and whereas she was *tahor*, an item touched by the blood was *tamei*. As people might not understand this nuance and they may conclude that if she is *tehorah*, so are her clothes, *Chazal* decided to make the woman *temei'ah* as well. When the *kesem* was discovered on something that was not susceptible to *tumah*, there was clearly no need for this *taharos*-related edict. Nowadays, although we do not keep our clothing and vessels in a state of *taharah*, the original edict of *kesamim* still applies, and a woman is *temei'ah* if she finds a *kesem*. However, there is certainly no need to extend the edict more than when it was originally enacted.

There is a disagreement regarding something that is not susceptible to most forms of *tumah*, but is susceptible to *tumas nega'im*.[113] Can this object become *tamei* from a *kesem*? Most *Poskim* say anything attached to the ground, such as a toilet, bathtub, or something similar, will be

110. שו"ת מעיל צדקה ס' ס"ב ועיין בחוו"ד ס ק"צ אות ט' בביאורים.
111. גמ' נדה נ"ח ע"א ושו"ע ס' ק"צ סע' י'.
112. ועיין מש"כ בגמ' נדה נ"ח ע"א ובתוס' ד"ה כר' נחמי–ה ועיין בס"ט ס' ק"צ סוף ס"ק צ"ג ובפ"ת ס' ק"צ ס"ק י"ז.
113. תוס' נדה נ"ח ע"א ד"ה כר' נחמי–ה ורא"ש פרק האשה ס' ב'.

tahor, even if the *kesem* is larger than a *gris*.[114] The Noda B'Yehudah adds that something that is *supposed* to be attached to the ground is treated as if it is connected even if it happens to be detached at the moment.[115] According to this, a *kesem* discovered on a detached toilet seat is also *tahor*.

Another disagreement that is very relevant to *kesamim* is whether paper is susceptible to *tumah*.[116] Within this disagreement, it is important to note that there are many types of paper. Rav Moshe Feinstein says regular paper is susceptible to *tumah*,[117] but toilet paper is disposable, so it is not susceptible to *tumah*. (The halachos of *kesamim* and toilet paper only apply when the woman cleaned herself after she waited for the drops to finish falling. Any blood discovered before this time, that is, during the time that she is actually relieving herself and immediately thereafter, renders her *temei'ah*, since, as we discussed earlier (Basic Overview, How a Woman Becomes a Niddah, headline "Mistaken Sensations [page 12]), she may have experienced a *hargashah* that was covered over by the physical sensation of relieving herself.)

Rav Yosef Shalom Elyashiv disagrees, giving several reasons why *kesamim* discovered on toilet paper are problematic. One reason is that we know that it came from her body, and blood that is *vadai migufah* (certainly from her body) renders her *temei'ah*. Another reason is based on the *Sidrei Taharah*,[118] which says that something that is not susceptible to *tumah* that is on top of something that is susceptible to *tumah* when the *kesem* is found, will be *tamei* in regard to *kesamim*. Therefore, since the woman is holding the toilet paper when wiping, we must be concerned about the *kesem*. Also, Rav Yosef Shalom Elyashiv says the fact that something is created to be disposable is not a reason to consider it something that is not susceptible to *tumah*.

In the United States, *Poskim* generally do not examine toilet paper unless there is concern that it might be a *re'iyah* (i.e., she either felt a *hargashah* or there is concern that this is her period), as they rule that toilet paper is not susceptible to *tumah* and the *kesem* is therefore *tahor*. In Eretz Yisrael the practice is to treat these as regular *kesamim*.

Rav Moshe Feinstein holds that sanitary pads are not susceptible to *tumah*. Rav Yosef Shalom Elyashiv is quoted as saying that they are susceptible to *tumah*, while others say pads are only a problem when

---

114. רמב״ם, רשב״א, מרדכי, סמ״ג, סמ״ק, שו״ע ורמ״א ס׳ ק״צ י׳, ועיין בפ״ת שם ס״ק יז׳– כא׳ מש״כ בשם הס״ט, חת״ס, נו״ב ושאר גדולי הפוסקים בענין זה.
115. נו״ב יו״ד מהדורא תנינא ס׳ קט׳, מובא בפ״ת ס׳ ק״צ ס״ק י״ט.
116. עיין בפ״ת ס׳ ק״צ ס״ק י״ח.
117. אג״מ יו״ד ג׳ ס׳ נ״ג.
118. ס״ט ס׳ ק״צ ס״ק צ״ג מובא בפ״ת ס״ק י״ז.

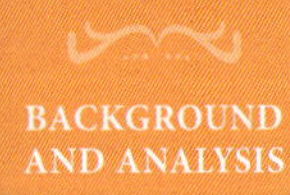

they are attached to underwear. *Poskim* in the United States generally are lenient regarding stains found on pads unless there is concern for a *re'iyah*, and in Eretz Yisrael, blood found on pads is generally treated as a *kesem*.

Teliyah

The forth leniency of *kesamim* is that a *kesem* is *tahor* if the blood that the woman found can be conceivably attributed to a source other than uterine bleeding.[119]

The Mishnah tells a story of a woman who found a *kesem*, and she also had a scab that had already healed.[120] Rebbe Akiva ruled that she was *tehorah* on the chance that the scab had bled again and then rehealed. When he saw his students looking at each other in astonishment, he told them that in regard to *kesamim* we are lenient and can even use a *teliyah* like this, because the *passuk* speaks of a woman who discovered "*dam*," implying that it was not a *kesem*. If a woman who is ostensibly *temei'ah d'Oraisa* wants to attribute the blood to a source other than the uterus, there has to be a strong possibility that that source actually produced the blood. When dealing with a *kesem*, though, the *teliyah* can be more lenient, as the possibility of the source of the blood being from something else can be more remote.

For example, if a woman finds a *kesem* that could have originated from a wound, an animal, or any other external source, *a Rav* will be lenient and attribute the blood to the external source even if he is not completely sure where the blood originated.

In general, a woman should consult a *Rav* if she would like to attribute a *kesem* to an external source.

Kesamim Do Not Create Vestos

The fifth leniency of *kesamim* is that they do not create *vestos*.[121] A *vest* is based on the concern that blood that was discovered is part of a pattern. A *kesem*, however, is sporadic in nature, and is not expected to repeat itself month after month.

See Background and Analysis, Vestos (page 162) for a discussion of *vestos*.

119. מש׳ נדה נ״ז ע״א וגמ׳ שם נח׳ ע״א ועיין שו״ע ס׳ ק״צ ס׳ י״א-ל״ב.
120. נדה נ״ח ע״ב.
121. ס׳ ק״צ סע׳ נ״ד.

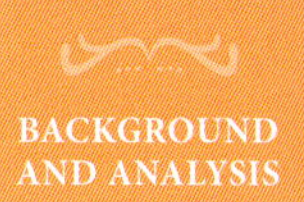

HARCHAKOS

Introduction to Harchakos

The Gemara tells a story about a woman who complained that although her husband was a tzaddik, he died at a young age.[122] Eliyahu HaNavi asked her how he behaved with her during the times she was bleeding each month. She replied that he did not even touch her small finger. Then Eliyahu HaNavi asked how he acted when she was in middle of *shivah nekiyim*. She answered that he ate and drank with her and slept in the same bed as her. When she said that, Eliyahu HaNavi answered, "*Baruch HaMakom shehargo* — Blessed is God Who killed him."

Rav Yosef Shalom Elyashiv explains Eliyahu HaNavi's questioning of the woman as follows: *mid'Oraisa* a woman is *temei'ah* for niddah only 7 days. *Shivah nekiyim* are observed based on the stringency of Rav Zeira, who says the Jewish women accepted to keep *shivah nekiyim*, which is really the halachah of a *zavah gedolah* (as discussed in Advanced Rulings, Taharah, headline "Understanding Shivah Nekiyim Mid'Oraisa [page 313])

Eliyahu HaNavi was therefore asking the woman if they were lenient, which was against the accepted halachah, to which the woman said that they were. In fact, in that time many women would go to the mikvah

122. גמ' שבת י"ג סוע"א וע"ב.

after the 7 days of niddah and would immerse again after *shivah nekiyim*. In this way they would immerse after the *d'Oraisa* and then again after the *d'Rabbanan* to remove the stronger *tumah* as early as possible, while observing all *harchakos* until the second immersion.

The Gemara is stressing that although they were lenient regarding the newly accepted stringency, they were nevertheless deserving of punishment for their disregard of this area of halachah.

These halachos of how a man must restrict the way that he acts with his wife when she is a niddah are called *harchakos* (literally, distances). The Torah explicitly says that a man may not have intimate relations with his wife while she is a niddah.[123] Such an act is punishable by *kareis* and is included in the three cardinal sins that a man must forfeit his own life rather than transgress.

Reasons for Harchakos

This story tells us that a husband may not touch his niddah wife in any way, even her smallest finger, even when the reason for doing so has nothing to do with deriving pleasure.[124] The *Rashba* explains that in a husband-and-wife relationship, every touch, or even just passing items back and forth, is an act that has the potential to bring to intimacy.[125] Passing items to a woman with whom a man is less familiar than his wife is not considered an act that has this potential, and is therefore permitted.

The *Rosh* gives a different reason for *harchakos*.[126] *Chazal* established *harchakos* for a niddah as an added protective "fence," because, unlike by other women with whom one is prohibited to have relations, *yichud* with a wife who is a niddah is allowed. They thus established *harchakos* to counteract this leniency.

Histaklus and Hirhur

Rabbeinu Yonah[127] says that the prohibition of gazing at one who is forbidden to a man is the prohibition of "*lo sasuru acharei eineichem*."[128]

---

123. ויקרא טו:יט–ל, יח:יט, כ:יח.
124. יו"ד ס' קצ"ה סע' ב'.
125. שו"ת הרשב"א חלק א' ס' אלף קפ"ח.
126. קיצור הל' נדה להרא"ש (סוף מס' נדה אחרי הל' מקואות) "ומשעת ראייתה... אחר."
127. דרישה אה"ע ס' כ"א ס"ק א'.
128. במדבר טו:לט.

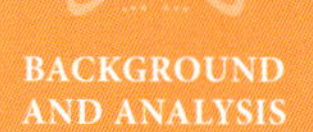

The Rambam appears to rule that gazing per se is a Rabbinical prohibition,[129] and that "*lo sasuru acharei eineichem*" is coming to forbid excessive materialism of any kind.[130] "*V'Nishmarta mikol davar ra*"[131] teaches that there is a prohibition of *hirhur*, as so to not come to *keri* (seminal emission) at night.[132] *Chazal* say looking at the clothes of one who is prohibited to him is prohibited because it causes *hirhur*.[133] A husband's *hirhur* about his wife who is *tehorah* is permitted before marital relations, but not when he is not with her.[134]

There is no prohibition to gaze at parts of the body that are not usually covered when a woman is a niddah.[135] However, *hirhur* is still an issue.[136] A husband may look at normally uncovered places (such as her face) even in order to derive pleasure, as long as he does not bring himself to the point of *hirhur*.

The *Rambam* says it is permitted for a husband to gaze at his wife when she is a niddah. [137] The *Raavad* qualifies that by saying that he may not view areas that are normally covered.[138] The halachah follows the *Raavad*, and a husband may not look at these areas.[139] However, it is unclear what the circumstances of the halachah are. Is the husband not allowed to look specifically when he wants to derive pleasure, or may he not look at areas that are normally covered even when pleasure is not on his mind?[140]

The *Tzlach*[141] and *Pri Megadim*[142] say a husband may not look at places that are normally covered when his wife is a niddah even when he does not want to have pleasure. The basic understanding is that it is only prohibited for the husband to look if he wants to have pleasure,

---

129. רמב״ם הל׳ איסו״ב כ״א, ב׳.

130. ספר המצוות להרמב״ם מצוה לא תעשה מ״ז.

131. דברים כג:י׳.

132. גמ׳ ע״ז דף כ׳ ע״ב.

133. שולחן ערוך אבן העזר סימן כ״א א׳ וז״ל: "ואסור להסתכל בבגדי צבעונים של אשה שהוא מכירה אפי׳ אינם עליה שמא יבא להרהר בה."

134. והוא פשטא דגמ׳ עבודה זרה דף כ׳ ע״ב "ת״ר ונשמרת מכל דבר רע שלא יהרהר אדם ביום ויבוא לידי טומאה בלילה", וכן משמע מהבית שמואל (אה״ע ס׳ כ״א ס״ק ז׳) "ובלא תשמיש אסור וכו׳", ועיין מש״כ בזה באה״ע ס׳ כ׳ ב׳עזר מקודש׳ ד״ה "ואולי האיסור שלא להרהר" ומשמע שאפלו אין אשתו עמו מותר להרהר אחריה אם היא טהורה "כי אין התאוה שולטת רק במה שאין בידו" ע״ש שהעריך בענין זה.

135. רמ״א סימן קצ״ה ז׳ וז״ל "אבל מותר להסתכל בה במקומות הגלוים אף על פי שנהנה בראייתה."

136. ס׳ קצ״ה בט״ז ס״ק ו׳ לענין האיסור עליו שלא ישב במטה המיוחדת לה.

137. רמב״ם הל׳ איסו״ב כא, ד ומג״מ שם שכתב להקל.

138. השגת הראב״ד שם שהחמיר.

139. ס׳ קצ״ה סע׳ ז׳.

140. ועיין בבדה״ש בביאורים שנשאר בצ״ע, ובשיעורי שבט הלוי שהעריך בזה.

141. צל״ח ברכות דף כ״ד ד״ה שוק.

142. פרמ״ג מש״ז ס׳ ע״ה ס״ק א׳ ד״ה במש״כ רש״י.

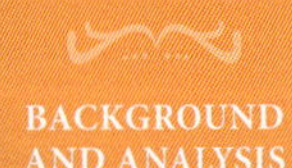

but that incidental looking would be permitted even if he sees places that are normally covered.[143]

A woman should be careful while changing her clothes when her husband is around when she is a niddah. She should use common sense, and he has to be honest with himself, but she does not have to be zealously careful about changing her clothes around her husband to the same degree that she would be around other men.

Rav Moshe Feinstein says she must cover whatever is part of "*shok* (upper part of the arm)," that is, *das Moshe* (the basic level of dignity mandated by Moshe Rabbeinu for all women), when she is around her husband, but is not required to cover her hair around her husband.[144] Apart from that, she may "dress down" to however she usually dresses when she is in the comfort of her home. Rav Yosef Shalom Elyashiv says she must dress around her husband like she would around strange men — *das Yehudis* (the basic level of dignity that applies to each woman according to her standing in her community). If she lives in a place where she wears long sleeves down to the wrist outside the home, Rav Elyashiv holds she must dress this way while a niddah around her husband, as well.

The Way a Woman Should Should Dress When a Niddah

Chazal say a woman should dress down during her niddah days.[145] On the other hand, the Gemara says she should dress up a bit so her husband will not become disgusted by her.[146] She should therefore dress in a way that looks good, but is not provocative.[147] This is her responsibility, and she should be careful about this.

Kalus Rosh (Frivolity)

A husband and wife may not have *kalus rosh* when the wife is a niddah.[148] This does not mean that they are prohibited to have a good

143. ספר טהרת הבית עמ׳ קסג.
144. אג״מ יו״ד ב׳ ס׳ ע״ה.
145. אבות דר׳ נתן פרק שני.
146. שבת ס״ד ע״ב שיטת ר׳ עקיבא, שו״ע ס׳ קצ״ה סע׳ ט׳.
147. ועיין בשערים מצויינים בהלכה ס׳ קנ״ג ס״ק כ״ד שזה מדובר אפ׳ בשוק כדי שלא תתגנה על בעלה.
148. בעלי הנפש להראב״ד שער הפרישה, מסכת אבות פרק ג׳ משנה י״ג ורבינו יונה שם, שו״ע ס׳ קצ״ה סע׳ א׳ ורמ״א.

time and laugh with each other. However, frivolous behavior which may lead to intimacy must be avoided.[149] The couple may play board games together.[150] They may not speak about matters of marital relations, but may tell each other how they feel about one another.[151] They may not joke about marital relations, or talk about what they miss about marital relations.

Negiah (Touching)

When discussing forbidden relationships in *Parashas Acharei Mos*, the Torah says, "*Lo sikrevu legalos ervah* — You shall not come close to uncover nakedness."[152] The *Rambam* explains that this *passuk* is telling us that aside from actual relations with a woman who is forbidden to him, "*lo sikrevu* — you shall not come close" is stating another Torah prohibition — that a person may not do something that brings him and her "closer together," through physical closeness, for example, hugging and kissing.[153]

The Ramban disagrees,[154] stating that physical closeness with a woman who is forbidden to him is not included in the Torah's prohibition of "*lo sikrevu*." The only prohibition that the Torah is telling us in these *pessukim* is actual relations, and not other types of intimate behavior. (The *Ramban* explains that physical closeness is either forbidden because it is a partial violation, or it is a Rabbinical prohibition.)

This disagreement tremendously impacts the halachah. We know that there are three severe *aveiros* (sins) that are forbidden to the point of *yehareg v'al yaavor* (one must allow themselves to be killed rather than transgress them), and the halachah is like the opinion of the Ri MiGash, who says that actions that lead to any of these three prohibitions are also *yehareg v'al yaavor*. The *Rivash* says the obligation to give up one's life as delineated by the Ri MiGash also includes Rabbinical prohibitions that lead a person to perform one of these three *aveiros*.[155] The Rama disagrees,[156] saying there is no obligation of *yehareg v'al yaavor* in the

149. עיין בב״ח ס׳ קצ״ה ובש״ך שם ס״ק ב׳.
150. שו״ת באר משה חלק א׳ ס׳ נ׳, חוט שני.
151. שו״ת באר משה חלק ה׳ ס׳ קמ״ו.
152. ויקרא יח:ו.
153. הל׳ איסו״ב כא, א ובספר המצוות להרמב״ם לא תעשה שנ״ג.
154. השגות הרמב״ן על ספר המצוות שם.
155. שו״ת ריב״ש ס׳ רנ״ה.
156. רמ״א יו״ד קנ״ז א׳.

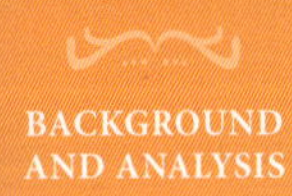

case of a Rabbinical prohibition. The halachah follows the Rama's position.

This being the case, it comes out that kissing a niddah is *yehareg v'al yaavor* according to the *Rambam*, and a Rabbinical prohibition according to the *Ramban*. The *Rama* says every Torah prohibition that is connected to an *aveirah* that is *yehareg v'al yaavor* is also *yehareg v'al yaavor*.[157] The *Shach* explains that the Rama holds like the Rambam.[158] The Shulchan Aruch[159] also rules like the Rambam regarding forbidden relationships, and he also rules like the Rambam in regard *to hilchos niddah*.[160]

The Rashba was asked if a man may touch his own mother, and answered that the prohibition of touching a woman who is prohibited to him is only said regarding one with whom closeness may lead to illicit relations. Otherwise, it is permitted.

Similarly, the Shach, when discussing the Rambam's opinion that touching a woman who is forbidden to him is a Torah prohibition, writes that a woman is allowed to go to a male doctor who will touch her while examining her.[161] He explains that even according to the Rambam, the Torah prohibition only applies to touching that is done in an affectionate and lustful way. A doctor does not derive any pleasure at all when he touches a woman for medical purposes, so his touching her will certainly not lead to illicit relations.

Practically speaking, it appears that touching when there is no chance of pleasure should be permitted. Rav Moshe Feinstein did not write that a man is allowed to shake hands with a woman. Although touching a woman in a situation in which there is no pleasure could be permitted *lechatchilah*, shaking her hand in an affectionate and lustful or pleasurable way is *yehareg v'al yaavor*. Therefore, the permissibility of such touching in each individual case would need to be decided on its own as to whether it is permitted *lechatchilah* or *yehareg v'al yaavor*. Rav Moshe Feinstein did not want to print a letter stating that it is permitted when the case straddles such a fine line.

In summary, touching any woman who is forbidden to a man in an affectionate way is *yehareg v'al yaavor*,[162] and if the contact is not one of affection, it is permitted *lechatchilah*.

---

157. שם.
158. ש"ך יו"ד ס' קנ"ז ס"ק י'.
159. שו"ע אה"ע ס' כ' סע' א'.
160. יו"ד ס' קצ"ה סע' טו', טז, יז' לענין אם הנדה או בעלה חולה.
161. ס' קצ"ה ס"ק כ'.
162. עיין ביו"ד ס' קנ"ז סע' א' וברמ"א שם, ומש"כ בש"ך ס"ק י'.

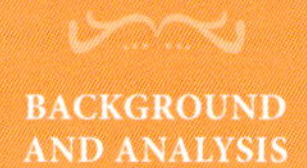

Indirect Touching

One of the *harchakos*, as discussed earlier, is that a woman who is a niddah may not prepare water for her husband is to wash his face, hands, or feet, as this is considered an affectionate action. The *Taz* explains that "washing" means pouring the water over her husband while he bathes.[163]

It is apparent from the *Taz* that this is only prohibited because of the halachah that a woman cannot wash her husband. However, the connection established by pouring the water is an indirect form of *negiah* and would otherwise be permitted.

Others explain that washing means filling up a bath for her husband to bathe in. Apparently, they hold that this must be the prohibition because the kind of washing that the *Taz* is talking about would be forbidden because of the connection, regardless of the affection involved in the washing.

What is an application of this disagreement? Everyone would agree that it is forbidden for a couple to touch each other through their clothing. That is considered direct touching, not indirect touch. (The only question in that case would be whether it is *yehareg v'al yaavor*, since it is only a Rabbinical prohibition because the touch is through the intermediary of the clothing. In fact, the *Pischei Teshuvah* specifically brings sources that say that a husband may not touch the clothing that his wife is currently wearing, even if it is hanging loosely.[164])

One explanation of the Taz's leniency permitting touching through an intermediary object is that he is discussing a scenario of a husband touching his wife in an indirect way, such as poking her with a pen.[165] Others explain that it means that he touches something that is touching something else that touches her.

The halachah is that indirect "contact," such as if the couple is standing on a shaky floor tile, even if they feel each other, is generally permitted, as that is truly indirect and inadvertent contact. Most other *direct* forms of touching through an intermediary object are only permitted in extenuating circumstances, such as if the wife needs to be given a shot and no one but the husband is around to help her.

163. ס׳ קצ״ה ט״ז ס״ק ח׳.

164. ס׳ קצ״ה ס״ק ג׳ בסוף, ועיין בשו״ת מנחת יצחק חלק ב׳ ס׳ כז מש״כ בזה, ועיין בספר מגלת אסתר על ספר המצוות לא תעשה שנ״ג.

165. עיין בשו״ת עולת יצחק חלק ב׳ ס׳ קפ״ח, ועיין בספר פתחי תשובות קצ״ה, ב׳ מש״כ בזה בהערה 20 ע״ש.

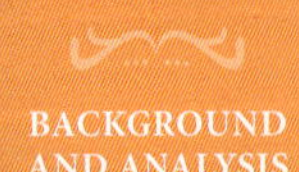

Touching When One Spouse Is Sick

A husband touching his wife when she is a niddah, even if it is not in an affectionate way, is at least Rabbinically prohibited, even according to the more lenient opinions, as discussed above. Touching in an affectionate way is, according to the *Rambam*, a Torah prohibition.

The *Shulchan Aruch* says a husband cannot touch his wife to assist her, even if she is ill.[166] This is based on the Rambam's position that touching a niddah is a Torah prohibition and is *yehareg v'al yaavor*. The Shach questions this statement: even according to the *Rambam*, touching her is only *yehareg v'al yaavor* when it is done in an affectionate way, so it is not necessary to be stringent not to assist her, and certainly not when she is sick.[167] The *Toras HaShelamim* explains that the Shulchan Aruch is ruling like the Rashba, that every touch can easily be affectionate in the case of a husband and wife.[168] So according to this position, even when she is ill, non-affectionate *negiah* does not apply.

The Rama disagrees, saying that a husband may assist his sick wife with basic functions.[169] He understands that non-affectionate *negiah* is a Rabbinical prohibition, and therefore permitted when she is sick. The only exception to this leniency is taking her pulse, which the husband may only do when she is literally in danger.[170] The *Poskim* explain that the reason why the Rama is stringent in the case of taking her pulse when there is no immediate danger is because he has to hold her for a long time.[171]

Directly Handing an Object

Tosafos in *Kesubos* says that a husband may not directly hand something to his wife when she is a niddah because he may come to touch her.[172] It is permitted for a man to hand something to other women, as even if he does inadvertently touch them, no prohibition has been transgressed when he had no intention of deriving pleasure. In regard to a wife, however, every touch is intrinsically an action of closeness.

---

166. יו״ד ס׳ קצ״ה סע׳ טז׳ ״אשה חולה והיא נדה, יט אסור לבעלה ליגע בה כדי לשמשה, כגון להקימה ולהשכיבה ולסמכה״ ע״כ.
167. ס׳ קצ״ה ס״ק כ׳.
168. ס׳ קצ״ה ס״ק ט״ו.
169. יו״ד ס׳ קצ״ה סע׳ ט״ז ברמ״א.
170. ס׳ קצ״ה סע׳ י״ז.
171. ס׳ קצ״ה ש״ך ס״ק כ׳ ועיין בספר פתחי תשובות ס׳ קצ״ה י״ז מש״כ בזה.
172. תוס׳ כתובות ס״א ע״א ד״ה מחלפא.

The halachah is like the opinion of Tosafos.[173] This is essentially a new Rabbinical edict. The reason for this edict is to prevent one from transgressing the prohibition of *negiah*, which is a Rabbinical prohibition according to the *Rama*, and a Torah prohibition according to the *Shulchan Aruch*.

Throwing an Object

Although the *Shulchan Aruch* does not mention it, the *Rama* adds that a husband also may not throw something to his wife.[174] The Rama understands that the edict is one of "directly relating to each other," and the *Shulchan Aruch* holds that *Chazal* only prohibited interactions that may result in the couple touching one another, in this case by passing something in close proximity.

The *Poskim* discuss the halachah if the husband threw something by mistake. The *Badei HaShulchan* says his wife should not catch it, because in doing so she will be completing his action.

Kol Ishah (Hearing a Woman Sing)

The *Shulchan Aruch* says,[175] based on the Gemara,[176] that Hashem's Name or *pessukim* may not be said around a woman who is singing, even if she is *tehorah*. However, many families sing the Haggadah and Hallel together at the Seder, and *zemiros* on Shabbos. Rav Yisrael Yaacov Fisher explains that the *kol* (voice) that is prohibited is a *kol* that the man is not used to hearing.[177] Therefore, family members may sing *zemiros* and the Haggadah in the the presence of family members, even when someone among them is a niddah.

There is a debate among the *Poskim* as to how the halachah of *kol ishah* applies to a husband and his wife who is a niddah.[178] The custom appears to be that we are lenient and allow him to say Hashem's Name

173. ס׳ קצ״ה סע׳ ב׳.
174. ס׳ קצ״ה סע׳ ב׳.
175. שו״ע או״ח ס׳ ע״ה סע׳ ג׳ ורמ״א ומ״ב שם ס״ק י״ז וי״ח.
176. עיין גמ׳ ברכות כ״ד ע״א בדברי שמואל, ועיין בחידושי הרשב״א (ברכות כ״ד ע״א ד״ה והא דאמר שבאשתו אסור לשמוע קול זמר שלה בשעת ק״ש אבל קול דיבורה מותר.
177. שו״ת אבן ישראל חלק ט׳ ס׳ ס״ג על שו״ע או״ח ס׳ עה׳ סע׳ ג׳.
178. עיין בס׳ קצ״ה פ״ת ס״ק י׳ שמסתפק בזה, ועיין בספר בארות יצחק עמ׳ שי״ד שהקל בזה, וכן הקל הפרדס רימונים מקשה זהב ס״ק ח׳ כיון שרגיל לשמוע קול זמר שלה, ובמשמרת הטהרה בשם ר׳ אלישיב הקיל במקום שהיא לא תשיר עבודו. אבל בלו״ש ס״ק ב׳, ובערוך השלחן ס׳ קצ״ה ס״ק כג׳, ובקיצור שו״ע ס׳ קנ״ג ס׳ ו׳, ובאגר״מ חלק ב׳ ס׳ ע״ה כתבו לאסור דאין הבדל בין אשת איש לאשתו נדה שיש לשניהם דין ״קול באשה ערוה״.

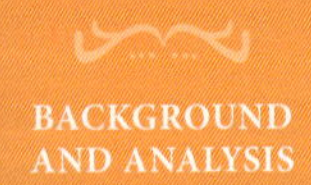

or *pessukim* when she is speaking. However, she should not sing in front of her husband when she is a niddah, except for *zemiros* along with family members.

Eating Together at the Same Table

The Gemara says, "*Lo yochal hazav im hazavah* — A *zav* shall not eat with a *zavah*."[179] The *Poskim* explain that this either means eating at the same table[180] or eating from the same plate.[181] There is no problem to eat at the same table when there is a *heker* (sign) on the table.[182]

The Heker

The *heker* must have a bit of height,[183] and must be something that is not being used for this meal.[184] Alternatively, the *heker* can be something that is generally not on the table, even if it is being used at this meal. As a rule, the *heker* should always be placed between the husband and the wife.[185]

The *Poskim* disagree whether or not a *heker* is necessary at a meal that also includes other people.[186] Rav Shlomo Zalman Auerbach says when there are others around, the *heker* may be smaller than usual, so it does not draw attention,[187] for example, a napkin or bottle cap. No other *heker* is necessary if a person or an empty chair is between the couple,[188] even when no one else is around. The couple sitting across from each other with nothing between them is generally not an effective *heker*.[189]

179. משנה שבת י״א ע״א וגמ׳ שם י״ג ע״א.
180. השגת הראב״ד על הרמב״ם פרק יא מהל׳ איסו״ב הל׳ יח, הרא״ש שבת פרק א׳ ס׳ לב׳, ובס׳ קצ״ה ג׳.
181. רמב״ם הל׳ איסו״ב פרק יא הל׳ יח, ושו״ע ס׳ קצ״ה בט״ז ס״ק ב׳.
182. ס׳ קצ״ה סע׳ ג׳.
183. חוט שני ס׳ קצ״ה, ג׳
184. ס׳ קצ״ה בט״ז ס״ק א׳, ועיין בתורת השלמים מש״כ בזה, ועיין בשו״ע ס׳ פ״ח לענין ההיכר לענין בשר וחלב.
185. וכן פסק בחוט שני, אבל בשיעורי שבט הלוי כתב דכל שמונח היכר על השולחן שיזכיר להם שהיא נדה סגי בכך.
186. עיין בפ״ת ס׳ קצ״ה ס״ק ה׳.
187. וכ״כ בשו״ת שבט הלוי להקל לצורך גדול, וכ״ה במשמרת הטהרה בשם הרה״ג ר׳ אלישיב במקום שאחרים אוכלין ביניהם יש להקל.
188. קובץ תשובות להרה״ג ר׳ אלישיב ס׳ פז׳.
189. ועיין מש״כ בזה בשיעורי שבט הלוי.

Eating from the Same Dish

The *Taz* says the prohibition of a couple eating from the same dish means that they may not both eat directly out of the same plate.[190] However, they may both take food from the same serving bowl, transfer it to their individual plates, and eat the food from there.

Rav Moshe Feinstein says a plate that is meant for strangers to eat out of is not included in this prohibition.[191] Rather, this prohibition refers to a plate that is part of a personal setting, which another person would not eat out of. According to Rav Moshe Feinstein, a niddah couple can take cut-up pieces of cake off of a serving platter at a *kiddush* one after another and eat them without transferring them to individual plates, since at a *kiddush* it is normal for people to eat straight from the serving platter. It is also normal for strangers to eat straight out of a large bowl of popcorn, so the couple may take directly from the bowl without transferring the popcorn to smaller plates. According to Rav Moshe Feinstein, in each situation the couple must ask themselves if they would partake from this bowl with a stranger or not.

Most *Poskim* disagree with Rav Moshe Feinstein, saying that the halachah applies any time that the couple is taking food from the same dish, until it is first put down on an individual plate.

Leftovers

The *Rishonim* note that that eating leftovers is another issue derived from the Gemara that tells us that a *zav* may not eat with a *zavah*.[192] The halachah is that the husband may not eat his wife's leftovers, but the wife may eat her husband's leftovers, even in front of him, as long as he is completely finished eating from the plate.[193] The *Acharonim* say that "leftovers" are the remnants of the one portion of food that she took for herself, but if she took one food item out of various food items, the remaining untouched items are not her "leftovers."[194] When a woman takes popcorn from a bowl, and some pieces fall back into the bowl from her hand, there may be an issue of leftovers. However, if she has a few kinds of food on her plate and does not touch one kind of food,

190. ס׳ קצ״ה ס״ק ב׳.
191. שו״ת אג״מ יו״ד א׳ ס׳ צ״ב.
192. סמ״ק ס׳ רצ״ג, ספר יראים ס׳ כ״ו, ובשו״ע ס׳ קצ״ה סע׳ ד׳ וברמ״א שם וברמ״א סע׳ ג׳ ובש״ך ס״ק ח׳.
193. ס׳ קצ״ה סע׳ ד׳ ברמ״א ובט״ז ס״ק ה׳.
194. אג״מ יו״ד חלק א׳ ס׳ צא, בדי השלחן ס׳ קצ״ה ס״ק נ״א.

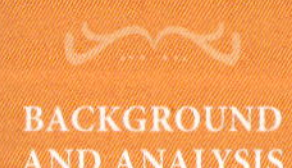

the husband may eat it when she is done eating (if she is still there, by transferring plates; if she has gone, even from her own plate). Rav Moshe Feinstein says if someone took butter and put some back from the knife onto the stick of butter, there may be an issue of leftovers as well.[195]

Rav Moshe Feinstein adds that the couple may not split an individual portion between them.[196] This means, for example, that they cannot split a can of soda or a small roll, even if they put the two halves onto individual dishes. The *Poskim* in Eretz Yisrael say this is fine, as long as they put it onto individual plates.

It comes out that Rav Moshe Feinstein is more stringent in regard to leftovers, but more lenient in regard to eating off of one plate. Rav Moshe Feinstein understands that the focus is on the food being eaten, while most *Poskim* focus on the people who are eating.

One can follow either opinion, but cannot follow the leniencies of both opinions.[197] Those who follow the ruling of Rav Moshe Feinstein hold that the halachah is subjective. One must ask themselves if they would eat the food (i.e., share a plate or eat leftovers) from a stranger in this circumstance. If the answer is yes, they can eat from their spouse. If not, they should avoid sharing the food or eating the leftovers.

Serving Food

The Gemara lists three expressions of closeness that a woman may not do for her husband when she is a niddah: preparing a drink for him, preparing his bed for him to sleep in, and washing his hands and feet.[198]

The *Poskim* discuss the definition of "preparing a drink for him."[199] Is she not allowed to prepare it, or may she not serve it to him, by putting it in front of him? The halachah is that she may not serve any individual serving directly in front of him, but she may prepare whatever she wants. This prohibition applies to food and drink alike.[200] A niddah wife may not serve a meal directly in front of her husband. She may, however,

195. אג״מ יו״ד חלק א׳ ס׳ צב.
196. אג״מ שם.
197. וזה לפי ששני דינים אלו, שיורי מאכל וקערה אחת, שניהם נלמדים מדין א׳- ״לא יאכל הזב עם הזבה״.
198. גמ׳ כתובות ס״א ע״א ״אמר רב יצחק בר חנניא אמר רב הונא: כל מלאכות שהאשה עושה לבעלה - נדה עושה לבעלה, חוץ ממזיגת הכוס, והצעת המטה, והרחצת פניו ידיו ורגליו״ ע״כ.
199. ועיין בהגהות מיימונית הל׳ איסו״ב פרק יא׳ אות נ׳, שו״ע ס׳ קצ״ה סע׳ י׳, ועיין מש״כ בתורת השלמים שם ס״ק י״ב מדברי הט״ז.
200. ועיין בס׳ קצ״ה בב״ח בשם מהר״ש אוסטרייך, ש״ך ס״ק י״ג.

serve her husband in a slightly different way, called a *shinui*.[201] Two examples of *shinui* are given in the *Shulchan Aruch*: The first is that the wife serves him the item, but instead of placing it down directly in front of him on the table, she places it off to the side.[202] The second example is that she serves him with her left hand; this is considered enough of a change from the norm.[203] However, many *Poskim* do not feel that serving with the left hand applies nowadays, when most people do not even notice which hand a person serves with.[204]

The prohibition against serving only applies "in front of him," which the *Acharonim* explain means when her husband looking.[205] If he looks away when she is serving, however, she may place the food directly in front of him.

The *Poskim* say that just as the wife may not serve her husband, he, too, may not serve her directly.[206] In the event that one of them served the other one directly, the food does not become prohibited, and it may be eaten.[207]

Sending Wine

The *Shulchan Aruch* also says a husband may not send a cup of wine to his wife (that is, give it or request from another person to give it to her) when she is a niddah.[208] This prohibition even applies to a *kos shel brachah* (cup of wine used for the performance of a mitzvah),[209] for example, Kiddush wine. In many families, everyone gets some of the Kiddush wine after Kiddush was made. When the wife is a niddah, instead of passing it to her, the husband may simply put the cup down on the table, and the wife can then pick it up and drink. In some families the person making Kiddush pours some of the wine into other cups and sends them around the table. The husband may pour for everyone, including his wife, and pass the cups around. The reason

201. ועיין בגמ׳ כתובות דף ס״א עמוד א׳ ״שמואל מחלפא ליה דביתהו בידא דשמאלא אביי מנחא ליה אפומא דכובא רבא אבי סדיא רב פפא אשרשיפא״.
202. שו״ע ס׳ קצ״ה סע׳ י׳.
203. שם.
204. עיין בשו״ת צ״צ בפסקי דינים ס׳ י׳, ועיין בחוט שני ובשיעורי שבט הלוי שסוברים שביד שמאל נקרא שינוי אם רגילה להניחו בפניו ביד ימין בשעת טהרה.
205. עיין ברמ״א ס׳ קצ״ה סע׳ י׳ ״בפניו״, והאחרונים מתירים גם באופן זה שהבעל הסתכל בצד בשעת ההנחה.
206. וכ״כ בספר האשכול ס׳ ס״ט, חכמ״א כלל קט״ז ס׳ י׳, ערוך השלחן סע׳ יד׳, שיעורי שבט הלוי.
207. וכן הסכמת רוב אחרונים, וכ״ה בשיעורי שבט הלוי.
208. בעלי הנפש להראב״ד שער הפרישה, שו״ע ס׳ קצ״ה סע׳ יג׳.
209. כ״כ בשו״ע ס׳ קצ״ה סע׳ יג׳.

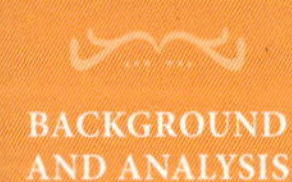

this is permitted is because even though she will drink from one of the several cups that were poured, there is no one cup in the group that was designated specifically for her.

The *Poskim* discuss whether this prohibition includes all alcoholic beverages, or just wine, and most are stringent that no alcoholic beverage be sent.[210] Some are lenient, however, regarding non-wine alcoholic beverages. All agree that sending non-alcoholic drinks is permitted. (Of course, even these drinks may not be served directly without a *shinui*.) Sending pitchers or bottles of wine to her is also fine; the only issue is sending an individual cup that is intended specifically for her.[211]

Sitting on a Bench

The *Terumas HaDeshen* says a couple may not sit together on a bench that is not attached to the ground when the wife is a niddah.[212]

Several reasons are brought in explanation of this prohibition. Some say the reason is because they feel each other's weight as the bench shakes, which is comparable to touching.[213] Another reason is that a bench is similar to a bed.[214] A third reason is that this may cause *hirhur*.

The Rama qualifies this prohibition in two ways.[215] First, he says that this prohibition only applies when the bench shakes. Second, the couple may sit together on a bench if it is attached to the wall even if it is shaky.[216]

Rav Moshe Feinstein says the seat of a car also is also treated as being attached to the ground (because of the car's sheer weight), so the couple may sit next to each other in the back seat of a car even if they feel each other's movements.[217] He is quoted as saying, however, that if they are sitting in close proximity to each other, they should put something between them, such as a pillow or hatbox, so they do not accidentally touch.[218] He adds that this should be done on an airplane as well. A couple should be especially careful when flying to put a pillow

---

210. ועיין בתורת הבית להרשב״א בית שביעי שער שני לענין מזיגת כוס של יין ״שהוא מרגיל לערוה״, ועיין בס׳ יג׳ שהביא השו״ע הדינים בשוה, ועיין בצ״צ בפסקי דינים ס׳ י״ג שהחמיר בכל משקה חשוב.

211. עיין בספר פתחי תשובות ס׳ קצ״ה סע׳ י״ג מש״כ בזה שהוא דבר פשוט שאין זה דרך חיבה לשלוח בקבוק.

212. שו״ת תרומת הדשן ס׳ רנ״א.

213. וכ״כ הש״ך בנקודות הכסף ס׳ קצ״ה סע׳ ה׳.

214. וכן משמעות הט״ז ס׳ קצ״ה ס״ק ו׳ ע״ש.

215. ס׳ קצ״ה סע׳ ה׳ ברמ״א.

216. שם.

217. אג״מ יו״ד חלק ב׳ ס״ס ע״ז.

218. ואם נגעו שניהם בבת אחת בכר ה״ז נגיעה ע״י דבר אחר ומותר בשעת הדחק.

or hatbox between them, because it is very common to fall asleep on an airplane and fall onto the person in the adjacent seat. The practice in Eretz Yisrael is not to sit together in the back seat of a car.[219]

A couch with one cushion is also a problem if the couple can feel each other's weight or if they are touching. A couch with separate cushions is fine if they cannot feel each other. If they can, it is an issue.

Preparing the Bed

A woman who is a niddah may not prepare her husband's bed for him to sleep in, in his presence.[220] Making his bed in the morning as part of the regular housework is not included in this prohibition and is allowed, even if he is standing there.[221]

Sleeping in One Bed

One of the things that the woman told Eliyahu HaNavi in the Gemara quoted above is that her husband slept in her bed when she was a niddah.[222] We learn from here that a couple may not sleep together in the same bed when the wife is a niddah.[223] The Maharam adds that they may not even sleep in two beds that are touching each other.[224] The Arizal says the amount of space between the beds must be far enough that the beddings do not touch.[225] Others say the beds should be one arm's length (an *amah*) apart,[226] so if someone stretches during the night, they will not touch their spouse. When there is not enough room, it is enough that the beds are separated so they are not touching one another.[227]

---

219. וכ״ה בשיעורי שבט הלוי ס׳ קצ״ה ה׳, ודלא במש״כ במשמרת הטהרה בשם הרה״ג ר׳ אלישיב שהקל בזה ע״ש.
220. גמ׳ כתובות ס״א ע״א, תוס׳ כתובות דף ד׳ ע״ב ד״ה והצעת המטה, שו״ע ס׳ קצ״ה סע׳ יא׳.
221. שיעורי שבט הלוי, וכן דעת רוב אחרונים.
222. גמ׳ שבת י״ג ע״א בסוף ובע״ב.
223. ס׳ קצ״ה סע׳ ו׳.
224. מרדכי שבת פרק א׳ סו״ס רל״ח ורמ״א ס׳ קצ״ה סע׳ ו׳.
225. ספר קב הישר פרק י״ז בשם האר״י ז״ל, שערים מצויינים בהלכה ס׳ קנ״ג ס״ק כ״א.
226. שיעורי שבט הלוי ס׳ קצ״ה סע׳ ו׳ ס״ק ב׳ בשם י״א.
227. עיין בפ״ת ס׳ קצ״ה ס״ק י״א.

Sitting on Each Other's Bed

The *Rishonim* add that a husband may not sit or lay on his wife's bed when she is a niddah because this may lead to *hirhur*.[228] This only applies when she is in the city — i.e., she intends to sleep at home that night, as opposed to when she is out of town on business or hospitalized, such as after childbirth.[229] She also may not lie on her husband's bed in front of him because of *hirhur*. She may, however, sit on his bed, even in his presence.[230]

Preparing Water

The Gemara also says that a woman who is a niddah may not wash her husband's face, hands, or feet.[231] The *Poskim* point out that this halachah cannot mean actually scrubbing him, for this is surely prohibited, as it is *negiah*. Pouring water on him is also clearly prohibited, and is not what the Gemara is referring to.[232] The prohibition is *preparing* water for him to bathe with,[233] which also includes preparing water for his *netilas yadayim*.[234] She also may not start his shower or bath.[235] She may, however, turn on the boiler to heat the water. Preparing his *negel vasser* is also allowed.[236]

Traveling Together

The *Terumas HaDeshen* says a couple may not travel together in a wagon through "gardens and orchards" while the wife is a niddah. This is forbidden as a pleasure ride is considered an act of closeness.

Going on a trip together is problematic only when the point of the drive is the trip itself, for example, going for a drive as a way to spend time together.[237] If the couple has a destination in mind, there is no problem driving there together.[238] It comes out that the couple may go

---

228. בעלי הנפש להראב״ד סוף שער הפרישה לענין שכיבה, ובטור יו״ד ס׳ קצ״ה לענין ישיבה, ובשו״ע ס׳ קצ״ה סע׳ ה׳.
229. פ״ת ס׳ קצ״ה ס״ק ט׳.
230. ס׳ קצ״ה בט״ז ס״ק ו׳.
231. גמ׳ כתובות דף ס״א ע״א.
232. בטור ס׳ קצ״ה סע׳ י״ב ובב״י שם.
233. ס׳ קצ״ה בש״ך ס״ק טז׳.
234. אשל אברהם מבוטשאטש או״ח ס׳ ד׳, ספר חזקת טהרה, חוט שני.
235. שו״ת מנחת יצחק חלק ז׳ ס׳ ע׳, וכן הסכמת רוב אחרונים.
236. הסברה הוא שאין בזה חיבה בהכנת מים אלו כיון שאין הנאה ברחיצה זו ועושים הרחיצה רק להעברת רוח רע ולכן היקלו בכגון זה.
237. שו״ת רב פעלים יו״ד חלק ז׳ ס׳ יז׳, וכן משמע מלשון הרמ״א ס׳ קצ״ה סע׳ ה׳.
238. פותח שער ס׳ טו׳ סמ״ב, טהרה כהלכה ע׳ רי״א.

on vacation together when the wife is a niddah, but should not drive in a roundabout way toward their destination. Some argue that going on a walk together is a problem, but Rav Yosef Shalom Elyashiv allows this.[239]

Yichud with a Niddah and Chuppas Niddah (A Chuppah When the Kallah Is a Niddah)

The halachah is that a couple may remain secluded together when the woman is a niddah.[240] Although there is generally a prohibition for a man to have *yichud* with a woman who is prohibited to him, *Tosafos* explains that a niddah is different because, unlike other women who are forever forbidden, a wife who is a niddah is only prohibited for a limited time.[241] The only exception, says the Gemara,[242] is by a *chuppas niddah*, since the husband does not yet have *pas b'salo* (lit. bread in his basket; a sense of contentment as though he has it already).[243] Practically speaking, a couple who had a *chuppas niddah* needs one *shomer* (lit. guard; another person who is present) during the day and two *shomrim* at night.[244] A boy and girl are usually used to save the couple from embarrassment, although another couple may serve as the *shomrim* instead.

The *Terumas HaDeshen* says a couple who voluntarily did not consummate the marriage in the first few nights (because of a custom) is permitted to have *yichud* if she later becomes a niddah, because they have demonstrated that they have self-restraint.[245] The Shach disagrees, saying that voluntarily separating is not enough.[246] The question dealt with by the *Poskim* is a different one, of a couple who tried to consummate the marriage, and the woman got her period before they were successful. Are they permitted to have *yichud*, or must they have a *shomer* until she is *tehorah*? Rav Shlomo Zalman Auerbach says the couple is permitted to remain alone together (without the need for *shomrim*) if they have attempted marital relations three times,[247] while others say that their having attempted even once is sufficient.[248]

---

239. וכן כתב בשיעורי שבט הלוי ס' קצ"ה סע' ה' אלא שחושש לשיטת הערוך השלחן אם הולכים בהרים לטיול, וכ"כ בספר משנת השלחן בשם הרה"ג ר' אלישיב.
240. משנה וגמ' סוטה ז' ע"א וגמ' סנהדרין ל"ז ע"א.
241. סנהדרין ל"ז ע"א בתוס' ד"ה התורה.
242. גמ' כתובות ד' ע"א, ובתוס' יומא י"ח ע"ב ד"ה יחודי.
243. ס' קצ"ב סע' ד'.
244. ס' קצ"ב סע' ד' ברמ"א.
245. תרומת הדשן ס' רנ"ג.
246. ס' קצ"ב בש"ך ס"ק י"א.
247. דבר הלכה הוספה (חדשה) לסי' ב' ס' י"ב מכתב מגיסו.
248. שו"ת ציץ אליעזר חלק ו' ס' מ'.

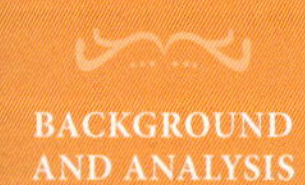

Some are even more lenient, saying that a couple that was alone together in the *yichud* room (i.e., she was *tehorah* at that time, and the *yichud* room was locked, as usual) may also remain alone together afterwards, even if she became *temei'ah* before any attempts at marital relations.[249] Rav Yitzchak Berkovits is uncomfortable with this ruling, but a *Rav* may rule this way if he feels the couple will observe halachah properly.

Rav Eliezer Moshe Horowitz says a couple at a *chuppas niddah* does not need *harchakos* as long as *yichud* is prohibited.[250] This ruling is based on the *Rosh*, which says that the whole reason for *harchakos* is as an added "fence" because *yichud* is permitted for a husband and his wife who is a niddah. If, however, we would understand like the Rashba that the reason for *harchakos* is to prevent the couple from coming too close, they would need to keep *harchakos* even though *yichud* is prohibited as well. Rav Moshe Feinstein is also quoted as saying that we follow the *Rosh* and rule that in the case of a *chuppas niddah* there are no *harchakos*. In Yerushalayim the *Poskim* are stringent, while some in the United States are lenient like Rav Moshe Feinstein.

Regarding a *chassan* putting the ring on the *kallah*'s finger by a *chuppas niddah*, some are stringent to drop it on her finger instead of putting it onto it,[251] understanding that directly placing the ring on her finger as usual is considered handing something to one's wife who is a niddah. This stringency is a very far stretch, because the couple really is not married until he lets go of the ring.[252] The practice in the United States is to allow the *chassan* to put the ring straight onto her finger as usual,[253] while some in Eretz Yisrael are stringent. In Eretz Yisrael the practice is that the *chassan* gives the *kesubah* to someone else who gives it to the *kallah*. According to Rav Eliezer Moshe Horowitz's ruling that *harchakos* are not kept by a *chuppas niddah*, he should be technically permitted to give it straight to her. However, most are stringent regarding passing the *kesubah*, even outside of Eretz Yisrael.

---

249. כך שמעתי מהרה״ג ר׳ ירוחם פיטר וכ״ה משמעות הי״א ברמ״א ס׳ קצ״ב סע׳ ד׳ וז״ל: ״יש אומרים אם היתה טהורה כשנשאת ולא בא עליה, ופירסה נדה אחר כך א״צ שימור עוד, והמחמיר תע״ב״.

250. חידושי רבי אליעזר משה הורוויץ מס׳ שבת דף י״א ע״א ד״ה מפני הרגל.

251. שו״ת יביע אומר חלק ה׳ אבה״א ס׳ י׳ ד״ה ״אולם״, חוט שני ס׳ קצ״ב סע׳ א׳ אות טז׳.

252. ועיין בספר משנת השלחן ס׳ קצ״ה סע׳ ב׳ שהרה״ג ר׳ אלישיב הקיל שלא לשנות נתינת הטבעת, וכן דעת רוב אחרונים.

253. משנת השלחן ס׳ קצ״ב סע׳ ד׳ תשובה קפ״ב בשם הרה״ג ר׳ אלישיב, שיעורי שבט הלוי.

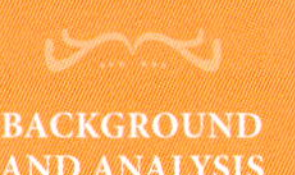

BACKGROUND AND ANALYSIS

HOW A WOMAN BECOMES A NIDDAH

Miscellaneous Laws

Niddah D'Oraisah

Period

Bedikah, Relations and Restroom

Niddah D'Rabbanan

Stains

Other forms of Tumah

HARCHAKOS

Intimate Separations

Eating Restrictions

Seats and Bedding

Additional Restrictions

TAHARA

The Five Day Wait

Rechitzah, Hefsek, Moch and Bedikahs

Shivah Nekiyim

Mikveh Preparations & Immersion

VESTOS

Understanding Vestos

Calculating Basic Vestos

Conduct on a Vest

Vestos Stringencies

Birth control and Vestos

Additional Vestos concepts

TAHARAH

Niddah and Zavah Mid'Oraisa

The Torah discusses two related *parshiyos* of *tumah* — the *parashah* of niddah[254] and the *parashah* of *zavah*.[255] A *niddah mid'Oraisa* is a woman who bleeds during her "*yemei niddah* (days of niddah)." *Mid'Oraisa* she will be *temei'ah* for 7 days including the day of the *re'iyah*, whether or not she continues to bleed during this time. After 7 days of *tumah* she can immerse in the mikvah, provided that the bleeding has stopped.

254. ויקרא טו:יט.

255. ויקרא טו:כה, ע' רש"י שם ד"ה ימים רבים.

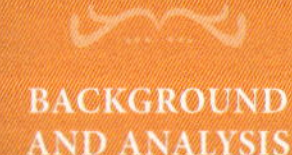

Niddah D'Oraisa

Sunday	Monday	Tuesday	Wednesday	Thursday	Friday	Shabbos
1	2	3	4	5	6	7
Bleeding	*Bleeding*	*Bleeding*	*Bleeding*	*Bleeding*	*Bleeding*	*Bleeding* *Mikvah immersion after the 7th day*
YIMEI NIDDAH						
8	9	10	11	12	13	14
YIMEI ZIVAH						
15	16	17	18			
YIMEI ZIVAH						

***Summary:** During Yimei Niddah, a woman is Teme'ah for 7 days, whether she bleeds one day or all seven days. Mikveh immersion occurs after the 7th day.*

The Torah discusses two types of *zavah* — a *zavah gedolah* and a *zavah ketanah*.[256] A *zavah* is a woman who went through the 7 days of niddah and continued to bleed, *or* she bleeds within the 11 days after the niddah days have finished, during the "*yemei zivah* (days of *zivah*)."[257]

A woman is a *zavah ketanah* if she bleeds 1 or 2 days during the *yemei zivah*. She is called a "*shomeres yom keneged yom*," and must be blood-free for 1 day, after which she may immerse in the mikvah and become *tehorah*.

256. רש״י שם ד״ה בלא עת נדתה, או כי תזוב, על נדתה.
257. נדה ע״ב ע״ב - ע״ג ע״א, רש״י שם בפרשת ויקרא, ועיין ברמב״ם איסורי ביאה פרק ו׳ הל׳ ב׳-ו׳, מ״מ שם הל׳ ד׳, ש״ך ס׳ קפ״ג ס״ק ד׳.

Zavah K'Tanah

Sunday	Monday	Tuesday	Wednesday	Thursday	Friday	Shabbos
1	2	3	4	5	6	7
Bleeding	*Bleeding*	*Bleeding*	*Bleeding*	*Bleeding*	*Bleeding*	*Bleeding*
YIMEI NIDDAH						
8	9	10	11	12	13	14
Bleeding	*Blood-Free Day* *Mikvah immersion after the blood-free day*					
YIMEI ZIVAH						
15	16	17	18			
YIMEI ZIVAH						

Summary: During Yimei Zivah, a woman is considered a Zavah Ketanah if she bleeds one or two days. She must observe one blood free day and can then immerse in a Mikveh.

A woman who bleeds for 3 days or more during *yemei zivah* becomes a *zavah gedolah*. She is *temei'ah* for an additional 7 days in which she makes sure that she is blood-free, called *shivah nekiyim*, which does not include the 3 or more days in which she bled. Only then may she immerse in the mikvah.

These are the basic halachos of a *zavah ketanah* and a *zavah gedolah* which were observed in the days until the time of the *gemarra*.

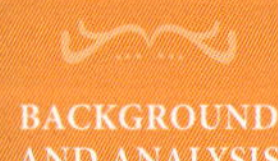

Zavah Gedolah

Sunday	Monday	Tuesday	Wednesday	Thursday	Friday	Shabbos
1 *Bleeding*	2 *Bleeding*	3 *Bleeding*	4 *Bleeding*	5 *Bleeding*	6 *Bleeding*	7 *Bleeding*
YIMEI NIDDAH						
8 *Bleeding*	9 *Bleeding*	10 *Bleeding*	11 *Shivah Nekiyim*	12 *Shivah Nekiyim*	13 *Shivah Nekiyim*	14 *Shivah Nekiyim*
YIMEI ZIVAH						
15 *Shivah Nekiyim*	16 *Shivah Nekiyim*	17 *Shivah Nekiyim* *Mikvah immersion after the Shivah Nekiyim*	18			
YIMEI ZIVAH						

During Yimei Zivah, a woman is considered a Zavah Gedolah if she bleeds on three days. She must observe Shivah Nekiyim, after which she can immerse in a Mikveh.

Rav Zeira's Stringency

The Gemara cites Rav Zeira, who says that the daughters of Yisrael acted stringently with themselves, and each woman always treated herself as a *zavah gedolah* and observed *shivah nekiyim* upon discovering blood, irrespective of the amount of bleeding or the time of the month.[258] Doing so became more than a custom — it became a real halachah.[259] The halachah treats *shivah nekiyim* nowadays almost as a *d'Oraisa*, even though its roots are only a custom. It is considered to be so stringent, that even fulfilling the mitzvah of *piryah v'rivyah* (procreating) is not grounds to be lenient in respect to waiving the need

258. נדה ס"ו ע"א.

259. רא"ש נדה פרק י' ס' ו', רמב"ן הל' נדה פרק א'.

for *shivah nekiyim*, even when a woman will not be able to conceive because of the observance of *shivah nekiyim*.[260]

The *Poskim* give three main reasons for keeping *shivah nekiyim* irrespective of the time or amount of bleeding.[261] One reason is because the tradition regarding which colors are *temei'im* and which are *tehorim* has gotten weaker throughout the centuries. Nowadays the practice is to be *metamei* anything that is close to red. It is thus possible that a woman will bleed a color that is really *tahor* for a few days during her *yemei niddah*, and will only encounter a color that is truly *tamei* on the last day of the bleeding. She will thus mistakenly start counting her 7 days of *niddah d'Oraisa* from when she discovered the *tahor* colors, when in fact she should have started from the last day, because that is when she was actually *temei'ah*. For this reason *Chazal* established that a woman should keep 6 *nekiyim* (clean, blood-free days),[262] so she will always have a minimum of 7 days from the last day of her bleeding. Additionally, she may confuse *yemei niddah* and *yemei zivah*. She may consider herself to be in the *yemei niddah* when she is really in the *yemei zivah*. Then, if she bleeds for 3 days, or on 1 day when she should be keeping *shivah nekiyim*, she will require 7 clean days, and assume that she only needs 6. So *Chazal* established that she should keep *shivah nekiyim* every time she begins to bleed.

It comes out that there is no difference nowadays as to the time of the month in which the woman bleeds. Every woman who becomes *temei'ah* will always keep *shivah nekiyim*, even if if she is really only *temei'ah d'Rabbanan*. Again, this halachah of keeping *shivah nekiyim* is treated as a very strong *d'Rabbanan*, almost as a *d'Oraisa*.

(The *Rambam* explains *yemei zivah* differently from other *Rishonim*.[263] He says that every woman is on an eternal cycle of 7 days *yemei niddah*, 11 days *yemei zivah*, 7 days *yemei niddah*, 11 days *yemei zivah*, and so on, from the time she gets her first period until the time she stops getting her period. Since a woman will probably lose track of where she is holding, *Chazal* were stringent that every woman who becomes *temei'ah* should always keep *shivah nekiyim*.

There are many questions on the Rambam's approach.[264] One is that it comes out that a woman will almost certainly get her period during her *yemei zivah*, while the Torah seems to be clear that a *zavah* is a fluke

260. שו"ת חת"ס ס' קע"ט, ספר אמרי אברהם בשם הגרש"ז אויערבאך.
261. עיין טור ס' קפ"ג, ט"ז שם ס"ק ב'.
262. רבי בשדות, נדה ס"ו ע"א, ועיין תוס' הרא"ש שם, רבינו יונה ברכות כ"ב בדפי הרי"ף.
263. רמב"ם איסורי ביאה פרק ו' הל' ו'.
264. הל' נדה להרמב"ן, גמ' ערכין ח' ע"א.

occurrence. The many explanations of the Rambam's position will not be explained now.)

The 7 days of *shivah nekiyim* are *not* in addition to the 7 days of niddah.[265] The woman only has to stop bleeding, as soon as this may happen, and then begin to count the *shivah nekiyim* starting the following day.[266] However, there is another factor that sometimes prevents a woman from beginning the *shivah nekiyim*, which is the halachah of *poletes shichvas zera*. We will soon discuss this halachah.

Hefsek Taharah, Moch Dachuk, and Rechitzah (Washing)

The Torah says, "*V'safrah lah* — And she shall count for herself,"[267] which tells us that a woman who is *temei'ah* must change her established status from being *temei'ah* to being *tehorah*.[268] The way she does that is by performing a *hefsek taharah*. Once she does this, she changes her status from "bleeding," to "not bleeding."

The Gemara says if a woman wants to do a *hefsek taharah* at the end of a day on which she actually bled, she needs a *bedikah* toward evening to establish that the day is ending fixed in her *taharah* status.[269] One opinion in the Gemara says she also needs a *moch dachuk* throughout *bein hashmashos*.[270] The Shulchan Aruch[271] and Rama[272] argue about a woman who only does a *hefsek taharah*, without a *moch dachuk* — is this *hefsek taharah* acceptable *bedi'eved*? The Rama holds that as long as the *hefsek taharah* was done toward evening it is enough, and the absence of a *moch dachuk* will not invalidate her establishment of her status of *taharah*, even if the *hefsek taharah* was performed before *shkiah* on a day in which she had bled several hours before. However, the Rama says that when a woman does a *bedikas shacharis* (a *bedikah* performed before *Minchah ketanah*) on Day 1 of her bleeding (assuming she only bled 1 day), this does not count as a *hefsek taharah*.

265. רמ״א ס׳ קצ״ו סע׳ יא׳, ט״ז ס״ק ו׳, ב״ח.
266. ס׳ קצ״ו סע׳ א׳.
267. ויקרא טו:כח.
268. נדה ס״ח ע״א.
269. שיטת ר׳ יהודה שם בגמ׳.
270. נדה ס״ח ע״ב.
271. ס׳ קצ״ו סע׳ ב׳, רמב״ם הל׳ איסו״ב פרק ו׳ הל׳ כ׳, הל׳ נדה להרמב״ן פרק ב׳ הל׳ א׳, עיין ס״ט ס״ק ו׳, גר״א ס״ק ח׳, חזו״א ס׳ צ״ב ס״ק מ״ה, אג״מ יו״ד ב׳ ס׳ ע״ט.
272. שם, תורת הבית להרשב״א בית שביעי שער חמישי.

The *Rishonim* discuss whether the same halachos as those of "Day 1" apply if the woman continues to bleed on a later day.[273] The question is, what does the the Gemara mean when it discusses "Day 1"? Some say that this term is literal, that the blood discharged earlier in the day that is being discussed was the blood of the onset of the woman's period. Others understand that "Day 1" is non-specific, and is a term used as a reference to any day in which a woman bled a substantial amount, even at the end of the period; the term "Day 1" is used because she has bled today as she did on the 1st day of her period. According to the latter opinions (that maintain that "Day 1" is non-specific) it comes out that a *bedikas shacharis* would be ineffective for a woman to establish her status of *taharah* by performing a *hefsek taharah*, even *bedi'eved*, on any day she experienced substantial bleeding.

In summary, some hold that a *bedikas shacharis* will not work as a *hefsek taharah* on any day she had substantial bleeding, and she must perform a *bedikah* in the afternoon.[274] Others say that as long as it is not really the 1st day ("Day 1") of the period, even a *bedikas shacharis* will work as a *hefsek taharah*.[275] The *Shulchan Aruch* is stringent, and the *Rama* is lenient.[276]

The stringent position of the *Shulchan Aruch* is applicable when the woman bled substantially on the day that she wants to try to do a *hefsek taharah*,[277] not when she only stained a little or got a bad *bedikah*.[278] The *Chazon Ish* notes that another issue to keep in mind is *when* this "same day on which substantial bleeding occurred" begins. Rav Shmuel HaLevi Wosner says it starts from the morning, not from the night before.[279] One may be lenient even according to the *Shulchan Aruch*'s stringent position if the woman did not experience substantial bleeding during the day, in which case a *bedikas shacharis* would be an effective *hefsek taharah* according to everyone.

The Chavas Daas disagrees with the Rama,[280] saying that since nowadays we are unsure of which colors of blood are really *metamei*, it could very well be that any day that the woman bleeds is actually Day 1 of her *tumah*. We must therefore always be concerned about the *Shulchan Aruch*'s position and do a *hefsek taharah* toward evening.

273. רש״י נדה ס״ח ע״ב ד״ה מי איכא למ״ד, תוס׳ ד״ה אמרו ליה, מהרש״א שם.
274. תוס׳ ד״ה אמרו ליה בשיטת ר׳ יוסי בגמ׳, חוו״ד.
275. ש״ך ס׳ קצ״ו ס״ק ו׳.
276. ס׳ קצ״ו א׳–ב׳.
277. עיין ש״ך ס׳ קצ״ו ס״ק ו׳ בשם מ״מ, מחצית השקל.
278. שו״ת מהר״ש חלק ו׳ ס׳ מ״א, משמרת טהרה בשם ר׳ אלישיב.
279. וכן פסק הרי״י פישר.
280. חוו״ד קצ״ו ביאורים ס״ק א׳.

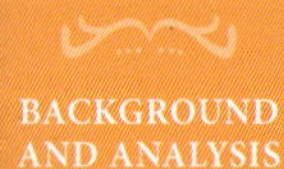

The halachah is the following. The *Shulchan Aruch* cites the *Rashba*, which says that ideally a woman should always do a *hefsek taharah* before *shkiah*, and then do a *moch dachuk*, which should be left inside throughout *bein hashmashos*.[281] However, there is room to be lenient if the day that the *hefsek taharah* is being done is not the 1st day of her period, especially if the woman has not bled at all on this day, since the morning.

A woman whose skin is irritated and is prone to cut herself from the *moch dachuk* should not do one.[282] A woman who recently gave birth should also not do a *moch dachuk*, because she will most likely irritate the skin and cut herself.

The ideal time to do the *hefsek taharah* is within the last few minutes of the day, close to *shkiah*.[283] The problem is that a woman will often do a few *bedikos* before she can produce a clean *hefsek taharah*. It is therefore recommended that a woman start trying to do a *hefsek taharah* a little bit earlier so she will not end up performing it after shkiah. It is not uncommon for women to call up a *Rav* saying that they were pressed for time and ended up doing a *hefsek taharah* a minute or two after *shkiah*, and asking what to do. To make sure that she does not come to such a situation, a woman should plan ahead, and start trying to do her *hefsek taharah* some time before *shkiah*.

A woman should ideally wash her entire body[284] with hot water[285] before doing a *hefsek taharah*. In the event that she is unable to wash her entire body, she should make sure to wash the external area where the *bedikah* is done.[286] On Shabbos, Tishah B'Av, and Yom Kippur, a localized cold-water cleaning should be done. On Yom Tov a localized warm-water cleaning should be performed.

---

281. קצ״ו א׳.

282. וכמש״כ בפ״ת קצ״ו ס״ק ח׳ בשם הנו״ב לענין בדיקות ז׳ נקיים וכ״ש הכא שקיל יותר.

283. ס׳ קצ״ו סע׳ א׳, ב״י, ב״ח, צמח צדק בפסקי דינים ס׳ קצ״ו.

284. פשטות דברי הרמ״א ס׳ קצ״ו סע׳ ג׳ וז״ל ״ומנהג כשר הוא כשהאשה פוסקת בטהרה שתרחץ ולובשת לבנים; אמנם אם לא רחצה רק פניה של מטה, די בכך״ עכ״ל, תורת השלמים ס״ק ו׳.

285. תורת הבית הקצר בית שביעי שער חמישי.

286. רמ״א שם, ועיין בחכמ״א כלל קי״ז סע׳ ח׳ דאפי׳ לכתחילה די שתרחץ רק אותו מקום ובכל מקום שעלול ליפול שם כתם, וכן כשפוסקת בטהרה בשבת יש לה לרחץ רק או״מ ועיין שו״ע או״ח ס׳ שכ״ו סע׳ א׳ ומ״ב ס״ק א׳, ו׳, וכן לענין יוה״כ די בכך ועיין שם ס׳ תרי״ג ומ״ב ס״ק ל״א.

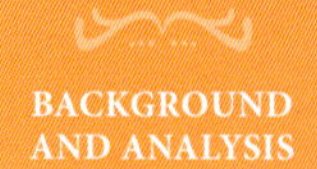

Chorin V'Sedakin (Cracks and Crevices)

Chazal say a *bedikah* must done in *chorin v'sedakin*.[287] According to most *Poskim*,[288] a *bedikas chorin v'sedakin* establishes that the last discharge that came out of her body was not blood, as a discharge remains in the cracks of the vaginal walls for a short while before leaving the body.

In another expression of the concept of *bedikas chorin v'sedakin*, the *Poskim* discuss whether a woman may do a second *bedikah* immediately after she just did one, or if she may do a *bedikah* after washing herself internally.[289] Must she wait some time before performing a new *bedikah*? They explain that the meaning of the need for *chorin v'sedakin* is to demonstrate that the woman has not bled in a while. This being the case, a woman who wants to do a *bedikah* right after having washed herself does not show that she has not recently bled, for any recent blood present within her body would have been washed away. According to this, she should wait before doing a *bedikah*. The same would be true regarding a *bedikah* immediately after one was just performed.

In short, the first explanation of the need for *bedikas chorin v'sedakin* is that a woman is required to show that no blood is present internally *right now* in one of the vaginal crevices, as blood on the inside of the body is *metamei* just like blood on the outside. The second reason for *bedikas chorin v'sedakin* is that she has to show she has not bled in a while.

The Chazon Ish holds that *lechatchilah* a woman should wait 15 minutes after washing herself before she attempts a *hefsek taharah*, and another 15 minutes between each attempt at a *hefsek taharah*; he is concerned for the second explanation of the need for *bedikas chorin v'sedakin*.[290] Other *Poskim* are lenient *bedi'eved* if she waited at least a minute or so, or even less.[291] However, whenever possible, a woman should leave some time to fulfill the *lechatchilah* of 15 minutes.

---

287. תורת הבית להרשב״א בית שביעי שער חמישי, ע״ש מש״כ בשם הראב״ד והרמב״ן.

288. ס״ט ס׳ קצ״ו ס״ק כ״ג ד״ה ועוד נ״ל, חזו״א ס׳ צ״ב אות כ״א ובס׳ פ״א, אבל בשו״ת רע״א ס׳ ס׳ ובנו״ב תנינא ס׳ קל״ה כתבו דהטעם של בדיקת חו״ס הוא דחיישינן שמא דם המקור יעבור דרך החו״ס בשעת הבדיקה ולכן חייבת לבדוק בהחו״ס, ויש נ״מ להלכה שלפי הס״ט וחזו״א חייבת להמתין בין בדיקה או רחיצה להבדיקה אבל לפי רע״א כל שבדקה ומצאה נקי מדם ה״ז טהורה, וכן אמר לי הר׳ דוד פיינשטיין שיש לסמוך על רע״א בזה.

289. שו״ת מהרי״ל דיסקין פסקים ס׳ כ״ב, אג״מ יו״ד ב׳ ס״א, מראה כהן בשם ר׳ אלישיב, חוט שני.

290. חזו״א ריש ס׳ פ״א.

291. בחוט שני הקיל אם חכתה ג׳ דקות, אבל הפוסקים בארה״ב סוברים אפ׳ לכת׳ כדעת הנו״ב ורע״א וכך אמר לי הרב דוד פינשטיין.

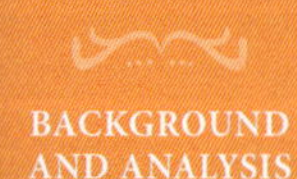

Lubricants

A woman may use a lubricant to help her with a *bedikah*,[292] but she must make sure that it does not ruin the color of the *mareh*. Rav Moshe Feinstein allows women to put the lubricant on the *bedikah* cloth before performing a *hefsek taharah*. Other *Poskim* maintain that putting other substances on the *bedikah* cloth ruins the *mareh*. They say that instead of applying the lubricant to the *bedikah* cloth, she should instead put a water-based lubricant (KY Jelly or Astroglide, but not Vaseline) inside her body, wait a few minutes, and then do the *bedikah*. This approach appears to be more ideal. Another problem with putting lubricants on the *bedikah* cloth is that it can cause the cloth to reach its saturation point, thus enabling less blood to stick to it.

The Bedikah

A woman should preferably buy *bedikah* cloths that were produced for the performance of *bedikos*, and not use homemade *bedikah* cloths. There are two basic kinds of cloths available: one is regular and the other is more elastic. The elastic one feels good inside but does not absorb the blood as well, and should preferably be avoided if possible.[293]

The *bedikah* cloth must be clean,[294] and the woman must inspect it before she uses it. It should be big enough to cover her finger, although no size is mentioned in halachah.[295] A tampon should not be used for a *bedikah*. Although a tampon would technically work for a *moch dachuk*,[296] using it for this purpose is discouraged.

How to Perform a Hefsek Taharah

A woman should put one foot up on a toilet seat or chair, and the other on the ground,[297] with the *bedikah* cloth wrapped around her

292. שו״ת מהרש״ם חלק א׳ ס׳ קמ״ו, דרכי תשובה ס״ק נ״ז, חוט שני.
293. בספר משנת השלחן קצ״ו ו׳ בשם הרה״ג ר׳ אלישיב.
294. ס׳ קצ״ו סע׳ ו׳.
295. עיין בשו״ע ס׳ קצ״ו סע׳ ו׳ לענין עד הבדיקה ולא הביא שיעור בזה, אבל בספר משנת השלחן כתב בשם הרה״ג ר׳ אלישיב שלכתחילה ״שיעור העד צריך להיות ג׳ על ג׳ אצבעות״ לא פחות ולא יותר אבל אינו מעכב בדיעבד, ובחוט שני כתב ששיעור הבדיקה היא שתוכל לכסות בעד כשני פרקים מהאצבע בקירוב.
296. גופי הלכ׳ במשנ״ב ס״ק א׳, יסוד הטהרה, שו״ת באר משה.
297. הגהות חתם סופר בשו״ע לס׳ קצ״ו.

finger. She should insert the cloth and gently press it against the vaginal walls to do a *bedikas chorin v'sedakin*.[298]

The cloth should then be put in a clean place to dry.[299] Wet *maros* look worse than dry ones do, and a woman is only helping herself by waiting for a *mareh* to dry instead of rejecting it right away, even if it initially looks *tamei*. If the *hefsek taharah* looks good, she should not attempt to do another one. If it is clearly not good, she should do another one, preferably waiting some time between each attempt. A woman should not try for a *hefsek taharah* too many times in one day because she may end up cutting herself in the process and end up losing more days waiting to heal than the 1 extra day needed to get a clean *hefsek taharah*.

A woman should bring every *bedikah* that she is not certain is *tehorah* to a *Rav*, even if she thinks it is *temei'ah*. Very often, a *Rav* can help her in ways she would not have thought of.

Specific intent is not necessary for a *hefsek taharah*;[300] a clean *bedikah* during the appropriate time establishes the woman's status as *tehorah*.

How to Perform the Moch Dachuk

The *moch* should be inserted before *shkiah*. It is advisable that when inserting the *moch dachuk*, the woman should move it around the sides of the vaginal canal, in effect doing a *bedikas chorin v'sedakin*, even though it is not required. This way if the *hefsek taharah* was not good, she will be able to use the *moch dachuk* as a *hefsek taharah* as well.

Poletes Shichvas Zera: The 5-Day Wait

The Gemara explains that the reason why all Jewish men separated from their wives 3 days before *Mattan Torah* (the Giving of the Torah) is because the women had to be *tehoros* by *Mattan Torah*, and not be *poltos shichvas zera* (emitting *zera* from their bodies).[301] We learn from the Gemara that the *tumah* of *poletes shichvas zera* disrupts the *shivah nekiyim*. [302] A *poletes* does not actually have to start the 7 days again; she just loses the days in which the *zera* may have emerged from her body.

298. תורת הבית להרשב״א בית שביעי שער חמישי, טוש״ע ס׳ קצ״ו ו׳.
299. עיין ט״ז ס׳ קפ״ח ס״ק א׳ מ״ש בשם הב״ח, שו״ת חת״ס ס׳ קמ״ה, שו״ת מהרש״ם.
300. שו״ת עבודת הגרשני ס׳ ע״ט.
301. שבת פ״ו ע״א.
302. נדה ל״ג ע״א.

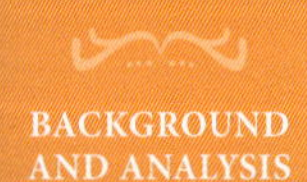

She has to continue the 7 days for an extra number of days equivalent to the number of days she was *polet.*

If a women emits even a small amount of *zera* from her body, this *zera* disrupts the entire date on which it was emitted.[303] However, only *zera* that is still potent and able to impregnate disrupts *shivah nekiyim*;[304] *zera* emitted from her body after this point does not affect the *shivah nekiyim*, as it is no longer potent.[305] The halachah is that *zera* remains potent and can impregnate for up to 6 *onos*, a 72-hour period of time.[306] Therefore, a woman who had marital relations cannot begin counting *shivah nekiyim* for 6 *onos* after marital relations.

The *Shulchan Aruch* says a woman must wait until the 4th day after marital relations (the day on which marital relations took place is Day 1) before performing a *hefsek taharah* and beginning *shivah nekiyim*.[307] Since the 72 hours always end during the 4th day after marital relations, and the *shivah nekiyim* have to be 7 complete days from sundown, she can perform a *hefsek taharah* at the end of Day 4, and begin counting the next day (Day 5) as the 1st day of *shivah nekiyim*. Although the 72-hour wait that the concern of *poletes shichvas zera* requires is 3 days, practically, it will always be a minimum of 4 days.

The Rama says to add a 5th day to the count brought by the *poletes shichvas zera* concern, in case the woman had marital relations around the time of *bein hashmashos* and thought that it happened during the day, while it was really already night.[308] In such a case, the woman thinks the 6 *onos* end a few minutes before *shkiah* on Day 4 of her counting when in reality her body can conceivably still emit potent *zera* a few minutes into Day 5 of her mistaken calculation.

The Rama also says that any woman who was allowed to have marital relations must wait this time.[309] Every woman who was permitted to have marital relations, whether or not she had marital relations right before her period began, must wait 5 days before making a *hefsek taharah.*

303. נדה ל״ג ע״ב.
304. שבת פ״ו ע״א, ע״ב, טוש״ע ס׳ קצ״ו סע׳ י״א, ש״ך ס״ק י״ז, ט״ז ס״ק ה׳.
305. ט״ז ס״ק ה׳.
306. שיטת חכמים בשבת פ״ו ע״ב, טוש״ע ס׳ קצ״ו י״א, ש״ך ס״ק יז׳, ט״ז ס״ק ה׳.
307. ס׳ קצ״ו י״א, שיטת ר״ת בתוס׳ נדה ל״ג ע״א ד״ה רואה וז״ל ״אשה ששמשה וראתה מיד אין לה להתחיל לספור נקיים עד אחר יום ד׳ דבעינן ו׳ עונות שלמות וכן פסק ר״ח״ עכ״ל.
308. ס׳ קצ״ו י״א ברמ״א, ת״ה סימן רמ״ה והאגור בשם ר״י מולין וש״ד וכ״כ מהרא״י ומהרי״ק שורש ל״ה.
309. שם ברמ״א וז״ל ״יש שכתבו שעכשיו אין לחלק בין שמשה עם בעלה ללא שמשה, וכל אשה שרואה, אפילו כתם, צריכה להמתין ה׳ ימים עם יום שראתה בו ותפסוק לעת ערב ותספור ז׳ נקיים וכן נוהגין במדינות אלו ואין לשנות״.

In summary, the Shulchan Aruch holds a woman can make a *hefsek taharah* on the 4th day, counting the day she became *temei'ah* as the 1st day, and the Rama holds she performs a *hefsek taharah* on the 5th day. The day that the *tumah* begins is considered the 1st day of the cycle, even if the bleeding only began a few minutes before *shkiah*. Towards the end of the 5th day the woman washes herself during the day, does a *hefsek taharah* before *shkiah*, and inserts a *moch dachuk* from before *shkiah* through *bein hashmashos*. That night and the following day will be Day 1 of *shivah nekiyim*.

When a Woman Does Not Need 5 Days

We noted above that as long as a woman was permitted to have marital relations before she became *temei'ah*, she must wait 5 days. Conversely, if marital relations were forbidden, she may count the 5 days from whenever she was last permitted. If this was more than 5 days prior to the onset of the bleeding, she may perform a *hefsek taharah* as soon as she stops bleeding.

Therefore, a *kallah* does not have to wait 5 days when preparing to become *tehorah* for her wedding, because she was prohibited to her *chassan* before she got her period and is therefore definitely not a *poletes*, so the Rama's provision does not apply.[310]

A *chassan* and *kallah* wait only 4 days before a *hefsek taharah* after *bi'ah rishonah*, because the 5-day wait was not insitituted for the *tumah* of *dam besulim*.[311] A woman who has not gone to the mikvah for one full cycle also does not need to wait 5 days, because when she got her period she was *temei'ah*, and it was prohibited for her to have marital relations.[312] Such a woman can attempt to do a *hefsek taharah* whenever she wants.

The *Poskim* are lenient when the day before the woman got her period was a prohibited day because it was a *vest* for 24 hours, from night to day, or if she got her period during *bein hashmashos* of Motzaei Tishah B'Av or Motzaei Yom Kippur.[313] These halachos are complicated, and a woman should ask a *she'eilah* should the circumstances arise.

310. ט״ז ס׳ קצ״ו ס״ק ז׳.
311. ס׳ קצ״ג ט״ז ס״ק ד׳ בשם מהר״ל מפראג (הגהות הטור ס׳ קצ״ו).
312. שו״ת דובב מישרים ס׳ ח׳, שו״ת הר צבי ס׳ קנ״ז, מנחת שלמה חלק ב׳ ס׳ עב ענף א׳, מנח״י חלק ג׳ ס׳ פ״ה.
313. אג״מ יו״ד ד׳ סימן י״ז וז״ל ״הנה לע״ד מסתבר שא״צ להמתין מיום הראייה אלא ד׳ ימים שהצריכו להמתין כדכתב הרא״ש (נדה פ״ד סימן א׳) שמא תפלוט ש״ז, ואם פלטה סותרת מעיקר הדין ויש מקום לגזור בלא שמשה אטו שמשה כמבואר לקמן, ויום הראשון שצריכה להמתין רק מחמת חשש דשמא תשמש בין השמשות, נמנה גם מימי האבלות, כיוון שהוא מחמת איסור אף שאינו מחמת איסור נדה, דכל שלא שייך שתשמש אינה צריכה

A woman may only circumvent the 5-day wait when the reason why the couple did not have marital relations was because it was halachically prohibited. If the couple was stringent not to have marital relations, this is not enough to get around the 5 days,[314] unless the stringency is something brought in the *Poskim*. If the couple thought that the wife was *temei'ah* because she discovered blood, and therefore separated, and they later find that the blood turned out to be *tahor* for any reason, the woman cannot begin her count of 5 days from when they separated.[315] The 5 days may only be started from when the wife is actually prohibited to her husband, even in a case that they separated and started keeping *harchakos* because they thought she may have been prohibited.

There are situations in which keeping the 5th day can cause other complications.[316] One example is a woman who might not be able to become pregnant if she does not go to the mikvah a day earlier. In all such cases, a competent *Rav* should be consulted to determine if a couple may be lenient in regard to the 5 days of the *Rama*. [317]

Wearing White Clothing during Shivah Nekiyim

When a woman becomes *temei'ah*, she counts the day on which the bleeding began as Day 1 of the 5 days, does a *bedikah* on Day 5 for a *hefsek taharah*, and counts the *next* day as Day 1 of the *shivah nekiyim*. By far the most common, serious mistake that women make in *hilchos niddah* is that they start counting Day 1 of *shivah nekiyim* on the day they did their *hefsek taharah*![318]

In the times of *Chazal* a woman wore a complete set of white clothing during *shivah nekiyim*. Nowadays, women's underwear is tight and blood will not pass through to the outer garments without staining the underwear. A woman should wear white underwear throughout *shivah nekiyim*.[319] In Eretz Yisrael many women are careful to sleep on white sheets during the *shivah nekiyim* as well,[320] even a *kallah* in the

---

להמתין חמישה ימים, אלא ארבעה בלבד ככלה, עי׳ לעיל אות י״ח. וכן נפטרו מלמנות יום החמישי כשראתה דם תיכף בתחילת מוצאי יו״כ ובתחלת מוצאי ט׳ באב״ עכ״ל.

314. טה״ב עמ׳ תכ״ב.

315. משנת השלחן בשם ר׳ אלישיב.

316. עיין בספר פתחי תשובות עמ׳ תט״ז- תי״ט ט״ז אופנים שדנין האחרונים אם אפשר להקל בדין של הרמ״א.

317. טהב״י בשם החזו״א, משמרת הטהרה בשם ר׳ אלישיב, ועיין באג״מ יו״ד ב׳ ס׳ פ״ד שכתב שם דיכולה להפסיק בטהרה אפ׳ קודם ליום ד׳ וז״ל ״יש להתיר לה אם יפרוש ג׳ ימים קודם הוסת ותפסוק מלראות ביום השני לנדתה לעשות הפסק טהרה ביום ההוא ולספור ז׳ נקיים תיכף ולטבול בליל עשירי״ ע״ש.

318. עיין ס׳ קצ״ו י״ב.

319. טור בשם הרא״ש, ס׳ קצ״ו ג׳.

320. ע״פ מרדכי בשם רוקח, שו״ע ס׳ קצ״ו ג׳.

days before her wedding.[321] In the United States many do not even teach about the need for a white sheet.[322] A guest should not ask her host to borrow a white sheet even if it is her custom to sleep on it, as this is a lack of *tznius* (modesty).

Rav Akiva Eiger (based on the *Rosh*) says a woman must inspect the white underwear or sheet.[323] It is said in the name of Rav Moshe Feinstein that a woman does not have to check her underwear; she may change in the dark and not look for *kesamim*. Most *Poskim* rule like Rav Akiva Eiger,[324] unless there are extenuating circumstances.

Bedikos during Shivah Nekiyim

During *shivah nekiyim* a woman must perform two *bedikos* every day.[325] The first *bedikah* should be done in the morning,[326] and the second should be done close to *shkiah*.[327] All *bedikos* of *shivah nekiyim* must be inserted as deeply in the woman's body as possible and pressed along the vaginal walls.[328] If this is too difficult, then at least the *hefsek taharah* and *bedikos* of Days 1 and 7 must be done in this manner, while the other ones may be simple *bedikos*.[329] A woman who only did one *bedikah* on Day 1 and one on Day 7 may immerse in the mikvah *bedi'eved*.[330] However, this halachah is only *bedi'eved*; a woman should never miss a *bedikah lechatchilah*.[331]

The *Noda B'Yehudah* says if a woman did *bedikos* every day besides Day 7, she must do a *bedikah* on "Day 8" and make Day 2 into Day 1, and Day 8 into Day 7, and in this way achieve the minimum requirement of performing *bedikos* on Day 1 and Day 7.[332] However, this will not work if the woman missed Day 2 as well, in which case she may have to push off her *tevilah* by a few days. In this case, she may be advised to immerse in

---

321. הגרש״ז אוערבאך.
322. אג״מ יו״ד ד׳ ס׳ י״ז אות כ״ז, שיעורי שבט הלוי.
323. ס׳ קצ״ו ד״ה להיות בודקת לכתחילה: עצמה וחלוקה.
324. ס״ט ס״ק ט׳, שיעורי שבה״ל.
325. עייו תוס׳ תוספות נדה ז׳ ע״ב וז״ל ״צריכה לבדוק בכל יום״ עכ״ל, טור בשם סמ״ג וז״ל ״ובכל ז׳ ימי הספירה צריכה להיות בודקת לכתחילה פ״א ביום ובספר המצות כתב פעמיים אחת שחרית ואחת ערבית״ עכ״ל, שו״ע ס׳ קצ״ו סע׳ ד׳.
326. וז״ל הב״י ס׳ קצ״ו ״פעם אחת בשחרית כשעומדת ממטתה״ עכ״ל, ובאחרונים כתבו שתבדוק מיד בבוקר עד חצות ואם לא בדקה עד חצות הפסידה בדיקת שחרית.
327. ובאחרונים כתבו שבדיקת ערב אפשר ממנחה קטנה עד שקיעה.
328. ס׳ קצ״ו סע׳ ו׳.
329. שם בשו״ע.
330. ס׳ קצ״ו סע׳ ד׳ בשם סמ״ג.
331. ס׳ קצ״ו סע׳ ד׳ וז״ל ״בכל יום מז׳ ימי הספירה צריכה להיות בודקת לכתחלה פעמים בכל יום, אחת שחרית ואחת סמוך לבין השמשות״ עכ״ל.
332. נו״ב תניינא יו״ד ס׳ קכ״ח.

the mikvah without fulfilling the Noda B'Yehudah's position. A woman should be in contact with a *Rav* should this situation arise.

A woman who has a cut, or is prone to get cuts due to her sensitive skin, should cut down to one *bedikah* a day if this will help.[333] If the skin is especially sensitive, she should do only one *bedikah* on Day 1 and one on Day 7, *lechatchilah*.[334] Rav Nissim Karelitz says a woman who is unable to get a clean *bedikah* should go to a *bodekes* who will do the *bedikah* for her. Alternatively, the *bodekes* can put a Q-tip near the cervix and wait a moment to see which color discharges are coming out; this can serve as the *bedikah*. A woman in this situation should do this for a *hefsek taharah*, and then once on Day 1 and once on Day 7.

The Raavad says a woman who did one *bedikah* throughout the entire *shivah nekiyim* may immerse in the mikvah.[335] The *Poskim* rely on the *Raavad b'makom igun*, which is defined as a situation in which a woman will not be able to get a clean *bedikah* for some time.[336] A woman who finds herself in this situation should ask her *Rav* for guidance.

A woman who has a questionable *bedikah* should label the *mareh* (for example, "Day 4, afternoon *bedikah*") and bring it to the *Rav* as soon as possible, after it dried. It is not a good idea to save a week's worth of *maros* and bring the *Rav* the whole stack at once. In the beginning of the marriage, a couple should bring anything with color to a *Rav*; they will not lose by asking. As time goes on, a person learns what is a *she'eilah* and which colors are clearly fine.

The Rama says there is a difference between the first 3 days and the last 4 days of *shivah nekiyim* in that in the first 3 days the halachah will not attribute a *kesem* that the woman discovers on white underwear to a source other than her uterus (as discussed in Advanced Rulings, Taharah, headline Attributing a Kessem to a Makkah during Shivah Nekiyim (page 333).[337] The only *teliyah* that would be effective during the first 3 days is a *makkah* that clearly bleeds. Also, we are still lenient when there is a stain that is smaller than a *gris*. Rav Moshe Feinstein counts these 3 days from the time that the woman stopped bleeding,

333. ובזה מקיים השיטות המובאים בבית יוסף ס׳ קצ״ו וז״ל ״ובכל שבעת ימי הספירה צריכה להיות בודקת לכתחלה פעם אחת ביום. כן כתבו הרמב״ן (פ״ב ה״ד, פ״ט הכ״ג) והרשב״א (שם כד.) והרא״ש (פ״י סי׳ ה) דלכתחלה מיהא צריכה לעשות כן וכן כתבו הגהות מיימוניות פרק ו׳ (איסו״ב אות ד) בשם התוספות (ז: ד״ה ר״א) ומדכתבו סתם תבדוק בכל יום משמע דלכתחלה אינה צריכה לבדוק יותר מפעם אחת ביום״ עכ״ל.

334. נו״ב תניינא יו״ד ס׳ קכ״ט.

335. רא״ש בשם הראב״ד, שו״ע ס׳ קצ״ו סע׳ ד׳.

336. שו״ת רע״א, שו״ת חת״ס ס׳ קע״ח, תשובת בית אפרים מ״ח, ערוך השלחן ס׳קצ״ו סע׳ כ״ה וכ״ו.

337. ס׳ קצ״ו סע׳ י׳.

which is not necessarily the day of the *hefsek taharah*; at that point the woman is no longer considered to have a *mayan pasuach* (lit. an open spring; a situation in which she is no longer considered to be expecting to bleed).[338] Once 3 days pass, she is considered one who has a *mayan sasum* (lit. a closed spring: a situation in which she is not expecting to see blood), and it is easier to attribute the *kesem* to something else.

When to Immerse in the Mikvah

A woman becomes *tehorah* and permitted to her husband after she completes the *shivah nekiyim* and immerses in a kosher mikvah. The Gemara says that the principle of *miktzas hayom k'kulo* (a part of a day is considered like the whole day) states that a woman should be allowed to immerse during Day 7 of her *shivah nekiyim*,[339] although she would be prohibited to her husband until the night.[340] The concern with permitting a woman to immerse during the day is that the couple will have marital relations during the day, and then she will begin to bleed. This uproots the *shivah nekiyim* before they were completed, and the couple is liable to *kareis* retroactively. A woman should therefore not immerse in the mikvah during the day. The exception to this rule is a *kallah* before her wedding, who will not see the *chassan* until the night of the wedding.[341]

A woman who cannot immerse in the mikvah at night may be able to immerse during the 8th day.[342] This is what was done in parts of Eretz Yisrael during the Gulf War. A couple who think that they are in a situation that will permit the wife to immerse during the day should call their *Rav*, who will advise them how to proceed.

A woman must immerse in the mikvah after *tzeis hakochavim* following *shivah nekiyim*. Many *Poskim* hold that women should not immerse earlier than 40 minutes after *shkiah* in Eretz Yisrael, unless the mikvah will be closed by that time. If one does not want to be stringent, they can easily keep the 20–25-minute *zman* (time) in Eretz Yisrael.

A couple who keeps Rabbeinu Tam on Motzaei Shabbos should keep it for *tevilah* as well.[343] The problem is that it may be difficult for a

338. עיין פ״ת ס״ק י׳.
339. עיין נדה ס״ז ע״ב.
340. טור קפ״ג, ואפי׳ טבלה ביום השמיני – ס׳ קצ״ז ה׳ ברמ״א בשם האגור, ועיין גר״א שחולק ע״ז אם הוא ביום שאחר יום שביעי.
341. ס׳ קצ״ז סע׳ ג׳ ברמ״א בשם מהרי״ל.
342. ס׳ קצ״ז סע׳ ד׳.
343. שו״ת שבה״ל חלק ד׳ ס׳ ק״ז.

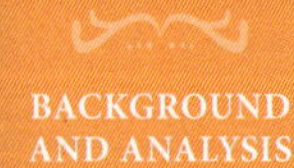

woman to find a mikvah in Yerushalayim on Friday and Yom Tov nights that is open so late. Under pressing circumstances, a woman in this situation may immerse before Rabbeinu Tam,[344] but the couple remains forbidden to each other until after *tzeis hakochavim* of Rabbeinu Tam.

Chatzitzah D'Oraisa and D'Rabbanan

A woman must do *chafifos* and then immerse her entire body, including her hair, all at the same time under the water.[345] If any part of her body or hair is not underwater, the *tevilah* is invalid, and the woman remains a *niddah d'Oraisa*. For this reason another woman must watch her while she immerses, to make sure that every strand of hair is under the water.[346]

There must be no *chatzitzah* on the woman's body or hair when she immerses, that blocks the water from touching that area.[347] A *chatzitzah d'Oraisa* is something that covers most of a person's body, that she or most women care not to have it there. A *chatzitzah d'Rabbanan* is when only one, not both, of these two criteria exist: either a substance that the person does not care about covers most of the body, *or* it covers only a small part of the body but the person or most people do not care to have it there.

The Rambam[348] and Geonim[349] disagree as to whether "the majority of the person's body" includes the hair. The Geonim and the Raavad hold that the hair is considered its own entity, while the Rambam holds that hair is viewed as part of her body. The Shulchan Aruch rules like the Geonim and the Raavad.[350] So, if most of the woman's hair *or* most of her body has something covering it, it is a *chatzitzah d'Rabbanan*, even if she does not mind that it is there.

344. פ״ת ס׳ קצ״ו ס״ק י״ג בשם חמודי דניאל, תשובות חכ״צ ס׳ י״א.

345. ז״ל הרא״ש מסכת נדה הלכות מקוואות "וצריכה שתטבול כל גופה בבת אחת ולא אבר אבר. כדדרשינן בסיפרא (פרשת אמור) דכתיב ורחץ בשרו במים ובא השמש וטהר מה ביאת שמשו כולו כאחת אף רחיצתו כולו כאחת" עכ״ל, שו״ע ס׳ קצ״ח סע׳ א׳.

346. ס׳ קצ״ח סע׳ מ׳.

347. עיין גמ׳ סוכה ה׳ ע״ב, ו׳ ע״א, וז״ל גמ׳ נדה ס״ז ע״ב "אמר ר׳ יצחק, דבר תורה: רובו המקפיד עליו - חוצץ, רובו ואינו מקפיד עליו - אינו חוצץ. וגזרו על רובו שאינו מקפיד - משום רובו המקפיד, וגזרו על מיעוטו המקפיד - משום רובו המקפיד" ע״כ, שו״ע ס׳ קצ״ח סע׳ א׳ וז״ל "צריכה שתטבול כל גופה בפעם אחת; לפיכך צריך שלא יהיה עליה שום דבר החוצץ. ואפילו כל שהוא, ואם דרך בני אדם לפעמים להקפיד עליו, חוצץ אפילו אם אינה מקפדת עליו עתה, או אפילו אינה מקפדת עליו לעולם כיון שדרך רוב בני אדם להקפיד עליו, חוצץ; ואם הוא חופה רוב הגוף, אפילו אין דרך בני אדם להקפיד בכך, חוצץ. הגה: ולכתחלה לא תטבול אפילו בדברים שאינם חוצצין, גזרה אטו דברים החוצצים".

348. רמב״ם מקוואות פרק ב׳ הל׳ ט״ו.

349. השגת הראב״ד שם.

350. ס׳ קצ״ח סע׳ ה׳.

The most common situation of *chatzitzah d'Oraisa* is something covering most of the woman's hair that she does not want there, such as baby oil. It is not common to have something covering most of the body that she does not want there. Practically, the only times a woman will be a *niddah d'Oraisa* after immersing is if there was a *chatzitzah d'Oraisa* or if she immerses in the mikvah without fully submerging.

A *chatzitzah* is considered something that is "cared about" if the person on whose body it is present cares about it, or if most people care about having this substance on their body even if this person happens not to; the halachah is stringent both ways.[351] The Rama says a woman should ideally remove everything from her body, even something small that she generally does not care about.[352]

Included in "caring" is that in most situations a person would not want this object or substance to be there.[353] If a woman would remove her rings while doing a normal activity, then her rings are *chatzitzos* for *tevilah*.[354] In the days that women kneaded dough on a daily basis, rings were considered a big problem.[355] Nowadays, when most women knead dough at most once a week, and often even less, there may be room to be lenient. If it turns out that a woman immersed in the mikvah wearing her rings, as with any *she'eilah* of a *chatzitzah*, a competent *Rav* should be consulted.

Some women get very nervous when preparing for the mikvah to the point that it can be debilitating. On the one hand, the severity of the halachos requires performance of *chafifos* in the best manner possible. However, now that we understand the development of these halachos, we can understand the differences between a *chatzitzah d'Oraisa*, *chatzitzah d'Rabbanan*, and what she is required to do *lechatchilah* according to the *Rama*.

A woman must return to the mikvah to immerse again even if she only discovers a *chatzitzah d'Rabbanan* after the immersion, but she can feel calm knowing that in most cases of *chatzitzah* she is dealing with prohibitions that are not *d'Oraisa*, and therefore do not carry a liability to *kareis* in case she was inadvertently intimate with her husband after an improper immersion.

If a *she'eilah* arises before or after immersion, a *Rav* must be consulted.

---

351. ס' קצ"ח סע' א', ש"ך ס"ק ב', ט"ז ס"ק ג'.
352. רמ"א ס' קצ"ח סע' א' בשם הגהות ש"ד.
353. עיין ס' קצ"ח סע' א', ש"ך ס"ק א', ט"ז ס"ק ב'.
354. פ"ת ס' קצ"ח ס"ק יד'.
355. ט"ז קצ"ח ס"ק כג'.

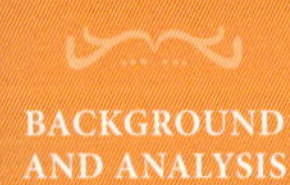

Iyun and Chafifah

Iyun, which means that a woman's body must be inspected before *tevilah* to make sure that no *chatzitzos* are present, is required *mid'Oraisa*.[356] A woman who immersed in the mikvah without *iyun* must immerse again. A woman should not rely on the mikvah lady to inspect her, but should check herself thoroughly before entering the mikvah.[357]

Ezra HaSofer also established that women should do *chafifos* before immersing in the mikvah, to remove any potential *chatzitzos*.[358] A woman should wash her entire body, as well as her *beis hastarim* (which we will soon discuss),[359] with hot water.[360] She should thoroughly comb all accumulations of hair on her body with a strong comb.[361] *Lechatchilah* a comb should be used; *bedi'eved*, if a woman used her fingers and removed any *chatzitzos* and knots, it is enough.[362] She should also comb her eyebrows and eyelashes.[363]

The obligation of *chafifah* with hot water can, according to the letter of the law, be fulfilled with a shower, and does not specifically require a bath.[364] The reason why women generally take a bath is to get rid of scabs, which will generally come off after a good soaking.[365] Practically speaking, all women, even those who do not have scabs, soak in a bath before *tevilah*, and they take off whatever *chatzitzos* they can. Scabs should be removed as much as possible, and whatever remains will not be a *chatzitzah*.

356. ב״ק פב׳ ע״א, ס׳ קצ״ט א׳.
357. ס״ט ס׳ קצ״ט ס״ק ה׳, ועיין ש״ך ס״ק יא׳, פ״ת ס׳ קצ״ט ס״ק ב׳.
358. ב״ק פ״ב ע״א, ס׳ קצ״ט סע׳ א׳.
359. ס׳ קצ״ט סע׳ א׳.
360. ס׳ קצ״ט סע׳ ב׳.
361. ס׳ קצ״ט סע׳ א׳ ״ולסרוק שיער ראשה יפה במסרק שלא תהיינה שערותיה נדבקות זו בזו״ ע״כ.
362. עיין ירושלמי סוף פרק כל שעה.
363. עיין ב״י ס׳ קצ״ט, חכמ״א.
364. עיין בספר החינוך מצוה קעה וז״ל ״מדין תורה היתה צריכה כל אשה לעיין כל גופה סמוך לטבילתה שלא יהא דבר חוצץ בגופה, ודיה. ועזרא ובית דינו תיקנו שתהא חופפת בכל מקום שיער שבה במים חמים, ומסרקת או מפספסת שערותיה בידיה או במסרק אם יש לה יפה יפה, כדי שאם היו שערותיה נקשרים תתיר אותם. ובנות ישראל החמירו על עצמן לשטוף כל גופן בחמין, וכל המשנה ממנהגן ימתח על העמוד״ עכ״ל.
365. עיין ס׳ קצ״ז סע׳ ט׳ ״דם יבש שעל המכה, חוצץ; וריר שבתוכה, אינו חוצץ. יצא הריר מתוכה, כל תוך ג׳ ימים לח הוא ואינו חוצץ; לאחר מכאן, יבש הוא וחוצץ. לפיכך אשה בעלת חטטים צריכה לחוף במים עד שיתרככו״ ע״כ.

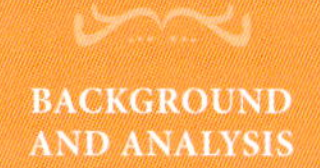

Common Chafifah Issues

A woman should cut her nails because there may be dirt underneath.[366] In Yerushalayim the practice is to cut the nails down to the skin.[367] Rav Moshe Feinstein says a woman may cut her nails to the length that she usually wants it, such that people would consider the nails "cut."[368] In the event that a woman forgot to cut her nails before Shabbos for a *tevilah* on Friday night, a non-Jew can cut them normally, with scissors.[369] The same applies to a *tevilah* on Yom Tov. If a non-Jew is not available, the woman should clean underneath the nails very well.[370]

A woman who shaves should preferably do so before the day of the *tevilah* so she will not have little hairs stuck to her skin. There is no obligation for a woman to shave.[371] No part of the body, including hair — even if it is supposed to be removed in the near future — can ever be considered a *chatzitzah*.[372]

A hangnail that is partially detached may be a *chatzitzah* and should be removed.[373] The only way for it to be a real *chatzitzah* is if it snags in her clothing when she is getting dressed.[374] A slice in the nail is generally not an issue. A woman should *lechatchilah* nevertheless file her nails before going to the mikvah.

Beis HaStarim and Common Chafifah Questions

A woman must also clean her nose, mouth,[375] and teeth,[376] as well as anywhere else that is considered *beis hastarim*.[377] There are various definitions of "*beis hastarim*": some say it refers to an internal cavity that can be seen from the outside;[378] others say it refers to an internal area

366. עיין ס׳ קצח׳ סע׳ כ׳, ט״ז ס״ק כ״א, ודלא כמש״כ בש״ך ס״ק כ״ה בשם ראב״ן, וז״ל אג״מ יו״ד חלק ב ס׳ פ׳ ״ולטבילה אף אם עבר הזמן שדרכה להתגלח פשוט שאינו חוצץ מצד שעומדות להתגלח כיון דמ״מ הרי מגופה הן״ עכ״ל.
367. עיין בחכמ״א כלל קי״ט ס׳ י״ב, ועיין בחוט שני.
368. אג״מ יו״ד חלק ב ס׳ פ׳.
369. ס׳ קצ״ח סע׳ כ׳ בנקוה״כ.
370. ט״ז קצ״ח ס״ק כ״א, שו״ת חכם צבי ס׳ פ״ב.
371. פ״ת ס׳ קצ״ח ס״ק י״ב.
372. דלא כש״ך ס׳ קצ״ח ס״ק כ״ה בשם ראב״ן, שו״ע ס׳ קצ״ח סע׳ כ״ב, ט״ז ס״ק כ״ב, חכמ״א כלל קיט׳ סע׳ ט״ז.
373. ס׳ קצח סע׳ כ״א.
374. בשם הרה״ג ר׳ ישראל יעקב פישר.
375. ט״ז ס׳ קצ״ט ס״ק א׳.
376. ס׳ קצ״ח סע׳ כד׳.
377. נדה סו׳ ע״ב, תוס׳ קידושין כה׳ ע״ב ד״ה כל הראוי, ס׳ קצ״ט א׳.
378. עיין פרדס רימונים פתיחה לסימן קצ״ח, רע״א ס׳ ס׳, שו״ת חת״ס ס׳ קצ״ב, פ״ת ס׳ קצ״ח ס״ק ט״ז.

that is "used";[379] while others explain that it refers to internal areas that can be accessed by water.[380] Something that is further within the body cavity is considered "internal," does not require *chafifah*, and does not create an issue if a *chatzitzah* is found there.[381]

Not doing a proper *chafifah* on the body or the hair invalidates the *tevilah*, but forgetting to properly clean *beis hastarim* does not.[382] A woman who forgot to brush her teeth or blow her nose and does not find a *chatzitzah* afterwards is *tehorah*, as those areas are considered *beis hastarim*.[383] If a woman did not do the other *chafifos* on her hair and body, however, she must immerse in the mikvah again, even if no *chatzitzos* were later discovered.[384]

A woman should contact a *Rav* if she finds a *chatzitzah* after immersing in the mikvah. Sometimes the *Rav* can help her out by attributing the *chatzitzah* to something that occurred after the *tevilah*.[385] A woman does not have to look for *chatzitzos* after she immersed, since she is now assumed to be *tehorah*.[386]

Many *Poskim* hold that contact lenses are a real problem of *chatzitzah d'Rabbanan*,[387] so a woman wearing contact lenses should remember to remove them. Hair conditioner coats the hair, and there is a disagreement whether a woman may use it before going to the mikvah. A woman should ideally not use conditioner before *tevilah*, unless using it is the only way to keep her hair untangled.[388] The *Rosh* and *Rashba* say anything a woman specifically wants on her body is not a *chatzitzah*.

Hair dyes are generally not a problem,[389] especially since they do not have any substance.

Lice are *chatzitzos*.[390] A woman whose head is itchy should go to a professional to get out every bug. Nits are only a problem for those who are repulsed by them. Some Yerushalmi women do not mind nits.

---

379. עיין שו״ת נו״ב קמ״א ס׳ ד׳.
380. רע״א בשם החו״ד, אבנ״ז ס׳ רנ״ה.
381. נו״ב יו״ד ס׳ ס״ד, חת״ס ס׳ קצ״ב.
382. ס׳ קצ״ח כ״ה.
383. ס׳ קצ״ח כ״ו.
384. בעלי הנפש להראב״ד שער הטבילה, שו״ע ס׳ קצ״ט סע׳ א׳, ש״ך ס״ק א׳ וב׳, ט״ז ס״ק ד׳.
385. ס׳ קצ״ח כ״ו.
386. עיין שיעורי שבט הלוי ס׳ קצ״ח מ״א.
387. במנח״י חלק י׳ ס׳ פ״ט החמיר בזה אפ׳ בדיעבד, ובאג״מ יו״ד א׳ צ״ח התיר בדיעבד כיון שאינם דבוקים והוא בבית הסתרים.
388. אהל שרה ס׳ ב׳ הל׳ ט׳ בשם הגרשז״א.
389. שו״ת פני אריה ס׳ ו׳.
390. ס׳ קצ״ח סע׳ מ״ז, עיין ס״ט ס״ק פ״ח, פ״ת ס״ק כ״ה.

Most American women care very much, so nits would be an issue for Americans.

Dandruff and dead skin should be removed as much as possible, and anything that remains afterwards is not a *chatzitzah*, since she does not care about its presence.

When to Perform Chafifos

The Gemara says *chafifos* should be done close to the *tevilah*.[391] There are two opinions as to when is the optimal time for *chafifos* to be performed. *Rashi* says a woman should do *chafifos* during the day because at night she will be in a rush to go to the mikvah.[392] The *She'iltos* says *chafifos* should ideally be done at night, close to the time that she will immerse in the mikvah.[393] The *Shulchan Aruch* says that ideally, a woman should start preparing by day, and do as much as she can.[394] She should then continue her preparations through *bein hashmashos*, and immerse in the mikvah immediately after *bein hashmashos*. If immersing immediately is not possible, or if she prepared at home and at the end of *bein hashmashos* she walked to the mikvah, which made a separation between the preparations and the *tevilah*, she should comb out her hair again at night when she is ready to immerse, as per the opinion of the Rosh.

A woman who works or simply cannot do many of the *chafifos* during the day should try to do at least something to fulfill Rashi's opinion. If she is doing all of the *chafifos* at night, she must spend an hour preparing for *tevilah*, so that she will not rush through the process to get home more quickly.[395] A woman who did even part of the *chafifos* during the day, however, is not bound by this time requirement.

For a Friday-night *tevilah*, a woman should do all her *chafifos* during the day on Friday,[396] tie up her hair, and immerse in the mikvah at night. On a Motzaei Shabbos *tevilah*, she should do *chafifos* on Friday to fulfill

391. נדה ס"ח ע"א.
392. נדה ס"ח ע"א ורש"י ד"ה הא דאפשר.
393. תוס' שם ד"ה כך.
394. ס' קצ"ט סע' ג', ע"פ הרא"ש מקוואות ס' ל"ז
395. רמ"א ס' קצ"ט סע' ג', ש"ך ס"ק ו' וז"ל "עוד כתב מהרש"ל שם על מה שנהגו מקדם להתחיל לחוף ביום ועתה תקנו לחוף בלילה ותעסוק בחפיפה דוקא שעה אחת שלא תהא מהומה לביתה שרי אפי' לרש"י מאחר דאיכא חשש איסור שלא ירגישו בטבילותיהן" עכ"ל, ס"ט ס"ק י"ג, ערוה"ש סע' י"ד. ר' משה פיינשטיין מיקל יותר - עיין חלק ג.
396. ס' קצ"ט סע' ה'.

Rashi's opinion, and then do a basic overall *chafifah* on Motzaei Shabbos before *tevilah* to fulfill the view of the *She'iltos*.[397]

Since a Friday-night *tevilah* does not allow one to perform *chafifos* at night, a woman may only immerse in the mikvah Friday night when this day is the correct time for her to immerse, and her husband is in town.[398] A woman should not plan ahead to immerse in the mikvah on Friday night if it is not the first opportunity for her to immerse.[399] If her husband is out of town and she wants to immerse any night of the week, she may,[400] besides for Friday night. The same applies to a woman after birth who is taking her time getting a *hefsek taharah*. If it works out that she gets a clean *hefsek taharah* on Friday night then she may immerse the following Friday night; otherwise she should not plan it.[401]

A woman should not push off a *tevilah* unless it is an absolute emergency.[402] Some women do not like going to the mikvah on Friday night because then they will not be able to wear makeup on Shabbos. Such a woman should either get Shabbos makeup if her *Rav* permits it, or have a little self-sacrifice, but she should go. Sometimes it is simply impossible to immerse in the mikvah on time. However, one should not push off a mikvah night without calling a *Rav* first. Pushing off the *hefsek taharah* is the same as pushing off the *tevilah*, and should not be done.[403]

Tevilah

The Ashkenazi custom is that the woman immerses, makes a *brachah*, and then immerses again.[404] An Ashkenazi woman thus immerses twice. Sefaradim say the *brachah* and then immerse only once. Immersing extra times is a nice custom for someone who has the custom to do so,[405] but is unnecessary according to halachah.

397. רמ״א ס׳ קצ״ט סע׳ ד׳.
398. רמ״א ס׳ קצ״ז סע׳ ב׳.
399. ס״ט ס׳ קצ״ז, שו״ת מהר״ם שיק ס״ק ק״ד, שיעורי שבט הלוי, חוט שני.
400. שדי חמד, ועיין בשו״ת שבות יעקב חלק ג׳ ס׳ ע״ז.
401. ס׳ קצ״ז ב׳ ברמ״א.
402. עיין נדה ל׳ ע״א, תוס׳ יומא ח׳ ע״א ד״ה דכולי עלמא להני תנאי אמרינן טבילה בזמנה מצוה, ב״י ס׳ קצ״ז, שו״ע ס׳ קצ״ז סע׳ ב׳, ט״ז ס״ק ב׳–ג׳, ובספר פתחי תשובות שהחיוב הוא גם לקיים עונתו ולפו״ר.
403. עיין פ״ת ס׳ קצ״ז ס״ק ג׳ מש״כ בשם הנו״ב.
404. עיין ס׳ ר׳ וברמ״א, של״ה בשער האותיות דף קא׳.
405. עיין ספר חסידים ס׳ שצד׳ שנשים רגילות לטבול שלוש פעמים, שו״ת מעשה אליהו ס׳ כ״ט שיש לטבול שבעה פעמים.

While saying the *brachah* in the mikvah, the woman should put her arm across her stomach and look out of the water.[406] She does this because of the opinions that the halachah is concerned for *libbah ro'eh es ha'ervah* (her heart seeing nakedness) by women, and not only by men. Some *Poskim* are stringent that she should cover her hair while saying the *brachah*.[407] Most, however, are not.

Some husbands do not touch their wives until they specifically say that they immersed in the mikvah.[408] According to the letter of the law, as soon as the wife breaks the *harchakos*, the husband knows she immersed and can assume that she is *tehorah*.[409]

The Rama says not to take a shower in the mikvah building after going to the mikvah,[410] so one does not mistakenly think it is the shower that is *metaher*. Because of this, a woman may shower when she gets home after breaking the *harchakos*, but does not have to wait until after marital relations.

The reader is referred to Basic Overview, Taharah, headline "Preparations and Immersing in the Mikvah" (page 54), which discuss the *chafifah* and immersion process in greater detail.

406. ש״ך ס׳ ר׳ ס״ק א׳, ט״ז ס״ק ג׳.
407. חסד לאלפים או״ח ס׳ ב׳ ה׳, בא״ח פרשת שמיני אות י״ט.
408. חוו״ד, חוט שני.
409. לחו״ש.
410. רמ״א ס׳ ע״ה, ש״ך ס״ק קנ״א.

VESTOS

Extra Bedikos

A woman has the status of being *tehorah* from the time she immerses properly in a mikvah until she knows that she actually becomes *temei'ah* again.[411] The halachah is not concerned that her status may change at any minute and she may suddenly become a niddah without warning. Since the Torah allows us to rely on something that has been established as one's status, a woman does not have to unnecessarily suspect that she may have just become a niddah at any given time. The Gemara mentions that it is commendable to do extra *bedikos* just to make sure she is still indeed *tehorah*.[412] However, these extra *bedikos* should not be done around her husband.[413] The *Rambam* says a woman should do extra *bedikos*,[414] but the *Rama* says she should not.[415]

The *Poskim* nowadays say not to do extra *bedikos* for several reasons.[416] First, we are *metamei* shades of blood that *Chazal* were not, because we

411. משנה נדה ט"ו ע"א.
412. משנה נדה י"ג ע"א.
413. נדה י"ב ע"א ותוס' ד"ה בעי.
414. עיין רמב"ם הל' איסורי ביאה פרק ח' הל' יא' ובפרק ד' הל' טז' ובהשגות הראב"ד שם, ועיין בדברי המחבר יו"ד ס' קפ"ד סע' א'.
415. רמ"א יו"ד קפ"ד א'.
416. אג"מ יו"ד חלק ב' ס' ע"ה, ובשע' שבט הלוי וחוט שני.

are not certain about many shades of *tamei* and are therefore more stringent than they were in the days of yesteryear. Also, women's skin is more sensitive than ever before; extra *bedikos* often irritate it and cause the woman to discover blood, which in fact came from a *makkah* she caused herself unnecessarily. As a matter of practice, a woman should never do an unnecessary *bedikah*. Nevertheless, the Gemara introduces the concept of *vestos* which require *bedikos*, as we will now learn.

Vestos: An Introduction

The Gemara says that once a woman immerses in a mikvah she is assumed to be in a state of *taharah* and is permitted to her husband without a *bedikah*.[417]

Another Gemara says[418] that the Torah's stating "*V'hizartem es Bnei Yisrael mitumasam*" — that Bnei Yisrael should be careful about contracting *tumah*,[419] tells us that a couple must separate on the *onah* close to the *vest*. A woman must also do a *bedikah* during the *vest*, to make sure that her period has not begun.[420]

Tosafos understand that once a *vest* arrives, a woman loses her status of *taharah*; therefore, according to the opinion in the Gemara that *vestos* are *d'Oraisa*, if a *vest* passes without a *bedikah* she is certainly *temei'ah*, and according to the opinion that *vestos* are *d'Rabbanan* she must perform a *bedikah* on the *vest* because she is *temei'ah* due to a *safeik* (and if 7 days pass after the *vest*, her husband can assume that even if she did see blood on the *vest*, she may have counted *shivah nekiyim* and therefore has a status of *taharah* due to a *sfeik sfeika* [doubt about a doubt — maybe she didn't see blood on the *vest*, and even if she did, maybe she counted *shivah nekiyim*]).[421]

Rashi understands that according to the opinion in the Gemara that *vestos* are *d'Oraisa*, there is a halachah that she must perform a *bedikah* on the *vest* and she is *temei'ah* due to a doubt about her status until she performs a *bedikah*. According to the opinion that *vestos* are *d'Rabbanan*, she maintains her status of *taharah* but we learn from the passuk stating "*V'hizartem es Bnei Yisrael mitumasam*" that she must perform a *bedikah* on the vest.[422]

417. נדה ט״ו ע״א.
418. גמ׳ שבועות י״ח ע״ב.
419. ויקרא טו:לא.
420. נדה ט״ו ע״א.
421. שם ד״ה אפילו.
422. שם ד״ה דאורייתא וד״ה וסתות.

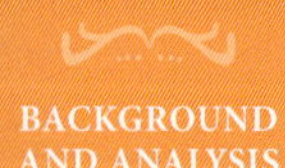

In summary, Tosafos understand that the occasion of a *vest* (the *onas havest*) creates a real question on her established status of *taharah*. If *vestos* would be *d'Oraisa*, the woman would be prohibited when the *vest* arrives. However, since the halachah is that *vestos* are *d'Rabbanan*, she only has an obligation to do a *bedikah*.

The Rambam holds the woman's status of *taharah* remains intact even when she forgets to do a *bedikah*.[423] Tosafos are concerned that her period may have begun, so a woman who did not do a *bedikah* at the time of the *vest* cannot rely on her established status of *taharah*. The Shulchan Aruch rules like the Rambam,[424] while the Rama rules like Tosafos regarding a missed *bedikah* on a *vest kavua* and on an *onah beinonis*.[425] Therefore, a woman who forgot to do a *bedikah* on one of the above days may not be together with her husband until she has done a *bedikah*.

Prohibited Behavior during a Vest

Since a woman may expect to get her period, the couple is prohibited to engage in marital relations during the time of the *vest* even though she is not actually *temei'ah*.[426] The *Shulchan Aruch* says *harchakos* need not be kept during the *vest*.[427] The *Shach* says it is best to avoid hugging and kissing,[428] and one who is careful with this will be blessed; and the Taz says that hugging and kissing are actually prohibited.[429] The *Acharonim* discuss whether the "blessing" of the Shach applies to also not sleeping in the same bed.[430] Some are stringent, and this is a good stringency to observe if one is able to, but the basic halachah is that it is not a problem.

---

423. רמב״ם הל׳ איסורי ביאה ד׳ ט׳.
424. ס׳ קפ״ד סע׳ ט׳.
425. שם ברמ״א.
426. נדה ט״ז ע״א.
427. ס׳ קפ״ד סע׳ ב׳.
428. שם ס״ק ו׳ כמש״כ הב״ח.
429. שם ס״ק ג׳.
430. סתימת רוב הפוסקים להקל ובפרט שחו״נ שרי מעיקר הדין וכ״ה בשולחן גבוה ס״ק ה׳ ובספר זבחי צדק ס״ק ח׳. אמנם בשו״ע הרב ובשעי׳ שבט הלוי ובחוט שני פסקו להחמיר, ובספר פתחי תשובות הביא סברה להחמיר ״דחיישינן שמא תפרוס נדה ולא תדע כיון שהם ישנים ונמצא יושן עם אשתו נדה שהוא אסור עכ״פ דרבנן״.

Bedikos during a Vest

A woman must do a *bedikah* on a *vest* to show that her period has not come during the time it was expected to come.[431] The *Chazon Ish* says it is enough for a woman to do one *bedikah* during the *onas havest*.[432] Rav Moshe Feinstein writes to do a few *bedikos* throughout the *onas havest*,[433] and Rav Shmuel HaLevi Wosner says similarly.[434] However, Rav Moshe Feinstein verbally said that the letter stating that one needs to do a few *bedikos* was to his nephew, and does not apply to everyone.[435] Practically speaking, a woman should do one *bedikah* during a *vest*, in accordance with the opinion of the Chazon Ish, because she may irritate and cut herself by doing more.

The *Bach* says if a woman missed a *bedikah* during the *onah*, doing a *bedikah* afterwards will not help establish that she did not bleed.[436] Perhaps the period came on the day that it was expected, and she only bled a little bit, which then fell away. The *Chavas Daas* says a woman has to do a *bedikah* throughout the entire *onah*, for perhaps she bled a little bit which fell away before the next time that she did a *bedikah* later on in the day.[437] The *Chavas Daas* therefore says a woman should be wearing a *moch dachuk* throughout the entire *onas havest*. Combining these two laws would come out that a woman needs a *moch dachuk* throughout every *onah* that she has, and if she did not have one she would be *temei'ah*, even *bedi'eved*. Most *Poskim* disagree with both of these premises, and the accepted halachah is that one *bedikah* is sufficient. If it was omitted, then, for a *vest she'eino kavua*, she is permitted without any further *bedikah*, and for a *kavua*, she is required to do a *bedikah* when she remembers, and then she is permitted.

Rav Moshe Feinstein says a woman should wear white underwear on the day of the *vest* so she will know if any blood came out. Some people do this, and it also helps bring us closer in line with the opinions of the Bach and Chavas Daas.[438] In practice we are not stringent like the opinions of the Chavas Daas or Rav Moshe Feinstein in this matter, and

431. ס׳ קפ״ד סע׳ ט׳, ר״ן פרק ב׳ דשבועות לדעת הרי״ף והרמב״ם הל׳ איסו״ב ד׳ ט׳, יב, יג׳.
432. חזו״א יו״ד ס׳ פ׳ ס״ק כ״ב.
433. אג״מ יו״ד חלק ג׳ ס׳ מ״ח.
434. שיערי שבט הלוי דלכתחילה צריכה ג׳ בדיקות.
435. מפי השמועה ע״י נאמנו של מו״ר שליט״א
436. ועיין ש״ך ס׳ קפ״ד ס״ק כ״ג.
437. ס׳ קפ״ד ס״ק ט׳.
438. אג״מ יו״ד חלק ג׳ ס׳ מ״ח, ובספר פתחי תשובות הביא בשם גדולי הוראה דסגי גם בבגד צבעוני דגם ע״ז ניכר אם יש דם.

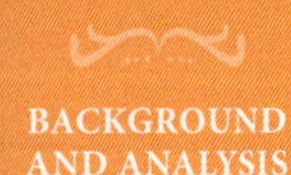

a woman should not perform a *moch dachuk* on any *vest*, and she is not required to wear white undergarments either.

The best time to do the *bedikah* is later rather than earlier. On a daytime *onah*, a woman should preferably perform the *bedikah* right before *shkiah*, if she can. On a nighttime *onah*, the ideal time for a *bedikah* is right before *neitz*. But, a woman does not have to wake up from her sleep in the middle of the night to do a *bedikah*. Instead, she should do it before she goes to sleep. If she happens to be up before *neitz*, she can do another one then, but she does not have to.

As mentioned earlier, if a woman realized after her *vest kavua*, or after an *onah beinonis*, that she did not do a *bedikah*, she is considered *temei'ah* until she does a *bedikah*, even though the *vest* has already passed.[439] If a woman forgot to do the *bedikah* on a *vest she'eino kavua*, she is nevertheless considered *tehorah* once the *vest she'eino kavua* has passed and remains *tehorah* afterwards. Therefore, she should *not* do a *bedikah* when she remembers. We will soon see which *vestos* have the status of *vestos kevuim*.

At the end of the *onah* a husband should ask his wife if she did a *bedikah*. This seems to be an actual halachah,[440] not just a good idea.

What Creates a Vest

Even though a woman bleeds for several days, the *vest* is only defined by the day of the onset of the period, which is the *onah* in which the bleeding began.[441] Also, a *vest* is only established from when the period began, not from when blood is discovered as a *kesem*[442] or on a bad *bedikah*.[443] This applies even if the blood she discovered on a *bedikah*

---

439. ס׳ קפ״ד סע׳ ט׳ וז״ל ׳עבר הוסת ולא בדקה ולא הרגישה, טהורה בלא בדיקה. י״א שאסורה עד שתבדוק, אם יש לה וסת קבוע, או שהוא יום ל׳ אף על פי שאינו קבוע. (והכי נהוג, וכן הוא לקמן סימן קפ״ט)׳, ובס׳ קפ״ט סע׳ ד׳.

440. עיין ס׳ קפ״ד סע׳ יא׳ ובפ״ת ס״ק כ״ז בשם החו״ד.

441. ס׳ קפ״ד סע׳ ה׳, ו׳.

442. ס׳ ק״צ סע׳ נד׳.

443. עיין שו״ע ס׳ ק״צ סע׳ נ״ד וז״ל ״אין בכתמים משום וסת. כיצד, מצאה כתם בר״ח, אפילו שלש פעמים, לא קבעתו ולא עוקרתו. חוץ מכתמי עד הבדוק לה, שהם מטמאים עד בכל שהן, והרי הן כראיות לכל דבר״ ע״כ ונראה מדבריו שכתמי עדי בדיקות הרי הן כראייות לכל דבר והיינו אפילו לוסתות. ומכח זה י״א דכל שמצאה דם על עד בדיקה חיישינן לחודש הבא משום וסתות, וכ״ה בחוט שני. אבל הלבוש דייק מזה שהביא המחבר דין של עדי בדיקות אחר ציור שראתה כתמים ג׳ פעמים ביום ידוע שגם בעד בדיקה לא חיישינן לוסת אא״כ ראתה כן ג׳ חדשים ביום ידוע, וז״ל ״אין בכתמים משום וסת. כיצד, מצאה כתם בראש חדש אפילו ג׳ פעמים, לא אמרינן משום זה שכן תמצא כתם בכל ר״ח, דזה לא שייך ולא קבעתו ולא עוקרתו, חוץ מכתמי עד הבדוק לה שהיא מקנחת בו גופה והם מטמאים בכלשהו כמו בראיית עצמה והוי לה כראייה לכל דבר, שהרי אנו רואין

cloth happened before the onset of a period, or if she became *temei'ah* due to staining before the onset of the period.[444] The only exception is when a woman discovers blood on a *bedikah* cloth on a *vest*. In this scenario, she will count that day as the *vest* for the following month. Obviously, this does not apply if the bad *bedikah* is attributed to something else, like a *makkah*.[445]

An Onah

The Gemara says the obligation to separate applies for the amount of time of an *onah*.[446] Rashi explains that an *onah* is from sunrise until *shkiah* or *shkiah* until sunrise.[447] The halachah is like the opinion of the Chavas Daas,[448] who says there is no *bein hashmashos* in regard to *vestos*, so if her period comes a minute after *shkiah* the *onas havest* will be at night. He explains that women's cycles are caused by the sun and the moon. Therefore, the *onah* — day or night — in which a woman begins to bleed will be the *onah* in which the couple must separate the next month. Although the previous period may have commenced in middle of a specific day or night, *vestos* are observed the *entire* day or night of subsequent months.

Yom HaChodesh

The Gemara discusses the *vest* of *yom hachodesh*.[449] Using the information we just presented, the calculation is as follows: the date on which the period began is marked on the calendar, with the *onah* in which the period occurred. That same Hebrew date the following month is observed as a *vest* during the same *onah* in which the period occurred.

שביום זה יצא דם מגופה ג׳ פעמים וזה הוא וסתה״. והרה״ג ר׳ בורקביץ אמר שאין בעד בדיקה משום וסת אא״כ מצא דם בעד שעשתה בעונת הוסת שאז איגלאי מילתא שוסת זה מקויים לחודש הבא ואז אין לחשוש אפילו לתחילת ראייתה בחודש זה.

444. שו״ת שבה״ל חלק ג׳ ס׳ קי״ח, שו״ת עמק התשובה חלק א׳ ס׳ קכ״ה, טה״ב עמ׳ ת״ע, ודלא כמש״כ באג״מ יו״ד חלק ג׳ ס׳ מ״ו דאם ראתה כן ג׳ פעמים איגלאי מלתא דכן הוא פתיחת המקור שלה, והמחמירים חוששין רק אם מצא כתמים תוך עונה לראייתה.

445. ס׳ קפ״ז סע׳ ו׳, וברמ״א ס׳ קצ״ו סע׳ י׳.

446. נדה ס״ג ע״ב.

447. רש״י שם ד״ה אסורה לשמש, וז״ל ״ורבי יהודה לטעמיה דאמר כל עונת וסתה אסורה ועונה הוי או יום או לילה ומי שוסתה בלילה ואפילו בסופה אסורה כל הלילה ואם וסתה ביום ואפי׳ בסופו כל היום אסורה״.

448. חוו״ד ס׳ קפ״ד ביאורים אות ה׳.

449. נדה ט׳ ע״ב, יב ע״א, טוש״ע קפ״ד סע׳ א׳.

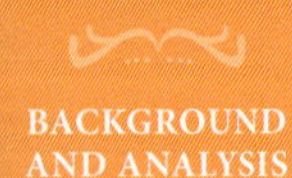

If the Onas HaVest Changes

The *Shulchan Aruch* says a *vest* only becomes a *vest kavua* when the period that reoccurred three times in a row on the same day began in the same *onah* each time.[450] When a woman has an old *vest* that was never "uprooted," it is kept in the upcoming month in the same *onah* in which her period occurred *last* month. A *vest* is really, according to the letter of the law, only the 12-hour period in which the period occurred during the previous month.

When a woman gets her period one month during the daytime and the following month at night, all of the *vestos* that she will keep in the coming month —the *onah beinonis*, *yom hachodesh*, *haflagah*, and whatever old *vestos* she may still have — will be at night. The reason for this is because the last *re'iyah* was at night.

However, when a woman established a *vest kavua* and then deviated from it once or twice, she must keep this *vest kavua* — this date or this *haflagah* — as long it has not been "uprooted." The *onah* that this *vest* will be kept on is the *onah* in which the woman bled three (or four) times and established the *vest kavua* (even if the last time she saw in a different *onah*). For example, if a woman has a *vest kavua* for the 23rd of the month at night and sees one month on the 25th of the month during the day, the next month she is required to separate from her husband on the 23rd at night, as well as the 25th during the day.

Creating a Vest Kavua

A woman who gets her period on the same date each month three times in a row creates a *vest kavua* for this date. "The same date" means that she begins to bleed on the same date[451] and *onah*[452] every month. She must now be concerned that her period will come on this date. If one month her period comes on a different date, she must be concerned for two dates as a *yom hachodesh* the following month: the date of her *vest kavua*, as well as this second date as a *vest she'eino kavua*.[453]

---

450. ס׳ קפ״ט סע׳ י״ג.

451. נדה ס״ד ע״א תוס׳ ד״ה איתמר, שו״ע ס׳ קפ״ט סע׳ ב׳.

452. בעלי נפש להראב״ד, שו״ע ס׳ קפ״ט סע׳ י״ג.

453. כ״ה לשון המשנה נדה ס״ג ע״ב ״היתה למודה להיות רואה יום ט״ו ושינתה להיות רואה ליום כ׳ זה וזה אסורין. שינתה פעמים ליום כ׳ זה וזה אסורין. שינתה ג׳ פעמים ליום כ׳ הותר ט״ו וקבעה לה יום כ״.

This continues until her *vest* becomes "uprooted" by the period's not arriving on this *vest kavua* date for 3 months in a row.[454] If this happens, she moves either to a new *vest kavua* or to a *vest she'eino kavua*, depending on the dates on which her period began during this time.

The same holds true for *haflagos*. A woman must be concerned that her next period will come the same amount of days (and in the same *onah*) following her last one as her last one came following the one before it. After four periods (three *haflagos*) this pattern is established as a *vest kavua*.[455]

Once established, a *vest haflagah kevuah*, too, must be observed until it is "uprooted" by the period's coming under different circumstances three times in a row. This means if a woman gets her period 3 months in a row after identical intervals and on the same *onah*, she keeps that interval as her *vest kavua* for the upcoming 3 months.

A *vest she'eino kavua* is "uprooted" after one time that the period did not occur on this date or after this *haflagah* (in the same *onah*).[456] If a woman gets her period during the nighttime of the 15th of one month, and in the next month it occurs under different circumstances, she does not keep that day again.

If the woman established a *vest kavua*, she must deviate from the *vest* three times in order to uproot it.[457] This being the case, when a *vest kavua* is created, this date or *haflagah* should be marked on the calendar for the next 3 months, so the couple will clearly know which days to observe as *vestos*.

In the event that a new *vest kavua* is not created, the woman will always have to be concerned that the old *vest kavua* may occur again.[458] For example, if, over a span of 7 months, she gets her monthly period on Days 5, 5, 5, 4, 2, 3, 5 she must continue t6o be concerned for Day 5 for the following 3 months, since she deviated from the vest kavua three times, but has not established a new vest kavua.

454. ס׳ קפ״ט סע׳ ב׳ וז״ל ׳שכיון שקובעתו בשלושה פעמים אינו נעקר בפחות מג׳ פעמים, שכל זמן שלא עקרתו ג״פ צריכה לחוש לו׳.
455. ס׳ קפ״ט סע׳ ב׳.
456. ס׳ קפ״ט סע׳ ב׳.
457. ס׳ קפ״ט סע׳ ב׳.
458. ס׳ קפ״ט סע׳ י׳, וש״ך ס״ק מ״א.

Vest Kavuah (Yom Hachodesh) with Deviations

Month:	*1*	*2*	*3*	*4*	*5*	*6*	*7*
Actual Period Began *(Date of the month)*	5 Nissan *During the Day*	5 Iyar *During the Day*	5 Sivan *During the Day*	4 Tamuz *During the Night*	2 Av *During the Night*	3 Elul *During the Day*	5 Tishrei *During the Day*
	3 Consistent Days of the Month VEST KAVUAH CREATED			*3 Inconsistent Days of the Month* VEST KAVUAH UPROOTED			

Upcoming Month:	*2*	*3*	*4*	*5*	*6*	*7*	*8, 9, 10*
Vest (Expected Period)	5 Iyar *During the Day*	5 Sivan *During the Day*	5 Tamuz *During the Day*	5 Av *During the Day*	5 Elul *During the Day*		5 Cheshvan, Kislev, Teves *During the Day* — *Vest Kavuah reinstated for subsequent 3 months*
				Vest Kavuah observed, in addition to Vest She'eino Kavuah			
Additional Vest She'eino Kavuah				4 Av *During the Night*	2 Elul *During the Night*	3 Tishrei *During the Day*	

The Reason for a Vest SheEino Kavua

The Mishnah discusses a woman who generally gets her period and established a *vest* on "Day 15," and then alters her pattern to a different day.[459] The Mishnah could mean that she established a *vest* that her period will come on the *date* of the 15th of the month,[460] or, the Mishnah may mean that her *kevi'us* is that her period came following a 15-day lapse after the previous one.[461] This shows us that both the date (called

459. נדה ס״ג ע״ב וז״ל המשנה ״היתה למודה להיות רואה יום ט״ו ושינתה להיות רואה ליום כ׳ זה וזה אסורין. שינתה פעמים ליום כ׳ זה וזה אסורין. שינתה ג׳ פעמים ליום כ׳ הותר ט״ו, וקבעה לה יום כ׳, שאין אשה קובעת לה וסת עד שתקבענה ג׳ פעמים, ואינה מטהרת מן הוסת עד שתעקר ממנה ג׳ פעמים״.

460. היא פשטות לשון המשנה שהכוונה ליום טו׳ או כ׳ לחודש, שאם מדובר באשה שראתה טו׳ ימים אחרי ראייתה הקודמת ה״ה זבה וזה דבר שלא מוסכם שתהא אשה קובעת וסתות בימי זיבתה.

461. נדה ל״ט ע״א שיטת שמואל, וז״ל הגמ׳ ״היתה למודה להיות רואה יום ט״ו (יום ושינתה ליום כ׳ זה וזה אסורין לשמש, שינתה פעמים ליום כ׳ זה וזה אסורין. ואמרת לן

the *yom hachodesh*, or *vest hachodesh*) as well as the amount of time that elapsed from one period to the next (called a *haflagah*) are considered to be catalysts that cause the period to come.

Any time a woman gets her period we assume she may be starting to create a *vest kavua*. The next month she must be concerned for the *vest hachodesh* and the *haflagah* as counted from this date, as a *vest she'eino kavua*.[462]

Vest Haflagah

A *haflagah* is calculated by counting the dates between the last two periods, beginning with the date that the first period began, and ending with the date that the second period began. This number of dates is then used to calculate the *haflagah* for the upcoming month. The *onah* for the *vest haflagah* will always be the same *onah* as the last *re'iyah*. This means that if one period came at night, and the next month it came during the day, the woman would not count the number of *onos* between the two *re'iyos* (resulting in an odd number) and keep the *vest haflagah* at night during the next month.[463] Rather, the second *re'iyah* establishes how many *dates* are between the two *re'iyos*, and the *onah* in which the *vest* last occurred will be observed as the upcoming *onas havest*.

If a woman gets her period one month during the day after a *haflagah* of 31 days, and the next month the period begins after a 28-day *haflagah* at night, she should keep both *haflagos* the upcoming month (Day 28 is kept as the halachah, and Day 31 as the stringency of the Beis Meir). Both *vestos* are kept by night, since the last *re'iyah* was at night. (It should be noted, however, that there are other opinions regarding these circumstances, as well.)

Don't forget that the *vest haflagah* is always calculated from the day and *onah* in which the period actually began, and not from the day that she was expecting it to come.[464]

עלה אמר רב יהודה אמר שמואל: ל״ש אלא ט״ו לטבילתה שהן כ״ב לראיתה, דהתם בימי נדתה קאי לה, אבל ט״ו לראיתה, דבימי זיבתה קאי לא קבעה״.

462. ס׳ קפ״ט סע׳ ב׳.

463. כ״ה בשו״ת נו״ב מהדורא תניינא ס׳ פ״ג ודלא כמש״כ הרב דוד טעוויל שם, ודלא כמש״כ בשו״ע הרב ס׳ קפ״ט סוס״ק ל״ו.

464. ס׳ קפ״ד סע׳ ו׳.

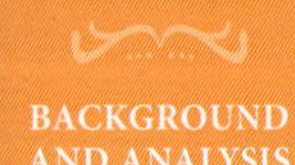

Onah Beinonis

The Gemara discusses "the *onah* of most women," which is called "the *onah beinonis*."[465] The *Shulchan Aruch* says every woman who does not have a *vest kavua* must keep this *onah*. A woman who has a *vest kavua*, however, does not have to keep *onah beinonis*.[466] The *Shulchan Aruch* says a woman who does not have a *vest kavua* must be concerned for a *vest* every 30 days, as well as for the other *vestos* she has from previous months (the *haflagah* and the *yom hachodesh*). The Shach disagrees, and says that *onah beinonis* is really *yom hachodesh*, and there is no new *vest* "of 30 days" called *onah beinonis*.[467] The accepted halachah is not like the Shach's position; we keep the *onah beinonis* on Day 30.

Sunday	Monday	Tuesday	Wednesday	Thursday	Friday	Shabbos
			1 Nov *12 Chesvan*	*2 Nov* *13 Cheshvan*	*3 Nov* *14 Cheshvan*	*4 Nov* *15 Cheshvan*
5 Nov *16 Cheshvan*	*6 Nov* *17 Cheshvan* DAY 30 ***Onah Beinonis DAY***	*7 Nov* *18 Cheshvan* ***Yom Hachodesh DAY***	*8 Nov* *19 Cheshvan*	*9 Nov* *20 Cheshvan*	*10 Nov* *21Cheshvan*	*11 Nov* *22 Cheshvan*
12 Nov *23 Cheshvan*	*13 Nov* *24 Cheshvan*	*14 Nov* *25 Cheshvan*	*15 Nov* *26 Cheshvan*	*16 Nov* *27 Cheshvan*	*17 Nov* *28 Cheshvan*	*18 Nov* *29 Cheshvan*
19 Nov *1 Kislev*	*20 Nov* *2 Kislev*	*21 Nov* *3 Kislev*	*22 Nov* *4 Kislev*	*23 Nov* *5 Kislev*	*24 Nov* *6 Kislev*	*25 Nov* *7 Kislev*
26 Nov *8 Kislev*	*27 Nov* *9 Kislev*	*28 Nov* *10 Kislev*	*29 Nov* *11 Kislev*	*30 Nov* *12 Kislev*		

465. גמ׳ נדה ט״ז ע״א, רש״י שם ד״ה בתוך ימי עונתה.
466. ס׳ קפ״ט סע׳ א׳ וי״ג.
467. ש״ך ס׳ קפ״ט ס״ק א׳ ול׳.

Onah Beinonis for a Woman Who Has a Vest Kavua

The halachah is that according to the letter of the law, an *onah beinonis* is only for someone who does not have a *vest kavua*.[468] The *Beis Yosef*, however, says a woman who has a *vest kavua* for a day that is earlier than the *onah beinonis* should be concerned for the *onah beinonis* as well in the event that her *vest* passed without incident.[469] This ruling is not brought in the *Shulchan Aruch*. However, Rav Yosef Shalom Elyashiv says one should be concerned for it nevertheless.

Most women who have a *vest kavua* today established it from a *mayan pasuach* as a stringency. The halachah is that on such a *vest kavua*, the *onah beinonis is* kept if the *vest kavua* as a stringency passed without incident, since the *vest kavua* is only being kept as a stringency.

The Onas Ohr Zarua

The *Ohr Zarua* says that besides for separating during the *onah* in which the period began, the couple must also separate during the previous *onah*.[470] For example, if her period came during the day, the couple must separate on the following month during the previous night, and during the day on which the *onah* occurs.

The question is: The Gemara itself originally said that the couple must separate in the *onah* preceding the *vest*, and rejected this possibility.[471] How, then, can the Ohr Zarua bring this as a halachah?

The Bach and the Shach defend the Ohr Zarua's position. The Bach answers this question by explaining that the Ohr Zarua does not mean to tell us the actual halachah; rather, he is suggesting this only as a stringent custom.[472] The Shach answers differently:[473] In the times of *Chazal*, women bled at the exact same time of the month each month, down to the hour. Nowadays, women's cycles are much more sporadic; they bleed at different times of the day and even on different days of

468. ס׳ קפ״ט סע׳ א׳ וז״ל ״אשה שאין לה וסת קבוע חוששת ליום ל׳ לראייתה שהוא עונה בינונית לסתם נשים ואם יש לה וסת קבוע לזמן ידוע מכ׳ לכ׳ או מכ״ה לכ״ה חוששת לזמן הידוע״ ע״כ, ובט״ז ס״ק א׳ וז״ל ״קא משמע לן דאין צריך לחוש לסתם עונה שהוא שלשים יום אלא זמן הידוע לחוד כיון שיש לה וסת קבוע״, עכ״ל.

469. ס׳ קפ״ד, חידושי הרמב״ן למס׳ נדה ט״ו ע״ב, אשכול ס׳ ל״ג, חו״ד ס״ק ב׳ ובס״ק כ׳, בית מאיר, לחו״ש ס״ק ל״ד.

470. או״ז חלק א׳ ס׳ שנ״ח.

471. שם בנדה ס״ג ע״ב.

472. ב״ח ס׳ קפ״ד ד״ה ונראה.

473. ס׳ קפ״ד ס״ק ז׳.

the month. Because their cycles are inexact, the Ohr Zarua said that it is appropriate to be concerned for the previous *onah* as well.

Rav Akiva Eiger[474] and the Chavas Daas[475] disagree, saying that the Gemara does not require separation in the *onah* before the period occurred, and there is no reason to keep the *onas Ohr Zarua*. However, nowadays, when nearly all women do not have a specific time when they get their period, it makes sense to follow the *onas Ohr Zarua*.[476]

Most *Poskim* say *bnei Torah* should keep the *onas Ohr Zarua* as a stringency,[477] like the *Bach* says. Some say not to keep the *onas Ohr Zarua* during the first year of marriage.[478] In a scenario where a woman has four *vestos* in a row, the couple need not observe the *onas Ohr Zarua* for each *vest*. If her wedding night or a mikvah night comes out on the *onas Ohr Zarua*, it need not be observed.[479] The custom in Hungary was to only keep the *onas Ohr Zarua* for a *vest kavua*.[480]

Rav Moshe Feinstein takes the *Shach* even further and says that since women nowadays get their period in an irregular pattern, every woman should observe the whole halachic day that her period fell on as a *vest*, and she should add the *onas Ohr Zarua* to the *onah* before that, for a total of a 36-hour *vest*.[481] Most people in Eretz Yisrael do not follow this position, although some follow Rav Moshe Feinstein in the United States.

In practice, the halachah is that the *onah* in which the woman's period came the previous month is the *onas havest*, and the *onah* before that (the *onas Ohr Zarua*) is observed as a stringency. Refraining from hugging and kissing is a stringency,[482] and does not need to be kept on the *onas Ohr Zarua*, which is a stringency itself.

474. חידושי רע"א ס' קפ"ד ד"ה וסתה.
475. ס' קפ"ד ביאורים בסוף אות ג'.
476. עיין באג"מ יו"ד חלק ג' ס' מ"ח וז"ל "וביום הוסת של חשבונה שרגילה לראות בין בוסת קבוע ובין בוסת שאינו קבוע צריכה לפרוש מבעלה כל היום אם היא רגילה לראות בין ביום ובין בלילה וכדמצוי ביותר אצל הנשים שלנו דעונה דידה כעונה אריכתא דמי דהיינו כל המעת לעת ואם רגילה תמיד לראות או ביום או בלילה תפרוש רק אותה עונה בלבד, וראוי להחמיר ג"כ חומרת האו"ז המובא בש"ך יו"ד סימן קפ"ד סק"ז לפרוש עונה אחת סמוכה לעונת הוסת אם לא במקום הצורך".
477. הוא דעת קצור שו"ע ס' קנ"ה סע' ב', חת"ס יו"ד ס' ק"ע, לחם ושמלה, בספר משנת השלחן בשם הרה"ג ר' אלישיב, שיעורי שבט הלוי, חוט שני.
478. כ"ה במשמרת הטהרה פ"ו בשם ר' שלמה זלמן אויערבאך דהוא חשיב במקום מצוה כל שנה ראשונה דכת' ושמח את אשתו, ודלא כמ"ש בחוט שני שיש להחמיר אפילו בשנה ראשונה, וכן פסק הרה"ג ר' אלישיב להחמיר.
479. עמש"כ שו"ת חת"ס ס' ק"ע, שו"ת ר' יונתן שטייף ס' קפ"ב, חכ"א כלל ק"ח ס' ג', לחו"ש ס"ק א'.
480. שו"ת תשורת שי ס' ער"ה, שו"ת פרי השדה חלק א' ס' ע', שערי טוהר שער ג' ס' א'.
481. באג"מ יו"ד חלק ג' ס' מ"ח.
482. כמ"ש בש"ך ס' קפ"ד ס"ק ו' בשם הב"ח ודלא כט"ז שפסק שחו"נ אסור מצד הדין.

The Stringency of the Chavas Daas

The *Chavas Daas* says *onah beinonis* is calculated by counting 30 days from the day *after* the *re'iyah*.[483] This means that *onah beinonis* is Day 31, not Day 30, from the onset of the period.

The halachah is that according to the letter of the law, *onah beinonis* is Day 30, and there is a stringency to observe Day 31 as an *onah* as well.[484]

Sunday	Monday	Tuesday	Wednesday	Thursday	Friday	Shabbos
					1 Dec 13 Kislev	2 Dec 14 Kislev
3 Dec 15 Kislev	4 Dec 16 Kislev	5 Dec 17 Kislev	6 Dec 18 Kislev	7 Dec 19 Kislev Ohr Zaruah DAY	8 Dec 20 Kislev DAY 30 Yom Hachodesh Onah Beinonis NIGHT	9 Dec 21Kislev Chavas Daas NIGHT
10 Dec 22 Kislev Ohr Zaruah DAY	11 Dec 23 Kislev DAY 33 Haflagah NIGHT	12 Dec 24 Kislev	13 Dec 25 Kislev	14 Dec 26 Kislev	15 Dec 27 Kislev	16 Dec 28Kislev
17 Dec 29 Kislev	18 Dec 30 Kislev	19 Dec 1 Teves	20 Dec 2 Teves	21 Dec 3 Teves	22 Dec 4 Teves	23 Dec 5 Teves
24 Dec 6 Teves	25 Dec 7 Teves	26 Dec 8 Teves	27 Dec 9 Teves	28 Dec 10 Teves	29 Dec 11 Teves	30 Dec 12 Teves

483. חוו״ד ס׳ קפ״ט ס״ק י״ב בביאורים, וכ״ה הו״א של הש״ך ס׳ קפ״ט ס״ק ל׳.
484. כ״ה בפרי דעה בפתיחה שער ח׳, טהרת ישראל ס׳ ה׳, אג״מ חלק ג׳ ס׳ נ׳, משמרת טהרה בשם ר׳ אלישיב, חוט שני.

The Pleissi

The *Pleissi* says that unlike by other *vestos* in which according to halachah a couple must only separate on the actual *onas havest*, *onah beinonis* requires separation for the complete date (night and then day) of the 30th day following the *re'iyah*.[485] He explains that the *onah beinonis* is built on a concern that since the woman has not displayed a particular pattern, she might begin to behave like the "average woman" and will bleed on Day 30. Since this is not related to her personal experience, there is no reason to assume that the period will arrive in a particular *onah* within Day 30. We therefore are concerned about the entire 24-hour period.

Sunday	Monday	Tuesday	Wednesday	Thursday	Friday	Shabbos
					1 Dec 13 Kislev	2 Dec 14 Kislev
3 Dec 15 Kislev	4 Dec 16 Kislev	5 Dec 17 Kislev	6 Dec 18 Kislev	7 Dec 19 Kislev Ohr Zaruah DAY	8 Dec 20 Kislev DAY 30 Plaisee DAY Yom Hachodesh Onah Beinonis NIGHT	9 Dec 21Kislev
10 Dec 22 Kislev Ohr Zaruah DAY	11 Dec 23 Kislev DAY 33 Haflagah NIGHT	12 Dec 24 Kislev	13 Dec 25 Kislev	14 Dec 26 Kislev	15 Dec 27 Kislev	16 Dec 28Kislev
17 Dec 29 Kislev	18 Dec 30 Kislev	19 Dec 1 Teves	20 Dec 2 Teves	21 Dec 3 Teves	22 Dec 4 Teves	23 Dec 5 Teves
24 Dec 6 Teves	25 Dec 7 Teves	26 Dec 8 Teves	27 Dec 9 Teves	28 Dec 10 Teves	29 Dec 11 Teves	30 Dec 12 Teves

485. כרתי ופלתי ס' קפ"ט ס"ק ט"ו, שו"ע הרב ס' קפ"ט ס"ק א'.

Outside of Eretz Yisrael,[486] the *Pleissi* is generally not taught. In Eretz Yisrael, however, it is an accepted practice.[487]

The question is how the *onos* of the *Pleissi* and the *Ohr Zarua* fit in with each other. In the case of a woman who got her period during the day, her *vest* the following month will be during the day. The night before would be an *onah* according to both the *Pleissi* and the *Ohr Zarua*; there is only one realistic stringency, even according to both positions. However, if her period came at night, the *onas havest* the next month will be at night, the following day would be forbidden according to the *Pleissi*, and the day before would be the *onas Ohr Zarua* — thus, there are two separate stringencies, occurring on two different days. In this case, the only thing forbidden during the day is marital relations, as refraining from hugging and kissing is unnecessary on an additional *onah* that is only kept as a stringency. Additionally, whatever the extenuating circumstances the couple has to permit marital relations during the day will be enough to permit them not to observe the *onos* of the *Ohr Zarua* or the *Pleissi*, as well.

It should come out that there is not really that much of a difference in practice between these two additional *onos* that should prevent someone from keeping the *onos* of the *Ohr Zarua* and the *Pleissi* simultaneously. However, Rav Yosef Shalom Elyashiv says that keeping both the *Pleissi* and *Ohr Zarua* for an *onah beinonis* is a *tarti d'sasri* (two concepts that conflict with each other).[488] He explains that keeping the *Pleissi* means keeping *onah beinonis* as a *din* — we have reason to be concerned that she might specifically see on Day 30, not because of her own *vest*. However, the Ohr Zarua applies his stringency to a woman's personal *vestos*, not to *dinim*. When she is expected to bleed according to her own private pattern on a certain date, we are cautious and refrain from marital relations for an *onah* beforehand. When we think it might come on a specific date, however, not connected to her private pattern, there is no point in also fearing that it might come earlier than that. Rav Yosef Shalom Elyashiv therefore held that keeping both the *Pleissi* and the *Ohr Zarua* on an *onah beinonis* is considered *ksil b'choshech holeich* — self-contradictory conduct.

In the United States the *Ohr Zarua* is taught in regard to all *vestos*. In Eretz Yisrael the *Ohr Zarua* is observed for all *vestos* besides for the *onah beinonis*, for which the *Pleissi* is kept instead.

486. טה"ב עמ' ע"ח, וכ"ה פשטות לשון השו"ע, ב"ח, ס"ט סוס"ק ל"א.
487. שיעורי שבט הלוי, משנת השלחן בשם ר' אלישיב.
488. כ"ה במשנת השלחן בשם ר' אלישיב.

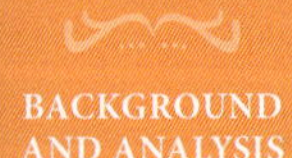

The *Poskim* say that even someone who keeps Day 31 as a *vest* should not keep the *Pleissi* or *Ohr Zarua* on this day. The Chavas Daas's stringency only applies to the *onas havest* itself.[489]

Yemei HaMevuchim

Based on the situation that existed in the times of the Gemara that nearly all women had a *vest kavua*, the Gemara cites Rebbi Meir, who says that a woman who does not have a *vest kavua* can never get married, because she may begin to bleed at any time, including during marital relations.[490] Rebbi Chaninah ben Antignos disagrees, saying that she may get married and live a regular married life with her husband as long as she does *bedikos* before marital relations.

The halachah is like the position of Rebbi Chaninah ben Antignos: a woman who does not have a *vest kavua* may get married and live a regular life.[491] The *Pleissi* explains that the reasoning for this is that we are not so stringent as to forbid her to marry; however, when a woman knows that she usually gets her period between certain days, intimacy is forbidden during those days, even according to Rebbi Chaninah ben Antignos, because she is anticipating her period during this time and does not know exactly when it will begin.[492] These days are called *yemei hamevuchim*.

The *Chazon Ish* explains that the reason for *yemei hamevuchim* is that it could be that the woman established a *vest* from a *mayan pasuach* that she was not aware of.[493] According to some *Poskim*, intimacy is forbidden throughout the days in which it would be normal for her period to come.[494]

Rav Moshe Feinstein disagrees, saying that marital relations are not restricted; however she needs *bedikos* before marital relations during the days of *yemei hamevuchim*.[495]

The basis for the argument is, as stated, that we are concerned that a woman who does not have a *vest kavua* will begin bleeding during

489. כ״ה במשנת השלחן בשם ר׳ אלישיב תשובה ע״א.
490. נדה י״ב ע״ב.
491. ס׳ קפ״ו סע׳ ב׳.
492. כו״פ ס׳ קפ״ד ס״ק ב׳, ובנו״ב דין ימי מבוכה כדין וסת, ועיין בספר פתחי תשובות ס׳ קפ״ד סע׳ ב׳ הערה 26 דיש נ״מ ביניהם אם עברו ימים אלו ולא בדקו אם דנין אותה כלא בדקה בוסת קבועה וצריך בדיקה או כושא״ק ומותרת לבעלה מיד, ע״ש.
493. חוט שני בשם חזו״א, אג״מ יו״ד חלק ב׳ ס׳ ס״ז.
494. ס״ט קפ״ד ס״ק ד׳, ערוה״ש סע׳ כ״ג, שו״ת מנח״י.
495. אג״מ יו״ד חלק ב׳ ס׳ ס״ז בסוף.

marital relations on days that she is prone to see blood. Therefore, most *Poskim* say a woman should do an external wipe with a colored tissue before being intimate, so she will discover if she is bleeding. In this way, she is taking precautions to avoid discovering blood during marital relations. Since the wipe was done on colored paper, any blood discovered on the wipe will not render her *temei'ah*, because it is a *kesem* on colored tissue and is not susceptible to *tumah*. It should be noted, however, that while a woman is bleeding, even if she is not *temei'ah* from the bleeding, the couple should refrain from intimacy until the staining subsides.

Since it is difficult to calculate exact days that we will consider *yemei hamevuchim,* the following rule of thumb is recommended for women who are expecting their period to come sometime in the next few days, but without definitive days of *vestos*: a woman should perform an external wipe before marital relations on any day that is not a *vest* once the first *vest* passed during any month. She should continue performing external wipes before marital relations until her period comes or she gets a positive pregnancy test.

Vest Achilah and Birth Control Pills

There is another *vest* called a *vest achilah,*[496] which can be established from something a woman ate that affected the pattern of her cycles.[497]

The most common application of this happens when a woman takes birth control pills that alter her cycle. This usually happens when a woman takes active hormone pills (generally starting a week before going to the mikvah) which, when she stops taking them (and switches to placebos), cause her to get her period within a certain amount of time. When she stops taking the pills, she should treat the days after as *yemei hamevuchim* because she knows that she will get her period sometime after she stops taking the pills, although she does not know exactly how long afterwards the period will begin.[498] If she detects a

496. נדה ס"ג ע"ב, רמ"א ס' קפ"ט סע' כ"ג.

497. ועיין ברמ"א ס' קפ"ט סע' כ"ג לענין אם צריך וסת אכילה להיות מורכב ליום כמו וסת הקפיצות או לא, וז"ל "אכלה שום וראתה, אכלה בצל וראתה, אכלה פלפלין וראתה, יש אומרים שקבעה לה וסת לראיה ע"י כל אכילת דברים חמים. (הרא"ש פרק האשה ומרדכי ריש שבועות). וי"א שכל זה שתראה ע"י מאכל דינו כמו שתראה ע"י קפיצה ושאר מעשה שהיא עושה, שמקרי ראיה ע"י אונס ואינה קובעת וסת אלא עם הימים. (ב"י לדעת הרשב"א) וי"א שדינו כוסת שתראה על ידי מקרה שבגופה וקובעת אותו אפילו בלא ימים שוים. (ב"י בשם תוספות)" עכ"ל.

498. דאם עדיין לא קבעה וסת ליום ידוע אחר נטילת הכדור יש לחוש לאותם ימים כמו ימי מבוכים.

pattern of beginning to bleed after beginning the placebos, she should call her *Rav* to determine if a *vest* was established. In such a case, she may be advised to keep the *vest* and disregard the intermediary days of *yemei hamevuchim*.

Pills and Vestos

Sunday	Monday	Tuesday	Wednesday	Thursday	Friday	Shabbos
1 DAY 1 *Period Begins*	2 DAY 2	3 DAY 3	4 DAY 4	5 DAY 5 *Rechitzah Hefsek Moch*	6 DAY 1 *Shiva Nekiyim* DAY 1 *Active Pills*	7 DAY 2 *Shiva Nekiyim*
8 DAY 3 *Shiva Nekiyim*	9 DAY 4 *Shiva Nekiyim*	10 DAY 5 *Shiva Nekiyim*	11 DAY 6 *Shiva Nekiyim*	12 DAY 7 *Shiva Nekiyim* *Mikveh Night*	13 *Tehorah*	14 *Tehorah*
15 *Tehorah*	16 *Tehorah*	17 *Tehorah*	18 *Tehorah*	19 *Tehorah*	20 *Tehorah*	21 *Tehorah*
22 *Tehorah*	23 *Tehorah*	24 *Tehorah*	25 *Tehorah*	26 *Tehorah* LAST DAY *Active Pills*	27 *Tehorah* *External wipe required before Intimacy* *Treated as Yimei HaMevuchim*	28 *Tehorah* *External wipe required before Intimacy* *Treated as Yimei HaMevuchim*
29 *Tehorah* *External wipe required before Intimacy* *Treated as Yimei HaMevuchim*	30 *Onah Beinonis observed*					

A woman in such a case no longer has to be concerned for her regular *vestos*,[499] because her catalyst to begin bleeding has been established to

499. שו"ת שבט הלוי חלק ד' ס' צ"ט, ספר נשמת אברהם בשם הגרש"ז אויערבך, משנת השלחן בשם ר' אלישיב, חוט שני.

be the pills that she is taking.[500] Any *vest kavua* that this woman had created previously would be temporarily uprooted for as long as she is on a cycle of taking pills. A *vest she'eino kavua* would not be calculated during these times, as well, as the pill has been established to be the catalyst to bring her period about.

A Re'iyah on a Mayan Pasuach

The *Poskim* discuss a case of a woman who gets her period on one of the days before her *vest*, and the bleeding continues through the day of the *vest*.[501] If one month a woman gets her period on Day 15, and the next month it begins on Day 14 and the bleeding continues into Day 15, does the fact that the woman continued bleeding on the day of the *vest* (called a *mayan pasuach*) tell us anything about Day 15? On the one hand, the onset of the period was on Day 14, so perhaps the *vest* is only established from then. On the other hand, since the woman was bleeding on the day of the old *vest* (Day 15), perhaps the old *vest* is not "uprooted."

The halachah is that a *re'iyah* from a *mayan pasuach* will not help to establish a new *vest*, but it will keep an old *vest* relevant in coming months.[502] In such a case, the woman should keep Day 14 *and* Day 15 the next month, but she has only accrued one *re'iyah* on Day 15 with regard to establishing a *vest kavua*. Although the second month's *re'iyah* from a *mayan pasuach* keeps the *vest* relevant in the future, it is not considered to be a second *re'iyah* on the old *vest*.

500. ובאג"מ וכן בספר לבושי עוז בשם ר' אלישיב כ' שאם אפשר טוב לכת' לראות שהכדורים אלה מונעים או מעכבים וסתה אבל בשעת הצורך יש לסמוך על החזקה שכדורים אלה מונעים או מעכבים וסתות של סתם נשים.

501. עיין ברמ"א ס' קפ"ד סע' ב', ובש"ך ס' קפ"ט ס"ק ל"ט, ובנוב"י ובכו"פ, ובחו"ד.

502. כ"כ הטור ס' קפ"ט סע' ל"ב וכ"ה בש"ך קפ"ט ס"ק ע"א ובנקוה"כ שם, וכן בט"ז ס' קפ"ט ס"ק י"ט, וכשיטת החו"ד ס' קפ"ד ס"ק ב'.

Vest Kavuah (Yom Hachodesh) *Mayan Pasuach*

Month:	*1*	*2*	*3*
Actual Period Began *(Date of the month)*	3 Nissan *During the Day*	5 Iyar *During the Night*	4 Sivan *During the Night*
Actual Bleeding Concluded *(Date of the month)*	7 Nissan *During the Day*	10 Iyar *During the Day*	8 Sivan *During the Day*

Upcoming Month:	*2*	*3*	*4*
Vest *(Expected Period)*	3 Iyar *During the Day*	5 Sivan *During the Night*	4 Tamuz *During the Night*
Additional Vest *Mayan Pasuach*			5 Tamuz *During the Night*

Summary: An ordinary yom hachodesh is observed the same onah in which the bleeding commenced the previous month (months 1 and 2 in our example). It is uprooted when that onah is passed without the period commencing. In month 3 the bleeding began on the 4th of Sivan and continued until 8 Sivan. Therefore, the prior vest of 5 Iyar at night was not "uprooted" as bleeding did occur on 5 Sivan at night, albeit from a continuation of the bleeding (a mayan pasuach) that began on 4 Sivan at night.

Establishing a Vest from a Mayan Pasuach

The Gemara says a woman who bleeds on the day of the *vest* from a *mayan pasuach* can establish a *vest* when the third *re'iyah* was from a *mayan pasuach*.[503] After the first or second time she bleeds from a *mayan pasuach*, it will not establish the *vest*, but it will keep it alive,

503. נדה ל"ט ע"ב "דאמר ר"ל: אשה קובעת לה וסת בתוך ימי זיבתה ואין אשה קובעת לה וסת בתוך ימי נדותה, ורבי יוחנן אמר אשה קובעת לה וסת בתוך ימי נדותה, ה"ד? לאו כגון דחזאי ריש ירחא, וחמשא בירחא, וריש ירחא, וחמשא בירחא, והשתא חזאי בחמשא בירחא, ובריש ירחא לא חזאי, וקאמר אשה קובעת לה וסת בתוך ימי נדותה - אלמא, מריש ירחא מנינא! א"ל: לא, הכי א"ר יוחנן, כגון דחזאי ריש ירחא, וריש ירחא, ועשרין וחמשה בירחא, וריש ירחא, דאמרינן דמי יתירי הוא דאתוספו בה" ע"כ.

as stated above. However, the third *re'iyah* from a *mayan pasuach* will establish the *vest*.

If a woman gets her period one month on Day 15, and the next month she begins bleeding on Day 14 and continues on Day 15, the dates on which she must be concerned during the following month are Day 14 and Day 15. Yet, she needs two more times in which the onset of the period begins on Day 15 to create a *vest kavua* for Day 15. If she gets her period on Day 15 during the third month, the woman now has two *re'iyos* from a *mayan sasum* on Day 15. If she now bleeds on this day during the third month, even from a *mayan pasuach*, she will create a *vest kavua*.[504]

This scenario creates a *vest kavua* as a stringency. Whenever a *vest* is kept as a stringency, only marital relations are forbidden; other forms of intimate touch are permitted, and a *bedikah* should be performed. Furthermore, the fact that the *vest* is only kept as a stringency means that there is no need to add additional levels of stringency to it, and there is no need to keep the *onas Ohr Zarua* in the *onah* before the *onas havest*.

The Beis Meir

If a woman gets her period one month after a *haflagah* of 37 days, she keeps the following haflagah 37 days after the second *re'iyah*. If the next month she bleeds on the 33rd day through the 37th day, the next month she should keep the 27th day as the *haflagah* and the 28th as a *haflagah* as a stringency.

The halachah is like the position of the Ramban[505] and the Beis Meir,[506] that when the period comes one month on a shorter *haflagah* than it came in the previous one, the woman keeps the shorter number of days as the new *haflagah*, but must also keep the longer *haflagah*, since it was never "uprooted."

The new *re'iyah* starts the count again, so we consider that day as Day 1 of her cycle. This being so, a period that arrives on a shorter *haflagah* than the previous time(s) does not "uproot" the longer *haflagah*

504. כ״כ החזו״א ס׳ פ״ה ס״ק מ״ד מ״ה נ״ב , ובחוט שני עמ׳ קכ״ב סע׳ ג׳, ובשע׳ שבה״ל ס׳ קפ״ט סע׳ י״ג, ובשו״ע הרב מבואר שדוקא בהפסיקה בנתיים וראתה הפעם השלישית באותו יום לחודש אבל אין קובעין וסת ממעיין פתוח אם תחילת ראייתה הייתה קודם לכן.

505. הל׳ נדה לרמב״ן פרק ו׳ הל׳ א׳.

506. עיין ס׳ קפ״ט סע׳ י״ד, בית מאיר על הגליון, ס״ט, כו״פ ס״ק י״ח, לחו״ש ס״ק כ״ט.

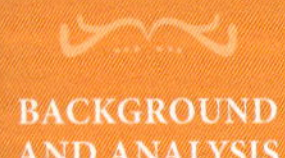

until that amount of days passes from the onset of the period and the woman is clean from blood on that day.

In our case, the woman should continue to keep the 28th day after the last *re'iyah* as a stringency, even though her period came on the second *haflagah* of 27, until she passes the 28th day without discovering blood.

The Ramban and Beis Meir thus hold that a shorter *haflagah* does not "uproot" a longer *haflagah*, since the longer *haflagah* does not become "uprooted" until this interval passes again and the *onas havest* passes blood-free.

The Shach disagrees, and holds that a shorter *haflagah* does "uproot" a longer *haflagah*.[507] Most Rishonim do not seem to agree with the Shach. The halachah is like the opinion of the Beis Meir, that a *vest* of a shorter *haflagah* does not "uproot" a longer *haflagah*, and the longer *haflagah* is kept as a stringency.[508]

Haflagah (Interval) *Bais Meir*

Month:	*1*	*2*	*3*
Amount of Days Since Last Period	35 Days	37 Days	33 Days

Upcoming Month:	*2*	*3*	*4*
Vest Haflagah *(Expected Period)*	35 Days	37 Days	33 Days
Additional Vest *Bais Meir*			37 Days

Summary: An interval date which is longer than the previous interval date will uproot the shorter interval. The Beir Meir says that a shorter interval (the 33 day interval) will not uproot the longer interval (the 37 day interval). His reasoning is that when the period arrives on the 33rd date, the month is "reset"; therefore date 37 is not uprooted, as it has not "passed."

507. ש״ך ס׳ קפ״ט ס״ק ל״א, פרישה, ב״ח ד״ה וע״ש כיצד, חת״ס ס׳ קס״ו אות ג׳.

508. משמרת טהרה בשם רב אלישיב.

When to Drop the Beis Meir

It turns out that a woman can have lots of *vestos*. She can carry old *vestos* for *yom hachodesh* if they were from a *mayan pasuach*, and she can carry the *Beis Meir* for many months forward. The *Poskim*[509] say that anyone keeping a *vest* as a stringency can drop the *onas Ohr Zarua* and any other stringency in *vestos* for the *vest* that is kept as a stringency.[510]

Rav Yosef Shalom Elyashiv says if a woman has shorter *haflagos* than the previous ones for 3 months, which did not "uproot" the longer *haflagah*, she may then stop being concerned about the longer *haflagah*.[511] Also, when a woman began to bleed after a fluke *haflagah* that was very long relative to her normal period length and is therefore not expected to return, she need not be concerned about the *Beis Meir*. For example, if a woman normally bleeds after approximately 30 days and one month her period came after 52 days, she need not be concerned about this *haflagah* after 52 days during the next month (or 2 months, as it may be), even if she only got a period with a shorter *haflagah* in between.

Also, if a woman creates a *vest kavua* for a *haflagah* that is shorter than the longer *haflagah*, she need no longer remain concerned about the longer *haflagah*.[512]

Vest for Yemei HaShavua

The *Rishonim* discuss another *vest*, called a *vest kavua l'yemei hashavua* — a *vest* for the day of the week.[513] If a woman gets her period, for example, every 29th day (and every *re'iyah* begins the same day of the week) during the same *onah*, she creates a *vest kavua* after just three *re'iyos*, instead of the four that are usually needed to establish a *vest haflagah*.[514]

This *vest* really only applies after seeing two *haflagos* of Day 22, Day 29, Day 36, and the like, and is one of the more common fluke *vestos kevuos* that women nowadays establish.

509. ונראה שיש להתיר חיבוק ונישוק על וסת לחומרה ואין אפי׳ תע״ב.
510. משמרת טהרה בשם רב אלישיב.
511. כ״ה סתימת האחרונים, משמרת טהרה בשם רב אלישיב, שבט הלוי חלק ה׳ ס׳ קז׳ שיש לסמוך על הש״ך בכה״ג, ויש מחמרין אם המשיכה ליום ההפלגה הארוכה דכל שראתה מקודם הוה תוספת דמים, וכ״ה בחזו״א.
512. הל׳ נדה לרמב״ן פרק ו׳ הל׳ ב׳, וכ״ה סתימת האחרונים.
513. רשב״א בשם רבותיו, טור ושו״ע ס׳ קפ״ט סע׳ ו׳.
514. חוו״ד, פ״ת ס״ק ד׳.

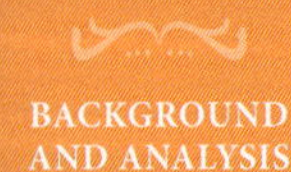

Rare Vestos

A woman who thinks she has a *vest* for consecutive numbers, or non-consecutive numbers in some form of sequence or pattern, should discuss the matter with her *Rav*.[515] These cases are rare nowadays, but they do happen, and the *Rav* will examine the woman's calendar to see if there is in fact some pattern.

Vest HaGuf

A *vest haguf* means a woman feels specific and significant sensations after which she gets her period within a certain time frame.[516] Most women have sensations around the time they get their period called premenstrual syndrome (PMS), but these symptoms are generally not considered the *vest haguf* that *Chazal* were discussing.[517]

The amount of time between the symptom and the *re'iyah* must be the same each month in order to establish this symptom as a *vest haguf*. Also, a *re'iyah* that happens more than 24 hours after the sensation is not seen as being linked to the sensation, and this is not considered a *vest haguf* either.[518]

A *vest haguf* is very rare. There are certain *vestos* that are created because a woman performs an action that *causes* the period to come, while others are an indication that the period is imminently coming. A woman who suspects that she has one should discuss the matter with her *Rav*.

The *Poskim* discuss whether a woman who has a *vest haguf kavua* should be concerned about *onah beinonis*.[519] A woman should discuss the matter with her *Rav* if the situation arises.

.515 עיין בשו"ע ס' קפ"ט סע' ז'– יב'.

.516 נדה ס"ג ע"א במשנה, שו"ע ס' קפ"ט סע' י"ט וז"ל "יש קובעת וסת על ידי מקרים שיארעו בגופה כגון שמפהקת, דהיינו כאדם שפושט זרועותיו מחמת כובד, או כאדם שפותח פיו מחמת כובד, או כאדם שמוציא קול דרך הגרון, וכן אם מתעטשת דרך מטה, או חוששת בפי כריסה ובשיפולי מעיה, או שאחזוה צירי הקדחת, או שראשה ואיבריה כבדים עליה, בכל אחד מאלו אם יארע לה שלשה פעמים, וראתה, קבעה לה וסת, שבכל פעם שהיא חוששת מהם, אסורה לשמש. ומיהו בפיהוק או עיטוש של פעם אחד אין הוסת נקבע, אלא כשעושה כן הרבה פעמים זה אחר זה. ואם אירע לה שלשה פעמים, שבכל פעם עשתה כן הרבה פעמים, הרי זה וסת. וכל אלו הוסתות שבגופה אין להם זמן ידוע, אלא בכל פעם שיקרה לה זה המקרה, הוא וסת".

.517 פרדס רימונים, שו"ת שבט הקהתי חלק ג' ס' רל"ח.

.518 חוו"ד ס' קפ"ז ס"ק ט"ו, סוג"ב ס' ז' ס"ד, אג"מ יו"ד א' ס' פ"ד, חוט שני.

.519 מסתימות לשון המחבר ס' קפ"ד סע' י"ב משמע שאפי' קבעה וסת הגוף צריך לחוש לעו"ב וז"ל "היה לה וסת לימים ולוסת מוסתות הגוף כגון קפיצה וכיוצא בה כיון שהוסת תלוי במעשה אימור לא קפצה ולא ראתה אבל חוששת לעונה בינונית שהיא ל' יום" עכ"ל, אבל הש"ך שם ס"ק ל"ב חולק עליו וז"ל "דבריו צל"ע דודאי אם יש לה וסת לימים ולוסת מוסתות הגוף חוששת לעולם לוסתה ולא שייך לומר אימור לא ראתה ואין

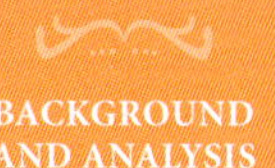

A Mesulekes Damim Nowadays

A *mesulekes damim* does not have *vestos*.[520] The classic examples are a woman who is pregnant and one who is nursing. The Gemara says a pregnant woman is only considered a *mesulekes damim* once she is sure that she is pregnant, which is from the third month.[521] Most *Poskim* say a woman must keep old *vestos* even after she knows that she is pregnant, having taken a pregnancy test.[522] The way this halachah is stated can be very misleading, because most women do not take pregnancy tests until they have missed their period, so any *vest she'eino kavua* that a woman had has in general already passed by the time she discovers that she is pregnant. In such a case, the woman does not have to be concerned for any *vestos* the next month, as long as she does not bleed after getting the positive pregnancy test. The only exception to this would be a *vest kavua* for *yom hachodesh*, which is rare in any case. If the situation arises, though, a woman who has a *vest kavua* for *yom hachodesh* should keep that *yom hachodesh* the first 3 months of pregnancy.[523]

In the days of the Gemara a woman after birth would not bleed for 24 months, whether or not she was nursing. Nowadays, it is common for women to stain, and often to even get a regular period during the months that they are nursing. A woman who gets her period during the time she is nursing must follow the halachos of a regular woman, and should keep all of the regular *vestos*.[524] A woman who does not get her period is not concerned for any *vest*, and maintains her status of a *mesulekes damim*.

Ro'eh Machmas Tashmish

The *Rif* says a woman who does not have a *vest kavua* must do three *bedikos* to establish that she is not a *ro'eh machmas tashmish* (one who bleeds as a result of marital relations). The Shulchan Aruch rules like

---

צריך לחוש לעונה בינונית כיון דיש לה וסת והכי משמע לקמן סימן קפ״ט ס״ס י״ט וכ״מ בדרישה סימן קפ״ט סעיף כ״ט דביש לה וסת לימים ולוסתות הגוף שוב אינה חוששת כלל רק לוסתה ע״ש״ עכ״ל, ויש שדייק מדבריו דאין לחוש לעו״ב כשקבעה וסת הגוף מורכב לימים אבל אם קבעה וסת הגוף עצמו צריך לפרוש גם בעו״ב, וי״א שאפי׳ אם לא מורכב ליום ידוע אין לחוש לעו״ב.

520. משנה נדה ז׳ ע״א, בעה״נ להראב״ד שער תיקון הוסתות, תורת הבית להרשב״א בית שביעי שער שלישי, טוש״ע קפ״ט סע׳ ל״ג ול״ד.

521. נדה ז׳ ע״ב , ח׳ ע״ב.

522. שו״ת נו״ב קמא אבה״א ס׳ ס״ט, שו״ת חת״ס ס׳ קס״ט, ודלא כמ״ש באג״מ יו״ד חלק ג׳ שנשתנו הטבעים שבדרך כלל אין מעוברת רואה דם בזמננו אפ׳ תוך ג׳ חדשים, ע״ש.

523. שאפי׳ קבעה וסת הפלגה אין חוששין כל שלא ראתה עוד, שעו׳ שבה״ל.

524. אג״מ יו״ד חלק ג׳ ס׳ נ״ב.

the Rif. [525] Such a woman must do a *bedikah* before and after marital relations, and her husband must check himself as well, to demonstrate that marital relations do not cause her to begin to bleed.

The *Terumas HaDeshen* says a woman who knows that she does not get her period before a certain date does not need to do these *bedikos* during the times that she knows that it will not come.[526] Even if she did, these *bedikos* do not count toward the *bedikos* necessary to establish that the woman is not *ro'eh machmas tashmish*.

The Shach disagrees, saying that one should not do *bedikos* for *ro'eh machmas tashmish* at all.[527] Many *Poskim* rule like the Shach and never require *bedikos* for *ro'eh machmas tashmish*.[528]

Those *Poskim* who require these *bedikos* say that they must be done during times when the woman is not a *mesulekes damim* (i.e., pregnant or nursing),[529] and should also not be done before a *vest*, because she is not expected to discover blood during that time. She also should not do these *bedikos* on the *vest* itself (aside from the fact that marital relations are prohibited on the *vest*) since even if she discovers blood, it was not necessarily caused by marital relations, because she is expecting her period to come on the *vest* anyway.

Many women are either pregnant or nursing for several years early in their marriage and therefore do not get a chance to carry out these *bedikos*. Some *Poskim* say if one did not do *bedikos* right away for *ro'eh machmas tashmish* in the beginning of marriage, she should not do them at all. This is how many *Poskim* in America rule.[530] They reason that there is no purpose in checking for *ro'eh machmas tashmish* when the couple has been intimate for years, and intimacy clearly does not serve as a catalyst for bleeding to occur, as she is clearly not seeing blood because of marital relations.

Many disagree, saying that these *bedikos* should be done as required whenever it becomes relevant for the couple, even if it takes a few years after marriage to establish that the woman is not a *ro'eh machmas tashmish*. Practically speaking, we do not require these *bedikos* if they were not performed early on in the marriage.

---

525. ס׳ קפ״ו סע׳ ב׳.
526. תה״ד ס׳ רמ״ז, טוש״ע קפ״ו ג׳.
527. ס קפ״ו ש״ך ס״ק א׳.
528. שערים מצויינים בהלכה, ע״ש מש״כ.
529. פ״ת ס׳ קפ״ו ס״ק ד׳ בשם מהר״ם פדוא״ה, תורת השלמים, ס״ט ס״ק ד׳.
530. הגרש״ז אויעורבאך.

SECTION THREE

Section Three is an in-depth analysis of *hilchos niddah* for the advanced user.

This section is unique in terms of presentation style and is intended for those who have a clear understanding of each topic.

The reader is encouraged to read and fully understand Sections One and Two before reading Section Three.

Presentation of the background of each section is limited, as the primary focus of this section is on questions one may have and final rulings on each topic.

For a more advanced presentation of the background for each halachah, as well as more details in terms of the development of the practical application of the halachah, the reader is referred to Section Two.

Supporting information is presented in the form of footnotes. These footnotes are intended to clarify a *psak* (halachic ruling) or to give further details about a particular topic. In certain instances, various viewpoints on a particular *psak* or conflicting viewpoints are presented. These should not be taken as *psak halachah*, as the ultimate ruling follows the main text.

HOW A WOMAN BECOMES A NIDDAH

Teaching Taharas HaMishpachah (Laws of Family Purity)

תניא, היה ר"מ אומר: מפני מה אמרה תורה נדה לשבעה — מפני שרגיל בה, וקץ בה, אמרה תורה: תהא טמאה שבעה ימים, כדי שתהא חביבה על בעלה כשעת כניסתה לחופה. (נדה דף לא עמוד ב)

- Rebbi Meir says *taharas hamishpachah* is a major contributor toward a happy marriage. It must be noted that even if someone thinks they have acquired the secret to a happy marriage without *taharas hamishpachah*, they must nevertheless follow all of *hilchos niddah*. Halachah is the fiber of life, and *aveiros* are the fiber of destruction. Rebbi Meir is telling us the fringe benefits of following a *chok* (mitzvah whose reason is unknown to man), not the ultimate reason, which we cannot know. Therefore, we cannot adapt the halachah at will when we think the reason does not apply.
- A *chassan* or *kallah* should learn the halachos according to their abilities, using methods that will give them an understanding of

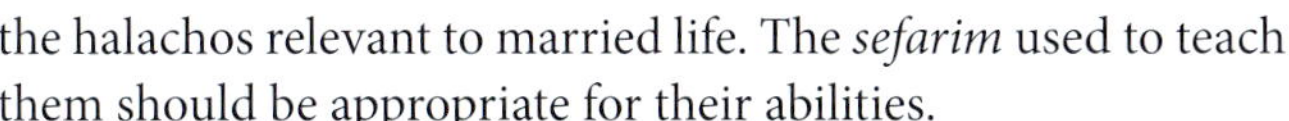

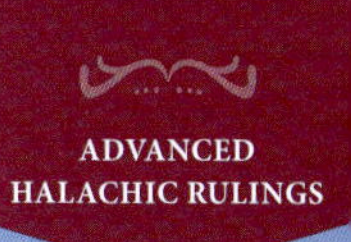

the halachos relevant to married life. The *sefarim* used to teach them should be appropriate for their abilities.

- A *chassan* or *kallah* should be tested to ensure that they have a clear understanding of the halachos.
- A *kallah* teacher should be clear as to the reasons behind the halachos she is teaching (for example, a *poletes shichvas zera* requires a 5-day wait, and the like). She should be equipped to answer questions that a *kallah* is almost certain to pose.
- A *chassan* or *kallah* teacher should be prepared to teach more than the basic do's and don'ts of the halachos.
- A person who is teaching a *chassan* or *kallah* should provide more than they can find in a *sefer* of halachic rulings. He or she is preparing someone for marriage, and along with this comes tremendous responsibility.

Ruling on One's Own She'eilos

1. The halachah does not forbid a person from ruling on his wife's *maros*,[1] even though there is a *yetzer hara* (evil inclination) to be lenient and no *sefarim* to use as references.
2. The *Pischei Teshuvah* says a man may not rule when his wife has a *she'eilah* in regard to *tevilah*,[2] because at that point she has the status of being prohibited to him and this ruling will give her a status of *taharah*.[3] Rav Nissim Karelitz points out that he may rule on a simple *she'eilah* that is found in the *Shulchan Aruch*.
3. The practical halachah is like the position of the Aruch HaShulchan, that the husband may even rule on *she'eilos* regarding her *tevilah*.[4]

---

1. Brought by the *Shach* 188:7.

2. 188:6, in the name of the *Chochmas Adam*.

3. Interestingly, the Shach does not differentiate between his ruling on a regular *bedikah* and his ruling on a *hefsek taharah*, which by definition changes the woman's status to that of *taharah*.

4. Rav Yosef Shalom Elyashiv, Rav Shmuel HaLevi Wosner, and most *Poskim*, as related by Rav Yossi Stilerman.

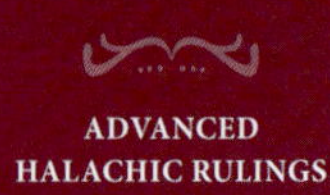

Illicit Relationships

- The Gemara says a Jew who has relations with a non-Jew is liable to *kareis*.[5] The Torah does not mention it because the Torah was not given to those who have thrown off its yoke.

- Rav Yaakov Kaminetzky says someone who marries a non-Jew is worse than someone who marries a Jew and does not keep the halachos of *taharas hamishpachah*.

- Rav Yosef Shalom Elyashiv says a *Rav* should never overtly rule that an unmarried woman should go to the mikvah to avoid *kareis*, because it may appear as though the *Rav* is sanctioning her behavior.[6] However, in certain situations, a friend should advise her to go to the mikvah to avoid unnecessary prohibitions.

- According to Rav Yosef Shalom Elyashiv and the *Sefer HaAkeidah*, a community is forbidden to allow unmarried women into the mikvah. However, this does not mean they have to check the marriage status of each woman.

- A Jewish woman married to a non-Jew should not be encouraged to go to the mikvah,[7] because it would seem that the *Rav* approves of the marriage by encouraging the couple to keep *taharas hamishpachah*. She should be shown the beauty of a Jewish marriage.[8]

- A nonobservant postmenopausal woman who is married to a Jew should be encouraged to immerse in the mikvah,[9] even if she will not be separating from her husband for the required

5. *Sanhedrin* 82a.

6. The *Acharonim* speak out against unmarried women or women during *shivah nekiyim* immersing in the mikvah before Yamim Nora'im. They say that allowing them to immerse opens the gates to illicit relationships.

7. Even though it would keep the couple away from each other physically for at least 12 days a month.

8. They also may want to discuss conversion, and in such a case, it may be a viable option. One should always seek guidance from a *Rav* who deals with conversions when dealing with such delicate circumstances.

9. This halachah also applies to a woman before menopause. However, a premenopausal woman must wait the minimum of 7 days from the onset of her period, so she at least fulfills the requirements of *niddah d'Oraisa*.

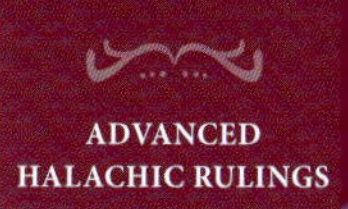

time for *poletes shichvas zera*, and even if she will not perform any *bedikos*.[10]

Bleeding from External Sources

- The *Chazon Ish* says a woman who bleeds from a polyp in the uterus is *tehorah* because this is not the normal way for blood to come out. *Rabbanim* rely on this ruling when it can be determined that they are not dealing with the uterine lining shedding.
- The Pleissi is lenient in regard to period bleeding from a prolapsed uterus,[11] but most *Poskim* are stringent even when the uterus is visible on the outside of the woman's body.
- A woman who has a prolapsed uterus should do a *hefsek taharah* and one *bedikah* on Day 1 and Day 7 of the *shivah nekiyim*.[12]
- A woman who has a prolapsed uterus is more prone to *makkos* than most women. She will probably bleed throughout the month because of *dam makkah*, so she should utilize the services of an experienced *bodekes* to help her determine whether the bleeding is *dam makkah* or *dam niddah*. Generally, a *Rav* will attribute the bleeding to a *makkah*, since we know the source of the bleeding is a cut cervix. A woman in this circumstance should contact a *Rav* for practical guidance.
- A woman is a *niddah d'Oraisa* even when something was done to her that caused her to bleed. This means a woman is a niddah even if something caused the lining to shed, such as ingesting horemone pills which trigger the period to come. If the bleeding comes from a *makkah*, such as when something cut the woman internally — even on the uterus itself — the woman is *tehorah*.
- Many *Rabbanim* are lenient when a woman bleeds from intrauterine procedures, on the assumption that the procedure

---

10. The reason for this ruling is that she will be *tehorah mid'Oraisa* and is currently in a marriage sanctioned by *Chazal*.

11. The reason for this is because he holds that a woman's bleeding with a prolapsed uterus it is not called *derech re'iyah*.

12. She may have to have these *bedikos* performed by a *bodekes*, depending on the severity of the situation. *Rabbanim* often advise women who have a prolapsed uterus to get into a Kegel exercise regiment which focuses on strengthening pelvic content. Often, after a few months of serious training, the uterus will rise back to its original place in the abdominal cavity.

cut the uterus. Rav Yosef Shalom Elyashiv says that in certain cases, the lining may have shed and one should be stringent. Always consult a competent *Rav* for a practical halachic ruling, providing specifics of the procedure.

- An IUD is an intrauterine device used as a contraceptive. It has been proven that IUDs do not cause miscarriages of already fertilized embryos, but only prevent fertilization. This being the case, even Rav Yosef Shalom Elyashiv allows them.[13] IUDs are known to sometimes cause mid-cycle bleeding, especially in the early months of usage. Such blood is *tamei* according to most *Poskim*. As we said, bleeding that was "forced" causes one to be a *niddah d'Oraisa*.[14]

Dam Makkah

- One may not be *metaher* blood that comes from the uterus unless he is certain that it is from a cut.
- Rav Yisrael Yaakov Fisher was *metaher maros* by sight, because he was able to determine when the blood was *dam makkah*.[15] Rav Yosef Shalom Elyashiv and Rav Nissim Karelitz are against doing so.[16]

---

13. A couple who would like to use any sort of contraceptive device or pill should consult with a competent *Rav* who has experience in these matters.

14. In such a case, the endometrium is forced to be expelled and she is therefore *temei'ah* — see *Shulchan Aruch* §183, "*Bein B'Oness Bein B'Ratzon*." If the device would cause cuts on the walls of the uterus, the woman is *tehorah*, as is the case with any *makkah*. Very often, the string attached to the IUD causes vaginal abrasions which bleed. One may need to consult a *bodekes*.

15. Rav Yisrael Yaakov Fisher was legendary for his expertise in this area, often determining medical information that even doctors had overlooked by looking at a *mareh*. Rav Yitzchak Berkovits says that if someone is on the level of Dayan Fisher he can be *metaher* a *mareh* by sight. Rav Moshe Feinstein (*Igros Moshe*, vol. 3, *siman* 146) and others say if a *Rav* is sure from the look of the *mareh* that it was caused by a *makkah* and the woman says she feels pain, he may rely on his expertise. It is interesting to note that Rav Shmuel HaLevi Wosner writes that a *Rav* who knows colors well can rule that blood he sees on the *mareh* is from a *macholes* or another animal. In theory, most *Rabbanim* have more experience with *dam makkah* than they have with *dam macholes* and he would agree that halachically, a *Rav* may be *metaher dam makkah* by sight. Some say that determining that blood originated from an animal is simpler than determining *dam makkah*, as the color is very different from *dam niddus*. Practically speaking, Rav Berkovits says that although it is permitted to do so, the general rule is that one should not judge that a *mareh* is *dam makkah* by sight. Rather, the woman should be sent to a *bodekes*.

16. Rav Yosef Shalom Elyashiv says that in the event that a woman lives with her husband based on the ruling of a *Rav* who ruled that a *mareh* is *tahor* because he determines by

- The custom is like the position of Rav Yosef Shalom Elyashiv, and one should never be *metaher* a *mareh* by sight, based on the estimation of the person looking at it that this must be *dam makkah*.
- If a woman says she cut herself when doing a *bedikah*, she should be sent to a *bodekes*. If she is unable go to a *bodekes* but can feel the cut and produce blood, she is believed. It is harder to permit her simply based on her declaration that she has a *makkah* in the form of a cut that is too high for her to reach.
- If a woman discovers blood on a *bedikah* cloth, a *Rav* should only attribute it to a cut that is known to be there *and* it bleeds.[17]
- Bleeding caused by contraceptive pills is always *dam niddah* because it is hormonal bleeding. It is not considered *dam makkah*.[18]

---

sight that the woman has an internal cut, the husband is possibly in a situation of sin. See the last page in *Chut Shani* for a letter written by Rav Nissim Karelitz against a *Rav* who was permitting *maros* by determining the color to be *dam makkah* without another *teliyah*.

17. The Mishnah in *Niddah* says Rebbi Akiva was *metaher* a *kesem* because the woman had a *makkah* that had already healed but it could have opened up. He explained to his students that the reason he was lenient was because she saw a *kesem*, not a *re'iyah*. I asked Rav Dovid Feinstein about a woman who experiences bleeding and goes to a *bodekes*, who sees a scab: is the *bodekes* required to scratch at the scab to determine if it could open up when the woman does a *bedikah*, or is it enough that she sees the scab? He replied, "You cannot be lenient unless you are certain that the *makkah* she sees could have produced the blood she found." Some *bodkos* have enough experience to tell the *Rav* that the *makkah* they found could have produced blood for a certain amount of time, while other, less experienced *bodkos* cannot tell how much blood the *makkah* would produce, or how long ago the *makkah* could have produced such blood.

18. Women might take two kinds of birth control pills: a single-hormone (progesterone) pill or a double-hormone (estrogen and progesterone) pill. Single-hormone pills cause an effect on the hormone levels within the body by producing high levels of progesterone, similar to pregnancy, which trick the body into thinking that the woman is pregnant. This in turn prevents ovulation as long as the woman continues taking the pill. In addition, single-hormone pills thin the uterine lining, thereby preventing a fertilized egg from implanting, and increase the amount of mucus in the cervix, which helps prevent sperm from reaching the uterus. Dual-hormone pills prevent ovulation and increase the amount of mucus in the cervix, which prevents fertilization.

A woman who takes single-hormone pills will push off her period until she stops taking the pills. If she is nursing and is not expecting to get her period, she can continue on this protocol for a long period of time, and it would prevent her from getting her period and from getting pregnant. This pill is often used for a *kallah* who wants to push off her anticipated period until after the wedding to prevent a *chuppas niddah*.

A woman may take dual-hormone pills for contraceptive purposes. (This is usually gauged on a 28-day cycle, starting on Day 5 or Day 6 of her cycle: 21 days of hormones followed by 7 days of placebo pills which remind her to take pills daily.) These pills allow her to regulate her cycle to some degree and prevent pregnancy with 99.9-percent accuracy.

Colors of Discharges

- The Mishnah states that only four shades of red are *tamei*, and everything else is uterine discharge, but not *dam niddah*.[19]
- Black is also a *tamei* color because it was originally red blood, which oxidized.
- Blue, green, brown,[20] pink, and amber are *tahor* colors. The practice is to also be *metaher* orange, although the Shelah is stringent.
- Even though most discharges are clinically blood, the Torah is only *metamei* the colors that *Chazal* called *dam niddah*. The practice nowadays is to be *metamei* any color that is reddish or black (based on the *Rosh*).
- A woman who discovers green may have an internal infection. Just as nose discharges should not be green, uterine discharges should not be green. This woman should be referred to a doctor. Pink may be the sign of internal fungus, and the woman should be sent to a doctor.

A *kallah* may be told to use double hormones to regulate her cycle for the upcoming wedding. It should be noted that certain pills also thin the uterine lining to the point that there is little or no bleeding even once one starts the placebo pills. A woman who is taking these pills may avoid becoming a niddah for months on end.

A woman may bleed as a result of pills for various reasons, some of which we will discuss here. A woman's body is often not welcoming to foreign hormones and may thus discharge blood the first few months she takes the pills (called "breakthrough bleeding"). If a woman takes single-hormone pills for too long she may bleed, whether or not she is nursing, since the body cannot hold off the period indefinitely. Many women stain when they stop taking the 21-day double hormone pills and switch to the 7-day placebo, since their bodies detect a drop in the hormone levels.

In all such cases, a woman is likely to become a niddah (possibly *d'Rabbanan*, if she only stains from the pills, as opposed to getting a full period) since the endometrium was forced to bleed, and since the bleeding is not due to a cut which is releasing blood.

19. *Niddah* 19a.

20. This halachah should not be taken literally; many *Rabbanim* prohibit various shades of brown. As always, unless something is clearly *tahor*, the *mareh* should be brought to a competent *Rav* who specializes in *maros*. It should be noted that the color brown is comprised of various shades of red, black, and yellow, or red, yellow, and blue, and in other cases red and green in specific proportions. In each variable, red and brown are relatively comparable, and therefore a *Rav* should be shown brown *maros* until the couple learns to determine on their own which colors are clearly brown and which have a reddish hue, which should be presented to the *Rav* as the *she'eilos* arise.

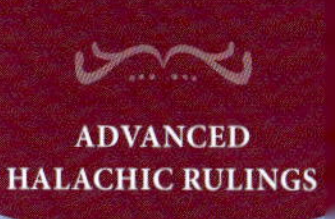

Checking Maros

- *Maros* should be checked in the shade of the sun ("*bein chamah l'tzeil* — between sunlight and shade"), not in florescent lighting (which lightens the color) or incandescent lighting (which darkens the color). The lights in the room should be turned off before a *mareh* is checked.

- *Maros* should not be checked with light that is filtered through glass, for example, a window or glasses,[21] as the glass may distort the light to some degree.[22]

- A wet *mareh* generally looks worse than a dry one. The *Bach* says to check *maros* once they dry. This ruling is generally followed unless the *mareh* is clearly *tamei* or *tahor*, or if the *Rav* needs to give a time-sensitive ruling.

- One should use his discretion before ruling at night about a *mareh*.[23] A ruling should only be given at night if it is a mikvah night or another pressing situation. Otherwise, it is always best to wait until morning and rule in the correct lighting.

- Someone who needs to rule at night should find the best light possible. Some *Rabbanim* have special "natural daylight lamps," for these situations.

- If a *Rav* checks a *mareh* on a mikvah night and is unsure whether the *mareh* is *tahor* or not, he should not allow the woman to immerse in the mikvah until a clear ruling is determined.

- If a *mareh* turns red after it was declared *tahor*, the practice is to be follow the opinion of the Shach, who holds that it is *tamei*.[24] For this reason, many *Rabbanim* discard or throw *maros* into a pile after giving a ruling.[25]

---

21. Those who use loupes to check *maros* should be careful to use "achromatic" lenses, which do not distort the light.

22. Rav Yaakov Blackman.

23. Rav Shmuel HaLevi Wosner, Rav Nissim Karelitz, and others say that a *Rav* may check if a *mareh* is a *she'eilah* at night, or if it is simply *tahor*. If there is no *she'eilah*, he may be *metaher* at night. If he realizes he is dealing with a real *she'eilah*, he should push off ruling until he sees the *mareh* in the proper light the next morning.

24. Rav Nissim Karelitz.

25. In practice, *maros* usually fade *from* red, not *to* red, but we would rule like the Shach in theory.

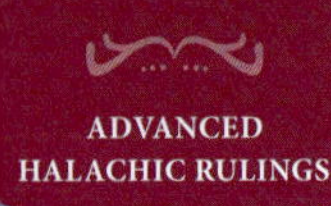

- If a *mareh* looks *tamei* and then fades to a *tahor* color, the woman is *temei'ah*, unless the person looking at it determines that what was seen as *tamei* the first time was not seen in the proper light.[26]
- If a *Rav* is *metamei* a woman out of a *safeik*, because he is unable to confidently be *metaher* the *mareh*,[27] when she immerses in the mikvah she should recite a *brachah*.[28]
- *Rabbanim* who check *maros* with a loupe are determining, through the use of the loupe, which color they are seeing when they are not confident that they can be *metaher* the *mareh* based on the naked eye alone. If the color red is not visible to the naked eye without a loupe the *mareh* is *tahor*.[29]
- Many women are embarrassed to show *maros* to a *Rav*. They should be encouraged to show them, and it should be explained to them what they stand to gain by having a *Posek* look at the *mareh*. If necessary, they can give it to the *Rav*'s wife, who can show it to the *Rav* on their behalf.[30]

A Lost Mareh

- If a woman or the *Rav* lost a *mareh*, the woman should be asked questions to determine if there was a real *she'eilah*, or she was just asking to be sure the color she saw was OK.
- A case of a real *she'eilah* on a *bedikah* cloth is a *safeik d'Oraisa* (a doubt about a *mitzvah d'Oraisa*), because the halachah is concerned about a *hargashah* and the woman has a reason to think that she is *temei'ah*, more than one who does not have a

26. Rav Nissim Karelitz.

27. In such a case, the *Rav* may be advised to send the woman to another *Rav* for his ruling. If no one else is available (which is rare nowadays, as a *mareh* can be sent by mail to anywhere in the world), she counts *shivah nekiyim* as though she is a niddah.

28. Rav Nissim Karelitz.

29. This halachah should not be taken at face value. Many years of learning and practice are required to determine what is and what is not considered visible to the naked eye.

30. Some *Rabbanim* have drop boxes where a woman can leave a marked envelope, and the *Rav* calls the number on the envelope and relates the ruling. In general, a couple should have a relationship with a *Rav* whom they are comfortable bringing their *she'eilos* to. Both husband and wife should share the responsibility of bringing *she'eilos* to their *Rav* and developing a relationship with him.

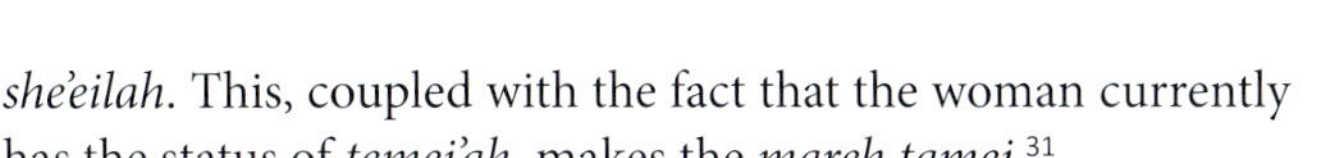

she'eilah. This, coupled with the fact that the woman currently has the status of *temei'ah*, makes the *mareh tamei*.[31]

- If she was pretty certain that the *mareh* was *tahor*, but was presenting it to the *Rav* for his confirmation, the *Rav* may be *metaher* the *mareh*.[32]
- See Advanced Rulings, How a Woman Becomes a Niddah, headlines "When the Size or Color Cannot Be Determined or the Kesem Was Lost" (page 221) regarding if the *she'eilah* was on a *kesem*.

Chacham SheHorah (A Rav Who Already Ruled)

- When a person comes to a *Rav* with a *mareh* that was previously shown to another *Rav*, the second *Rav* may not issue a different ruling until he consults with the first *Rav* to ask if he allows him to change the ruling.[33]
- Rav Nissim Karelitz says if a *Rav* rules stringently about a *mareh* because he is not confident enough to permit it, but he does not render a final ruling that the *mareh* is prohibited, the questioner may ask another *Rav* for his ruling.[34]
- The *din* of *chacham shehorah* only applies when dealing with an item, like a *mareh*, and does not apply to a personal ruling.[35] If someone asks his *Rav* where to light Chanukah candles, or

---

31. *Chochmas Adam*; *She'arim HaMetzuyanim B'Halachah*; Rav Nissim Karelitz.

32. The *Pischei Teshuvos* cites the *Sefer Tehillah L'Dovid*, which says that in the event that a woman loses her *hefsek taharah* before she had a chance to inspect it, she remains *temei'ah* and must perform another *hefsek taharah* the next day (unless she inserted the *moch dachuk* before *shkiah*). Since she had not yet inspected the *bedikah*, the *bedikah* does not count. Thus, since she has not proven that she has the status of a *tehorah* by producing a clean *hefsek taharah*, she is unable to begin the *shivah nekiyim*.

33. See *Chut Shani* 188:2 for a short yet detailed explanation of *hilchos chacham she'horah*.

34. There are times that a person brings a *mareh* to a *Rav* and the *Rav* says that he "cannot say that this is OK." By some *Rabbanim* that means "It is *tamei*," and by others it means "I cannot confidently say that this is *tahor*, so you should be stringent out of a *safeik*." In the latter case, the *Rav* may recommend that they show the *mareh* to someone else.

35. Once a *Rav* says that something is prohibited, it is prohibited, and another *Rav* may not argue with his ruling. This is the *din* of *chatichah naaseh neveilah* in *issur v'heter* (*Ramban*; *Rashba*; and *Rosh*). Other reasons for the *din* of *chacham she'horah* are out of respect for the *Rav* who issued the first ruling, and so the Torah does not get distorted with one *Rav* saying one thing and another *Rav* arguing with the first ruling (*Ran*).

whether he should keep 1 or 2 days of Yom Tov in Eretz Yisrael, he may then present the same *she'eilah* to another *Rav*.

- A second *Rav* may override the ruling if the first *Rav* made a mistake in his ruling. However, if the first *Rav* has a different *mesorah* than the second Rav, this not considered a mistake in ruling, and does not allow another *Rav* to rule against the first ruling.[36] This applies frequently when dealing with *she'eilos* on *maros*, which is a topic that is ruled primarily based on *mesorah*.

- A person may ask a *Rav* what "he thinks" about something (for example, "What would the Rav say in a particular case?") without asking for a ruling, if he wants to "shop around." However, if the *Rav* gives a ruling that a certain item is prohibited, it becomes prohibited.

- Rav Nissim Karelitz says that when someone is dealing with a *she'eilah* that is not relevant right now, they can ask different people for the halachah to get the consensus of *Poskim*, after which they can decide which ruling they would like to adopt. In general, unless someone is qualified to render halachic decisions himself, he is encouraged to adopt one *Rav* to follow in all situations, as the Mishnah says, "*Aseh lecha Rav*."

- If someone brings a *mareh* and the *Posek* knows that according to his *mesorah* the *mareh* is *tamei* while another *Rav* would be *metaher* it, he should rule, and not defer to another *Rav*.[37]

- Many *Poskim* say that when a *Posek* is not certain that a *mareh* is definitely *tamei*, but he does not want to take responsibility and be *metaher* it, he should send the woman to someone else.

Hargashos With Blood and Without Blood

- A woman who experiences a *hargashah* and discovers blood is *temei'ah mid'Oraisa* if she discovers the blood within a half hour after the *hargashah*, since she has the combination of blood and a *hargashah*.

---

36. Some *Rabbanim* have a policy to tell people who bring them *maros* that they will look at the *mareh*, but it becomes property of the *Rav* once it is shown to him. This is to prevent people from "shopping around."

37. Many *Rabbanim* will practically defer a *she'eilah* to a *Rav* with a more lenient *mesorah* rather than rule stringently on the *mareh*, if the situation warrants such action.

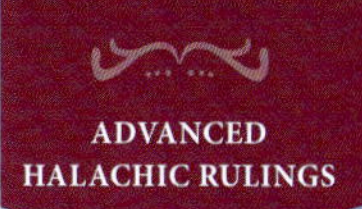

- Such a woman may count her 5 days from the time she experienced the *hargashah*. She does not have to wait to start counting from the time she discovered the blood.
- The *Terumas HaDeshen* says if a woman had a *hargashah* and did not discover any blood, she is nevertheless *temei'ah* because we assume blood was discharged, and for some reason was not found.
- Most *Poskim* agree that if a woman feels an internal wetness and found nothing, she is *tehorah*. Rav Moshe Feinstein, however, is stringent. The custom is not to follow this stringent position.[38]

Note: The internal wetness being discussed is an internal feeling, not an external sensation of moisture, which all agree is not called a *hargashah*.

- Practically speaking, if a woman experiences a *hargashah* of her whole body shaking or her *mekor* opening[39] (but not if she experiences internal wetness) and finds nothing, she is *temei'ah mid'Rabbanan*, as per the opinion of the Terumas HaDeshen, and must go through the entire *taharah* process.
- Rav Shmuel HaLevi Wosner holds such a woman must immerse in the mikvah, but does not make a *brachah* on the *tevilah*.
- Rav Nissim Karelitz disagrees, saying that she must make a *brachah*.
- It comes out that according to Rav Shmuel HaLevi Wosner, the halachah is only being *metamei* this woman due to a *safeik*, not as a definitive *tumah d'Rabbanan*.
- Rav Nissim Karelitz says a *hargashah* of internal wetness means that the women felt blood leaving her cervix, not that she felt pains at the site of the cervix.

---

38. The whole concept of feeling internal wetness as a *hargashah* is in itself a novelty of the Noda B'Yehudah, with which the Chasam Sofer disagrees. Therefore, the halachah is lenient when she thinks she felt internal wetness and did not find any blood.

39. *Sefer Mishnas HaShulchan* explains the *hargashah* of the opening of the *mekor* as a similar sensation to what one feels at the onset of urination. Most women nowadays realize that they got their period by actually discovering blood or by feeling an external sensation of wetness, not by feeling the cervix "release" the blood.

- Practically speaking, a woman who *knows* that she had an internal wetness should do a *bedikah*.[40] If she is not completely sure, she should not do anything.
- Realistically, most women nowadays do not experience the *hargashos* described by *Chazal* and will not become *temei'os* from experiencing *hargashos*.

Proving That a Hargashah Does Not Cause Bleeding

- If a woman experiences a *hargashah*, does a *bedikah*, and finds *tahor* colors, she establishes that this type of *hargashah* does not cause blood to come out by her, and no longer has to do a *bedikah* for that type of *hargashah*.
- The *Chazon Ish* says this status must be created with three *hargashos*, no matter when they happen in the woman's monthly cycle. If the woman experiences a *hargashah* and finds nothing, this will not count toward establishing this, and she is *temei'ah*, like any woman who experiences a *hargashah* and finds nothing. The woman must find *tahor* colors to which she can attribute the *hargashah* in order to establish that this *hargashah* is *tehorah*.
- The *Poskim* note that almost all women who call with *she'eilos* that they felt a *hargashah* are imagining the sensation, because they heard something in a *shiur* or from their friends.[41]

---

40. The *Baruch Tam* explains that just as a person does not feel blood flowing through their veins, because the blood and their body temperature are equal, so too a woman does not feel her period until the blood leaves her body and drops to a lower temperature. A similar comparison would be to someone preparing a baby bottle — the correct temperature is when one sprays the milk on their wrist and does not feel the liquid. This is because they do not want to upset the baby by giving them something too hot or cold, and they want to imitate the mother's milk, which is body temperature. Interestingly, women of yesteryear were able to feel as the blood exited their cervix as their bodies were much more sensitive to this feeling.

41. Some *Rabbanim* have a habit of asking every woman who bring them a *she'eilah* if she had a *hargashah*. It seems to be a mistake in practice nowadays when nearly all women do not have *hargashos*, because it only serves to confuse the woman, without any constructive purpose.

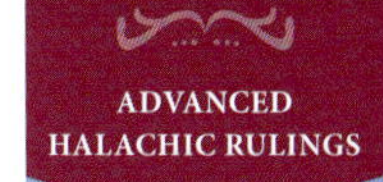

The Three Cases When a Hargashah Is Suspected

- The *Pischei Teshuvah* says that in three cases the halachah is concerned that the woman experienced a *hargashah* and we do not apply any of the leniencies of *kesamim*, because an external sensation may have masked the sensation of the *hargashah*. These cases are: when a woman discovers blood after marital relations or after urinating, and when she discovers blood when something, such as a *bedikah* cloth, was inserted into her body.

- This concern for a *hargashah* when discovering blood after urinating or after marital relations only exists when the blood was discovered within the amount of time the Mishnah terms "*osyom*."[42]

- Rav Moshe Feinstein says *osyom* after urinating means that the woman left the toilet in a haste before the drops finished falling, such as when she rushed to get a pot off the fire or a child who is screaming.

- The *Darchei Teshuvah* says the leniencies of *kesamim* are applied if a woman discovered blood after marital relations if her husband had waited inside her after he was *mazria* (reached the climax of intercourse) and was *poreish b'eiver meis* (withdrew when no longer erect). This wait is longer than the *shiur osyom*, meaning that the blood that was discovered was found after this amount of time.

- The halachah is concerned for a *hargashah* on blood discovered on a *bedikah* cloth, even if it was only found after the *shiur osyom*. See below for discussion about when the *bedikah* cloth was an *eid she'eino baduk*.

- Blood that is discovered on the husband's *eiver* after marital relations is not treated with the leniencies of *kesamim*, even when it is only found after the *shiur osyom*. This is a case of a foreign object that entered the woman's body, similar to a *bedikah* cloth.

- A woman is *temei'ah mid'Oraisa* if she stuck her finger in her vaginal area and discovered even a small drop of blood.[43]

---

42. Rav Yosef Shalom Elyashiv says the *shiur osyom* after marital relations is 2 minutes, and the *shiur osyom* after using the restroom is 1 minute (*Mishnas HaShulchan*). Rav Yitzchak Berkovits does not rule like this, although many *Poskim* in Eretz Yisrael rule this way.

43. Rav Nissim Karelitz.

- For something to be suspected to have masked a *hargashah* it must actually enter the woman's body. There is no concern for a *hargashah* when a foreign object was only present in the area called *bein hasfasayim* (between the vaginal lips).[44]

- A woman who discovers a substantial amount of blood (the size of 6–7 *gris* in Eretz Yisrael, or the size of half of a dollar bill in the United States) is *temei'ah mid'Oraisa* even when she is certain that she did not experience a *hargashah*.[45] See Basic Overview, How a Woman Becomes a Niddah, Headline "Niddah D'Oraisa", page 10.

Blood Discovered After Using the Restroom

- There are three primary opinions regarding the scenario of a woman who discovers blood after using the restroom, under circumstances in which the halachah is not concerned for a *hargashah*:

1. Rav Yosef Shalom Elyashiv says it is *vadai migufah* (and he is concerned for a *hargashah* up to a minute after she finished urinating) so she is *temei'ah mid'Oraisa*. According to this opinion it makes no difference what color the tissues are, because leniencies of *kesamim* are anyway not relevant.
2. Rav Nissim Karelitz and others say the following:

- If *oso makom* was the only place where the woman wiped,[46] the blood is considered *vadai migufah*, but the halachah is, as cited in the *Gilyon Maharshah*, that all leniencies of

44. If a woman discovers blood on her underwear that was tight or thin to the point that it entered bodily crevices, all leniencies of *kesamim* still apply.

45. In general, it may be reasonably assumed that a woman who experiences this amount of bleeding has gotten her period, and is not just experiencing heavy staining. Practically speaking, a lot is dependent on the *Rav* to whom the *she'eilah* is brought. Often one can be lenient even regarding stains larger than the *shiur* of 6–7 *gris* when he concludes that this was not her period, just heavy staining.

46. Rav Nissim Karelitz (*Chut Shani* 191:1:4) understands the *din* of *vadai migufah* as stated in the *Gilyon Maharsha*, that the leniencies of *kesamim* are applied, but says *vadai migufah* includes *bein hasfasayim*. The *Sidrei Taharah* (*siman kattan* 57) and *Pleissi* (183:1) also cite opinions that extend the *din* of *vadai migufah* to include *bein hasfasayim*, while others extend *vadai migufah* even further than that, as long as they undoubtly presume the blood came from the woman. Rav Nissim Karelitz further holds (*Chut Shani* 190:10:5) the *din* of an item that is not susceptible to *tumah* with regard to *kesamim* as stated in the *Sidrei Taharah* excludes an item that is not susceptible to *tumah* but is held by a person who is susceptible to *tumah*. According to Rav Nissim Karelitz, if a woman wipes only *oso makom* she loses the leniency of an item that is not susceptible to *tumah* as well as

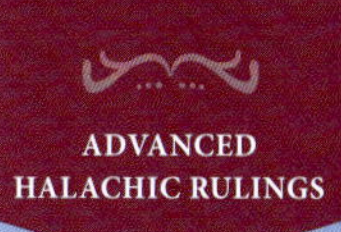

kesamim besides for that of the size of a *gris* are applied. According to this opinion, it makes a difference whether or not toilet paper is considered to be susceptible to *tumah*, the toilet paper's color, and whether or not pastel is considered "colored," and the answers to these questions determine the *psak*.

- If she also wiped other areas besides *oso makom*, all the leniencies of *kesamim* are applied, including that of the *gris*. However, she loses the leniency of something that is not susceptible to *tumah*, because the fact that she wiped herself shows us that the blood originated from her body, and she is holding the toilet paper in her hand, which is susceptible to *tumah*.[47]

3. Rav Yitzchak Berkovits and others (*She'arim HaMetzuyanim B'Halachah*) say the blood is not considered *vadai migufah* unless she only wiped the vaginal opening, which practically never happens because she is wiping away urine from the urethra (so the case is almost never one dealing with *vadai migufah*), so all leniencies of *kesamim*, including that of the *gris*, would be applied. According to this opinion, it also makes a difference whether or not toilet paper is considered to be susceptible to *tumah*, the toilet paper's color, and whether or not pastel is considered "colored."

› Practically speaking, when a woman wipes herself after using the restroom and discovers blood, all leniencies of *kesamim* apply even though we may reasonably assume that it came from her, unless we think the sensation of urination masked her *hargashah* because the blood was discovered *osyom*.

› Practically speaking, blood found in a cup used for a urine sample is generally *metamei*, as it is generally discovered *osyom*.

---

the leniency of the *gris*. Some *Poskim* in Eretz Yisroel opine like Rav Nissim Karelitz on one or both of these *psakim*.

47. Practically speaking, Rav Yitzchak Berkovits does not agree with this ruling at all. He holds the *kesem* is always viewed on whatever it was found. Even when we know that it came from the woman's body, we still apply all the leniencies of *kesamim*, including that of something that is not susceptible to *tumah*, when applicable. We are also not stringent like the opinion of the Sidrei Taharah to exclude an item that is not susceptible to *tumah* but is held by someone who is susceptible.

- Rav Moshe Feinstein says that in order to be concerned about a *hargashah* after urinating, the woman must discover the blood before the drops finish falling to be considered *osyom*.[48]
- If the blood was not found *osyom*, the laws of *kesamim* will be applied, even though it seems to have originated *migufah*. We will even apply the leniency of *teliyah* whenever there is a chance that the blood came from an external source.[49]

Tampons

- The laws of a *re'iyah* apply to blood that is discovered on a tampon, because it is thick enough to mask a *hargashah*. This halachah even applies to smaller or narrower tampons.

Note: For this reason, a woman who is staining is advised to use a pad, not a tampon.

Kesamim

- *Rashi* says the edict of *kesamim* was instituted because the woman may have had a *hargashah* and is *temei'ah mid'Oraisa*.[50] *Chazal* were thus *metamei* blood when it is experienced without a *hargashah*, as a woman may have felt a *hargashah* without being aware of it.
- *Tosafos* says *kesamim* are a "protective fence" for the Torah prohibition of niddah.[51] A woman would therefore be *temei'ah mid'Rabbanan* even if she certainly did not have a *hargashah*, as the blood is niddah blood even if there was no *hargashah*.
- The *Sefer HaEshkol* says *Chazal* only instituted the edict of *kesamim* in regard to the laws of *taharos*, but not to make a

---

48. Rav Yitzchak Berkovits says that whenever a *she'eilah* after using the restroom arises, a *Rav* should assume the woman waited for the drops to finish falling and should not question her as to whether or not she waited. We can rely on the fact that in general women wait and do not rush off the toilet.

49. Some examples of external sources are hemorrhoids, a urinary tract infection, a bladder infection, scratches, cuts, pimples, and bleeding from the rectum. Once blood is not considered to be *vadai migufah*, we assume that it may have come from anywhere, and apply all the leniencies of *kesamim*.

50. *Niddah* 58:71, "*Mid'Rabbanan*."

51. Ibid., "*Modeh Shmuel SheHi Temei'ah Mid'Rabbanan*."

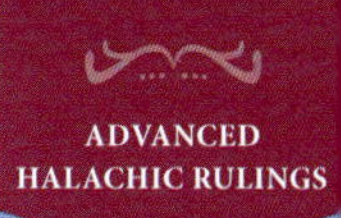

woman *temei'ah* to her husband. His proof is that *kesamim* are not mentioned in the *Rif.*

- Practically speaking, the halachah is like the position of Tosafos, and one may not rely on *Rashi* or the *Sefer HaEshkol* even in extremely extenuating circumstances.[52]

Gris

- The *Chasam Sofer* says *Chazal* extended the law of *kesamim* to include not only *tumah* and *taharah*, but also to make a woman forbidden to her husband. However, when the *kesem* is less than a *gris*, it is not included in this extension, as this was the amount of blood produced by a commonly found bug called a *macholes.*
- Although the *macholes* does not exist nowadays, the halachah is almost never *metamei* a *kesem* smaller than a *gris*[53] unless the case is one where we are concerned about a *hargashah*, which changes it from a *kesem* to a *re'iyah d'Oraisa*, or if the *kesem* is *vadai migufah* (see above).
- A *kesem* must be larger than a *gris* in order for it to be *tamei*. A *kesem* up to and including the size of a *gris* is *tahor.*
- Rav Moshe Feinstein says a *gris* is the size of a penny.
- Many *Poskim* in Eretz Yisrael say a *gris* is the size of a one-shekel coin.[54]

Shaas Metzias HaKesem

- *The Shulchan Aruch HaRav (siman 190)* says a *kesem* is viewed in the state in which it is found - *shaas metzias hakesem.* This

52. Don't forget, a woman who had a *re'iyah* or a *hargashah* is *temei'ah mid'Oraisa* and loses all leniencies of *kesamim*. It is up to the *Rav* to determine that this is only a *kesem* and that there is no need to be concerned about a *hargashah* or a *re'iyah.*

53. The *Poskim* discuss whether there is a place to be stringent if someone finds a *kesem* that is less than the size of a *gris*. Rav Shmuel HaLevi Wosner and others say that if someone finds a *kesem* that is less than the size of a *gris*, she should never be stringent, nor should a man be stringent for his wife, because they have obligations towards each other which should not be negated because of a stringency that is explicitly against the directive of *Chazal.*

54. Realistically, a shekel is the size of a penny without the rim. Many *Poskim* in Eretz Yisrael use an old telephone coin called an *asimon* to measure a *gris.*

means we view the *kesem* in the state in which the woman found the stain, not in the state it is in when it reaches the Rav.

- If a woman discovered a *kesem* on colored underwear and swiped it with a bedikah cloth to determine the color, we view the *bedikah* cloth, but give the ruling as though this blood is on the colored underwear, because that is *shaas metzias hakesem.*[55]
- If a *kesem* is thick, one does not spread it out to see if it is a *gris.* Rather, one views it as it comes.[56]
- If a woman wipes her body with something that is not susceptible to *tumah* (for example, toilet paper, according to Rav Moshe Feinstein) and discovers blood, we view the blood on what it was "found", not as though it was found on her body (which is susceptible to *tumah*), even though we know the blood originated from her body, since shaas metzias hakesem was on an item that is not susceptible to *tumah.*

Calculating the Gris

- The *Rambam* says the leniency of the *gris* does not apply to a *kesem* that is found on the woman's skin, and it is *tamei* even if it is smaller than a *gris.*
- Tosafos disagree, saying that a *kesem* found on the woman's skin must also be at least a *gris* in order to be *tamei*, but two separate *kesamim* are combined toward this *gris.*
- Practically speaking, the halachah is not stringent like the Rambam, but is stringent like Tosafos.[57]
- A *kesem* found on skin should be brought to a *Rav* by placing clear tape over the blood and bringing the tape. This way the *Rav* can see the size as well as the color.

---

55. This applies even if the underwear is black (as opposed to green or blue), in which case we may mistakenly say that she did not actually "discover" the *kesem* until she swiped it, because the depth of the color masks the color completely.

56. Rav Yosef Shalom Elyashiv; *Aruch HaShulchan*; see *Pischei Teshuvah* 190:9.

57. *Toras HaShelamim* 190:9; *Bach*, ibid.; *Chochmas Adam*; Rav Moshe Feinstein; Rav Yosef Shalom Elyashiv; Rav Nissim Karelitz; *Shulchan Aruch* 190:8, "*Yesh Omrim.*"

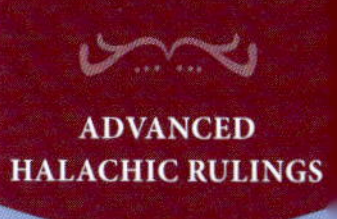

- If a *kesem* went through clothing, we view each layer independently and do not add all the stains up toward a *gris*.[58]

- If a *kesem* is found on a folded cloth, and when the cloth is viewed while folded, one sees a *gris*, but when the cloth is straightened out the *gris* gets divided and each new *kesem* is smaller than a *gris*, the *kesamim* are not combined to form a *gris*. The exception is when there is a *tiny* fold in the cloth that separates the parts of the *gris*. In such a case, the halachah is stringent, because *shaas metzias hakesem* was when the *gris* was fully intact.[59]

- The *Pischei Teshuvah* says if one *kesem* is found partially on a white background and partially on colored clothing, the *Rav* should combine the parts that are on the white background and discount the part on the colored background, even if the colored area splits the *kesem* in two.[60]

- If two *kesamim* are found on clothing and each is smaller than a *gris*, they are not combined to form a *gris*, even if they are very close to each other. If there is a *tahor* color that surrounds the two *kesamim*, however, they are joined together to become a *gris*, since we can determine that the *kesem* was only one stain[61] when it emerged from the woman.[62]

- If a *kesem* is partially *tamei* and partially *tahor*, we only add the *tamei* parts toward the *gris*, even if the *tamei* parts of the stain are not touching one another, as long as they are connected through the *tahor* colors.

- The size of a *gris* applies even to a *kesem* of black blood.[63]

---

58. Rav Yosef Shalom Elyashiv; Rav Nissim Karelitz.

59. Rav Yosef Shalom Elyashiv is stringent in all such cases and says to view the *kesem* as it comes, even though the *kesem* covers the folds. Rav Nissim Karelitz is lenient if a *kesem* traverses folds in a cloth, unless the folds are sewn together. See *Pischei Teshuvah* 190:16.

60. *Sidrei Taharah* 190:21; Rav Yosef Shalom Elyashiv.

61. The reason for this ruling is we assume the *kesamim* arrived at the same time if they are part of the same stain. If the *Rav* determines that the two *kesamim* left her body at two separate times, he may be *metaher*. A classic case in which a *Rav* can be *metaher* is if she saw a stain that is less than a *gris* on her underwear and later sees a second stain that is connected with a *tahor* color to the first stain.

62. *Hagahos Rav Akiva Eiger* 190:10; Rav Yosef Shalom Elyashiv; Rav Nissim Karelitz.

63. *Aruch HaShulchan*; Rav Moshe Feinstein. See *Pischei Teshuvah* 190:12.

- If a *bodekes* sees a cut, but also sees that the uterus is bleeding, we will not say that half the *gris* came from the cut and half from the uterus. Rather, the woman is *temei'ah*.[64]

Kesamim on Colored Clothing

- The Gemara in *Niddah* says *Chazal* did not include in the edict of *kesamim* stains that are discovered on colored clothing.[65]
- Rashi says the reason for this leniency is because the stain's color is not discernible on colored clothing.[66]
- The *Rambam* says *Chazal* did not include stains discovered on colored clothing in the edict even if the color is discernible. The only *kesem* that is *tamei* is one that is found on white clothing.[67]
- Rav Yosef Shalom Elyashiv rules like Rashi, that if a *kesem* is found on colored clothing but the blood is recognizable, it is *tamei* if the clothing is susceptible to *tumah* and the blood stain is larger than a *gris*. Pastel colors are not dark enough to mask the color of blood,[68] so *kesamim* found on such colors are *temei'im*.[69]

---

64. There are many reasons for this ruling. One is that the object inserted by the *bodekes* is almost certainly masking a *hargashah* if she is able to see the cervix. We also know this blood is *vadai migufah*, in which case all the leniencies of *kesamim* apply besides for that of the *gris*.

65. 61:72, "*Shittas Rebbi Nassan Bar Yosef*."

66. Ibid, "*Lehakel*."

67. *Hilchos Issurei Biah* 9:7.

68. It is said that Rav Yosef Shalom Elyashiv recommends that women wear dark green (not pastel) underwear because it distorts the color, but one can still see if she had a *re'iyah*. He says not to wear black or deep red underwear when she is *tehorah* because she can get her period and not realize it, because the color is completely distorted (Rav Nissim Karelitz).

69. Rav Nissim Karelitz. He is also stringent in the event that the *kesem* is floating on top of colored clothing in a manner in which it can be easily viewed; in this case, the leniency of a *kesem* on colored clothing does not apply and it must be dealt with as a *kesem*. Rav Yitzchak Berkovits is not stringent in such a case.

A case once arose of a pair of underwear that was white on one side and had polka dots the other. Rav Berkovits said he would be lenient about a *kesem* that was found on the white side, directly opposite the polka dots, and whatever is opposite the dots will not be counted toward the *gris*, being that the polka dots are visible through the cloth. He said this leniency only when the cloth was single-ply (the colored and white were the same cloth), not on two-ply underwear, where one full cloth is white, as is often the case. In *Chut Shani* 190:10:13:4, Rav Nissim Karelitz is stringent in such a case. In *Shu"t B'Tzeil HaChochmah* it says that in the above case, if the *kesem* originally was on the side of the

- Rav Moshe Feinstein rules like the Rambam, that the background is considered colored as long as is not "white," and any *kesem* found is *tahor*. Pastel colors are considered colored in this regard.
- Practically speaking, the custom is to be lenient like Rav Moshe Feinstein.
- This leniency only applies to clothing, not to people. A *kesem* found on a dark-skinned woman may be *tamei*.[70]
- Rav Nissim Karelitz says this leniency applies to colored vessels (which are susceptible to *tumah*) as well as to clothing.

Toilets and Bathtubs

- Rav Yosef Shalom Elyashiv says *Chazal* instituted that *kesamim* are *temei'im* when they are found on anything that is susceptible to *tumas nega'im* in the Old City of Yerushalayim.[71] Outside the Old City and outside of Eretz Yisrael, he is lenient about anything that is attached to the ground. This means anything attached to the ground in the Old City, including toilets, toilet seats, and bathtubs, would be considered susceptible to *tumah* in regard to *kesamim*.
- The custom is not to be stringent and follow this opinion, so the leniencies of *kesamim* are applied to anything found on a bathtub, toilet, or toilet seat (even if it is currently not attached) and it is *tahor*, unless the case is one in which the halachah is concerned about a *hargashah*.
- If a woman discovers blood in the toilet and did not look in the toilet beforehand, we presume the toilet is an *eid she'eino baduk* and the relevant halachos apply, even if the person before her flushed. See below for the laws of *eid she'eino baduk*.

---

cloth that is colored and then went to the side that is white, she is *tehorah*, because the *kesem* landed on the colored cloth. Rav Nissim Karelitz is stringent in that case as well because he says *shaas metzias hakesem* was on the white cloth. Again, Rav Berkovits is lenient in all such cases.

70. 610. *Minchas Yitzchak*.

71. The *Chavas Daas* says the edict of *kesamim* was established because *Chazal*, in the times of *tumah* and *taharah*, found it difficult that the item on which the *kesem* was found was *tamei* yet the woman from whom it came was *tehorah*. Therefore, they only instituted the edict of *kesamim* on items that are susceptible to *tumah*. There is a disagreement whether or not this also includes things that are susceptible to *tumas nega'im*.

Toilet Paper

- There are three basic opinions regarding a *kesem* found on toilet paper:

  1. Rav Moshe Feinstein holds that *paper* is susceptible to *tumah*, but *toilet paper* is disposable and therefore not susceptible to *tumah*. A *kesem* found on toilet paper is *tahor* even if the *kesem* is larger than a *gris* (as long as there is no suspected *hargashah* or *re'iyah*).[72]
  2. Rav Shmuel HaLevi Wosner and Rav Nissim Karelitz follow the Sidrei Taharah, who says toilet paper is not susceptible to *tumah* (like Rav Moshe Feinstein), but the woman holding it is, and therefore the laws of *kesamim* are applied when blood is discovered on toilet paper.
  3. Rav Yosef Shalom Elyashiv holds that toilet paper is susceptible to *tumah*, so the laws of *kesamim* apply to it.[73] He says we are not concerned about the *Sidrei Taharah* quoted above, in any case.

- Some quote Rav Yosef Shalom Elyashiv as saying that blood found on toilet paper has the status of a *re'iyah* because he is stringent like the Sidrei Taharah,[74] who says when we know the blood is *vadai migufah* it is considered a *re'iyah*, so the *dinim* of *niddah d'Oraisa* apply.[75]

---

72. Rav Reuven Feinstein told me that baby wipes are generally considered not susceptible to *tumah*, as they are classifiably *peshutei kli eitz* (simple items that are not vessels). I asked if there were any types of baby wipes that we would be more stringent about, and he said the only one that he can think of is a baby wipe that is totally made from cloth, without any synthetic materials. I asked if the *din* applies because wipes are disposable, and he said, "No, it is because they are *peshutei kli eitz*."

73. The *Sefer Mishnas HaShulchan* says that Rav Yosef Shalom Elyashiv holds toilet paper is susceptible to *tumah*, but he also holds that if a woman wipes with something that is not susceptible to *tumah*, she is still *temei'ah* because we view the *kesem* as it was found on her body. Practically speaking, the accepted halachah is not like these rulings, but there are many reasons why Rav Yosef Shalom Elyashiv is stringent about blood found on toilet paper: it is on something that is susceptible to *tumah*, it is *vadai migufah*, it is a *kesem* on her body since the *kesem* originated on her body, or because we will be concerned about a *hargashah* as the blood is generally found within the *shiur osyom* after using the restroom.

74. To avoid confusion: Rav Yosef Shalom Elyashiv is stringent like the Sidrei Taharah that blood that is *vadai migufah* is *tamei d'Oraisa* even if it is only a drop of blood, like a *re'iyah*. He is *not* stringent like the Sidrei Taharah regarding an item that is not susceptible to *tumah* that is held by someone who is susceptible to *tumah*.

75. According to this opinion, in such a situation it would take a *Rav* to determine if the blood is actually *vadai migufah* or not. See "*Vadai MiGufah*" above. Yet other opinions say we must be concerned about a *hargashah* when blood is found after using the restroom,

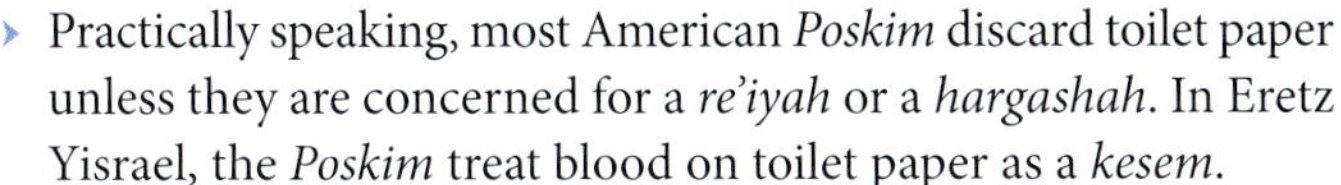

- Practically speaking, most American *Poskim* discard toilet paper unless they are concerned for a *re'iyah* or a *hargashah*. In Eretz Yisrael, the *Poskim* treat blood on toilet paper as a *kesem*.
- Practically speaking, we hold that toilet paper is not susceptible to *tumah*. However, Rav Yitzchak Berkovits does check toilet paper and treats blood on it as a *kesem*, because he holds that when one lives in Eretz Yisrael they should take on its *Rabbanim*'s rulings.
- Women should be taught never to look in the toilet[76] or at the toilet paper.[77]

Toilet Water

- There is a disagreement whether or not filthy water is susceptible to *tumah*.[78]
- Rav Yaacov Blau and other *Poskim* are lenient in regard to toilet water, so according to them, any *kesem* found in toilet water can be flushed.
- Practically speaking, Rav Yitzchak Berkovits holds we are concerned for the opinion that toilet water is susceptible to *tumah*, even if there is urine in the water, and a *kesem* found in the water should be brought to a *Rav*.[79] If there is solid human waste in the water, the water is considered *mayim seruchim* (dirtied water) and is not susceptible to *tumah*.
- If the water was flushed or dyed, or if the woman cannot get the blood onto a cloth, the halachah is to be lenient.

---

so the status of the toilet paper becomes irrelevant (if it was used after the restroom), and they do not allow any leniencies of *kesamim*.

76. If a woman has a hard time not looking, she should be taught to go to the bathroom with the lights off.

77. Rav Shmuel HaLevi Wosner; Rav Nissim Karelitz.

78. The *Pischei Teshuvos* (190:10) brings that most *Poskim*, including the Maharsham, the Minchas Yitzchak, and Pardes Simchah are lenient regarding toilet water. See *Pischei Teshuvos* 191:7 for a detailed synopsis of the topic of toilet water.

79. Rav Yosef Shalom Elyashiv; Rav Nissim Karelitz.

Pads

There are four opinions regarding how to view *kesamim* on pads:

1. Rav Moshe Feinstein says pads are not susceptible to *tumah*, so all *kesamim* on pads are *tehorim*, whether or not the pad is attached to the underwear, unless there was a suspected *hargashah* or *re'iyah*.[80]
2. Rav Yosef Shalom Elyashiv holds that pads are nullified to the underwear upon which they are stuck, and the laws of *kesamim* apply. If the pad is not attached to the underwear, Rav Yosef Shalom Elyashiv agrees that it is not susceptible to *tumah*.
3. Some *Poskim* hold that pads are susceptible to *tumah* whether or not they are attached to underwear.[81]
4. The *Sidrei Taharah* says that even if pads are not susceptible to *tumah*, a pad that rests on underwear which is susceptible to *tumah* must be dealt with as something that is susceptible to *tumah*,[82] even if it is not attached to the underwear.[83]

- *Poskim* in Eretz Yisrael tell women who have staining issues not to attach the pads (as per Rav Yosef Shalom Elyashiv's opinion). If the pad was attached when a woman found a *kesem*, they treat it as a *kesem*. Otherwise they discard it.[84]
- In the United States, the *Poskim* are generally lenient in regard to a *kesem* found on a pad. They are only *metamei* when the pad contains an amount of blood that indicates that the woman is having a *re'iyah*.
- Practically speaking, pads are not susceptible to *tumah*. Rav Yitzchak Berkovits does check pads, because he believes that someone living in Eretz Yisrael should follow the opinions of the *Poskim* of Eretz Yisrael.

---

80. Rav Shlomo Zalman Auerbach in *Otzros HaTaharah*.

81. See *Pischei Teshuvos, siman* 10, *he'aros* 138–139.

82. It is possible that if the woman is wearing synthetic underwear with a pad that is not attached, some opinions will be stringent if she finds a *kesem*, because the pad is susceptible o *tumah*. The Sidrei Taharah would be lenient because the underwear in such a case is not susceptible to *tumah*.

83. Rav Nissim Karelitz.

84. *Poskim* in Eretz Yisrael are lenient, as opposed to the Sidrei Taharah, regarding pads, but are stringent and follow his position regarding toilet paper, because according to them, pads have a lesser status of being susceptible to *tumah* than toilet paper.

Nylon and Synthetic Clothing

- Rav Moshe Feinstein says nylon and synthetic clothing is made from earth and is therefore not susceptible to *tumah*, even if it is a full item of clothing. (The Chazon Ish, Rav Yosef Shalom Elyashiv, Rav Shmuel HaLevi Wosner, and Rav Nissim Karelitz agree.)
- The Minchas Yitzchak says nylon clothing is susceptible to *tumah*. (Rav Shlomo Zalman Auerbach followed this ruling.)
- Practically speaking, the halachah is lenient like the Chazon Ish, Rav Moshe Feinstein, Rav Yosef Shalom Elyashiv, and Rav Shmuel HaLevi Wosner.[85]

Wearing Colored Clothing and Towels

- When a woman is not in *shivah nekiyim*, she should avoid wearing white underwear or any garment that may render her *temei'ah* unnecessarily if a blood stain would be found on it. Similarly, she should use colored bedding.
- The most common issues with *kesamim* are when they are found on nightgowns and towels, and therefore women should be careful to use colored towels and nightgowns.

Sleeping on White Sheets during Shivah Nekiyim

- During *shivah nekiyim*, many people in Eretz Yisrael follow a stringency (based on the custom brought in the *Shulchan Aruch*) to sleep on white sheets, even if the woman is sleeping in white underwear.
- In the United States most women are not taught to specifically sleep on white sheets, unless the woman is not sleeping in underwear.

85. A classic *she'eilah* is about synthetic underwear, which is not susceptible to *tumah* according to this ruling.

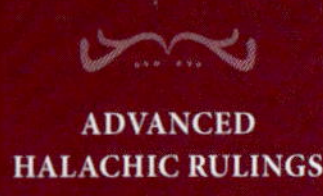

ADVANCED HALACHIC RULINGS

Tights

- Tights generally have a white stripe made from cotton, which is susceptible to *tumah*. Therefore, the laws of *kesamim* apply, especially because this stripe is directly near *oso makom*[86]. However, the nylon section is not susceptible to *tumah*, so if the *kesem* is found on that section, it is *tahor*.[87]

Attributing the Kesem to a Different Source

- The Gemara says one may attribute a *kesem* to something when the "source" of the staining resembles the *kesem* to a certain degree. However, if it is clear from the circumstances that the source one is trying to attribute the *kesem* to did not actually create the *kesem*, this is not a valid *teliyah*. For example, one cannot attribute a *kesem* to horseradish that the woman ate when the *kesem* is clearly blood. However, if this source is a possibility, the *teliyah* is valid.[88]

- Rav Shmuel HaLevi Wosner says that in the case of a valid *teliyah*, which also contains the possibility that the *teliyah* is false — for example, the *Rav* wants to attribute the *kesem* to paint, and the *kesem* does look like paint to a degree, but there is a chance that the *kesem* is really blood — the woman is not required to send the *kesem* to a laboratory to determine if it is paint. The halachah allows one to attribute to a legitimate

---

86. Some *poskim* are lenient regarding a *kessem* found on tights, for one of the following reasons: the cotton is part of the tights is part of the larger synthetic article of clothing and therefore not mekabel tumah; if the white stripe is not made out of cotton it is not mekabel tumah; if the white stripe is only white on one side, but colored on the second side (single ply) they consider it "colored clothing" and applicable leniencies apply; or, if the blood soaked through colored underwear the kessem is treated as though it was found on the colored underwear and those leniencies apply.

Practically, Rav Berkovits is lenient when the white strip is not made out of cotton, or if it is made out of cotton but is one-ply, two color cotton, or if she was wearing the underwear for a long period of time and it can be assessed that the blood sat on colored underwear and only later soaked through. He is not lenient if the blood soaked straight through colored underwear onto the tights.

87. Rav Shmuel HaLevi Wosner says when the majority of an article of clothing is nylon, even if there is a section that is susceptible to *tumah*, all *kesamim* found on such an item are *tehorim*, no matter where the *kesem* is found. Rav Yitzchak Berkovits is stringent in regard to such an article of clothing if the *kesem* is found on the section that is susceptible to *tumah*.

88. Rav Shmuel HaLevi Wosner; Rav Nissim Karelitz.

possible source, and there is not even a need to compare the two colors to each other to determine whether the *teliyah* is accurate.[89]

- If a woman wearing white underwear finds a *kesem* on something outside the underwear (such as on her white skirt) and sees that the underwear are clean, if she knows that the underwear remained tightly on her the whole time (for example, she did not go to the bathroom) then she remains *tehorah*, because the stain clearly came from an outside source, even if she does not have any specific *teliyah*.[90]

- Rav Shmuel HaLevi Wosner says if a woman finds a *kesem* on the inside of her underwear (which is not soaked through to the outside), she cannot attribute it to an external source, since the *kesem* is clearly from the inside and did not originate from an exterior source.

- A *kesem* found on tights by a woman who is wearing clean underwear is *tahor,* as stated above. This is because the blood could not have possibly come from her body. If the underwear is not clean, the *kesem* found on the tights will make her *temei'ah* if there is no *teliyah*. This is relevant if she is wearing colored underwear and white tights. The *kesem* on the underwear is *tahor* because the underwear is a colored garment, but the *kesem* on the tights is *tamei*, as it is probable that the blood came from her body.

- Rav Shmuel HaLevi Wosner says a *Rav* cannot attribute if he can tell by sight that the *teliyah* is false.

- Rav Nissim Karelitz says a woman who is dealing with *kesamim* (such as working in a blood laboratory) has a legitimate *teliyah* if she later finds a *kesem* on herself. This holds true even if she was careful not to get blood on herself, because we assume that she simply was not careful enough while dealing with the *kesamim*.

- Rav Nissim Karelitz says if a woman notices blood in a toilet that she did not check before she sat down, and there are girls in the house who menstruate, the woman can attribute the blood to them. This is the same as the *din* we find in the *Shulchan Aruch* that if a woman has daughters who sit on their mother's bed,

89. Rav Nissim Karelitz.

90. *Sidrei Taharah* 190:45; Rav Shmuel HaLevi Wosner.

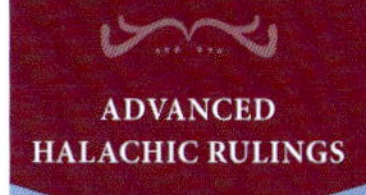

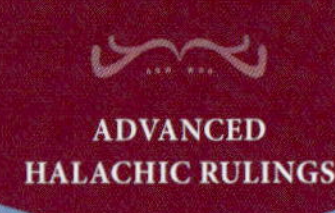

she can attribute *kesamim* found on the bed to her daughters (assuming the blood could have reached the bed from one of her daughters).

- A *Rav* can attribute a *kesem* to a chronic condition that is known to cause bleeding.[91]

Common Teliyos

- A woman who has children around the house — or a Kindergarten teacher — is considered like someone who went through a *shuk shel tabachim* (marketplace of butchers), and can attribute most *kesamim* discovered on clothing to the children.
- Rav Nissim Karelitz says a woman who works in an environment where it is common to draw blood from patients — for example a doctor, nurse, or lab technician — may attribute her *kesamim* to the work environment.[92]
- A woman who has chronic nosebleeds can attribute most *kesamim* to nosebleeds if the blood could have dripped to the location where the *kesem* was found.
- A woman who has a condition that commonly causes bleeding,[93] such as hemorrhoids, a urinary tract infection, a bladder infection, scratches, cuts, pimples, or bleeding from the rectum, can attribute most *kesamim* to that condition.[94]

---

91. Examples include: a woman who consistently stains after performing exercises and a *bodekes* determines that the cervix is causing abrasions because of the exercise, any medical condition that is known to cause non-uterine bleeding, and a pap smear.

92. Obviously the *teliyah* must make sense, even in such situations. If a woman finds a *kesem* on white underwear during *shivah nekiyim* and always works wearing clothing plus a lab coat, which are all free of *kesamim*, she would not have a legitimate *teliyah*. See *Pischei Teshuvah* 190:26 in the name of the *Sidrei Taharah* that a *teliyah* in reference to clothing must makes sense regarding the layout of the clothing and the possibility of the *kesem* to reach the location on the clothing from the place of *teliyah*.

93. This stipulation must be met in order to have a valid *teliyah*. A woman who has a urinary tract infection that is painful but does not cause bleeding does not have a valid *teliyah*. In every case the *Rav* must determine that the *teliyah* makes sense to the degree that this blood could have originated at the place of the *teliyah* and reached the place where the blood was discovered. The *Rav* must take into account how much blood the *teliyah* produces compared to how much blood was discovered.

94. Rav Yosef Shalom Elyashiv; Rav Shmuel HaLevi Wosner; Rav Nissim Karelitz.

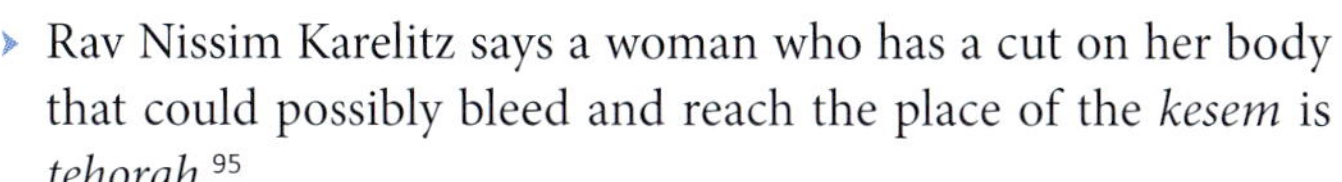

- Rav Nissim Karelitz says a woman who has a cut on her body that could possibly bleed and reach the place of the *kesem* is *tehorah*.[95]

- Rav Nissim Karelitz says when a woman has a cut that cannot reach the place of the *kesem*, but she touched the cut and knows she had blood on her hand, she may attribute the stain to the cut.[96]

- Rav Nissim Karelitz says when the woman is not sure about whether she touched the cut, or when she knows she touched a cut that can possibly cause bleeding, but is not sure that blood got on her hand before touching the place the *kesem* was found, she cannot attribute the stain to the cut. The exception to this is when she touched a cut that was bleeding at the time she touched it. In this case, she may attribute the blood to it even if she later does not see blood on her hand, since it is common for blood to transfer to a hand.

- Rav Nissim Karelitz says if a woman shaves with a sharp razor and subsequently discovers a *kesem* she may attribute the *kesem* to the razor,[97] because it is very common for shaving to cause small cuts which produce large amounts of blood.

When the Size or Color Cannot Be Determined or the Kesem Was Lost

- If it cannot be determined whether a *kesem* was larger or smaller than a *gris*, or if it cannot be determined whether the color of the *kesem* was *tamei* or *tahor*, such as when the *kesem* was

95. In other words, if a woman had a cut that healed, but it could bleed if it is pressed, she has a valid *teliyah* (*Lechem V'Simlah, siman kattan* 14; *Pischei Teshuvah* 190:25 in the name of the *Sidrei Taharah*, based on the Mishnah in *Niddah* 58:72).

96. Although the general rule is that we do not attribute *tumah* from one location to another, as the Gemara says in *Niddah* 58a, *Tosafos* ("*U'Mi Mechazkinan*") says in the event that a woman touched an area of blood with her hand which normally could not stain the place where the blood was actually discovered, this no longer falls under the category of "from one location to another," since blood was known to be on her hand.

97. This scenario is referring to a case in which the woman shaved an area that leads us to believe that the *kesem* may have come from the shaving. If a woman shaved her underarms with a razor and finds a *kesem* on her thigh, she must determine that the *kesem* could have reached her thigh from her underarm. If she touched her underarm after shaving and then touched her thigh and her hand had some blood on it, or if the underarm was bleeding when she touched it, even if she does not know that there was any blood on her hand, she has a *teliyah* (based on Rav Nissim Karelitz).

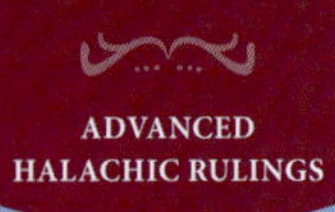

lost after being discovered, the woman remains *tehorah*. This is because a *kesem* is *tamei mid'Rabbanan*, and in the case of a *safeik d'Rabbanan* we rule leniently.[98]

- If a woman sees blood go down the drain while she is in the shower and is not sure of the color or size, she remains *tehorah*.
- A *Rav* may not be lenient when he is unsure whether or not the *kesem* is the size of a *gris*, or whether the color is *tamei*. The reason for this is because he is not dealing with a *safeik d'Rabbanan*, but with a lack of knowledge.[99] As stated, if the determination of the size cannot be made because the *kesem* is lost or because of another impossible situation, the halachah is to be lenient. When the determination cannot be made because of lack of skill on the part of the *Rav*, he cannot be lenient.
- A practical tip that may be used when it is difficult to determine whether or not a *kesem* is the size of a *gris*: imprint a penny into silly putty and maneuver that area to conform to the *kesem*.

Eid SheEino Baduk (An Unchecked Bedikah Cloth)

- In general, any blood wthat is found on a *bedikah* cloth is *tamei*, so long as it is visible to the naked eye.
- The *Shulchan Aruch* says blood discovered on an *eid she'eino baduk* may be attributed to a *macholes*, so the woman remains *tehorah* when the blood is smaller than a *gris*. The *Taz* explains that the reason for this is because the laws of *niddah d'Rabbanan* are applied to an *eid she'eino baduk*.
- The *Chasam Sofer* says one may only attribute the stain to a present-day insect,[100] and not to the *macholes* of *Chazal*, which allows up to a *gris*.

---

98. Rav Akiva Eiger 190:46; *Chochmas Adam*; Rav Yosef Shalom Elyashiv; Rav Nissim Karelitz.

99. *Teshuvos Imrei Yosher* §88; *Mishmeres HaTaharah* 3:9; Rav Shmuel HaLevi Wosner. Rav Wosner is stringent (based on the *Maharil*) when a woman had a *kesem* but was unable to determine whether it added up to a *gris* — even if the *kesem* is subsequently lost — because he says that there was the opportunity to determine the status of the *kesem*, so the question is one of a lack of knowledge, even when the *kesem* later gets lost. Rav Yitzchak Berkovits agrees with most other *Poskim*, who say that when the *kesem* is present, this is considered a lack of knowledge and one must be stringent. However, if the *kesem* is lost, one may be lenient.

100. The *Chasam Sofer* says a *kesem* nowadays is ruled *tahor* as long as it is smaller than a *gris*, even though a *macholes* today does not produce blood the size of a *gris*. The

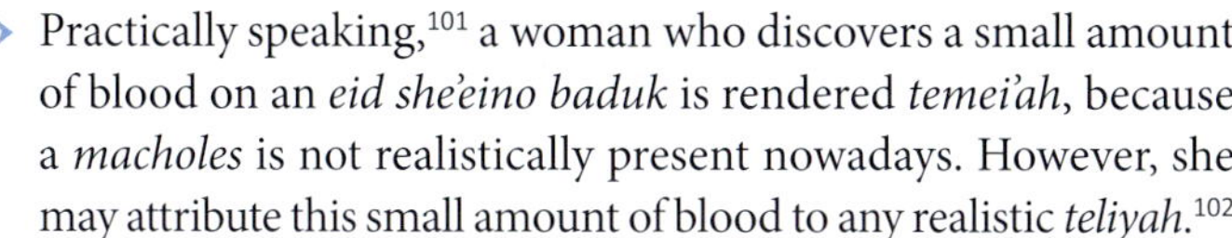

- Practically speaking,[101] a woman who discovers a small amount of blood on an *eid she'eino baduk* is rendered *temei'ah*, because a *macholes* is not realistically present nowadays. However, she may attribute this small amount of blood to any realistic *teliyah*.[102]

- Since an *eid she'eino baduk* is only *tamei mid'Rabbanan*, this *bedikah* will not create a future *vest* even if it was performed on a *vest*,[103] just like all other *kesamim*[104] which do not create *vestos*.[105]

- When a woman does a *bedikah* with an *eid she'eino baduk*, the *Rav* may be lenient and allow her to remain *tehorah* if she can produce a valid *teliyah*.[106]

- Whenever the *dinim* of an *eid she'eino baduk* are applied to something other than an *eid bedikah*, such as a toilet, the *Rav* may be *metaher* as much blood as is common to find in such a situation.[107]

---

reason for this is that *Chazal*, who instituted the edict of *kesamim*, included in this edict the leniency of the *gris*, and that applies nowadays as well. However, in the case of an *eid she'eino baduk*, which is dealing with an actual *teliyah*, one can only attribute the blood to a *macholes* that exists and could possibly have created the *kesem*.

101. Explained by Rav Mati Friedman.

102. Rav Nissim Karelitz.

103. See Basic Overview, How a Woman Becomes a Niddah, Headline "Leniency 5: Even When Problematic, Blood Discharged as a Kessem Does Not Create a Vest", (page 17), which says that *kesamim* do not create *vestos*, because a *kesem* — that is, whatever caused the woman to experience a *kesem* that is *metamei* — is not indicative that the woman will get her period next month.

104. See Advanced Rulings, Vestos, page 379, for a discussion regarding which *bedikos* create *vestos*.

105. Rav Yosef Shalom Elyashiv.

106. Rav Shmuel HaLevi Wosner explains that he is not lenient if something looks like blood on an *eid she'eino baduk* as easily as he would be in the case of a *kesem*, because once the woman does a *bedikah* the issue becomes one of a *safeik d'Oraisa*, even though the concept of *eid she'eino baduk* downgrades the *bedikah* to a *d'Rabbanan* (according to the *Chavas Daas*).

107. As stated above, the Chasam Sofer holds that the *teliyah* of a *gris* is not a *teliyah*, it is a *din*. On the other hand, a real *teliyah* is needed in the event that one is trying to actually attribute the blood to something, such as in the case of an *eid she'eino baduk*, so one may only attribute it to a *macholes* that is common. That means that in the case of an *eid she'eino baduk* on an *eid bedikah*, a *Rav* can be *metaher* small dots that are common to find on a cloth. When dealing with a toilet that is *eino baduk*, the halachah allows for a *teliyah* on a much larger amount of blood. The reason for this is because it is common for larger amounts of blood to be found in the toilet, for example, when the restroom was previously used by someone who has hemorrhoids or another source of blood.

Vadai MiGufah (When the Blood Definitely Came from the Woman's Body)

- When a small amount of blood definitely came from a woman *without* her experiencing a *hargashah*:[108]
  - *Rashi*, according to the *Sidrei Taharah*,[109] and Rav Yosef Shalom Elyashiv say that this blood is *tamei mid'Oraisa*.[110]
  - *Tosafos* and most others say that this blood is considered a *kesem*, unless it is enough blood to be considered a *re'iyah*.
- Practically speaking, the halachah is like the position of Tosafos; see upcoming headlines for the practical application of these *halachos*.
- Rav Shlomo Miller (of Toronto) points out that *vadai migufah* means that the only place that the woman touched is *oso makom* (the vaginal opening), and nowhere else.[111] Rav Yitzchak Berkovits agrees with this ruling.
- The leniencies of *kesamim* apply to a stain even when it is clear that the blood came from the woman.[112] A classic example of this is a stain found on underwear, up to the size of a *re'iyah*.

---

108. This disagreement is based on the Gemara that states that in order for a woman to be *temei'ah mid'Oraisa*, she must experience both blood and a *hargashah*. Without that combination she will be *tehorah mid'Oraisa* and possibly *temei'ah mid'Rabbanan* if she only experiences either blood or a *hargashah*, as mentioned above in the name of the *Terumas HaDeshen*. The *Aruch HaShulchan* and others explain the reality of *niddah d'Oraisa* today — when women generally do not have *hargashos* — to mean that she experiences bleeding *b'derech re'iyah*, i.e., she got her period. The case presented is that of a woman who discovers a minimal amount of blood that certainly came from her body, i.e., the blood is *vadai migufah*. The question is thus the following: What is the purpose of the *din* that a woman must experience a *hargashah*? Is it to establish that the blood certainly came from her (*Rashi*), or it is a *gezeiras hakasuv* (derived from the Scripture) that a woman must experience a *hargashah* and without it, she is *tehorah mid'Oraisa* (*Tosafos*)?

109. 190:93.

110. In *Mishnas HaShulchan*, Rav Yosef Shalom Elyashiv is quoted as saying that all the laws of *niddah d'Oraisa* apply when the blood is *vadai migufah*, and can create and uproot *vestos*, even if the woman says she certainly did not have a *hargashah*.

111. Rav Shlomo Miller says a woman who does a wipe with a tissue generally touches more than just *oso makom*, and even Rav Yosef Shalom Elyashiv would apply the leniencies of *kesamim*. Some *sefarim* say to ask her exactly where she wiped to determine if the blood is *vadai migufah* or not. If the *Rav* holds like Rav Moshe Feinstein that tissues are not susceptible to *tumah* and that there was no *hargashah* because it was after *shiur oysom* and that blood that is *vadai migufah* retains the status of a *kesem* (like Tosafos), he certainly does not have to ask such questions.

112. There is a difference between saying that something definitely came from the woman, and saying that the blood is *vadai migufah*. A woman who discovers blood on her underwear becomes *temei'ah* (assuming the circumstances stand to make her *temei'ah* —

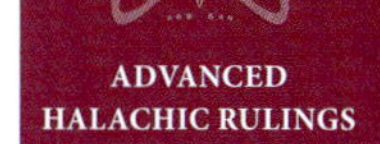

- Practically speaking,[113] blood that is categorically *vadai migufah* is treated with all of the leniencies of *kesamim* besides for that of the the size of a *gris*,[114] because we know that this blood definitely did not come from a *macholes*.[115] Blood found on underwear is treated with all leniencies of *kesamim* including that of the *gris*, as that is not considered *vadai migufah* even though we know with certainty that the blood originated from the woman.

---

see the five leniencies of *kesamim* discussed in Basic Overview, How a Woman Becomes a Niddah, Headline "Niddah D'Rabannan: Kessamim", page 13) because the blood came from her, beyond a reasonable doubt. Nevertheless, we will apply all the leniencies of *kesamim* including that of the *gris*, because we rule like Tosafos. I asked Rav Yitzchak Berkovits to give an example of a case of *vadai migufah* in which the leniencies of *kesamim* would apply, but not that of the *gris*, and he said, "Basically only an applicator."

113. Rav Yossi Stilerman pointed out that this is based on the *Machatzis HaShekel* §183.

114. Although Rav Yitzchak Berkovits is lenient regarding *vadai migufah*, he is not completely lenient in a case in which something was inserted vaginally, such as an applicator (for medications, or by a *bodekes* to determine if a woman is bleeding or not), even though it is too thin to mask a *hargashah*. I asked him why, as a medical applicator is usually plastic, and a long (Q-tip type) applicator is *peshutei kli eitz* and is not susceptible to *tumah*, but he still would not permit it. If even a drop of blood is found on an applicator he is stringent, even if the applicator is colored. His reasoning seems to be that in all cases *d'Rabbanan* we determine the status of the *kesem* based on the situation in which the *kesem* was found. However, when something is inserted directly into the vaginal canal the issue is not one of dealing with "finding" the *kesem* (i.e., outside the body), but is a circumstance that gives an inside view of what is going on inside the the woman's body, in which case the halachah is *metamei* even a drop of blood. This is not to say that every time a *kesem* is found the halachah will be stringent based on where the *kesem* was determined to have come from. For example, if a woman wipes with a colored tissue and discovers blood on the tissue, we know with almost certainty that the blood came from her and did not originate on the tissue. Similarly, if someone wipes her leg with a white cloth which is susceptible to *tumah* and there is more than a *gris* of blood but not in one spot, we will be lenient and not combine the stain to form a *gris*, even though it clearly originated on her body, where we would normally combine to form a *gris*, because at the time when the *kesem* was found it was on the tissue or the cloth. However in the case of the applicators, Rav Berkovits is not lenient because the applicator is inserted internally, and therefore, the *kesem* was not "found" anyplace. So his explanation of *vadai migufah* is that it is only when the woman touches the vaginal opening on the outside and not the surrounding area. In such a case, Rav Berkovits would apply all the leniencies of *kesamim* besides for that of the *gris*. All that being said, Rav Berkovits maintains that even in the case of applicators, although leniencies of *kesamim* are not applied, this is not treated as a *d'Oraisa*, because it did not mask a *hargashah* and, even though the blood certainly came from her, *vadai migufah* according to the *Gilyon Maharsha* is *d'Rabbanan*. So we are left with an anomaly in that applicators have the *din d'Rabbanan*, but none of the leniencies of *kesamim*. Truthfully, there will anyway be no problem according to Rav Berkovits, because he holds that even something that is inserted vaginally that *does* create *niddus d'Oraisa* (such as a *bedikah*) does not create a *vest* anyway.

115. As per the *Kreisee U'Pleisee* and *Gilyon Maharsha* §183.

Applicators

- The leniencies of *kesamim* are applied when an applicator is inserted into the vaginal canal, depending on where precisely it is used,[116] besides for the leniency of the *gris*, because an applicator is too thin to mask a *hargashah*, yet we know that any blood found on it is *vadai migufah*.

Note: It seems that Rav Yosef Shalom Elyashiv does apply the *dinim* of a *niddah d'Oraisa* to blood found on an applicator because it is *vadai migufah*.

Dam Chimud and Bedikos Before the Wedding

- A postmenopausal woman must immerse in the mikvah for *dam chimud* before the wedding, even if she immersed after her last period, but may do so even more than 4 days before the wedding, as long as the wedding preparations have begun.[117]
- The *Rama* says a woman should not immerse in the mikvah more than 4 days before the wedding, and in the event that she does, she must do *bedikos* between the *tevilah* and the wedding[118] to establish that there was no *dam chimud* after the *tevilah*.[119]

---

116. One type of applicator is a thin plastic device that women use to insert medication into their vaginal canal. Another type of applicator looks like a long Q-tip and is used by a *bodekes* to determine whether there is bleeding from the cervix. This applicator is also used by doctors to take strep cultures. In any event, when an applicator is used to check a woman internally, a speculum is generally employed to open the vaginal canal, and that would elevate the status of any blood found to a *d'Oraisa*, irrespective of the *din* of *vadai migufah*.

117. A regular woman must count *shivah nekiyim* after her last cycle before the wedding, and these same *shivah nekiyim* will count for *dam chimud*. A postmenopausal woman can count *shivah nekiyim* from the time that they start the wedding preparations, even if it is months before the wedding. Some say she can start counting from when they write the *Tennai'm*, while others say she must have received a present from the *chassan*, because such actions show he is serious about the *shidduch* (*She'arim HaMetzuyanim B'Halachah*). A woman who immerses in the mikvah for *dam chimud* should ideally immerse within 4 days of the wedding. If she immerses earlier, she may be required to do *bedikos* until the wedding.

118. Rav Yosef Shalom Elyashiv and Rav Shmuel HaLevi Wosner say she should ideally do two *bedikos* per day, although Rav Elyashiv says that according to the letter of the law she can do one, but should be stringent to do two *bedikos* a day.

119. Rav Mati Friedman noted that if for whatever reason such a woman immersed in the mikvah more than 4 days before the wedding, the *tevilah* is valid *bedieved*, as long as she immersed after the wedding preparations began. She would, of course, need to continue checking herself until the wedding, based on the *Rama*.

- A woman who goes to the mikvah within 4 days of her wedding may do *bedikos* until the wedding day as a stringency. The *Rama* says there is no need to do *bedikos* between the *tevilah* and the wedding unless the woman went to the mikvah more than 4 days before. Some *kallah* teachers do teach this,[120] although the general practice is to be lenient.

- The *She'arim HaMetzuyanim B'Halachah* says if a woman immerses in the mikvah more than 4 days before the wedding, she should do only one *bedikah* during those 4 days.

- Rav Yosef Shalom Elyashiv says a woman who did not do *bedikos* between the *tevilah* and the chuppah is permitted *bedi'eved* even if there was a separation of more than 4 days.

- The *Chavas Daas* says a woman does not need to do any *bedikos* after the wedding, even if *bi'ah rishonah* takes place more than 4 days from the *tevilah*. Rav Nissim Karelitz is stringent. However, the practice is to be lenient as per the opinion of the Chavas Daas.

- If the *chassan* was switched for another *chassan* after the *kallah* counted *shivah nekiyim*, she is required to count another *shivah nekiyim* because there is new *chimud* for the new *chassan*.[121]

- A woman should ideally not go to the mikvah more than 4 days before the wedding. If the wedding is on a Sunday night, she may go on Thursday night, but preferably not before.

---

120. This is based on the *Bach* and *Sidrei Taharah* (192:2:8), which are stringent and say she should do *bedikos* even if there is only 1 day between the *tevilah* and wedding. Rav Yitzchak Berkovits and most other *Poskim* do not follow this opinion, because the *Rama* explicitly says no *bedikos* are necessary unless there are 4 days between the *tevilah* and chuppah.

121. There is a story of a wedding in Yerushalayim where the *chassan* backed out of the wedding right before the *kabbalas panim*. The *mesader kedushin*, Rav Mordechai Eliyahu *ztz"l*, asked if anyone would step in and marry the *kallah* in place of the *chassan*. One of the *chassan*'s friends said he would do it, and the *kallah* agreed to marry him. He called his family and told them to come to the hall because he is getting married shortly. The *chassan* and *kallah* were told to take a walk to get to know each other a little and the wedding would commence when his family arrived. The *she'eilah* was whether the *kallah* needed new *shivah nekiyim* for *dam chimud*. Rav Mordechai Eliyahu ruled that she did, because there was new *chimud* for the new *chassan* (related by Dovid Wolpe and Motti Litwin; this is mentioned as a halachah in the *Pischei Teshuvah*. See also the *Taz* [192:1], where he discusses the difference between this situation and the cases of Yehudah and Tamar as well as Rus and Bo'az, where *tevilah* was not necessary because intimacy occurred right away, as opposed to a case of a switched *chassan*, in which there is time for the dam chimud to emerge.)

Note: A *kallah* should not go to the mikvah on Friday night or Motzaei Shabbos because it is a *tevilah shelo b'zmanah* (an immersion not in its mandated time) which is not recommended on these nights.[122] A *kallah* getting married on Sunday night should also not go on Wednesday night,[123] because she should immerse in the mikvah as close to the night of the wedding as possible. If she immersed on Wednesday night (for example, for convenience purposes), she does not need any *bedikos* before the wedding, even when the exact time of the *tevilah* on Wednesday night ends up being earlier than the time of the chuppah on Sunday night.[124]

- All *bedikos* that a *kallah* does should be inserted at a minimum until the first knuckle. She should be certain to insert the cloth internally, or the *bedikah* is invalid. She should also be especially

---

122. See Advanced Rulings, Taharah, Headline "A Delayed Mikvah Night in Regard to Shabbos and Yom Tov," page 368. In the event that a *kallah* has no choice but to immerse in the mikvah on Motzaei Shabbos, she may do so, according to nearly all *Poskim*. The *Noda B'Yehudah* (*Tinyana*, *siman* 117) actually says that a *kallah* before the wedding may immerse in the mikvah on Motzaei Shabbos *lechatchilah* because there is no concern that she is rushing to her house because she is not yet married, and no issue of *srach bitah* (her daughter may learn from her and do the same in her home). For this reason, a *kallah* does not need to start *chafifos* during the day (which is Rashi's opinion), as is generally the case with other women.

123. The *Rama* (192:2) says a *kallah* who immerses on "*leil dalet*" when the *bi'ah rishonah* will take place on Motzaei Shabbos is not required to do any *bedikos* between the *tevilah* and the wedding. Some understand "*leil dalet*" to mean Wednesday night, and say all women should immerse in the mikvah within 3 days of the wedding; although the accepted explanation is that it means Tuesday night, and all women should immerse in the mikvah within 4 days of the wedding (*Chochmas Adam* 115:3; *Sidrei Taharah* 192:2:7). The *Taz* explains that the reason women immersed on *leil dalet* is because in the days of the Gemara women would get married on *yom dalet* (as the Mishnah in *Kesubos* says, "*Besulah niseis l'yom revii* — A virgin is married on *yom revii*"); many women therefore immersed the same night as was done in the days of the Gemara. If in the days of the Gemara they married on *yom dalet* (Wednesday), they certainly immersed the night before, so *leil dalet* must refer to Tuesday night. The *Darchei Teshuvah* (*siman kattan* 22) says since a *kallah* can immerse in the mikvah during the day (because *srach bitah* is not applicable, nor is there a concern that she is going to interrupt the *shivah nekiyim*), there is no proof that in the times of *Chazal* they immersed on Tuesday night if they could have immersed on Wednesday (which leaves only three nights until Motzaei Shabbos). Therefore, he holds the *leil dalet* of the Rama allows for only 3 days between the *tevilah* and the chuppah, after which *bedikos* are required. Practically speaking, a *kallah* whose wedding will be taking place Sunday night should ideally not immerse in the mikvah on Wednesday night, in deference to the opinions that she needs 3 days between the *tevilah* and the chuppah, if possible. Another reason to immerse on Thursday night is to immerse as close as possible to the night of the wedding without immersing Friday night or Motzaei Shabbos, as explained above.

124. In other words, these 4 days are not calculated *me'eis l'eis* (24 hours).

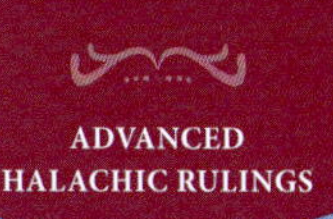

careful not to rip her *besulim* during the *taharah* process.[125] The *bedikah* should be performed in a manner that does not cause her pain.

The Women Who Count Shivah Nekiyim for Dam Chimud

- As a general rule, every woman, even one who is postmenopausal, requires *shivah nekiyim* before her marriage because of *dam chimud*. This halachah even includes a woman who had a hysterectomy.[126] This woman says a *brachah* on the *tevilah*.[127]
- Rav Shmuel HaLevi Wosner says a woman who had a hysterectomy needs *shivah nekiyim*, but does not need to do any *bedikos* because there is no chance of blood coming out from her *mekor*, since she no longer has a *mekor*.
- A *baalas teshuvah* who is married and now wants to have an Orthodox wedding with the same man does not need *shivah nekiyim* for *dam chimud*,[128] but she does need *shivah nekiyim* for her last period. This means she may immerse in the mikvah more than 4 days before the wedding *lechatchilah*. Also, she does not need to do *bedikos* before the wedding even though she is

125. In general, a woman can perform a regular *bedikah* without tearing her *besulim*, much as a woman can use a tampon and keep the *besulim* intact. The *besulim* allow for thin objects (such as a woman's finger) to be inserted into the vaginal canal, but tear when something thicker than 2–3 finger-widths (such as the male *eiver*) penetrate. When a *kallah* performs *bedikos*, she generally will not tear the *besulim* simply by inserting the *bedikah* cloth, even if she goes in all the way. However, since many girls mistakenly perform the *bedikah* on an angle or twist and turn the cloth when it is inside, or their skin is very dry and prone to irritation, a *kallah* should be taught to perform a simple *bedikah* up until the first knuckle (internally, not just between the lips of *oso makom*) while pressing into *chorin v'sedakin*.

126. It is not clear if this ruling is based on a *lo plug* (the halachah does not change based on specific circumstances) (*She'arim HaMetzuyanim B'Halachah*), or if there is a real concern that the postmenopausal woman will expel blood, or that the woman with the hysterectomy may still have part of her uterus intact.

127. Rav Yosef Shalom Elyashiv; Rav Shmuel HaLevi Wosner.

128. The reason for this *din* is since the woman thought she was married before and was living in a mindset in which marital relations were normal, not *znus* (immorality), she does not change into a *chimud* mentality now that she is marrying according to Jewish Law, since nothing really changed in the relationship between her and her husband.

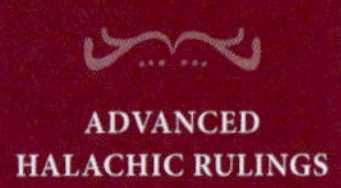

ADVANCED HALACHIC RULINGS

immersing more than 4 days before,[129] because *dam chimud* is not a concern.[130]

- The *Radvaz* and the *Toras HaShelamim* say a *kallah* who is pregnant at the time of the wedding still needs *shivah nekiyim* for *dam chimud*.[131]

- Rav Yosef Shalom Elyashiv says if a couple was intimate before the wedding, the *kallah* is still required to count *shivah nekiyim* for *dam chimud*, unless they lived as a couple, i.e., they moved in together. In the event that the couple was actually sharing a house together, the woman is required to count *shivah nekiyim* for her last period, but not for *dam chimud*.

- Rav Yosef Shalom Elyashiv says that in the case of a non-Jewish couple who were married and converted together, the woman does not need *shivah nekiyim* for *dam chimud* since they are already "married," but does need *shivah nekiyim* for her last period, if applicable.[132]

Postponed or Canceled Weddings

- If a wedding was postponed because of a snowstorm and the *chassan* and *kallah* know the wedding will eventually take place, the *kallah* does not need new *shivah nekiyim* for *dam chimud*. In the event that she got her period while waiting for the new wedding date, she needs *shivah nekiyim* for the *re'iyah*.

129. As cited in the *Rama* 192:2.

130. Rav Shmuel HaLevi Wosner.

131. It makes no difference whether the pregnancy happened under permissible circumstances, such as when a woman was married, became pregnant, divorced, and is now remarrying, or if she conceived out of wedlock; the woman needs *shivah nekiyim* for *dam chimud*. The *Poskim* explain that the laws of *mesulekes damim* apply to a pregnant woman in regard to some *dinim*, such as *vestos*, but regarding *dam chimud* she is not any better than a *ketanah* or a woman who had a hysterectomy.

132. Rav Yosef Shalom Elyashiv says a woman who got her period as a non-Jew and then converted does not need *shivah nekiyim* for the last period, because *niddus* of a non-Jew is not *metamei* like *niddus* of a Jewish woman. Therefore, if a woman converts and intends to marry the same man she was married to as a non-Jew, she does not need *shivah nekiyim* at all, unless she got her period after the conversion. It should be noted that such a couple must separate for 3 months before their new wedding to differentiate between a Jewish child and a non-Jewish child. See *Shulchan Aruch*, *Even HaEzer*, *siman* **13.**

Rav Yosef Shalom Elyashiv says if a woman started *shivah nekiyim* and then found out she may not be Jewish and underwent conversion as a stringency, she must restart *shivah nekiyim*, even though she was doing *bedikos* properly.

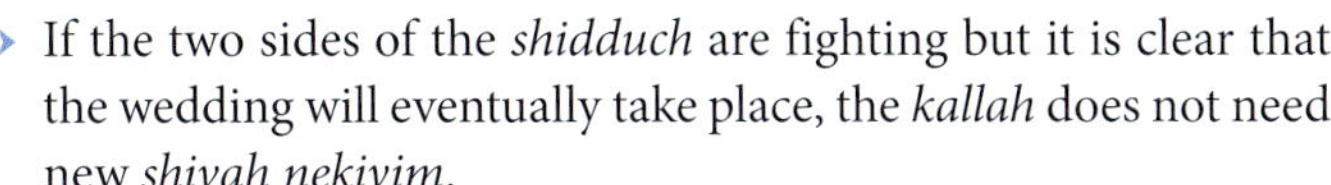

- If the two sides of the *shidduch* are fighting but it is clear that the wedding will eventually take place, the *kallah* does not need new *shivah nekiyim*.
- If the *chassan* and *kallah* think the wedding is really off, the *kallah* needs ew *shivah nekiyim* for *dam chimud* when they reconcile.
- The litmus test for these cases is whether the reservation for the hall was canceled.

Not Seeing Each Other the Week Before the Wedding

- The *chassan* and *kallah* not seeing each other the week before the wedding is an old custom. Some say it came about because of *dam chimud*. We teach it even though there is really no source for it in halachah, because it is a widely accepted custom and it has many benefits.
- Some people have a custom that the couple separates from when the *kallah* does a *hefsek taharah* before the wedding. In order not to publicize the day that the *hefsek taharah* was done, they just tell the *chassan* that the family custom is to separate two weeks before the wedding.
- Practically speaking, if the couple has to meet for any legitimate reason, there is no reason to stop them.

Note: Some people are careful not to talk, text, email, or send notes to each other during this time. Every couple can make their own boundaries, along with their *Rav*, but it is a good idea to implement something along these lines. It should be explained to an engaged couple what they stand to lose by having a *chuppas niddah* and they will generally be accepting of this time of separation.[133]

133. A quick calculation shows that a *tahor* couple should ideally get married toward the end of the woman's cycle so she gets her period shortly after becoming *temei'ah* from *dam besulim*. After the woman returns from the mikvah, the couple can resume the regular cycles of *tumah* and *taharah* immediately. A *chuppas niddah* couple cannot have *yichud* at the beginning of married life, and must wait for the woman to immerse in the mikvah (Night 13 of her cycle) before *bi'ah rishonah*. Then they have to separate for 11 days for *dam besulim* (4 days before *shivah nekiyim*, and the 7 days of *shivah nekiyim*; the 5th day of *poletes shichvas zera* is not needed), so, by the time the woman returns from the mikvah (Day 24 or Day 25 or so of her cycle, depending how long *bi'ah rishonah* takes) they only have a few more days until her *vestos* arrive. Sometime soon she will get her period (unless she is already pregnant), and they are going to have to remain separated for another 12

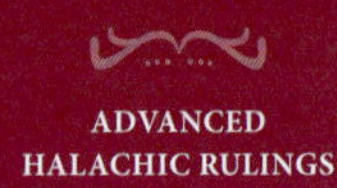

- Rav Shamshon Brodsky[134] related that in Europe the *chassan* and *kallah* had a meal together the night before the wedding. Nevertheless, separating the week before the wedding is an old custom and should be adhered to, unless there is a pressing need for the couple to meet one another.

Besulim Torn on a Bedikah

- Rav Moshe Feinstein says *dam besulim* is only *metamei* when it is torn through marital relations, because the whole reason that *dam besulim* is *metamei* is really because of *dam chimud*.
- The Minchas Yitzchak, Rav Shmuel HaLevi Wosner, and Rav Nissim Karelitz say *dam besulim* is *metamei* in whichever way they tear.
- A *kallah* who tears her *besulim* right before the wedding when doing a *bedikah* is *tehorah* according to Rav Moshe Feinstein, as the blood is only *dam makkah*. According to the *Minchas Yitzchak*, she is *temei'ah* and will have a *chuppas niddah*.
- Practically speaking, we rule like Rav Moshe Feinstein.

Removing the Besulim Before the Wedding

- The *sefarim* discuss removing *besulim* before the wedding,[135] saying that according to the Torah, this is not the ideal way. It is the *chassan*'s job to make his *kallah* into his *kli* (vessel) through *bi'ah rishonah*. Therefore, whenever it can be avoided, it should not be done by a doctor.[136]

---

days. It turns out that a *chuppas niddah* couple can have only 5 or so *tahor* days the first 5 weeks of marriage! This 1-week custom turns out to be very beneficial.

134. My great-uncle, who was an *alter Mirrer*, learned in Shanghai, and was a *mechutan* with Rav Nochum Partzovitz.

135. *Minchas Yitzchak*; *Chut Shani*; *Shiuri Shevet Levi*.

136. In rare cases it becomes necessary for a doctor or *bodekes* to remove the *besulim*, such as when the woman has thick *besulim* that will not rip through marital relations. Sometimes the *besulim*, which have the texture of an elastic membrane, have a thin, string-like part that covers over the vaginal opening in such a way that prevents the *chassan* from penetrating. Such cases require assistance in removing the *besulim*, but they are rare, and are the exception, not the rule. Some *Rabbanim* have a terrible practice of giving *chassanim* performance-enhancing pills to help them get through *bi'ah rishonah* more easily. Generally, when a *chassan* is having a hard time with *bi'ah rishonah* he (or the *kallah*) has not received proper guidance and must be (re)educated. Sending such a couple

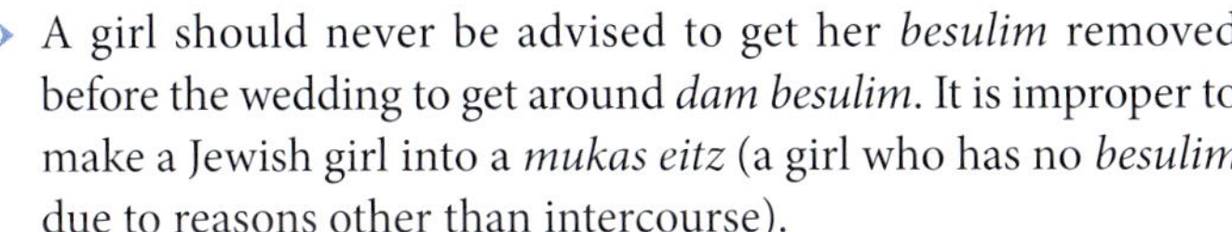

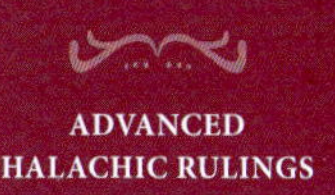

- A girl should never be advised to get her *besulim* removed before the wedding to get around *dam besulim*. It is improper to make a Jewish girl into a *mukas eitz* (a girl who has no *besulim* due to reasons other than intercourse).
- Some women have flexible *besulim* that never tear. Some women have even given birth with their *besulim* intact.

Note: Some women may need their *besulim* to be removed surgically. A common reason to suspect this is if a woman says that marital relations are painful long after the wedding. When the *besulim* are surgically removed, she does not become *temei'ah*, as per Rav Moshe Feinstein's opinion.

Bi'ah Gemurah Without Discovering Dam Besulim

There are several opinions regarding a situation in which *bi'ah gemurah* occurred but there was no *dam besulim*:

- The *Rosh* — A woman is *temei'ah* after *bi'ah rishonah* whether or not the couple discovers *dam besulim*.[137]
- The *Raavad* — A woman is *tehorah* when there is no *dam besulim* by *bi'ah rishonah*.[138]
- The *Rama* — If the *chassan* only did *he'arah*, the couple may rely on the *Raavad*. If there was a *gemar bi'ah*, the halachah is like the opinion of the Rosh.[139]
- *Gemara Yevamos* — There is a disagreement as to what is considered a *bi'ah gemurah*:[140]
    - Shmuel — *He'arah* means *neshikas ha'eiver* (lit. kissing of the organ; sexual contact).
    - Rabbah bar bar Chanah quoting Rav Yochanan — *Gemar bi'ah* is when the entire *atarah* is inserted.

---

to a doctor or a *bodekes* or introducing them to pills to tear the *besulim* may be detrimental in the long run. Sometimes a *bodekes* may be able to give proper education regarding intimacy when the girl has underlying fears and apprehensions about painful relations.

137. *Niddah* 10:1.

138. End of *Shaar HaPerishah*, "*Baalei HaNefesh*."

139. Chap. 193.

140. 55:72–56:71.

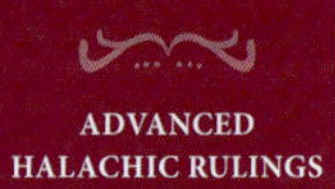

- Ravin quoting Rav Yochanan — The insertion of anything less than the entire *atarah* is not considered *gemar bi'ah*; it is still considered *he'arah*.[141]
- Rav Dimi and Rav Shmuel bar Yehudah quoting Rav Yochanan — When the *atarah* (crown of the male organ) is inserted it is considered *he'arah*. Anything more than that is considered *gemar bi'ah*.
- *Tosafos*[142] and the *Rambam*[143] — Anytime that the *eiver* penetrated deeply enough that had he been *mazria* she could have gotten pregnant, it is considered a *gemar bi'ah*. Anything less than that is considered *he'arah*.[144]
- The *Sidrei Taharah* — A *kallah* nowadays should be assumed to be *temei'ah* once *miktzas ha'eiver* more than the *atarah* entered.[145]
- *Chochmas Adam*— *Bi'ah gemurah* occurs when the entire *eiver* is inserted.[146]

› Practically speaking, the halachah is like the opinion of the Sidrei Taharah.[147]

› See Advanced Rulings, How a Woman Becomes a Niddah, Headline "First-Night Phone Calls", page 237) for the practical halachos that are derived from this discussion.

---

141. According to the Gemara's conclusion, Ravin agrees with Shmuel as follows: Shmuel holds that *neshikas ha'ever* is considered the initial stage of *he'arah* and Ravin is explaining that until the whole *atarah* enters it retains the status of *he'arah*, and, according to both Amora'im, is not considered *gemar bi'ah*.

142. *"Eino."*

143. *Hilchos Issurei Bi'ah*.

144. *Tosafos* and the *Rambam* give this definition for *gemar bi'ah*, but do not define how much of the *eiver* must enter to no longer be considered *he'arah*.

145. 193:3, "*Dayah V'Adayin.*"

146. *Klal* 115, *siman* 15.

147. Rav Yitzchak Berkovits rules like the Sidrei Taharah, Rav Yaacov Blau rules that until most of the *eiver* is still considered *he'arah*, and some *Poskim* in the United States rule like the Chochmas Adam. Practically speaking, Rav Berkovits is the most stringent in theory but is the most lenient in practice, because he holds that the issue is a *safeik d'Rabbanan*. Therefore, when a *chassan* calls and does not know what happened, the *Rav* should be lenient when they did not actually discover any blood, as explained in "First Night Phone Calls" below. Realistically, the *besulim* should be ripped once the *atarah* has entered, because the thickness of the *atarah* is what causes the *besulim* to tear. That being said, it is difficult to understand why some allow most of the *eiver* or more, since anything beyond the *atarah* does not change the dynamics so as to create more suspicion that the *besulim* ripped.

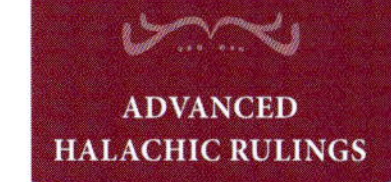

When There Are No Besulim

- The *dinim* of *dam besulim* do not apply to a *beulah* (a woman who had intercourse) or to a *mukas eitz*.[148]
- The halachah of *dam besulim* even applies to a *kallah* who was never married and is postmenopausal, unless there is a clear reason why she should not have her *besulim* intact.

Note: A wedding should be planned according to the status of the *kallah*. A *besulah* should ideally get married toward the end of her cycle so the *tumah* of *dam besulim* will soon be followed by her period. A *beulah*, or other woman with no *besulim*, could get married at the beginning of her cycle, to give the couple more time together.[149]

- Stitches that keep the vaginal canal closed are not called *besulim*, and any blood discovered is *dam makkah*.
- A *kallah* who is sure that she has no *besulim* does not have to be concerned about *dam besulim*.
- Most *kallos* today are assumed to have intact *besulim*; there might be a little blood, if any.
- A *kallah* should not be sent to a *bodekes* to check whether or not she has *besulim*; it is improper to introduce a girl to marriage though a *bodekes*. Unless there is reason to suspect otherwise, we assume that she does have her *besulim* intact.[150]

---

148. Rav Yosef Shalom Elyashiv.

149. That being said, some *Rabbanim* advise that every girl get married toward the end of her cycle, whether or not she is a *besulah*, to give her time to get back to herself after *bi'ah rishonah*, which can be physically and emotionally draining for some girls. This may not apply to a *beulah* or postmenopausal *kallah*. Each case should be presented to a knowlegable authority for direction when questions arise.

150. The *Poskim* point out that checking for *besulim* before marriage will not avoid *dam besulim* because most girls have *besulim*; they just do not bleed much of the time because they are "dried out" (like dead skin), so the doctor or *bodekes* cannot even help in most cases. This can be compared to ripping a cuticle. Although the cuticle is present and may possibly bleed when ripped, practically, in many cases there will be no blood. As noted, we are stringent like the Rosh that *bi'ah rishonah* will make a woman a niddah when we suspect she has *besulim*, irrespective of whether blood is actually found.

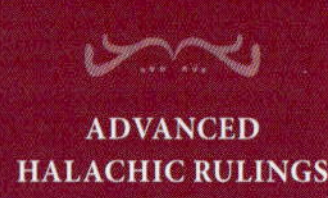

After Bi'ah Rishonah

- If the *chassan* maintains the connection after breaking the *besulim* (whether or not there was blood, if there was a *bi'ah gemurah*), he may continue until *gemar bi'ah*. The *kallah* becomes forbidden only once he has separated from her. If he separates before *gemar bi'ah*, he should not continue to *gemar bi'ah*.[151]

- Rav Nissim Karelitz says that after *bi'ah rishonah* the *chassan* may be *poreish b'eiver chai* (withdraw while still erected) even though his wife is about to be prohibited to him.

- Some teach that after *bi'ah rishonah*, a *kallah* should be taught to try to tear the remaining *besulim* by doing a thorough *bedikah*, with or without a *bedikah* cloth.[152] In this way she can avoid the chances that some *besulim* have been left intact, which can potentially be *metamei* her when she returns from the mikvah. However, she should be careful not to unnecessarily hurt herself.[153] Practically, it is not advisable for a newlywed woman to try to tear any potentially remaining *besulim*.

---

151. Rav Nissim Karelitz and other *Poskim*.

152. This *bedikah* should only be performed once the couple is certain that the woman is *temei'ah*, so as not to unnecessarily be *metamei* her because of an extra *bedikah*.

153. Practically, this extra *bedikah* often causes more irritation than anything else. The reason for this is that the *besulim* are shaped like an elastic ring around the vaginal opening. A regular *kallah* will generally not rip her *besulim* by inserting her finger unless, by chance, the skin happens to be dry or she has something wrapped around her finger, such as a *bedikah* cloth, in some cases. The reason for this is that *besulim* allow blood to exit the body and things to be inserted (for example, a finger or a tampon) approximately up to the thickness of a finger. During *bi'ah rishonah*, the *eiver*, which is approximately three fingers in width, breaks the *besulim*. This breakage occurs because of the thickness of what is being inserted, not the length.

(That said, a regular *kallah* should really do *bedikos* with her whole finger. However, out of the concern that she may accidentally break the *besulim* [either because she is going about it at the wrong angle, because she is excessively dry, or because the *bedikah* cloth causes the tear] and this [either having to go to a *bodekes* to perform the *bedikos* for her, or becoming *temei'ah* based on the *Minchas Yitzchak*] will cause her anguish before the wedding, *kallos* are advised to do *bedikos* only up to the first knuckle.)

Thus, performing another *bedikah* after *bi'ah rishonah* to remove the remaining *besulim* actually has a low rate of success, because a full *bedikah* generally does not remove *besulim* and has big chance of failure because she may irritate herself. On top of that, many *kallos* get confused about when to do this *bedikah* and end up doing it before the *chassan* is completely successful, often finding blood and being *metamei* themselves unnecessarily right in the beginning of marriage, before *bi'ah rishonah* occurs. This advice may be used by a *Rav* to guide a couple that clearly has been successful and now wants advice on how

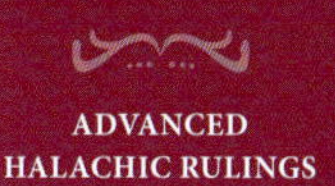

- If there was *dam besulim*, the *chassan* should wash his hands and make the following *brachah*, brought from the *Rosh*[154]:

בָּרוּךְ אֲשֶׁר צָג אֱגוֹז בְּגַן עֵדֶן שׁוֹשַׁנַּת הָעֲמָקִים, בַּל יִמְשׁוֹל זָר בְּמַעְיָן חָתוּם, עַל כֵּן אַיֶּלֶת אֲהָבִים שָׁמְרָה בְּטוֹהַר, וְחוֹק לֹא הֵפֵרָה, בָּרוּךְ הַבּוֹחֵר בְּזַרְעוֹ שֶׁל אַבְרָהָם.

- Rav Nissim Karelitz says the *brachah* on *dam besulim* is only recited one time — after *bi'ah rishonah* in the event that there was blood — and is not recited a second time even if the couple discovers more blood.

First-Night Phone Calls

- Even a minute amount of *dam besulim* is *metamei*. We do not treat it with the leniencies of *kesamim*, except that it does not create a *vest*.
- If a *kallah* discovers blood within a few minutes of marital relations, the couple should assume that it is *dam besulim* and she is *temei'ah*, even in the event that there was clearly not a *gemar bi'ah*.
- Blood that is discovered on the male *eiver* is treated as a *bedikah*, even when it is only discovered a few minutes after marital relations. The couple should assume that it is *dam besulim*, even if he has not completely entered her, and the woman is *temei'ah*.
- In the event that the couple achieved a *gemar bi'ah* they must separate from each other, even if they did not discover any *dam besulim*. The reason for this is because the *zera* may have concealed the *dam besulim* that came out.[155]
- Many *Poskim* (including Rav Yosef Shalom Elyashiv) say that entry anyplace from the *atarah* until the whole *eiver* is treated as a *safeik* as to whether this is considered *gemar bi'ah*. The couple would thus have to separate due to a *safeik*, even if she did not actually discover any blood.

---

the wife can avoid becoming *temei'ah* again when she returns from the mikvah, although even in such a case the *bedikah* serves little or no purpose.

154. Kesuvos 1:15.

155. *Rosh*.

- Practically speaking, the issue here is one of a *d'Rabbanan* (*dam besulim*), regarding a concern that is not so common (there was blood that was masked by the *zera*), as well as the fact that the Rama seems to agree with the Raavad that the couple does not have to separate when they did not discover blood, even when there was a *bi'ah gemurah*. Therefore, if it seems from the conversation there was no *bi'ah gemurah* and they did not find any blood, the couple can try again for a *bi'ah gemurah*. [156]

Dealing With the Pain of Besulim

- *Rabbanim* point out that some *kallos* are scared of the pain of *bi'ah rishonah*, and have a hard time consummating the marriage for a long time. It is generally hype that makes these women scared, as there is not anything to really be afraid of. There is more psychological fear than physical pain.[157]
- In general, pain that a *besulah* feels is not from the *besulim* tearing. It is from new muscles being used.[158]

When Dam Besulim Is Discovered Later On

- If a couple has *bi'ah rishonah* and the *besulim* tear, and when the woman returns from the mikvah they discover *dam besulim* again, the woman becomes *temei'ah* again.[159] If the source of the

156. Many *Rabbanim* ask the *chassan* if he felt like he entered a tight, narrow space, or if he simply felt pressure. If it sounds like there was no penetration and the couple did not actually find any blood, they allow the couple to continue trying. When such a *she'eilah* arises, it should be presented to a *Rav* knowledable in this area.

157. *Besulim* look like thin, dry skin, such as large cuticles. They varies in thickness from woman to woman, but are generally not thick or attached strongly enough to cause much, if any, pain. In general, the more a *kallah* is nervous about the pain, the more pain *bi'ah rishonah* will actually cause, because she is holding back and not allowing the *chassan* to penetrate, thereby causing *oso makom* to contract and causing him to hurt her more than if she relaxed and allowed him to enter.

158. Even though there may be a certain amount of pain associated with tearing the *besulim*, the Gemara in *Kesubos* says a girl in a heightened state of arousal during *bi'ah rishonah* will override any pain associated with *besulim*. The more a *kallah* tries to fight the pain, the more pain she will cause, by tightening the pelvic muscles. The more she embraces the moment, the less pain she will experience.

159. Practically, a woman who discovers *dam besulim* after the second *bi'ah* becomes *temeiah*, although practically, most *besulim she'eilos* after the first night are treated as *kesamim*, and one may be lenient regarding leniencies of *kesamim* and the *shiur osyom* after marital relations.

blood is another *makkah*, she is *tehorah*. This is the reason why some suggest that the *kallah* tear the remaining *besulim* herself after *bi'ah rishonah* by doing a full *bedikah* once the relationship has clearly been consummated.

- Rav Moshe Feinstein and Rav Nissim Karelitz say that in the event that there was blood by *bi'ah rishonah*, even when there was no *bi'ah gemurah*, the couple does not have to be concerned about *dam besulim* again when she returns from the mikvah, even though there may then be *bi'ah gemurah*.[160] If they actually discover blood after marital relations the second time, however, she is *temei'ah*.
- A *kallah* who bleeds both the first and second times is *temei'ah* both times. However, if the blood is because he cut her (as is often the case on the perineum), and not because of *besulim*, she is *tehorah*. A *bodekes* can tell where the blood came from.[161]
- Rav Nissim Karelitz says in the event that there is *dam besulim* after the second *bi'ah* that is *metamei* her, the *chassan* nevertheless does not make a *brachah* on that blood. The *brachah* is made only when he makes her into his *kli*, and not when *dam besulim* occurs.

---

160. Rav Moshe Feinstein explains that we see that *Chazal* were concerned that the *zera* could have masked *dam besulim*, which is why a *kallah* is *temei'ah* even if there was only *gemar bi'ah*. This demonstrates that the discussion is not one of a lot of blood, since *zera* can conceal it from sight. In the event that the couple saw blood after the *bi'ah rishonah*, even if it was only caused by *he'arah*, the halachah is lenient for the second *bi'ah*, and we assume that all the *dam besulim* came out the first time. Practically speaking, a couple should be advised against looking for blood after the second *bi'ah*. See *Chut Shani* 193:1.

161. Although a *bodekes* usually helps a woman, she can become an inadvertent liability regarding *dam besulim* in particular, as follows: If a woman has a *she'eilah* regarding *besulim* after the second *bi'ah* and goes to a *bodekes*, who sees the *besulim* are ripped, she will be *temei'ah* because the *besulim* were ripped through marital relations, which is *metamei* according to everyone. Whereas normally any blood that a woman discovers after the second *bi'ah* is treated with the leniencies of *kesamim*, a *bodekes* who sees that the *besulim* were torn through *bi'ah* makes the *Rav* certain that the blood the woman found came from *dam besulim*, to which the leniencies of *kesamim* do not apply, and even a minute amount of blood is *metamei*.

In certain cases, *Rabbanim* will be lenient if the woman did a *bedikah* before finding blood after the second *bi'ah*, because torn *besulim* may be treated like any other *makkah* (according to Rav Moshe Feinstein, not the *Minchas Yitzchak*), and since the *besulim* did not necessarily tear through *bi'ah*, we may, in certain circumstances, attribute the blood to the *bedikah* cloth irritating that area, rather than to *dam besulim*. The only foolproof system is for the woman to be advised not to look for blood after *bi'ah rishonah*.

- Blood that was discovered after the second *bi'ah*, but it was discovered some time after *bi'ah gemurah*, is treated as a *kesem*, and all the laws of *kesamim* apply.

Avoiding Dam Besulim the Second Time

- After the couple experienced *bi'ah gemurah*, or if blood was discovered after the first *bi'ah* even without *bi'ah gemurah*, the woman should wear dark underwear, not look for *kesamim* during or after marital relations, and use a colored towel to avoid unnecessary complications.

Note: The husband may be advised to be *poreish b'eiver meis* after marital relations the second time, so any blood that may be discovered will have the status of a *kesem*.[162]

Taharah After Dam Besulim

- After *dam besulim* a woman needs to wait 4 days and then may begin to count *shivah nekiyim*. The 5th day that is generally necessary because of the Rama's stringency[163] need not be kept after *dam besulim*, because *dam besulim* is *tumah d'Rabbanan* and was not included in the edict of the Terumas HaDeshen and Rama.[164]
- Rav Shmuel HaLevi Wosner says this *din* applies even if the woman discovers *dam besulim* when she returns from the mikvah after the second *bi'ah*.
- If a woman got her period after becoming *temei'ah* from *dam besulim*, she requires the regular 5 days before beginning *shivah nekiyim*, because she is now dealing with *tumah d'Oraisa*, even though the original *tumah* was *d'Rabbanan*. However, she may begin counting 5 days from the original *tumas besulim*.[165]

---

162. *Darchei Teshuvah*

163. 196:11.

164. The Maharal of Prague.

165. Rav Yosef Shalom Elyashiv; Rav Shmuel HaLevi Wosner; Rav Nissim Karelitz.

Saying "Nitmeisi — I Am Temei'ah"

- Rav Shmuel HaLevi Wosner holds that in the event that a woman is *temei'ah* because she said "*Nitmeisi*," a *brachah* is said on her eventual *tevilah*, or at the very least she should fulfill her obligation by hearing someone else's *brachah*. Rav Yosef Shalom Elyashiv and Rav Nissim Karelitz maintain that a *brachah* should not be said.

- Rav Nissim Karelitz says a woman who is *temei'ah* because she said "*Nitmeisi*" does not keep *vestos* the following month on the date she said she was *temei'ah*, even though she is *temei'ah* to her husband in all matters.

- Women must be taught not to joke about being a niddah.

- If a woman thought — and said — that she was *temei'ah* and later finds out that she was actually *tehorah* the whole time (because the blood was only from a *makkah*, it was a good color, or the like), she remains *tehorah*. A mistake is better than an *amaslah* (a legitimate reason as to why she said something untrue).[166]

- Rav Shmuel HaLevi Wosner says that for an *amaslah* to be valid, the husband has to believe that what she is saying now is true, and that what the woman said before was a lie due to the reason that she is now presenting.[167]

- Practically speaking, if the woman has a valid reason for why she said she is *temei'ah*, she is believed. Joking around is not a valid reason, however; in this case she is *temei'ah*.[168]

- Rav Nissim Karelitz says if a woman says "*Nitmeisi*" and afterward says that it was all a joke, and then says a real *amaslah*, she is believed if she can explain why she said it was a joke and did not reveal the real reason.

- If the husband realizes when his wife says "*Nitmeisi*" that she is joking, she remains *tehorah*. However, she should never do this in the first place.

- The *She'arim HaMetzuyanim B'Halachah* says if a woman says, "Today is a *vest*," and then changes her mind, she remains

166. Rav Nissim Karelitz.

167. See 16:185:2.

168. Rav Nissim Karelitz and most other *Poskim*.

tehorah and is not required to perform a *bedikah* that day simply because of her statement.[169]

- The woman's keeping *harchakos*, even in front of other people, is not considered saying "*Nitmeisi*." She remains *tehorah* even if her husband thought she was *temei'ah*.

- A woman who is in a situation in which she is presumed to be a niddah (see footnote[170]) is not required to pretend in public that she is *temei'ah*. She may, in many circumstances, want to, however, in order to avoid *maras ayin* (doing something that can cause the onlooker to think that one is sinning) or publicly advertising her status.

- If a woman got a good *hefsek taharah* but lied to her husband and told him it was *tamei* because she wants to surprise him with an "early" mikvah night, this is considered a joke. The woman is forbidden to her husband until she goes to the mikvah again on the night that her husband thinks she is supposed to go to the mikvah.[171]

- See Advanced Rulings, Taharah, Headline "Poletes Shichvas Zera After a Prohibited Day" (page 302), regarding whether a woman who says "*Nitmeisi*" keeps 5 days for *poletes shichvas zera* or not.

Pesichas HaKever

- There is a disagreement between the Noda B'Yehudah, and the Tiferes L'Moshe, and Rav Boruch Frankel whether the principle of *ein pesichas hakever b'lo dam* (there is no opening of the uterus without blood) applies when a woman's *mekor* is opened up from

---

169. He explains that the reason is that a woman who claims that she is *temei'ah* is imposing upon herself a status of being prohibited to her husband. When she says that today is a *vest*, she does not create for herself a status of being prohibited; she is telling her husband to possibly *expect* her to become prohibited to him.

170. The classic two cases of this halachah are a woman who becomes *tehorah* relatively immediately after giving birth, and a couple who has not yet successfully consummated their relationship after their wedding. The postpartum woman does not have to keep *harchakos* in public, but she may want to avoid any public acts of breaking *harchakos* (for example, passing her baby to her husband at the *pidyon haben*). The newlywed couple may be advised to actually keep *harchakos* even though the woman is still *tehorah*, so as not to advertise the fact that they are having difficulties with *bi'ah rishonah*.

171. Rav Mati Friedman. This may be only theoretically, and not practically, because it may be possible to consult with her *Rav* to verify his ruling if she had brought him a *mareh* at the beginning of the *shivah nekiyim*. This is not something to play around with.

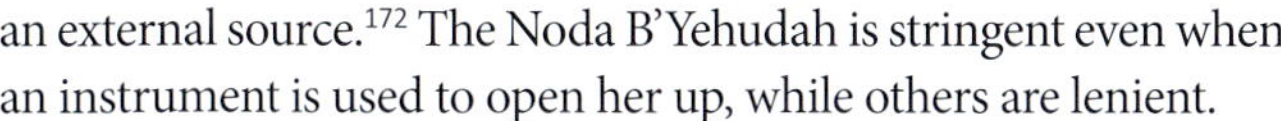

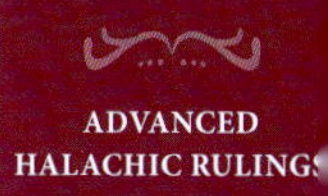

an external source.[172] The Noda B'Yehudah is stringent even when an instrument is used to open her up, while others are lenient.

- Practically speaking, the halachah is stringent like the Noda B'Yehudah, whether the cervix opened due to internal, natural means, or externally through the use of an instrument.[173]
- Rav Moshe Feinstein says we only need to be stringent in regard to *pesichas hakever* when an instrument that is thicker than a small finger was used to open the cervix. This is approximately three-quarters of an inch (18 millimeters) in diameter.[174]
- Rav Yosef Shalom Elyashiv and Rav Nissim Karelitz say the Noda B'Yehudah's *din* of *ein pesichas hakever b'lo dam* also applies even to a *mesulekes damim*, such as a pregnant, nursing, or postmenopausal woman.
- Practically speaking, routine checkups and internal ultrasounds are not *metamei* because they do not go past the cervix. If blood is discovered on these instruments, however, the woman may be *temei'ah* even if the amount of blood is less than a *gris*, because the entrance of a foreign object may have masked a *hargashah*. However, a woman in this scenario does not become *temei'ah* because of *pesichas hakever* alone.[175]
- Rav Nissim Karelitz says a woman is *temei'ah* even if she produces a clean *bedikah* immediately after *pesichas hakever*.

---

172. The Gemara in *Niddah* (21:71) cites a disagreement about whether or not the halachah is *ein pesichas hakever b'lo dam*. Rashi and the Rambam rule that there is *pesichas kever b'lo dam*, while the Raavad, Ramban, and Rashba rule that there is no *pesichas kever b'lo dam*. The Shulchan Aruch (188:3) and Rama (194:2) rule *ein pesichas kever b'lo dam*, and the *Pischei Teshuvah* 194:4 brings the opinion of the Noda B'Yehudah that the *din* of *ein pesichas kever b'lo dam* is not limited to when the *mekor* opens from the inside to allow something to exit, and even includes circumstances when the cervix is opened from the outside.

173. The cervix is a muscle which is generally closed and is comprised of the internal OS and the external OS. The internal OS is the internal part of the cervix which opens into the uterus, while the external OS is the cervical opening into the vaginal canal. Most *Poskim* hold that the internal OS must be opened in order to be *metamei* a woman due to *pesichas hakever*.

174. Other *Poskim* are stringent if the cervix was opened as little as 8 millemeters, although most agree that anything less than that is not *metamei* because of *ein pesichas hakever b'lo dam*. Some *Poskim*, as brought in *She'arim HaMetzuyanim B'Halachah*, are lenient unless the instrument is the thickness of two fingers (approximately 35 millimeters).

175. Depending on the specifics of the procedure, a *Rav* should be consulted regarding practical cases of *pesichas hakever*. When asking a *she'eilah*, be sure to provide information as to which procedure was performed, which instruments were used, whether the cervix was opened, what day of her month the woman is up to, and all such relevant information.

- Pap smears often do go past the cervix,[176] but the instrument used is too thin to be *metamei*. Any bleeding found may be attributed to *dam makkah*.

- Internal photography and IUDs enter the uterus,[177] and, depending on the circumstances, may open the *mekor* too much.[178] These instruments may be *metamei* depending on the specifics of the procedure. Before committing to any procedure, one should ask the doctor for specifics of the procedure and the instruments being used, and consult with a *Rav*.

Labor Issues Regarding Niddah

- Rav Moshe Feinstein says a woman in labor is *temei'ah* from the time she is dilated more than three-quarters of an inch (which is the diameter of a small finger), because of *pesichas hakever*, as per the opinion of the Noda B'Yehudah.

- Rav Nissim Karelitz says a woman who is fully dilated to the point where the baby will certainly come at any moment should assume that she is *temei'ah*. If the dilation proves to be part of false labor, she is *tehorah* again.

- Practically speaking,[179] one may be lenient and follow the opinion that dilation itself is not *metamei* — although it is clear that *pesichas hakever* causes bleeding, and that bleeding will

---

176. A pap smear is a test performed to determine if the cervical cells are behaving normally. A doctor uses a special stick or brush to remove a few cells from inside and around the cervix. The tip of the brush is very thin and enters part of the cervix to remove some cells. Rav Yitzchak Berkovits as well as most other *Rabbanim* are lenient regarding pap smears, in that they do not cause *pesichas hakever*, and any blood found can be attributed to a *makkah*, since the objective of the procedure is to rip cells away from the cervix (i.e., cause a *makkah*).

177. An IUD is an intrauterine device commonly used as a contraceptive. It is shaped like a grappling hook and is inserted by a doctor past the cervix, into the uterus. Since the body recognizes a foreign device, it generally does not allow implantation of a fertilized embryo to occur. IUDs may or may not contain hormones affecting the way they interact with the body and menstrual cycle. Most IUDs look more or less alike and require similar procedures for insertion and extraction.

178. Nowadays, inserting an IUD generally does not open the cervix past the point of *pesichas hakever*, so the woman does not become *temei'ah* from the procedure unless she discovers blood afterward, which is considered *dam niddah* (*d'Oraisa* or *d'Rabbanan*, depending where it is found), and not *dam makkah*, since the body commonly releases blood in response to a foreign insertion. A woman should not do any extra *bedikos* after inserting an IUD.

179. This ruling of Rav Yitzchak Berkovits was explained by Rav Yossi Stilerman. The ruling is based on the *Chavas Daas* 194:1, which says that *pesichas hakever* is *metamei* when something leaves the uterus, not when the uterus simply opens.

come when the baby comes out, she does not become *temei'ah* the moment the uterus opens.[180] Once the baby emerges, however, the women is *temei'ah* because of *pesichas hakever* and as a *yoledes*, even in the event that there is no blood.

- Practically speaking, a woman during childbirth — even when she is fully dilated — does not become *temei'ah* unless she either (1) discovers blood, (2) is unable to walk because the baby descended low into her pelvis (not because she is in too much pain), or (3) the baby is delivered, even if no blood is seen.

- An internal examination is generally performed when a woman in labor comes to the hospital.[181] If there is any blood on the glove used to check her, she becomes a *niddah d'Oraisa*. This holds true even if there is only a drop on a colored glove, because this examination is similar to a *bedikah* in that the foreign object inside of her will mask the *hargashah*. A woman should ask to see the glove after the internal examination has been performed.[182] If there is no blood on the glove, she remains *tehorah*.[183]

- Rav Yossi Stilerman pointed out that a woman becomes *temei'ah* in the event that the membrane is stripped[184] and blood is

---

180. Rav Yosef Shalom Elyashiv. Many *Poskim* are stringent when a woman is dilated and in labor, but rule that dilation itself is not *metamei* if she is not experiencing actual labor. Rav Nissim Karelitz explains that it is common for the uterus to dilate a few centimeters toward the end of the pregnancy, which means that dilation in itself is not *metamei*. Rather, the *Poskim* who are *metamei* a woman in active labor do so out of concern that *pesichas hakever* at that stage caused blood to discharge. Practically speaking, Rav Yitzchak Berkovits is lenient regarding dilation, even when it is experienced in active labor.

181. The objective of the internal exam is to determine how dilated the cervix is and how effaced (thin; stretched) the uterus is, to determine how far into labor the woman may be.

182. As a general rule, a woman is not obligated to look and be *metamei* herself unnecessarily, and in fact should not usually do so. But in a case in which it is so common to find blood, she is obligated to find out what is happening in her body. Therefore, during *shivah nekiyim* and when a doctor does an internal exam for a woman in labor, a woman must look at the *eid bedikah* or at the glove to see if there is any blood. Besides for these situations, a woman should be careful not to be *metamei* herself unnecessarily.

183. When a woman gets an internal exam to determine dilation and effacement, a hand is inserted into her body past the cervix. However, *ein pesichas hakever b'lo dam* itself is at this point not *metamei*, because the dilation which began already will cause blood to come out when the baby is born. She does not become *temei'ah* before this point because of dilation or because of the internal check unless blood is found.

184. "Stripping the membrane" is a form of induction in which a doctor or nurse inserts two fingers past the cervix and strips away the mucus that is blocking the cervix. The procedure can generally be performed successfully once the woman is dilated the width of two fingers, and usually leads to the onset of contractions and labor. Realistically, in the event that there is no blood on the glove when the stripping occurs, the procedure was not performed successfully. The procedure should only be performed under Rabbinic

discovered on the glove.[185] If there is no blood, she remains *tehorah*.[186]

- The mucus plug is not *metamei* when it comes out unless it has blood on it.[187] All leniencies of *kesamim* apply to that blood,[188] and its color is generally not problematic.
- Most doctors ensure that a woman will give birth within 24 hours of her water breaking, because of fear of infection.[189] The water breaking is not *metamei*,[190] and all the leniencies

---

guidance, as should any form of induction (such as ingesting castor oil, administering Pitocin, or breaking the water). Membrane stripping is a painful procedure, as is any procedure that forces the cervix open. Rav Yosef Shalom Elyashiv says one should be stringent regarding any procedure for which the doctor used an instrument thicker than the width of a finger, and assume there was *pesichas hakever*. The difficulty with this ruling is that a woman will certainly know if the doctor inserts such an instrument past the cervix, as she will certainly experience excruciating pain if there was *pesichas hakever*, as she would if the doctor strips the membrane. See *She'arim HaMetzuyanim B'Halachah* and *Teshuvah M'Ahavah*, vol. 1, *siman* 116.

185. Since it is common to see blood after stripping the membrane, the woman should ask to see the glove.

186. Similar to when an external exam of the cervix is performed, a woman does not become *temei'ah* if the doctor (unsuccessfully) stripped the membrane because of *ein pesichas hakever b'lo dam*, because the woman is already dilated, so no extra *pesichas hakever* occurred, and we know she will eventually become *temei'ah* when the baby is born (Rav Yossi Stilerman).

187. The mucus plug is the glob of mucus that caps the cervix throughout pregnancy and prevents bacteria from entering the uterus. It is generally discharged sometime toward the end of pregnancy, when the cervix starts dilating, anywhere from a month to a few minutes before delivery. Many women do not notice when it passes and there is no need to deliver the baby within a certain time frame afterward, as there is once the water breaks. A woman who spots the mucus plug and sees blood on it should bring it to her *Rav*.

188. I asked Rav Yitzchak Berkovits whether the leniencies of *kesamim* apply to the mucus plug, besides for that of the size of a *gris*, because the plug is *vadai migufah*, in which case all leniencies of *kesamim* besides for that of the size of a *gris* are applied, because the blood certainly did not come from a *macholes*. He said a mucus plug is not expected to come with any blood, and although the plug itself is *vadai migufah*, the blood is not.

189. This refers to the amniotic fluid which is discharged within 24 hours of delivery. Most women begin to experience contractions followed by the water breaking, though sometimes the water breaks first, after which contractions generally begin. Some doctors rush to induce a woman whose water is broken, as this poses possible risks to the mother and baby. As always, a *Rav* should be consulted regarding such matters.

190. Some *Poskim* are stringent regarding niddah when the water breaks if they feel that the woman will deliver the baby imminently. However, they will be lenient when it seems clear that the woman still has time until the delivery. Some women experience their water breaking months before the actual delivery and must receive medical assessment and intervention to stem the onset of early labor and delivery. In such a case, most *Poskim* agree the woman is not a niddah simply because the water broke (Rav Nissim Karelitz).

of *kesamim* apply to any blood that is discovered. Although some are stringent (such as Rav Nissim Karelitz), the practice is that she remains *tehorah* (as per Rav Shmuel HaLevi Wosner's opinion).

- A woman who cannot walk because she is in pain remains *tehorah*. She becomes *temei'ah* when the reason that she cannot walk is that her legs are physically separated too far apart because of the baby's descent into her pelvis.

The Tumah of a Yoledes (One Who Gives Birth) and Mapeles (One Who Miscarries)

- The Torah says a woman who gives birth to a boy is *temei'ah* for 7 days, immerses in the mikvah, and then has 33 days of *dam tahor* in which she is *tehorah* even if she is bleeding. If she has a girl, she has 14 days of *tumah*, then *tevilah*, followed by 66 days of *dam tahor*. Nowadays, a woman also has to count *shivah nekiyim* because of the blood she saw during childbirth.
- Rabbeinu Tam rules that a woman cannot start counting *shivah nekiyim* during her *yemei tumah*. According to Rabbeinu Tam, a woman who gave birth to a boy will never immerse in the mikvah before 14 days, and a woman who gave birth to a girl will never immerse before 21 days.
- The Rif rules that once a woman stops bleeding, counts *shivah nekiyim*, and immerses in the mikvah, she is permitted to engage in marital relations even if she starts bleeding again, as long as it is during *yemei taharah*.[191]
- The Ramban, Raavad, and Roke'ach rule that any blood, whether it is seen during *yemei tumah* or *yemei taharah*, is included in the stringency of Rav Zeira, and a woman requires *shivah nekiyim* to get out of her *tumah* status.
- The *Rambam* says there are places that allow a woman to have marital relations during *yemei tehorah* even if she is bleeding. He rules if that is someone's custom they may follow it; otherwise, one may not.
- The Shulchan Aruch rules a woman may begin counting *shivah nekiyim* during *yemei tumah* — unlike the opinion of Rabbeinu Tam

191. This explanation of the *Rif* is according to the Maharam MiRuttenberg.

— and one may not engage in marital relations when there is *dam tahor.*[192]

- Nowadays, a regular niddah or a woman who gives birth to a boy must wait 12 days to go to the mikvah (besides a *kallah*, or other specific situations in which a woman does not need to wait 5 full days before doing a *hefsek taharah*; see Advanced Rulings, How a Woman Becomes a Niddah, Headline "Taharah After Birth", (page 249), while a woman who gives birth to a girl has to wait 14 days before she can go to the mikvah. This halachah is usually not relevant as most women are unable do a *hefsek taharah* so soon after delivery.

- A woman who miscarried less than 40 days after conception is a regular niddah,[193] not a *yoledes* or *mapeles*.

- A woman who miscarried "a form or a bone" after being pregnant for 40 days must wait 14 days before she may go to the mikvah. Practically, the implementation of this *din* is uncommon because it takes a woman some time to become clean after a miscarriage.

- Rav Yisrael Yaakov Fisher says that even when an ultrasound shows the baby has no heartbeat, one should not rush to do a D&C because of the small chance that the medical equipment was not accurate and the baby may survive. A rav must be certain that the fetus is not viable to allow the woman to proceed with a D&C.

- A D&C is allowed when a woman is hemorrhaging, because that is a threat to the mother's life.

- The *Rama* says that when a woman miscarries and there is "a form or a bone," a *pidyon haben* is not performed for the next child.

- Rav Yosef Shalom Elyashiv says a *pidyon haben* is not performed for a second child when the first pregnancy miscarried after 40 days of pregnancy.

---

192. It is not clear whether the Shulchan Aruch agrees with the Ramban, Raavad, and Roke'ach that this is a *din*, or he agrees with the Rambam that this is a custom. The reason for this uncertainty is that the Shulchan Aruch (190:42) rules that one may attribute a *kesem* to *tahor* blood, even though the *yoledes* is *temei'ah* nowadays. If the reason the *yoledes* is *temei'ah* is because of a *din* (as per the Ramban), then one should not be allowed to attribute the blood to anything because the attribution is going to cause her to be *temei'ah*. If it is only a stringency or custom (as per the Rambam), the ruling of the Shulchan Aruch makes sense, because her stringency is not a reason to cause one not to attribute the blood to something. See *Shulchan Aruch* and *Shach* in 190:42 for added clarity about this subject.

193. Rav Yosef Shalom Elyashiv says the 40th day is considered "after 40 days" in this regard, because part of a day is considered a day.

- Practically speaking, a *pidyon haben* may be performed for a child born from the second pregnancy if an ultrasound performed by an expert showed that the first baby stopped developing before 40 days, and a margin of error was allowed.
- The 40 days are calculated from the last time that the woman went to the mikvah,[194] unless the date of conception is known,[195] such as when the couple or medical staff were tracking the woman's ovulation. This *din* only applies to an actual miscarriage of a "form or a bone," not just a late period.

C-Sections

- A C-section birth is not *metamei* at all as long as no blood is vaginally discharged.[196]
- Any blood that is discharged vaginally is *tamei niddah* — not *yoledes* — and therefore requires 5 days and *shivah nekiyim*, as opposed to 14 total days for a woman who gives birth to a girl.
- Nowadays it is almost certain that a woman who has a C-section will discharge blood vaginally and be *temei'ah niddah* once the surgery is complete,[197] although it is hard to determine at exactly which stage of surgery she becomes *temei'ah*. A couple should observe all *harchakos* once the surgery commences.

Note: A bris is not performed on Shabbos and a *pidyon haben* is not held for a boy born via C-section.[198]

---

194. Based on *Rashi, Niddah* 30:71.

195. The reason for this *din* is the assumption that most women ovulate on or after the night they go to the mikvah, so that night is a good barometer to gauge the age of the miscarried child. The exception to this rule is if the last time she went to the mikvah was due to a *kesem*. In such a case we would calculate the 40 days from the last time she went to the mikvah after a regular *re'iyah*, because that is the normal time for women to ovulate and conceive.

196. Based on *Shulchan Aruch* 194:14.

197. Rav Yosef Shalom Elyashiv; *Nishmas Avraham*; *Pischei Megadim*.

198. See *Chut Shani* 194:6.

Taharah After Birth

- A woman after birth should try to get a *hefsek taharah* whenever she thinks she is able to do so.[199] She should preferably wait until she is certain that she stopped bleeding so she does not perform too many *bedikos* in an area that recently sustained trauma, because that can cause a *makkah* unnecessarily.
- A woman should not use a *moch dachuk* after childbirth because it often causes irritation — i.e., a *makkah*.[200]
- A woman should be very careful not to hurt herself with *bedikos* after birth. If *bedikos* are painful she should contact her *Rav*, who may limit the amount of *bedikos* she should perform.
- Stitches may be a *chatzitzah*, so she may have to wait for them to be removed, fall out, or get absorbed before she can go to the mikvah (see Advanced Rulings, Taharah, Headline "Stitches", page 351)
- A woman after birth may immerse in the mikvah on Friday night if it is a *tevilah b'zmanah* (immersion at the correct time), but should not specifically schedule it to happen on Friday night for convenience. (See Advanced Rulings, Taharah, Headline "A Delayed Mikvah Night in Regard to Shabbos and Yom Tov," (page 368) for the halachos of *tevilah shelo b'zmanah*.)

---

199. A few noteworthy additions regarding this matter: Some doctors will not allow a woman to immerse in the mikvah before the 6-week checkup. Some *sefarim* advise a woman to wait a few months before going to the mikvah after childbirth. While practical halachah allows a woman to immerse whenever she is able to undergo the *taharah* process, she should be sure to consult with a medical professional before going to the mikvah to be sure she has properly healed and that all *chatzitzos*, such as stitches, have been removed (or have dissipated).

Many women use a single-hormone birth control pill after birth while nursing, and can "nurse clean" for a year or so (sometimes less and sometimes more, depending on the woman). Often, however, there is breakthrough bleeding when a new cycle of birth control is begun. This bleeding often occurs a few days after introducing hormones to the body and lasts a few days. While a woman may want to wait until after she is completely ready to go to the mikvah to, with her doctor's guidance, initiate birth control, often this is a mistake. A woman who was ready to become *tehorah* before the 6-week checkup and only starts the birth control afterwards may stain during *shivah nekiyim* and lose more time unnecessarily. It may be advisable, with a doctor's consent, for her to begin the birth control earlier, even if she will not go to the mikvah for another few weeks. In this way the body can become acclimated to the new hormones.

200. This means to say that a woman should not use a *moch* for the *taharah* immediately following the birth, especially if she has stitches (which must be removed before the *tevilah*). Any subsequent *taharah* processes may require a *moch*, especially if the *hefsek taharah* is performed on Day 1 of the new period. In such a case, a *Rav* should be consulted for guidance.

HARCHAKOS

The Twenty Ways That a Niddah Couple May Not Interact

Prohibition	לשון המראה מקום	מ״מ
1. Marital relations	ואל אשה בנדת טמאתה לא תקרב לגלות ערותה	ויקרא יח׳ יט׳ ושו״ע ס׳ קצה׳ ס׳ א׳ וס׳ קפג׳
2. Thinking about prohibited behaviors	ומצד ההרהור יבוא לידי הרגל עבירה	שו״ע ס׳ קצה׳ בט״ז ס״ק ו׳
3. Looking at parts of her body that are normally covered	לא יסתכל אפ׳ בעקבה ולא במקומות המכוסים	שו״ע ס׳ קצה׳ ס׳ ז׳
4. Frivolous behavior	לא ישחוק ולא יקל ראש עמה	שם ס׳ א׳
5. Touching one another	לא יגע בה אפילו באצבע קטנה	שם ס׳ ב׳
6. Directly handing an object	לא יושיט מידו לידה שום דבר ולא יקבלנו מידה	שם
7. Throwing an object	וכן ע״י זריקה מידו לידה או להיפך אסור	שם ס׳ ב׳ ברמ״א

8. Hearing her sing	צ"ע אי מותר לשמוע קול זמר שלה	שם בפתחי תשובה ס"ק י
9. Eating at one table	לא יאכל עמה על השלחן אא"כ יש שום שינוי	שו"ע שם ס' ג'
10. Eating off of one plate	עוד ראיתי שטות גדול שמניחין חתיכות קטנות בקערה א' הוא נוטל אחת והיא נוטלת אחת	שם בט"ז ס"ק ב'
11. Eating her leftovers	אסור לו לאכול משיורי מאכל שלה	שם ס' ג' ברמ"א ושו"ע ד'
12. Serving without a shinui	סוכה גוזמל הרוסא וינפב — 'גה	שם ס' י'
13. Sending wine	לשלוח לה כוס של יין אסור	שם ס' יג'
14. Sitting together on a shaky seat	ואסור לישב על ספסל ארוך שמתנדנדת ואינו מחובר לכותל	שם ברמ"א ס' ה'
15. Preparing the bed	אסורה להציע מטתו בפניו	שם ס' יא'
16. Sleeping on attached beds	אם שוכבים בב' מטות והמטות נוגעות זו בזו אסור	ס' קצה' ס' ו' ברמ"א
17. The husband on his wife's bed	לא ישב במטה המיוחדת לה אפ' שלא בפניה	שם ס' ה'
18. The wife on her husband's bed	ונראה דכ"ש שהיא לא תישן במטה שלו דיש טפי הרהור... אבל ישיבה בעלמה מותר	שם ט"ז ס"ק ו'
19. Preparing water to wash	אסורה ליצוק לו מים לרחוץ	שם ס' יב'
20. Vacationing together	לא ילך עם אשתו בעגלה אחת... אם הולך רק דרך טיול	שם ס' ה' ברמ"א

The Prohibition of Marital Relations

- The prohibition of marital relations that exists in regard to a niddah is when there is entry to the place where *zera l'vatalah* (wasted seminal discharge) is no longer applicable. Anything less than that is called *neshikas ha'eiver*, and is not the *d'Oraisa* prohibition of marital relations.[201]
- In order not to be considered *zera l'vatalah*, a man must be *mazria* into the vaginal canal, not just between the external lips of *oso makom*.

A Niddah during Marital Relations

- If a woman realizes during marital relations that she is bleeding, her husband has to get into a position of being supported by his arms that are fully stretched out down towards the bed so their bodies are not touching, as if he was doing a push-up, not touching her with the rest of his body, but without moving at all internally.[202] He should wait until his erection subsides and be *poreish b'eiver meis* so he will not have pleasure when he comes out.
- The *Chavas Daas* says even when a woman thinks she felt something leave her body during marital relations, she does not have to be concerned that she is a niddah, because many foreign sensations occur during marital relations.[203] In the event that blood is discovered afterwards, the couple is not blamed

201. Although this action is not the *d'Oraisa* prohibition of marital relations, it is almost certainly the *d'Oraisa* prohibition of affectionate touching, which is prohibited when the wife is a niddah.

202. The husband must separate from his wife in a way that does not touch her at all, as any *negiah*, especially in an affectionate way, is prohibited when she is a niddah, yet he should not be *poreish b'eiver chai*. He should wait in that position and then be *poreish b'eiver meis*.

203. The Chavas Daas draws a distinction between when a woman *knows* that blood is emerging from her, and when she *thinks* she feels a *hargashah*. In the latter case he says there is no way to know for certain if it was a *hargashah* of bleeding or a different feeling, and the husband therefore does not have to be *poreish b'eiver meis*. He seems to be lenient even if she suspects that she felt one of the *hargashos* delineated by *Chazal*. Nowadays that women do not have such *hargashos*, it seems clear that a man does not have to be *poreish b'eiver meis* unless they are certain that blood is emerging, and not just when his wife says that she felt something.

for not having realized, and they are considered as though it was not in their control.

- The case of a woman realizing that she became *temei'ah* during marital relations is not at all common. Sensations felt during marital relations are nothing to be concerned about (and, according to the *Chavas Daas*, a woman should not be taught to look out for them). In any case, the room should always be dark during marital relations, so blood cannot be seen.

- The most common case of the need to be *poreish b'eiver meis* is when a woman discovered blood, forgot about it, and remembered during marital relations. In this scenario, her husband must get into the position discussed earlier so he will not have pleasure from touching her body, and be *poreish b'eiver meis*.

- The same is true in the event that an *onah beinonis* or a *vest kavua* passed and the woman neglected to do a *bedikah*. Since she is considered *temei'ah* until she does a *bedikah* and it comes out clean, her husband must push himself up and be *poreish b'eiver meis*. The same applies the night of the *onah beinonis* or *vest kavua* if the couple forgot it was the *vest* and initiated marital relations.

- See the *Rama* 185:4 regarding the atonement necessary for a couple who had marital relations when it was prohibited.

- Rav Shmuel HaLevi Wosner says a couple that had marital relations while the woman was a niddah should repent and do good deeds, give charity, and learn Torah,[204] specifically focusing on relearning *hilchos niddah*.

Histaklus: Other Women

- Every woman must cover the following areas of her body when she is around any man other than her husband:
    - *Ervah b'etzem*, which is from the collar bone down to the knees, including the knees (which is called *shok* in the Gemara). Additionally, she must cover her *zero'a*, which is

---

204. Rav Nissim Karelitz says a couple that had marital relations while the woman was a niddah are deserving of *kareis*. They should therefore learn more Torah, because the Torah is life-giving, as it says in *Mishlei* (3:18), "*Eitz chaim hi lamachazikim bah* — It is a tree of life to those who grasp it."

her arm from the top to the elbow, including the elbow.[205] These areas constitute *das Moshe* and apply to all women.

- She must cover her hair.
- *Das Yehudis*, to whatever the standard of her community is, such as covering from the elbow to the wrist and from the knee to the foot.

› Rav Moshe Feinstein says hair may be showing up to a *tefach* (approximately 4 inches) because it is not *ervah b'etzem*. This means a square *tefach* can be seen *bedi'eved* without violating *das Moshe*. She cannot show a *tefach* of hair all around her head.

› A woman who goes against the standard in her community violates *das Yehudis*, and can be divorced without receiving her *kesubah* monies. (This is according to the ruling in the Gemara; nowadays this is not implemented).

› A man may not look at the parts of a strange woman that are *ervah b'etzem*, even if he is not doing it to derive pleasure. Therefore, he should *lechatchilah* avoid situations in which he will be exposed unnecessarily to women who expose these areas.

› By a strange woman, everything else, including areas that may be uncovered (face and hands) and whatever is considered *das Yehudis*, is included in the prohibition of "*histaklus*." *Histaklus* does not mean "seeing"; it means "gazing." It is forbidden to view those areas of a woman's body with the intention to derive pleasure, but is not forbidden to see them with no intention to derive pleasure.

› Looking at a person in a way that is prohibited is the prohibition of "*lo sikrevu*" (*Vayikra* 18:6). Looking at a picture of something prohibited is the prohibition of "*lo sasuru*" (*Bamidbar* 15:39).

› A woman may use a male doctor because doctors generally do not view their patients as human beings, but rather as a sort of medical specimens.[206]

---

205. *Kesubos* 72b.

206. Obviously a woman must stop using a doctor who she feels is acting inappropriately (even, according to Rav Nissim Karelitz, if it is *pikuach nefesh*!). In additon, if a woman does use a male doctor, she must not act in forbidden ways that are not necessary for her health, for example, she may not shake hands with her gynecologist.

Histaklus: One's Niddah Wife

- Rav Moshe Feinstein says a woman who normally walks around the house with her forearms uncovered may do so when she is a niddah. This also applies to her legs below the knees and her hair (*das Yehudis)*.[207] But, no matter what she wears when she is *tehorah*, she must cover from her knees to her neck (and her arms down to the elbows[208]) when she is a niddah because this area is called *shok*, and is *ervah b'etzem*.[209]
- Rav Yosef Shalom Elyashiv says a woman has to dress in front of her husband when she is a niddah in the way she would if a strange man were in the house, so she must cover whichever areas are considered "covered areas" (*das Moshe*) and anything she would normally cover when around strange men (*das Yehudis*).
- In Eretz Yisrael and Europe, *chassanim* and *kallos* are taught according to Rav Yosef Shalom Elyashiv's position. People in the United States are generally taught Rav Moshe Feinstein's opinion. American women may wear basic pajamas,[210] and in Eretz Yisrael the women buy slippers so that the husbands cannot even see their wives' toes.[211]
- Rav Shmuel HaLevi Wosner says that although the Rama says the husband may look at parts of his wife's body that do not have to be covered, it cannot be to the point where it causes *hirhur*, as this is prohibited in and of itself.[212]
- Rav Moshe Feinstein says a woman may uncover her hair around her husband when she is a niddah even though she

207. These areas fall into the category of *das Yehudis*. Therefore, if she normally dresses in a lax manner when she is *tehorah*, she can continue to dress that way when she is *temei'ah*, as long as she does not uncover *ervah b'etzem*, which is considered *das Moshe* and cannot be compromised, even if she normally is not careful to keep those areas covered.

208. *Mishnah Berurah, Orach Chaim* 75:2.

209. Rav Dovid Feinstein.

210. Clearly, the couple has to be honest with themselves regarding these halachos.

211. The *Shulchan Aruch* and *Poskim* do not discuss the way a man should dress when his wife is a niddah, and there are seemingly no restrictions on her to look at his "covered areas" while she is a niddah. That said, a person should always adhere to general rules of *tznius* and self-dignity, and the couple must be careful never to come to frivolous behavior while the wife is a niddah.

212. *Sidrei Taharah*.

generally keeps it covered when she is *tehorah*, because her husband saw her hair when they were single, and hair is not *ervah b'etzem*.[213]

- Rav Shmuel HaLevi Wosner and other *Poskim* disagree with this ruling, and maintain that a woman must cover her hair when she is a niddah so her husband does not see it.
- Rav Shmuel HaLevi Wosner and Rav Nissim Karelitz say it is best for the husband not to be present at the time his wife gives birth, because it is hard to avoid gazing at her "covered areas."[214] Rav Moshe Feinstein rules that the husband may be present during childbirth, but should avoid *histaklus* of her "covered areas."
- The *Pischei Teshuvah* cites the Noda B'Yehudah, who allows a husband to serve as his wife's "mikvah lady" to watch her immerse in the mikvah if no one else is around to serve that function. We rely on this ruling in extenuating circumstances when there is no other choice.[215] The reason for this ruling is that we can assume that he will not stumble when she is about to be *tehorah*.

Kalus Rosh

- Many *Poskim* define *kalus rosh* as the couple losing themselves to the point that they forget what the wife's status is, or they discuss something that generally leads to intimacy.[216]
- A couple may tell jokes and have a good time when the wife is a niddah.

---

213. Although it is praiseworthy for a woman to strive to attain the level of Kimchis, who said about herself that the walls of her home never saw her hair uncovered (as well as the rest of her body, adds the Ramban), she does not have to cover her hair when she is a niddah, according to Rav Moshe Feinstein.

214. Religious hospitals in Eretz Yisrael have differing guidelines regarding whether to allow the husband to remain in the delivery room or not once active labor has commenced. Many hospitals allow him to remain in the room, behind a curtain. In secular hospitals there are generally no restrictions on the part of the hospital. In all cases it is up to the husband to avoid *histaklus*.

215. Rav Shmuel HaLevi Wosner.

216. An example of this is brought in *Shu"t Be'er Moshe*, which says that a niddah wife should not dance in front of her husband, even in *tznius* clothing, because this is a form of *kalus rosh*.

- They may not speak intimately, or make light of intimate things.
- Rav Nissim Karelitz and Rav Shmuel HaLevi Wosner say a man may send flowers to his wife for Shabbos or after birth, and may also give her presents, because these acts generally do not lead to *kalus rosh*.[217]
- They cannot talk about what they miss from the *tahor* days or what they wish they could be doing had she been *tehorah*.
- A couple may not talk passionately when the woman is a niddah, but they may talk about things that bring them closer as a couple. The husband may tell his wife how appreciative he is of everything she does for him, as long as the conversation does not lead to intimacy.[218]
- A couple should not have a "romantic dinner" when the wife is a niddah. This refers to an atmosphere that generally leads to intimacy.[219]
- Rav Nissim Karelitz says that playing games together is permitted,[220] unless play generally leads them to *kalus rosh*.[221]
- Rav Yosef Shalom Elyashiv and Rav Shmuel HaLevi Wosner say a niddah couple should be stringent not to play games together, even if the game generally does not lead to intimacy.
- Practically speaking, the halachah is lenient as per the opinion of Rav Nissim Karelitz, unless the game is of the nature that generally leads to *kalus rosh* or intimacy.
- Rav Nissim Karelitz says the prohibition of *kalus rosh* with a niddah applies to both the husband and the wife.

---

217. Rav Shmuel HaLevi Wosner says an intimate gift "such as something a man may present to his wife before going go the mikvah" should be avoided. Some *Poskim* do not allow a husband to send any gift to his niddah wife, regardless of its nature, just as the *Shulchan Aruch* prohibits sending a cup of wine. Most *Poskim* disagree and say the only presents that should be avoided are those that are comparable to wine (i.e., presents that may lead to *kalus rosh* or intimacy), but all other presents may be sent.

218. Rav Nissim Karelitz.

219. The example would include when the couple sets up a special table with a tablecloth and candles during the week.

220. For example, board games, cards, and dreidel.

221. Some European *Poskim* do not allow a husband and his niddah wife to play board and card games. The reason may be that in refined European cultures playing a board game with a woman signifies the initiation of something intrinsically intimate, whereas Americans simply view it as "having a good time."

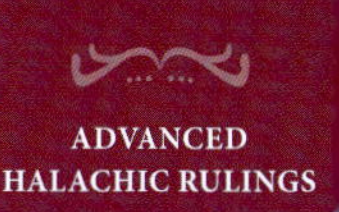

- The *Pischei Teshuvah* says that included in *kalus rosh* is the prohibition for a man to smell his wife's perfume when she is a niddah, even when she is not wearing it (for example, when it is on the nightstand).
- Rav Nissim Karelitz says a man may smell his wife's deodorant even if it is scented.

Touching a Stranger of the Opposite Gender

- Touching a stranger of the opposite gender with the intention to derive pleasure is *yehareg v'al yaavor*.
- Touching a strange woman without any intention to have pleasure is permitted *lechatchilah*. An example would be helping an old woman across the street or shaking someone's hand.
- Accidentally touching a strange woman's hand is not prohibited even *mid'Rabbanan*. No atonement is necessary if such an action happened.
- Before shaking a woman's hand, one must realize that there is a very fine line between incidental touching which is permitted *lechatchilah* and intimate touching which is *yehareg v'al yaavor*. If someone is really sure there is no pleasure, he may shake hands with a strange woman. Whenever someone is not absolutely sure, he must avoid shaking her hand.
- Shaking a non-Jewish woman's hand is prohibited and has the same applications as above.[222]

Touching One Another; Directly Handing or Throwing an Object

- The *Shulchan Aruch*[223] says touching one's spouse in an intimate manner is prohibited *mid'Oraisa* when the wife is a niddah.[224] Elsewhere the *Shulchan Aruch* implies that any form of touching

222. Rav Shmuel HaLevi Wosner. He adds that a man should not shake any woman's hand even if it is not in a way that will give him pleasure.

223. *Even HaEzer* 20:1.

224. *Rambam*.

is prohibited *mid'Oraisa*.[225] Directly handing something to one's spouse is prohibited *mid'Rabbanan*.

- The *Rama* says touching affectionately, directly handing objects to each other, and throwing objects to each other are all prohibited *mid'Rabbanan*.[226]
- We will soon see that the distinction between whether these actions are prohibited *mid'Oraisa* or *mid'Rabbanan* applies in regard to helping a sick spouse.
- A couple must be certain not to touch one another when they are doing something within close proximity of each other, as non-affectionate touching is at least Rabbinically prohibited.[227]
- Rav Shmuel HaLevi Wosner says a niddah couple should not walk under the same umbrella or read from the same book since they may accidentally touch one another. If they certainly will not touch, it is permitted.[228]
- Rav Shmuel HaLevi Wosner says the prohibition of touching one another applies even when the other spouse is sleeping.
- The prohibition of handing one's spouse something applies even when other people are around.[229]
- Rav Shmuel HaLevi Wosner says a niddah couple should be careful to avoid touching each other's clothing. Even contact between their clothes should be avoided.

Indirect Touching

- The *Taz* says that if not for the prohibition of preparing water to wash, a woman would be allowed to pour water on her husband.

225. *Yoreh Dei'ah* 195:17.

226. *Ramban*.

227. Rav Nissim Karelitz cites a Medrash (*Shemos Rabbah* 16:2) that says that women are compared to grapes, based on the *passuk* that says, "*Eshtecha k'gefen poriah* — Your wife is like a blossoming grape vine." This teaches us that just as a nazir, who is forbidden to drink wine, must also refrain from coming in contact with grapes, a man who must stay away from marital relations with a niddah must also distance himself from touching her.

228. Rav Nissim Karelitz.

229. Rav Moshe Feinstein; Rav Shmuel HaLevi Wosner.

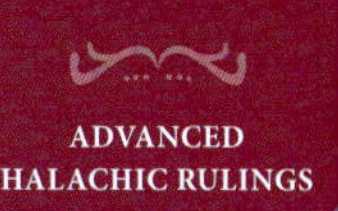

- From the *Taz* we see that touching one another through another object is permitted,[230] and may be relied upon in extenuating circumstances.[231] In such a case, one spouse can touch the other spouse with an item, but cannot directly hand that item from one to the other.[232]
- This *Taz* may *only* be relied upon in extenuating circumstances, as we will soon see.
- The *Megillas Esther* and Rav Nissim Karelitz say gloves and clothes are considered like skin when it comes to *negiah*, and it is therefore prohibited for a couple to touch each other's clothing while they are wearing it. It is permitted to touch clothing that the other person is not wearing.[233]

Practical Cases of Indirect Touching

- A man can give his wife injections while she is a niddah if she cannot do it herself and there is no one else is available to do it for her. He can do it without directly touching her.[234] This is even permitted if she is not ill.
- Rav Moshe Feinstein says a man may not push his wife in a wheelchair when she is a niddah.
- Rav Nissim Karelitz says that based on the *Taz*, the husband may push his wife in a wheelchair in extenuating circumstances, for example, if no one else is around to help her, and the couple avoids *kalus rosh*.
- Practically speaking, one may rely on Rav Nissim Karelitz's opinion when necessary.

---

230. Rav Nissim Karelitz.

231. Rav Shmuel HaLevi Wosner explains that while the Taz holds that touching through another object is permitted, the Shach disagrees. Rav Wosner himself rules like the Shach, while Rav Nissim Karelitz and Rav Yitzchak Berkovits rule like the Taz, but only in extenuating circumstances.

232. This is because directly handing something is a connection between one person and the other through touching an item; this is not called a connection.

233. It is certainly permitted for a man to do the laundry when his wife is a niddah. The prohibition against the husband's touching his wife's clothing is only while she is wearing it.

234. It seems that the woman should not hold the other end of the needle with her hand, because that would be completing a connection between the two of them.

- Rav Shmuel HaLevi Wosner says a man may electronically raise the hospital bed for his wife after she gives birth even if there are no extenuating circumstances, since it is a very indirect way of causing movement that affects her. In extenuating circumstances, he can even raise the bed manually.
- Rav Yitzchak Berkovits allows a man whose wife is snoring to shake her for a short period of time with a book if this will cause her to stop snoring, to allow him to fall sleep.

Carrying Heavy Items Together

- A niddah couple may not carry anything together; this halachah is taught *lechatchilah.*
- Rav Shmuel HaLevi Wosner says it is prohibited for a niddah couple to carry something together, even if the item is very heavy.
- Rav Nissim Karelitz says that in extenuating circumstances, an item that needs to be carried by two people may be carried by a niddah couple.[235]
- One may rely on Rav Nissim Karelitz's opinion only in extenuating circumstances. For example, a couple may carry a carriage together up many flights of stairs if there is no one else to help the husband.

Other Forms of Passing

- The Tashbetz says a child may be passed from one spouse to the other, since the child is really going on its own because a living being carries its own weight.[236]
- The age from which a baby may be handed from one spouse to the other is when the child can roll over or really move on their own from one person to another.

235. Immediately after bringing this leniency, Rav Nissim Karelitz quotes the Chayei Adam, who says a niddah couple cannot carry an object together even if many people are helping to carry this item. Seemingly, he wants to emphasize that a niddah couple may only be lenient and carry an item together in extenuating circumstances, or he certainly would have been lenient when the item is so heavy that many people are required to carry it.

236. *Pischei Teshuvah* 195:3.

- Rav Shlomo Zalman Auerbach is quoted as saying that once the baby reached this age, the couple may hand the baby to each other even if the child is sleeping or fighting not to go.[237]

- If the husband is not at all involved in handing the object to his wife, she may place something on him and may even directly take an item off of him. An example is when the husband falls asleep with a baby who has not reached the age of carrying itself on him; the wife may take the baby off.

- Even if the wife is passive, her husband cannot place something on her just as he cannot place something in her hand. However, he can take something off of her if she is completely passive.

- Rav Nissim Karelitz says when the *wife* falls asleep with the baby, the husband *cannot* take the baby off of her, unless it is absolutely necessary (for example, explains Rav Yitzchak Berkovits, when there is a danger to the baby).

- The Chidda says a niddah couple may serve as *kvatter* at a bris by putting one pillow on top of another one, with the baby resting on the top pillow. Instead of taking the baby directly from his wife, the husband instead takes the top pillow and the baby off the bottom pillow.

- The *Darchei Teshuvah* and Rav Shmuel HaLevi Wosner say a niddah couple may not place one pillow on top of another in order to serve as *kvatter*.

- Practically speaking, when nobody knows about the woman's status other than her husband, the fact that she is a niddah should not be advertised to everyone at the bris.[238] If a couple is offered to serve as *kvatter* when the woman is a niddah, ideally, they should respectfully decline. If this is not possible, the options that they have are to give the baby to an intermediate person, or to put the child on a chair.

- Rav Shmuel HaLevi Wosner says when one spouse is holding a child, the other spouse may not feed the child or give the child a kiss.

- Rav Yosef Shalom Elyashiv and Rav Nissim Karelitz say that in extenuating circumstances, when one spouse is holding a child,

237. This ruling is not in agreement with the *Pischei Teshuvah* 195:3.

238. Related by Rav Yossi Stilerman.

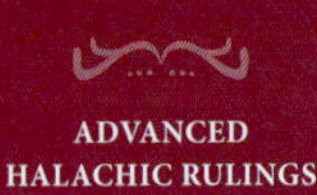

the other spouse may feed the child or give them medicine or ear drops.

- Rav Nissim Karelitz says the couple should refrain from washing a baby together when a woman is a niddah because it is very difficult to avoid contact.
- Practically speaking, a couple may interact with the same child so long as they are careful not to touch each other or come to *kalus rosh*.
- Rav Shmuel HaLevi Wosner says although it is true that a living being carries its own weight, *lechatchilah* a niddah couple should not walk with a child, each one holding one hand.

Havdalah

- One spouse may not light the Havdalah candle that the other spouse is holding.[239]
- A woman who is a niddah may hold the Havdalah candle while her husband makes the *brachah*.[240]
- One spouse may smell the *besamim* (spices) that the other spouse is holding. However, Rav Yosef Shalom Elyashiv is stringent, and equates the husband's smelling *besamim* that his wife is holding to his smelling her perfume, which is prohibited. Similarly, Rav Shmuel HaLevi Wosner is stringent.

Throwing an Object to One's Spouse

- Some (based on the *Pischei Teshuvah*) permit throwing an object in the air indirectly — not straightforwardly — in the spouse's direction, so that the spouse can move over and catch it.
- Rav Nissim Karelitz, Rav Shmuel HaLevi Wosner, and Rav Yitzchak Berkovits (based on the *Sidrei Taharah*) do not like this leniency, because it turns the whole prohibition of handing and throwing objects into a joke. Rav Berkovits therefore says one should teach that it is prohibited, although it may be done when necessary.

---

239. Rav Nissim Karelitz.

240. Rav Moshe Feinstein; Rav Yosef Shalom Elyashiv; Rav Nissim Karelitz; Rav Shmuel HaLevi Wosner.

- Rav Yossi Stilerman said that indirectly throwing something that is delicate or expensive, in which case it is understood that it *must* be caught or it will break, is prohibited according to everyone.[241]
- The *Pischei Teshuvah* says that included in the prohibition of one spouse throwing something to the other is that they may not blow something off each other's clothing.

Indirectly Passing or Throwing an Object

- Rav Yosef Shalom Elyashiv, Rav Nissim Karelitz, and Rav Shmuel HaLevi Wosner say a husband may not put something into or take something from a bag that his niddah wife is holding.[242] He also may not take a key from his wife's purse that is hanging from her shoulder. He also may not throw something into the bag she is holding.
- Rav Shmuel HaLevi Wosner says the husband may not place something into or take something out of her clothing or pocket.
- Rav Nissim Karelitz says the husband may certainly put something into or take something from a wagon or stroller that his niddah wife is pushing. This is because she is simply pushing it, but is not actually supporting the stroller.

241. For example, a man may not indirectly throw his phone towards his wife, because it is understood that if she will not catch it, it will break.

242. Many *Poskim*, including Rav Yitzchak Berkovits, are lenient regarding touching through an intermediate object in extenuating circumstances, and it would seem that these same *Poskim* should really be lenient in regard to directly handing something through an intermediate object, which is certainly more lenient than touching. The reason they are stringent in cases such as taking or passing something from a handbag is because touching through an intermediate object is only permitted when there is an urgent need, and it is very rare that one would need to pass something through an intermediate object without having the option to use an intermediary person or to place the item on the ground. It seems to me that if one can think of a case that should allow for passing through an intermediate object, they certainly have what to rely on. Rav Nissim Karelitz actually brings (195:2:7) that indirect throwing would be permitted in extenuating circumstances, although he does not elaborate on what such a case would be. It must be remembered, though, that doing an unnecessary act, such as serving as *kvatter* by a bris, is certainly not considered an extenuating circumstance. One should consult with a competent *Posek* before implementing such a ruling.

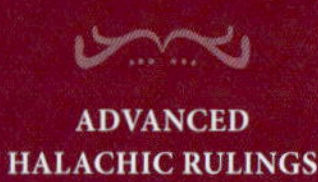

- Rav Nissim Karelitz says one may not hand something to their spouse with the wrong hand.[243] One may also not directly hand something in front of other people if the wife is a niddah.[244]

- Rav Nissim Karelitz says when one spouse opens a door, the other spouse may hold the door to keep it open. This is not called "handing something," since the door supports itself on its hinges.

- In the event that something was accidentally directly handed from one spouse to the other, there is no prohibition to use that item (as is the case regarding something that was affected by a *melachah* on Shabbos).

Kol Ishah: All Women

- It is prohibited to say *divrei Torah* when a woman is singing, even if she is not a niddah.

- Rav Yisrael Yaakov Fisher says that when a man is used to hearing his wife (or other relative) sing, he can say *divrei Torah* when she sings, as long as she is *tehorah*.

- The prohibition of *kol ishah* applies whenever the prohibition of *yichud* applies, no matter how bad the woman's voice sounds.

- A man may stay in a place where women are singing if he is not paying attention and is focused on other things. He may also learn in that place if he cannot go somewhere else easily, as it says, "*Eis laasos laHashem heifeiru Torasecha*" — we sometimes need to be lenient in order to enable doing a mitzvah (a *Rav* should always be consulted to decide when one may be lenient and when not). This means that generally, when women start singing he can tune them out, but cannot specifically go somewhere that women are singing.

- If someone's great-aunt came for a meal, for example, and begins to sing, the solution is to sing along with her so that there will

243. Rav Yitzchak Berkovits explains this *din* as follows: the main prohibition is a direct connection of passing between the husband and his wife, with the emphasis of the prohibition being on the husband. However, if one of them is passive, there may be room for leniency. A woman may put something on her husband or take something off him (such as his lap) if he is passive and not actively involved in the action. If she is passive, he may take something from her lap but may not place something on her, as this is akin to passing it to her.

244. Rav Moshe Feinstein.

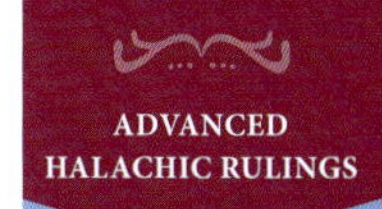

be at least two voices singing, which is less problematic. This is not *lechatchilah*, but may be relied on when necessary.

- Rav Yosef Shalom Elyashiv says *kol ishah* is not an issue with sisters, daughters, or mothers even though they are prohibited to a man. Thus, a woman may sing in front of her brothers. This applies even after they are married.
- It is permitted for a choir to sing *zemiros* at a *Kiruv Shabbaton* because of the following reasons: (1) there are more than one voice, thus removing the focus from the prohibited voices, (2) a mitzvah does not cause *hirhur*, and (3) this is a situation of "*eis laasos*" (see above).
- Rav Yisrael Yaakov Fisher says one may give a Torah lecture in front of women whose hair is uncovered.
- Practically speaking, this applies even in a situation in which women are dressed immodestly, because of "*eis laasos*."
- Rav Yaakov Kaminetzky told stories and avoided saying real *divrei Torah* in front of immodestly dressed women.

Kol Ishah: One's Niddah Wife

- A man should be stringent and not listen to his wife singing when she is a niddah — even if he is used to hearing her voice —because of the concern that he might come to *hirhur*.
- When a woman is singing children's songs to the kids, the husband should not pay attention if it may cause *hirhur*. It seems that this would be permitted because there is little concern that nursery songs will cause *hirhur*. Sefaradim are stringent not to listen to a niddah wife singing, no matter what she is singing.
- It seems that a woman can sing *zemiros* when she is *tehorah*, but not when she is a niddah.[245]
- Practically speaking, a family may sing *zemiros* together.[246] The Soloveitchik families used to sing the Haggadah together, regardless of whether one of the women at the table happened to be a niddah.

245. Rav Shmuel HaLevi Wosner.

246. In this scenario there is more than one voice and it is a mitzvah endeavor, although it is not "*eis laasos*."

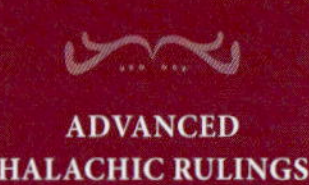

- Some teach that a niddah may sing *zemiros* with the family, but no other songs. If one was taught this way, they may do so.
- The Minchas Yitzchak, Rav Yosef Shalom Elyashiv, Rav Shmuel HaLevi Wosner, and Rav Nissim Karelitz say a wife may play a musical instrument when she is a niddah, and her husband may listen to her play. She should not specifically play for him (for example, a serenade) because this is a form of *kalus rosh*, as well as a form of affection.
- Rav Nissim Karelitz says a man may have pleasure from hearing his wife's voice when she is a niddah (as long as it does not lead to hirhur).

Recordings of Women Singing

- There is a disagreement whether or not it is permitted for a man to listen to a recording of a woman singing. Rav Ovadia Yosef says if the man knows what she looks like it is prohibited, and if he does not, it is permitted.
- It seems that it should be permitted to listen to a recording in which the woman singing is no longer alive.
- Rav Moshe Feinstein says it is a *davar meguneh* (disgusting thing) to listen to a recording of a deceased woman singing. It is therefore prohibited, but not because of *kol ishah*.

When a Heker Is Necessary

- A niddah couple may not eat at the same table without some sort of *heker* between them.
- Rav Yosef Shalom Elyashiv says this only applies if they are eating a meal together, not if they are having a snack.
- Rav Shmuel HaLevi Wosner says they need a *heker* when they are having drinks together.
- Rav Nissim Karelitz says when a husband makes Kiddush for his wife on Shabbos morning and they eat a piece of cake together, it is considered a snack, not a meal, and no *heker* is necessary.

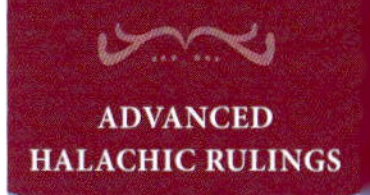

- Rav Nissim Karelitz says there is no need for a *heker* if only one of them is eating, even if the spouse is sitting with them at the table.
- A *heker* is not necessary if the couple is sitting with an empty chair between them.
- Rav Yosef Shalom Elyashiv says there is no need for a *heker* if someone is sitting between them.
- Rav Nissim Karelitz says if the woman sits in a different seat during her niddah days, that itself is a valid *shinui*,[247] and no other *heker* is necessary.[248]
- Rav Nissim Karelitz and Rav Shmuel HaLevi Wosner say a *heker* is still needed in the event that a couple is eating a meal together and one of them is holding their plate in the air instead of making use of the table, as the normal thing is to use the table to eat a meal. If the husband and wife are eating together but there is no table at all in front of them, they do not need any *heker*, because that is not called eating "together."[249]
- Rav Shmuel HaLevi Wosner and Rav Nissim Karelitz say a couple that is using a *heker* for meat and dairy may use the same *heker* for niddah, because in both cases they are using an item that serves to remind them not to eat "together." It is not necessary to have two reminders to refrain from the same act.
- Rav Shmuel HaLevi Wosner says if the couple is sitting across the table from each other, such as when they are sitting at the opposite heads of the table, and there is a distance between them, they do not need any *heker*. If the table is small and they are across from each other, they still need a *heker*.

---

247. It is not clear why Rav Nissim Karelitz says that the woman is the one who must switch her seat, and not the husband. If the reason is to serve as a reminder for the man (as Rav Nissim Karelitz himself holds) it seems that when a man is sitting in a different seat than usual, it would certainly serve to remind him of her status, and therefore serve as a valid *heker*. Practically speaking, many *Rabbanim* say that the man's switching his seat is a valid *heker*, and the reason Rav Nissim Karelitz says the wife should switch her seat is that most men generally have a designated seat at the head of the table and are not going to switch their seats as easily as a woman would. That said, if he would switch his seat, it certainly would serve as a valid *heker*.

248. *Beis Yosef*; *Sidrei Taharah*.

249. This often happens at a smorgasbord, where people stand together eating without making use of a table.

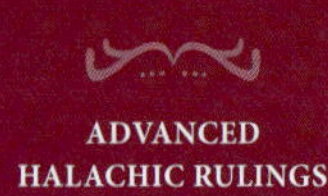

What Serves as a Valid Heker

- The *heker* can be something that is normally on the table but is not being used for this meal, or something that is generally not on the table that is being used for this meal.[250] For example, they can bring out a honey dish and make use of it during this meal if they only use honey on Rosh HaShanah.
- Many *Poskim* (including Rav Shmuel HaLevi Wosner) say the *heker* must be noticeable to both the husband and wife. Rav Nissim Karelitz, however, says the prohibition is on the husband; as long as he knows about the *heker* they may eat together even if his wife is unaware which item he is using.
- Rav Yosef Shalom Elyashiv and Rav Nissim Karelitz say the *heker* must be between the husband and wife and have some height.
- Rav Shmuel HaLevi Wosner says the *heker* does not have to be directly between the couple or their plates; it may be placed a bit to the side, as long as it is recognizable to both of them. Also, something is acceptable as a *heker* even when it does not have any height to it, such as a ring.
- Rav Nissim Karelitz and Rav Shmuel HaLevi Wosner say another *heker* is needed if the couple generally use placemats when eating. If they do not generally use placemats, then placemats are a good *heker*. It is enough for only one of them to use a placemat; they do not both need to use them. One spouse eating on the tablecloth and the other eating on the bare table is a valid *heker*.
- Rav Shmuel HaLevi Wosner and Rav Nissim Karelitz say if there is something that is always on the table (like a vase) and it is moved between the couple, it serves as a valid *heker*, even though they are used to seeing this item on the table.

250. This is learned from the *din* of *lechem* (bread) or *kankan* (pitcher), which means that something that is always on the table but is not currently being used, such as bread, or something that is not normally on the table but is now being used, such as a new pitcher, is valid as a *heker*.

When Others Are Around

- The *Pischei Teshuvah* says there is a disagreement whether a *heker* is needed when other people are around.
- Rav Shlomo Zalman Auerbach says when others are around the *heker* can be less noticeable, like a matchbox, napkin, or bottle cap, but a *heker* should ideally be used.
- Rav Shmuel HaLevi Wosner says *lechatchilah* a *heker* should be used when others are around. If the situation is one in which using a *heker* is embarrassing around other people, there is room to be lenient.

Note: If a couple is lenient regarding this halachah, they should recognize that it is the only one of the twenty *harchakos* that some *Poskim* are lenient about when other people are around.

Eating from One Plate

- A niddah couple may not eat off of *ke'arah achas* (one plate) without each spouse first transferring the food to their own, individual plate.
- Two definitions are given for *ke'arah achas*, which a niddah couple may not eat together from:

1. The *Poskim* of Eretz Yisrael say that all foods, even something that is normally eaten straight from the serving dish (for example, hors d'oeuvres), must be placed on individual plates, or someone else must take between the husband and the wife.
    - Example: A husband and wife can take cake that is meant to be put on plates (for example, birthday cake) one after the other and eat it only if they first transfer it to their individual plates. Similarly, one spouse may not take cake that is meant to be eaten by hand (for example, *kiddush* cake) immediately after the other one unless they put it down first on an individual plate, or if someone else takes a piece of cake between them.
2. Rav Moshe Feinstein explains that the prohibition of *ke'arah achas* applies only to food that is not normally eaten directly from the plate. If the food on the serving dish is something that is meant to be directly eaten by many people, the couple may take some of it one right after the other, even if this dish

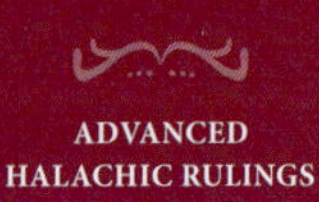

is generally eaten by hand. If the food on the serving dish is something that is generally eaten only after transferring it to a private plate, it must be transferred before being eaten.

- Example: *Kiddush* cake, which is meant to be eaten by hand by many people, may be taken by one spouse after the other and eaten without first placing it on individual plates. Birthday cake, which is normally eaten from a plate, must be transferred to individual plates before consumption.

- Practically speaking, Americans should be taught according to Rav Moshe Feinstein's opinion, and people living in Eretz Yisrael should be taught according to the opinion of the *Poskim* in Eretz Yisrael.

- Rav Shmuel HaLevi Wosner and Rav Nissim Karelitz say if either the husband or the wife takes food from a plate and puts it in front of themselves on an individual plate or napkin or on the table, it is no longer called *ke'arah achas*.[251] If they take from a serving plate food that is normally eaten only from an individual plate, and place the food on the table just to permit eating from the same plate, it is still included in the prohibition of *ke'arah achas*.[252]

- Rav Shmuel HaLevi Wosner says that in the event that one spouse transfers food to an individual plate, the other may then eat directly from the serving plate because they are essentially eating from two separate plates. The first spouse may no longer make use of the commandeered plate.

- Rav Nissim Karelitz says when one spouse eats from one area of a multi-sectional dish, the other spouse may eat from a separate area. Each section is viewed as its own *ke'arah achas*. The opposite is also true: if two foods are on one plate and one spouse eats from one food, the other cannot eat from the other

---

251. Based on the *Taz* 195:2.

252. An example of this *din*: a husband and wife are eating chicken, which is normally only eaten from individual plates — they need to transfer the chicken and then eat it (according to all opinions). Rav Shmuel HaLevi Wosner is saying they cannot simply place the chicken on the table for a second and then eat it with their fingers, saying they transferred it to individual settings. In order to permit eating food that is on the same (serving) plate, the food must actually be transferred to an individual plate before being consumed.

food even if it is sitting on the plate separately from the foods that have been eaten from,[253] unless it is first transferred.[254]

Note: Although Rav Nissim Karelitz is stringent regarding *ke'arah achas*, he almost certainly would be lenient regarding leftover food. If the wife eats from a piece of chicken and does not touch the rice, although the husband may not eat the rice from her plate while she is eating, he may eat it once it is transferred to another plate after she is finished eating (as per the opinion of the *Poskim* in Eretz Yisrael).

- The husband may eat his portion if his wife simply tasted his food, even if she did not transfer it to a different dish. The *dinim* of of *ke'arah achas* and leftovers do not apply to this portion.

Leftover Food

- The *Shulchan Aruch* says a woman may eat her husband's leftovers. However, the husband may not eat his wife's leftovers.
- Drinking her leftovers from her cup is also forbidden.
- Regarding leftover drink, the *Rama* offers various options that permit him to drink her leftovers:
  1. If she has left the room
  2. If the drink has been poured into another cup
  3. If someone else drinks in between the wife and the husband
  4. If he does not know that she drank from this cup
- Regarding the application of these leniencies to leftover food, there is a debate among the *Poskim*. The *Poskim* of Eretz Yisrael say that all the above leniencies apply. Therefore, when another person eats from the woman's food after she ate from it, the husband may then also partake from it. Or, if he transfers her portion to another plate, he can eat from it, even though no one else ate from it in the middle. Also, the husband may eat his wife's leftovers if she left the room completely, even without transferring it to another plate.

253. In the above case, the prohibition would be *ke'arah achas*, which would prohibit the couple from partaking of the food at the same time. However, according to most *Poskim*, the untouched food would not fall into the category of leftovers if the woman does not eat from the food at all. Therefore, no *shinui* (such as the husband waiting for his wife to leave the room, transferring plates, or the like — see below) is required before eating such food.

254. Rav Shmuel HaLevi Wosner.

- Rav Moshe Feinstein agrees that if the food is such that most people would eat other people's leftovers in such a situation, for example, portions of food that she has not touched, like the rice when she ate the chicken, then these leniencies do apply.[255] Also, items that others would be happy to continue eating (perhaps a portion of roasted potatoes) may be transferred similarly. (Rav Yitzchak Berkovits explains that this is only true if the portions have been first moved from her plate onto an independent plate; then, he can transfer it to his plate.) However, according to Rav Moshe Feinstein, if the food is such that most people would not eat others' leftovers, for example, if she has bitten from a piece of chicken, the leniencies of transferring the food onto another plate or someone else eating in between the spouses do not apply, and there is no way to permit him to eat this food in front of her. Additionally, Rav Moshe Feinstein says that any food that is meant for one person may not be split between a niddah couple. For example, a can of soda or a roll is generally meant to be consumed by only one person; it may not be split between the couple, even if they transfer it to two separate plates or cups.
- Rav Shmuel HaLevi Wosner and the *She'arim HaMetzuyanim B'Halachah* say that "tasting" food is not called "eating," and thus does not render everything else in the dish leftovers.
- If the woman eats a small portion, that is called "eating" from the food, and renders the rest "leftovers." If she just tastes the food, the rest of the food remains permissible.
- As we said, according to Rav Moshe Feinstein a half-eaten piece of chicken may not be transferred to a new plate and eaten. If the item can be cut to make it look like new, in a way that a stranger would now eat it, it is permitted. An apple that can be cut and salvaged may be transferred to a different plate and eaten by the husband, but he may not eat the apple core she bit from.
- A break-apart roll or a large roll that is meant to be shared by many people may be cut up to share, even according to Rav Moshe Feinstein.

255. Explained by Rav Yossi Stilerman.

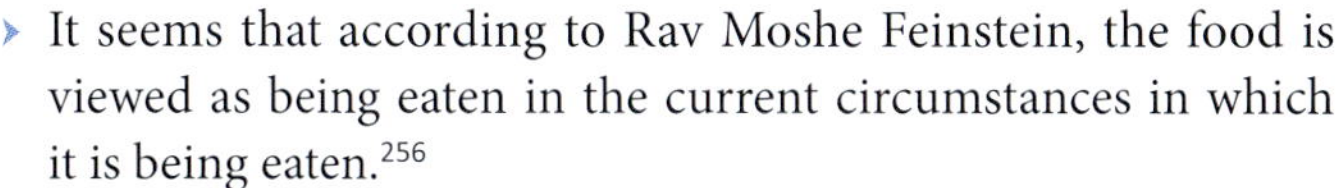

- It seems that according to Rav Moshe Feinstein, the food is viewed as being eaten in the current circumstances in which it is being eaten.[256]
- The *Minchas Yitzchak* says the leniency of transferring food to another plate to allow the man to eat his wife's leftovers only applies to food that needs a utensil to be eaten. If no utensil is necessary to eat this food, another leniency (such as the woman leaving the room) must be employed.
- Rav Shmuel HaLevi Wosner says a woman does not have to tell her husband that she ate from a particular food; there is no affection when he does not know she ate from it. Also, the husband may certainly eat from a portion that was brought for her if she subsequently decided not to touch it. There is no need to transfer the food to another plate in such cases.
- Rav Yosef Shalom Elyashiv says when a woman is drinking from a cup, her husband cannot sneak a sip of her drink, even if she does not know about it, because the prohibition of drinking leftovers is on the husband.

Sharing Cups, Silverware, and Toothbrushes

- Rav Yosef Shalom Elyashiv says a man may use his wife's cup and utensils without washing them, even if they are dirty and a stranger would not use them; there is no issue of leftovers.[257]
- The *Be'er Moshe* and many other *Poskim* say a man may use his wife's toothbrush after she uses it, even though a stranger would not use it.
- Rav Shmuel HaLevi Wosner says a man may smoke his wife's leftover cigarettes or finish her partially consumed medication.[258]

256. It seems that even according to Rav Moshe Feinstein, who says that splitting a can of soda is prohibited because of *ke'arah achas*, a couple may split — that is, pour the contents into two separate cups and drink it in this way — an individual portion of fountain soda when they are in an amusement park (where they charge an exorbitant amount of money per drink) because it is normal for people to split fountain sodas in amusement parks.

257. *Shach* 195:9, "*V'Darkei Moshe*."

258. *Shu"t Yad Eliyahu*.

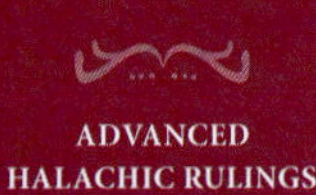

How to Eat Leftovers

- According to Rav Moshe Feinstein, in order for one to be allowed to eat his wife's leftovers after transferring them to a different plate, the items must look like they are now going to be served, and in their new state can be served to a stranger. If he can do this, he can eat it.

- The husband may eat his wife's leftovers when she has finished eating and left the room. This means that she left for good, not just that she is in the kitchen serving the next course.[259] This applies even according to Rav Moshe Feinstein, as long as the food being eaten looks like it is going to be served, and in its new state can be served to a stranger.

- According to Rav Moshe Feinstein, if the woman is done eating one item on her plate — even food that can be made to look like it is going to be served, even to a stranger — the husband may not transfer the item onto his plate, because a stranger would never take food from a strange woman's plate. The husband may, however, transfer the food to a third plate and eat it or transfer it from there to his plate.[260] For example, if a woman has rice on her plate that she is finished eating from, her husband can transfer it to a third plate and eat it or transfer it from there to his plate.

- If other people eat from the food, the husband may also partake from it. This is only according to *Poskim* in Eretz Yisrael, not according to Rav Moshe Feinstein.[261]

---

259. Even though Rav Shmuel HaLevi Wosner is lenient as long as the wife is not in front of the husband, most *Poskim* are not lenient unless she really left the room for good.

260. Rav Yitzchak Berkovits seems to understand Rav Moshe Feinstein's ruling as meaning that the husband first has to make the food look like it is going to be served even to a stranger, and only then may he eat the food. He must therefore first transfer it to a third plate, a place where a stranger would eat the food, and then he may eat or transfer the food to his plate.

261. I would have assumed that even Rav Moshe Feinstein would agree that this would be permitted for "intimate" foods, because the fact that others are eating from it must mean that it is not that intimate. However, it seems that a food is determined to be intimate whether or not someone else eats from it. The fact that someone ate from the intimate food just to allow the husband to eat it is inconsequential, even if that was not their intention. If a niddah ate part of an apple and then her son took a bite, her husband cannot partake of that apple unless he first makes it look like it is going to be served even to a stranger by slicing and displaying it on a plate.

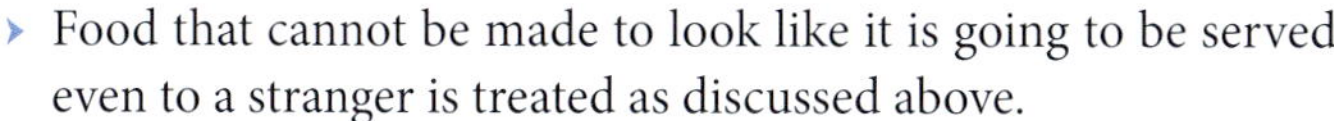

- Food that cannot be made to look like it is going to be served even to a stranger is treated as discussed above.

The Woman Serving

- A woman may prepare her husband's food, but must serve individual portions with a *shinui*.[262]
- A woman may put the serving plate directly in front of her husband; the issue is only regarding an individual serving.[263] The same applies to bottled drinks — she may place the bottle directly in front of him. However, she may not directly serve him an individual cup to drink.[264]
- If the husband looks away when his wife is serving him, she does not need to use another *shinui*. Rav Shmuel HaLevi Wosner does not agree with this ruling, but Rav Yitzchak Berkovits holds that it is fine.
- Rav Shmuel HaLevi Wosner and Rav Nissim Karelitz say if the woman always serves with the right hand, serving with the left hand is a valid *shinui*.
- Practically speaking, serving with the left hand is not called a *shinui* nowadays. It used to be that people would only serve with the right hand, but today no one notices which hand one is using to serve.
- A valid *shinui* is when the woman places the item on the table but out of her husband's direct reach, and he has to extend his arm to get the food.[265]
- Rav Nissim Karelitz says a woman may put a few individual servings in front of her husband, even though one of them is for him. She may also serve an individual serving that is not ready to be consumed, such as a tea that does not yet have sugar, if he is going to add it after it is served.

---

262. While there seems to be a disagreement whether the prohibition of serving food refers to the prohibition to prepare *and* serve, or it refers only to the act of serving, Rav Yitzchak Berkovits and most other *Poskim* hold that the prohibition refers to the serving, not to the preparation (195:16:3).

263. *Shach*; *Pischei Teshuvah*.

264. Rav Nissim Karelitz.

265. Rav Nissim Karelitz.

The Man Serving

- Rav Nissim Karelitz and many other *Poskim* say the husband may not serve his wife directly in front of her; all the halachic ramifications of the wife serving the husband apply (see above).
- Rav Yitzchak Berkovits used to rule leniently in regard to this halachah because men would traditionally not serve their wives,[266] so *Chazal* never said it was prohibited. Practically speaking, he is stringent today, as many *Poskim* prohibited the husband serving his wife unless there is a a valid *shinui*.

What Is Included in "Serving"

- Some European *Poskim* say a woman cannot mix her husband's drink, like coffee or tea. The halachah is not like this; the prohibition does not allow *serving* drinks, and does not apply to preparing them.
- Practically speaking, pouring and serving all drinks and food in front of the husband (or his wife, according to many) is prohibited in regard to all types of drinks, even water.
- Rav Ovadia Yosef says that Sefaradim are lenient in regard to serving drinks that are not alcoholic.
- Rav Nissim Karelitz says the couple may serve each other salt, spices, and medicines, because they are not considered important like food and drinks.[267]
- Rav Nissim Karelitz says any food that is not ready to be eaten the way it was served may be served directly, without a *shinui*.[268]

266. Rav Nissim Karelitz and Rav Yitzchak Berkovits hold that in the days of *Chazal* it was not normal for a man to be involved in food preparation to any degree. For this reason, the *Shulchan Aruch* does not mention that a man should not serve food to his wife, because it simply was never done. However, if it would become normal for the man to serve (as is the case nowadays in some homes), it would be prohibited for him to serve her without a *shinui*.

267. For this same reason Rav Nissim Karelitz is lenient regarding water, although Rav Yitzchak Berkovits and many others are not.

268. Examples include tea that requires sugar or turkey that needs carving. Rav Nissim Karelitz seems to understand that the leniency of serving food that is intended for many people (i.e., on a serving plate) applies to food that is not ready to be eaten from the serving plate, until it is transferred to an individual plate.

- Food that was served in the wrong way may be eaten. The item does not become prohibited (as is the case regarding an item that was affected by a *melachah* that was performed on Shabbos).[269]

Sending Alcoholic Beverages

- A man may not send wine to his wife when she is a niddah. This means he may not tell someone to bring alcohol to his wife, and may not put individual alcoholic beverages close to his wife, even if he does not place them directly in front of her.
- Rav Yosef Shalom Elyashiv and Rav Shmuel HaLevi Wosner say that using a *shinui* does not permit one to serve the alcoholic drink.
- Rav Nissim Karelitz says this prohibition applies even when the wife is not present, because there is a certain amount of affection when a woman knows who sent her the wine.
- Rav Shmuel HaLevi Wosner says the prohibition applies to a *kos shel brachah* as well as regular alcoholic beverages.
- "Wine" in this context means grape juice, beer, schnapps, and all other alcoholic beverages. This is based on the *Rashba*, which says that this prohibition of sending wine is because it may lead to frivolous behavior.
- A man may send his wife Kiddush wine in the following ways: A woman may drink her husband's leftovers, so the man can put the cup down without sending it to her. Alternatively, he may fill many cups for many people and put the serving dish with these cups in front of her, and she can take one of them, since no single cup was designated for her.[270]
- At a bris, another person may bring the *kos shel brachah* to the mother of the baby, but the husband may not tell someone to bring it to her. He may say to someone, "The halachah is that the mother should drink some wine."
- If someone is a guest and the host makes Kiddush and passes individual cups around the table, the husband may indirectly pass one of the cups to his wife (without putting it directly

269. Rav Yosef Shalom Elyashiv; Rav Shmuel HaLevi Wosner.

270. Rav Nissim Karelitz.

in front of her, but he can put it closer to her) even though the cup is intended for her. Such an action is not considered *sending* alcohol to his wife; he is simply indirectly *passing on* what someone else sent.[271]

- One spouse can serve or send a full bottle of wine to the other; the prohibition only applies to individual servings.
- Depending on the circumstances, a bottle of beer may be considered an individual serving.[272]
- The husband may send one cup of wine to his wife if everyone is supposed to drink from this cup; in this case, the cup is not specifically for her, but is communal. This does not work if a baby is the only one who will be drinking from it besides for the couple.
- Practically speaking, sending alcohol as well as serving food to each other are prohibited from the husband to the wife and the wife to the husband.[273]

Shaky Benches, Couches, and Tables

- The *Rama* says a niddah couple may not sit on the same bench that is shaky and is not attached to the floor.
- A niddah couple may not sit on a couch together if they can feel each other, even if they are sitting on separate cushions. They may both sit on one couch if they cannot feel each other.
- Rav Shmuel HaLevi Wosner says a very heavy couch is considered like a seat that is attached to the floor, so the couple may sit on it together even if they feel each other's movements, as long as they leave some space between them (so they do not accidentally touch).[274]

---

271. *Shu"t Shevet HaKehasi*, vol. 5, end of *siman* 107.

272. Most *Poskim* define "a cup that is designated for her" to mean a serving that she would drink straight from the bottle or cup. Therefore, in a setting in which people drink beer straight from the bottle, it should be treated as an individual serving which should not be sent from husband to wife or vice versa.

273. Rav Shmuel HaLevi Wosner.

274. Based on the *Beis Lechem Yehudah*.

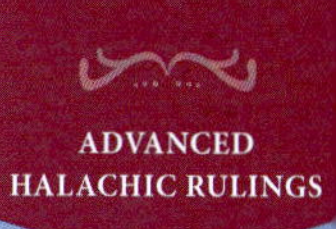

- Rav Nissim Karelitz says if someone else is sitting between the couple on the shaky bench,[275] or there is a large item on the bench between the couple, this is not considered a "shaky bench"; thus, the couple may sit there together even if they feel each other's movements. The item must be large enough to "split" the bench into two separate sitting areas; placing a small item between them will not help.
- Practically speaking, the leniency of someone or something splitting between the couple is only applicable in regard to a seat, such as a chair, couch, or bench. This leniency does not apply to a couple sitting together on the same bed, which is prohibited.
- Rav Shmuel HaLevi Wosner says a couple may eat together at a shaky table even though they may feel the other's movements of the table, because they do not intend to cause or feel the shaking.

Cars, Airplanes, and Boats

- Rav Moshe Feinstein says a niddah couple may both sit on a bench that is attached to the floor or a car bench that is attached to the car, even if they feel each other's movements.
- Rav Yosef Shalom Elyashiv says a niddah couple may not sit together in the back seat of a car if they can feel each other, unless they place something or someone between them.
- In the United States the practice is to follow the opinion of Rav Moshe Feinstein, that a car is considered like a seat that is attached to the ground, so people are not particular about not feeling the spouse's movements. The only potential prohibition is incidental or accidental touching, so precautions should be taken.
- Rav Nissim Karelitz says the Chazon Ish holds a niddah couple may sit next to each other on a bus, but they should not do so unless they can be certain not to touch, even accidentally.
- Practically speaking, the couple may sit next to each other on an airplane or bus. Rav Moshe Feinstein says to put something

275. Many *Poskim* (*Shaarei Tohar*) say the minimum age of a person sitting between them is at least that of a small child who "splits" the couple, and that a baby would not help in this area.

between them, like a pillow or hat box, to make sure that no accidental touching will occur.

- Rav Shmuel HaLevi Wosner says a niddah couple may not go on a small boat together for several reasons: it is an affectionate act, they can feel each other's movements, and it is considered like a "trip" (see Advanced Rulings, Harchakos, Headline "Vacations," page 288).

Making the Beds

- The *Shulchan Aruch* says a niddah may not make her husband's bed, which includes fluffing the bedding, in preparation for him to sleep in it, since this is an act of intimacy.[276]
- Rav Nissim Karelitz says if the woman is making the bed so the room looks cleaner, it is permitted even if she does so right before he goes to sleep.
- Rav Shmuel HaLevi Wosner says the reason that this is presented as a prohibition on the woman is because this is something she should be doing when she is *tehorah*. The prohibition applies to the husband as well.[277]
- Rav Shmuel HaLevi Wosner says she may not employ a *shinui* to prepare his bed for sleeping.
- A woman may make her husband's bed in the morning, even in front of him, as this is considered "housework," which is permitted.[278]
- Rav Nissim Karelitz and Rav Shmuel HaLevi Wosner say there is no need to mess up the bed in the event that it was wrongly prepared to sleep in.

---

276. Some explain the origins of this *din* as follows: In the days of *Chazal* (and up until recently) most people were very poor and lived in small living quarters. Their beds were taken apart during the day to allow space for the household furniture and for use of the common areas of the home. At night, the women would move the furniture away and set up the beds in preparation for sleep. This act, brought in the Gemara, is intimate in nature, and prohibited when she is a niddah. By extension, any interaction she has with the bed in preparation for his sleeping in it is prohibited.

277. *Chochmas Adam*; *Aruch HaShulchan*; Rav Shmuel HaLevi Wosner; Rav Nissim Karelitz.

278. Rav Nissim Karelitz; Rav Shmuel HaLevi Wosner.

Separating the Beds

- The *Rashba* says a niddah couple must separate their beds because two people sleeping close to each other is itself a form of affection, even if they are lying on individual beds.
- Rav Shmuel HaLevi Wosner says a niddah couple may not sleep in the same bed even if there is plenty of room on the bed and they are very far from each other. They must be on two individual beds that are separated.
- Rav Shmuel HaLevi Wosner says the actual halachah is that it is sufficient to separate the beds even the smallest amount. The point is that they are not touching one another.
- The various opinions regarding how far to separate the beds are as follows:
  - The beddings cannot touch.[279]
  - They should be separated the width of a person.
  - They should be separated to the point where the people in the beds will not inadvertently touch if they stretch their arms during the night.
  - The beds should be an *amah* apart.
- Practically speaking, a person may be lenient when there is not enough room for the wider opinions, as long as the beds are not touching, and can rely on the opinions that say even a small amount is enough to consider the beds separated.[280] This, however, should only be done when necessary.
- It is not necessary to put a night table between the beds. Rav Nissim Karelitz says — as a piece of advice — that if there is not enough room to separate the beds an *amah*, the couple should put something between the beds as an added *heker*. Rav Shmuel HaLevi Wosner brings this practice as a custom.
- The *Minchas Yitzchak* says both spouses may lean on the headboard if it is also attached to the wall. If the headboard is attached to one of their beds they can both lean on it as well. A couple should not buy such a headboard, but if they did,

279. Arizal, *She'arim HaMetzuyanim B'Halachah*.

280. *Mekor Chaim*, brought in the *Pischei Teshuvah*.

they may use it. Even if they feel each other's movements while leaning on the headboard, it is fine.[281]

- Rav Yosef Shalom Elyashiv, Rav Shmuel HaLevi Wosner, and the *Chazon Ish* say the issue of the beds touching is only relevant when both spouses are in their beds. The beds may be touching when one spouse is sleeping in their bed and the other bed is empty.
- A niddah couple can sleep on the same bunk bed — one on top and the other on bottom — as long as they do not feel each other's movements.[282]
- Practically speaking, the halachah is like the opinion of Rav Yosef Shalom Elyashiv in regard to bunk beds, as long as they do not feel each other, because there is no affection when they are sleeping separately. If they do feel each other, it is considered like a shaky bench.

A Husband on His Wife's Bed

- A husband may not lie or sit on his wife's bed when she is a niddah. This prohibition applies whenever she can easily come home.[283]
- A man is allowed to sit on another woman's bed. The reason for is that a man has a lesser degree of *hirhur* for a strange woman than he has for his own wife.[284]
- A man may sleep on his wife's bed when she is in the hospital, since she cannot come home easily, aside from the day she is being released.

---

281. This seems to be based on the *Taz* that says that indirect touching is permitted in extenuating circumstances. In fact, this case is a lesser version of indirect touching because there is no intention to touch one another when they are simply leaning on the headboard, as there is when he is poking her with a pen or administering a shot. In the event that they already bought the beds, they may be lenient, but one should not buy such a headboard *lechatchilah*.

282. Rav Yosef Shalom Elyashiv.

283. Rav Berkovits says this *din* applies even if he is not lying down for his own confort, such as if he would like to lie with a child who is lying in his wife's bed.

284. For this reason, the Mishmeres Taharah allows a man to sit on his wife's bed if his intent is not for the pleasure of sitting, but for the necessity of sitting, such as if he sits on her bed to tie his shoes.

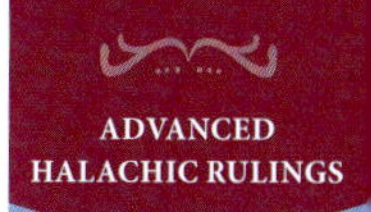

- Rav Shmuel HaLevi Wosner says a husband may sleep in his wife's bed when she traveled far away, but if she left the city and can return easily, he may not.[285]
- Standing, leaning on, or touching the spouse's bed is fine. The issue at hand is the man's *hirhur*, and that does not apply in these situations.[286]
- Rav Shmuel HaLevi Wosner says that in order for the bed to be considered "hers," the woman must sleep in the bed; simply stating which bed she wants to sleep in does not make it designated for her.
- Practically speaking, a bed is considered "hers" even if she has not yet slept in it during these days in which she is a niddah,[287] as long as it was designated for her.

A Woman on Her Husband's Bed

- A woman may not lie on her husband's bed in front of him, although she may sit on it, even in front of him.
- Rav Yosef Shalom Elyashiv says a woman may lie on her husband's bed while he is not in the room, even if he knows she is lying on his bed.[288]

---

285. Based on the *Pischei Teshuvah*.

286. Rav Nissim Karelitz.

287. Some (Rav Shmuel HaLevi Wosner in 195:5:4) teach that her bed only becomes *her* bed when she sleeps in it. Rav Yitzchak Berkovits holds once it is decided whose bed it is, it becomes their bed for that niddah cycle until they decide to switch beds during the woman's days of *taharah*.

The *Shulchan Aruch* says when the wife is *temei'ah* due to *dam besulim*, the husband may sleep in the bed where *bi'ah rishonah* took place even though it is her bed. If the case of the *Shulchan Aruch* is dealing with *dam besulim* and it is assumed that most *kallos* are not *temei'os* before *bi'ah rishonah* occurs, it seems logical that the classic understanding of "her bed" is the bed that is designated for her and not that this is the actual bed that she slept in, alone, during the time she was *temei'ah*. When asked to define "her bed," Rav Yitzchak Berkovits said, "The one that is understood to be hers." Rav Nissim Karelitz mentions that one should designate one bed as hers and one as his during days that she is *tehorah*, and the husband should avoid her bed during the time she is a niddah.

288. This is in contrast to the ruling of the husband eating her leftover food, where most *Poskim* say if the wife ate from something and the husband does not know about it, she is not obligated to tell him, but if he happens to know that the food is hers he cannot eat the leftovers. Regarding a woman lying on her husband's bed, she may lie there even if he knows that she is in his bed, and in this case there is no concern for *hirhur*.

- The *Chochmas Adam* says a woman may not lie or sit on her husband's bed in front of him, but most *Poskim* are not concerned about sitting.[289]

Beds and Bedding

- Rav Yosef Shalom Elyashiv, Rav Shmuel HaLevi Wosner, and Rav Nissim Karelitz say if the couple visits their parents or in-laws often and each has a bed in the room that they prefer, this bed is considered "theirs." If they visit infrequently, they can pick whichever bed they prefer for each specific visit.
- Rav Yosef Shalom Elyashiv says a couch that is sometimes used by the husband to lie on and sometimes used by the wife to lie on, may be used by a niddah couple to sit or lie on, but not at the same time if they can feel each other. The reason for the permissibility in this case is since it is not designated for one person's use.
- Rav Yosef Shalom Elyashiv says a niddah couple should not switch sheets because sheets are intimate items.
- Practically speaking, a niddah couple may switch sheets, pillows, and covers while she is *temei'ah*.[290]
- Rav Shmuel HaLevi Wosner says if it becomes necessary for a niddah couple to switch beds when the wife is a niddah, they may switch just the mattresses. There is no need to switch the bed frames or box springs.

---

289. His reasoning is because the Taz is the one who says that we extrapolate the halachah that a woman should not sit or lie on her husband's bed from the *din* in the *Shulchan Aruch* that he should not sit on her bed (which the *Shach* and *Taz* explain to mean sitting or lying on her bed). The *Chochmas Adam* says if she cannot lie on his bed, then seemingly it should also say that she cannot sit on his bed. If there is more *hirhur* when she is on his bed than when he is on her bed, it seems that if he cannot sit on her bed, she certainly cannot sit on his bed. Rav Shmuel HaLevi Wosner says most *Poskim* allow a wife to sit on her husband's bed, and that is the way he rules. Practically speaking, most *Poskim* (including Rav Yitzchak Berkovits) do not follow the Chochmas Adam's opinion.

See *Shiurei Shevet HaLevi* 262, where Rav Shmuel HaLevi Wosner explains that the concern is generally for the man's *hirhur* which only applies when he sees his wife lying on his bed because that is reminiscent of marital relations, not when she is only sitting on it. Regarding him sitting on her bed, he says the man cannot lie or sit because any contact with her bed causes *hirhur*, and that is the reason behind these prohibitions and most of the *harchakos* in general.

290. Rav Nissim Karelitz.

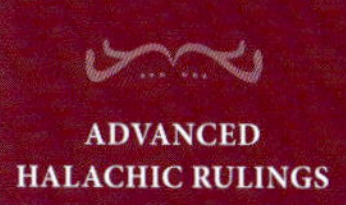

- Rav Nissim Karelitz says a couple should decide which bed is the husband's and which is the wife's. If they need to switch for any reason, they have to physically change the beds and the mattresses.[291]

Preparing Water for Washing

- A woman may not prepare her husband's shower or bath, but she can put on the boiler to heat the water for him to bathe.
- Rav Shmuel HaLevi Wosner says she may prepare the soap, towels, and anything else necessary for bathing. The prohibition applies only to preparing the water.
- Rav Yosef Shalom Elyashiv says this prohibition applies only in front of him; it is permitted not in front of him.
- Practically speaking, this means she may not prepare the water while she is in view of her husband. It is permitted even when they are both in the house, or if he knows that this is being done for him, as long as he does not actually see her doing it.
- Rav Shmuel HaLevi Wosner and Rav Nissim Karelitz say a woman cannot prepare water for her husband to wash his hands, even if it is cold water.[292] The ways that she may prepare his water are either not in front of him, or with a *shinui*, such as with the left hand.[293]
- Rav Shmuel HaLevi Wosner says a niddah wife may prepare any water being used for a mitzvah, or to remove *ruach ra* (bad spirit, which is present on the hands before one washes upon awakening in the morning).
- Practically speaking, it is prohibited for a woman to prepare water for her husband to wash *netilas yadayim*.[294] It would

291. Not all *Poskim* are stringent, as Rav Nissim Karelitz is in regard to this *din*; many (Rav Shmuel HaLevi Wosner and others) allow the couple to switch just mattresses, while some (see *Sugah B'Shoshanim*, chap. 13, "*Shenistapeik BaZeh*") allow them to make a one-time decision to switch without requiring any actual moving of the furniture. Interestingly, those who are stringent like Rav Nissim Karelitz and require the couple to move the entire bed, have to rely on Rav Nissim Karelitz's leniency, which allows for them to carry something heavy together (see Advanced Rulings, Harchakos, Headline "Carrying Heavy Items," page 262).

292. *Shulchan Aruch* 195:12.

293. Speculatively speaking, Rav Yitzchak Berkovits would not like this *shinui* of Rav Nissim Karelitz, just as he does not like this *shinui* for serving food. See below.

294. Rav Nissim Karelitz.

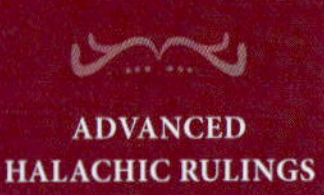

seem that this should have been permitted, because there does not seem to be much affection involved, but this halachah is explicitly stated in *hilchos netilas yadayim*. It is permitted for a woman to prepare her husband's *negel vasser*, because it is there to remove *ruach ra*, not to wash himself.[295]

- Rav Shmuel HaLevi Wosner says it is permitted for one spouse to prepare water for the other to wash for medical purposes.
- Practically speaking, this prohibition also applies to the husband.[296]

Vacations

- The *Rama* says, "A man should not go with his wife in one wagon or on one boat if he is going only as a way of strolling, for example, in gardens."
- The prohibition is: (1) traveling, (2) alone,[297] and (3) for the scenery or with no expressed purpose. All three conditions must be met for the trip to be prohibited.
- If the couple has a specific destination, the trip is permitted.[298]
- A couple cannot "take a drive," but can go on vacation together. The prohibition here is affection, which leads to intimacy. Having a good time while the wife is a niddah is permitted.
- The couple may go to an amusement park or museum when the woman is a niddah. These days are meant to be spent together

295. Although the *Shulchan Aruch* brings the prohibition to prepare water for washing her husband's hands, feet, and face, Rabbeinu Yonah (*Shach*) says even if he is washing only his feet the woman should not prepare the water if it is done in an affectionate way. That said, most *Poskim* agree that the prohibition to prepare water applies even when the water is sufficient to only wash a small area of the husband's body, such as his hands.

296. *Sefer HaEshkol*; *Chochmas Adam*; *Aruch HaShulchan*; Rav Shmuel HaLevi Wosner; Rav Nissim Karelitz.

297. *Chochmas Adam*; Rav Shmuel HaLevi Wosner. Rav Wosner is lenient when others are with the couple, but says the niddah couple should put something between them.

298. Rav Nissim Karelitz has a completely different understanding of the topic than most other *Poskim*, which is a stringency and a leniency that most others do not agree with. He says that when the couple is traveling on separate seats, like in a car, it is not called "a trip," even if they are both in the front seats; the prohibition is only when they are sitting on the same bench or seat together. He also holds that the presence of other people with them does not permit the trip. Practically speaking, Rav Yitzchak Berkovits is not lenient or stringent like this approach.

doing things and growing closer. “Dating” to a specific place is fine.

Taking a Walk

- Rav Moshe Feinstein says that going on a secluded walk is permitted.
- Rav Shmuel HaLevi Wosner permits a couple to go on a hike if the reason they are going is to see the outdoors, but does not allow them to go if their intention is simply to get away from other people and go somewhere alone where it is romantic and secluded. Some (*Aruch HaShulchan*) prohibit walks altogether.

When the Husband Is Sick

- The *Shulchan Aruch* says when the husband is sick his wife may help him if there is no one else around. However, she may not perform affectionate acts.
- Rav Shmuel HaLevi Wosner says “helping” means even directly touching him, as long as it is not in an affectionate way. She may help him herself, and does not need to extend herself monetarily to hire someone else to help him.
- Rav Shmuel HaLevi Wosner and Rav Nissim Karelitz say this leniency only applies when the husband is really sick or injured. In the event that he just has a cold or something nondebilitating, she cannot touch him. He must be ill to the point that he cannot function on his own.
- Rav Shmuel HaLevi Wosner says a wife can definitely do anything to help her husband when there is a threat to his life.
- Rav Shmuel HaLevi Wosner says if a man is sick and he has the option of a strange woman helping him (for example, a nurse), or his wife when she is a niddah, it is preferable for a stranger to attend to him, because there is less affection by a stranger. His wife may only help him if no one else can assist him.
- Rav Shmuel HaLevi Wosner says in the event that a woman realizes that it will be necessary to help her husband for some

time,[299] she should ideally use an intermediary cloth,[300] as opposed to direct touching, whenever possible. (Rav Yosef Shalom Elyashiv concurs.)[301]

- Practically speaking, a woman may be lenient and help her husband only in extenuating circumstances, if he really needs help, he is truly ill, and there is no one else around to help him.[302]

When the Wife Is Sick

- The *Shulchan Aruch* says when a wife is sick, her husband may not touch her to help her, even when no one else is around to assist her.
- The Rama says her husband may help her in the event that she really needs it.
- The Gra and others say the *Shulchan Aruch* (which is based on the *Rambam*) would be stringent even in a situation of danger to her life!
- The *Shach* and the *Aruch HaShulchan* say even the *Shulchan Aruch* would allow the husband to save his niddah wife if there is a danger to her life.
- Practically speaking, a husband may help his sick wife for short periods of time when she needs it,[303] and certainly if there is a danger to her life.

---

299. *Shu"t Radvaz.*

300. The *She'arim HaMetzuyanim B'Halachah* says that in the event that one spouse must touch the other because one of them are sick, they should first touch through an intermediary object, and if that is not possible, use an intermediary cloth, and only then, when circumstances require, may they directly touch.

301. This is brought in *Pischei Teshuvah* regarding a woman who is sick and the husband is allowed to take her pulse. The *Sefer Mekor Mayim Chaim* says that although he may take her pulse, he should use an intermediary cloth whenever possible.

302. For example, there was a man who broke his leg, and Rav Yitzchak Berkovits allowed his wife to help him move around the apartment when he really needed it, like to get to the restroom. This only applies if there is no one else available to help and the action with which he requires help is one that is necessary.

303. This is based on the *Rama*, which says a husband cannot take his wife's pulse unless there is a real danger (*Shach*), even though he may help her around the house even if she is not in great danger. The classic understanding is that taking the pulse takes some time, which may change the mood to an amorous one. Therefore, when the husband is sick and cannot move, the wife may touch him for a longer time, as long as she is really helping him and it does not become an excuse to display her affection for him. When the wife is

- Rav Shmuel HaLevi Wosner says in the event that a woman is sick and her husband finds it necessary to help her, he should try and hire someone to help her if possible.[304] However, he does not need to spend more than he can afford on such a helper.[305]
- Rav Nissim Karelitz says in the event that a husband must take his wife's pulse or help her for a long period of time,[306] he should ideally use an intermediary cloth or glove, whenever possible.
- Rav Shmuel HaLevi Wosner says that even under the circumstances in which a husband may help his wife, he may not do anything affectionate, such as washing her, unless this is absolutely necessary for her health.
- A woman in labor who discovered blood or otherwise became *temei'ah* may be helped by her husband down the stairs in the event that there is no one else around to do so. He does not have to wake up a neighbor in middle of the night to help her, as doing so is considered difficult.
- However, if there is an option for the woman to be helped by someone else other than her husband, it is forbidden for the husband to help her.

---

sick and the husband is healthy, he can help her, but the halachah is more stringent, and he may only touch her for short periods of time because a man's mind tends to wander to thoughts of frivolous behavior more quickly than a woman's does. Also, the *Shach* says that in the event that the man is sick, there is less cause for concern, because he has less strength and is less inclined to initiate an intimate action.

304. *Shu"t Radvaz.*

305. This is Rav Shmuel HaLevi Wosner's understanding of the *Rama*, based on the *Radvaz*, that a husband must spend money on hired help to avoid having to physically help his wife himself. Many others say that just as a woman is not obligated to pay for hired help when her husband is sick, he similarly does not have to pay for hired help when the wife is the one who is sick. They maintain that the reason that the *din* of a woman being sick is mentioned in a separate *se'if* from the *din* of the man being sick is because the Shulchan Aruch needed to separate them because of his view that when the woman is sick her husband should not help her. However, the Rama holds that the *din* is the same in both cases, and the same would apply regarding hired help — that there is no requirement to extend oneself financially in either case.

306. Rav Shmuel HaLevi Wosner makes the obvious observation that taking the pulse nowadays can be done with a machine, which certainly involves less affection than taking it by hand, as was done in the times of *Chazal*. This *din* would certainly be more lenient regarding these halachos.

Places That a Niddah Should Avoid

- A woman should not go to a cemetery during the days that she is actually bleeding (either because of menstrual bleeding or because of childbirth),[307] unless the situation is an embarrassing one.[308]
- During *shivah nekiyim* a woman may go to a cemetery even though she is still a niddah until she immerses in a kosher mikvah.[309]
- Rav Shmuel HaLevi Wosner says a woman who is bleeding can go to shul, pray, say *Birchas HaMazon*, and say the Name of Hashem.[310] However, she should not gaze at the parchment of the *Sefer Torah*.

Harchakos on Tishah B'Av and Yom Kippur, and during Aveilus (Mourning)

- The *Shulchan Aruch* says since marital relations are prohibited on Yom Kippur, a man should treat his wife as though she is a niddah, and should not sleep in the same bed.[311]
- The *Mishnah Berurah* says a person should keep *harchakos* throughout the entire Yom Kippur, both by night and by day.
- The *Shulchan Aruch* says since marital relations are prohibited on Tishah B'Av, a man should not sleep in the same bed as his wife.[312]
- The *Mishnah Berurah* says a person should keep *harchakos* the night of Tishah B'Av, but does not need to keep *harchakos* during the day.

---

307. In such a case, the woman should ideally stand further than 4 *amos* from the *kevarim*, if possible (Rav Shmuel HaLevi Wosner).

308. See *Rama* 195:17 and *Orach Chaim* 88.

309. If one does not understand the *din* this way (which is the understanding of the Chayei Adam), single girls would never be able to go to cemeteries because they do not go to the mikvah, and are therefore *temei'os* all the time.

310. *Pri Chadash*.

311. *Siman* 615.

312. *Siman* 554.

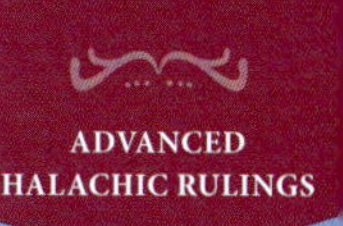

- The *Shaar HaTziyun* explains that the reason we are stringent and keep *harchakos* throughout the entire Yom Kippur, but only during the night of Tishah B'Av, is because women get dressed up on Yom Kippur to go to shul, and there is a stronger *yetzer hara* than on Tishah B'Av, when the women are not dressed up. If a woman for any reason does get dressed up on Tishah B'Av, the couple should keep *harchakos* for the entire Tishah B'Av.
- Practically speaking, on Yom Kippur all *harchakos* should be kept. On Tishah B'Av night, only marital relations, sleeping in one bed, and hugging and kissing are prohibited.[313] During Tishah B'Av day, only marital relations are prohibited. If the woman is dressed up, the couple should not sleep in one bed or hug or kiss either.
- During *aveilus*, marital relations, sleeping in one bed, and hugging and kissing are prohibited. Everything else is permitted.

Harchakos When There Is a Pending She'eilah

- Rav Shmuel HaLevi Wosner says that in the event that a couple has a *she'eilah* on a *mareh* or a *kesem* or whether a *tevilah* was valid, they must keep all *harchakos* until they get an answer.[314]
- Practically speaking, this is the halachah, unless it is clear that the couple is just nervous about something and does not have an actual *she'eilah* that can ultimately be determined.

Family Issues Regarding Yichud and Negiah

- Touching and *yichud* with immediate family members is permitted because there is no desire for immorality.
- Rav Yosef Shalom Elyashiv says a family of *geirim* (converts) can touch and have *yichud* with one another because there is no affection.

---

313. Tishah B'Av is different from Yom Kippur regarding *harchakos* since the prohibition on Tishah B'Av is a derivative of *hilchos aveilus* (the laws of mourning), which do not apply on Yom Kippur.

314. Although most *she'eilos* regarding *tevilah* and all *she'eilos* on *kesamim* are *d'Rabbanan*, the *she'eilah* is one that is "*efsher l'vrurei*," meaning, the answer can be determined (as opposed to *she'eilos* whose answers cannot be determined), so it may not be discounted as a *safeik d'Rabbanan*.

- Rav Moshe Feinstein says a half-sister is considered the same as a full sister in regard to *yichud*, and is permitted. An adopted sister is a stranger unless she was adopted from a very young age.
- Having *yichud* with a young (under bas mitzvah) strange girl is prohibited *mid'Rabbanan. Yichud* with an older (over bas mitzvah) strange girl is prohibited *mid'Oraisa*, but is not *yehareg v'al yaavor*.

Yichud with a Niddah

- A man may have *yichud* with his wife even when she is a niddah. The only exception is when they are newly married and they have not yet had marital relations, in which case the concern of *yitzro takfo* (his *yetzer hara* overwhelming him) exists, because there is no *pas b'salo*.
- Rav Shlomo Zalman Auerbach says once the couple had three attempts at marital relations, they may have *yichud* if the woman becomes *temei'ah*.
- Practically speaking, the couple may be lenient if they had only one attempt at marital relations.
- Some are even more lenient and say that once the couple was alone together in the *yichud* room during the wedding, they can have *yichud* even if the wife becomes *temei'ah* afterwards and no marital relations were attempted. Rav Yitzchak Berkovits does not like this ruling, however. A *Rav* may be lenient, but he should drive home the severity of the prohibition of breaking *harchakos*.[315]
- Rav Yosef Shalom Elyashiv says when a couple was already intimate and the wife subsequently refused to go to the mikvah (i.e., she is a *moredes* [rebel]), *yichud* remains permitted even though marital relations are prohibited (because she is still a niddah) and the man may not feel like he has *pas b'salo*.

---

315. Rav Dovid Feinstein and Rav Dovid Cohen permitted continued *yichud* in such cases, where there was *yichud* in the *yichud* room but no attempts at marital relations were made.

The Shomrim When There Is a Chuppas Niddah

- Since *yichud* is prohibited when there is a *chuppas niddah*, the couple needs one child during the day and two children at night to serve as *shomrim* until the woman becomes *tehorah*.
- The best-aged children to use as *shomrim* are children between the ages of six and nine,[316] who will notice if any sort of intimate behavior happens and will go around telling other people what they saw.
- Technically speaking, the *chuppas niddah* couple may use another couple as *shomrim*. Ideally, however, children should be used.[317] By day, only one *shomer* (child or adult) is necessary.
- The *shomrim* do not have to stay up all night.[318]
- The *Chazon Ish* says that at night the niddah couple may leave the door to their bedroom slightly ajar.[319]
- Practically speaking, the couple must leave the door to the bedroom wide open if no one else is inside.
- Rav Yosef Shalom Elyashiv says when there is a *chuppas niddah* only one *shomer* is required in the *yichud* room even if the chuppah takes place at night, because it is not normal to have marital relations in the *yichud* room.
- Rav Yosef Shalom Elyashiv says *yichud* is not forbidden for a couple that was illicitly living together as husband and wife before the wedding in the event that the woman is a niddah

316. The *Poskim* vary in their opinions on which age *shomrim* is best to use in the case of a *chuppas niddah*; the range is anywhere from 5–12. Rav Shmuel HaLevi Wosner says this is a very subjective halachah, and he cites the *Beis Shlomo* (*Orach Chaim* 48), which says that the litmus test for a child knowing when intimacy takes place is if the child is embarrassed to be seen without any clothes on; the *shomer* must be at least that age. He also says (from the *Bach*) that a child who is nine years or older should not be used as a *shomer* because from that age there is the concern the child would be involved in the intimate activity. The Chazon Ish and others are not concerned that the child will become involved in any frivolous activity because the *kallah* will serve as a *shomeres* for her husband.

317. *Chazon Ish*; Rav Nissim Karelitz. Rav Nissim Karelitz explains that it is best to use children, because of *tznius*.

318. Although the *shomrim* do not have to stay awake throughout the entire time that *yichud* is prohibited for the *chuppas niddah* couple, Rav Shmuel HaLevi Wosner says they must stay in close proximity to the couple, to the point where they can see what happens between the couple at all times.

319. Rav Yosef Shalom Elyashiv.

on the wedding night; therefore, no *shomrim* are necessary. Otherwise, *shomrim* would be necessary even if the couple was intimate before the wedding, as they do not have *pas b'salo*.

Harchakos by a Chuppas Niddah

- The *Rashba* says the reason why *Chazal* instituted *harchakos* for married couples is because every interaction between a married couple may lead to intimacy. Extra restrictions are therefore necessary to prevent them from becoming intimate.
- The *Rosh* says the reason for *harchakos* is because the couple is permitted to remain alone together when the wife is a niddah, unlike others with whom *yichud* is forbidden. *Chazal* therefore implemented extra *harchakos* so the couple does not come too close on days that it is forbidden.
- Rav Eliezer Moshe Horowitz[320] and Rav Moshe Feinstein[321] say a couple that had a *chuppas niddah* does not have to keep *harchakos*, because *yichud* for them is forbidden.[322]
- A *Rav* in the United States may rely on Rav Moshe Feinstein's ruling, and may teach the couple not to keep *harchakos* if they had a *chuppas niddah*, assuming that there will be *shomrim* around until the woman immerses in the mikvah.
- According to this ruling, the *chuppas niddah* couple does not need to keep *harchakos* until the woman goes to the mikvah.[323]

320. Found in the back of *Gemara Shabbos* 11a.

321. Rav Moshe Feinstein is purportedly quoted in a *kuntres* (pamphlet) called *Kol Torah*, which can be found online at hebrewbooks.org. It is also generally not the common practice of *Rabbanim* to rely on such a ruling, even in the United States. Nevertheless, Rav Yitzchak Berkovits says one may rely on this ruling if necessary.

322. Based on the *Rosh*.

323. I asked Rav Yitzchak Berkovits whether one should only be lenient under the chuppah and allow the *chassan* to put the ring on the *kallah*'s finger (which is clearly permitted according to almost everyone, because they are not married yet!) and to directly hand her the *kesubah*, being that she is only an *arusah* (a woman after *eirusin*, which is the first step of *kiddushin*/marriage, who may not have to keep *harchakos*), because the *Birchos Nissu'in* (the blessings on the marriage which are recited under the chuppah) have not yet been said. He said that according to many *Poskim*, the woman is a *nesuah* (one who is after *nisu'in*, which is the second step of *kiddushin*/marriage) because she is standing under the chuppah, and in either case does not have to keep *harchakos*. Practically speaking, Rav Berkovits is lenient regarding this ruling.

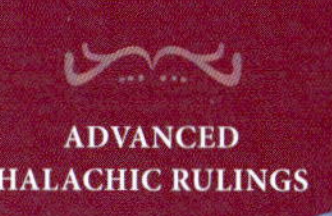

- Rav Yosef Shalom Elyashiv and Rav Shmuel HaLevi Wosner say the *chassan* by a *chuppas niddah* may put the ring directly on his *kallah*'s finger, as long as he is careful not to touch her.[324]

- Rav Nissim Karelitz says the *kallah* by a *chuppas niddah* should point her finger upward, and the *chassan* should drop the ring onto her finger.

- In Eretz Yisrael, most *Rabbanim* rule like the Rashba that *harchakos* need to be kept when there was a *chuppas niddah*, but most *Rabbanim* allow the *chassan* to put the ring on the *kallah*'s finger in the normal fashion.

324. Rav Yosef Shalom Elyashiv says to take extra steps to prevent other people from realizing that the *kallah* is a niddah by a *chuppas niddah*. This includes being creative in planting *shomrim* in the *yichud* room so everyone does not realize that *yichud* is not taking place until a later date.

TAHARAH

Understanding the 5-Day Wait

- The *Raavad*[325] — *Poletes shichvas zera* is only *metamei* for *taharos* purposes. It is not *metamei* a woman to her husband, nor does it disrupt *shivah nekiyim.*
- The *Rosh*[326] — *Poletes shichvas zera* disrupts the day of *shivah nekiyim* on which the woman is *poletes.* Being that *zera* can impregnate a woman for 72 hours after marital relations, a woman cannot start counting *shivah nekiyim* until Day 5 of her *re'iyah.*
- The *Rambam*[327] — Even if the woman is *poletes* after 72 hours, the *zera* does not disrupt *shivah nekiyim* because it no longer has the ability to impregnate her at that point. Anything that emerges after this time is considered like water.

325. Brought in the *Rosh.*

326. *Perek Bnos Kusim.*

327. The Rambam is not arguing with the Rosh; he is simply adding this point, that when a woman is *poletes* after 72 hours, the *zera* has already become impotent and is therefore inconsequential.

- The *Shulchan Aruch*[328] — A woman should not count *shivah nekiyim* for the first 4 days after marital relations because she may be *poletes shichvas zera* and thereby disrupt that day.[329] She should count 4 days, perform a *hefsek taharah* on Day 4, and the 5th day is "Day 1" of the *shivah nekiyim* (like the *Rosh*).

- *Rama*[330] —

  1. Regardless of whether or not a woman actually had marital relations before her *re'iyah*, she must wait before starting *shivah nekiyim*.

  2. Every woman, even if she becomes *temei'ah* from a *kesem*, must count 5 days — the day that she became *temei'ah* and another 4 days — before beginning her *shivah nekiyim*. The reason for this extra day is out of concern that the woman may have marital relations after *shkiah* (for example, Sunday night, which is in essence Monday), during *bein hashmashos*, and will mistakenly think it was before *shkiah* (Sunday). If she counts only 4 days according to her calculations (and does a *hefsek taharah* on Wednesday,) she will be *poletes* after starting *shivah nekiyim* (a few minutes into Wednesday night, which is in essence Thursday). Every woman must therefore always count 5 days so there will not be room to err in this halachah.

Poletes Shichvas Zera

- Every man had to distance himself from his wife for 3 days before *Mattan Torah* so his wife would not be *temei'ah* as a *poletes shichvas zera*.[331]

- Nowadays, *poletes shichvas zera* disrupts the day of *shivah nekiyim* on which the woman was *poletes* because it creates an issue of counting "clean days," and is not an issue of actual

---

328. *Rosh* on 196:11.

329. For clarity's sake: A woman must wait 4 days as opposed to 3 (in the opinion of the Shulchan Aruch) because although 72 hours is only 3 days, the only case in which a woman would be allowed to count only 3 days is when her husband was *mazria* exactly at the moment of *shkiah*. If he was *mazria* before *shkiah*, that would disrupt that day and then another 3 days. If he was *mazria* a minute after *shkiah*, that would disrupt 3 days and another minute, which disrupts the 4th day as well, because *zera* disrupts the entire day in which the woman is *poletes*.

330. *Terumas HaDeshen*.

331. *Rashi* on *Parshas Yisro*.

tumah. A woman may complete her *shivah nekiyim* once she has part of the day of each of the 7 days, even if she was *poletes* afterwards.[332]

- *Poletes shichvas zera* does not uproot a *hefsek taharah*, only *shivah nekiyim*. This means a woman can do a *hefsek taharah* even during the times she may be *poletes shichvas zera*. This halachah should only be applied *bedi'eved*, as the ideal time for the *hefsek taharah* is on Day 5 between *Minchah ketanah* and *shkiah*.

Poletes Shichvas Zera After a Permitted Day

- The halachah is like the opinion of the Terumas HaDeshen, that a woman who is halachically permitted to have marital relations must wait 5 days before doing a *hefsek taharah*, whether or not she actually had marital relations.[333]
- Thus, in the event that a couple refrained from marital relations but it was a permitted day, the woman must still wait 5 days before commencing *shivah nekiyim*.
- The *Noda B'Yehudah* says a woman who immersed in the mikvah and then began to bleed must wait the full 5 days before

332. The exception to this rule is a woman who was illegitimately with her husband before she immersed. If they were together before she had a part of the day of Day 7, she must wait 72 hours (4 days; she does not need 5 days because *Chazal* did not establish a decree for a case that is so infrequent [*Shach* 196:23]) and then count the missing days of *shivah nekiyim* before she may immerse in the mikvah. If they were together after she had a part of the day, she can immerse in the mikvah from that night (196:12). Alternatively, if she immersed on Day 7 of *shivah nekiyim* and was then with her husband, she does not need a new *tevilah* because of *poletes shichvas zera*, although such a woman would need a new *tevilah* for going to the mikvah on Day 7.

333. Interestingly, Rav Nissim Karelitz is lenient in the case of any woman who, if she waits the regular 5 and 7, is scheduled to immerse in the mikvah on Shabbos after a Yom Tov (where there will be a break between the *chafifah* and *tevilah*); this woman may count *shivah nekiyim* after a 4-day wait. While Rav Nissim Karelitz is lenient in this regard, the majority of *Poskim* consider the stringency of the *Terumas HaDeshen* as a *din* that applies across the board. Rav Shmuel HaLevi Wosner says that in such a case there is a possibility to be lenient, and every *Posek* should rule as he sees fit according to the individual situation.

See *Dagul M'Revavah, siman* 197, "*V'Nireh D'Dam*," which says that a woman who waited the regular 5 and 7 should certainly immerse in the mikvah on Friday night (assuming that the *tevilah* is on time and her husband is in town) because although the 5-day wait is the innovation of the Terumas HaDeshen, it has become part of the standard halachah.

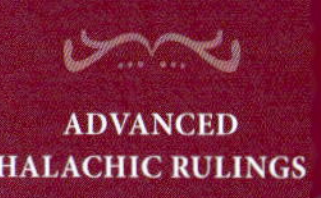

starting *shivah nekiyim*, because she was *tehorah* and permitted to her husband.

- The *Sidrei Taharah* says a woman who bleeds in the mikvah, or even within a few hours after she came home from the mikvah, does not need to wait 5 days before starting another *shivah nekiyim*, as long as she was not yet intimate with her husband.[334]

- Rav Yosef Shalom Elyashiv says even when a doctor says that the couple cannot or should not have marital relations for medical reasons, this is not enough to dispense with the 5 days of the Rama. A woman must wait 5 days unless she was prohibited the entire time she was *tehorah* and then got her period.

- Rav Shmuel HaLevi Wosner and Rav Nissim Karelitz say that even in the event that the woman's husband was out of town for months before, and came back right after she started bleeding, the couple cannot be lenient regarding the 5 days, because she was *tehorah* to him even though he was out of town.[335]

- If a couple separated because they were unsure of the wife's *taharah* status, such as if they are waiting for a ruling on a *mareh* (for example, of a *bedikah* done on an *onas havest*), and it turns out that the woman is *tehorah*, they do not count the day they separated because it turns out they separated as a mistake, since the woman was really *tehorah* the whole time.[336]

- Rav Shmuel HaLevi Wosner says if a couple separated due to a mistake, such as if the woman thought she was *temei'ah* (for example, she thought that a *mareh* was *tamei*), and they later found out that she was *tehorah* the whole time, they may count the 5 days from the time they thought she was *temei'ah*.

- Practically speaking, the halachah is not like Rav Shmuel HaLevi Wosner's opinion because the woman was *tehorah* the entire

334. *Chochmas Adam*; *Me'il Tzedakah*; *Chazon Ish*; Rav Yosef Shalom Elyashiv; Rav Shmuel HaLevi Wosner; Rav Nissim Karelitz. See *Pischei Teshuvah* 196:16 in the name of the *Noda B'Yehudah* and the *Sidrei Taharah*. Rav Elyashiv is lenient on the night of the *tevilah*, as long as the woman did not have marital relations. However, if she begins to bleed the next morning, even if she did not yet have marital relations, she needs to wait 5 days and then count *shivah nekiyim*, like a woman who bleeds on a regular permitted day.

335. *Shach* 196:20, and not like the *Bach*.

336. Rav Moshe Feinstein; Rav Yosef Shalom Elyashiv.

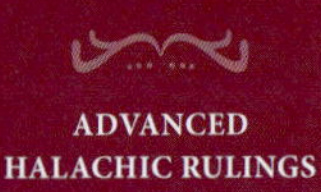

time,[337] to the extent that she does not even need an *amaslah* once she realizes she is *tehorah*.[338]

Poletes Shichvas Zera After a Prohibited Day

- Rav Moshe Feinstein says that in the event that a woman got her period on a date that the couple was entirely forbidden to have marital relations, like Tishah B'Av[339] or Yom Kippur, *and she got her period during* bein hashmashos,[340] she may count the prohibited day as Day 1.[341]

---

337. Sometimes a woman may experience staining for a few days, which may or may not eventually lead to a period. In the event that a *Rav* is lenient and advises her to wear a pad (which cannot become *tamei*) for a few days, and allows the couple to break *harchakos*, and the woman actually gets her period after some time, the 5 days must be started from the time that the woman gets her period and actually becomes prohibited, rather than when she started experiencing the staining. In this case, since the woman was trying to be *tehorah* in the event that the staining has cleared up, she cannot count those days toward the 5 days of *poletes shichvas zera*.

338. Ironically, in some ways stricter *dinim* apply to a woman who thinks she is *temei'ah* than to a woman who knows she is lying to her husband. The first woman made a mistake and she is thus not considered *temei'ah* when she discovers her error. Yet, at the same time, she may not use these days as *tamei* days, and include them in her 5-day count. The second woman wanted to make herself prohibited. She is thus considered *temei'ah* with all its implications, including allowing her to count 5 days from the time that she told this to her husband, even though she knows she was being untruthful.

339. I asked Rav Dovid Feinstein if a woman who begins bleeding on *Motzaei Tishah B'Av Nidcheh* (Sunday night) can count Shabbos and Sunday as prohibited days since the *Rama* says one should not engage in marital relations on that Shabbos unless it is the night when the wife must immerse in the mikvah. Since marital relations on such a Shabbos are prohibited according to the *Rama*, this practice is kept in *Klal Yisrael* even more stringently than the *onas Ohr Zarua* on a standard *vest*, regarding which many *Rabbanim* are lenient even though it is kept as a stringency. Rav Dovid Feinstein agreed unless the couple was lenient that year for any reason, and with the understanding that the woman must have gotten her period during *bein hashmashos*.

340. A woman who got her period before *shkiah* did not have 24 prohibited hours before. If she got it after *bein hashmashos*, she had the opportunity to have marital relations, and this leniency would not be applicable.

341. Rav Yosef Shalom Elyashiv and Rav Nissim Karelitz are stringent in such cases, reasoning that although marital relations are prohibited on these days, the prohibition is not because the woman is a niddah; rather, marital relations are prohibited because of an outside reason. It may be that in the event that a woman or her husband are in *aveilus* and she then gets her period, perhaps Rav Moshe Feinstein would be lenient that she does not need a 5-day wait from the onset of the period because marital relations are prohibited, but Rav Yosef Shalom Elyashiv and Rav Nissim Karelitz would be stringent. Practically speaking, Rav Moshe Feinstein is lenient in such a case; see *Igros Moshe, Yoreh Dei'ah* 17:21.

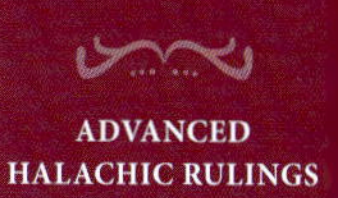

- The same is true if she observes a *vest* for 24 hours, like a woman who began to bleed during the day and *always* keeps the *onas Ohr Zarua* or the *Pleissi*, or she keeps Rav Moshe Feinstein's 24-hour *vestos*. In these cases, marital relations are already forbidden from the night before. If the woman begins to bleed in these circumstances after a 24-hour prohibited time frame during *bein hashmashos*, she can count the previous day as the start of the 5-day count.
- This leniency is really only relevant if the couple holds the *vest* as a *din* (such as if they are never lenient not to keep the *onas Ohr Zarua* for anything), and not just as a stringency.
- According to these *Poskim*, these leniencies only work if the woman gets her period during *bein hashmashos* after the prohibited day, otherwise she was technically able to have marital relations and cannot count these days toward her 5.
- A woman who did not do a *bedikah* on an *onah beinonis* retains the status of being prohibited, and can count 5 days early from the *onah beinonis* even if she gets her period a few days later. This should not be done *lechatchilah* because she has a *mitzvah d'Rabbanan* to do a *bedikah*, but may be applied *bedi'eved*.
- A woman who says "*Nitmeisi*" does not have to count 5 days from the time she gets her period, but may count the days of *poletes shichvas zera* from the time she said "*Nitmeisi*," because she is halachically *temei'ah*.[342]
- This applies only if her husband did not know she was lying.[343]
- If the woman who said "*Nitmeisi*" realizes she is pregnant and that her scheme was not necessary, she has a valid *amaslah* that she wanted to go to the mikvah early and does not need to immerse in the mikvah simply for saying "*Nitmeisi*."

---

342. Rav Nissim Karelitz.

343. Practically speaking, this ruling is not to be implemented. If a couple did not yet perform the mitzvah of *pru u'revu* (the mitzvah to procreate) a *Rav* may rely on Rav Moshe Feinstein's opinion and allow 4 and 7, and should not advise the woman to lie to her husband. The question arises why Rav Shlomo Zalman Auerbach and other *Poskim* decided that it would be better for a couple to wait a full cycle (almost 6 weeks!) on the chance that the woman would bleed less than 5 days and have the opportunity to have marital relations before ovulation, rather than for her to tell her husband a halachah-guided white lie. Perhaps they held that it would be better for the couple's *shalom bayis* that the wife should be a niddah for such a long time, rather than to shake the foundations of the home with a lie. Alternatively, perhaps they do not agree that saying "*Nitmeisi*" creates enough of a prohibition to allow the woman to start the count.

- If a couple was illegitimately intimate before the wedding, we would be lenient and allow a *hefsek taharah* after 4 days of bleeding because the *hefsek* is taking place before the wedding, even though there may be a real concern that she may be *poletes shichvas zera*.

- See Advanced Rulings, How a Woman Becomes a Niddah, Headline "*Taharah* After *Dam Besulim*," (page 240) for *dinim* regarding *taharah* after *dam besulim*.

A Re'iyah during Bein Hashmashos

- Practically speaking, although many *Poskim* do not allow a woman to count the previous day as day 1 of the 5-day count, unless there are extenuating circumstance, a woman who got her period during *bein hashmashos* may begin counting the day *before* as Day 1 of her *re'iyah*. Stringencies are not placed upon stringencies; because she was not able to have marital relations during *bein hashmashos*, since she got her period during this time,[344] the Rama's stringency of waiting 5 days does not apply.[345]

- The amount of time for this halachah is 20 minutes after *shkiah* in Eretz Yisrael. The amount of time in the United States is the earliest time that people would do *melachah* on Motzaei Shabbos.[346]

- Regarding *vestos*, a woman in this scenario counts the night as the *onas havest* for the upcoming month, since the *re'iyah* happened after *shkiah* (as per the opinion of the Chavas Daas).

- This ruling may be relied upon practically when the couple has not been intimate during *bein hashmashos*. We will soon see that some *poskim* only allow a woman to immerse after 4 days of *tumah* after passing a day in which intimacy was forbidden.

Poletes Shichvas Zera and Pru U'Revu

- The *Chazon Ish*, Rav Moshe Feinstein, and Rav Yosef Shalom Elyashiv say a woman who ovulates early can refrain from

---

344. Presumably, this leniency would not be applicable if the couple had marital relations any time during *bein hashmashos*, even if the bleeding began later during *bein hashmashos*. In this scenario, an additional day is needed before a *hefsek taharah* is allowed.

345. *She'arim HaMetzuyanim B'Halachah*; Rav Nissim Karelitz.

346. Approximately 42–50 minutes.

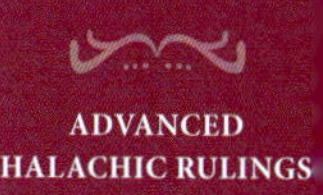

marital relations for 24 hours — starting at *shkiah* — before her period and perform a *hefsek taharah* on Day 4 of her bleeding, when the couple did not have marital relations for 24 hours before the *re'iyah*. This ruling may only be implemented in extenuating circumstances, such as in a case in which it is necessary for the facilitation of *pru u'revu*. A competent *Rav* should be consulted first.

- It is said that Rav Shlomo Zalman Auerbach told women who ovulated early not to go to the mikvah one month,[347] so when they bleed the second month they will already have been *temei'os*, and can do a *hefsek taharah* as soon as they can.[348]

Poletes Shichvas Zera during Shivah Nekiyim

- A couple that erred and had marital relations during *shivah nekiyim* uproot 6 complete *onos*, which, practically, is 4 days of *shivah nekiyim*. This sometimes happens if the wife is more religious than the husband and is trying to keep halachah while he is not interested, and they have been intimate during *shivah nekiyim*.[349]

  For example: A woman who counted 2 complete days of *shivah nekiyim* and had marital relations on Night 3 would disrupt Days 3, 4, 5, and 6. She would therefore have to add extra days — Days 7, 8, 9, 10, and 11 — to complete her *shivah nekiyim*, and then immerse on Night 12 of *shivah nekiyim*, for a total of 16 days (5 and 11) from the *re'iyah* until *tevilah*.

- Rav Nissim Karelitz says that in a case of *poletes shichvas zera* during *shivah nekiyim* there is no need for the woman to produce an additional clean *hefsek taharah* before she completes the missing days, because there is no concern for blood, only for *zera*.

---

347. Many couples have a hard time going a full cycle and then another 11 days of niddah. Also, many women cannot get a good *hefsek taharah* on Day 4 of their cycle. One should always consult a competent *Rav* (with lots of experience!) and a good doctor when these situations arise, before deciding not to immerse in the mikvah for an entire cycle. *Poskim* who use this ruling, as opposed to allowing her to wait only 4 days, hold this method is halachically preferable.

348. *Minchas Yitzchak*; Rav Shmuel HaLevi Wosner.

349. Rav Shmuel HaLevi Wosner says that in such a case a *Rav* should not be lenient and minimize *shivah nekiyim*, but may be lenient regarding the 5-day wait and other leniencies. See *Shiurei Shevet HaLevi* 196:12.

- The *Poskim* are lenient in regard to a woman who had an intrauterine insemination (IUI) procedure or any other similar procedure during *shivah nekiyim*,[350] and the *din* of *poletes shichvas zera* does not apply. There are two reasons for this leniency. The first is that *poletes shichvas zera* is only a problem when it happens through marital relations,[351] and the second is that *poletes shichvas zera* only applies to the *zera* that did not make it into the cervix.[352]

Hefsek Taharah

- The Torah says, "*V'safrah lah,*" which teaches us that a woman should count her days toward becoming *tehorah*.
- The way that she establishes that she is no longer bleeding is by doing a *hefsek taharah*. Even *mid'Oraisa*, a niddah would need a *hefsek taharah* before immersing in the mikvah,[353] even though a niddah in the times of *Chazal* did not count *shivah nekiyim*.

---

350. IUI is a form of assisted fertilization. It is generally performed by a doctor who takes a semen sample and injects it via a cathether past the cervix around the time of ovulation.

351. The *Poskim* discuss whether a woman who does intrauterine insemination, which places sperm inside the woman, during *shivah nekiyim*, disrupts *shivah nekiyim*. Rav Shlomo Zalman Auerbach is lenient, while Rav Yosef Shalom Elyashiv is stringent. Most *Poskim* agree that only *zera* that emerges from the husband with a *hargashah* is *metamei* the man from whom it came (regarding *tumah* and *taharah* purposes), but anything that emerges on its own or through a medical procedure is not *metamei* the man. That said, maybe Rav Shlomo Zalman Auerbach, who is lenient in this case, is lenient because the *zera* is inserted with a catheter and does not enter the woman with a *hargashah*.

352. This is evident from the *Shulchan Aruch* 196:13, which says that possibly, a woman can wash herself internally and will not have to wait days for *poletes shichvas zera*. The Rama disagrees because he says that we are not familiar with the complete cleansing process nowadays. If *zera* that makes it into the cervix is part of *poletes shichvas zera* which disrupts *shivah nekiyim*, then the woman's washing herself would not help; the *Shulchan Aruch* would not discuss being lenient when a woman does it, and the Rama would have answered that douching does not work, now that we do not know how to do it nowadays.

353. In general, the halachah is in accordance with the opinions that a woman must perform a *hefsek taharah* no matter the circumstances, and a woman who did not do a *hefsek taharah* (and the minimum *bedikos* of *shivah nekiyim*) may not immerse in the mikvah. However, in the event that a woman who is married to a Jew agrees to immerse in the mikvah without any *bedikos*, Rav Yitzchak Berkovits is lenient and allows her to go to the mikvah when she is unwilling to go through the proper *taharah* process. The reason for this is because some opinions hold that immersing in the mikvah without doing a *hefsek taharah* and *bedikos* will render a woman *tehorah mid'Oraisa*. This being the case, it is therefore better for her to be *tehorah mid'Oraisa* according to some opinions, than to be *temei'ah* and liable to *kareis* according to everyone. However, if such a woman is in an illegitimate relationship, such as if she is married to a non-Jew, Rav Berkovits would not be Lenient to allow her to immerse even with the proper *bedikos*, because such a woman

- A woman who did not perform a *hefsek taharah* cannot start *shivah nekiyim*. She may be able to count the first *bedikah* she did during *shivah nekiyim* as the *hefsek taharah* in the event that she missed the actual *hefsek taharah*, but there must be a *bedikah* counted as a *hefsek taharah* somehow.

- The most common mistake that couples make in *hilchos niddah* is that they count the day the wife did the *hefsek taharah* as Day 1 of the *shivah nekiyim*.[354] A *chassan/kallah* teacher should be sure to stress that Day 1 is the day *after* the *hefsek taharah*.

- A woman who counted incorrectly, immersed in the mikvah without counting a complete *shivah nekiyim*, and was intimate with her husband, must separate for 4 days (for *poletes shichvas zera*)[355] as soon as she recognizes the mistake. She is then required to add on the extra day(s) to complete the missing day(s) of *shivah nekiyim*. This is discussed in Advanced Rulings, Taharah, Headline "Poletes Shichvas Zera during Shivah Nekiyim" (page 305).

- If a woman performed a *hefsek taharah* without having in mind that this *bedikah* was for a *hefsek taharah*, it still counts for a *hefsek taharah* if necessary, as long as she did a full check in the *chorin v'sedakin*.[356]

---

should not think we agree with her illegitimate lifestyle. In the first case, since the woman is legitimately married and wants to immerse, we should allow her. This approach is really based on a statement of Rav Moshe Feinstein, who says that a child born to *baalei teshuvah* (returnees to religion) who had not been keeping *taharas hamishpachah* at the time of conception possibly may not have a status of a *ben niddah* (child of a woman who was niddah at the time of his conception) if his mother went swimming in the ocean before he was conceived. This holds true even if the woman was wearing a tight bathing suit, as this is only a *chatzitzah d'Rabbanan*. Moreover, the *tevilah* was *metaher* the woman even though she did not have any intention to become *tehorah* (198:48). In this case it seems clear that the woman did not perform a *hefsek taharah* before swimming.

354. Women confuse the fact that a *re'iyah* begins "Day 1" of the cycle even if it was a few minutes before *shkiah*, while *shivah nekiyim* starts after *shkiah*, even though the *hefsek taharah* was performed before *shkiah*.

355. That is, assuming she was intimate after immersing in the mikvah at the wrong time. If no intimacy occurred, the woman does not need to wait 4 days; she can just finish the *shivah nekiyim* and immerse in the mikvah on time.

356. There is a disagreement among the *Poskim* regarding this *din*, and Rav Yitzchak Berkovits rules like those who hold that this *bedikah* is valid (*Shu"t Avodas HaGershani* 79). This scenario is common by women who do *bedikos* in order to clean up on the day of the *hefsek taharah*, and then forget to perform the *hefsek taharah* itself. If the last *bedikah* the woman did was *tehorah*, she may proceed to count *shivah nekiyim*. The reason that some are stringent is because she may not have done the *bedikos* properly if she was not intending to use them as her *hefsek taharah*. In either case, even those who are stringent agree that if a woman did proper *bedikos* intending to use them during *shivah nekiyim*,

- The *Sidrei Taharah* says a woman should be careful not to perform too many *bedikos* while attempting to get a clean *hefsek taharah*,[357] as she may irritate herself and cause internal cuts.[358]

- SeeAdvanced Rulings, Taharah, Headline "A Bedikah Performed at Night" (page 330), regarding a *hefsek taharah* that was done after *shkiah*.

Separating the Hefsek Taharah and the Shivah Nekiyim

- A *hefsek taharah* should ideally be done on Day 5 after the commencement of bleeding, between *Minchah ketanah* and *shkiah*. However, someone who stopped bleeding before Day 5 and is in a *bedi'eved* situation (for example, she is traveling) may perform the *hefsek taharah* even a few days earlier. *Bedi'eved*, the *hefsek taharah* and *shivah nekiyim* do not need to be connected to each other.[359]

- Since most women bleed for approximately 5 days, the most common case of making an early *hefsek taharah* is of a woman who became *temei'ah* through a *kesem* or through a bad *bedikah*. Keep in mind that this is *bedi'eved*, and ideally the *hefsek taharah* should be on Day 5 to connect it to the *shivah nekiyim*, and should ideally be performed between *Minchah ketanah* and *shkiah*.

- If a woman performed a *hefsek taharah* and subsequently saw a *kesem* that was larger than a *gris* on colored underwear, she may proceed with *shivah nekiyim* even though the *kesem* would

---

and a *Rav* afterwards says one of the original *bedikos* is *temei'ah*, she may use a subsequent *bedikah* as her *hefsek taharah*, since it was certainly performed correctly.

357. 196:24.

358. Many *Rabbanim* say a woman should not try more than four or five times to get a clean *hefsek taharah*, or she most certainly will cause an internal *makkah*. If a woman cut herself inside, she must still produce a clean *hefsek taharah* in order to continue counting *shivah nekiyim*. This even applies when she certainly has an internal cut, and there is something to which she can attribute the blood. In the event that a woman cuts herself, a *bodekes* can perform the *bedikah* for her.

359. Nearly all *Poskim* agree with this. There is a lone opinion (*Shiyerei Taharah*) that says that just as *poletes shichvas zera* disrupts *shivah nekiyim*, it also uproots the *hefsek taharah*. This opinion holds the *hefsek taharah* should be performed in a way that it does not conflict with *poletes shichvas zera*, and a *hefsek taharah* that was not performed in this manner does not count, even *bedi'eved*. As stated, nearly all *Poskim* disagree with this ruling and hold that *poletes shichvas zera* does not uproot the *hefsek taharah*, meaning that the *hefsek taharah* can be done before Day 5 when necessary.

have made her *temei'ah* had she changed into white underwear after performing the *hefsek taharah*.

Moch Dachuk

- The Rashba requires a *moch dachuk* in all situations,[360] in order not to confuse people regarding which day requires the *moch dachuk* (maybe only the day she started bleeding[361]). Therefore, every woman should use a *moch dachuk* after the *hefsek taharah* starting from *shkiah*,[362] and should keep it in throughout *bein hashmashos* until *tzeis hakochavim*.[363]
- Practically speaking, a woman should *lechatchilah* use a *moch dachuk* unless there is a reason not to. *Bedi'eved*, a clean *hefsek taharah* is acceptable without a *moch dachuk*, even if there was blood on the day of the *hefsek taharah*.[364]

---

360. The reason for the *moch dachuk* is to establish that *shivah nekiyim* started free from blood.

361. The *Shulchan Aruch* and the Gra are stringent, saying that a woman requires a *moch dachuk* even *bedi'eved*, if she only bled 1 day. The Chavas Daas understands "bled 1 day" to mean any day she had substantial bleeding. The Rama is lenient if no *moch dachuk* was performed even if she actually only bled 1 day.

362. In the event that a woman cannot keep the *moch dachuk* in for the entire *bein hashmashos*, it would not be effective to keep it in for part of *bein hashmashos*. If she missed inserting the *moch dachuk* by *tzeis hakochavim*, she is no longer required to perform a *moch dachuk*. The Gra holds that *bein hashmashos* begins at *shkiah*, while Rabbeinu Tam holds that it begins three-quarters of a *mil* before *tzeis hakochavim*. In Eretz Yisrael, where everyone follows the Gra's opinion, there is no reason to put in a moch after *shkiah*. Outside of Eretz Yisrael, where many people rely on Rabbeinu Tam's opinion for certain things, there is reason to put in a *moch* until three-quarters of a *mil* before *tzeis hakochavim*. (If *tzeis hakochavim* is 48 minutes after *shkiah*, *bein hashmashos* would start 39 minutes after *shkiah* according to this opinion.) Therefore, one who could not insert the *moch* at *shkiah* in America should insert it when she can, provided it is not very close to *tzeis hakochavim*.

363. Rav Moshe Feinstein, the Minchas Yitzchak, Rav Shmuel HaLevi Wosner, and Rav Nissim Karelitz say that a woman should not go into a *reshus harabbim* (public area, where carrying in prohibited) on Shabbos with a *moch dachuk*, because it constitutes carrying. However, most *Poskim* say that a woman can use a pad or tampon in a *reshus harabbim* on Shabbos because it is used as an article of clothes, to prevent staining her clothes with blood.

364. This is based on the *Rama*, which says that a *hefsek taharah* without a *moch dachuk* works even on Day 1 of the *re'iyah*, and is in disagreement with the Chavas Daas, who requires a *moch dachuk* if the woman bled on the day of the *hefsek taharah*, even when it is not the 1st day of the period. Practically speaking, most *Poskim* say to try to be stringent like the Chavas Daas and always require a *moch dachuk*, but will be lenient *bedi'eved* like the Rama (Rav Yosef Shalom Elyashiv).

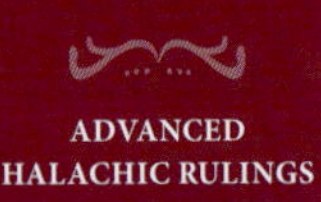

- Rav Yosef Shalom Elyashiv says a woman who became *temei'ah* through a *kesem* is not required to use a *moch dachuk*.[365]
- A woman should avoid using a *moch dachuk* in the event that it causes irritation.

The Bedikas Shacharis as a Hefsek Taharah

- The *Rama* says a *bedikas shacharis* will always work as a valid *hefsek taharah*, unless the woman bled for only 1 day and did the *bedikas shacharis* that day.[366]
- The *Dagul M'Revavah* says a *bedikas shacharis* is defined as a *bedikah* performed before *Minchah ketanah*.
- A working woman who finds it difficult to perform a *hefsek taharah* at work should wash and perform a *hefsek taharah* in

---

365. Rav Yosef Shalom Elyashiv also says that a woman who becomes *temei'ah* through a *kesem* and then gets her period a few days later should consider the onset of the period as "Day 1" regarding the *bedikas shacharis* and *moch dachuk*. The onset of her period is also calculated for *vestos* (according to most *Poskim*, besides for Rav Moshe Feinstein), although the counting of 5 days before the *hefsek taharah* begins when she became *temei'ah*, according to everyone. Rav Yosef Shalom Elyashiv is not lenient regarding these halachos when a woman experienced bleeding that is *vadai migufah*, because he holds that such bleeding is considered a *re'iyah d'Oraisa* (like the Sidrei Taharah). Presumably, most other *Poskim* who disagree regarding a *kesem vadai migufah* and treat it as a *d'Rabbanan* will be lenient regarding a *bedikas shachris* and the *moch dachuk bedi'eved*.

It is interesting to note that Rav Nissim Karelitz, who is always stringent regarding blood discovered on a *bedikah* cloth and treats it as a *re'iyah d'Oraisa* (regarding *vestos* and other halachos), is stringent that any blood found on a *bedikah* cloth requires a woman to treat the day as the 1st day of her *re'iyah*. Such a ruling is interesting, because if a woman attempts to clean internally in the morning on Day 5 of her period and discovers some blood on the cloth, Rav Nissim Karelitz would require her to treat the rest of the day as the 1st day of the *re'iyah*, which is a tremendous novelty. That would mean such a woman would be required to perform a *bedikah* after *Minchah ketanah* or the *hefsek taharah* done in the morning would be invalid, even according to the Rama. Again, most *Poskim* are lenient in this case as well.

366. The Chavas Daas says a woman who bled for a few days should only do a *bedikah* after *Minchah ketanah* if she bled the day of the *hefsek taharah*, even though it is not "Day 1" of the cycle. He also says that a woman who bleeds the day of the *hefsek taharah* requires a *moch dachuk*. This is because the Chavas Daas understands "Day 1" to mean the day of substantial bleeding (as the *Shach* and *Taz* say, "since she now has *mayan pasuach*"). He also says that since we are no longer experts on the shades of colors of blood, it is possible that the last day of the flow is actually the 1st day of *tamei* blood, so in essence it really may be Day 1 of the period. As a rule, the practice is to try to fulfill the Chavas Daas's opinion and require a *moch dachuk*, especially if the woman bled substantially during that day. *Bedi'eved*, one may be lenient even when the woman only did a *bedikas shacharis* and did not insert a *moch dachuk*, as long as it is not the actual 1st day of her period (Rav Yosef Shalom Elyashiv and Rav Nissim Karelitz).

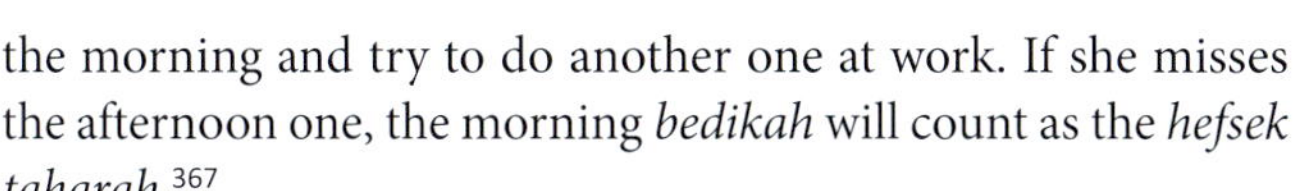

the morning and try to do another one at work. If she misses the afternoon one, the morning *bedikah* will count as the *hefsek taharah*.[367]

- How much blood must be discovered to be called "having bled on that day"? Some say even the smallest amount, while others say that a real *re'iyah* is required.
- Rav Yisrael Yaacov Fisher says a *re'iyah* at night is not called a *re'iyah* for that day. If the woman is clean from *alos hashachar* (the rising of the morning star; daybreak), a *bedikas shacharis* will count for her, even on Day 1 of the *re'iyah* (which began the night before the *hefsek taharah*).

Hefsek Taharah and Moch Dachuk After Accepting Shabbos

- The *Terumas HaDeshen* says a woman cannot do a *hefsek taharah* on Friday after accepting Shabbos in order to start counting *shivah nekiyim* on Shabbos, even if it is still day. For her, it is already the next day, Shabbos.
- The Agur, in the name of the Maharil, says that the woman may perform a *hefsek taharah* even after she has already accepted Shabbos.
- The halachah is that one should ideally follow the Terumas HaDeshen's opinion, so on Fridays a woman should *lechatchilah* do a *hefsek taharah* before accepting Shabbos. *Bedi'eved*, however, a *hefsek taharah* may be performed anytime before *shkiah*. In the event that a woman performs an early *hefsek taharah* and subsequently stains after accepting Shabbos, she may nevertheless perform another *hefsek taharah* even though she already accepted Shabbos.
- The halachah does not follow the Terumas HaDeshen's view in regard to a *moch dachuk*, however, and a woman who did an early *hefsek taharah* should not use a *moch dachuk* from when she accepted Shabbos through *tzeis hakochavim*, which, for someone who makes early Shabbos, can be up to two and a

367. The simple explanation is that a *bedikas shacharis* works according to most *Poskim* (albeit *bedi'eved*) if it was not the 1st day of her bleeding. That being said, women nowadays wait 5 days after the onset of the period before attempting a *hefsek taharah*, so it is rare to actually have a case where a *bedikas shacharis* (*hefsek taharah*) is performed on the day that she started bleeding.

half hours. The woman should only use the *moch dachuk* from *shkiah* through *tzeis hakochavim*.[368]

Washing Before the Hefsek Taharah

- Ideally, a woman should wash herself before performing a *hefsek taharah*.[369] The reason for this is so she will not find old *kesamim* once she starts *shivah nekiyim*.[370]
- The woman should preferably wash the lower half of her body with warm water, when permitted (not on Shabbos or Yom Tov).
- She could just wash the external vaginal area, and does not need a full shower.
- The *Poskim* say she may use a baby wipe when necessary.
- On Yom Tov she should wash the external vaginal area with warm water.
- On Shabbos, Tishah B'Av, and Yom Kippur she should wash the external vaginal area with cold water.
- The *hefsek taharah* is effective *bedi'eved* even if she did not wash herself at all.[371]
- Rav Yosef Shalom Elyashiv says a woman should wait 10–15 minutes after washing herself internally before doing the *bedikah*, if time allows.[372]
- If the woman did the *bedikah* without waiting after washing herself, the *bedikah* is valid *bedi'eved*.

---

368. Rav Yosef Shalom Elyashiv.

369. *Rama*.

370. *Toras HaShelamim*.

371. Ibid.

372. Rav Yosef Shalom Elyashiv does not actually differentiate between an internal and an external washing, although there should really not be any reason for a woman who only washed externally to wait afterwards before performing the *hefsek taharah*, since the point of waiting is so the internal *bedikah* will show that blood has not come for some time (which is the reason for *chorin v'sedakin* [*Sidrei Taharah*]). Rav Nissim Karelitz says one should wait 3–8 minutes after washing, and he does differentiate between an internal wash (which requires a wait *lechatchilah*) and an external wash. Rav Nissim Karelitz actually advises that women should *lechatchilah* wash internally before beginning to count *shivah nekiyim*.

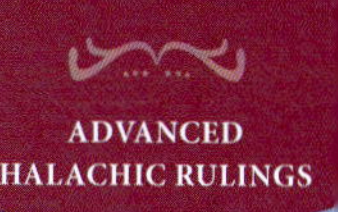

Understanding Shivah Nekiyim Mid'Oraisa

- Niddah — When a woman discovers blood during *yemei niddah*, she counts 7 days including the day of the *re'iyah*, and then goes to the mikvah. It makes no difference if she continues to bleed during those 7 days or not.
- *Zavah ketanah* — A woman who bleeds 1 or 2 days during *yemei zivah* is required to count 1 "clean" day, after which she may immerse in the mikvah. This woman is called a *shomeres yom keneged yom* (one who observes 1 clean day after bleeding 1 or 2 days during *yemei zivah*).
- *Zavah gedolah* — A woman who bleeds for 3 or more days during *yemei zivah* is required to count *shivah nekiyim*, after which she may immerse in the mikvah.

Calculating Yemei Niddah and Yemei Zivah

- *Rashi* — A woman has 7 *yemei niddah* followed by 11 *yemei zivah*. She then reverts back to *yemei niddah*, no matter how long the next cycle is in coming. She has one 11-day opportunity to have *dam zivah* every cycle.
- The *Rambam* — A woman is on eternal 7- and 11-day cycles from her first period until menopause.

For example:[373] If a woman gets her period every 30 days, she will be a niddah after the first *re'iyah* according to everyone. When she bleeds again on Day 30, she will be a niddah according to Rashi because she surpassed her *yemei niddah* after Day 18. According to the *Rambam*, she will be a *zavah* because Day 30 falls in *yemei zivah*: 7 *yemei niddah* +11 *yemei zivah* =18 +7 *yemei niddah* =25 +11 *yemei zivah* = 36. Day 30 falls between Days 25 and 35, which is during *yemei zivah*.[374]

373. This is the simple explanation of the *Rambam*. See *Chavas Daas* for an alternative explanation.

374. The Commentaries ask the following question on the *Rambam*: The concept of *zavah* by definition means a fluke *re'iyah*, which is an occurrence that is out of the ordinary. How could the Rambam say that every woman is on an eternal 7–11-day cycle, if the second period of most women (*onah beinonis*) will always fall during *yemei zivah*? The Chavas Daas answers that the Rambam is not discussing a case in which a woman has a *re'iyah* on a *vest*; in such a case he agrees it would be *dam niddah*, and not *dam zivah*.

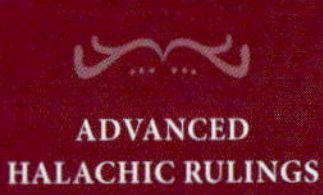

The Three Stringencies[375]

1. Although the Mishnah states that *mid'Oraisa* there are only five *tamei* colors of blood, *Chazal* were stringent and were *metamei* any color that is "similar to red," so as not to confuse *tahor* colors with *tamei* colors.[376]
2. The Enactment of Rebbe B'Sados — A woman who bleeds for 1 or 2 days must keep an additional 6 *nekiyim* on the chance that the last day of the *re'iyah* was during *yemei niddah*.[377] If she bleeds for 3 or more days, she should keep 7 *nekiyim* on the chance that the *re'iyah* was during *yemei zivah*. The reason for this stringency is so women will not confuse *yemei niddah* and *yemei zivah*.
3. Rav Zeira's Stringency — Jewish women accepted to keep *shivah nekiyim* after every *re'iyah*. The reason for this stringency is so women will not confuse the 6 *nekiyim* of a 1-day or 2-day *re'iyah* with 7 *nekiyim* of a *zavah gedolah* by a 3-day *re'iyah*.[378]

Rav Zeira's Stringency

- The stringency of Rav Zeira of keeping *shivah nekiyim* in every case of niddah — including *niddah d'Rabbanan*, as we are concerned about *zavah gedolah* — is universally kept and treated as a *din d'Oraisa*, even though it is a decree of *Chazal*.
- One may never be lenient and minimize the *shivah nekiyim*, even in a case that it is for the purpose of *pru u'revu*. However, one may be lenient regarding the Terumas HaDeshen's requirement of waiting 5 days of *poletes shichvas zera*, as discussed above in Advanced Rulings, Taharah, Headline "*Poletes Shichvas Zera*" (page 302).

---

375. See also *Niddah* 66:71 and *Shulchan Aruch* 183 and 16:2.

376. Some learn that this is a part of the edict of Rebbe B'Sados, while others explain that this is simply what happened as a result of the tradition getting lost throughout time. The Gemara says that many Tanna'im would not rule because they felt they were not capable of discerning *tamei* colors from *tahor* colors.

377. Rebbe B'Sados is concerned that the blood that came during the first few days of the *re'iyah* was not comprised of *tamei* colors, and the woman is really only becoming *temei'ah* on the last day of her *re'iyah*. If she is a niddah, she now needs an additional 6 days before she can go to the mikvah.

378. 183:16:2; see *Tosafos*, the *Rosh*, and the *Ran*.

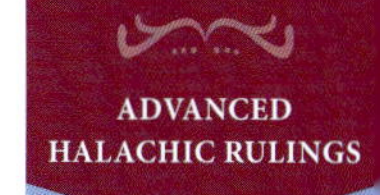

The Bedikos of Shivah Nekiyim

- The Mishnah asks what the halachah is *bedi'eved* if a woman only does *bedikos* on Days 1 and 7. Rebbi Eliezer says she is considered *tehorah*, Rebbi Yehoshua says she only has Day 1 and Day 7, and Rebbi Akiva says she only has Day 7.[379]
- The Gemara brings a disagreement regarding Rebbi Eliezer's opinion as to the minimum amount of *bedikos* that a woman may do during *shivah nekiyim*. Rav says Rebbi Eliezer holds it is enough if she did a *bedikah* on Day 1 *or* Day 7, and Rebbi Chaninah says she needs at least Day 1 *and* Day7.
- *Tosafos* — A woman should *lechatchilah* check herself every day of *shivah nekiyim*.
- The *Mordechai* — A woman should *lechatchilah* do two *bedikos* every day of *shivah nekiyim*.
- The *Raavad* — We rule like Rav. And, the woman does not actually need the one *bedikah* to be on Day 1 or Day 7. Rather, one *bedikah* anytime during *shivah nekiyim* suffices.
- The *Mordechai* and the *Smak* — The halachah is like Rebbi Chaninah's opinion, that *bedikos* are needed on Day 1 *and* Day 7. The minimum is that the woman may not go 5 days without a *bedikah*.
- The *Shulchan Aruch* brings the *Raavad* as the *din*, and the *Mordechai* as an additional opinion, but concludes that "one should not be lenient."[380]
- The *Pischei Teshuvah* says a woman for whom *bedikos* are painful may do only *bedikos* on Day 1 and Day 7, *lechatchilah*.

The Variables If a Woman Missed a Bedikah

- *Lechatchilah*, a woman must do two *bedikos* a day during *shivah nekiyim* plus the *hefsek taharah* and *moch dachuk*, for a total of sixteen *bedikos* each month.[381]

379. *Niddah* 68:72.

380. 196:4.

381. A *Rav* should impress the importance of performing mitzvos *lechatchilah* versus *bedi'eved*.

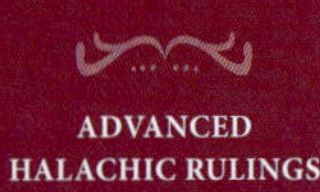

- If a woman is having a hard time with *bedikos* (i.e., due to extenuating circumstances or she cut or may cut herself) a *Rav* should be lenient for her in the following order, as deemed necessary on a case-by-case basis:

  1. She should stop inserting a *moch dachuk*.
  2. She should do only one *bedikah* every day (preferably in the morning, according to Rav Yosef Shalom Elyashiv and Rav Shmuel HaLevi Wosner[382]).
  3. She should do one *bedikah* on Day 1, Day 3, and Day 7.[383]
  4. She should do one *bedikah* on Day 1 and Day 7.
  5. She should do one *bedikah* on Day 1 and on a middle day.
  6. She should do one *bedikah* on Day 1 or Day 7.
  7. She should do one *bedikah* anytime during *shivah nekiyim*. (This ruling is to be implemented in a situation of *makom igun* only.)

A Woman Who Only Missed Day 1 or Day 7

- The *Noda B'Yehudah* says a woman must do *bedikos* on Day 1 *and* Day 7 specifically. It is not sufficient to just do two *bedikos* sometime during the 7 days. It is not even sufficient to do one of the two in the middle. She must perform a *bedikah* on the first and last day of the *shivah nekiyim*. Therefore, a woman who did all of the *bedikos* on every day except for Day 7 should not go to the mikvah the night she was supposed to. Rather she should do a *bedikah* on Day 8, thereby making Day 2 into Day 1 and Day 8 into Day 7; in this way she will have had done *bedikos* on Day 1 and Day 7.

- The *Noda B'Yehudah* also says that if the woman did *bedikos* on Day 1 and Day 3, she can do a *bedikah* on Day 8, and does not

382. Although one would think that performing the afternoon *bedikah* is more important, Rav Shmuel HaLevi Wosner explains that the morning *bedikah* is more important, because that sets the day as one of the *shivah nekiyim*, so it should be done as early as possible. Therefore, a woman who does two *bedikos* a day should do the morning *bedikah* as soon as possible, from *neitz* (*bedi'eved* from *alos hashachar*). Also, a woman who is doing one *bedikah* a day should only do the morning *bedikah*.

383. In this way the woman has Day 1 and Day 7, and also does not have more than 5 days without a *bedikah*. This advice is often given to cover for the event that the woman will miss the *bedikah* on Day 7; now she at least has two *bedikos* during *shivah nekiyim*. Days 1 and 7 are specifically those days. Day 3 may be substituted with any of the middle days of *shivah nekiyim*.

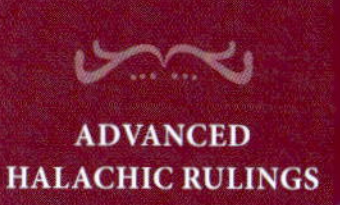

have to wait until Day 9; in this way she has a beginning and end to her *shivah nekiyim*. He explains that the requirement for Days 1 and 7 is that a) there is a *bedikah* on the first and last day, and b) there is no gap bigger than 5 days between *bedikos*. Having done a *bedikah* on Days 1, 3, and 8 fulfills these two requirements

- The *Dagul M'Revavah* says the reason a woman requires *bedikos* on Day 1 and Day 7 is so as not to have 6 days without a *bedikah* from the *hefsek taharah* (based on the *Smag*). Therefore, he says a *bedikah* on any day from Day 1 to Day 6 would suffice as the first of the two, since there is a gap of less than 6 days from the *hefsek taharah*.[384]
- Rav Yosef Shalom Elyashiv and Rav Shmuel HaLevi Wosner say a woman who missed a *bedikah* on Day 1 should not rely on the Dagul M'Revavah's opinion. Rather, she should consider her first *bedikah* (i.e., Day 2) as Day 1, and add the extra days to complete her *shivah nekiyim*.
- Practically speaking,[385] although Rav Yitzchak Berkovits agrees with the ruling of the Noda B'Yehudah theoretically, and holds that the halachah should be like this, it would be a stringency that leads to a leniency in that it will almost definitely put a strain on the couple's *shalom bayis*. He therefore usually tells women to rely on the opinion of the Dagul M'Revavah.
- Rav Yosef Shalom Elyashiv says a woman who did *bedikos* for the first 6 days of *shivah nekiyim* and missed Day 7 may immerse on time.[386]

A Woman Who Did Bedikos on Day 1 and Day 7

- The *Rama* says a woman who did *bedikos* on Day 1 and Day 7 may immerse in the mikvah *bedi'eved*.[387]

384. The Noda B'Yehudah is the author of the *Dagul M'Revavah*. The commentaries raise the issue that he contradicts himself between these two works in regard to this *din*.

385. This also seems to be the ruling of Rav Yosef Shalom Elyashiv, brought in *Mishnas HaShulchan*.

386. Although ideologically Rav Yosef Shalom Elyashiv holds such a woman should wait an extra day so she has *bedikos* on Day 1 and Day 7, practically, he says to allow her to immerse on time so as not to cause a strain on her *shalom bayis*.

387. The *Pischei Teshuvah* says this may be done *lechatchilah* if a woman usually gets hurt from doing *bedikos*. Always consult with a competent *Rav*.

- Rav Yosef Shalom Elyashiv and Rav Shmuel HaLevi Wosner say if a woman did *bedikos* on Day 1 and another *bedikah* during *bein hashmashos* after Day 7, she may immerse on time. The reason for this is that the halachah may be that a woman only needs one *bedikah* during *shivah nekiyim*, and even if she needs two *bedikos*, maybe *bein hashmashos* is part of Day 7 (this is a *sfeik sfeika* [doubt about a doubt]).

- Rav Shmuel HaLevi Wosner and Rav Nissim Karelitz say a woman who performed a *hefsek taharah* and *moch dachuk* and a *bedikah* on Day 7 may immerse on time, if necessary. The reason is because the *moch dachuk* was inside her body after *shkiah* on Day 1 of *shivah nekiyim*, and can thus count as a *bedikah bedi'eved* (even though it is a *bedikas laylah* [a *bedikah* performed at night]). It may be counted together with the *bedikah* she performed on Day 7, so it is considered as though she did *bedikos* on Day 1 and Day 7.[388]

A Woman Who Did a Bedikah on Day 1 and a Middle Day

- A woman who only did two *bedikos* during the whole *shivah nekiyim* including Day 1 — for example, she did *bedikos* on Day 1 and Day 6, and forgot to do a *bedikah* on Day 7 — should rely on the opinion of Dagul M'Revavah and Rav Yosef Shalom Elyashiv, and may immerse on time, as stated above.

- Rav Yosef Shalom Elyashiv says a woman who did a *bedikah* on Day 1 and another *bedikah* on Day 7 during *bein hashmashos* may immerse that evening because of a *sfeik sfeika* (a doubt about a doubt) — perhaps the *bedikah* was performed during the day, and, even if it was not, perhaps the halachah is like the opinion that a *bedikah* done on Day 1 is sufficient. The same applies if the *bedikah* of Day 1 was performed during *bein hashmashos* and another *bedikah*, on another day, was also performed.

388. Rav Nissim Karelitz allows one to be lenient in such a case if there are other reasons to do so. In general, such cases include a childless couple, or a couple who will have *shalom bayis* issues if the woman will not immerse in the mikvah on time.

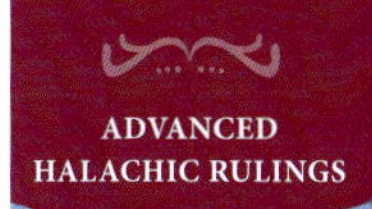

A Woman Who Only Did One Bedikah on Day 1

- The *Chavas Daas*, *Chochmas Adam*, and *Aruch HaShulchan* say that in a situation of *makom igun*, such as if the woman has cuts, one may be lenient as per the opinion of the Raavad, even if the woman just did one *bedikah* any time during *shivah nekiyim*.
- Practically speaking, a *Rav* should be consulted for guidance in such situations.
- In the event that a woman did only one *bedikah* in the entire *shivah nekiyim* — even if it was on Day 1 — and the situation is not one of extenuating circumstances, the woman must add extra days to her *shivah nekiyim* to complete them, counting the day she did her *bedikah* as Day 1.[389]
- Rav Yosef Shalom Elyashiv and Rav Shmuel HaLevi Wosner say a woman who immersed in the mikvah after doing only one *bedikah* during *shivah nekiyim*, even if it was on Day 1 or Day 7, should return to the mikvah to immerse again in the event that she was already with her husband. If the couple were not yet together, the woman should do the necessary *bedikos* and immerse again.[390]

A Woman Who Did Only One Bedikah on One of the Middle Days

- In a scenario of *makom igun* or extenuating circumstances, a *Rav* may allow this woman to immerse in the mikvah.
- If it is not a situation of *makom igun* or extenuating circumstances, this woman must add extra *bedikos* on extra days, and in this way complete *shivah nekiyim*.
- If a woman who only did one *bedikah* during the middle days of *shivah nekiyim* (and there were no extenuating circumstances) was already with her husband, she must still wait 6 *onos* and

389. Refer to End Note on page 416 for a more detailed discussion.

390. Rav Shmuel HaLevi Wosner says to immerse again but without a *brachah*, since there is a disagreement whether the *tevilah* is required.

add *bedikos* on extra days to complete the *shivah nekiyim*.[391] Practically, she must wait 4 days.[392]

- Rav Shmuel HaLevi Wosner says that in the event that a woman in this scenario immersed in the mikvah but was not yet with her husband, she must add *bedikos* on extra days to complete the *shivah nekiyim*. However, she may immediately start the counting since she was not yet intimate with her husband; she does not need to wait 6 *onos*, and the stringency of the Terumas HaDeshen of *lo shamshah attu shamshah* (we do not differentiate between cases in which they were intimate and those in which they were not intimate) is not applied in this case.

Extra Bedikos

- The Mishnah says it is commendable for women to check themselves frequently.[393]
- Practically speaking, nowadays women should not do unnecessary *bedikos*, around the time of marital relations or otherwise.[394] There are several reasons for this. One is that the practice nowadays is to be stringent to be *metamei* colors that *Chazal* were not, and we should not add extra stringencies on top of that. Another reason is in order to minimize the emotional difficulty that a woman may have to go through, as

391. Rav Shmuel HaLevi Wosner. See the *Chasam Sofer* brought in the previous footnote, which is more lenient.

392. She does not need to wait the extra 5th day for *poletes shichvas zera* because it is not a common case, and therefore not included in the *din* of the *Terumas HaDeshen*.

393. *Niddah* 13:71.

394. Some *Poskim* say that a woman should do a *bedikah* when she finds a *kesem* that is smaller than a *gris* on colored clothing or on something that is not susceptible to *tumah*. They reason that although she was saved from becoming *temei'ah* because of *Chazal*'s leniency, at this point she has to check to see if she is bleeding. Rav Shmuel HaLevi Wosner writes against such practices, and Rav Yitzchak Berkovits agrees with Rav Wosner. (Although Rav Wosner is stringent if she finds a *kesem* on the day of the *vest*, Rav Berkovits is lenient in such a case as well.) He says that whenever someone finds a *kesem* and is *tehorah* because of one of the leniencies of *kesamim*, she should avoid doing *bedikos* — unless the situation is one in which *bedikos* are a necessity, such as it is the day of her *vest* or during *shivah nekiyim* — and should also refrain from marital relations for 12–24 hours until she clears up or gets her period. The woman can also be advised not to look for more *kesamim*, but must be consciously aware if she gets her period.

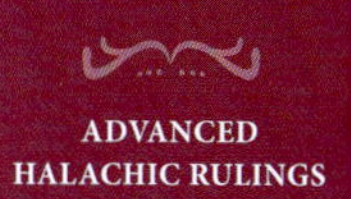

the concern exists that the woman will cut herself by doing too many *bedikos*.[395]

- As a general rule, women should be taught to never do *bedikos* unless the *bedikah* is one that is specifically required by halachah, or she is explicitly advised to do so by a competent *Rav*.[396]

The Obligation of the Bodekes

- There is a disagreement whether or not a *bodekes* who is checking a woman internally for a cut must also check the cervix to see if blood is emerging. The reason to do so would be, as the Mishnah says,[397] that it is commendable for women to check themselves frequently.
- Rav Yisrael Yaakov Fisher says that the *bodekes* should just check if there is a cut, and she does not have to check the cervix to see if any blood is currently coming out.[398]

---

395. Rav Nissim Karelitz.

396. In general, a woman who is unsure whether or not to perform a *bedikah* usually has much more to lose by performing an extra *bedikah* than she stands to lose if she misses a necessary *bedikah*. In the event that a *moch dachuk* was not done, the woman will almost never have to wait another day, especially when the *hefsek taharah* was clean. A woman who missed a *hefsek taharah* only stands to lose 1 day (or possibly 2, if the second night is a Friday night and it is a delayed *tevilah*, according to those who are stringent in such a case). A missed *bedikah* during *shivah nekiyim* will only impact the count of a woman who is only doing *bedikos* on Day 1 and Day 7 and she missed one of those days. (Even in that case the woman will lose only up to a week.) A missed *bedikah* on a *vest she'eino kavua* it is not a problem *bedi'eved*, and the woman can perform a missed *bedikah* for a *vest kavua* as soon as she remembers. In contrast, a woman who performs an unnecessary *bedikah* while she is *tehorah* and finds a drop of blood on the cloth is *temei'ah* and requires 5 and 7. It is important for a woman to understand the risk she is taking by performing an extra *bedikah* versus calling a *Rav* to seek his guidance when the need arises.

397. *Niddah* 13:71.

398. When a woman goes to a *bodekes*, the *bodekes* can check externally for a *makkah*, and if she finds a *makkah* she is not required to do an internal examination. Once she does an internal examination with a speculum, however, it is usually impossible for the *bodekes* not to see the cervix. The standard procedure for a *bodekes* is to check for a *makkah* and to then swab the cervix to determine if blood is coming out at this time as well, whether or not there is a *makkah*. Based on this ruling of Rav Yisrael Yaacov Fisher, a *Rav* can tell the *bodekes* to check externally for a *makkah*, and if she does not find one, to check internally, but to avoid swabbing the cervix if at all possible. In many cases it is necessary for the *bodekes* to swab the cervix to determine if there is a *makkah* because the cervix is actually the most common place to find a *makkah*, and checking the discharge is required. Otherwise, it should be avoided if possible.

- Some *Poskim* tell *bodkos* to check the cervix to determine what color discharges are coming out at the moment.
- Practically speaking, the halachah is like Rav Yisrael Yaacov Fisher's opinion, but many *bodkos* always check the cervix.

Kesamim during Shivah Nekiyim

- Rav Moshe Feinstein says *kesamim* during *shivah nekiyim* disrupt *shivah nekiyim mid'Rabbanan.*[399] The reason that women wear white underwear during *shivah nekiyim* is so they can see what color the stain is in case they have a *hargashah*.
- Rav Moshe Feinstein says a woman does not have to check her underwear during *shivah nekiyim*, just like she never has to be on the lookout for *kesamim*.
- Rav Akiva Eiger[400] and the *Sidrei Taharah* say a woman must check her clothes during *shivah nekiyim* to make sure she is clear of *kesamim*.[401] This means she also has to check her white underwear.[402]
- Practically speaking, the halachah is like Rav Akiva Eiger's opinion unless there are extenuating circumstances.[403]

---

399. Others disagree and hold that *kesamim* during *shivah nekiyim* disrupt *shivah nekiyim mid'Oraisa*.

400. Based on the *Rosh*.

401. I asked Rav Yitzchak Berkovits about a woman who has a *she'eilah* on a *hefsek taharah* and will not have the time to get to a *Rav* and do another one before *shkiah*. Should she do a second *bedikah* and put it in an envelope, and if the first *hefsek taharah* is good she will discard the envelope, and if it is bad she will open the envelope and see if that *bedikah* is *tehorah*? He answered that she may not do this. Since the halachah is like Rav Akiva Eiger's opinion, that a woman must check her underwear during *shivah nekiyim*, she must certainly check her *bedikos*. Even Rav Moshe Feinstein is only lenient in regard to *kesamim*, not *bedikos*.

402. Rav Shmuel HaLevi Wosner; Rav Nissim Karelitz.

403. This means that a woman should not be advised to change in the dark and not look at her underwear during *shivah nekiyim* to avoid *kesamim*. Practically speaking, in extenuating circumstances a *Rav* may employ other methods to get a woman to the mikvah, such as advising her to wear a pad which is not susceptible to *tumah*. It is said that Rav Moshe Feinstein would advise women who were staining due to an IUD or pills to minimize *bedikos* of *shivah nekiyim* to avoid becoming *temei'os* from the *bedikos*. A competent *Rav* should be consulted for practical *she'eilos*; one should never minimize the number of *bedikos* without direction from a competent *Rav*.

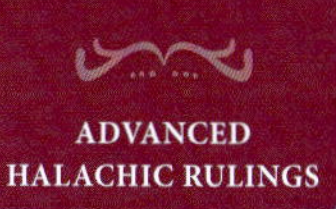

- If a woman did an unnecessary *bedikah* outside of a *vest* or *shivah nekiyim*, she may discard it without checking, unless she already saw that there was a *she'eilah*. In that case it should be brought to a *Rav*. During *shivah nekiyim*, one may not discard an unnecessary *bedikah* without checking it.

- If a woman really has a new *re'iyah* — not just a *kesem* — during *shivah nekiyim* after a good *hefsek taharah*, she can create a new *vest*. This *din* only applies after Day 3 of *shivah nekiyim*, at which point she is considered as having a *mayan sasum*. See Advanced Rulings, Vestos (page 379) for more on how to calculate *vestos*.

Pads during Shivah Nekiyim

- According to Rav Moshe Feinstein's opinion that *kesamim* during *shivah nekiyim* are *d'Rabbanan*, a woman who is having a hard time becoming clean can technically wear a white pad[404] or synthetic underwear throughout *shivah nekiyim* to avoid issues of *kesamim*. This woman remains *tehorah* as long as she can successfully perform her *bedikos*.

- A woman who is in extenuating circumstances may be advised to rely on this ruling when necessary, but should not do such a thing without seeking guidance from a *Rav*.

White Underwear during Shivah Nekiyim

- After the *hefsek taharah* a woman should put on white underwear beginning at *shkiah*.[405] There is no need to change into white underwear before *shkiah*, even if the *hefsek taharah* was performed earlier in the day.[406]

---

404. See "*Kesamim*," page ## for the *dinim* of pads.

405. Rav Yitzchak Berkovits explains that wearing white underwear is a *din* of *shivah nekiyim* which starts at *shkiah*, and is not a *din* of *hefsek taharah*.

406. Rav Shimon Eider brings that women should change into white underwear from the time they do the *hefsek taharah*, even if the *hefsek taharah* was done earlier in the day. He bases his ruling on the *Shulchan Aruch*, which says that a woman should change into white underwear after doing the *hefsek taharah*. He deduces that this means that white underwear is necessary whenever a *hefsek taharah* is done. The reason most *Poskim* do not seem to hold like this is because the *Shulchan Aruch* says this halachah right after stating that the *hefsek taharah* should be performed right before *shkiah*, so by default the white underwear will have been worn from *shkiah*.

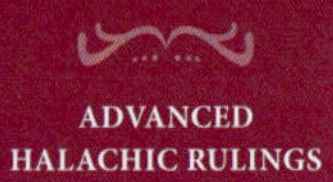

- The white underwear must be worn until *tzeis hakochavim* after *shivah nekiyim*. A woman who leaves to the mikvah after this time may first change into colored underwear. Otherwise, she should leave her house wearing white and may change into dark underwear after immersing.

- The *Poskim* say that the underwear should be white, and not, says Rav Shmuel HaLevi Wosner, a worn-out, musty sepia color. It must also not be worn out or ripped. Women should be taught by their *kallah* teachers to buy new white underwear from time to time.

- Rav Moshe Feinstein says synthetic underwear is not susceptible to *tumah*. Rav Yitzchak Berkovits added that even if there is a strip of cotton in the middle, it is nullified to the underwear.

- In extenuating circumstances, a *Rav* can suggest that a woman wear synthetic white underwear to avoid a problem with *kesamim*.

- Women should not wear synthetic white underwear during *shivah nekiyim* without being guided by a *Rav* to do so, because *shivah nekiyim* will become a joke. When the situation deems itself necessary, a *Rav* can advise a woman, on a case-by-case basis, to wear synthetics, and he should stay on top of the particular situation.[407]

- Some *Rabbanim* tell women to wear dark underwear during *shivah nekiyim* when they are staining and the origin of the blood is clearly from a cut. Many *Poskim* tell women to wear pads or synthetics, but to make sure they are wearing white to fulfill the dictum "*yemei libun* (days of whitening)."[408]

- A woman may immerse in the mikvah even if she did not wear white underwear during *shivah nekiyim* for whatever reason.[409]

---

407. Not only will it become a joke, but women will purposely miss *bedikos* if they spot on synthetic underwear, to avoid coming to a possible *d'Oraisa* issue if any blood is found on the *bedikah*.

408. Rav Yitzchak Berkovits.

409. *Chochmas Adam*; Rav Yosef Shalom Elyashiv. These *Poskim* are actually only lenient if a woman did not wear white underwear because of a situation that was beyond her control, however, if she was negligent and purposely did not wear white underwear, they advise that she be penalized by being told to start counting again. Rav Yitzchak Berkovits would not be stringent in such a case if she was negligent. Rav Shmuel HaLevi Wosner expounds and says that a *Rav* should even be lenient if the woman wore colored underwear negligently, and actually discovered a *kesem* larger than a *gris* that would have been *metamei* her had she followed halachah and worn white.

Sleeping on White Sheets

- Most *Poskim* in Eretz Yisrael say a woman should sleep on white sheets during *shivah nekiyim*,[410] even when the woman is sleeping in white underwear.[411] This practice is based on the *Shulchan Aruch*.
- In the United States most women are not taught to sleep on white sheets, unless the woman is not sleeping in underwear.[412]
- A woman whose family custom is to use white sheets should keep this custom, even in the United States.

What to Use for the Bedikah

- The *Shulchan Aruch* says all *bedikos* should be performed with a white, clean, and soft cloth.
- Rav Yosef Shalom Elyashiv says that although the *Shulchan Aruch* does not say the size of the cloth, it should be three fingers squared,[413] no more or less. *Bedi'eved*, any size cloth is acceptable to use for a *bedikah*, as long as it gets the job done.
- Rav Nissim Karelitz says the minimum size of the *bedikah* cloth is one that can be wrapped around the finger, and cover from the tip of the finger to the second knuckle.
- A woman may use a tampon for a *moch dachuk lechatchilah*, and as a *hefsek taharah bedi'eved*.
- Rav Yosef Shalom Elyashiv, Rav Shmuel HaLevi Wosner, and Rav Nissim Karelitz say a *bedikah* that a woman performed

---

410. Some even use white pillowcases. However, most *Poskim* say that this is a big stringency. Some say that a woman should wear white pajamas, even if she is wearing white underwear; however most say that this is a stringency.

411. There was a *kallah* who asked if she should put a white sheet on her bed before she is married, because she slept in the same room as younger siblings and wanted to avoid raising any eyebrows. Rav Shlomo Zalman Auerbach is quoted to have told her to retain her custom and use the sheets. See Background and Analysis, Taharah, headline "Wearing White Clothing during Shivah Nekiyim" (page 150), where Rav Yitzchak Berkovits is quoted as saying that someone who has a custom to use white sheets should adhere to the custom, but not if it will lead to others understanding that she is in middle of *shivah nekiyim*, such as if she is a guest in someone else's house and forgot to bring her own sheet.

412. Rav Moshe Feinstein.

413. Rav Shmuel HaLevi Wosner says the *bedikah cloth* should ideally be 7–8 centimeters squared.

only with her finger — without any cloth —does not count for a *bedikah*, even *bedi'eved*.[414]

- Rav Nissim Karelitz says a *bedikah* performed with paper or tissues counts *bedi'eved*, as long as the material is absorbent.[415]

Depth of the Bedikah

- The minimum depth of a *bedikah* is when the first knuckle is inserted into the vaginal canal, and not just when the *bedikah* cloth goes into the external lips. Anything less than that is called a "wipe," and is invalid as a *bedikah*.
- Ideally, a woman should do the *bedikah* as deeply as she can go, being careful not to irritate herself.[416]

Position While Performing the Bedikah

- The *Chasam Sofer* says a woman should ideally perform all *bedikos* while standing with one foot raised and placed on a chair and the other foot on the ground.
- Rav Shmuel HaLevi Wosner says if a woman needs to, she can do *bedikos* while lying on her back. If she feels that she can perform the *bedikah* more easily while sitting (on a toilet), she may do so.[417]

---

414. *Sidrei Taharah*.

415. He adds that in such a case the woman should be careful that the paper does not rip and fall apart inside her. If it does, the *bedikah* is invalid.

416. Rav Shmuel HaLevi Wosner and many other *Poskim* clearly say that a woman should insert the *bedikah* cloth as deeply as possible and should not be worried that she may hit the cervix, because the cervix is deeper than her finger could ever reach (*Shu"t Chasam Sofer* 179). Rav Yitzchak Berkovits said that the *Rambam* discusses doing a *bedikah* to the place where the male *eiver* reaches at *gemar bi'ah* and said that it appears that the *eiver* reaches a point in her body deeper than a woman could possibly ever do a *bedikah*. That being said, most *bodkos* and gynecologists assert that the cervix is definitely within reach of a probing finger and that a *bedikah* cloth that touches the cervix could easily cause a *makkah*. *Bodkos* say that they see women all the time who have cuts on the outside of the cervix caused by *bedikah* cloths. A proof that the finger could easily reach the outside of the cervix is when a pregnant woman is induced through "membrane stripping," the doctor reaches *into* the cervix to strip the membrane. If the doctor can reach into the cervix, they certainly could reach the outside of the cervix. Practically speaking, a woman should do *bedikos* as deeply as possible but should be careful not to cause herself unnecessary cuts, and should certainly not go too deep, so as to avoid cutting her cervix.

417. Rav Nissim Karelitz.

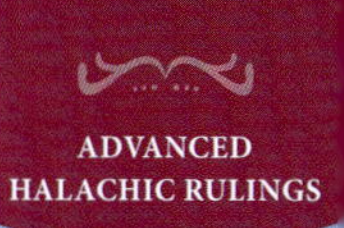

Lubricants

- Rav Moshe Feinstein says a woman may use lubricants for performing a *bedikah*.
- Rav Yosef Shalom Elyashiv says lubricants should ideally be avoided because they make it harder for the *Rav* to see exactly what color the *mareh* is.
- Practically speaking, a woman may use water-based lubricants when necessary.[418] She should ideally put the lubricant inside her body, instead of on the cloth. She should then wait 10 minutes, thus facilitating a more comfortable *bedikah* without ruining the *mareh*.

Washing, Swimming, and Bathing during Shivah Nekiyim

- Rav Yosef Shalom Elyashiv and others say a woman should not sit in a bath or swim during *shivah nekiyim*, unless she performs a *bedikah* before entering the water.
- Practically speaking, a woman may *lechatchilah* go swimming or bathe during *shivah nekiyim*. If she does, she is not required to do any extra *bedikos*. She should avoid doing a purposeful internal cleansing.

Chorin V'Sedakin

- The *Sidrei Taharah* and the *Chazon Ish* say a *bedikas chorin v'sedakin* shows that blood has not emerged in the past few minutes.[419]

418. KY Jelly or Astroglide (water-based versions), but not Vaseline.

419. Others explain that the *bedikas chorin v'sedakin* actually shows that she did not bleed at the moment of the *bedikah*. They explain that if a woman performs a superficial *bedikah*, there is always the possibility that some blood trickled out of the uterus and flowed through the cracks and crevices of the vaginal canal, just beyond the reach of the *bedikah* cloth.

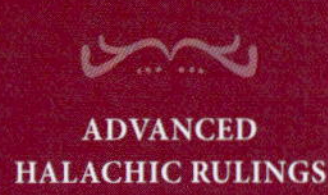

- If a *bodekes* puts a Q-tip or applicator next to the cervix and waits a little to see which color discharges are coming out,[420] this counts as a *bedikah lechatchilah.*[421]

- Rav Yaacov Blau says women should be taught to insert the *bedikah* cloth straight in, dab along the walls internally, and then remove the cloth directly without twisting it. In this way, the woman fulfills the obligation of *bedikas chorin v'sedakin*, and she will not cut herself unnecessarily. A woman should be taught "in, around, and out," and she should not twist the cloth as she is inserting it, and she should not "layer" the cloth by dabbing it against the vaginal walls in ascending or descending stages.

- A *bedikah* that is done without checking *chorin v'sedakin* but is left inside for "a while" is counted as a valid *bedikah*. Rav Moshe Feinstein says the amount of time for this is *lechatchilah* 15 minutes, and *bedi'eved* even 30 seconds.[422]

- The same halachah applies to the *moch dachuk*. If it remains inside the woman's body for 15 minutes before *shkiah* (or even 30 seconds *bedi'eved*), or she checked *chorin v'sedakin* with the *moch dachuk* before *shkiah*, it will serve as a new *hefsek taharah* in the event that the *hefsek taharah* comes out not good. Again,

---

420. Rav Akiva Eiger; *Pischei Teshuvah* 198:16.

421. Some *bodkos* perform the *bedikah* with an applicator next to the cervix, while others use a *bedikah* cloth to perform the *bedikah*, pressing into the crevices, just as the woman herself would do.

422. This is based on a disagreement between the Rashba and Noda B'Yehudah as to the reason for the requirement to perform a *bedikas chorin v'sedakin*. The Rashba (*Toras HaBayis* 305) says the requirement to check *chorin v'sedakin* is because the vaginal walls may contain blood and such a *bedikah* will reveal that blood. The Noda B'Yehudah (*mahadurah kamah*, no. 55) says the *bedikas chorin v'sedakin* was only required for *kodshim* in the times of the Beis HaMikdash, but not for a niddah, and therefore a niddah does not require a *bedikas chorin v'sedakin* even for the *hefsek taharah* and *bedikos* of *shivah nekiyim* (this is the opinion of the Raavid).

The Chavas Daas (196:4) rejects the position of the Noda B'Yehudah and says that a woman needs a *bedikas chorin v'sedakin* for the *hefsek taharah* and *bedikos* on Days 1 and 7 of *shivah nekiyim* for many reasons: 1. The statement that a woman does not need a *bedikas chorin v'sedakin* except for *kodshim* was said in regard to a woman who has a status of *taharah*, but a niddah, who has a status of *tumah*, needs *bedikas chorin v'sedakin*. 2. A superficial *bedikah* will not show that blood is not present when the *bedikah* is performed unless the *bedikah* cloth is left inside the body for the amount of time it generally takes to perform a *bedikah*.

That said, if one leaves the cloth inside the body for 30 seconds, Rav Berkovits says to rely on the *bedikah* even for a *hefsek taharah* or *bedikos* of *shivah nekiyim*, since even the more stringent positions agree that such a *bedikah* is valid as a *bedikas chorin v'sedakin*.

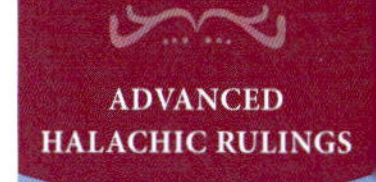

this is provided that the *moch dachuk* was inserted fully, before *shkiah*.

- If a woman did not do the *bedikah* in *chorin v'sedakin*, but she walked around with the *bedikah* inside her, even a little bit, it is a valid *bedikas chorin v'sedakin*.
- The 30-second amount of time may be relied upon in the event that a woman washed herself and wants to now do a *bedikah*, or between two *bedikos* where the first one came out not good. This discussion is all regarding *bedi'eved* situations, for example, if it getting close to *shkiah*. *Lechatchilah*, however, a woman should wait 10–15 minutes between one *bedikah* and the next, or between a *rechitzah* and the *bedikah*.[423]

When to Perform Bedikos during Shivah Nekiyim

- The Beis Yosef says the morning *bedikah* should be performed between *neitz hachamah* and *chatzos*. If a woman needs to do it earlier, she may do it from *alos hashachar*, *bedi'eved*.
- The afternoon *bedikah* should be performed between *Minchah ketanah* and *shkiah*.
- Rav Shmuel HaLevi Wosner says a woman need not do two afternoon *bedikos* in the event that she did not do the morning *bedikah* before *chatzos*. She should only do the afternoon *bedikah* for that day, after *Minchah ketanah*.[424]

---

423. When a woman goes to a *bodekes* to perform a *hefsek taharah* for her, the standard practice is to clean the woman internally from any blood and to then perform the *bedikah*. I asked Rav Dovid Feinstein how long the *bodekes* should wait after cleansing the woman internally before performing the *hefsek taharah* and he said, "She can do it right away without waiting." I asked whether the *din* of *chorin v'sedakin* requires her to wait, and he said, "As long as she produces a clean *hefsek taharah*, it is OK even if she does not wait." It sounds like he understands the concept of *chorin v'sedakin* like those who hold that a *bedikas chorin v'sedakin* shows blood has not been missed during the *bedikah* (as explained in the above footnote), and not that blood has not come for some time.

424. Some *Poskim* advise a woman who did not perform the morning *bedikah* on Day 1 or Day 7 to do the *bedikah* whenever she remembers, even if it is between *chatzos* and *Minchah ketanah*. In this way she can be certain to have performed a *bedikah* on a day on which it would be a problem if she did not. Rav Shmuel HaLevi Wosner and others say the woman loses the *bedikah* of that day if the *bedikah* is performed between *chatzos* and *Minchah ketanah*. The only thing such a *bedikah* counts toward is "*kol hayad hamarbeh livdok*" (the opinion that says that one should do many *bedikos*) which is not something we generally encourage. Practically speaking, Rav Yitzchak Berkovits says a woman should always perform the *bedikos* at the correct times but we would allow a *bedikah* to be performed between *chatzos* and *Minchah ketanah b'dieved*, such as if a woman is

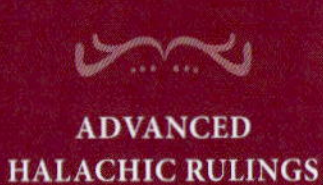

A Bedikah Performed at Night

- A *bedikah* performed at night will only be relied upon in extenuating circumstances (for example, to save the couple from a *chuppas niddah*).[425] An example would be a situation in which the *Rav* wants to use the *moch dachuk* as the only *bedikah* of *shivah nekiyim*.

- Rav Yosef Shalom Elyashiv says a woman may rely on the latest *zman shkiah* on the calendar, but cannot do a *hefsek taharah* even a minute later.

- A *hefsek taharah* done after *shkiah* is invalid to allow that night and the following day to be Day 1 of *shivah nekiyim*. However, it can serve as an early *hefsek taharah* for tomorrow (*bedi'eved*, as a woman should ideally do a *hefsek taharah* between *Minchah ketanah* and *shkiah*), with Day 1 being 2 days from now in case she misses a *hefsek* the day after the night *bedikah*.[426] In Eretz Yisrael, this includes a *hefsek taharah* done even a minute after *shkiah*.[427]

- Rav Nissim Karelitz says a *bedikah* that was inserted before *shkiah* and removed after *shkiah* counts as though it was performed before *shkiah*, because there is clear evidence that she was clean from before *shkiah*.[428]

- Rav Yosef Shalom Elyashiv and Rav Nissim Karelitz say that in the event that a woman is unsure whether her *hefsek taharah* \was performed before or after *shkiah*, the *bedikah* does not

---

doing *bedikos* only on Days 1 and 7 and performed one or both of those *bedikos* between *chatzos* and *Minchah ketanah*.

425. Tosafos (*Niddah* 69:71, "*Shivah*") hold a *bedikah* performed at night is invalid, while Rashi (*Pesachim* 81:71) holds such a *bedikah* counts.

426. Rav Yosef Shalom Elyashiv. This is also the opinion of the Sefer HaEshkol, Lechem V'Simlah, Noda B'Yehudah, and the Chazon Ish.

427. Rav Moshe Feinstein is quoted as being lenient and allowing a *hefsek taharah* up to 8 or 9 minutes after *shkiah* in New York City. Some Chassidishe *Poskim* allow a *hefsek taharah* that was performed 13 minutes after *shkiah*, and some even allow up to 20 minutes after *shkiah* (Satmar and Klausenberg). Practically speaking, I asked Rav Dovid Feinstein how long after *shkiah* a *bodekes* should be allowed to perform a *bedikah* for a woman who needs the service, and he told me, "10 minutes, *bedieved*."

428. Based on this ruling, in the event that the *hefsek taharah* was *tamei* and the *moch dachuk* was *tahor* and the *moch dachuk* was inserted before *shkiah* and she inserted it in a manner that is considered a *bedikas chorin v'sedakin*, the *moch dachuk* may serve as a valid *hefsek taharah*, as discussed above.

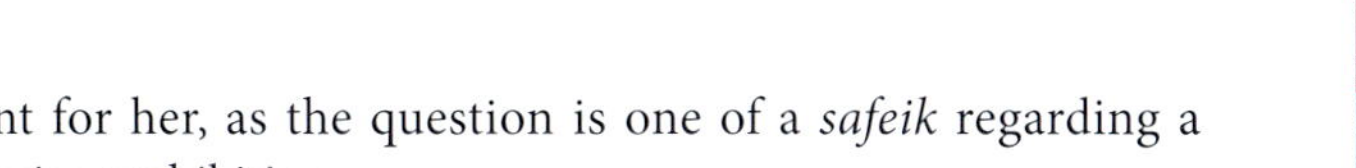

count for her, as the question is one of a *safeik* regarding a *d'Oraisa* prohibition.

- If a woman cannot, for whatever reason, perform one of the *bedikos* during *shivah nekiyim*, she should not do a *bedikah* before *alos hashachar* or after *tzeis hakochavim*. Such a *bedikah* will be invalid, and she will become *temei'ah* in the event that she discovers blood, even less than a *gris*.

Counting Shivah Nekiyim Out Loud

- The *Shelah* says it is a mitzvah for women to count each day of *shivah nekiyim* out loud, the same way a person counts *sefiras ha'omer*. He says the reason for this is because the Torah says, "*V'safrah lah*," which he understands to mean that the woman should count out loud.[429]
- The *Noda B'Yehudah* and the *Radvaz* say there is no need to verbally count *shivah nekiyim*; a woman's need to count these days is not like counting *sefiras ha'omer*.
- The *Sefer HaChinuch*, the *Sefer HaEshkol*, and the *Ramban* all explain that "*V'safrah lah*" means that the woman should be mindful that she is in *shivah nekiyim*.
- Even according to the *Shelah*, a woman's counting is valid *bedi'eved* even when she did not count out loud.
- Practically speaking, the halachah is like the opinion of the Sefer HaChinuch, that a woman does not have to actually count at all.[430] The halachah has always clearly been like the opinion of the Sefer HaChinuch, and there is no room for inventing new customs in *Klal Yisrael*.[431]

---

429. Tosafos in *Kesubos* (72:71, "*V'Safrah Lah*") ask why a woman counting *shivah nekiyim* (a *zavah gedolah*) does not make a *brachah* on the *shivah nekiyim*. Tosafos answer that she can possibly stain during *shivah nekiyim* and have to start again, so *Chazal* did not require her to make a *brachah* that could potentially be *l'vatalah* (for naught). The Shelah learns from this *Tosafos* that although the woman is not required to make a *brachah*, she is required to count each day of *shivah nekiyim* out loud. Practically speaking, as stated above, most hold there is no place for counting out loud.

430. Rav Yosef Shalom Elyashiv.

431. Rav Yitzchak Berkovits is against the practice some women have to say *"Hayom yom rishon l'libuni* — Today is the first day of my whitening," for example.

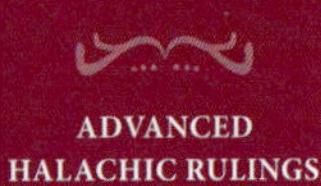

A Woman Who Got Distracted during Shivah Nekiyim

- Most *Poskim*[432] hold there is no issue if a woman got distracted from the fact that she was in *shivah nekiyim*.[433]
- Rav Yosef Shalom Elyashiv and Rav Nissim Karelitz are stringent (as per the opinion of the Me'il Tzedakah), saying that a woman's getting distracted from the fact that she is in *shivah nekiyim* breaks the *shivah nekiyim*. However, she needs to have gotten distracted for 1 complete day, from *shkiah* to *shkiah*, to invalidate that day.[434] If she got distracted but had part of the day, the day counts and she does not have to add an extra day to complete the *shivah nekiyim*.
- Practically speaking, we are not stringent even regarding a woman who got distracted for more than 24 hours.
- Women should be taught not to get distracted from the fact that they are in *shivah nekiyim*, even when they feel sure that a *bedikah* is not good. In any case, a woman can only know that a *bedikah* is not good when she hears that ruling from a *Rav*.
- Women should be taught that many very bad-looking *maros* are really *tehorim*. They should bring all their questions to a *Rav* and should not give up hope.[435]

A Woman Who Lost Count of Shivah Nekiyim

- If a woman forgot which day she did a *hefsek taharah* and began counting *shivah nekiyim*, she may only go to the mikvah when she knows for certain that she has 7 clean days in a row with

---

432. This is the opinion of the Lechem V'Simlah, Oneg Yom Tov, Chazon Ish, Tepliker Rav, and others.

433. The definition of "getting distracted" in these cases means that the woman completely gave up hope of going to the mikvah as scheduled, such as if she found a bad *kesem* and assumes that it is *tamei*. Those who are stringent suspect that she may not check herself properly if she has no hope of going to the mikvah, and that is problematic during *shivah nekiyim*.

434. This is also the opinion of the overwhelming majority of *Poskim*, including the ones who are stringent and hold that there is even a concept of getting distracted from the fact that one is in *shivah nekiyim* in the first place. They hold that only when a woman got distracted for 1 complete day does she lose that day and must make it up.

435. Rav Nissim Karelitz.

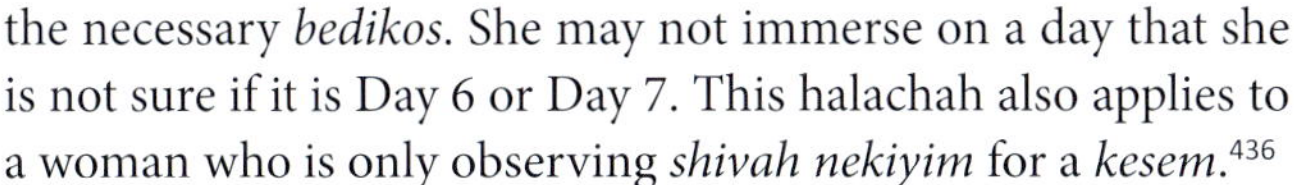

the necessary *bedikos*. She may not immerse on a day that she is not sure if it is Day 6 or Day 7. This halachah also applies to a woman who is only observing *shivah nekiyim* for a *kesem*.[436]

Attributing a Kesem to a Makkah during Shivah Nekiyim

- One may only attribute a *kesem* found during the first 3 days of *shivah nekiyim* to a cut that is known to bleed. This is a degree more stringent than the conventional attribution of *kesamim*, where one may even attribute a *kesem* to a cut that they do not know if it presently bleeding.[437]
- Rav Nissim Karelitz says if a woman touched blood that came from an external place, and she knows she became dirty from the blood and later found a *kesem*, she may attribute her *kesem* to the external source, even during the first 3 days of *shivah nekiyim*.[438]
- These "first 3 days of *shivah nekiyim*" begin the day after the woman stops bleeding substantially.[439] If a woman bled for only 1 day, and then has a *kesem* on Day 2 of *shivah nekiyim* (i.e., she has 4 days from the *re'iyah* or *kesem* until her *hefsek taharah*, and then 2 days into *shivah nekiyim*), she has already been clean from substantial bleeding for 5 or 6 days. A *Rav* may thus

---

436. Rav Yosef Shalom Elyashiv. See *Pischei Teshuvah* 196:17.

437. Rav Yosef Shalom Elyashiv says one may attribute a *kesem* that was found on outer clothing if the undergarments are clean. It seems that the rule of not attributing a *kesem* to a different source during the first 3 days of *shivah nekiyim* only applies when the *teliyah* is a necessary component in being *metaher* the woman. However, if objectively speaking it is understood that the woman is *tehorah* (such as if it is simply not possible that the *kesem* miraculously went through her underwear to her outside clothing), one can be lenient even during the first 3 days of *shivah nekiyim*, even if there is no clear cause to attribute the stain to (Rav Nissim Karelitz; see *Pischei Teshuvah* and *Panim Me'iros*).

438. What should be apparent from the language of the *Poskim* is that during the first 3 days of *shivah nekiyim* one may not attribute a stain to a far-fetched *teliyah*. However, if a *teliyah* actually presents itself to be viable, it may be used anytime during the *shivah nekiyim*. The definition of "viable" seems to be that there is something that has a source that produces blood and it is somewhat likely that the *kesem* came from that source.

439. For the source of this *din*, see *Pischei Teshuvah* 196:10, that the Chasam Sofer and Sidrei Taharah hold that if a woman does a *bedikah* (before the *hefsek taharah*) and sees a *kesem* 3 days after that *bedikah*, she may attribute the *kesem* to any type of *makkah*, since she certainly stopped bleeding from the time of the *bedikah*. Practically speaking, *Poskim* are lenient even in the event that the extra *bedikah* was never performed, as long as she did not bleed a lot in the past 3 days.

attribute a *kesem* that she discovers[440] to a *shuk shel tabachim* (lit. marketplace of butchers; i.e., she was in a place where blood is commonly found) or other, similar, lenient attributions.[441]

- The custom is like the opinion of the Aruch HaShulchan,[442] that a *Rav* should not ask a woman which day she is up to. He should assume she is past Day 3 of substantial bleeding, so he can be lenient and attribute a *kesem* to some cause.
- Even in a case in which one may attribute a *kesem* to a *makkah*,[443] a woman must still produce a clean *hefsek taharah* and the necessary minimum *bedikos* of Day 1 and Day 7. A woman who is having difficulty producing clean *bedikos* because of a cut or irritation may go to a nurse or *bodekes*, who can produce a valid *hefsek taharah* and *bedikos* of Day 1 and Day 7 for her, using a *bedikah* cloth or Q-tip. A woman who for whatever reason cannot get all three of these *bedikos* through a *bodekes* must at least have the minimum required *bedikos*, as discussed above.[444]

When to Perform Chafifos

- The *Gemara Niddah* 66b says a woman should perform *chafifos* close to the time she will be immersing in the mikvah.

---

440. The *Pischei Teshuvah* says a woman who is counting *shivah nekiyim* because of a *kesem* or *dam chimud* may attribute a *kesem* to a cut even if it is not known to bleed, even during the first 3 days of *shivah nekiyim*. The explanation for this seems to be as we are saying, that a woman may attribute a *kesem* to a *makkah* — even one that does not bleed — as long as she is not substantially bleeding, because there is not such a need to prove that her *mayan* is *sasum*.

441. *She'arim HaMetzuyanim B'Halachah*.

442. 60:39.

443. Some *Rabbanim* tell women who are staining during *shivah nekiyim* because of a *makkah* to wear dark underwear during the duration of *shivah nekiyim*, because they are going to attribute the staining to the *makkah* anyway. This ruling has a basis in *Teshuvos Rebbe Akiva Eiger*, *Tinyana*, *siman* 34, which permits this *b'makom igun*. See *Shiurei Shevet HaLevi* 190:10:9 (which says not to do this on Day 1 and Day 7), and *Igros Moshe*, vol. 3, *siman* 95. Rav Yitzchak Berkovits says to advise a woman in this situation to wear a white pad or synthetic underwear during this time, as *Chazal* clearly say that she should wear "white." This is also the ruling of Rav Yosef Shalom Elyashiv, quoted in *Mishmeres Taharah*. Since the woman is wearing something that cannot become *tamei*, and a valid *teliyah* exists (which are two *tzirufim*), a *Rav* may be lenient for this woman, while still fulfilling the letter of the law. In any case, the woman must be advised not to miss the minimum *bedikos*, as well as the *hefsek taharah*.

444. *Chavas Daas*; *Avnei Millu'im*; Rav Yosef Shalom Elyashiv; Rav Shmuel HaLevi Wosner.

› The *Gemara Niddah* 67b–68a says a woman should perform *chafifos* on *erev Shabbos* or *erev Yom Tov* for a *tevilah* on Shabbos, Motzaei Shabbos, or Yom Tov. The Gemara asks: If she can distance the *chafifah* from the *tevilah* on Motzaei Shabbos, shouldn't she be allowed to do that every day of the week? Accordingly, a woman should be allowed to do *chafifos* on Sunday for a Monday-night *tevilah*. The Gemara answers that whenever it is possible, one should perform the *chafifos* close to the *tevilah*, and if it is not possible, she should not.[445]

Note: This means that when a woman can perform *chafifos* on time, she must; only in a case of a Motzaei Shabbos or Motzaei Yom Tov *tevilah* did *Chazal* allow women to perform *chafifos* not immediately prior to *tevilah*.

› The Gemara asks: one Gemara says that a woman should perform *chafifos* during the day and immerse at night, while another Gemara says she should perform *chafifos at* night — which one is preferred? The Gemara answers that whenever it is possible, one should perform the *chafifos* close to the *tevilah*, and if it is not possible, she should not — in other words, the different *dinim* are explaining the differentiation between a regular *tevilah* and a *tevilah* after Shabbos or Yom Tov.

› *Rashi* explains that a woman should ideally perform her *chafifos* during the day. However, in a case of a Motzaei Shabbos or Motzaei Yom Tov *tevilah*, she should perform *chafifos* on the night of the *tevilah*.

› *Tosafos* brings the *She'iltos*, which, in contrast to the above opinion, says that ideally a woman should perform *chafifos* at night, unless it is a Friday- or Yom Tov-night *tevilah*, in which case she should perform *chafifos* during the day.

› The *Rosh* says that on a regular night, in order to satisfy both opinions, a woman should start *chafifos* during the day, continue through *bein hashmashos*, and end after *tzeis hakochavim*, at which point she may immerse in the mikvah.

445. This fundamental concept in the Gemara is important when answering *she'eilos*, particularly in *hilchos niddah*. Some people have a hard time understanding the concept of "*lechatchilah*" and "*bedi'eved*," and it is incumbent on the *Rav* to explain to them that *lechatchilah* is usually the way to go, unless there is something out of the ordinary. This particularly comes into play regarding being lenient with *bedikos* during *shivah nekiyim*, OCD behavior in regards to *chafifah* and *tevilah*, and many other areas of halachah.

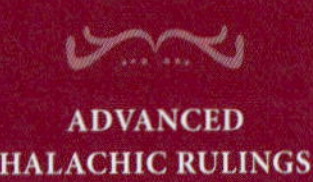

- The *Shulchan Aruch* says the halachah is like the opinion of the *She'iltos*. A woman who is able to start earlier should try to fulfill Rashi's opinion.[446]
- The *Rama* says the halachah is like the opinion of the *She'iltos*, and it is a nice custom to also fulfill Rashi's opinion.
- The *Shach*[447] and *Taz*[448] say the halachah is like Rashi's opinion.

Chafifos for Tevilah That Falls on Motzaei Shabbos or Yom Tov

- A woman whose *tevilah* falls on Motzaei Shabbos or Motzaei Yom Tov should perform all her *chafifos* on *erev Shabbos* or *erev Yom Tov*, and shower and comb out her hair on Motzaei Shabbos or Motzaei Yom Tov.[449] In this way, she fulfills both opinions — she does the *chafifos* on the day before (*erev*) as per Rashi's opinion, and she does the *chafifos* on the night of her *tevilah*, as per the *She'iltos*.[450]
- This also applies to a *tevilah* on Motzaei Yom Tov after a 2-day Yom Tov.
- A woman who will immerse in the mikvah on the second night of Yom Tov should perform all *chafifos* on *erev Yom Tov*, and should tie her hair up until the *tevilah*. She should also clean her mouth the night of the *tevilah*.[451] She will not perform any other *chafifos* on Yom Tov itself.

---

446. 199:3.

447. 199:6.

448. 197:5.

449. The *Poskim* discuss that the woman must also redo anything that may have ruined her *chafifah* achievements. The examples given are brushing her teeth and removing any makeup that she may have applied after initiating the *chafifos* on Friday. Most *Poskim* advise women who have begun *chafifos* on Friday for a Motzaei Shabbos *tevilah* to avoid putting on any difficult-to-remove makeup, such as eyeliner, so as not to disqualify what has already been accomplished. See *Rama* 199:6, which says that a woman should be careful between the *chafifah* and *tevilah* to avoid any *chatzitzos*.

450. Although the She'iltos would really hold that the woman should do everything on Motzaei Shabbos or Motzaei Yom Tov, he agrees that once she has already done the *chafifos* once on *erev Shabbos* or *erev Yom Tov*, it only takes a short time to do full *chafifos* now to bring her to the desired level of preparedness to immerse in the mikvah.

451. Rav Shmuel HaLevi Wosner says that a woman should use a dry toothbrush to clean her mouth and may use (precut) dental floss if she knows that it will not cause her gums to bleed.

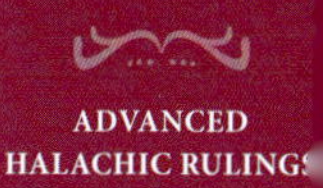

- *Chafifos* that are performed within one *onah* of the *tevilah* are considered *chafifos* that are adjacent to the *tevilah*.
- A woman may do *chafifos* on *erev Shabbos* or *erev Yom Tov* at a time that is most convenient for her. She does not have to wait until the last hour in the day, because she is anyway not doing the *chafifah* through *bein hashmashos*.
- A woman who will immerse in the mikvah on Motzaei Yom Tov after a "3-day Yom Tov" performs some *chafifos* on the day before the 1st day (i.e., *erev Shabbos* or *erev Yom Tov*)[452] and performs the majority of the *chafifos* on Motzaei Shabbos or Motzaei Yom Tov. She should ensure that she takes her time during this preparation and does not rush through it.
- In general, a woman is not obligated to take off from work to do *chafifos* at a better time.
- No matter when a woman does *chafifos*, she should always shower and comb her hair in the mikvah building, aside from when she immerses on Shabbos or Yom Tov.
- In the event that a woman does not have time on *erev Shabbos* or *erev Yom Tov* to do most preparations for a Motzaei Shabbos or Motzaei Yom Tov *tevilah*, she should at least do something on *erev Shabbos* or *erev Yom Tov*, and the rest on Motzaei Shabbos or Motzaei Yom Tov.
- When a woman is going to the mikvah, her husband may miss davening with a minyan to watch their children during a Friday-night *tevilah* if this is necessary to allow her to immerse.[453] This should not be done during the week, however, if he can go to another minyan.

---

452. The reason for this is to fulfill the opinion of the Shach that a woman should do *chafifos* on *erev Shabbos* or *erev Yom Tov* even though it is separated from the *tevilah* by more than 3 days. Most others disagree and hold that there is no reason to do anything on *erev Shabbos* or *erev Yom Tov* because it is so far removed from the *tevilah* that it is not considered a valid *chafifah*.

453. Rav Shmuel HaLevi Wosner says that even someone who is learning in *kollel* should take off to help his wife so she can immerse on time.

Prioritizing Tevilah on Time

- The *Chasam Sofer* says that there are many reasons a woman should immerse in the mikvah on time:[454]
  - *Tevilah* on time is a mitzvah according to many opinions.[455]
  - A woman should remove her *tumah* from her body as soon as possible.[456]
  - In this way, the couple can fulfill the mitzvah of *pru u'revu*.[457]
  - Her husband will have *pas b'salo*, knowing his wife attaches importance to mikvah night.[458]
- Rav Shmuel HaLevi Wosner[459] and Rav Nissim Karelitz say that even if marital relations will for any reason be impossible on the night of the *tevilah*, a woman should immerse on time because there is a mitzvah to hug and kiss,[460] and she is committed to her husband in this regard.[461] This applies even to a *tevilah* on Friday night.[462]

---

454. *Siman kattan* 96.

455. This is the opinion of the Rach, brought in the *Taz* (197:3; *Shach*, ibid.). The *Taz* there explains that although Rabbeinu Tam disagrees and holds there is no mitzvah to immerse in the mikvah on time, he only argues that the *tevilah* itself is not a mitzvah, but he certainly agrees that there is a mitzvah to immerse to be permitted to her husband so that he can fulfill the mitzvah of *pru u'revu*.

456. *Yerushalmi Niddah* 2:4.

457. Rav Yosef Shalom Elyashiv. The *Pischei Teshuvos* and Rav Shmuel HaLevi Wosner explain that the mitzvah of *pru u'revu* in this context is not referring to having children; it refers to the *mitzvah d'Oraisa* of marital relations and the souls that are created during copulation. Every woman, even one who is no longer having children, should therefore immerse in the mikvah on time, to maximize the amount of time the couple will have together.

458. The *Poskim* discuss whether a couple can have *yichud* if the wife did not immerse on time and her husband does not have *pas b'salo*. See *She'arim HaMetzuyanim B'Halachah*, *siman* 162, "*Ishah*."

459. Rav Shmuel HaLevi Wosner (*Shiurei Shevet HaLevi* 196:11) cites a *passuk* regarding *bikkurim* in *Parashas Korach* that says, "*Kol tahor b'veischa yochal oso* — Each pure one in your house shall eat it." *Chazal* learn from there that the woman, who is considered "*beischa*," has a mitzvah to be in a *tahor* state whenever possible.

460. The *Gedolei HaPoskim* say hugging and kissing are a part of the *mitzvah d'Oraisa* of marital relations. This is therefore a *mitzvah d'Oraisa* unto itself.

461. *Shach* 197:3.

462. Rav Yosef Shalom Elyashiv.

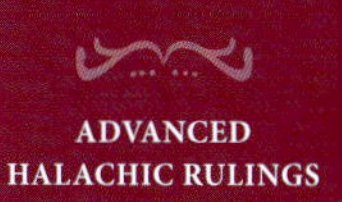

- A woman should prioritize going to the mikvah for the above reasons even when she is pregnant, nursing, or menopausal.[463] Immersing on time is not only for couples who are trying to conceive.

Pushing Off Going to the Mikvah

- Women should be taught that they must call a *Rav* if they ever want to push off going to the mikvah, push off the *hefsek taharah*, or miss any *bedikos* of *shivah nekiyim*, for any reason.[464]
- If a woman is really unable to go to the mikvah,[465] she may delay going. The woman will follow the halachos of someone who is going on time, which allow for a *tevilah* on Motzaei Shabbos *lechatchilah*.
- In almost all cases — including, for example, Seder night of a 3-day Yom Tov at her in-laws' house — a woman should be encouraged to go to the mikvah on time.
- In many cases the woman can just go to the mikvah later on that night.
- The *Rav* should always ask if the couple has children yet, and take that into consideration.

Hiding Mikvah Night

- The Rama says that in the event that a woman tells people when she is going to the mikvah, her husband transgress "*Arur shochev im beheimah* — Cursed is one who lies with an animal."
- A woman may say a white lie to hide when she is going to the mikvah.

463. For example, the woman became *temei'ah* through a fluke *kesem*, *pesichas hakever*, or another form of *niddus*.

464. Many teach this as a blanket rule: a couple should call a *Rav* any time they want to apply a *bedi'eved* ruling. This includes missing *bedikos* during *shivah nekiyim*, and immersing with some sort of *chatzitzah* (for example, nail polish or makeup).

465. A *Rav* should use ingenuity to get someone to the mikvah on time. *Rabbanim* have set women up to run to the mikvah in middle of a sister's or daughter's wedding, or to go to the mikvah in middle of the night.

- Rav Yosef Shalom Elyashiv says that a woman's telling anyone when she is going to the mikvah — even her mother — is a complete lack of *tznius* and is against halachah.
- Rav Yosef Shalom Elyashiv says that in the event that a woman forgot to cut her nails for a Friday-night *tevilah* and already accepted Shabbos, it is preferable that her husband cut them for her than for her to ask her mother or friend.[466]
- Even if someone will certainly realize that a woman went to the mikvah, she should still go. Even though others will figure out that she went to the mikvah, this is not enough of a reason to push off going, unless a large amount of people will figure out she is going.[467]
- A woman should never actively tell someone that she is going to the mikvah. If they figure it out, they figure it out.
- If a woman refuses to go to the mikvah because many people will figure it out but one person knowing can make the whole difference, she should *hint* to that person. She may say, "I have something important to take care of, do you mind covering for me . . ." Although the person knows she is going, she did not explicitly *say* so.
- Practically speaking, if a woman has a choice of telling one person who can cover up for her so many people will not figure out she is going, or not saying anything to anyone, it is better to keep quiet, and whoever figures it out, figures it out.
- A *Rav* cannot force a woman to go to the mikvah when she does not want to go. But he should know whom he is dealing with, and in which direction to guide the couple. It is important for every couple to be close to a *Rav* who knows them personally.

---

466. This ruling is based on the *Noda B'Yehudah*, brought in the *Pischei Teshuvah*, that when a woman is going to the mikvah and there is no one around to be her "mikvah lady," her husband may fill that capacity. The reason is that no man will stumble when his wife will be *tehorah* in just a few moments. This is also based on the opinion of the Taz, who holds that touching through an intermediate object is permitted. The halachah relies on the *Taz* in extenuating circumstances, and this case is considered one of extenuating circumstances because the woman's only other option is to tell someone she is going to the mikvah that night, which is a very serious issue. Obviously, the best-case scenario is if the mikvah attendant can cut her nails for her or if it can be done by a non-Jew.

467. Rav Shmuel HaLevi Wosner.

Chatzitzos

- The *Shulchan Aruch* says that a *chatzitzah d'Oraisa* is something that covers most of one's body, *and* she or most women do not want it to be there.
- A *chatzitzah d'Rabbanan* is something that covers most of her body and she does not care that it is there, *or* something that covers a small part of her body and she does care that it is there.
- The *Rama* says *lechatchilah* a woman should even remove a small thing that she does not care about.[468]
- The *Rambam* says hair is part of the body, so in order for something to be considered as covering most of the body it must cover most of her hair *and* her body.[469]
- The Geonim say hair is viewed independently, so something that covers most of the woman's hair *or* most of her body and she or most women care that it is there, is a *chatzitzah d'Oraisa*.[470]
- The *Shulchan Aruch* says one should follow the opinion of the Geonim.[471] Therefore, anything that covers most of the woman's hair that she does not care about is a *chatzitzah d'Rabbanan*. A substance that the woman cares is there creates a *chatzitzah d'Oraisa*.

---

468. Rav Shmuel HaLevi Wosner explains the Rama's reasoning to mean that *this woman* may not care about the presence of this *chatzitzah*. But since most women may care, this would constitute a *chatzitzah*. Also, this woman may not be aware of what is considered a *chatzitzah* and what is not, so the Rama advises everyone to remove everything.

469. *Hilchos Mikvaos* 2:15.

470. The Acharonim argue whether, when the halachah discusses "hair," we are discussing hair on the head, which is what comes to mind when one says "hair" (*Tiferes L'Moshe*), or it refer to any area on the body that has hair (*Sfas Emes*). The difference would be according to the Geonim's opinion, which is that something that covers most of her hair it is a *chatzitzah* (*d'Rabbanan*) even if she does not care. Is all body hair taken into account, or only hair on the woman's head? Rav Shmuel HaLevi Wosner and others say "hair" refers to the hair on the head, and all other hair is considered part of the body in regard to *chatzitzos*.

471. 198:5, *Raavad* and *Gra*.

Immersing in Clothing

- The *Shulchan Aruch* says that a woman may immerse in loose clothing.[472] This may be relied on in the event that a woman is going to the mikvah in a public place, like a beach.
- This should not be done *lechatchilah* whenever avoidable, but should be implemented whenever necessary.

"Caring" about a Chatzitzah

- Something that most people in a woman's social environment care about, *or* something that she cares about, is considered a *chatzitzah*.
- Some women exhibit signs of OCD in regard to *chatzitzos*, and some will even go to the point they will not immerse in the mikvah for fear that they are immersing with *chatzitzos*. A *Rav* should explain to women what is a *she'eilah* and what is not a *she'eilah*. Being normal in this area and not being overly careful is what defines the aspect of "caring" about the presence of a *chatzitzah* in the first place.
- A woman should understand that some things are only done *lechatchilah* but will not invalidate the *tevilah* at all (the Rama says that this is the halachah regarding to something that covers a small area of the body and she does not care that it is there.) Most other things may be a *chatzitzah d'Rabbanan* but she will not be have done an *aveirah* that is punishable with *kareis* by immersing that way. A real *chatzitzah d'Oraisa* is very rare, because most people know if there is something that is covering most of their body or hair that they do not want there.
- Rav Nissim Karelitz says that a *chatzitzah* is defined as something that sticks to the body and separates the body from the water. If something is on the body but it does not have any substance (for example, a tattoo), it is not a *chatzitzah*.
- "Caring" about the presence of the *chatzitzah* means that one cares on a regular basis, not just once a year. If this woman or most women only take off their rings for a once-a-year painting, rings will not be a *chatzitzah*, *bedi'eved*.

472. 198:6.

- Taking something off for a once-a-week event is not called "caring" about its presence. If a woman bakes challah and removes her rings only once a week, it is not considered "caring" about the presence of her rings, as long as it is established that most women do not care about this on a more frequent basis (see below, "Rings and Piercings").[473]
- "Caring" means that this object bothers her and she does not want the *chatzitzah* to be there,[474] or she does not want the *chatzitzah* to get ruined,[475] or she usually removes it for halachic purposes,[476] or she is embarrassed to have it there.[477]
- The *Beis HaLevi* says that just caring about the presence of something for the purpose of immersing in the mikvah is not considered "caring" in that it can upgrade something that covers most of the body to a *chatzitzah d'Oraisa*. If this would not be so, there will never be a case of a *chatzitzah* that covers most of the body and the woman does not care about it, because everyone wants to immerse in the mikvah in the most *lechatchilah* fashion.
- Rav Nissim Karelitz says that every *she'eilah* of *chatzitzah* must be considered with all the surrounding information, such as how large the *chatzitzah* is and on what part of her body it is. If someone (or most people) would not care about its presence based on its size or location, it is not a *chatzitzah*.[478]

---

473. Rav Moshe Feinstein (*Igros Moshe*, vol. 1, 60:97) explains that the "caring" in this case is not that the woman removes her rings (for example) once a week. Rather, one must determine whether the action of baking challah, which creates a situation that forces her to remove the rings, is a normal occurrence for most women (or just for her) more than once a week. So, if a woman (or most women) removes her rings more than once a week, but does not do so because she intrinsically cares not to wear her rings, that will not constitute "caring."

474. *Rambam*.

475. *Raavad*.

476. *Noda B'Yehudah*.

477. See *Rashi*, *Sukkah* 6:71; ibid., *Eiruvin* 4:72; *Rambam*, *Mikvaos*, chap. 9, Mishnah 3; Raavad, *Sefer Baalei Nefesh; Shu"t Noda B'Yehudah* 141:64; and *Shu"t Chasam Sofer*, *siman* 192 for more information on "caring" about *chatzitzos*.

478. See 16:198:18.

When a Chatzitzah Is Found After Tevilah

- Practically speaking, in the event of a real *chatzitzah* — even *d'Rabbanan* — the woman must return to the mikvah and immerse again with a *brachah*, even if she was already with her husband.
- If there was a *chatzitzah d'Oraisa* and the couple had marital relations, they transgressed the prohibitions of *niddah d'Oraisa* and are liable to *kareis*. If the *chatzitzah* was a *chatzitzah d'Rabbanan*, they violated the prohibitions of *niddah d'Rabbanan* and are not liable to *kareis*.
- Rav Shmuel HaLevi Wosner says that in the event that the woman did not fulfill the opinion of the Rama and remove a substance that was on a small part of her body that she does not care about, the *tevilah* remains valid. This holds true even when a woman purposely disregarded the Rama's opinion. A *Rav* can allow someone to disregard the Rama's opinion in extenuating circumstances.

Taking a Bath

- The custom is to take a bath as preparation for *tevilah*,[479] because this is the most thorough way to clean oneself, and because soaking in hot water loosens scabs, dried blood, and sweat.[480]
- A woman who does not have a bathtub, or has a bathtub that is unfit for use and she cannot take one in the mikvah, may take a long hot shower.
- It is best not to ask a neighbor to use their bath before immersing in the mikvah, for reasons of *tznius*.

---

479. See *Sefer HaOrah L'Rashi*, which says the preferred method of performing *chafifos* is in a bath, rather than a shower. Practically speaking, the She'arim HaMetzuyanim B'Halachah says he did not find any *Poskim* that require a woman to sit in a bath; as long as she showers until the skin is soft, that is enough. In conclusion, he says not to change the custom (which is to sit in a bath), but if there is a reason for a woman not to use a bath, the *chafifos* are certainly valid if she showers.

480. Rav Shmuel HaLevi Wosner says a pregnant woman should not sit in a hot bath for a prolonged period of time because it may hurt the fetus.

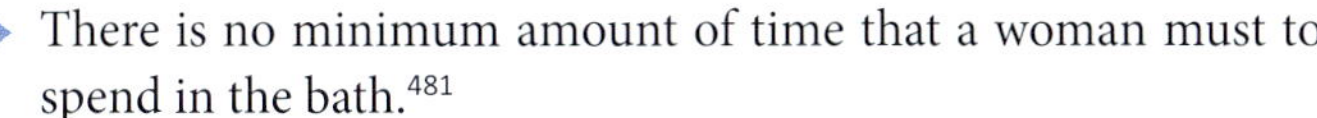

- There is no minimum amount of time that a woman must to spend in the bath.[481]

Amount of Time One Must Spend on Chafifos

- The halachah does not give a minimum amount of time that a woman must spend in the bath or on her *chafifos* when she started the *chafifah* process during the day.[482] Some recommend a half hour (for the bath alone),[483] but, practically speaking, the woman may do whatever works for her, as long as she gets the job done well.
- A woman who did not begin her preparations during the day and does all *chafifos* at night must spend 1 hour on her *chafifos*.
- Rav Moshe Feinstein says that the hour that the woman must spend at night is a precaution to ensure that she does the *chafifos* without rushing to get home. Therefore, it is acceptable for a woman to spend less than an hour on *chafifos* if she is able to do a very thorough job. The only amount of time that must be spent is the amount of time that this woman would normally spend if time was not an issue and she was not rushing to go anywhere.

---

481. That being said, the woman should be careful to sit in the bath long enough to soak the skin to the point that dried sweat, dirt, and blood are easily removed. Some *kallah* teachers teach that a woman must be in the bath for a half hour. This, however, should not be taught, since the halachah does not gives any minimum time requirement for the *chafifah* process as a whole, and certainly not for the bath alone.

482. If a woman does not have time to do the majority of *chafifos* during the day, she can be advised to do one *chafifah* (such as cutting her nails) during the day and finish the *chafifos* at night. In such a case, she is not required to spend an hour at night, since she began during the day. Rav Yaacov Blau explains the reason for this ruling as follows: Since the woman started *chafifos* during the day, she had an awareness that she is going to immerse in the mikvah at night, so she naturally minimized her interaction with anything that can potentially be a *chatzitzah* later on. The minimum amount of time spent on *chafifos* later on will therefore be sufficient to remove any *chatzitzos*, and she is not required to spend an hour on her nighttime *chafifos*.

483. See *Darchei Teshuvah*, in the name of the Gaon M'Batatch and the *Shevet Levi*, and *Shu"t Pri HaSadeh*, vol. 4, *siman* 134. It should be noted that the Chasam Sofer recommends that a woman spend an hour on *chafifos* even if she is doing them during the day.

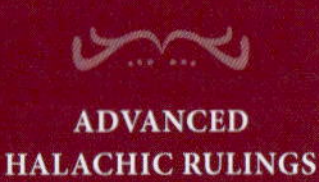

A Woman Who Did Not Perform Chafifos

- A woman who did not perform *chafifos* on her body or hair must immerse in the mikvah again after she performs them, even if she does not find any *chatzitzah* after immersing.
- If a woman failed to do *chafifos* on *beis hastarim*, a second *tevilah* is not necessary, as long as no *chatzitzos* are later discovered.[484]
- A Friday-night tevilah must be pushed off until after Shabbos in the event that *chafifos* were not done; the halachah does not rely on *chafifos* performed by a non-Jew.

Iyun

- The *Shulchan Aruch* says a woman must check over her body before she immerses in the mikvah to make sure there are no *chatzitzos*.[485] This is called "*iyun*."
- The *Taz* says that a woman's performing *chafifos* before going to the mikvah fulfills her obligation of *iyun*.[486] She can be certain that there is nothing on her, and it is as though she visually checked over her entire body.
- The *Sidrei Taharah* says that aside from the *chafifah* process, a woman must visually check over her body to make sure she did not miss anything. If she consciously looked over her body during the *chafifah* process, no further *iyun* is necessary.[487]
- The *Shach* says a woman should perform *chafifos* as well as *iyun* before *tevilah*.[488]
- Practically speaking, a woman should follow the opinion of the Shach and Sidrei Taharah, and should look over her body just before she immerses in the mikvah.

---

484. The reason why *chafifas beis hastarim* does not invalidate the *tevilah bedi'eved* is because *chatzitzos* in the *beis hastarim* are uncommon (199:11). A woman must check after the *tevilah* to see if there was any *chatzitzah* if she skipped *chafifos beis hastarim*.

485. 199:1.

486. 199:4.

487. Rav Nissim Karelitz.

488. 199:11.

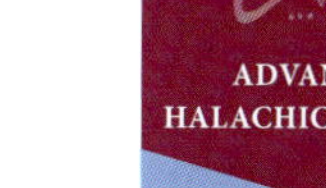

- A woman should be careful to do *iyun* before a *tevilah* on Shabbos or Yom Tov because the *chafifah* and *tevilah* are not performed in the same *onah*.
- In the event that a woman is not sure whether she did *iyun*, she may rely on the Taz's position that *chafifos* are enough.
- The mikvah attendant can assist the woman with *iyun* and thus fulfill her obligation for her.
- Rav Yosef Shalom Elyashiv says that doing *iyun* does not remove the woman's *chafifah* obligation. A woman who only did *iyun* without performing the necessary *chafifos* is still *temei'ah* after the *tevilah*, just like any woman who does not perform the necessary *chafifos*.

Chafifah on Hair and Shaving Hair

- Rav Shmuel HaLevi Wosner says there are five reasons why women in some communities shave their heads:
    1. They are concerned that the hair will knot and create a *chatzitzah* for *tevilah*.
    2. The *Zohar* says that hair is one of the places that attract *tumah*.
    3. The *Darchei Teshuvah* says that there may be dry sweat on her scalp, which is a *chatzitzah*.
    4. The *Shach*, in the name of the *Raavan*, says that hair is intended to be cut and therefore constitutes a *chatzitzah*.[489]

489. The Shach seems to be concerned about the opinion of the Raavan, who says that something that is intended to be removed must be removed. This means that a woman would have to shave whatever is normal for her to shave, and she must cut her nails. The Taz and many others are not concerned about the Raavan's opinion, and they hold that if something is part of the body, it cannot be considered a *chatzitzah*. This means that in the event that a woman shaved one leg and forgot to shave the other one she would need a new *tevilah* according to the Shach (as a stringency), but not according to the Taz. The halachah is generally like the opinion of the Taz, especially if the couple already had marital relations. It is difficult to say that a woman who did not follow the Raavan's opinion did not immerse in a *lechatchilah* way, because a woman will invariably miss a few hairs every time she shaves. That being the case, according to the Raavan a woman will always be *temei'ah mid'Rabbanan*, because she is going to have a small amount of *chatzitzah* that she cares about. Even if we would say that she does not care about such small amounts of hair, it is difficult to say that according to this position, most women do not fulfill the opinion of the Rama *lechatchilah* most times they immerse.

5. They are concerned that hair will float on top of the waters and invalidate the *tevilah*.

- Rav Shmuel HaLevi Wosner and Rav Nissim Karelitz say that many Sefaradi women are careful to shave all pubic hair before going go the mikvah because they are concerned that there may be dry sweat in that area, which constitutes a *chatzitzah*. In the event that a woman who is generally careful to remove pubic hair immersed without shaving, her *tevilah* is valid *bedi'eved* (as per the Birchei Yosef's opinion).

- Practically speaking, women in communities that are not accustomed to remove the hair on their heads or pubic hair should comb out their hair using a strong brush or comb that really gets the knots out, so as to avoid any *chatzitzos*.

- A woman should run her fingers through any area on her body that has hair to make sure there are no *chatzitzos* or knots. Such areas include her eyebrows and eyelashes.

- Rav Yosef Shalom Elyashiv and Rav Nissim Karelitz say that a woman may immerse in the mikvah with hair that she intends to cut after going to the mikvah, because hair is part of the body and thus does not constitute a *chatzitzah* even if it will certainly eventually be removed.[490]

- Rav Shmuel HaLevi Wosner says a woman may cut her hair to go to the mikvah during *sefirah*, during the Nine Days, and on Chol HaMoed.

- A woman may cut or shave her hair on the day that she goes to the mikvah.[491]

---

490. *Chasam Sofer* 198:12.

491. Some *Poskim* maintain that a woman should not cut her hair or shave the day she goes to the mikvah (*Beis Lechem Yehudah, siman kattan* 6), and some even go so far to say she should not cut her hair 3 days before going go the mikvah (*Shu"t Avnei Tzedek, siman* 107), out of concern that small hairs will get stuck to her body and create a *chatzitzah*. Practically speaking, although the *Rama* (198:24) says she should not do things that easily cause *chatzitzos* the day she goes to the mikvah, most *Poskim* maintain that shaving does not easily cause *chatzitzos* that will not be easily removed during the *chafifah* process. That said, some *Rabbanim* advise women who want to get a waxing (which may leave residual wax on the body) to do it a few days before going go the mikvah so they will not find a *chatzitzah* later on; this is what Rav Yitzchak Berkovits advises as well, as he says she must avoid anything sticky the day she goes to the mikvah (such as sticky dough). Many *Poskim* say this is all advice, not practical halachah, and that practically speaking, a woman may shave or cut her hair the day she goes to the mikvah if she feels it is necessary, but she must be careful to remove all *chatzitzos* subsequently.

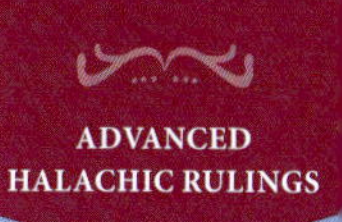

Cleaning the Nose and Internal Chatzitzos

- Rav Akiva Eiger explains that the nose has three parts:
  1. The outside of the nose, which is considered part of the body. *Chafifos* must be performed on this area, and water must reach there during *tevilah*.
  2. Inside the nose, in a place that is visible on the outside, which is considered *beis hastarim*.[492] The woman must remove any visible residue (by blowing her nose before the *tevilah*), and water must be able to enter this part of the nose, although water does not need to actually enter during *tevilah*.
  3. Inside her nose, which is not visible from the outside, is considered internal, so no *chafifos* are required here, and water does not need to be able to enter.
- Rav Shmuel HaLevi Wosner says that an internal birth control device may fall into one of two categories:
  1. Some devices are in the uterus (IUD). A woman is not required to remove this device before *tevilah*, even *lechatchilah*.
  2. Other devices are inside the vaginal canal (for example, NuvaRing). This type of device should be removed *lechatchilah*,[493]

492. From the words of Rav Akiva Eiger ("*Lo nitnah Torah l'malachei hashareis* — The Torah was not given to angels") and the tone of the *Poskim*, it seems this area refers to the inside of the nose that is visible from the outside when someone looks directly at her (a relatively small area). If someone would look up her nose with a flashlight, most of what they would see is considered internal, and no *chafifah* is required in those areas. However, some understand the *Chochmas Adam* (*klal* 119) to mean that a woman should remove nose discharges that are higher up in the nose, but can be easily removed with her finger. Practically speaking, she should certainly remove readily seen dry nose discharge. Anything else should be removed *lechatchilah* but is not a problem *bedi'eved*.

493. Truthfully, an internal birth control device should fall into the category of the inside of the nose which is not visible, and the woman should not have to remove it *lechatchilah* However, Rav Shmuel HaLevi Wosner says to be concerned about the stringent opinions because there is not a clear definition of what is considered internal enough that water does not need to be able to enter. However, a *Rav* may certainly be lenient *bedi'eved* if she already immersed in the mikvah or is having a hard time removing the device.

It may be that the *Poskim* are more stringent *lechatchilah* in regard to the the vaginal canal as opposed to the inside of the nose because it is an area that is "used" for marital relations and *bedikos*. In this respect it is similar to the inside of the mouth, which is internal but is used for eating, and the outer areas of the nose and ears, which are visible and "used" in the respect that no one wants residue to be seen in these areas.

Perhaps another reason to be stringent *lechatchilah* in cases of birth control devices as opposed to nose discharges is because nose discharges are created by the body, while birth but does not invalidate the *tevilah* if it was not removed, *bedi'eved*. This ruling may be relied upon if a woman was intimate with her husband after immersing in the mikvah with the NuvaRing; otherwise she should immerse again.

- Rav Shmuel HaLevi Wosner says if a woman forgot to remove a *bedikah* cloth and immersed in the mikvah with it inside, she does not have to immerse again if she was already with her husband, but she should immerse again otherwise.[494]
- Rav Moshe Feinstein says that anything that is not attached in *beis hastarim* will not be a *chatzitzah*.[495]
- Most *Poskim* in Eretz Yisrael disagree with this.

Other Internal Chatzitzos

- A woman does not need to take off her nail in order to remove a splinter that is underneath it, as long as the splinter is not protruding. This applies even if the splinter is visible and she

---

control devices are foreign influences introduced into the body, and one should be more wary of creating a foreign *chatzitzah*.

494. There is a disagreement among the Acharonim regarding what the difference is between something "external," "*beis hastarim*," and something "internal" in regard to the vaginal area. (This disagreement would presumably carry over to other areas of the body as well.) The Noda B'Yehudah (*Shu"t Noda B'Yehudah* 141:64; *Tinyana, siman* 135; *Pischei Teshuvah* 198:16) seems to hold that the area the male organ reaches during intercourse is considered *beis hastarim* and water needs to be able to enter. Water need not be able to enter anything more internal; only anything that is visible from the outside must come in contact with the water. Rav Akiva Eiger (*Shu"t* 271:60) says that whatever area the water would normally be able to reach easily, but is unreachable because of the natural contours or narrowness of the body (such as a closed mouth; see *Pischei Teshuvah* 198:16), is considered *beis hastarim*. Anything that is generally unreachable for the water is considered internal. This seems to mean that water does not need to be able to enter the vaginal canal, which is generally closed during *tevilah*. The last opinion, that of the Rama MiPano (*siman* 110), is that whatever is generally internal but is visible at times to the outside (such as teeth and gums) is considered *beis hastarim*. He holds that anything more internal than that is considered internal and water need not be able to enter. This would mean that water must be able to enter the external area of *oso makom*, but certainly not the vaginal canal. Practically speaking, the *Poskim* seem to rule like the Noda B'Yehudah even *bedi'eved*, and will not allow a woman to immerse in the mikvah if she has a *chatzitzah* in the vaginal canal (such as stitches after birth). The reason Rav Shmuel HaLevi Wosner is lenient *bedi'eved* if she immersed with a *bedikah* cloth is because he holds that something that is not attached in *beis hastarim* does not invalidate the *tevilah bedi'eved* (like Rav Moshe Feinstein's opinion).

495. *Igros Moshe, Yoreh Dei'ah* 68.

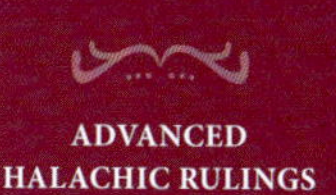

can see it directly.[496] The splinter is considered internal, even though it is not covered by skin, and the woman may immerse in the mikvah without removing the splinter.[497]

- Anything that is really inside of the body — not just in cavities — is considered to be part of the body and is not a *chatzitzah*. Some examples are pacemakers and plates that were inserted inside the body.[498]
- Anything the skin completely grows over — even if it can be seen — is called part of the body and is not a *chatzitzah*.

Stitches

- Stitches, even within *beis hastarim*,[499] are generally considered a *chatzitzah* when they need to be removed by a doctor. This applies even when they are on the woman's body for longer than 30 days.[500]
- There is a disagreement among the *Poskim* regarding stitches that dissolve and are absorbed into the body. Rav Nissim Karelitz says they are a *chatzitzah*. Rav Shmuel HaLevi Wosner says they are not a *chatzitzah*, even before they are completely absorbed.
- Rav Nissim Karelitz says that if a woman has stitches in an area of her body where she does not really care about their presence, she may immerse in the mikvah with them.[501]
- Practically speaking, most American *Poskim* rule like Rav Shmuel HaLevi Wosner, and are lenient to allow a woman to

496. This is the opinion of the Shach (198:16), unlike the simple explanation of the *Shulchan Aruch*, which seems to say that if the splinter is visible it is a *chatzitzah*, even if it is internal.

497. Rav Shmuel HaLevi Wosner. The reason for this *din* seems to be the fact that most people will not remove their nail to remove a splinter. Therefore, a semi-exposed splinter is not considered something that most people care about.

498. Rav Shmuel HaLevi Wosner.

499. If the stitches are in the mouth or vaginal canal (for example), they are a *chatzitzah*. However, if they are really internal, such as in the uterus or body cavity, they are not (Rav Nissim Karelitz).

500. Rav Yosef Shalom Elyashiv; Rav Shmuel HaLevi Wosner.

501. Although Rav Nissim Karelitz cites this halachah, it is hard to practically think of a location where someone gets stitches (or even one stitch) and does not think from time to time that they would like the stitch(es) removed.

immerse in the mikvah even before the stitches dissolve. See footnote.[502]

Rings and Piercings

- Rings are generally removed by most women more than once a week.[503] Therefore, a woman may immerse in the mikvah with the rings *bedi'eved* only when water can get underneath the rings.[504] A ring that is on a woman's finger too tightly to allow water to get in is considered something that covers a small area of the body that people care about, and she cannot immerse with it even *bedi'eved.*
- All other body piercings are subjective, and are dependent on how often a woman (or most women) removes that particular piece of jewelry.[505]

---

502. Many American *Poskim* are lenient if a woman has dissolvable stitches that are mostly dissolved. The reason is either that the stitches are part of her body at a certain point, or she no longer cares about their presence after a certain point. However, this ruling is a bit hard to understand, because almost no one who has stitches resigns themselves to having them remain on their body, no matter where on their body the stitches are located. I asked Rav Dovid Feinstein what the *dinim* of stitches are, and he said, "There is no *heter* (permissiblity) in the world" to immerse in the mikvah with any stitches, even dissolvable, no matter where they are on the body, even in *beis hastarim.*

503. This halachah, as well as most of the following cases, are all *bedi'eved*, based on the *Rama* that even a small *chatzitzah* that one does not care about should be removed *lechatchilah.*

504. A classic *she'eilah* is when a woman cannot, for whatever reason, remove her ring from her finger. Most *Poskim* say that a ring constitutes a *chatzitzah d'Rabbanan* in the event that it is not removed before *tevilah.* Rav Shmuel HaLevi Wosner, however, explains that it depends on how tightly the ring is attached to the finger. Everyone agrees that a ring that is on so tightly that it cannot be swiveled on the finger at all (i.e., it is literally stuck like glue) is a *chatzitzah* even *bedi'eved.* However, if the woman can swivel the ring around on the finger even though she cannot take it off, she should immerse in the mikvah while wearing the ring (if there is no alternative way to remove the ring) and should swivel the ring around her finger while she is under the water (*Sefer Mishnas HaShulchan*). The reason for this ruling is based on a disagreement between the Shach (198:56) and the Sidrei Taharah (ibid., *siman kattan* 10), regarding how loose something must be in order to no longer be considered a *chatzitzah.* The Shach holds that the object must be very loose, and we try to follow the Shach's opinion whenever possible. However, the *Sidrei Taharah* says as long as the object is not "choking her," it is considered loose and the woman may immerse with it *bedi'eved.* Rav Wosner says one should rely on the *Sidrei Taharah* in extenuating circumstances. See *Pischei Teshuvah* 198:13.

505. An example is when a woman has a second earring higher up on her ear. If most women and this woman do not remove their second earring more than once a week, the *tevilah* is valid *bedi'eved* if she immersed without removing it. Otherwise, it constitutes

- Rav Shmuel HaLevi Wosner says that as part of the *chafifah* process a woman should clean inside the hole of any piercing after removing the jewelry, to ensure that there is no dirt in the hole during the *tevilah*.[506]

Calluses, Blisters, and Dry Blood

- In Eretz Yisrael people are careful to remove calluses,[507] and in the United States they are not. Therefore, in Eretz Yisrael the mikvah lady will shave the calluses to the skin, while in the United States the mikvah lady often will not even check for calluses.
- Rav Shmuel HaLevi Wosner and Rav Nissim Karelitz say that a blister is part of the body and is therefore not a *chatzitzah*, as long as it is intact.[508]
- Rav Shmuel HaLevi Wosner says that a woman should remove scabs that come off easily, but should not remove any scab that will cause further bleeding.[509]

---

a *chatzitzah*. The same halachah applies to all other body jewelry. See *Rebbe Akiva Eiger* 198:23, "*HaShirim V'HaNezamim*" in the name of the *Tashbatz* and the *Bach*.

506. This should be taught and performed *lechatchilah*, but if a woman immersed in the mikvah and later remembers that she did not clean her earring hole, she is not required to immerse again as long as no specific *chatzitzah* has been discovered, just like any time a woman misses a *chafifah* in the *beis hastarim* (Rav Nissim Karelitz).

507. Rav Yosef Shalom Elyashiv, Rav Shmuel HaLevi Wosner, and Rav Nissim Karelitz are lenient regarding calluses, as are most *Poskim* in the United States. They hold that since a callus is part of the body it cannot be considered a *chatzitzah*, even if the woman will eventually remove it. *Teshuvos V'Hanhagos*, vol. 1, *siman* 520 says one should be stringent regarding calluses, and this seems to have become the adopted custom in many mikvaos in Eretz Yisrael.

508. Rav Shmuel HaLevi Wosner and Rav Nissim Karelitz say that a woman who has a blister should preferably not pop it, since this demonstrates that she does not want the blister on her body anymore, which may create an issue of *chatzitzah*. In the event that the blister was popped, they maintain that the excess skin is now considered unwanted and creates a *chatzitzah*, and must be removed with sterile scissors before *tevilah*, removing as much skin as possible. If removing the excess skin is painful, the woman should not remove it before *tevilah*, because in this case she would prefer that the skin remain intact.

509. The *Shulchan Aruch* says that dry blood that is on a wound is a *chatzitzah* and must be removed before *tevilah*. According to the *Smag*, this is referring to excess blood on top of the scab. According to the *Mordechai*, it refers to the scab itself, which he holds must be removed before one immerses in the mikvah. Practically speaking, most *Poskim* say a woman should remove any excess blood (which will anyway come off in a bath) and any easily removable scabs that do not cause additional bleeding (*Chazon Ish*); since these are things that a woman wants off of her body, she cares about their presence. Most

Hair Conditioner, Shampoo, Deodorant, and Scented Soaps

- Hair conditioner coats the hair with molecules of an invisible substance. Some *Poskim* say that hair conditioner creates a *chatzitzah d'Oraisa* (according to the Geonim) and should never be used before *tevilah*, even *bedi'eved*.

- Practically speaking, women should *lechatchilah* not use hair conditioner before immersing in the mikvah. *Bedi'eved*, if a woman has tangled hair, she may use conditioner and then rinse it out of her hair,[510] even though many *sefarim* are against it.

- The *Shevet HaKehasi* says that in the event that a woman immersed in the mikvah and later finds residue of shampoo in her hair which was not completely washed out before going go the mikvah, she is *tehorah* (*bedi'eved*) because shampoo is wet and allows the mikvah water to reach the hair.

- All residual deodorant must be removed before *tevilah*. A woman who finds deodorant after the *tevilah* must immerse again, as is the case whenever a *chatzitzah d'Rabbanan* is discovered after a *tevilah*.

- It seems from the *Taz* that there is no problem to use scented soaps during *chafifos*,[511] as long as no residue is left on the skin.[512]

Baby Oil

- Baby oil is a *chatzitzah*.[513] If it covers most of the hair it is a *chatzitzah d'Oraisa* (according to the Geonim). If it covers a

---

women want a scab that is not ready to fall off on its own to remain, because it protects the body from infection and seals the wound so additional bleeding does not occur. Some *Rabbanim* advise women to remove all scabs before going go the mikvah (based on the *Mordechai*), but doing so often causes bleeding and creates additional *chatzitzah she'eilos*.

510. The reason for this ruling is based on the opinions that something that covers the body (or hair) but is specifically intended to remain there and the woman has no intention of removing it, does not create a *chatzitzah*.

511. 199:2.

512. Rav Shmuel HaLevi Wosner.

513. *Aruch HaShulchan*; Rav Shmuel HaLevi Wosner. Rav Wosner explains that although the *Shulchan Aruch* says that certain liquids are not *chatzitzos* when they are wet (for example, ink and milk), oil is different. Since the nature of oil is to deflect water away from the body, oil is a *chatzitzah* regardless of whether it is wet or dry.

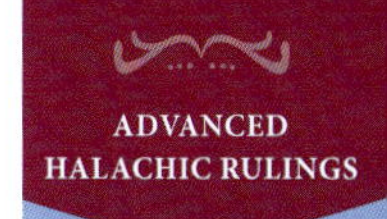

smaller area of the body it is a *chatzitzah d'Rabbanan*. In either case, the woman must immerse again if she finds baby oil on herself after the *tevilah*, even if she was already with her husband.

Hair Dye

- Dyed hair is generally not a problem for *tevilah*.[514] In the event that the woman wants the dyed part to grow out, the dye will be an issue, and she may have to cut her hair or dye it again. In the event that there is substance to the dye, she should consult a *Rav*.

Eye Chatzitzos and Contact Lenses

- A woman should be careful to remove all discharges from in and around her eyes before she immerses in the mikvah.
- If a woman immersed with eye discharge that was later found outside the eye, she must immerse again because an external eye discharge is a *chatzitzah*, whether it was wet or dry during the *tevilah*.[515]
- If a woman immersed in the mikvah with eye discharge that was later found inside the eye, and it is a wet discharge, she is not required to immerse again.[516]
- Rav Shmuel HaLevi Wosner and Rav Nissim Karelitz say if a woman immersed in the mikvah with eye discharge that is found inside the eye and it is a dry discharge (i.e., it has started going green), she should immerse again if easily possible, as per the opinions that such discharge is a *chatzitzah*.[517] If it is difficult for her to immerse again (for example, the mikvah is already closed), or she was already with her husband, she need not immerse again.[518] In such a case the halachah relies on the

514. *Shu"t Pnei Aryeh, siman* 6.

515. *Shulchan Aruch* 18:7.

516. Ibid.

517. *Tosafos*; *Smag* in the name of Rabbeinu Tam and the *Rambam*.

518. *Shach* 198:13 in the name of the *Raavad*, *Rashba*, *Rambam*, Rabbeinu Tam, and the *Rambam*; *Sidrei Taharah*; *Aruch HaShulchan*.

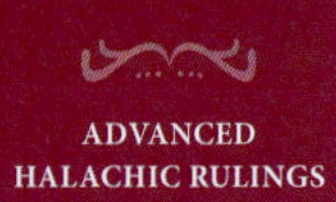

opinions that such discharge is not a *chatzitzah* since it is found inside the eye.[519]

- Rav Moshe Feinstein, the *She'arim HaMetzuyanim B'Halachah*, and Rav Shmuel HaLevi Wosner say that a woman should *lechatchilah* remove her contact lenses before *tevilah*. If she immersed while wearing them, however, the *tevilah* is valid *bedi'eved*, since lenses are not attached to the eye and the eye is considered *beis hastarim*, so lenses are not *chatzitzos d'Rabbanan* (even if she removes them every night). The woman does not need another *tevilah* in the event that she was already with her husband. If she was not, however, she should return to the mikvah to immerse again.

Nails, Hangnails, and Cuticles

- Practically speaking, women nowadays are told to cut their nails, out of concern that there is dirt underneath.[520]
- A woman should cut her nails for *tevilah* with scissors, not by ripping or biting the nails.[521]
- A woman who forgot to cut her nails for a Friday-night *tevilah* should have a non-Jew cut her nails, even with scissors or a nail clipper. If this is not possible, she should clean underneath very well, and immerse in the mikvah with long nails.[522]
- Rav Yisrael Yaakov Fisher says hangnails are only a problem when they bother the woman because they hurt or get stuck in

519. The crux of the disagreement here is whether a dry *chatzitzah* inside the eye is a problem for niddah (*Shulchan Aruch*; *Tosafos*; *Smag* in the name of Rabbeinu Tam and the *Rambam*), or only for *taharos* (*Shach* 198:13 in the name of the *Raavad*, *Rashba*, Rabbeinu Tam, and the *Rambam*; *Sidrei Taharah*; *Aruch HaShulchan*).

520. *Shulchan Aruch* 198:18; Rav Shmuel HaLevi Wosner; Rav Nissim Karelitz. This is in contrast with the opinions (Shach in the name of the Raavan) that the nail must be cut even if it is clean underneath, since nails are something that will be cut. The *Poskim* discuss whether a woman must cut her toenails before going to the mikvah. The consensus among most *Poskim* is that *lechatchilah* she should cut them. However, in the event that she forgot to cut the toenails, they will not constitute a *chatzitzah bedi'eved* even if there is dirt under the nails. The reason for this ruling is because most women do not care if dirt gets under their toenails. The *Poskim* also point out that although the Arizal says (based on Kabbalah) that in a regular situation one should not cut their fingernails and toenails on the same day, a woman who needs to cut her nails for the mikvah should not be concerned about this if it will interfere with her mikvah preparations in any way.

521. *Shulchan Aruch, Yoreh Dei'ah* 390:7.

522. *Mishnah Berurah* 340:3.

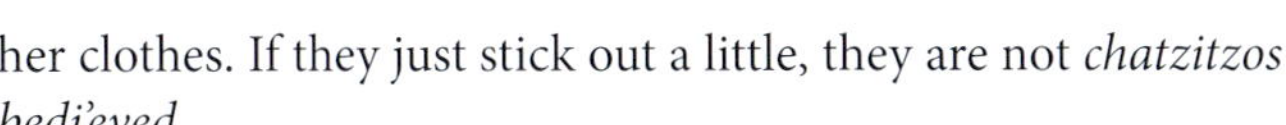

her clothes. If they just stick out a little, they are not *chatzitzos bedi'eved*.

- Rav Moshe Feinstein and Rav Nissim Karelitz say a woman should cut her nails to the length that is normal to cut it, such that most people would consider the nails "cut."[523] There is no need to cut the nails all the way down to the skin.
- Many *Poskim* say that as long as the woman cannot see the nail from the other side of her finger, they are short enough.
- Rav Nissim Karelitz says a woman who cut her nails properly within 3 days of preparing for the mikvah has no reason to cut them again during the *chafifah* process.
- Rav Yosef Shalom Elyashiv and Rav Nissim Karelitz say cuticles that are hanging away from the skin and were not trimmed correctly for *tevilah* are not *chatzitzos bedi'eved*. The reason for this is because the water gets under the cuticles.

Nail Polish

- Nail polish should *lechatchilah* be removed before every time a woman goes to the mikvah. This is based on the *Rama*, which says that even a small amount of *chatzitzah* that one does not care about should be removed.
- In the event that a woman immersed in the mikvah while wearing nail polish, the halachah depends on how well the nails are done. If the polish is chipped to the degree where most women would remove the polish, the *tevilah* is invalid because the case is one of a small substance that most people care about. If the woman just got a manicure, however, the *tevilah* will count *bedi'eved*.[524] A *Rav* must always be consulted before this *din* is practically applied.[525]

523. The *She'arim HaMetzuyanim B'Halachah* quotes the *Achiezer* (3:33), which says that a woman who refuses to immerse in the mikvah if she is required to cut her nails may be allowed to retain her nails, as long as she cleans thoroughly under them before the *tevilah*.

524. This leniency is based on the *Beis HaLevi*, which says that just wanting something to be off for the mikvah is not called "caring" about it, and the *Rashba* and *Rosh*, which say that whatever a woman wants to be there is not a problem, even if it is a small *chatzitzah*.

525. Rav Mati Friedman pointed out that it may be difficult to actually apply this *din*, being that most women do not actually want their nail polish on for weeks on end without removing it. In certain circumstances, such as if a woman got acrylic nail polish or a

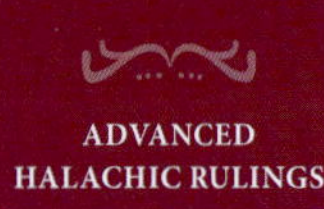

Makeup

- Rav Shmuel HaLevi Wosner says that makeup in ancient times was powder that was not stuck to the skin, as it is today. This is why the *Shulchan Aruch* seems to be lenient in regard to makeup. Ideally, this is not to be relied upon nowadays.[526]

- Practically speaking, even *bedi'eved* a woman may not immerse in the mikvah while wearing makeup, because makeup gets smudged in the water, and most women care about their makeup.[527] Therefore, all makeup must be removed before *tevilah*, and it is a *chatzitzah* even *bedi'eved*.[528]

Pens, Pencils, Markers, and Tattoos

- Marks from pens, pencils, or markers are not *chatzitzos bedi'eved*, because there is no substance left when they make a mark on the skin.[529]

---

permanent manicure, a *Rav* can certainly be lenient if the woman is adamantly against removing it for *tevilah*.

526. *Bach* 198:17; *Sidrei Taharah*, end of *se'if kattan* 33.

527. That being said, the *Pischei Teshuvos* says if someone immersed with waterproof makeup, the *tevilah* is valid *bedi'eved*.

528. Rav Shmuel HaLevi Wosner says there is room to be lenient if a woman is adamant about not removing her makeup before going go the mikvah, based on the *Shach* (198:14), which says that makeup (*kachol*) that a woman put on her face for beautification is not a *chatzitzah*, because she wants the makeup on her for beautification and because it has no substance. The *Taz* (198:17) implies that both qualities must be met: that there is no substance and that the woman specifically wants the dye to remain for beautification purposes. The *Sidrei Taharah* (*se'if* 33) says the main reason to be lenient is because there is no substance.

The *Poskim* discuss whether makeup today has the same status as the *kachol* of yesteryear which was a more powdery substance and did not stick to the skin as well as makeup does today. Rav Wosner is lenient in extenuating circumstances, but Rav Yitzchak Berkovits does not like this leniency because allowing *kachol* was specifically when it was applied for beauty and the woman was careful not to remove it. However, being that a woman is only *tehorah* once she emerges from the mikvah (based on Kabbalah) and at that point the makeup will certainly smudge, one should not allow a woman who is wearing any type of makeup to immerse in the mikvah, even in extenuating circumstances. It seems that even a woman who claims that her makeup is applied so well that it will not smudge in the water certainly should not be allowed to immerse while wearing such makeup. This is because the Shach's reasoning is that makeup (*kachol*) is not a *chatzitzah* because it is not attached very well to the skin, but this woman refutes the very basis that would allow a *tevilah* with makeup, for she claims that the makeup is, in fact, stuck well to the skin.

529. Rav Nissim Karelitz explains that something "that has no substance" is something that, when rubbed hard, does not produce any substance. Although it stains the skin (or

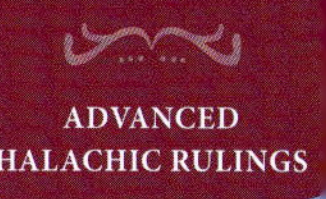

- Tattoos are not *chatzitzos*.[530]
- The *Poskim* say that there are certain nonpermanent tattoos that a person is permitted to get, as they coat only the skin, without actually soaking into the skin or vandalizing it. These tattoos are real *chatzitzos d'Rabbanan*, since they are nonpermanent and there certainly is substance to them.

Glitter and Paint

- Glitter and paint are *chatzitzos* because they have substance, and most people are careful to remove any and all traces of these substances from their bodies.
- The *Shulchan Aruch* says that if a professional's body is always covered with a substance that is specific to that profession, this substance is not considered a *chatzitzah* for them, because every person in this profession does not care about the presence of this particular substance.
- If a preschool teacher, an artist, or a painter claims that she does not care about glitter or paint on her skin, and she generally walks around without completely removing these substances, the *Shulchan Aruch*'s principle may be applied, and if these substances were not removed before the woman immersed in the mikvah, her *tevilah* is valid *bedi'eved*. This halachah only applies if the woman would walk around in public covered in the same amount of glitter or paint as was on her body during the *tevilah*.[531]

Cotton Balls

- In the United States, a woman who needs cotton balls in her ears may immerse in the mikvah with them inside, based on Rav Moshe Feinstein's opinion that cotton balls are not considered attached to the ears, and since the ears are *beis hastarim*.
- In Eretz Yisrael the practice is that women soak the cotton balls in their ears in codfish oil before immersing, because the

hair), it does not fill the ridges of the skin with a substance.

530. This ruling is for someone who has already gotten one illegitimately, as getting a tattoo may be prohibited *mid'Oraisa*.

531. Rav Nissim Karelitz.

dinim of water apply to oil as well, thus mitigating any issue of *chatzitzah*.

Fillings and Loose teeth

- The Avnei Nezer holds that items that a woman needs on her body for medical purposes, such as bandages, stitches, and fillings, should be considered things that one does not care about, since the woman wants them there for the time being.
- The Chayei Adam maintains that inasmuch as the woman wants them off as soon as possible, these items are considered things that are on a small part of her body that she cares about.
- Rav Yosef Shalom Elyashiv says that anything that a woman completely resigned herself to having in her body, and is there for 30 days (like a filling), is not a *chatzitzah*. The reason for this is because the woman has accepted that this object will be part of her for a long time and therefore does not mind its presence.
- This halachah applies even if the woman immersed in the mikvah on the 30th day, and has an appointment to remove this object the next morning.[532]
- We are generally stringent as per the Chayei Adam's opinion in regard to things like bandages, casts, and stitches. In the case of fillings, we are lenient, because Rav Moshe Feinstein writes that today's fillings are better than they used to be and women are not as conscientious and eager to have them removed. However, a temporary filling which she is planning on removing is considered an item that she cares about unless it will be there for 30 days, in which case she has resigned herself to maintaining this item in her mouth.

532. *Yesod HaTaharah*. The reason for this ruling is because the halachah in such cases really depends on the woman's mindset. Therefore, even when the woman knows that she is getting the item removed the next morning, she has already resigned herself to having the item in her mouth for a long enough time that she demonstrates her willingness to have this item in her body. Rav Yosef Shalom Elyashiv is quoted as saying (*Pischei Teshuvos* 198:328) that in the case of a woman who is set to have something in her mouth for less than 30 days, her husband may tell her before her scheduled *tevilah* that her appointment was changed to a later time, one that is after 30 days from the date that this temporary object was put in. Once the woman hears this and does not object to the new appointment date, she shows that she accepted it and may immerse with the item in her mouth. Practically speaking, Rav Yitzchak Berkovits says one may rely on this ruling when necessary, with the guidance of a *Rav*.

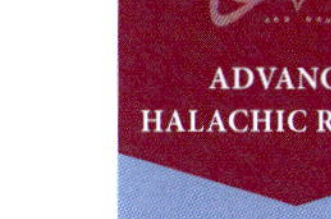

- Rav Shmuel HaLevi Wosner and Rav Nissim Karelitz say that a loose tooth in a woman's mouth is not considered a *chatzitzah*, even though the woman will certainly remove it after immersing in the mikvah. This tooth is part of her body at the time of *tevilah*.

Casts and Splints

- A cast or splint is a *chatzitzah* even if it will be on the woman's body for more than 30 days, because no one resigns themselves to wearing a cast for the rest of their lives.[533]
- A doctor will sometimes put on a removable cast, which he will then allow the woman to remove before going to the mikvah. This is a great idea to implement when possible. If a splint can be removed before the *tevilah*, the woman may immerse when it is removed.
- Rav Shmuel HaLevi Wosner says that a woman may immerse in the mikvah with a cast or splint that has been made loose for the *tevilah*.[534]

Braces, Retainers, Teeth Bonding, and Oral Hygiene

- If a woman did not check her teeth before going to the mikvah — although the *tevilah* is fine if she does not find a *chatzitzah* — she is obligated to check her teeth afterwards.

533. Rav Shmuel HaLevi Wosner; Rav Nissim Karelitz; *Teshuvos Teshuvah M'Ahavah*. Although the Ksav Sofer leans toward being lenient regarding a cast that is meant to remain for a long period of time, most *Poskim* maintain that no one actually wants a cast on their body, so it remains a *chatzitzah* as long as it is on her. The *Poskim* are lenient and only rely on the *Ksav Sofer* in a case in which it is evident that the couple will not keep *hilchos niddah* if the woman will not immerse.

534. This concept is a disagreement between the Shulchan Aruch (198:23), the Rama (ibid., 1; *Sidrei Taharah, se'if kattan* 4), the Shach, and the Bach (see *Shach*, ibid., *siman kattan* 28) regarding whether something that is loose must be removed for *tevilah*. The Rama and others are stringent, and the Rama's position should be fulfilled whenever possible. However, the Acharonim (Rav Shmuel HaLevi Wosner and others) say that one may rely on the *Shulchan Aruch* in a case of need. This ruling is, practically speaking, very difficult to implement, because a doctor generally will not allow a cast to come into contact with water at all, and it is rare that a cast can be made loose enough to allow water to enter underneath.

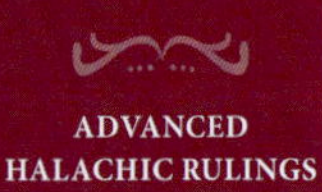

- Braces are a *chatzitzah* even if they are implanted for more than 30 days, because most people do not like having braces.[535]
- A woman should be careful not to get floss shreds between her teeth when flossing before immersing in the mikvah.[536]
- Teeth bonding is not a *chatzitzah*, as it is intended to last a few years.[537]
- Permanent retainers are not *chatzitzos* because most people do not mind having them, so they are considered something that covers a small area that one does not care about.[538]
- Removable retainers must be removed before one immerses in the mikvah, and are *chatzitzos* if left in the mouth.[539]

---

535. Rav Yosef Shalom Elyashiv. Some *Poskim*, among them the She'arim HaMetzuyanim B'Halachah, say that braces are not a *chatzitzah*. He explains that anything that a woman cannot remove on her own, either because it is too difficult or because a professional is required, does not constitute a *chatzitzah* because she accepts its presence on her body. Therefore, the *chatzitzah* is now considered like part of her body (*Shu"t Mahari Assad*, *siman* 229). The problem with this line of reasoning is that there are many things that require a professional to remove and yet are considered *chatzitzos*, for example a cast or stitches, because a woman does not accept that these things are part of her body. In fact, most people who have stitches, casts, or braces say that they have a semi-constant awareness that the item is on their body, which shows they do not completely accept them.

536. Rav Shmuel HaLevi Wosner. It should be noted that although *kallah* teachers teach women to floss before going go the mikvah, some Acharonim (such as Rav Nissim Karelitz) point out that there is no obligation to floss before going go the mikvah, and the *chafifah* in the woman's mouth can be achieved simply by brushing her teeth. This is especially important because in the event that a woman forgot to floss before Shabbos, it should not be done on Shabbos if it will cause her gums to bleed. She also should not brush her teeth on Shabbos because of *sechitah* (squeezing). Rather, she should carefully clean her teeth with a toothpick or gently use a dry toothbrush and look over her teeth for any *chatzitzos*.

537. Teeth bonding is performed by a cosmetic dentist who bonds teeth together to create a more uniform smile. The bonding should last at least 5 years, and most dentists claim it can last up to 12–15 years. In any case, the procedure is deemed permanent regarding *tevilah*.

538. A permanent retainer is a thin metal strip that is cemented behind the teeth, generally after one has braces removed, which keeps the teeth from shifting back to their pre-braces position. The strip is intended to be implanted for life. Realistically, it usually has to be recemented in place every 3–5 years.

539. Presumably, even Rav Moshe Feinstein would agree that removable braces are a *chatzitzah* even though they are in *beis hastarim*, since the braces literally attach to the teeth.

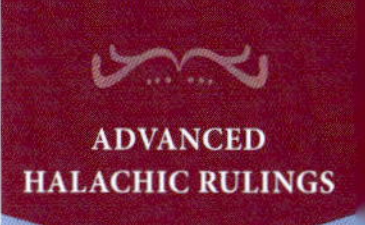

Eating on the Day of Tevilah

- The Rama says that a woman should not eat between the *rechitzah* and the *tevilah*.[540]
- Practically speaking, this means that a woman should not eat anything from the time she washed out her mouth until she immerses in the mikvah.[541]
- Most *Poskim* maintain that a woman can drink between *chafifos* on her mouth and the *tevilah*, because liquids generally do not cause *chatzitzos*.[542]
- Some teach that this halachah means that a woman may not eat from when she starts the *chafifos*. This ruling really does not make much sense, because a *tevilah* on Motzaei Shabbos means the woman cannot eat from the time she started *chafifos* on Friday.[543] Or, this would mean that she may not eat at a wedding if she is going to the mikvah afterwards and began the *chafifah* process earlier in the day.
- The *Shulchan Aruch* brings a custom that is accepted in *Klal Yisrael* that a woman does not eat things that can get stuck in the teeth on the day of *tevilah*, for example, meat (and chicken, says Rav Shmuel HaLevi Wosner). Orange juice with pulp,

540. 198:24.

541. A woman should *lechatchilah* finish her preparations and go to the mikvah without eating anything after cleaning her mouth for the final time before immersing. When *tevilah* falls on Shabbos or Yom Tov, she should cleanse her mouth before Shabbos or Yom Tov and immerse at night, as she would regularly. In the case of a *tevilah* on the second night of Yom Tov or on a Yom Tov that follows Shabbos, or the opposite, the woman may eat on Yom Tov or Shabbos even though she performed *chafifos* on *erev Shabbos* or *erev Yom Tov*, and should rinse her mouth before going to the mikvah. The *she'eilah* arises in a case of a woman who is going to the mikvah on Friday night and wants to make an early Shabbos: may she eat after she finishes the *chafifos*, before *tevilah*? Practically speaking, the *Poskim* encourage women in this situation to make Shabbos at the regular time (i.e., not early Shabbos) and go to the mikvah before the meal. However, this is not always practical, for example, if one is attending a *Shabbos sheva brachos*. In such a situation, a woman may make Kiddush and eat challah (preferably without the crust), fish, soup, and other basic foods (but not chicken or meat), and go to the mikvah later on. This ruling may be implemented when necessary.

542. Rav Shmuel HaLevi Wosner; Rav Moshe Halberstam; *Badei HaShulchan*.

543. The *Sidrei Taharah* (198:49) actually says that a woman who is immersing in the mikvah late Friday night, after the *seudah*, should not eat between the *chafifos* and the *tevilah* because she may find a *chatzitzah* after the *tevilah*. That being said, it seems clear from the *Poskim* that the intention of the Rama is that the woman should not eat between the *chafifos on her mouth* and the *tevilah*, but she may certainly eat between starting the *chafifah* process and the *tevilah*.

peanut chews, popcorn, cheese, pasta, and similar foods have also become a sort of part of this custom, and a woman should ideally stay away from these things so she does not have *she'eilos* after the *tevilah*.[544]

Immersing in the Mikvah during the Day

- *Mid'Oraisa* a woman may immerse in the mikvah during the day of Day 7, because part of a day is considered like the whole day. However, *Chazal* were concerned about the possibility that she would be with her husband while it is still daytime and subsequently bleed between that time and nightfall. This uproots *shivah nekiyim* retroactively, thereby making their marital relations illicit, for which they are liable to *kareis*.
- *Chazal* even forbade going during the day on Day 8 or subsequent days. This is because of *srach bitah* — that a woman's daughter will think that it is permitted to immerse during the day on Day 7 *lechatchilah*, and will eventually be with *her* husband after she immerses on Day 7.
- The practice is like the opinion of the Dagul M'Revavah, that a *kallah* on the day of her wedding who was unable to complete her *shivah nekiyim* earlier may go to the mikvah on Day 7, as long as the couple does not have *yichud* until after *shkiah*.[545] In such a situation, the chuppah should ideally be scheduled for after *shkiah*.[546]
- In the event that a wedding is a daytime wedding, someone else (generally, a child) should be in the *yichud* room like in the case of a *chuppas niddah*, and the couple is permitted to have *yichud* once *shkiah* comes.

---

544. Rav Shmuel HaLevi Wosner. Rav Yosef Shalom Elyashiv and Rav Nissim Karelitz are of the opinion that only the foods that are mentioned in the *Shulchan Aruch* may not be eaten on the day one goes to the mikvah. However, Rav Yitzchak Berkovits holds like Rav Wosner in this regard, and advises women to stay away from any food that easily gets stuck in the teeth.

545. Rav Shmuel HaLevi Wosner says such a *kallah* should be sure to do her evening *bedikah* of Day 7 between *Minchah ketanah* and *shkiah* to fulfill all of her *bedikos lechatchilah*, even though she already immersed. Rav Dovid Feinstein is quoted as saying that *yichud* may occur before *shkiah* as marital relations are unlikely to occur before nightfall.

546. Rav Yosef Shalom Elyashiv; Rav Shmuel HaLevi Wosner; Rav Nissim Karelitz. See *Pischei Teshuvah* 197:10.

- Rav Yisrael Yaakov Fisher says Day 7 starts from *alos hashachar*, not *neitz hachamah*, and a woman can technically immerse in the mikvah from *alos hashachar* if she will not see her husband until *shkiah*. This is only to be relied on in extenuating circumstances, as a woman is rarely allowed to immerse on Day 7.
- The *She'arim HaMetzuyanim B'Halachah* says that a *kallah* may immerse in the mikvah on Day 8, after she completes *shivah nekiyim*, *lechatchilah*. *Bedi'eved*, she may immerse on Day 7, if necessary, as explained above.
- Rav Moshe Feinstein says that in a place where there is no mikvah in the neighborhood, a woman may go to the mikvah on Friday that is Day 7, as long as she does not return home until after her husband has left to shul,[547] and he will not return until *tzeis hakochavim*.[548]
- The *Shulchan Aruch* says a woman may not go to the mikvah on Shabbos day.[549]
- During the Gulf War, when it was dangerous to go out at night, women went to the mikvah the day after they were supposed to

---

547. Although the Shulchan Aruch, Shach, and Taz seem clearly against allowing any woman to immerse in the mikvah during the day, the *Sidrei Taharah* explains that they are stringent only regarding cases in which she comes home and sees her husband before *tzeis hakochavim*. In such a case, *Chazal* decreed that a woman may not immerse in the mikvah during the day because she may be intimate during the day, begin to bleed, and uproot *shivah nekiyim* retroactively. The second reason is because of *srach bitah*, as explained in the *Shulchan Aruch*. However, the *Sidrei Taharah* says if the woman will come home after nightfall, one may be lenient and allow a *tevilah* during the day, even if the reason is so they will not fail to fulfill the mitzvah of *onah* (this is not only in extenuating circumstances).

Rav Shmuel HaLevi Wosner says he asked the Chazon Ish about a couple who was traveling far away on a boat that was to leave before nightfall after Day 7 of *shivah nekiyim*. The Chazon Ish was stringent not to allow the woman to immerse in the mikvah during the day, even though it would be impossible for her to immerse for many weeks afterwards. Rav Wosner says he tried to get the Chazon Ish to be lenient, but to no avail. Rav Wosner himself is lenient in a case in which it would be impossible to immerse in the mikvah for quite some time, but not like the Sidrei Taharah, who is lenient even if the couple will miss just one night together.

While Rav Moshe Feinstein rules like the Sidrei Taharah, a competent *Rav* should be consulted before actually allowing a woman to immerse in the mikvah during the day.

548. This ruling was relied upon very often by women who were in the Catskill Mountains for Shabbos in the summer, and were not within walking distance of a mikvah.

549. The reason for this, as explained in the *Shulchan Aruch*, is that immersing on Shabbos day includes two leniencies: immersing during the day, as well as distancing the *chafifah* from the *tevilah*, since doing *chafifos* on Shabbos is prohibited.

go (Day "8" of *shivah nekiyim)*, except in the case of a Friday-night *tevilah*, when they went during the day on Sunday. This was the ruling in Eretz Yisrael, as opposed to Rav Moshe Feinstein's leniency which was implemented in the Catskill Mountains in America.

- If a woman immersed during the day (Day 7 or Day 8 of *shivah nekiyim*) and had no valid reason for doing so, the *tevilah* counts *bedi'eved*,[550] although she should hide the fact that she immersed from her husband until nightfall, even if she immersed on Day 8.[551]
- Rav Yosef Shalom Elyashiv says a woman (even one who is not experiencing extenuating circumstances) may go to the mikvah building during the day to do preparations, as long as she actually immerses after *tzeis hakochavim*.[552]

Tevilah When the Husband Is Out of Town

- A woman who counted *shivah nekiyim* when her husband is out of town may immerse in the mikvah whenever it is convenient for her, even a day or two before he comes home, but should not immerse on Friday night.
- A woman can have *shivah nekiyim* and a break before going go the mikvah. In such a case, she may wear dark underwear from after *tzeis hakochavim* after the last day of *shivah nekiyim* until she immerses in the mikvah.
- In Eretz Yisrael the custom is not to allow a woman whose husband is out of town to immerse in the mikvah.[553] In the

550. The *Shach* says that in the event that a woman immersed on Day 7 without a valid reason, she should immerse again at night, in deference to those who say that a *tevilah* during the day is invalid (*Haga'os Maimoni*; *Raavad, She'iltos*). Rav Shmuel HaLevi Wosner says she should not make a *brachah* on the second *tevilah* because there is a *safeik* whether or not she is obligated to do it.

551. A classic example of this is a woman who generally keeps Rabbeinu Tam, but for some reason immersed in the mikvah earlier than allowed. Such a woman should avoid coming in contact with her husband until after *tzeis hakochavim* of Rabbeinu Tam.

552. See *Shach* 197:6 in the name of the *Bach*.

553. Rav Yosef Shalom Elyashiv; Rav Shmuel HaLevi Wosner. Rav Yitzchak Berkovits says to advise a woman who is in a location where it is accepted not to allow a woman to immerse in the mikvah if her husband is out of town to do a *hefsek taharah* and all necessary *bedikos*, but not to go to the mikvah until her husband comes home. She should not push off her *hefsek taharah*, though, because it is better to be waiting on Day 7 than in

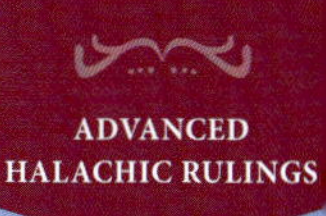

United States the custom is to allow it, but the woman should either: (1) sleep with a knife under her pillow, or (2) sleep with an article of her husband's clothing, or (3) sleep with a child or another woman in her room or bed.[554]

Taharah during Aveilus

- A woman may not immerse in the mikvah when either she or her husband is in *aveilus*,[555] because marital relations are prohibited then.[556]
- The woman should go through the entire *taharah* process, including the *hefsek taharah*, *moch dachuk*, and all *bedikos* of *shivah nekiyim*, but should not immerse in the mikvah until after *aveilus* is complete.
- The woman should not push off her *hefsek taharah*. Instead, she should wait on "Day 7" until the conclusion of *aveilus* to immerse in the mikvah.
- The woman may change into dark underwear once she finishes *shivah nekiyim*, even though she has not yet immersed in the mikvah.

A Mikvah Night on Yom Kippur or Tishah B'Av

- A woman does not go to the mikvah when her mikvah night falls on Yom Kippur or Tishah B'Av. (The mikvah will anyway

---

the middle of *shivah nekiyim*, because she is closer to a *taharah* status. The other reason for this ruling is because very often a woman thinks her husband will not be in town when she will be ready to go to the mikvah and circumstances change that allow him to be there on time, but she has not performed the necessary *bedikos* to allow her to immerse on time. This ruling is in contrast with the opinion that it is better for her to push off the *hefsek taharah* so she will immerse "on time."

Rav Shmuel HaLevi Wosner is lenient to allow her to immerse the night before her husband will come home if he is coming home during the day, to allow them to maximize their time together so she does not have to wait until the night to immerse in the mikvah. In such a case she should use one of the precautions of Rebbi Yehudah HaChassid (as delineated above) for that night.

554. Based on Rebbi Yehudah HaChassid and *Pardes Shlomo* in the name of the *Shvus Yaakov*.

555. The woman may not immerse in the mikvah even though it would allow the couple to break other *harchakos*, such as directly handing things to one another.

556. *Shu"t Maharim Shik*, *siman* 385.

be closed.) Rather, she should go on Motzaei Yom Kippur or Motzaei Tishah B'Av, doing most of her preparations on *erev Yom Kippur* or *erev Tishah B'Av* and some preparations the night of the *tevilah*.[557]

- A woman who is immersing on *Motzaei Tishah B'Av Nidcheh* (Sunday night) should do all of her preparations on *erev Shabbos*, and do touch-ups on *Motzaei Tishah B'Av Nidcheh* (Sunday night) if she is fasting. If she is not fasting for any reason she should do all *chafifos* on Sunday night.[558]

- Rav Yosef Shalom Elyashiv, Rav Shmuel HaLevi Wosner, and Rav Nissim Karelitz say that if a woman is supposed to go to the mikvah on Friday night of Tishah B'Av that falls on Shabbos (and the fast is therefore pushed to Sunday), she may do so, and marital relations are permitted.[559]

- See Advanced Rulings, Taharah, headline "A Vest on a Mikvah Night or on the Wedding Night" (page 395) for the halachos regarding a mikvah night that falls on a *vest*.

A Delayed Mikvah Night in Regard to Shabbos and Yom Tov

- A woman may not delay her mikvah night to Friday night, Yom Tov night, or Motzaei Shabbos or Motzaei Yom Tov. The only *tevilah* allowed during these times is a *tevilah* that is on time.[560]

---

557. *Dagul M'Revavah*; *Shach*; *Mishnah Berurah, siman* 551.

558. The reason for this ruling is that a woman who immerses on *Motzaei Tishah B'Av Nidcheh* (Sunday night) should really do her *chafifos* on *Motzaei Tishah B'Av Nidcheh*. However, experience has shown that after fasting women are prone to rushing the *chafifos* and making mistakes. Therfore, it is a good idea for a woman to do all of her preparations on *erev Shabbos*, and then she can get through everything on *Motzaei Tishah B'Av Nidcheh* (Sunday night) in a more timely fashion. If she is not fasting for any reason, she should do all *chafifos* on *Motzaei Tishah B'Av Nidcheh* (Sunday night).

559. For more information regarding this halachah, see *Mishnah Berurah* 554:40; *Magen Avraham*, ibid., *siman kattan* 20; and *Sidrei Taharah* 197:1 in the name of the *Shelah*.

560. See background, above. On a Friday-night *tevilah* a woman misses doing her *chafifos* at night, which is only allowed when she is immersing on time. On Motzaei Shabbos she does *chafifos* during the day on Friday (as per Rashi's opinion that *chafifos* must be done during the day), and she does *chafifos* before she immerses (as per the *She'iltos*, which says that *chafifos* must be done at night), but the Friday *chafifah* is too far removed from the *tevilah*, as *chafifos* are only considered close to the *tevilah* when they are performed within one *onah* of the *tevilah*. Rav Yosef Shalom Elyashiv says that a reason not to allow a delayed *tevilah* on Friday night is out of the concern that a woman

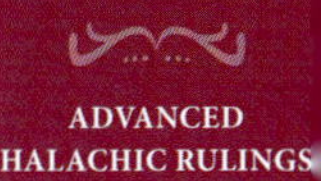

- A woman must have been in a situation in which she really did not have a choice but to push off her mikvah night — and not just a good excuse explaining why she could not go earlier[561] — in order to allow a delayed *tevilah* to take place on such a night.[562]
- A woman who pushed off her *hefsek taharah*[563] is also considered to have delayed her *tevilah*.[564] This means that she should not immerse in the mikvah on Friday night, or on Motzaei Shabbos in a place where a delayed *tevilah* is not allowed on Motzaei Shabbos.
- A woman who has a valid reason for not going to the mikvah on Friday night may go on Motzaei Shabbos. An example of a good excuse is that the woman was very ill or bedridden, and not just that she did not want to go because of the inconvenience.
- Practically speaking,[565] a *Rav* will often be lenient and allow a woman who pushed off going to the mikvah from Friday night

---

will squeeze her hair on Shabbos, which is prohibited *mid'Oraisa*. The halachah is lenient for a woman who is immersing on time, but this edict is not waived for a woman who is not immersing on time.

561. This is the opinion of the Terumas HaDeshen, unlike the Mordechai and the Agur (brought in the *Taz* 197:4), who are stringent even if the woman did not immerse on Friday night due to unavoidable circumstances.

562. Rav Nissim Karelitz says that if man was out of town and returns home on *erev Shabbos*, his wife may immerse in the mikvah on Friday night even though she finished *shivah nekiyim* beforehand. His reasoning is that in Eretz Yisrael the custom is that a woman does not immerse in the mikvah while the husband is out of town, so this woman legitimately waited (i.e., there were unavoidable circumstances) until her husband arrived back in town. Practically speaking, in the United States the custom is to allow a woman whose husband is out of town to immerse on Thursday night and to follow Rebbi Yehuda HaChassid and put a knife or article of his clothing under her pillow. If she did not immerse on Thursday night for whatever reason, she has what to rely on to immerse on Friday night, even though it is a delayed *tevilah*.

563. This unfortunately seems to be a common practice among women who do not want to immerse in the mikvah at certain times.

564. See *Pischei Teshuvah* 197:3 in the name of the *Noda B'Yehudah* that a woman who experienced unavoidable circumstances or made a mistake may immerse in the mikvah on Friday night even though the *tevilah* was delayed. The case given there is a woman who mistakenly miscalculated and found herself in a place where she was not able to perform the *hefsek taharah* on time. It seems clear from the case that had she pushed off the *hefsek taharah* purposely she would not have been allowed to immerse on Friday night, because this would have been considered delaying the *tevilah*.

565. Rav Yosef Shalom Elyashiv and other *Poskim* seem to hold that according to the letter of the law, a woman should not immerse in the mikvah on Motzaei Shabbos if it is a delayed *tevilah*, based on the *Rama* 197:2, which says that in a place where it is the custom to be stringent in this matter, a woman who delayed her *tevilah* should not immerse on Motzaei Shabbos because one should not do *chafifos* so far from the *tevilah*. That being

to go Motzaei Shabbos, because the woman and her husband probably are not the strongest couple, and another night apart may really hurt their *shalom bayis*.[566]

Immersing in a Public Place

- A woman may immerse in a lake that she knows is kosher for use as a mikvah, if she can ascertain that no one will see her immerse.
- If the woman is afraid someone will see her, she may wear clothing that is very, very loose.[567]

---

said, Rav Elyashiv holds that although Yerushalayim is considered a place where it is the custom to be stringent, a woman who has a valid reason may immerse on Motzaei Shabbos, even if the *tevilah* was delayed, because there is what to rely on in extenuating circumstances (and all cases of *shalom bayis* are considered extenuating circumstances). Rav Shmuel HaLevi Wosner and Rav Nissim Karelitz say the Rama was giving general instructions for places where the custom is to be stringent, but they do not consider themselves in a place where it is the custom to be stringent (possibly because that was never the custom in Bnei Brak). Rav Wosner explains the reason not to be stringent: Although a delayed *tevilah* on Motzaei Shabbos will require the woman to perform all *chafifos* on Motzaei Shabbos (not fulfilling Rashi's opinion that one must do *chafifos* during the day), one may rely on the *She'iltos* and allow any woman in extenuating circumstances to perform all *chafifos* at night. He reasons that this woman should not be any worse than a woman who has a hard time performing *chafifos* on time, and this is essentially the same scenario as any time during the week, when a woman is not obligated to delay the *tevilah* to fulfill all the opinions *lechatchilah*. Practically speaking, Rav Yitzchak Berkovits seems to rule like Rav Elyashiv (possibly because he is in Yerushalayim), and is lenient for a woman who has a good reason for not immersing on time, and says to follow the custom of the city both for stringencies and for leniencies.

See *Pischei Teshuvah* 197:6 in the name of *Teshuvos Even HaShoham* that in a city that does not have a custom to be stringent, a *Rav* should be lenient, which will probably be the *din* in most Jewish communities around the world.

566. Rav Shmuel HaLevi Wosner cites his rebbe'im that nowadays a *Rav* should try as best as he can to get every woman to the mikvah as soon as halachah allows, even if that means allowing her to immerse on Friday night in the case of a delayed *tevilah* in certain instances. In the United States, *Rabbanim* often allow a delayed *tevilah* to take place on Friday night, when they deem it necessary, due to *shalom bayis* and other considerations. The *Mishnah Berurah* (326:24) brings that the custom is not to allow women to immerse in the mikvah on Friday night when it is a delayed *tevilah*. What seems clear is that Rav Wosner is setting the tone for *Rabbanim* to understand that we live in a spiritually weak generation and although a *Rav* may want to penalize a woman who has been lax in halachah, it is best to minimize such occurrences so as to maximize the couple's time together.

567. Most *Poskim* hold a woman cannot immerse in a bathing suit that has elastic and sticks to the body tightly. If a woman needs to immerse in a public place and she feels that she must wear something to cover up because people may see her, she must be sure that whatever she is wearing is loose enough for the water to easily touch every area of

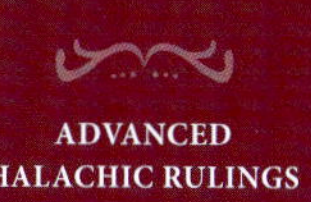

- A woman does not have to pick up her feet when she immerses in a regular mikvah. However, she has to pick up her feet during the immersion in a muddy area, so mud will not get stuck to the bottom of her feet.[568]

- Rav Mati Friedman pointed out that before someone immerses anywhere besides in an established kosher mikvah, she should call a competent *Rav* to make certain the place is kosher for *tevilah*.

Tevilah Without Intention

- The halachah is that a *tevilah* without intention is a valid *tevilah*.

- The woman must still do *chafifos* to validate the *tevilah*. Even if a woman went swimming in the ocean on Day 7 of *shivah nekiyim* before doing *chafifos*, she must immerse in the mikvah again at night *with a brachah*. If a woman did *chafifos* and then went swimming in the ocean,[569] she must immerse in the mikvah again, but does not make a *brachah*.

The Brachah and the Tevilah

- A woman says the following *brachah* upon immersing in a mikvah:

בָּרוּךְ אַתָּה אֲדֹנָי אֱלֹהֵינוּ מֶלֶךְ הָעוֹלָם, אֲשֶׁר קִדְּשָׁנוּ בְּמִצְוֹתָיו וְצִוָּנוּ עַל הַטְּבִילָה:

- Ashkenazi women immerse, say the *brachah*, and then immerse again.[570]

---

her body (*Minchas Yitzchak*; *Aruch HaShulchan*; *Badei HaShulchan*). Practically speaking, this should only be relied on when necessary and should not be done *lechatchilah* (Rav Shmuel HaLevi Wosner).

568. 198:30.

569. This *din* is brought for the theoretical understanding of the halachah aspect, not to be applied in the real world.

570. Rav Shmuel HaLevi Wosner brings three reasons why Ashkenazim immerse at least twice. One reason is to fulfill both opinions regarding whether the *brachah* should be said before or after the *tevilah*. The woman thus immerses, says the *brachah*, and then immerses again to fulfill all possibilities. Another reason to immerse twice is to ensure that the woman certainly immersed correctly, as the extra immersion helps guarantee

- Sefaradi women say the *brachah* and then immerse only once.
- A woman says the *brachah* regardless of whether she is immersing for *tumah d'Oraisa* or *tumah d'Rabbanan*. This includes a woman whom the *Rav* told to immerse in the mikvah because he "could not permit a questionable *bedikah*" even when he is not totally sure she is *temei'ah*. However, a woman who is only immersing because of a stringency[571] does not say a *brachah*.[572]
- Rav Nissim Karelitz says that a *kallah* does not say *Shehecheyanu* on her first *tevilah*.[573]
- Some have a custom to immerse extra times for added *kedushah* (holiness). This is a custom, not a halachah.[574]
- The halachah is that there is no concern of *libbah ro'eh es ha'ervah* (her heart seeing nakedness) by women. Yet, as per the opinions who hold there is a concern, a woman should put her arm across her midsection, below her heart, while saying the *brachah*.

---

that the water reached every area of her body. Alternatively, women immerse extra times for added *kedushah* (holiness).

571. Interestingly, if a woman says "I am *temei'ah*," and then changes and says "I am *tehorah*," and gives a valid reason why she lied, she is believed. Nevertheless, the *Rama* (185:3) says the husband has a right to be stringent on himself. Because of this *Rama*, the halachah is that the woman is allowed to start counting 5 days from when she said "I am *temei'ah*," even though she really has a valid *amaslah*. That being said, it would seem that although a woman in this scenario must go through the *taharah* process, she would not make a *brachah* on the *tevilah* since she is only immersing because of the stringency of her husband.

That said, there is a disagreement whether a woman who said "I am *temei'ah*" and did not give a valid *amaslah* — in which case she must immerse in the mikvah — must recite a *brachah* or not. Many maintain that since she knows she was never *temei'ah*, she should not make a *brachah*, while others say she should because *Chazal* were *metamei* her. Practically speaking, a *Rav* should be consulted if such a case arises.

572. Rav Nissim Karelitz.

573. *Shu"t Chasam Sofer*, *Orach Chaim* 400:55.

574. Rav Shmuel HaLevi Wosner says that the custom to immerse more than twice (three, five, seven, nine, ten, twelve, or fourteen times, which according to some is for added *kedushah*) also serves a higher purpose in that the woman can nearly be guaranteed that the water will reach all body crevices when she continuously emerges from and re-submerges in the mikvah waters. This is not to say that a woman who immerses twice (or once if she is Sefaradi) is not completely *tehorah*. Presumably, if a woman decides to immerse more than two times the mikvah attendant is not required to watch her immerse, because she is certainly *tehorah* according to halachah, and anything a woman does for added *kedushah* does not require the mikvah lady's supervision.

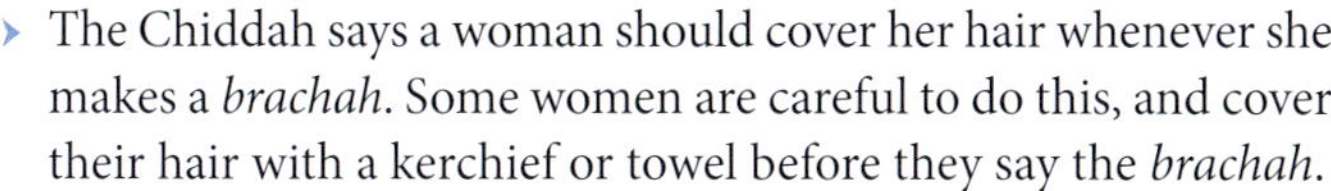

- The Chiddah says a woman should cover her hair whenever she makes a *brachah*. Some women are careful to do this, and cover their hair with a kerchief or towel before they say the *brachah*.
- A wig is clearly a good enough covering in everyday situations, for those who want to follow the Chiddah's opinion while saying *brachos*.
- Practically speaking, most women are not careful to follow the Chiddah's opinion.
- While immersing, the woman should lean forward slightly so that the water reaches the area at the bottom of the breasts which may press against the body.
- The woman's arms should be near her sides, not spread too far and not pressed against her body, just as they are while she walks.
- The woman should be careful not to seal her lips or close her eyes too tightly during the *tevilah* because it causes skin that is normally exposed (and requires contact with the water) to become concealed. Her lips and eyes may remain closed during the *tevilah*.

Attributing a Chatzitzah

- If a woman did *chafifos* immediately prior to the *tevilah*, and then later, after her *tevilah*, discovered a *chatzitzah*, she does not need to immerse in the mikvah again as long as there is a chance that the *chatzitzah* came about after she came out of the mikvah.
- The best *teliyah* of a *chatzitzah* is when the woman was busy with, eating, or touching this form of *chatzitzah* after she was immersed.
- A real, probable *teliyah* is needed in order to be lenient regarding a *chatzitzah* discovered after a Friday-night *tevilah*, or any other time when *chafifos* were not done during the same *onah* as the *tevilah*.

Common Chatzitzah Questions After Tevilah

- The most common *she'eilos* that arise after *tevilah* are questions regarding loose skin and broken nails.

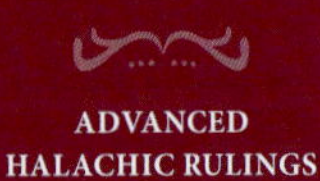

- Loose skin is generally not a problem, because the halachah assumes that it came loose from the towel that the woman dried herself with after the *tevilah*.
- A hangnails that snags in clothing is a problem when it bothers her, unless she did something after the *tevilah* that may have caused her nail to break. It is a good idea to teach women to scratch their nails (fingers and toes) on the tiled floor when they come out of the mikvah; this should take away most *she'eilos* on nails.
- A woman who has a cold should blow her nose right before she enters the mikvah. Anything found later on will be assumed to have emerged after the immersion.
- Lice are *chatzitzos* and must be removed before *tevilah*.
- Nits that have not yet hatched (and therefore do not yet itch) are not *chatzitzos*.
- Dandruff should be removed as much as possible. A woman may immerse with whatever she no longer cares about.
- Eczema and dead skin from sunburns must be removed as much as possible, and whatever remains on her skin is not a *chatzitzah*.[575]
- The *Ramban* says a woman should not second-guess herself after the *tevilah*, trying to figure out which halachah she may not have kept correctly or which stringency she may have missed.[576] On the contrary, she should feel confident that she immersed according to halachah, unless something specific turns up later on.

Showering After Tevilah

- Rav Moshe Feinstein says a woman may not shower in the mikvah building after she immerses.[577] However, a woman who

575. Rav Shmuel HaLevi Wosner. According to most *Poskim* the remaining skin must be in a state that would not be removed by most people, such as hanging, loose, or dead skin.

576. The example the *Ramban* gives is she should not doubt whether she closed her eyes or lips too tightly.

577. This edict of *Chazal* that a woman should not wash herself after *tevilah* in the mikvah building is so that one does not mistakenly think that the the bath — or in our case, shower — was what made her *tehorah*.

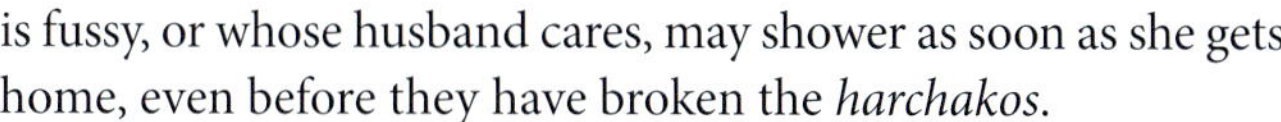

is fussy, or whose husband cares, may shower as soon as she gets home, even before they have broken the *harchakos*.

- The *Poskim* say that every woman, even one who is not fussy, may shower when she gets home after the couple have stopped keeping *harchakos*, for example, the woman handed something to her husband.[578]

- Rav Shlomo Zalman Auerbach would say that a man should shower *twice* on Friday, once before going the mikvah out of respect for the other men using the mikvah, and once afterwards in honor of Shabbos, unless the mikvah is very clean.

- Practically speaking, men can shower in the mikvah building after immersing; women should not.

- A person should wash their hands after immersing in the mikvah, as they would for *negel vasser*.

The Mikvah Attendant ("Mikvah Lady")

- The mikvah attendant must make sure that all of the woman's hair goes under the water.[579] In fact, this is one of the main reasons she is there.[580]

- The mikvah attendant must be a Jewish woman above the age of bas mitzvah.[581]

---

578. *Shu"t Shevet HaLevi*, vol. 5, *siman* 125.

579. The *Be'er Halachah* (75:2) says that a woman should be very careful not to immerse while any of her hair is floating on top of the mikvah waters. He says that a good idea for women who have long hair is to immerse with a loose hair net which ensures that the hair goes under the water. Practically speaking, most women do not immerse with a hair net, but some Chassidishe mikvaos have a policy that does not allow a woman (who does not shave her head) to immerse without a hair net. Rav Nissim Karelitz writes that a woman who immerses with a hair net should ensure that the net is not tight around her head.

580. If a woman immerses with a *chatzitzah*, it generally falls into the category of a *chatzitzah* that covers a small part of the body that one does not care about, because it is rare for someone to immerse with something covering most of her body, which she overlooked in her mikvah preparations. That being said, almost all cases of *chatzitzah* involve *tumah d'Rabbanan*. However, if a woman immerses and her entire body was not completely immersed in the mikvah at the same time — such as if even a strand of hair remains above water — she retains her status of a *niddah d'Oraisa* (*Beis Yosef*; *Sidrei Taharah*; Rav Shmuel HaLevi Wosner; Rav Nissim Karelitz).

581. Rav Shmuel HaLevi Wosner says to be careful that the mikvah lady is not a young girl of twelve. She should be someone who clearly displays signs of maturity because the issue at hand is one of *tumah* that is established to be *tamei*, so a bona fide *gedolah* is required to be certain that the niddah's status changed (*Pri Megadim*, *Orach Chaim*

- Rav Shmuel HaLevi Wosner says that the custom, based on the writings of the Arizal, is that the mikvah attendant says "Kosher" or "*Tehorah*" when she sees the *tevilah* performed correctly.[582] If for any reason she does not say this, it does not disqualify the *tevilah*.

- As stated above, the mikvah lady can assist the woman in doing *iyun*.

- Some women have a custom to look at the mikvah lady when they come out of the mikvah water. This is based on Kabbalah sources, and is brought in the *Rama*.[583] The woman does not have to look at the mikvah lady's face; merely seeing her is sufficient.[584]

- The mikvah lady should ideally be *tehorah* if possible; if not, it is also fine.[585]

- If a woman is immersing in a location where finding a mikvah lady is impossible, her husband may serve in that capacity.[586]

451:47:6). Rav Moshe Feinstein says the mikvah lady must also be someone who keeps *hilchos taharas hamishpachah*, so she is trustworthy in the matter.

582. The holy *sefarim* say that when the mikvah lady says "Kosher," the angels concur and say "Kosher." This should refute any potential thoughts later on that the *tevilah* was invalid because of a minor technicality. By doing everything that she was supposed to do, a woman can be confident that the *tevilah* changed her status to kosher.

583. The *Lechem V'Simlah* says the mikvah lady should approach the woman coming out of the mikvah and touch her. In many mikvaos, especially in Eretz Yisrael, the custom has become for the mikvah lady to shake the hand of the woman emerging from the mikvah. Many mikvah ladies in the United States do not do this, although most women are careful to look at the mikvah lady upon emerging from the water (which is nearly inevitable anyway).

584. The *Sidrei Taharah* (*siman kattan* 91) says this only applies to a woman who may possibly conceive on this night. A woman who knows that she will not be intimate, is taking birth control, or cannot conceive for whatever reason, does not have to be careful about this.

585. This is so the woman sees something *tahor* upon emerging from the mikvah. The *She'arim HaMetzuyanim B'Halachah* explains that when she comes out of the mikvah, a woman should not see something that itself cannot become *tahor* in a mikvah. She should therefore avoid looking at an animal or a non-Jew but may look at a niddah, since the niddah can immerse in the mikvah. Interestingly, although a non-Jew can immerse in a mikvah and convert to Judaism, a woman should nevertheless be careful to see a Jew first.

586. *Noda B'Yehudah*, brought in *Pischei Teshuvah* 195:2.

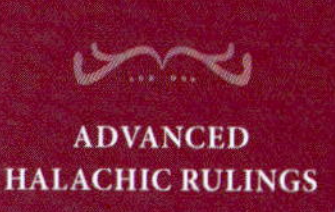

The Time for Tevilah

- A woman must immerse in the mikvah after *tzeis hakochavim*. In Eretz Yisrael, this time is 20 minutes after *shkiah* in the winter, and 25 minutes after *shkiah* in the summer. The time varies depending on where in the world the woman happens to be, and a woman should check her local calendar for the time of *tzeis hakochavim*.
- People who keep Rabbeinu Tam's *zman* as a stringency do not have to keep it for *tevilah*. A woman who keeps Rabbeinu Tam in regard to when night begins for halachic purposes, however,[587] should not immerse before that time.[588] In circumstances that require an earlier *tevilah*, such as Friday night, where the mikvah will close earlier than the time of Rabbeinu Tam, she should immerse earlier, but should not go home until the time of Rabbeinu Tam.
- A woman must observe these times even if she is immersing in the mikvah after *shivah nekiyim* have already ended, for example, on Day 8. She may not immerse after *shkiah* or during the day unless there are extenuating circumstances, as discussed above.

Saying "I Am Tehorah"

- The *Chavas Daas* says after a woman became a niddah and became *temei'ah*, she must explicitly tell her husband that she went to the mikvah or that she is now *tehorah*.

587. In extenuating circumstances, such as if the mikvah will close before that time, the woman may immerse earlier but should not see her husband before the time of Rabbeinu Tam.

588. Although Rabbeinu Tam himself holds that a woman can immerse in the mikvah from *shkiah*, the halachah does not follow his opinion in this area. If the woman keeps Rabbeinu Tam in regards to when is called night, she must wait for that time before immersing, even though Rabbeinu Tam himself would tell her to immerse earlier. This is in contrast to the *dinim* of *ke'arah achas* and leftovers (see "Chapter Three: *Harchakos*") which are both learned from the same *din* of *lo yochal hazav im hazavah*, for which one must follow the same *Posek* consistently.

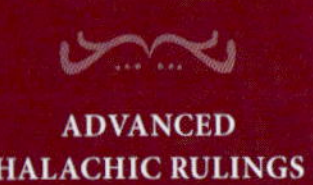

- The Lechem V'Simlah disagrees, and holds that the woman does not need to say anything;[589] once her husband knows that she is *tehorah* he may break *harchakos*.
- Practically speaking, most *Poskim* rule like the Lechem V'Simlah, saying that following the opinion of the Chavas Daas is a stringency.[590]
- Rav Nissim Karelitz says one should follow the opinion of the Chavas Daas, unless the couple makes up a certain sign between themselves to mean that she is *tehorah*.
- Rav Moshe Feinstein says that if a husband trusts his wife, she is trusted when she says that she went to the mikvah even if she is lax in other areas of halachah, even if she desecrates Shabbos in public.[591]

---

589. The *Lechem V'Simlah* explains that the *Chavas Daas* is only talking about a case in which a woman said, "I am *temei'ah*," and immediately contradicted her words by lying down next to her husband. However, in a regular case there is no requirement for her to say "I am *tehorah*" or "I went to the mikvah," since her husband expects that to be the case.

590. Rav Yosef Shalom Elyashiv; Rav Shmuel HaLevi Wosner.

591. This means to say that although a woman is considered a *mumar* (apostate) in certain aspects of halachah, since she is careful to keep other areas stringently, she is considered trustworthy in the areas in which she has proven herself.

VESTOS

An Onah

- *Mid'Oraisa*, all mitzvos that must be performed during the daytime can be done from *alos hashachar* until *tzeis hakochavim*. However, *mid'Rabbanan*, they may only be done from *neitz* until *shkiah* to ensure they are performed during the "day."
- *Vestos*, however, are entirely governed by *neitz* and *shkiah*, with no regard for *alos hashachar* and *tzeis hakochavim* at all. The *Chavas Daas* says that *vestos* are calculated from *neitz* and *shkiah*[592] because a woman's menstrual cycle is affected by light.[593]
- Practically speaking, in regard to *vestos* the halachah is like the Chavas Daas's opinion and does not allow any room for

592. A classic *she'eilah* is of a woman who accepted Shabbos and then discovered blood before *shkiah*. The halachah is that the upcoming *vestos* are to be kept as a daytime *onah*, as prescribed by the Chavas Daas. The reasoning behind the ruling is that sunlight is what affects the menstrual cycle, not the *"din"* of day or night (*Shu"t Ksav Sofer; Badei HaShulchan*).

593. Interestingly, chickens are also regulated by the sun and lay eggs at the crack of dawn. Chicken farmers therefore turn on the lights in the chicken coop many times during the night to trick the chickens into laying more eggs.

leniencies either way,[594] even if a woman got her period close to *neitz* or *shkiah*. (However, although the times of *neitz* and *shkiah* are absolute in regard to establishing *vestos*, leniencies in regard to the times of *neitz* and *shkiah* do arise in regard to the 5 days of *poletes shichvas zera*,[595] as is discussed in Background and Analysis, Taharah, headline "When a Woman Does Not Need 5 Days," (page 149).

- Rav Nissim Karelitz (as well as most other *Poskim*[596]) say that a woman who travels from one place in the world to another observes her *onas havest* according to the times of *neitz* and *shkiah* in the place where she is at the moment.[597] This ruling is based on the opinion of the Chavas Daas, that the reason we take the *onah* into account when establishing a *vest* is because sunlight causes changes in the menstrual cycle.

- The *vest* is always set at the *onah* in which the bleeding began, even though the woman continued to bleed into the following *onah*.[598]

---

594. To establish or break a *vest kavua*, or to permit marital relations at night by saying the *vest* was really during the day.

595. That is, a woman who had a *re'iyah* during *bein hashmashos* may be lenient and begin counting the day before as Day 1 of the *re'iyah* (as if the *re'iyah* was before *shkiah*) as she starts to count her 5 days. However, the *onah* in which one began bleeding is calculated from after *shkiah*, and the next month's *vestos* will all be at night. The same *re'iyah* is ironically calculated as having started during the day in one regard and the night in another regard.

596. Rav Shmuel HaLevi Wosner cites an opinion that one should be stringent if a woman traveled (eastward) to a location that shortened the hours of her cycle regarding *vestos*, but is not stringent if she traveled during *shivah nekiyim*. Practically speaking, most *Poskim* are not stringent in regard to *vestos* or *shivah nekiyim*.

597. This means to say that a woman who has a *vest* on Monday night who traveled from Eretz Yisrael to the United States will have a longer *vest* because she is traveling westward with the sun, extending her *onah*. The opposite is true as well if she travels east. In such a case, she shortens the *onas havest* and only needs to keep the *onah* in the place where she is presently located.

This *din* also applies to a woman who travels during *shivah nekiyim* to another country. As a rule, she always goes according to where she is presently located, even if she extended or shortened *shivah nekiyim* through her travels (*Minchas Yitzchak*; Rav Shmuel HaLevi Wosner).

598. The *Shulchan Aruch* cites the Raavad, who says that the *vest* for the next month is the *onah* of when she began bleeding, as well as the amount of time that the initial blood flow continued into the next *onah*. Practically speaking, the halachah is to only keep the *onah* of when she began bleeding, because the Raavad was talking about times when women had *hargashos* and knew how long their cervix opened to allow the initial flow to start. Nowadays that women generally no longer have *hargashos*, they must only keep the one *onah* of when they started to bleed.

The Onset of the Period

- The *Shulchan Aruch* says the *onas havest* is the *onah* in which the *re'iyah* started, as well as the time that the onset of the period continues into the next *onah*. For example, for a woman who began to bleed before *shkiah* and continues to bleed for an hour after *shkiah*, her next month's *onas havest* will be the day plus 1 hour.[599]

- Practically speaking, women should not be told to watch how long they bled for out of concern for the Raavad's opinion (even though the Shulchan Aruch rules like this) because women nowadays no longer have *hargashos*, and have no idea when the onset of the period really stopped and the *tosefes damim* (additional bleeding) started. The *onah* of the onset of the period creates the *vest* for next month, with no exceptions.

- Chabad Chassidim teach that a woman should count the amount of *onos* that she was clean for, which is between the *onah* in which the bleeding stops (from "last month") and the next onset of the period (of "next month").[600] She then calculates that same amount of *onos* from the next *onah* in which she stops bleeding, and has her *vestos* for the upcoming month. Other than in Chabad, this ruling is not followed.

- If a woman really has a new *re'iyah* — not just a *kesem* — during her *shivah nekiyim*, after a good *hefsek taharah*, this creates a new *vest* only after Day 3 of *shivah nekiyim*, as only then is she considered as having a *mayan sasum*.[601]

Spotting Before the Period Begins

- Rav Moshe Feinstein and Rav Nissim Karelitz say that a woman who experiences staining before her period comes counts the

599. 184:5:9, based on the *Raavad*.

600. Chabad Chassidim generally calculate from the *hefsek taharah* until the next *re'iyah*, unless the woman can establish that she stopped bleeding before the *onah* of the *hefsek taharah*.

601. In order to create a new *vest* a woman must bleed enough for it to be considered a new *re'iyah* (6–7 *gris* [half a dollar bill]), and not just enough to be *metamei* her such that she would need to start *shivah nekiyim* again. The situation must also dictate that she is having a new period, and not just heavy staining. Rav Nissim Karelitz is stringent, and says to count a *vest* if the woman had 1 clean day and then a substantial amount of bleeding. His ruling is a big novelty, though, and most *Poskim* disagree.

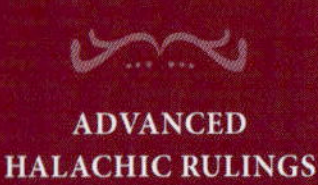

vest from the day that she began spotting when this staining is connected to the *re'iyah*. If the staining is separated by some clean time (Rav Nissim Karelitz says 1 day), the upcoming *vestos* are counted from the onset of the period.

- Practically speaking, *kesamim* do not create *vestos*, and the *vestos* are always counted from the onset of the period.[602]

Vestos for Beginners

- Beginners should only be taught the following *onos*: *onah beinonis* as Day 30, *yom hachodesh*, and *haflagah*. They should also be taught to watch out for *vest hashavua*. *Bnei Torah* should also be taught the *onas Ohr Zarua*, but not the *Pleissi* and the *Chavas Daas*.
- Rav Shmuel HaLevi Wosner says a beginner should be taught according to the opinion of the Pischei Megadim,[603] not like the opinion of the Beis Meir.[604]
- Those who can keep track should be taught the *Beis Meir* and Rav Yosef Shalom Elyashiv's halachah of establishing from a *mayan pasuach*.

Onah Beinonis

- The *Taz* says the *onah beinonis* is Day 30 after the last *re'iyah*,[605] counting the date of the onset of the period as Day 1.[606]

---

602. *Shu"t Shevet HaLevi*; Rav Yosef Shalom Elyashiv. This is Rav Elyashiv's ruling unless she establishes that she always spots and then gets her period within a day. In such a case he says to treat the *kesem* as a *vest haguf* of sorts and to be concerned about it as a stringency.

603. He holds that a *re'iyah* from a *mayan pasuach* will not continue a *vest she'eino kavua*. See Advanced Rulings, Vestos, headline "Establishing a *Vest* Due to *Mayan Pasuach*," (page 400).

604. He holds that a *re'iyah* that came early does not uproot a *re'iyah* that came later in regard to a *vest haflagah*. See Advanced Rulings, Vestos, headline "The Beis Meir: A Short Haflagah After a Long Haflagah" (page 402).

605. 189:17.

606. The *Shulchan Aruch HaRav* says an *onah beinonis* requires a *bedikah*, after which the woman is permitted to her husband on the *onah beinonis* itself. Practically speaking, nearly all *Poskim* rule like the simple explanation in the *Shulchan Aruch*, that marital relations are forbidden on the *onas havest* of *onah beinonis*, like any other *vest*.

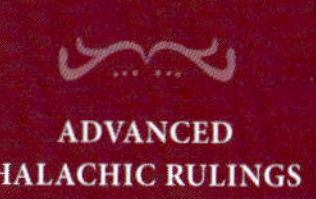

- The *Shach* and *Toras HaShelamim* say the *onah beinonis* is the same day as the *yom hachodesh*.[607]
- The *Chavas Daas* says the *onah beinonis* is Day 31 after the last *re'iyah*. He says that a woman counts 30 days starting the day *after* the last *re'iyah* (which is the original thought of the Shach).[608]
- Practically speaking, the halachah is like the opinion of the Taz, and Day 31 is observed as a stringency.[609]
- Rav Yosef Shalom Elyashiv says one may be lenient and not keep the Chavas Daas's opinion of keeping Day 31 as a *vest* when there is a good reason not to do so. Some examples are a mikvah night and when one is traveling away or arriving home from their travels. This ruling is practically only relevant when Day 31 is not also the *yom hachodesh*, as it is after a month that has only 29 days.
- Rav Nissim Karelitz and Rav Shmuel HaLevi Wosner say that even if a woman consistently gets her period at *haflagos* longer than 30 days,[610] and even has a *vest kavua* as such,[611] she must still keep the *onah beinonis* every month.[612]
- Rav Yaacov Blau says that if a woman established 3 months in a row that her period did not come at a *haflagah* of fewer than 30 days,[613] she may be lenient the following month, as per the opinion of the Shach,[614] to keep only the *haflagah* and the *yom*

607. 189:21.

608. 189:12.

609. Rav Yosef Shalom Elyashiv; Rav Nissim Karelitz.

610. *Shiurei Shevet HaLevi*, "*Mistaber D'Yeish Lachush*."

611. This means to say that she establishes that she consistently bleeds later than 30 days, not that she created a *vest kavua* for a *haflagah* longer than 30 days. Although such a woman essentially established that she will not bleed on Day 30, she must nevertheless observe the *onah beinonis*.

612. *Aruch HaShulchan*; *Sidrei Taharah*; *Shu"t Shevet HaLevei*; *Minchas Yitzchak*.

613. The *Pischei Teshuvos* also brings this from the *Imrei Baruch* in the name of the Maharil, the *Taharas Yisrael*, and Rav Moshe Feinstein (*Igros Moshe*, *Yoreh Dei'ah*, vol. 8, 2:72).

614. Rav Nissim Karelitz and Rav Shmuel HaLevi Wosner cite the *Terumas HaDeshen* (*Shulchan Aruch* 186:3), which says that when a woman never gets her period for less than a certain amount of days, she creates a *vest kavua* not to expect it before this amount of time. Rav Karelitz and Rav Wosner say the Terumas HaDeshen is only lenient regarding extra *bedikos* of a woman who is establishing that she does not bleed due to marital relations (which is what *siman* 186 discusses), but the woman does need to keep *onah*

hachodesh.[615] Once her period comes on or earlier than Day 30 one time,[616] she should revert to keeping *onah beinonis* as prescribed by the *Taz* (Day 30).

- Rav Yosef Shalom Elyashiv says a woman who establishes that her period did not come at a *haflagah* of fewer than 30 days should keep *onah beinonis* on Day 30, but should not keep the *onos* of the *Chavas Daas* (Day 31), the *Pleissi*, or the *Ohr Zarua*.[617]

Vestos from When a Woman Was Single

- Even if a woman kept a calendar from when she was single, she may generally discount her old cycles, unless it seems that she knew what she was doing according to halachah.
- The cycle before the wedding will carry forward for *yom hachodesh* and *onah beinonis*, but there is no *haflagah* to be carried forward.
- Ideally, a woman should be taught to keep a calendar from the time she gets engaged or even earlier, so the wedding can be planned accordingly.
- Depending on the specifics, a *kallah* who is taking birth control pills may not have to keep *vestos*. See "A *Kallah* Who Is Taking Birth Control Pills" below.

---

beinonis even when she established that she never begins bleeding before Day 35 of her cycle (for example). Other *Poskim* seem to learn the *Terumas HaDeshen* in its simplest form, that a *vest* was created, so there is no need to keep the *onah beinonis*.

615. Realistically, the only differences will be on a Hebrew month of 30 days, in which the *onah beinonis* and *yom hachodesh* are separate dates. The other difference would be if one holds the *Pleissi* or *Chavas Daas*, which are stringencies within *onah beinonis*.

616. Most *Poskim* who are lenient like Rav Yaacov Blau say that the woman should keep the *onah beinonis* as long as she got her period on Day 30 or earlier at least one time. The reason is because they hold the *vest* of the *Terumas HaDeshen* is a *vest l'shaos* (a *vest* dependent on time removed form an event, for example, 5 hours after immersion in the mikvah), which is uprooted after one time (*Shu"t Teshuras Shai*). The *Chavas Daas* (189:2) disgrees, and says a *vest l'shaos* is uprooted only after three times, and someone who keeps the *vest* of the *Terumas HaDeshen* should keep it until the woman's period comes on Day 30 or earlier three times, as with any *vest kavua*. Practically speaking, most *Poskim* are not lenient like the Chavas Daas regarding the *vest* of the *Terumas HaDeshen*.

617. This is Rav Yosef Shalom Elyashiv's ruling, although he recognizes that there is a disagreement among the *Poskim* in this regard and says one should ask a *she'eilah* when there is a need if they want to be more lenient.

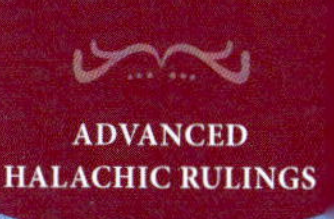

Calculating Vestos

A Woman Who Gets Her Period on Rosh Chodesh

- These are the main opinions mentioned in the *Poskim* regarding which *yom hachodesh* a woman should keep if she gets her period on 'ל of the Hebrew month and there is no 'ל in the upcoming month:
    - The woman skips next month's *yom hachodesh* (as there is no 'ל) and keeps the upcoming 'ל in 2 months' time.[618] She should keep the next 'כט of the month as the *onah beinonis*, as that is 30 days since her last *re'iyah*.
    - She keeps the next 'כט as the *onah beinonis*, since that is 30 days since her last *re'iyah*. She does not have a *yom hachodesh* the next month.[619]
    - She keeps the next 'כט as the *onah beinonis* and also keeps it as the *yom hachodesh*, since it is the last day in the month, just like 'ל was, which is the day of her last *re'iyah*.[620]
    - 'ל of the month is Rosh Chodesh, so she should keep the upcoming Rosh Chodesh ('א of the next month, in 31 days) as *yom hachodesh*.[621]
- Practically speaking,[622] the woman should keep the upcoming Rosh Chodesh (in 31 days) and the upcoming 'ל (in 2 months' time) as a stringency as *yom hachodesh*. She does not keep any stringencies beyond that, such as the *onas Ohr Zarua* or a *re'iyah* from a *mayan pasuach*. She of course also keeps the upcoming 'כט of the month as the *onah beinonis*.
- The *Bach* says that in the event that a woman gets her period on 'א of the month, then on 'ל, and again on 'א — all of which were the 1st day of Rosh Chodesh— she creates a *vest* for Rosh Chodesh even though the *re'iyos* were on different dates of the month.[623]

---

618. Rav Nissim Karelitz.

619. *Aruch HaShulchan*; *Shu"t Mahari Shteif.*

620. *Taharas Yisrael.*

621. *Shu"t Yad Sofer* and others.

622. Rav Yossi Stilerman.

623. 189:15.

- The halachah is like the opinion of the Bach, but the woman only creates a *vest* for the 1st day of Rosh Chodesh, not for both days.[624]

- In the event that a woman gets her period on Rosh Chodesh ('א of the month) and the following month has 2 days of Rosh Chodesh, she keeps only 'א as the *vest* yom *hachodesh*. She keeps 'ל as the *onah beinonis*, not as *yom hachodesh.*

Vest Kavua Nowadays

- It is almost impossible to find a woman who has a *vest kavua* nowadays, although 70 years ago in Yerushalayim it was more common.[625] The reasons for the change are that people nowadays have irregular schedules, eat processed foods, and live with lights on at night.[626]

- There is an opinion that nowadays we no longer need to be concerned about *vestos*. Being that the whole reason for a *vest she'eino kavua* is to see if the woman is establishing a *vest kavua*, which is so rare today, it makes sense to abolish *vestos* completely. Practically speaking, the halachah does not follow this opinion at all.

- In the event that a woman studies her dates and finds that she has a *vest kavua*, it is generally a fluke. However, she must observe each of her *vestos*, whether *kavua* or *eino kavua*, as detailed in the *Shulchan Aruch.*

- Some women claim that they had a *vest kavua* when they are single. This in itself is infrequent. Also, most girls do not know which colors are *tamei*, and are not tuned into the times of *neitz* and *shkiah*, in order to calculate when they began bleeding from a halachic standpoint.

---

624. *Aruch HaShulchan*; Rav Shmuel HaLevi Wosner.

625. In the times of *Chazal* it seems that nearly every woman had a *vest kavua*, with some women seeing at the exact same time, during the same *onah*, every single month. A woman who did not have a *vest kavua* was unique.

626. The *Chavas Daas* explains that light affects a woman's cycle. Women used to live on a very set schedule, operating from sunrise to *shkiah*, at which time they would go to sleep. Nowadays, electricity allows one to be active at all hours of the day and night. Another reason given is that women used to eat only natural foods, which would easily get digested and would keep their bodies on a natural schedule. Nowadays most women eat processed foods, and that affects the natural menstrual cycle.

Harchakos on a Vest

- According to the letter of the law, hugging and kissing are permitted on a *vest*, but a couple who is stringent will be blessed.[627] Along these lines, the couple may touch each other in an affectionate way but they are advised not to get too carried away. All other non-affectionate *harchakos*, such as passing and holding items, are permitted even on the *onas havest*.
- There is a disagreement whether a couple may sleep in the same bed on a *vest* (Rav Nissim Karelitz and Rav Shmuel HaLevi Wosner say to be stringent, and others are lenient). The couple can sleep in separate beds that are touching one another, but do not need to actually separate the beds.[628]
- All *harchakos* are permitted on the *onas Ohr Zarua* and on all other *vestos* that one keeps as a stringency (such as the *Pleissi*, the *Chavas Daas*, and so on), even touching affectionately. The worst that can happen is that the couple is not keeping a stringent custom.

Bedikos on the Vest

- The *Chazon Ish* says a woman is only obligated to do one *bedikas chorin v'sedakin* on the *onas havest*, although she may do more.[629] The *bedikah* should be performed toward the end of the *vest*.
- Rav Yosef Shalom Elyashiv says that on a *vest she'eino kavua* a woman is only obligated to do one *bedikah*. On a *vest kavua*

---

627. *Shach*. Some explain the Shach's promise that blessings will come on one who is stringent as follows: Since the couple knows that the woman may be getting her period on the *onas havest*, they should avoid hugging and kissing to the point where if she would get her period shortly, as anticipated, it will be difficult for them to get through the days that she will be a niddah. Meaning, a brief affectionate touch, hug, or kiss is permitted. It is the getting carried away that should be avoided.

628. It seems that sleeping in the same bed is, at most, touching in an affectionate way, which is the only type of touching that if one refrains from it, they will be blessed. Nevertheless, Rav Yitzchak Berkovits is a bit more stringent when teaching this, because the couple is only a few steps from marital relations when sleeping in the same bed. This stringency is brought in *Shulchan Aruch HaRav*, quoting the *Ramban*. The *Pischei Teshuvos* explains another reason why it is good to be stringent: the woman may get her period while sleeping, and her husband may unknowingly touch her, which is prohibited *mid'Rabbanan* even when there is no intention to have pleasure (this is also the Ramban's opinion, as brought in *siman* 195, "*Harchakos*").

629. Rav Nissim Karelitz.

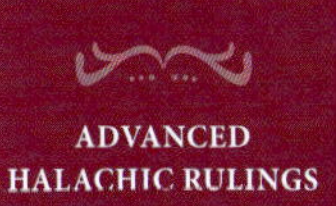

or *onah beinonis* (Day 30 only, not Day 31) she should do two *bedikos*, one at the beginning of the *vest* and one at the end.

- Rav Moshe Feinstein says a woman should do many *bedikos* throughout the *onah* of the *vest*.
- Rav Shmuel HaLevi Wosner says that when possible, a woman should do three *bedikos*: one in the beginning, one in the middle, and one at the end of the *vest*. If she does not, she should do one in the beginning and one at the end. If the woman really has a hard time with these *bedikos*, she can do one *bedikah* toward the end of the *vest*.
- The halachah is like the opinion of the Chazon Ish, and a woman should do one *bedikah* on the *onas havest*, whether it is a *vest kavua* or *eino kavua*. The reason for this leniency is to prevent women from cutting themselves unnecessarily.
- The ideal time to do the *bedikah* during a daytime *onah* is 20 minutes before *shkiah*.[630]
- The woman does not have to wake up before *neitz* to do a *bedikah* at the end of a nighttime *onah*. Rather, she should do the *bedikah* right before she goes to sleep. However, the *bedikah* must be performed after *shkiah*.
- If a woman wants to get up before *neitz* to perform the nighttime *bedikah*, it is commendable, but unnecessary.[631]
- For someone who keeps Rav Moshe Feinstein's "24-hour *onah*," the *bedikas havest* may be performed anytime during the 24 hours.[632]
- Many *Poskim* teach to do two *bedikos* on the *onas havest*. Some even rule that a woman who missed a *bedikah* on any type of *vest* must make it up during the next *onah* (after the *vest* has

---

630. If a woman performed a *bedikah* earlier in the day for a daytime *vest*, the *bedikah* is effective so long as it was performed after *neitz* (not *alos hashachar*), as we rule that *vestos* are calculated from *neitz* until *shkiah*.

631. Rav Nissim Karelitz, Rav Shmuel HaLevi Wosner, and many others hold a woman must perform the *bedikah* of a nighttime *onah* before *neitz* or when she goes to sleep, and then again in the morning when she wakes up, even if it is after *neitz*. Rav Yitzchak Berkovits holds if she checked before she went to sleep she is not required to wake up to perform a *bedikah* before *neitz* or to do another *bedikah* when she wakes up in the morning, as the morning is not even the *onas havest* anymore.

632. Rav Yitzchak Berkovits must be talking about someone who follows Rav Moshe Feinstein's rulings in regard to *vestos*, but follows the Chazon Ish's rulings in regard to the *bedikos*. Rav Moshe Feinstein holds to do many *bedikos* on the *vest*.

already finished),[633] even if it is a *vest she'eino kavua*. Practically speaking, we do not follow these *Poskim*.

- Rav Nissim Karelitz says the *bedikah* on the *vest* is to determine whether or not the period has arrived as anticipated. Therefore, a woman whose husband is out of town must perform the *bedikah* on the *vest*; she should not postpone the *bedikah* until just before her husband arrives home.

A Woman Who Is Unable to Perform Bedikos on Her Vest

- A woman who cannot perform *bedikos* on her *vest* because she has internal cuts should *lechatchilah* go to a *bodekes* who can perform the *bedikah* for her.
- If she did not go to a *bodekes* for any reason and a *vest she'eino kavua* passed, she is permitted to her husband even without a *bedikah*.
- A woman who did not perform a *bedikah* (or have one performed for her by a *bodekes*) on an *onah beinonis* or a *vest kavua* remains forbidden to her husband after the *vest* until a *bedikah* is performed, either by herself after her cuts have healed, or by a *bodekes*.
- A woman who has technical difficulties performing a *bedikah* on her *vest*, such as when she is traveling or does not have *bedikah* cloths, should try as best she can to extend herself and perform a *bedikah*, if at all possible. If she is unable to do so and missed the *bedikah*, she does not have to perform a *bedikah* after a *vest she'eino kavua*, but must perform a *bedikah* after a *vest kavua* or *onah beinonis*, as discussed.

633. Although it seems like an unnecessary stringency to follow the more stringent opinion of doing two *bedikos* on a *vest* and to add this *din* of making up a *bedikah* during the next *onah*, which can only serve to hurt her by doing a *bedikah* when it is not even a *vest*, *Rabbanim* often teach this way since women have a tendency to be lax in regard to these *bedikos*. *Rabbanim* do not want to make a distinction between a missed *bedikah* on an *onah beinonis* — in which case the couple remains prohibited to each other until the woman does a *bedikah* — and when the woman missed it for a *vest she'eino kavua*, because most people do not understand the difference and end up just being lenient in all cases.

Rav Shmuel HaLevi Wosner brings this *din* of doing a *bedikah* in the morning after a nighttime *onah*, and he adds that the woman should do *bedikos* on the *onas Ohr Zarua* and *Chavas Daas* (who considers *onah beinonis* as Day 31) as well. Practically speaking, most *Poskim*, including Rav Yizchok Berkovits, are lenient.

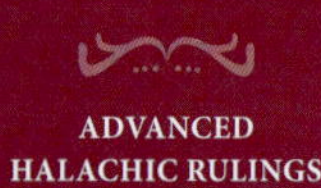

A Missed Bedikah on a Vest

- A *vest she'eino kavua* is kept out of concern that a woman is establishing a *vest kavua*. This being the case, a woman will not lose her status of *taharah* in the event that she missed the *bedikah*. Besides for missing a *mitzvah d'Rabbanan*, nothing else happens to this woman, and she should not do a *bedikah* when she remembers.
- The *onah beinonis* is in place of a *vest kavua*. If a woman misses a *bedikah* on this day — or on any *vest kavua* — she has to do a *bedikah* afterwards, when she remembers.
- The couple remains forbidden to one another after an *onah beinonis* or a *vest kavua* until the woman performs the *bedikah*. If she remembers during marital relations that she has not yet done a *bedikah*, her husband must be *poreish b'eiver meis*.
- Rav Nissim Karelitz says that a woman who missed a *bedikah* on an *onah beinonis* or a *vest kavua* is required to do a *bedikah* even if she remembers long after the *vest* passed, and even if she only remembers when she is no longer expecting her period, such as when she is pregnant.
- Rav Yosef Shalom Elyashiv says that when a woman missed a *bedikah* on an *onah beinonis* or a *vest kavua*, marital relations are prohibited until she does a *bedikah*, and hugging and kissing are permitted even before the *bedikah*.

Bathing and Swimming on a Vest

- Rav Nissim Karelitz says that a woman should refrain from taking a bath or swimming on the *onas havest*, unless she performs the *bedikah* of the *vest* before she begins bathing or swimming. After bathing or swimming, she should *lechatchilah* not do the *bedikah* of the *onas havest* afterwards for 8 minutes, and *bedi'eved* for 3 minutes.
- Rav Yosef Shalom Elyashiv says that a woman may swim or bathe on a *vest* after she has performed a *bedikah*. She may shower on a *vest*, even without performing a *bedikah*, since no water directly enters *oso makom*.
- Practically speaking, a woman may *lechatchilah* shower, swim, or bathe on a *vest*. If she does, she is not required to do any extra

bedikos, neither beforehand nor afterwards.[634] A woman should avoid intentionally cleansing herself internally on an *onas havest*.[635] See Advanced Rulings, Taharah, headline "Washing Before the *Hefsek Taharah*" (page 312) for a discussion about the how long a woman should wait before doing a *bedikah* after washing herself internally.

Saying "I Did a Bedikah" on a Vest

- Many *Poskim* hold that a woman must verbally state on an *onas havest* that she did a *bedikah*,[636] as she is to a certain degree considered like one who has a status of *tumah* once the *onas havest* arrives.[637]
- Practically speaking, a woman should tell her husband that she has performed the *bedikah* on each *vest*, whether *kavua* or *eino kavua*. This is a *mitzvah d'Rabbanan*, and is not a problem if it was not done.[638]

---

634. *Chazon Ish*.

635. Rav Yitzchak Berkovits says that women should not clean internally (douche) on a *vest* or during *shivah nekiyim*. Aside from the halachic aspect, doctors tell women that it is best if they never douche, because a woman's body naturally maintains a balanced pH level, and when a woman douches she throws the pH balance off and the body compensates by producing more yeast than necessary, which can lead to a painful yeast infection. In any case, it should be avoided during *vestos* and *shivah nekiyim*.

636. *Chavas Daas, Chiddushim, siman kattan* 32.

637. This seems to be the simple explanation of the *Shulchan Aruch* (184:11). The *Pischei Teshuvah*, ibid., *siman kattan* 27 quotes the *Chavas Daas*, which says she has to specifically tell her husband she is *tehorah*, even if she is lying next to him on the bed. However, the case that the *Shulchan Aruch* is talking about is a woman who had a *vest kavua*, who is now after the *vest* passed. According to the natural state of this woman she should be *temei'ah*, since she should have begun bleeding on the *vest*. Therefore, the Chavas Daas holds she should tell her husband why she is contradicting what he expects her status to be, by lying next to him. However, the Chavas Daas is not discussing the case of a woman who does not have a *vest kavua* who simply needs a *bedikah* on the *vest she'eino kavua* to be permitted to her husband, because even if she missed the *bedikah* on the *vest* and lay down next to him, he will not necessarily expect her to be *temei'ah*. Such a woman is not considered *temei'ah* (184:9), and if she missed telling her husband that she did a *bedikah* she is still permitted to him. It seems Rav Yitzchak Berkovits holds one should fulfill all the opinions on the topic by saying she did a *bedikah* if possible, but it is certainly not a problem in the event that she did not say, especially since if she did not do the *bedikah* itself this is not a problem in the case of a *vest she'eino kavua*.

638. Rav Shmuel HaLevi Wosner.

Marital Relations on a Vest

- The *Pardes Rimonim* says a couple that realizes in the middle of marital relations that it is an *onas havest* (whether *kavua* or *eino kavua*) should separate immediately — before the woman actually begins to bleed, which, since it is a *vest*, could occur at any moment — and the husband should not wait to be *poreish b'eiver meis.*

- The *Chavas Daas* says the husband must be *poreish b'eiver meis* in such a case,[639] so as not to have pleasure when he comes out.

- Rav Shmuel HaLevi Wosner says the husband should generally be *poreish* as soon as possible, as per the view of the Pardes Rimonim, unless that will cause him to be *mazria*, in which case he should wait to be *poreish b'eiver meis.*

- Practically speaking, in the event that a couple realizes that they are having marital relations illicitly on an *onas havest*, or if they realize while in the middle of marital relations that an *onah beinonis* or a *vest kavua* passed without the wife having done a *bedikah*, the husband must push himself up and be *poreish b'eiver meis.*

Immersing on a Vest

- It is prohibited for a woman to immerse in the mikvah on an *onas havest*, because marital relations are prohibited.[640]

- The *Chasam Sofer* says a woman may immerse in the mikvah on the *onas Ohr Zarua* because it is only kept as a stringency.

---

639. The *Chavas Daas* actually says the husband should only be *poreish b'eiver meis* if they are having marital relations on the *vest* when the wife knows that blood is emerging during marital relations. If, however, she says that she experiences a *hargashah* during marital relations, he does not have to be *poreish* at all. Practically speaking, many *Poskim* say he should be *poreish b'eiver meis* when the woman remembers during marital relations that it is a *vest*, even if she does not specifically know that she is currently actually bleeding.

640. *Aruch HaShulchan*; Rav Nissim Karelitz. Others say that the woman should immerse in the mikvah so they can maximize their time together in regard to hugging and kissing (which are not recommended anyway on a *vest*, but these *Poskim* waive that, being that it is a mikvah night). See *Pischei Teshuvah* 184:24. Practically speaking, Rav Yitzchak Berkovits is stringent, as are many other *Poskim*, not to allow a *tevilah* any time marital relations are prohibited according to halachah, but to allow a *tevilah* when marital relations are prohibited as a stringency (such as on *vestos* that are kept as a stringency, or Tishah B'Av that is *nidcheh* to Sunday).

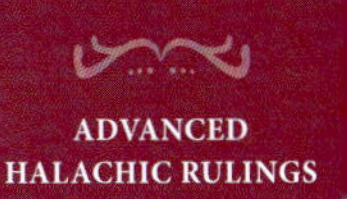

- Rav Shmuel HaLevi Wosner says a woman may immerse in the mikvah during *yemei hamevuchim*.[641]
- If a woman immerses in the mikvah on an *onas havest*, the *tevilah* is valid, but the couple must keep all *harchakos* as though she did not immerse, until after the *onas havest* passes. Once the *onas havest* passes, everything becomes permitted, and there is no need for the woman to immerse again.

When the Husband Travels Away

- The *Shulchan Aruch* says a husband who is leaving his wife for some time has an obligation to demonstrate extra affection towards her before he leaves,[642] even if this day is on the *onas havest*.[643]
- Rav Nissim Karelitz says that the extra affection that the *Shulchan Aruch* says can be done on an *onas havest* is hugging and kissing, not marital relations, which are prohibited on an *onas havest*.[644] The couple should be careful not to get too carried away with hugging and kissing, as marital relations are prohibited.
- Rav Nissim Karelitz says that in the event that a man is traveling away from his wife on an *onas Ohr Zarua*, he should be lenient regarding the *onas Ohr Zarua*, and marital relations are permitted.
- The *Rama* says that a man who is traveling for the purpose of a mitzvah, such as to learn Torah or to fund-raise for *tzedakah*,

641. The woman should follow the protocol of *yemei hamevuchim* and perform an external wipe with a colored tissue before marital relations.

642. 184:10.

643. The *She'arim HaMetzuyanim B'Halachah* brings from *Acharonim* the reason to be lenient in the case of a husband who is traveling away, because the wife may be nervous that her husband will be unfaithful while he is away from her. He is therefore allowed to show her that he is not abandoning her in any way. It therefore follows that when he is going for the purpose of a mitzvah, the wife will not think her husband is abandoning her for ulterior motives, because she sees he is fueled by the desire to do God's will.

644. Although the Rama cites an opinion that marital relations for one who will be traveling away are permitted on a *vest*, most Acharonim (and the Rama himself) hold that marital relations are prohibited, but other forms of affection are permitted and encouraged, even though it says that blessing will come to one who generally keeps *harchakos* on a *vest*. See Advanced Rulings, Vestos, headline "Marital Relations on a Vest" (page 393).

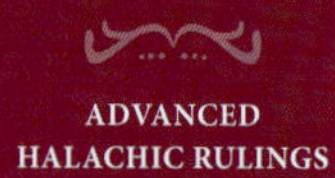

is not obligated to demonstrate extra affection. If he is going on a business trip, however, he is obligated to demonstrate extra affection before leaving.[645]

- Rav Shmuel HaLevi Wosner says that a husband who is leaving for the purpose of a mitzvah is not obligated to have marital relations, but still must show extra affection. The reason marital relations are not required is either because he is busy with a mitzvah, and one who is busy with one mitzvah is exempt from a different mitzvah, or because he may become delayed by his wife and may no longer be able to perform the mitzvah he is supposed to be leaving for.
- Rav Nissim Karelitz says that a man who is usually home — as opposed to someone who travels often — and leaves for even a few days has the status of one who is traveling, and thus the accompanying obligations.
- Rav Yosef Shalom Elyashiv says that a man who leaves the country, even for a short time, has the status of one who is traveling away.
- A husband is not obligated to show any extra affection the night before his wife goes on a trip, because she is the one doing the "abandoning."
- Rav Shmuel HaLevi Wosner says that one is considered "traveling away" if he will not return within one *onah*, he is traveling overseas, or he is leaving for a short time but does not know when he will return (such as if he leaves for short-term army service, in which a dangerous situation may arise).
- The *Rama* says that a man must delay his trip if he is leaving within an *onah* of his wife's going to the mikvah.
- The *Pleissi* says that a trip need not be delayed in the event that the wife is going to the mikvah on her *onas havest*, because marital relations are anyway not allowed on that night.
- Rav Shmuel HaLevi Wosner and Rav Nissim Karelitz say that when a couple is traveling together, the husband is not obligated to show extra affection.

645. Rav Shmuel HaLevi Wosner.

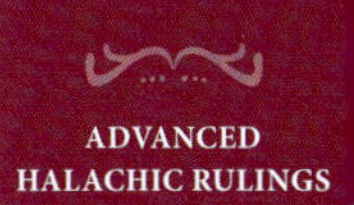

A Vest on a Mikvah Night or on the Wedding Night

- In the event that the wedding night occurs on a *vest*, the couple is permitted to have *yichud* and hug and kiss, but not have marital relations, unless the *kallah* is currently on birth control pills,[646] in which case the implications that are stated above would apply.
- The *Chasam Sofer* says marital relations are permitted on the *onas Ohr Zarua* if it is a mikvah night, but not when the mikvah night is the actual *onas havest*.
- See Advanced Rulings, Taharah, headline "A Vest on a Mikvah Night or on the Wedding Night" (page 395) regarding a mikvah night that falls on a *vest*.

The Onas Ohr Zarua

- The *Ohr Zarua* says that besides for observing the *onas havest*, a woman should keep the *onah before* the *vest*.
- The *Shulchan Aruch HaRav* and *She'arim HaMetzuyanim B'Halachah* say many people only observe the *onas Ohr Zarua* for a *vest kavua*.[647]
- Practically speaking, those who observe the *onas Ohr Zarua* should do so even for a *vest she'eino kavua*.[648]
- Rav Moshe Feinstein says the *onas havest* is always the entire date — night and day — of the *re'iyah*. In addition, one should

646. Rav Yosef Shalom Elyashiv.

647. The logic behind this opinion may be that a *vest kavua* tells with a certain amount of accuracy when a woman is expected to begin bleeding. The *onas Ohr Zarua* would then reinforce the *vest*, in case the woman deviates up to one *onah*. A *vest she'eino kavua* is an educated guess as to when the upcoming period may come, but it is certainly not accurate in terms of percentage because a woman keeps two *vestos she'einam kevu'im* a month, aside from the *onah beinonis*, and at best only one will be accurate in any given month. That said, the *onas Ohr Zarua* is only extending the guesswork another *onah*. On the other hand, it could be argued that since the halachah is trying to avoid the scenario of a woman beginning to bleed during marital relations, the best time to keep the *onas Ohr Zarua* is when there is even more guesswork, when she is only keeping *vestos she'einam kevu'im*, and not when there is a *vest kavua*. Practically speaking, the *Ohr Zarua* is kept for all *vestos*.

648. Rav Shmuel HaLevi Wosner and most other *Poskim*.

keep the previous *onah* for the *onas Ohr Zarua*, for a total of 36 hours.[649]

- Practically speaking, Rav Moshe Feinstein's "24-hour *onah*" is generally not taught, although some do observe it. A person who has a family custom to keep it should do so.
- Rav Nissim Karelitz says the Chazon Ish told the author of *Taharas Bas Yisrael* not to mention the *onas Ohr Zarua* in his *sefer*, because he held it is a stringency for *bnei Torah*, and should not be spread to the masses who may not be ready to accept it.
- Likewise, Rav Moshe Feinstein says *bnei Torah* should be taught about the *onas Ohr Zarua*, and others should not.[650]
- Rav Shmuel HaLevi Wosner says a woman should do *bedikos* on the *onas Ohr Zarua* as she would on the *onas havest*. Practically speaking, however, there is no obligation to do a *bedikah* on the *onas Ohr Zarua*,[651] and it should be taught that one should not to do it.
- Practically speaking, the *onas Ohr Zarua* should be observed by *bnei Torah* as a stringent custom for all *vestos*, unless someone keeps the *Pleissi* on an *onah beinonis*. See footnotes for a discussion on this topic.

When the Onas Ohr Zarua Should Not Be Kept

- The times to be lenient and not keep the *onas Ohr Zarua* are the following:
  - In a case of a woman who has a hard time keeping halachah
  - When the couple has *vestos* 4 days in a row, or when a *Rav* has another reason to be lenient, such as *shalom bayis*, a hard time getting to the mikvah due to staining, or the like

649. *Igros Moshe, Yoreh Dei'ah* 3:48.

650. Rav Yitzchak Berkovits often says that not all people learning Torah are *bnei Torah* and not all people who do not spend their entire days learning Torah are not *bnei Torah*. A *Rav* should use his intuition to determine whether a couple is ready to keep a stringency and when the time has come to be lenient.

651. Rav Yosef Shalom Elyashiv; Rav Nissim Karelitz.

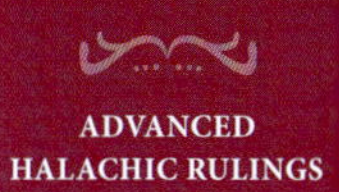

- On a mikvah night, the night of the wedding, or an *onah* that the husband is leaving or returning from a trip, after consulting with a *Rav*[652]

- Rav Yosef Shalom Elyashiv says whenever one is lenient regarding the *onas Ohr Zarua*, it should be treated as *yemei hamevuchim*, and a *bedikah* should be performed.[653]

- Practically speaking, if a couple is lenient regarding the *onas Ohr Zarua* that precedes the first *vest* of the month, the woman is not required to perform a *bedikah* or even an external wipe. If the couple is lenient regarding a subsequent *onas Ohr Zarua* that occurs after the first *vest* of the month, the woman should do an external wipe with a colored tissue before intimacy, until she becomes *temei'ah* or gets a positive pregnancy test. This halachah would not apply in the event of an unusually early *vest haflagah*.

- Rav Nissim Karelitz and Rav Shmuel HaLevi Wosner say *hataras nedarim* (annulment of vows) is not required for one to stop keeping the *onas Ohr Zarua*.

- A couple who are being taught to keep the *onas Ohr Zarua* should be taught to keep it starting from the beginning of their marriage.[654]

The Pleissi

- The *Sidrei Taharah* says when a woman gets her period during the day she keeps her *onah beinonis* during the day, and when she gets her period at night she keeps her *onah beinonis* at night, as with each *vest*.[655]

---

652. Rav Yosef Shalom Elyashiv; Rav Shmuel HaLevi Wosner.

653. This is in accordance with Rav Yosef Shalom Elyashiv's ruling regarding *yemei hamevuchim*.

654. Rav Yosef Shalom Elyashiv; Rav Nissim Karelitz. Some *chassan* and *kallah* teachers teach to keep the *onas Ohr Zarua* after the first year of marriage. Rav Yitzchak Berkovits is against this practice, as he holds that the fundamentals practiced in one's home from the beginning of marriage are the ones that stick, and most people will have a difficult time implementing a stringency later on. The tone set in the home from the beginning will be the foundation upon which the home is built, and that foundation should contain the stringencies and halachic viewpoints the home stands for.

655. 189:31.

- The *Pleissi* says the *onah beinonis* is always a complete Hebrew date of 24 hours. The *Pleissi*'s *onah* is always the night and the day of the *onah beinonis*. This means that whatever date the *onah beinonis* falls on — no matter if the period came during the day or the night — the woman will always keep the night and the following day, which is one complete Hebrew date.
- When keeping the *Pleissi*'s *onah*, the extra *onah* is kept as a restriction from marital relations, but does not require a *bedikah*. The regular *bedikah* of the *onas havest* should be performed in the *onas havest* of last month's *re'iyah*, as by all *vestos*.
- Rav Yosef Shalom Elyashiv says the *Pleissi*'s *onah* should only be kept as a stringency on Day 30, not on Day 31.

The Pleissi Versus the Ohr Zarua

- If the *onos* of the *Ohr Zarua*, the *Pleissi*, and the *Chavas Daas* are put together, a woman who gets her period at night will keep that night for *onah beinonis*, the day before for the *onas Ohr Zarua*, the next day for the *Pleissi*, and the next night for the *Chavas Daas*.
- Rav Yosef Shalom Elyashiv says one should not keep both the *onos* of the *Pleissi* and the *Ohr Zarua* on an *onah beinonis*, but should only keep the *Pleissi*, and one who keeps both is a "*ksil haholeich b'choshech* — a fool who walks in the dark."[656]

---

656. *Sefer Mishnas HaShulchan*, which brings Rav Yosef Shalom Elyashiv's rulings in *hilchos niddah*, states that on an *onah beinonis* one should only keep the *Pleissi*, not the *onas Ohr Zarua*, even if the *onas havest* is at night. This is in sync with how Rav Yitzchak Berkovits understands Rav Elyashiv's ruling.

In *Shiurei Shevet HaLevi* 189:1:5, Rav Shmuel HaLevi Wosner says one should keep the *Pleissi* and *onas Ohr Zarua* when the *onas havest* is at night. If the *vest* is during the day, the woman should only keep the *vest*, as well as the night before. It is not clear whether that night should be kept as the *Pleissi*, in which case it is halachically prohibited, or as the *onas Ohr Zarua*, in which case it is prohibited as a stringency in *vestos*. He seems to hold that it is as a *din* of the *Pleissi*, but will be lenient in extenuating circumstances.

Rav Mati Friedman pointed out that it could very well be that in the case of an *onah beinonis* when the *onas havest* was during the daytime, one should not keep the *Pleissi* at night and add the *onas Ohr Zarua* to the day before, because that would mean adding stringencies onto stringencies. It may be that Rav Yosef Shalom Elyashiv would agree that if the *onas havest* of the *onah beinonis* is at night, one should keep the *Pleissi* the following day and add the day before for the *onas Ohr Zarua*. This seems to be how Rav Wosner explains the topic, and is not the way that the *Mishnas HaShulchan* explains what Rav Elyashiv holds.

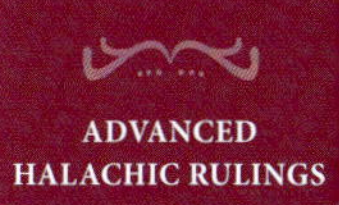

- Practically speaking, people in Eretz Yisrael keep Day 30 with the *Pleissi* and on Day 31 only keep the *vest* itself (i.e., the *Chavas Daas* without the *Pleissi*), unless Day 31 also happens to be the *haflagah* or another *vest* for which they keep the *onas Ohr Zarua* as well. This is really only applicable on a month that has 29 days.

Yemei HaMevuchim

- The *Chazon Ish* (based on the *Chavas Daas*[657]) says that the span of days within which a woman normally gets her period (for example, between 'ב and 'ו) is called *yemei hamevuchim*, and the couple is forbidden to have marital relations during these days.
- Rav Moshe Feinstein and the *Minchas Yitzchak* say a woman is not actually prohibited during these days, but she needs to do a *bedikah* before marital relations.[658]
- In the event that a woman begins to bleed during marital relations on a day that she had no reason to expect it, the couple had no control over it, and they do not need any atonement. However, an *onah* during which she was expecting to get her period is not a situation over which they had no control,[659] and

657. The Chavas Daas holds that a woman is prohibited during the span of the days she normally gets her period, even if she knows she did not establish a *vest* during this time. The Chazon Ish holds that she is prohibited thoughout all these days when she is not sure whether or not she established a *vest*. But in the event that she knows that she did not establish a *vest*, she does not have to separate during the days that she knows are not *vestos*. Practically speaking, the Chazon Ish is stringent like the Chavas Daas because most women do not keep calendars from their single days, so there is a chance she established a *vest* without knowing (*Chut Shani*).

658. The *Rif* says a woman who does not have a *vest kavua* should do *bedikos* three times before and after marital relations to determine if she is a woman who bleeds due to marital relations. The *Rosh* says she should always do *bedikos* as long as she does not have a *vest kavua*. The halachah generally follows the *Rif* in the case of such a woman, however, Rav Moshe Feinstein extends the *din* of the *Rosh* to include *yemei hamevuchim*.

659. Rav Yosef Shalom Elyashiv says a woman should do a *bedikah* before marital relations once her *onah beinonis* passes. Rav Reuven Feinstein says she should do an external wipe with colored tissues to determine that she has not begun to bleed, and if anything happens afterward, the couple is considered as though they had no control over the situation because the proper precautions were taken. Once the woman's *vestos* arrive she can be reasonably expected to get her period, and surely after the *vestos* pass she can be assumed to begin bleeding shortly. Although the *vestos* she established are generally kept as a concern for a specific cause (such as *yom hachodesh*, *haflagah*, etc.), nevertheless,

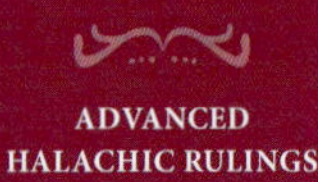

if she bleeds during marital relations on such an *onah* the couple requires atonement.

- Rav Yitzchak Berkovits says a woman should do an external wipe with colored toilet paper before marital relations during *yemei hamevuchim* so she will know if she began to bleed. She should use colored toilet paper so she will not become *temei'ah* if she finds a *kesem*, but will at the same time know if she started bleeding.[660] She must be careful to do a wipe — and not perform a *bedikah* — or she loses all the leniencies of *kesamim*!

- In the event that the color does not look good, the couple should refrain from marital relations until the issue clears up or the woman actually gets her period.

Establishing a Vest Due to a Mayan Pasuach

- Rav Yosef Shalom Elyashiv and Rav Shmuel HaLevi Wosner say that in the event that a woman gets her period one month on a certain day, and the next month on that day she has a *mayan pasuach* (she began to bleed during an earlier *onah* but is still bleeding during this *onah*), she should keep *vestos* from the second *re'iyah* according to the halachah and the *re'iyah* from the *mayan pasuach* as a stringency.[661] If she begins to bleed twice on this day from a *mayan sasum*, and the *re'iyah* during the third month on this day is from a *mayan pasuach*, the woman establishes a *vest* as a stringency. She should keep the new *vest* as a stringency, but also treat the last *vest she'eino kavua* as a *vest* for the upcoming month.

Example for *yom hachodesh*: If a woman gets her period twice on Day 28, then gets her period on Days 27 (or even 26, 25, etc.) and continues to bleed on Day 28, she creates a *vest kavua* for Day 28. She

---

a woman must take precautions so she will not begin to bleed during marital relations. Thus, we require an external wipe before marital relations.

660. A woman who finds some blood on the external wipe before marital relations during *yemei hamevuchim* should be advised not to come to a *safeik hargashah* by performing an unnecessary *bedikah*, looking in the toilet, or having marital relations. Most *Rabbanim* tell such a woman to wear a pad for 12 hours and call afterwards if she did not get her period. If the pad is clean, she may have marital relations if an external wipe shows that she is clean. If there is staining on the pad, the *Rav* may tell the couple to wait until she clears up or gets her period. This 12-hour buffer may change depending on the circumstances. In all circumstances such as these, a couple should seek the guidance of a competent *Rav*.

661. Based on *Pischei Teshuvah* 184:8.

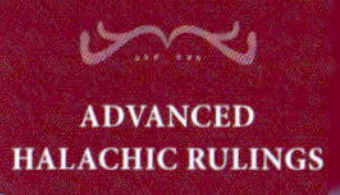

should keep Day 27 as a *vest she'eino kavua*, and Day 28 as a *vest kavua* as a stringency.

Example for *haflagah*: A woman gets her period twice after 35 days and then gets it again after 33 and continues bleeding into "Day 35." She should keep Day 35 as a *vest haflagah* as a stringency, and the *haflagah* of 33 days as a *haflagah eino kevuah*.[662]

- The *Pischei Megadim* is lenient regarding the entire concept of a woman establishing a *vest* due to a *mayan pasuach*.
- Practically speaking, one should be stringent as per Rav Yosef Shalom Elyashiv's opinion. A woman should do a *bedikah* on the *onas havest* on the month following the *re'iyah* from a *mayan pasuach* to determine if she is establishing a *vest* due to a *mayan pasuach*,[663] but should not keep another stringency on top of the *vest*, such as the *onas Ohr Zarua* or the *Pleissi*.
- Rav Yosef Shalom Elyashiv says that a woman does not establish a *vest* due to a *mayan pasuach* on a *vest* that is not kept after one *re'iyah*, such as a *vest hakefitzos* or *vest l'yemei hashavua*.

---

662. It seems that someone who keeps the *Beis Meir* should not keep this stringency of establishing a *vest* from a *mayan pasuach* for a *vest haflagah*, because the two contradict each other. The *Beis Meir* says that a short *haflagah* does not uproot a longer *haflagah* because the short date resets the clock, so that the longer *haflagah* was never passed, and was therefore never uprooted. That means that according to the *Beis Meir*, a woman who has a 35 day *haflagah* and then gets her period on Day 33 keeps both Day 33 and Day 35 the following month; Day 33 reset the clock and is the "main *re'iyah*," and Day 35, which was never uprooted, is observed as the old *vest haflagah*. A woman who is concerned about a *haflagah* from a *mayan pasuach* is in fact being concerned about the exact opposite. She is concerned that the period that came on the shorter *haflagah* is not really the main *re'iyah*, but is just additional bleeding. The "real *re'iyah*" only occurs later, on the longer *haflagah*. This means to say that not only does the shorter *haflagah* not reset the clock, but it is not even the real *re'iyah* to begin with, rather, it is only additional bleeding.

663. To clarify: A woman who gets her period onה' of the Jewish month creates a *vest she'eino kavua* forה' of the following month, during which she must do a *bedikah* in the *onah* in which she began to bleed (whether night or day). If the period that month comes onד' of the month and continues into ה', the woman has a *vest she'eino kavua* for ד' of the upcoming month, but did not uproot ה', since she was in fact bleeding during ה'. She should thus perform a *bedikah* on ד' of the following month, as that is her *vest*, but should also do a *bedikah* on ה', as she had a *re'iyah* from a *mayan pasuach*. The fact that she was bleeding on ה' does not count as a second *re'iyah* toward establishing a *vest* until she bleeds from a *mayan sasum* — that is, the bleeding starts on this date — although it does keep the *vest* alive. In the event that she bleeds twice from a *mayan sasum* (as long as the *vest* is kept alive by her bleeding from a *mayan pasuach*) and the third time from a *mayan pasuach*, the woman has created a *vest* as a stringency according to Rav Yosef Shalom Elyashiv. Someone who is concerned about this opinion should perform a *bedikah* on the *onah* of a *re'iyah* from a *mayan pasuach* to determine if a *vest* was established.

- Rav Shmuel HaLevi Wosner says that if a woman establishes a *vest* and then deviates from the *vest* for 3 months, but does not establish another day, and then bleeds on the originally established day from a *mayan pasuach*, the old *vest kavua* does not reawaken. This is in contrast to an old *vest kavua* reawakening if a new *kavua* has not been established and she bleeds again on the old *vest kavua*.

The Beis Meir: A Short Haflagah After a Long Haflagah

- The *Beis Meir* and the *Ramban* say that in the event that a woman's period occurred with a shorter *haflagah* than it did last month, it does not uproot the longer *vest*, but also does not uphold it.[664] The reason for this is if a woman begins to bleed one month — let's say after 35 days — and the next month gets her period after a shorter *haflagah* — say after 33 days — she never passed (i.e., undid) the longer *haflagah*, because Day 35 of the second *re'iyah* is really Day 3 of a new *re'iyah*, since a new onset of the period starts the count over again.[665]
- Rav Shmuel HaLevi Wosner says a shorter *vest* does uproot a longer *vest*, unlike the Ramban's opinion.[666]
- Rav Yosef Shalom Elyashiv says a longer *haflagah* stops being a concern when three shorter *haflagos* happen, even when they are three different amounts of days and do not create a *vest kavua*.[667]
- Practically speaking, one should not rely on Rav Shmuel HaLevi Wosner's opinion (which is based on the *Shach*) unless the shorter *vest* is a *vest kavua*, which is extremely rare. One should be concerned about the longer *vest* unless it was broken by an even longer one, a shorter *vest kavua*, or three *haflagos* that are shorter than the longer *vest*.

---

664. This is also the opinion of the Shulchan Aruch HaRav, the Sidrei Taharah, the Pleissi, and others. The *Shulchan Aruch HaRav* says the Shach and Rama, who disagree with this *din*, only said that a shorter *vest* uproots a longer *vest* because they never saw the words of the *Ramban* inside; had they seen the *Ramban*, they certainly would not have have disagreed with him. Practically speaking, Rav Yitzchak Berkovits agrees with this.

665. *Sidrei Taharah*; *Pleissi*; Rav Nissim Karelitz.

666. This is also the opinion of the Shach, Prishah, Bach, Chasam Sofer, and others.

667. *Shevet HaLevi* and others.

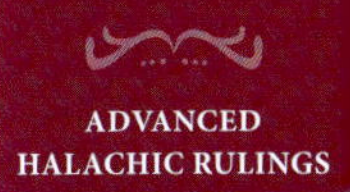

- Rav Yosef Shalom Elyashiv says that a woman who has a fluke *vest* (for example, she bled after 92 days) does not have to continually be concerned about the longer *vest*. She breaks it by deviating from the *vest* for 1 month, just like any other *vest she'eino kavua*.

Note: Although Rav Yitzchak Berkovits is stringent and follows the Ramban's opinion, many *Poskim* are lenient. It is important to note that Rav Berkovits is adamantly stringent because he holds that what used to be known as the "stringency of the *Beis Meir*" is actually a clear *Ramban*.

- Those who keep the *onas Ohr Zarua* keep it even on a *Beis Meir*.[668]
- The *haflagah* of the *Beis Meir* is calculated from the last *re'iyah*, not from the last *vest*, like all *vestos*.[669]

The Aviasif

- The *Aviasif* says an *onah* is 12 hours,[670] and is not based on actual day or night.[671]
- Practically speaking, the halachah does not follow the Aviasif's opinion.[672]

Which Vestos Should Be Kept While One Is Taking Pills

- A woman who is taking birth control pills (usually 21- or 28-day cycles) which regulate her cycle does not need to keep any *vestos*

668. Although Rav Yitzchak Berkovits says not to keep the *onas Ohr Zarua* for stringencies in *vestos*, he says to keep it for the *Beis Meir*, because he considers the *Beis Meir* as the actual halachah, and not as a stringency.

669. Rav Nissim Karelitz.

670. See *Shach* 194:7 and *Taz*, *siman kattan* 2.

671. The Shach in the *Nekudas HaKesef* explains the *Aviasif*, likes the explanation, and rules like the Aviasif. The Taz asks many questions on the *Aviasif*, and disregards this position.

672. Rav Shmuel HaLevi Wosner cites the Chasam Sofer and others who are stringent and follow the Aviasif's opinion. Practically speaking, the majority of *Poskim* are lenient.

that month if she will be taking the pills on her *vestos*.[673] Once she goes off the pill (or starts taking the placebo), she should treat the days until her period arrives as *yemei hamevuchim*, doing an external wipe with colored tissues (not a *bedikah*) before marital relations until she establishes three times in which *onah* her period will occur. She does not need to do any *bedikos* for *vestos* that month.

- If during the month that she is taking pills the woman has *vestos* from a period that came about while she was on pills (i.e., she took pills last month which regulated her cycle to some extent) and she is not taking pills this month on the *vest*, she should keep only the *onah beinonis*,[674] and need not keep the *vestos* of *yom hachodesh* and *haflagah*.
- If a woman has old *vestos* during the month that she starts taking pills, that is, *vestos* from a period that came about naturally when she was not on pills, and she is not taking pills on the *vest*, she should keep those *vestos* that month.
- If a woman establishes 3 months in a row that her period comes in a certain *onah* after she stops taking the pills (or starts the placebo), she creates a *vest achilah* for that *onah*. She should keep that *onah* in the following months as her *vest*, for all matters.

---

673. This is a common form of birth control, used by many women. In general, a woman takes one pill every day of the month from a certain day in their cycle (usually Day 4 or so) for a certain amount of days and gets her period 2–4 days after she stops taking the pill. Some companies make placebo pills (usually red or blue) for the time she should get her period, which do not actually affect the cycle at all; they just keep the woman in the mindset that she should be taking a pill every day of the year. The period usually arrives a certain number of hours after she stops taking the pills every month, and this ruling saves her a few *vestos* monthly.

674. This ruling very rarely actually comes into practice, as explained: A woman taking a dual-hormone pill which regulates the cycle generally starts taking the pill a few days into her cycle and continues taking them for 21 or 28 days, after which she starts taking placebos for around a week. If she is on a 21-day cycle of pills, she is going to stop taking the pills around Day 25 or 26 and get her period around Day 28, so keeping *onah beinonis* in this case will not apply, since it will never arrive. If she is on a 28-day cycle of pills, she will be taking the dual-hormone pills through *onah beinonis*, so she will not keep any of the standard *vestos* that month at all (unless she established that she bleeds a certain amount of *onos* after starting the placebo), so *onah beinonis* will not be kept that month at all either. This ruling becomes relevant the month after she stops taking the pills — since last month's period was induced by the pill, she only keeps *onah beinonis*. Also, if she decides to extend the 21-day cycle of pills a couple of days, causing her period to come after Day 30, but she will not be taking hormone pills on the *onah beinonis*, she should in fact keep *onah beinonis*.

- A woman who is taking a form of birth control that does not alter her cycle should keep all *vestos* as usual.[675]
- Rav Yosef Shalom Elyashiv says that after a woman stops taking pills she should keep the last *yom hachodesh* she experienced "naturally," before she started the pills, and should keep it as a *vest* for all matters.
- Practically speaking, one should follow Rav Yosef Shalom Elyashiv's opinion as a stringency, refraining from marital relations and doing a *bedikah* on that *onas havest*. The couple should not keep any stringencies on top of it, such as refraining from hugging and kissing, the *onas Ohr Zarua*, and so on.

A Kallah Who Is Taking Birth Control Pills

- Rav Yosef Shalom Elyashiv says if a *kallah* is currently taking birth control pills to push off her period and the *vest* in on the wedding night, she can assume that she will not bleed that night, and may have marital relations even without a *bedikah*, even if she has not yet established that this pill works for her.[676]
- Rav Moshe Feinstein says marital relations are forbidden in the event that the *kallah* went off the pill and it is a *vest*. If it is not a *vest* but she may nevertheless begin to bleed because it has been a long time since her last *re'iyah*, she should be careful. Rav Yitzchak Berkovits says a *kallah* in this situation should do an external wipe with colored tissues, similar to *yemei hamevuchim*.

675. Examples of forms of birth control that do not affect the woman's cycle are spermicides, sponge, diaphragm, and an IUD. The NuvaRing introduces a small amount of hormones directly into the woman's blood stream, and, while its makers do not claim that it sets her cycles on any sort of pattern, one side effect of using the NuvaRing is "changes in menstrual cycle." A woman who is using the NuvaRing should be treated like a woman who is on birth control pills, as both of these affect the body in a similar way. Practically speaking, a woman who wants to take any form of birth control should be sure to speak to their *Rav*, as the *Poskim* differ in their opinions regarding when to allow a woman to take contraceptives, and which contraceptives are permissible for use.

676. Most *Rabbanim* say they are against *kallos* taking pills before the wedding, for many reasons. It seems that many women miscarry the first few months after the wedding and *Rabbanim* attribute this to the artificial hormones that are still in her systems. Doctors argue this point and say pills have no long-term effect (more than 1 month) on pregnancies. Practically speaking, most *Rabbanim* prefer, in theory, that the *kallah* go "natural" but will not argue the point, because many *kallos* will try to do anything to prevent a *chuppas niddah*.

- Practically speaking, many *Poskim* say a *Rav* should preferably try to determine that a specific pill actually works for her.[677] Once she shows that it works for her to push off the period and avoid staining, even if it was just used for 1 month, it can be relied on that it will work in the future. This ruling may be used if at all necessary (for example, in the event of a short engagement) since pills in general have been proven to work.[678]

Vest HaGuf

- *Vest haguf* is a sign that a woman's period is coming. It does not cause the period, but it shows that she will bleed very soon.
- Rav Moshe Feinstein says that for a *vest haguf* to be called part of the *re'iyah*, the *re'iyah* has to occur within 24 hours of the symptom.
- Most *Poskim* say that PMS is not called a *vest haguf*,[679] as only the signs listed in the *Shulchan Aruch* can be considered a *vest haguf*.[680]

---

677. Although pills have a very good record of pushing off or regulating women's cycles (single versus dual hormones), it is not uncommon for some women to experience breakthrough bleeding or staining when they start taking pills, due to hormonal fluctuations in the body. This bleeding is usually experienced during the first 3 months of taking pills, at random times during the month, after which time the body generally regulates itself. For this reason, the *Poskim* prefer that a *kallah* who is planning on taking pills during her engagement show that these pills actually work for her by taking them for 3 months before the wedding. However, very often women experience cramping, bloating, irritability, etc. from taking pills and we want to limit these discomforts during the engagement. Some *Rabbanim* therefore prefer that the *kallah* take the pills toward the end of the engagement, either to regulate or push off her period, so she will be *tehorah* on the wedding night, without introducing too many foreign hormones into her blood stream. Practically speaking, since pills generally work for the majority of women, if she is currently taking a hormone pill (as opposed to a placebo) we will be lenient, allowing her to have marital relations even on a *vest*.

678. Rav Yosef Shalom Elyashiv.

679. PMS is defined as premenstrual symptoms that generally preceed the time a woman gets her period every month. Post-PMS is a group of symptoms a woman feels *after* getting her period. The symptoms are described as bloating, anger, irritability, tension, depression, crying, weight gain, nausea, headaches, cramping, oversensitivity, exaggerated mood swings, fatigue, tenderness, acne, sleep disturbances, and appetite changes.

Some symptoms of PMS are similar to the *vestos haguf* described in the *Shulchan Aruch*. A woman who gets such symptoms, immediately followed by her period, should consult a *Rav*.

680. See *Shulchan Aruch* 189:19.

Vestos for a Mesulekes Damim

- The *Raavad* says that a woman does not create a *vest kavua* during the times that she is a *mesulekes damim*, but she does have to keep a *vest* the month after having a *re'iyah*. If she bleeds three times in the same *onah* on the same *vest* she will not establish a *vest kavua*; it will be broken in 1 month if she deviates from the *vest*.

- The *Rashba* says since this woman is a *mesulekes damim*, she does not have to be concerned about something that is obviously a chance occurrence. Therefore, a *mesulekes damim* does not keep *vestos* at all.

- Practically speaking, the halachah is like the Raavad's opinion.

- Rav Moshe Feinstein says that if the *vestos* passed in the first month of pregnancy and no bleeding occurred, the woman does not have to keep any further *vestos*, since there was no *re'iyah* that month.

- Practically speaking, a *vest kavua* is rare nowadays, so once a woman passes her first month of pregnancy she generally has no *vestos* that she needs to keep. In the event that she does bleed during the pregnancy,[681] she would have to keep *vestos* the next month, as per the Raavad's opinion.[682]

- A woman who bled during pregnancy and knows that the reason is unrelated to a period does not keep *vestos* as a result of such discharge,[683] even if she became *temei'ah* as a result of the blood.

- Rav Moshe Feinstein says a woman who is nursing and gets her period is no longer a *mesulekes damim*.[684]

---

681. Rav Mati Friedman pointed out that a woman who is bleeding during pregnancy should contact her practitioner and *Rav* immediately!

682. Rav Yosef Shalom Elyashiv.

683. A case that would fall under this category is that of a woman who experiences a partial separation of the placenta which causes her to bleed. This blood is treated as a *re'iyah* (there are no leniencies of *kesamim*), but *vestos* are not applied, because the onset of such bleeding is not menstrual in nature.

684. Rav Yosef Shalom Elyashiv. It seems that in the times of *Chazal* a woman would not get her period for 24 months after having a baby, whether or not she nursed. That is no longer the case. Women today often stain or get a monthly period even while nursing, and certainly when they are not nursing postpartum.

- A nursing woman who stains right after she got home from the mikvah or is *temei'ah* because of a *kesem* need not keep a *vest*, as these types of bleeding are generally part of residual birth bleeding or a *kesem*, which do not create *vestos*.

- Rav Nissim Karelitz and most other *Poskim* are stringent in the case of a woman who tests positive for pregnancy before her *vestos* pass, and rule that she does not attain the status of a *mesulekes damim*, and therefore must continue to keep these *vestos*. Rav Yosef Shalom Elyashiv explains that a positive test does not uproot the *vestos* since it is common to bleed during the first month of pregnancy.

Vest HaKefitzos — When a Period Is Triggered

- *Vest hakefitzos* means a certain action caused the woman to begin to bleed. A *vest hakefitzos* is created by the woman getting her period after performing the same action 3 months in a row on the same date or cycle (for example, every Wednesday), during the same *onah*.[685]

An example of a *vest hakefitzos* is when a woman's period comes 3 months in a row immediately after an exercise class that takes place on a specific day of the month.

- Rav Nissim Karelitz says the onset of the period must occur within a day of the action of *kefitzos* in order for the onset of the period to be linked to it.

- Rav Shmuel HaLevi Wosner says an action of *kefitzos* must occur within the same *onah* in which the period started in order for it to be linked to the onset of the period. Otherwise, the action of *kefitzos* is no longer seen as connected to the onset of bleeding. The exception to this rule is when a woman already got her period twice on this date after *kefitzos* she has done during the same *onah*, and the third time is separated by 1 day.[686]

- Rav Nissim Karelitz says although the Shulchan Aruch rules that a woman can become a niddah even when an outside stimulus

685. This is how the Shulchan Aruch and Rama rule, like the Rambam, Rashba, and Raavad. *Rashi* and the *Tur* say a woman can establish a *vest hakefitzos* even if it is not attached to a certain day.

686. See *Chavas Daas* 189:23.

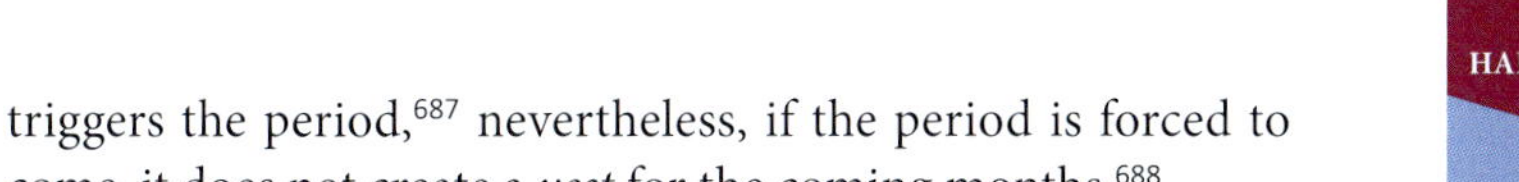

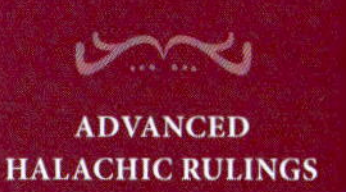

triggers the period,[687] nevertheless, if the period is forced to come, it does not create a *vest* for the coming months.[688]

- Rav Shmuel HaLevi Wosner says that in the event that a woman is *temei'ah* because of an internal exam or operation that forced her period to come, according to the letter of the law she does not need to keep that *re'iyah* as a *vest*, even if it occurred on or around her *vestos*. This *vest* is different from a regular situation where something caused her to bleed, such as if she jumped and caused herself to bleed, since it was forced upon her. However, she should keep *vestos* the next month from the date of the forced *tumah*, as a stringency. Also, in the event that the examination was performed around the time of her expected period, she should not keep a long *vest haflagah* from the first natural period, skipping the unnatural one, and counting the third period (which is the second natural one).

Three Bedikos to Establish That One Did Not Bleed as a Result of Marital Relations

- Most *Rishonim* (*Rashba*, *Rashi* [first explanation], *Ri*, *Raavad*, and *Rosh* [main explanation]) say that a woman — even one who does not have a *vest kavua* — is not obligated to do any *bedikos* before marital relations. The Gemara that says that a woman should do a *bedikah* is discussing doing a *bedikah* for *taharos*, and not to permit herself to her husband.
- Some Rishonim (Rabbeinu Chananel and Rabbeinu Tam [second explanation in *Rashi*]) say a woman who does not have a *vest kavua* requires a *bedikah* before marital relations throughout her life, since she may suddenly begin to bleed at any time, even when she is not dealing with *taharos*.

687. *Siman* 183.

688. Rav Nissim Karelitz differentiates between a woman who experiences a period caused by outside stimuli, and a woman who experienced an event that was so traumatic that it is not expected to happen again in the future. In the latter case, although the woman is *temei'ah mid'Oraisa* (whether naturally or produced by an unnatural stimulus), this experience is not counted toward a *vest hakefitzos*.

- Other *Rishonim* (*Rif*[689]) say a woman needs three *bedikos* before and after marital relations to establish that she does not bleed as a result of marital relations, unless she has a *vest kavua*.[690]

- The *Shulchan Aruch* says a woman should perform three *bedikos* to show that she does not bleed as a result of marital relations.[691]

- The Shach disagrees, saying a woman should not to do any *bedikos*.[692]

- Practically speaking, the halachah is taught like the ruling of the Shulchan Aruch, and these *bedikos* should be done; although in the United States, many do not teach this halachah at all.[693]

- Rav Shmuel HaLevi Wosner says the *bedikah* before marital relations should be done in the half hour before marital relations, and the *bedikah* after marital relations should be performed immediately afterwards.[694]

- In the beginning of the marriage, a *Rav* will assume that any blood that a woman discovers is *dam besulim* as long as there is still pain from marital relations.[695] Most *Poskim* say this assumption applies even for a woman who did not see any blood by *bi'ah rishonah*, but saw blood upon returning from the mikvah and from subsequent relations.[696]

---

689. *Kesubos*, "*Almanah Nizonis*."

690. The *Drishah* and *Sidrei Taharah* explain that the purpose of the *bedikah* before marital relations is to determine that the woman is *tehorah* at the onset of marital relations, while the *bedikah* after marital relations determines whether marital relations caused her to begin to bleed. Without the *bedikah* before marital relations there is a possibility that the woman began bleeding before marital relations, and that marital relations were not the cause of this bleeding.

691. *Rif*.

692. Most *Rishonim*.

693. The *She'arim HaMetzuyanim B'Halachah* (*Kuntres Acharon* 154:4) says these *bedikos* should not be done nowadays, and explains at length that since the chances of finding a woman who bleeds due to marital relations are so small, there no longer exists a legitimate concern that would require every woman to do *bedikos* to establish that this is not the case by her.

694. Rav Nissim Karelitz.

695. For this reason many *Poskim* advise not to do these *bedikos* for the first 6 months of marriage.

696. Rav Shmuel HaLevi Wosner; Rav Nissim Karelitz.

- A woman should wait to do these *bedikos* until *dam besulim* ceases to be a concern. In addition, she should do these *bedikos* after her *onas havest*.[697] She should not do *bedikos* on the *vest* itself,[698] and should not do them while she is pregnant or nursing.[699]

- Some teach to do these *bedikos* whenever she can, even if she is unable to perform the *bedikos* in the beginning of her marriage due to pregnancies or nursing, and even if she is already married for many years.

- Many other *Poskim* say a woman who did not do these *bedikos* right away should not do them at all, since at that point in her marriage it is a very distant concern that she will actually be a woman who bleeds due to marital relations.[700]

- Practically speaking, in Eretz Yisrael women should be taught to perform these *bedikos*, and a woman should perform one *bedikah* three separate times after marital relations (as soon after relations as possible), even if it takes a few years of marriage until she can perform them.

- Rav Yosef Shalom Elyashiv and Rav Nissim Karelitz say once a woman does these *bedikos* for one husband, she establishes that she is not a woman who bleeds due to marital relations, even if she marries another man later in life.

697. Rav Nissim Karelitz explains that until her *vestos* arrive, a woman is considered one who will not bleed, so a *bedikah* performed during this time is no indication that she did not bleed because of marital relations.

698. Marital relations are prohibited on the *vest*, so there is no way for her to perform these *bedikos*. The question arises in a scenario in which a woman performed the *bedikos* anyway and had marital relations illegitimately on a *vest* (intentional or unintentionally, such as if she later realizes it was a *vest*). Would the *bedikos* count for this woman, since she showed she does not bleed due to marital relations specifically on the date she is supposed to bleed — there can be no better way to show she does not bleed due to marital relations! On the other hand, perhaps we may reason that since the *bedikos* were *temei'os*, she would not be considered a woman who bleeds due to marital relations because any blood discovered on the *bedikah* cloth would be attributed to the *vest*, so the woman cannot use these *bedikos* from such a circumstance to be *metaher* herself either.

699. *Chasam Sofer*; Rav Nissim Karelitz.

700. Rav Shmuel HaLevi Wosner; Rav Yosef Shalom Elyashiv; see *Pischei Teshuvos*, p. 76.

The Onah to Keep the Month After a Missed Bedikah

- Rav Yosef Shalom Elyashiv and Rav Nissim Karelitz discuss a case in which a woman gets her period one month, and forgets to do a *bedikah* on the *onas havest* the following month like she was supposed to. She does not get her period during her *onah*, but begins to bleed at a different time. The following month, the woman only needs to keep the new *onah* (the *onah* in which she most recently began to bleed) and does not keep the old *vest* (the *onah* during which she never did a *bedikah* to establish that she did not bleed).[701]

- Rav Yosef Shalom Elyashiv discusses a case in which a woman established a *vest*, and then got her period on a new date for 2 months in a row. Then, the third month, she forgets to do a *bedikah* on the new *vest she'eino kavua*. Had she performed the *bedikah* as required, she would have created a new *vest kavua* and would have uprooted the old *vest kavua* by deviating from it three times and by setting a new *vest kavua*. However, the woman missed the *bedikah* on the third *vest* and it was therefore not established. This woman no longer has her new *vest she'eino kavua*, and she may disregard the old *vest kavua* as well for the time being, since she did not get her most recent period on either the *vest kavua* or the *vest she'eino kavua*. In such a case, she only keeps the *onah* in which her most recent period occurred, as a new *vest she'eino kavua*. However, if she gets her period on the old *vest kavua* in a subsequent month, she will reinstate the *vest kavua*, since she never created a new *vest kavua*, and will keep the *vest kavua* for the next 3 months.

---

701. In other words, although the woman failed to produce a clean *bedikah* on the *vest* to show that she uprooted this specific date as a cause for her *re'iyah*, since she also did not get her period on that date, she is not required to keep the old *vest* on top of the new *vest* on the date she begins to bleed.

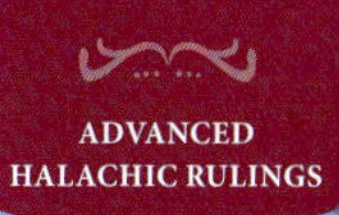

Bedikos That Cause Vestos

- In the event that a woman does a *bedikah* that comes out *temei'ah* on a day that is not a *vest*, this date is not counted as a *vest* for next month.[702]
- This woman can count 5 days and 7 days from the day of this *bedikah* that is *temei'ah*, because that is the time that she became *temei'ah*, even if the onset of her period only arrives a few days later. However, she calculates her *vestos* from the actual day of the onset of her period.
- When a *bedikah* done on the day of a *vest* comes out *temei'ah*, the woman continues to count this day as a *vest* for next month, even if the onset of her period only occurs a few days later.[703]

702. Although Rav Nissim Karelitz and the She'arim HaMetzuyanim B'Halachah hold that a *bedikah* counts for a *vest* both when it is a stringency and when it is a leniency, most *Poskim* disagree.

703. This halachah is based on the *Shulchan Aruch* (190:54) which says that even when a woman finds a *kesem* on the same day of the month 3 months in a row, it does not create a *vest*. However if she discovers blood on a *bedikah* cloth, this is considered a *re'iyah* for all matters pertaining to niddah. The simple explanation of the *Shulchan Aruch* is that whenever a woman discovers blood on a *bedikah* cloth she should create a *vest* on that date, whether or not it was a previous *vest*. (Discovering blood on a *bedikah* cloth is as though she had a *re'iyah*; see *Pischei Teshuvah, siman* 183 that the Chavas Daas and others hold that a bad *bedikah* has the status of a *safeik d'Oraisa*.) The *Levush* says that the *Shulchan Aruch* should be understood to mean that if a woman discovers blood on a *bedikah* cloth 3 months in a row on the same date, only then does she create a *vest* (the opposite *din*, but similar case to when she sees *kesamim* on the same date 3 months in a row), but if she discovers blood on a *bedikah* cloth on a random day she certainly does not create a *vest* for that date.

Rav Yitzchak Berkovits rules that if the cloth was the *bedikah* of the *onas havest*, she keeps the *vest* and counts that *vest* for the next month (the woman now has two occasions of this *vest*), even if her period arrives a few days later. Others say that she keeps the day she started bleeding as the *onas havest* for the upcoming months, and keeps the date of the bad *bedikah* (which was a previous *vest*) as a *vest* as a stringency. Almost everyone agrees that a bad *bedikah* on a random day will not create a *vest* for the upcoming month, as per the opinion of the Levush. Some disagree and say a *bedikah* is considered a *re'iyah d'Oraisa* in all matters, and that includes *vestos* as well.

When a Woman Does Not Know When She Got Her Period

- When a woman does not know whether she started bleeding before or after *neitz* or *shkiah*, she counts the *vest* as if it came during the later *onah*.[704]
- If the bleeding clearly came from before *neitz/shkiah*, for example, a woman only realized that she was bleeding a minute after *neitz* and her bed is wet with a lot of blood, the earlier *onah* should be kept, since circumstances indicate that the period began during the earlier *onah* even if she did not discover the blood until later.

Common Cases of Establishing a Vest Nowadays

- *Vest kavua l'yemei hashavua* — A woman who begins to bleed on the same day of the week during the same *onah* three times in a row, with the same intervals between all three *re'iyos*, creates a *vest kavua* for this day. This *vest* is established after three *re'iyos*, and not four that are necessary to create a regular *haflagah kevuah*.
- For example: A woman gets her period at intervals of 22 days, 29 days, or 36 days, etc. She creates a *vest* for that day of the week after three *re'iyos*, which is two *haflagos*.
- The *Chavas Daas* says when a woman has three *re'iyos* that create a *vest l'yemei hashavua* (two *haflagos* of 22, or 29, and so on), and then gets her period on that *haflagah* again, she shows that her *haflagah* is the *kevuah*, not the *yom hashavua*.[705] She will keep future *vestos* on that *haflagah*, and not according to the *yom hashavua*.[706]
- A *vest l'yemei hashavua* is one of the most common fluke *vestos kevuos*, and every *chassan* and *kallah* should be taught about it.

---

704. *Raavid*.For a thorough discussion about this *halachah* see End Notes.

705. See *Pischei Teshuvah* 189:4.

706. The difference is that when a woman establishes a *vest l'yemei hashavua*, she always keeps that *yom hashavua* for the next 3 months, even if she deviates from the *vest* 1 month. If her constancy is now the *haflagah*, she will keep the *haflagah* each month from the previous *re'iyah*, and it is not connected to any particular day of the week.

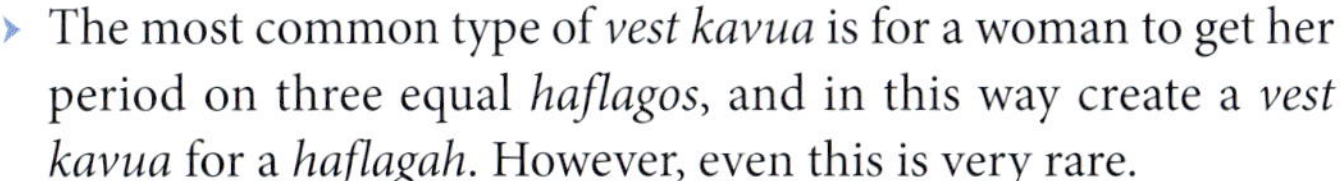

- The most common type of *vest kavua* is for a woman to get her period on three equal *haflagos*, and in this way create a *vest kavua* for a *haflagah*. However, even this is very rare.

Lost Calendar

- A woman who lost her calendar does not have to be concerned about *vestos* until she begins to bleed again, unless she knows when the bleeding started the month before, or knows that a certain *onah* is a *vest*.[707]
- The *Chavas Daas* says this even applies for a woman who has a *vest kavua* but cannot recall which date or *haflagah* it is.[708]

707. The Chavas Daas, She'arim HaMetzuyanim B'Halachah, and most other *Poskim* explain that the reason for this leniency is that *vestos* are *d'Rabbanan*, and the woman's losing her calendar creates a *safeik d'Rabbanan*, allowing one to be lenient. Rav Shmuel HaLevi Wosner also brings this reason in the name of *Teshuvos Mahari Assad*.

The Chasam Sofer, the Chazon Ish, and Rav Nissim Karelitz are stringent regarding this halachah, saying that the woman has to keep any day on which she may have a *vest* (similar to *yemei hamevuchim*). This stringency may be based on the opinion of the Chasam Sofer and the Noda B'Yehudah (*Pischei Teshuvah* 184:3), that marital relations during the *vest* are prohibited *mid'Oraisa*. See *Chut Shani* 189:1.

708. 184:4.

End Note from page 319

A Woman Who Only Did One Bedikah on Day 1: *A More Detailed Discussion*

The following *dinim* may be relevant in extremely extenuating circumstances. As always, an *extremely* competent *Rav* should be consulted before applying such *dinim*:

- In the event that a woman did only one *bedikah* on Day 1 – besides *b'makom igun* — and there are really, really extenuating circumstances — a *Rav* may can be lenient and allow her to immerse on time to save her from waiting another week.
- Rav Yosef Shalom Elyashiv says that "extenuating circumstances" in this situation means that the woman will violate something more severe (i.e., she will be with her husband illegitimately), or she will stop keeping the halachos of *taharas hamishpachah* completely.
- The *Chasam Sofer* says that in the event that a woman who is not *b'makom igun* did only one *bedikah on* Day 1 and immersed illegitimately, she need not immerse again if she was already with her husband.
- Discussing the same scenario, the *Avnei Shoham* says the *tevilah* always counts *bedi'eved* and she does not need to immerse again, even if she was not yet with her husband.
- The *Sefer Badei HaShulchan* points out that the wording in the *Chasam Sofer* allows such a woman who immersed too early without the required *bedikos* to remain in her state of *taharah*, when she was already "*lansah im baalah*." He explains this to mean that even according to the Chasam Sofer the woman need not immerse again (and she is not required to count *shivah nekiyim* again) if she already broke *harchakos*. If the Chasam Sofer meant "until they were intimate," he would have written "*shekvar shimshah im baalah*."
- Rav Yossi Stilerman said a woman who did only one *bedikah* may not immerse in the mikvah, even if that *bedikah* was performed on Day 1 or Day 7. The exceptions to this are only *b'makom igun*, such as when the woman has an internal cut, or

if she is a *kallah* and this will prevent her from having a *chuppas niddah*.

The following ruling should not be relied upon without calling a very competent *Rav* first Rav Yosef Shalom Elyashiv says that in the event that a *Rav* realizes that a woman who only did one *bedikah* the entire *shivah nekiyim* will violate the laws of her *niddah d'Oraisa* status if he does not allow her to immerse in the mikvah, he should let her go to the mikvah on time. This also applies if a woman only did a *hefsek taharah* without doing any *bedikos* at all during *shivah nekiyim*, because *mid'Oraisa* a woman only needs a *hefsek taharah*.

End Note from page 413, (**When a Woman Does Not Know When She Got Her Period**)

Raavid. The basis for this ruling is the *Shulchan Aruch* 184:4, which says "If she is prone to see her period at sunrise, and is unsure if the onset of this flow began before or after sunrise, she is forbidden (i.e. observes future *vestos*) during the day (as if the period began after sunrise)". The classic understanding of most Acharonim is that any woman who is unsure if her period started before or after *neitz* or *shkiah* keeps the later *onah* as the upcoming *onas havest*. The *Shach* cites the *Rosh*, who says *vestos* are *d'Rabbanan*, allowing one to be lenient so that the couple is only required to separate the next time during the day since "she was certainly bleeding during the day, after sunrise" which seems to imply the reason for this is that we establish that in *halachic* the woman was *certainly* bleeding during the day; it follows that *vestos* should be kept during the day.

The Taz says, since we know she was certainly bleeding during the day, we will attribute the onset of the bleeding to the day, because תולין הקלקלה במקולקל —we attribute the period to the time she expected her period.

The Shiurei Shevet HaLevi 184:4:3 cites the *Lechem v'Simlah*, which says that since this is a case where we know that she bled in at least one of the time periods we cannot be lenient in both the night and the day, rather, we would have to be stringent and assume that she bled over both time frames. However, since practically we attribute the period to the time she expected her period (due to then principle of תולין הקלקלה במקולקל) we assume that the bleeding oncly occurred at the later time.

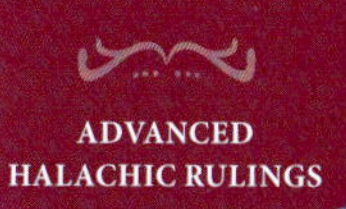

The Pri Dei'ah says the later *vest* carries with it an established state of *tumah*, and for that reason we cannot completely disregard the *vest*.

The following question arises: Why is it that the same Acharonim who are lenient when a woman loses her calendar because they say *vestos* are d'Rabbanan, also say that a woman who is unsure of whether she began to bleed before or after *neitz* should keep upcoming *vestos* during the day? A woman who loses her calendar and is not sure whether her period started on Monday or Tuesday night, may be lenient on both days because *vestos* are *d'Rabbanan*, yet the *safeik* that arises in her case is also a case where we *know* that she started to bleed on at least one of those days, and she certainly saw blood during the later *onah*!

The Razaah (Hasagos to the Raavid, Shaar *Vestos*) disagrees with the Raavid, saying that since there is a question as to when the *vest* should be observed, she is not required to keep any *vestos* that came about because of this period, even when the *safeik* is between two concurrent *onos*.

It would seem that the case of the *Shulchan Aruch* is specifically speaking about a woman who has a *vest kavua* during the day, as it says "אם רגילה לראות בהנץ החמה — If she is prone to see her period at sunrise." Such a woman has established that she *always* begins bleeding during the day due to a specific cause, such as *yom hachodesh*. When she is unsure when her period came during this month — before or after *neitz* — she should assume she bled during the day, because she is already prohibited during the day, as her *vest kavua* established that she is prohibited during the day. In other words, our lenient ruling only applies when there is a *safeik d'Rabbanan* which allows her to be lenient. Yet, in our case, she already has an upcoming *vest* during the day. As such, the *Shulchan Aruch* concludes that she is forbidden during the day, because the woman is already prohibited during the day.

The other explanation is since she already established a *vest* during the day, when she bleeds this month and is unsure when the bleeding started there is a very strong probability that her period came during the day, as it did during the previous months when she established the *vest*. This is why the Lechem V'Simlah says the reason is because she may attribute the period to the time she expected her period, because the day was "*mekulkal, blemished*" when it established the *vest*, and so now we are going to go with the *probable* time, which is during the day.

The Chavas Daas refutes this last point by saying that the Shach, who brings the reason for keeping the *Ohr Zarua* lived in a time when women had already stopped seeing blood at the same time each *vest*; therefore, he cannot be talking about our case that she sees blood at the same time each month.

Sugah BaShoshanim writes that the reason for the Raavid's opinion is based on another *Raavid*, which is actually the next paragraph in the *Shulchan Aruch*. The *Shulchan Aruch*'s case there involves a woman who sees the onset of her period for a few moments, which occurs between two *onos*. For example, she started bleeding during the day, at the end of the day, into the night, for a few minutes. The halachah is that she keeps the earlier *onah* as the *vest* — and also the later *onah* for the amount of time the initial bleeding continued. Therefore, he says, in our case (where she is unsure if the bleeding began during the night or the next day), even if the bleeding began during the night, there is still an element of *vestos* that should occur during the day. We will therefore be lenient and completely drop the night *vest*, and will extend the day *vest* to include the entire day.

The *Pleissi* and *Sidrei Taharah* explain the reason for the *Shulchan Aruch*'s ruling as follows: When the next month arrives, she should really not have to keep any *vestos* because it is a *safeik d'Rabbanan*. However, once the earlier *onah* passes without incident, we now assume that the period actually came in the later *onah* the previous month, because the *vest* is the time the blood should have come. Since it did not arrive in the earlier *onah*, the period must have occurred in the later *onah*.

Rav Binyomin Forst quotes Rav Yechezkel Roth, who says that if a woman established a *vest* at night and is then unsure when the period arrived, she should keep the nighttime *onah*. It seems very clear that he understands the topic in the same way as we explained above, and the reason the woman keeps the nighttime *onah* when she established a *vest* at night is because that is the time which has been established as "blemished"- i.e. it fell on a *vest*.

According to this understanding of the *Shulchan Aruch*, a woman nowadays who does not have a *vest kavua* and is unsure when her period started, before or after *shkiah*, should be lenient and not keep any *vestos* the following month, but should presumably still keep both times as *yemei hamevuchim*, performing an external wipe with a colored tissue before marital relations in order to establish that she is *tehorah* without risking that she become *tameiah*.

Practically speaking, however, Rav Yitzchak Berkovits is lenient only in a case in which the woman is unsure when the onset of the period was, provided the two possible *onos* are separated by at least one *onah*. If it is a 50/50 chance between two back-to-back *onos*, the woman should keep the later *onah*, which is the classic understanding of the *Shulchan Aruch*.

GLOSSARY

Alos hashachar — the rising of the morning star; daybreak

Amah (pl. amos) — a Biblical measurement of one arm's length

Amaslah — a legitimate reason as to why she said something untrue

Atarah — crown, of the male organ

Aveilus — mourning

Aveirah (pl. aveiros) — sin(s)

B'derech re'iyah — in the normal way of seeing blood

Bedi'eved — ex post facto

Bedikah — lit. a check; an internal check of the vaginal canal through the use of a cloth

Bedikah cloth — a clean, white cloth used to perform a *bedikah*

Bedikas shacharis — a bedikah performed before *Minchah ketanah*

Bein hasfasayim — between the vaginal "lips"

Bein hashmashos — the period of time between sunset and nightfall

Beis hastarim —internal cavities in the body that can be seen from outside the body and where water may enter

Besulim — hymen

Beulah — a woman who has had intercourse

Bi'ah — intercourse

Bi'ah rishonah — the first intercourse

Birchas HaMazon — Grace after Meals

Bodekes (pl. bodkos) — examination nurse(s)

Chafifah (pl.chafifos) — the cleansing process that a woman performs before immersing in the mikvah to remove any *chatzitzos*

Chai nosei es atzmo — a living being carries its own weight

Chassan — groom

Chatzitzah (pl. chatzitzos) — lit. an impediment; something that is on the body and can prevent mikvah waters from reaching there

Chatzos — halachic midnight/midday

Chibbah — affection

Chibbuk v'nishuk — hugging and kissing

Chorin v'sedakin — holes and crevices

Chuppas niddah — a chuppah that takes place when the *kallah* is a niddah

D'Oraisa — from the Torah

D'Rabbanan — from the Rabbis

Dam — blood

Dam besulim — virginity bleeding

Dam chimud — bleeding caused by longing/emotional excitement

Das Moshe — the basic level of dignity mandated by Moshe Rabbeinu on all women

Das Yehudis — the basic level of dignity that applies to each woman according to her standing in her community

Daven(ing) — pray(ing)

Derech re'iyah — in the normal way of seeing blood

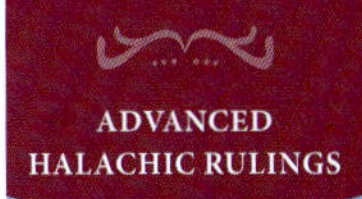

Din — law

Din (pl. dinim) — law(s)

Divrei Torah — words of Torah

Eid she'eino baduk — an unchecked *bedikah* cloth; a cloth that was used to perform a *bedikah* that possibly contained blood on it before the *bedikah* was performed

Ein pesichas hakever b'lo dam — there is no opening of the uterus without blood

Eiver — the male reproductive organ

Erev — the eve of

Geder/gedarim — Talmudic fence/boundary

Gemar bi'ah — completion of intercourse

Gris — a Talmudic measurement of approximately the size of a penny or a one-shekel coin

Haflagah — a *vest* of the length of a woman's most recent menstrual cycle

Harchakah (pl. harchakos) — lit. distance(s); action(s) that a couple may not take when the wife is a niddah

Hargashah — sensation; referring to a sensation that a woman feels upon getting her period

He'arah — surface-level contact, with little penetration

Hefsek taharah — a *bedikah* that is performed to establish that a woman has stopped bleeding, which allows the *shivah nekiyim* to begin

Heker — sign

Hirhur — thinking about that which is forbidden

Histaklus — gazing at that which is forbidden

Iyun — inspecting [one's body in preparation for immersing in the mikvah]

Kallah — bride

Kalus rosh — frivolity

Kareis — extinction of the soul and its denial of a share in the World to Come

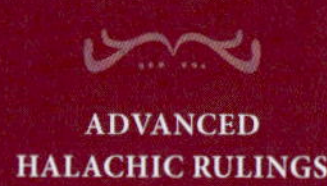

Kavua — fixed; routine

Kedushah — holiness

Kenissas atarah — penetration of the male organ

Kesem — stain

Klal Yisrael — lit. the Congregation of Israel; the Jewish nation

Kol ishah — lit. the voice of a woman; [hearing] a woman sing

Kos shel brachah — cup of wine that is used for the performance of a mitzvah (such as Kiddush or Havdalah)

Kvatter — a couple that passes the baby from the mother to the father at a bris

Lechatchilah — at the outset

Macholes — a type of louse

Makkah — cut; wound

Makom igun — a situation in which a woman will not be able to get a clean *bedikah* for a long time

Mareh (pl. maros) — questionable *bedikah* cloth(s) presented to a *Rav* for a halachic ruling

Mattan Torah — the Giving of the Torah

Mayan pasuach — lit. an open spring; a situation in which she is no longer considered to be expecting to bleed

Mayan sasum — lit. a closed spring; a situation in which she is not expecting to bleed

Mazria — climax of intercourse

Mekabel tumah — susceptible to impurity

Mekor — lit. source; the uterus

Melachah — a creative act that is prohibited on Shabbos

Mesorah — tradition

Mesulekes damim — a woman who does not get her period

Metaher — causes to become pure

Metamei — causes to become impure

Mikvah (pl. mikvaos) — ritual bath(s)

Minchah ketanah — approximately two and a half halachic hours before sundown

Minyan — a quorum of men for praying

Moch dachuk — a *bedikah* in which the *bedikah* cloth is left inside the woman's body for a period of time

Mukas eitz — a girl who has no *besulim* due to reasons other than intercourse

Negel vasser — [water for] washing one's hands upon awakening

Negiah — touching

Neitz (hachamah) — sunrise

Netilas yadayim — [water for] washing one's hands before partaking of bread

Nidcheh — delayed

Niddah — a woman who is impure due to uterine bleeding

Onah (pl. onos) — literally, time; the part of the day from sunset to sunrise, and the part of the day from sunrise to sunset

Onah beinonis — a *vest* of the average cycle of most women

Onas havest — the part of the day (from sunset to sunrise or sunrise to sunset) that one keeps as a *vest*

Osyom — immediate

Pas b'salo — lit. bread in his basket; a sense of contentment as though he has it already

Passuk (pl. pessukim) — verse(s)

Pesichas hakever — opening of the uterus

Pesichas hakever — the opening of the uterus

Poletes shichvas zera — a woman who who emits sperm after cohabitation

Poreish — separate; withdraw

Poreish b'eiver chai — withdraw while erect

Poreish b'eiver meis — withdraw when erection has expired

Posek (pl. Poskim) — halachic authority(/ies)

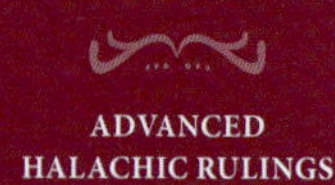

Pru u'revu — lit. be fruitful and multiply; the mitzvah to procreate

Psak — halachic ruling

Rav (pl. Rabbanim) — Rabbi(s)

Re'iyah — lit. seeing; blood that was seen

Rechitzah — lit. washing; washing the vaginal area before performing a *hefsek taharah*

Ro'eh machmas tashmish — one who bleeds as a result of marital relations

Ruach ra — bad spirit which is present on the hands before one washes upon awakening in the morning

Safeik — doubt

Safeik d'Oraisa — a doubt regarding a Torah law

Safeik d'Rabbanan — a doubt regarding a Rabbinical law

Sefer (pl. sefarim) — holy book(s)

Sefer Torah — Torah Scroll

Shaas metziyas hakesem — the state in which the stain was when it was found

Shalom bayis — harmony between husband and wife

She'eilah — halachic question that one asks a *Rav*

Shidduch — marriage partner

Shinui — change

Shiur (pl. shiurim) — Torah class(es); amount of time

Shiur osyom — immediate time frame

Shkiah — sunset

Shomer (pl. shomrim) — literally, guard(s); someone who is present to ensure that no intimacy takes place

Srach bitah — perhaps her daughter will learn from her behavior and do the same in her own home

Taharas hamishpachah — [laws of] family purity

Tahor/tehorah/tehorim/tehoros — pure

Tamei/temei'ah/temei'im/temei'os — impure

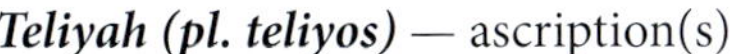

Teliyah (pl. teliyos) — ascription(s)

Tevilah — immersion

Tevilah b'zmanah — immersion at its [correct] time

Tevilah shelo b'zmanah —immersion not at its [correct] time

Tumah — impurity

Tzeis hakochavim — when the stars come out; nightfall

Tznius — modesty

Vadai migufah — certainly from her body, i.e., the uterus

Vest (pl. vestos) — a day on which we may assume that there is a significant chance that a woman will get her period

Vest achilah — a *vest* that is established due to something a woman ate that affected the pattern of her cycles

Vest hadilug — a predictably changing cycle

Vest haguf — a *vest* connected to a bodily sensation

Vest hakefitzos — a *vest* that is created when the period is caused by a specific action 3 months in a row

Vest kavua — a "fixed" *vest*; the set day that a woman gets her period each month

Vest kavua l'yemei hashavua — a *vest* that gets created when a woman gets her period on the same day of the week, in the same *onah*, three times in a row

Vest she'eino kavua — a "non-fixed" *vest*; a day that a woman got her period once and therefore there is a chance that she will get it again on the same day the following month

Yehareg v'al yaavor — one must give up their life rather than transgress

Yemei — days of

Yemei hamevuchim —days during which a woman anticipates that she will get her period, but she does not know precisely when it will be

Yemei niddah — days in which a woman is considered a niddah if she bleeds

Yemei zivah — days in which a woman is considered a *zivah* if she bleeds

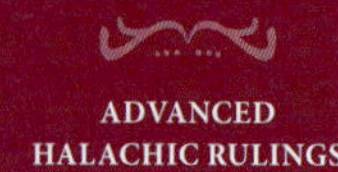

Yetzer hara — evil inclination

Yichud — halachos forbidding a man to remain secluded with a strange woman

Yichud room — a locked room where a couple spend time together immediately after the chuppah

Yoledes — a woman who gives birth

Yom hachodesh — a *vest* of the date of the Hebrew month

Zemiros — lit. songs; holy songs sung at the Shabbos meals

Zera — sperm

Zman — time

IN HONOR OF

MY DEAR WIFE

CERYSE MIZRAHI

OUR DEAR CHILDREN

SOPHIA, JACK, RALPH, MARCIA, SARAH

WITH MUCH LOVE,

EDIE MIZRAHI

לזכר נשמת

KALMAN BEN R' ELIMELECH
AHARON NASSON BEN R' YEHUDA
ELIMELECH HACOHEN
ROCHEL BAILA BAS R' DOV HALEVI

MAY THE MERIT OF THIS
LEARNING BE AN ALIYAH FOR THEIR *NESHOMOS*

DOVID AND CHAYALA LITVINTCHOUK

FOR MY GRANDPARENTS:

DANIEL AND JONAH WEISER
RAPHAEL AND JULIA TSHUVA

HAGGAI AND RIVKY WEISER

WITH SINCERE GRATITUDE FOR THE INVALUABLE GUIDANCE, INSPIRATION AND ENCOURAGEMENT OF

OUR REBBE, HARAV

REUVEN EPSTEIN, SHLITA

YOU HAVE BEEN A GUIDE,
COUNSELOR AND DEAR REBBI

THANK YOU FOR ALL YOU HAVE DONE AND CONTINUE TO DO FOR US ON A CONSTANT BASIS,

MOSHE AND BB ODES

IN MEMORY OF

MY GRANDPARENTS

CHAYA SARAH BAS ELIEZER HILLEL O'H

AVROHOM BEN GEDALYA O"H

CHAVA BREINDEL BAS TZVI O"H

****

IN RECOGNITION OF

MY REBBE

RABBI REUVEN EPSTEIN SHLITA

MAY YOU BE ZOCHEH TO BE MARBITZ TORAH FOR MANY YEARS TO COME,

YOUR TALMID,

SHIMMY AND DASSY ENGEL

TO

RABBI REUVEN AND MRS. GITTY EPSTEIN:

CONGRATULATIONS ON SUCH AN OUTSTANDING ACCOMPLISHMENT.

WE'D LIKE TO THANK YOU FOR ALL THE AMAZING EFFORT YOU HAVE PUT INTO THE COMMUNITY.

THANK YOU FOR ALL YOU HAVE TAUGHT US, FOR BEING AMAZING ROLE MODELS, AND MOST IMPORTANTLY FOR BEING OUR SHADCHAN!

WITH TREMENDOUS GRATITUDE,

MAYER AND LELI LOWY

לעלוי נשמת

YISROEL BEN YITZCHOK DAVID Z"L
MV"H MOSHE AHARON B"R MENACHEM A"H

NIFTAR T"Z MENACHEM AV

VZU' MARAS GITTEL RIYO B"R YOSEF ARYE A"H

SHLOMO ROSENBERG

AS A ZCHUS FOR

EFRAT BAT USHRA

ASAPH AND AUSHRA HAIMOFF

ספר זה נתרם לכבו
של המחבר הרה"ג

ר' ראובן שליט"א

ואתו עמו הרבנית החשובה מרת
גיטל תחי'.

הרב והרבנית שליט"א משימים לילות כימים להיות
לסיוע ולעזר
למשפחות בישראל שיהיו שרוים בשלום ובשלוה.
מעומק הלב נברכם
שיזכו להוסיף בעבודתם הקדושה

להרבות קדושה ושלום בישראל
ולזכות לרוות הרבה נחת דקדושה
מכל צאצאיהם ותלמידיהם, אכי"ר.

מתוך הערצה וידידות,
ה.ח.

הוקדש לעילוי נשמת

הרב ראובן בן משה יעקב ע״ה עפשטיין
נלב״ע טו׳ כסלו תשכ״ב למ״ק

בילא רבקה בת מנחם מענדל ע״ה עפשטיין
נלב״ע ד׳ תשרי תש״נ למ״ק

משה יצחק בן אליהו הכהן ע״ה אסשטיין
נלב״ע יג׳ אב תשס״ז למ״ק

הרב אברהם בן שימא ע״ה גורצמאן
נלב״ע יב׳ תמוז תשס״ז למ״ק

מלכה בת יהושע אהרן ע״ה זאקס
נלב״ע יז׳ תשרי תשמ״ו למ״ק
ת. נ. צ. ב. ה.

L'KOVOD

HARAV EPSTEIN,

YASHER KOACHACH TO YOU AND YOUR REBBETZIN FOR THE PERSONAL HADRACHA AND GUTSKEIT YOU DO FOR KLAL YISROEL!
YOU SHOULD ONLY GO M'CHAYIL EL CHAYIL AND HAVE THE STRENGTH TO CONTINUE YOUR AVODAS HAKODESH!

ARI AND HADASSA MONHEIT

לזכר נשמת

RACHEL BAS YOSEF ZEV
CHAIM DAVID BEN REB YITZCHAK MEIR HALEVI
AVRAHAM CHAIM ZEV BEN SHMUEL YITZCHAK HACOHEN
AHARON BEN YESHAYA HALEVI
YISROEL BEN YESHAYAHU HALEVI
MOSHE YOSEF BEN BARUCH ELIMELECH

EZRA "TINY" & ESTHER KAPNICK

In Loving Memory
of Our Dear Father

BEKHOR HAI

BEN YITZCHAK ZT"L

MIKEY KHAFIZOV

In Honor of

RABBI REUVEN EPSTEIN

And the Whole

YESHIVAS OHR YITZCHAK!

MORDY EISIG

SPONSORED IN MEMORY OF

CHAYA SARA BAS MORDECHAI

SOL AND WEINREICH

לעלוי נשמת

THE KEDOSHIM OF THE HOLOCAUST

HESHY BAUM

THIS DEDICATION IS
IN HONOR OF OUR DEAR PARENTS

ARIE & BREINA POLLAK
AND
DAVID & MIRIAM CYWIAK

MAY YOU ALWAYS HAVE MUCH NACHAS FROM US.

YEHUDA & ZAHAVA POLLAK

לעלוי נשמת

הינדא בת יהודה אריה
אליהו צבי בן שלמה
דאבע אסתר בת דוב נתן
פלארא מזל טוב בת יצחק
עמרם בן יוסף הכהן
איטה פריידל בת צבי
יצחק בן זאב הלוי

YEHUDA AND RIVKY FREUNDLICH

IN HONOR OF

RABBI REUVEN EPSTEIN,

WHO CONTINUES TO INSPIRE AND EDUCATE PEOPLE IN SUCH CRUCIAL AREAS OF LIFE.
AS A MERIT FOR THE BROOK HAVEN KOLLEL CENTER TO CONTINUE TO INSPIRE AND WELCOME NEW JEWS INTO THEIR CENTER

YOSEF AND ROOKIE SHAPIRO

IN HONOR OF

EDIT

LOVING WIFE. DEDICATED MOTHER. TIRELESS WORKER.

YOSSI SHECHTER

Donated in honor of

RABBI EPSTEIN

YOSSI AND JUDY KAUFMAN

DEDICATED IN HONOR OF
OUR CHILDREN,

SHIMI, ADINA AND AVI

FOR BRINGING SUCH LIGHT
TO OUR LIVES

REUVEN & GITTY EPSTEIN

לעלוי נשמת

GANENDEL SARA BAS SHMUEL LEV

YEHUDA ZUCKER

IN HONOR OF

YONA BEN BRYNA

DEDICATED BY:
MR AND MRS.
AKIVA LANDSBERG

לעלוי נשמת

PINCHUS ARYEH BEN YOSEF MOSHE
AND
YAAKOV MICHOEL BEN MEIR

CHAIM BARUCH
AND NAOMI NEUMANN

THIS DEDICATION IS
לעלוי נשמת
MY GRANDFATHER

MENACHEM MENDEL MUTTERPERL

MR. AND MRS. CHAIM
MUTTERPERL

לעלוי נשמת

AVRAHAM YEHUDA BEN R' YEHUDA
BEN YOSEF HALEVI A"H
MARAS BRACHA SIMA BAS R'
YITZCHAK A"H
V'KOL SHESH MILLION KIDOSHIM
SHENEHARGO AL KIDDUSH HASHEM

ELI & FRUMIT MARMORSTEIN

IN RECOGNITION
OF THE FINE JOB

RABBI EPSTEIN

IS DOING IN BEING
MECHANECH HIS TALMIDIM.

MAY HASHEM ASSIST YOU SO
THAT YOU MAY CONTINUE IN
YOUR AVODAS HAKODESH FOR
MANY YEARS TO COME.

GEDALYA AND CHANIE ENGEL

לזכר נשמת

AVRAHAM BEN GEDALYA

CHAVA BREINDEL BEN AVRAHAM

ELIEZER BEN AVRAHAM

CHAYA SARAH BAS ELIEZER HILLEL

AVRAHAM BEN BEN TZION YISHAI

MENACHEM DAVID BEN AVRAHAM
YITZCHOK

FRADEL BAS DAVID ARYEH FAIGA
BREINA BAS SHIMON CHAIM

HILLEL AND SARAH ENGEL

לעלוי נשמת

MARAS BRACHA SIMA BAS R'
YITZCHAK A"H
AVRAHAM YEHUDA BEN YOSEF
HALEVI
R' YITZCHOK AMRAM ELIYAHOU
BEN AVRAHAM ISHAI
YAAKOV BEN MOSHE
ELIEZER ZEV BEN TZVI CHAIM

LEZECHUS LEMOTZEI
ZIVUG HAGON B'KAROV

MOSHE BEN BAILA LEAH
SARAH BAS BAILA LEAH
ELIEZER ZEV BEN BREINDEL
NECHAMA

PHILIP MARMORSTEIN

"SOME PEOPLE MAKE IT HAPPEN
SOME PEOPLE WATCH OTHERS
MAKE IT HAPPEN
SOME SAY "WHAT HAPPENED?"

TO MY DEAR FRIEND AND
ONE-TIME CHAVRUSA WHO IS
CHANGING THE WORLD.

**RAV REUVEN
EPSTEIN**
שליט"א

KEEP MAKING IT HAPPEN!

DOVBER AND ROCHELLE COWAN,
LONDON, UK

IN HONOR OF

RABBI EPSTEIN

WITH MUCH APPRECIATION FROM YOUR TALMUD,

MORDECHAI AND
RIKI SENDEROVITS

לעלוי נשמת

NOTA TZVI BEN ELIYAHU

MOTI AND SHOSHI KOZLOWITZ

לזכר נשמת

MY GRANDFATHER

SHEVA BAS TUVIA AVRAHAM

MENACHEM AND
GITEL BRUKIRER

לעלוי נשמת

MY BROTHER-IN-LAW'S FATHER,

YAAKOV MENACHEM MENDEL BEN YECHIEL ROTTBLAT

A CHASHUVA YID WHO CAME TO ERETZ YISRAEL AS A LITTLE BOY FROM POLAND DURING THE WAR, KNEW THE CHAZON ISH AND WAS A CLOSE TALMID OF THE STEIPLER.

MAY THE ZECHUS OF THIS BOOK ELEVATE HIS NESHAMA TO THE HIGHEST.

MENASHE VAKHOVSKY

UPCOMING BOOK TITLES BY THE SAME AUTHOR

SUBSCRIBE AT MARRIAGEPRO.CO TO STAY UP TO DATE WITH THE LATEST CONTENT!

The Marriage Project is an online and in-person project dedication to providing high quality content for those in the dating, engaged and married stages of life. To date The Marriage Project's dating, marriage and relationship seminars have been attended by hundreds of thousands around the world.

More information about The Marriage Project can be found online at MarriagePro.co (not .com)